# Advanced Knowledge Application in Practice

edited by
**Igor Fürstner**

**Advanced Knowledge Application in Practice**
Edited by Igor Fürstner

**Published by InTech**

Janeza Trdine 9, 51000 Rijeka, Croatia



**Publishing Process Manager** Iva Lipovic

**Technical Editor** Teodora Smiljanic

**Cover Designer** InTech Design Team

Additional hard copies can be obtained from orders@intechopen.com

Advanced Knowledge Application in Practice, Edited by Igor Fürstner
p. cm.
ISBN 978-953-307-141-1

For EU product safety concerns:
IN TECH d.o.o., Prolaz Marije Krucifikse Kozulić 3, 51000 Rijeka, Croatia,
info@intechopen.com or visit our website at intechopen.com.

# Contents

# Preface

The world economy of today is more integrated and interdependent than ever before. The fact that in many industries historically distinct and separate markets are merging into one global market leads towards an environment that offers more opportunities, but is also more complex and competitive than it used to be.

One of the main factors that drive today's economy is technology. If technology is defined as a practical application of knowledge and the aim is to become really competitive on the global market, there is a need for something more, thus a cutting edge practical application of knowledge would be necessary what the most advanced technology currently available is - high tech.

If the classification of high-tech sectors is taken into consideration, it can be noticed that the research activity takes place not only in the so-called high-tech societies such as the United States, Japan, Germany, etc., but also in other regions.

This book is the result of research and development activities, covering concrete fields of research:

- Chapter one introduces a methodology for classifications of textile defects
- Chapter two describes some possibilities for predicting wear in real contacts
- Chapter three presents several applications of laser processing for on-line process monitoring
- Chapter four introduces the process of deposition of carbon films
- Chapter five lists the formability testing methods
- Chapter six investigates aluminum foams
- Chapter seven estimates the type of car driver
- Chapter eight investigates the human biomechanics in working activities
- Chapter nine presents cattle heart rate measurements
- Chapter ten discusses a control method for permanent magnet linear synchronous motor
- Chapter eleven introduces a control method for power systems
- Chapter twelve shows a model in the building of hydro acoustical antennas
- Chapter thirteen introduces a readout system for experiments
- Chapter fourteen gives a review on swarm robotics
- Chapters fifteen and sixteen present control possibilities in robotics
- Chapter seventeen shows a telerobotic application

- Chapter eighteen presents an aid for the blind in the learning process
- Chapter nineteen introduces a new approach for contour detection of the cornea
- Chapter twenty presents recent research results in phytoremediation

October 20, 2010

Editor

**Igor Fürstner**
*Subotica Tech – College of Applied Sciences*
*Subotica, Serbia*

# 1

# An Advanced and Automated Neural Network based Textile Defect Detector

Shamim Akhter[1, 2] and Tamnun E Mursalin[3]
[1]*National Institute of Informatics,*
[2]*American International University-Bangladesh,*
[3]*University Of Liberal Arts-Bangladesh*
[1]*Japan*
[2,3]*Bangladesh*

## 1. Introduction

All textile industries aim to produce competitive fabrics. The competition enhancement depends mainly on productivity and quality of the fabrics produced by each industry. In the textile sector, there have been an enlarge amount of losses due to faulty fabrics. In the Least Development Countries (LDC) like Bangladesh, whose 25% revenue earning is achieved from textile export, most defects arising in the production process of a textile material are still detected by human inspection. The work of inspectors is very tedious and time consuming. They have to detect small details that can be located in a wide area that is moving through their visual field. The identification rate is about 70%. In addition, the effectiveness of visual inspection decreases quickly with fatigue. Thus, to produce less defective textile for minimizing production cost and time is a vital requirement. Digital image processing techniques have been increasingly applied to textured samples analysis over the last ten years (Ralló et al., 2003). Wastage reduction through accurate and early stage detection of defects in fabrics is also an important aspect of quality improvement. The article in (Meier, 2005) summarized the comparison between human visual inspection and automated inspection. Also, it has been stated in (Stojanovic et al., 2001) that price of textile fabric is reduced by 45% to 65% due to defects. Thus, to reduce error on identifying fabric defects requires more automotive and accurate inspection process. Considering this lacking, this research implements a Textile Defect Detector which uses computer vision methodology with the combination of multi-layer neural networks to identify four classifications of textile defects. Afterwards, a microcontroller based mechanical system is developed to complete the Textile Defect Detector as a real-time control agent that transforms the captured digital image into adjusted resultant output and operates the automated machine (i.e. combination of two leaser beams and production machine), illustrated in Fig. 1.

The main purpose of this chapter is to present an advanced and automatic Textile Defect Detector as a first step for a future complete industrial Quality Information System (QIS) in textile industries of Least Development Countries (LDC). The chapter is organized as follows:

- Section 2 describes relevant previous efforts in the fields, such as textile fabric inspection systems, computer vision and machine learning systems for automated textile defects recognizing, electronic textile (e-textiles) systems etc.
- Section 3 provides the methodology and implementation of the proposed textile defect detectors. Software and hardware system implementation are two major parts. The software system implementation consists the textile image processing and the neural network designing issues. The hardware system consists micro-controller design and implementation issues.
- Section 4 provides the experimental comparison of the proposed implementation on the textile defects detection.
- Finally, Section 5 concludes with some remarks and plausible future research lines.

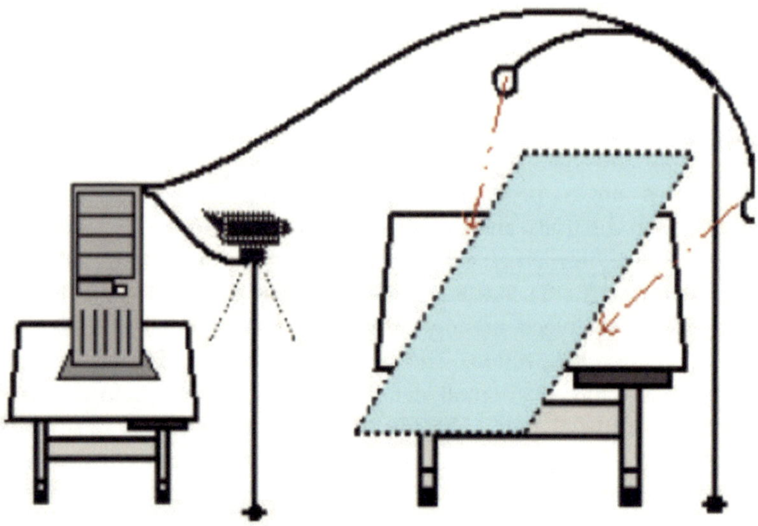

Fig. 1. Real-time Environment of Textile Defect Detector

## 2. Related work

Machine vision automated inspection system for textile defects has been in the research industry for longtime (Batchelor & Whelan, 1994), (Newman & Jain, 1995). Recognition of patterns independent of position, size, brightness and orientation in the visual field has been the goal of much recent work. However, there is still a lack of work in machine vision automated system for recognizing textile defects using AI. A neural network pattern recognizer was developed in (Zhang et al., 1992).

Today's automated fabric inspection systems are based on adaptive neural networks. So instead of going through complex programming routines, the users are able to simply scan a short length of good quality fabric to show the inspection system what to expect. This coupled with specialized computer processors that have the computing power of several hundred Pentium chips makes these systems viable (Dockery, 2001). Three state-of-the-art fabric inspection systems are - BarcoVision's Cyclops, Elbit Vision System's I-Tex and Zellweger Uster's Fabriscan. These systems can be criticized on grounds that they all work

under structured environments - a feat that is almost non-existent in list developed countries like Bangladesh.
There are some works in (Ciamberlini et al., 1996) based on the optical fourier transform directly obtained from the fabric with optical devices and a laser beam. Digital image processing techniques have been increasingly applied to textured samples analysis over the last ten years. Several authors have considered defect detection on textile materials. Kang et al. (Kang et al., 1999), (Kang et al., 2001) analyzed fabric samples from the images obtained from transmission and reflection of light to determine its interlacing pattern. Wavelets had been applied to fabric analysis by Jasper et al. (Jasper et al., 1996), (Jasper et al., 1995). Escofet et al. (Escofet et al., 1996), (Escofet et al., 1998) have applied Gabor filters (wavelets) to the automatic segmentation of defects on non-solid fabric images for a wide variety of interlacing patterns. (Millán & Escofet, 1996) introduced Fourier-domain-based angular correlation as a method to recognize similar periodic patterns, even though the defective fabric sample image appeared rotated and scaled. Recognition was achieved when the maximum correlation value of the scaled and rotated power spectra was similar to the autocorrelation of the power spectrum of the pattern fabric sample. If the method above was applied to the spectra presented in Fig.1, the maximum angular correlation value would be considerably lower than the autocorrelation value of the defect free fabric spectrum. Fourier analysis does not provide, in general, enough information to detect and segment local defects.
Electronic textiles (e-textiles) are fabrics with interconnections and electronics woven into them. The electronics consist of both processing and sensing elements, distributed throughout the fabric. (Martin et al., 2004) described the design of a simulation environment for electronic textiles (e-textiles) but having a greater dependence on physical locality of computation. (Ji et al., 2004) analyzed the filter design essentials and proposes two different methods to segment the Gabor filtered multi-channel images. The first method integrates Gabor filters with labeling algorithm for edge detection and object segmentation. The second method uses the K-means clustering with simulated annealing for image segmentation of a stack of Gabor filtered multi-channel images. But the classic Gabor expansion is computationally expensive and since it combines all the space and frequency details of the original signal, it is difficult to take advantage of the gigantic amount of numbers. From the literature it is clear that there exists many systems that can detect Textile defects but hardly affordable by the small industries of the LDC like Bangladesh.
In this research, we propose an automated Textile Defect Detector based on computer vision methodology and adaptive neural networks and that is implemented combining engines of image processing and artificial neural networks in textile industries research arena. In textile sectors, different types of faults are available i.e. hole, scratch, stretch, fly yarn, dirty spot, slab, cracked point, color bleeding etc; if not detected properly these faults can affect the production process massively. The proposed Textile Defect Defector mainly detects four types of faults that are hole, scratch, fresh as no fault and remaining faults as other fault.

## 3. The automated neural network based textile defect detector

The proposed textile defect recognizer is viewed as a real-time control agent that transforms the captured digital image into adjusted resultant output and operates the automated machine (i.e. combination of two leaser beams and production machine) through the micro-controller. In the proposed system as the recognizer identifies a fault of any type mentioned above, will immediately recognize the type of fault which in return will trigger the laser

beams in order to display the upper offset and the lower offset of the faulty portion. The upper offset and the lower offset implies the 2 inches left and 2 inches right offset of faulty portion. This guided triggered area by the laser beams will indicate the faulty portion that needs to be extracted from the roll. For this the automated system generates a signal to stop the rotation of the stepper motor and cut off the faulty portion. Whenever, the signal is generated the controller circuit stops the movement of the carrying belt and the defective portion of the fabric is removed from the roll. Then after eliminating the defective part again a signal is generated to start the stepper motor and continue the further process. Here, the whole system implementation is done in a very simple way. In addition to this the hardware equipments are so cheap that a LDC like Bangladesh can easily effort it and can make the best use of the scheme.
The methology that the whole system consists of two major parts - software and the microcontroller based hardware implementation. The major steps required to implement the Textile Defect Detector is depicted in Fig. 2.

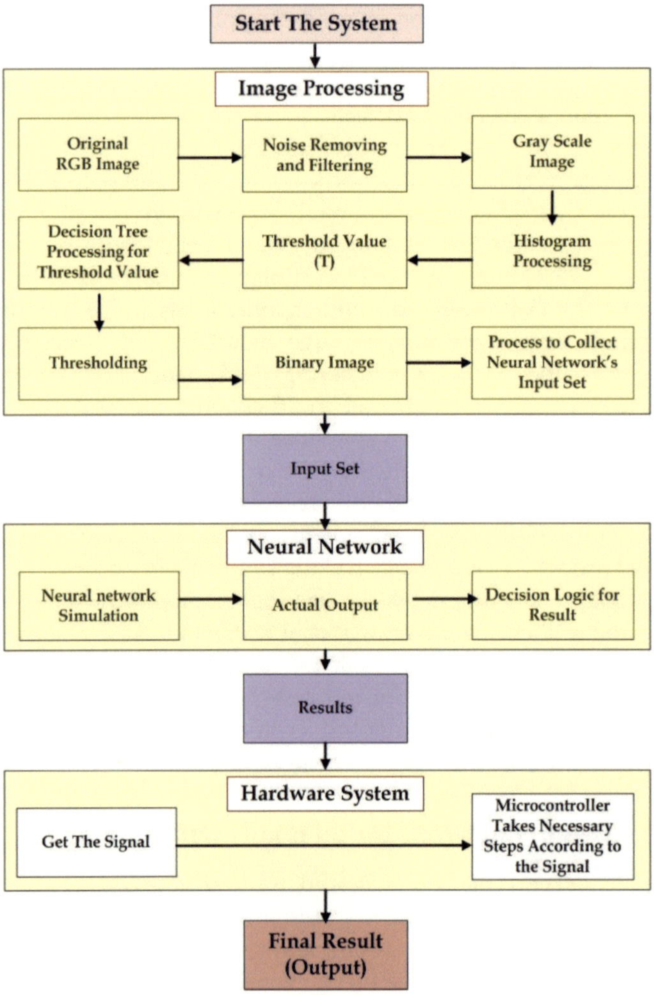


Fig. 2. Major components of the Textile Defect Detector

### 3.1 The software system

The software system can be a competitive model for recognizing textile defects in real world. Base on the research, the software system design is also separated into two additional parts. The first part focuses on the processing of the images to prepare to feed into the neural network. The second part is about building a neural network that best performs on the criteria to sort out the textile defects. Whenever, the software, detects a fault of any type mentioned above, sends/ triggers a signal to the hardware system.

#### 3.1.1 Processing textile image for the neural network input

At first the images of the fabric is captured by digital camera in RGB format (Fig.3 and Fig.5) and passes the image through serial port to the computer. Then, noise is removed using standard techniques and an adaptive median filter algorithm has been used as spatial filtering for minimizing time complexity and maximizing performance (Gonzalez et al., 2005) to converts digital (RGB) images to grayscale images ( left in Fig. 4). A decision tree is constructed based on the histogram of the image in hand to convert the gray scale image in a binary representation. As we know from the problem description that there are different types of textile fabrics and also different types of defects in textile industries hence different threshold values to different pattern of faults there is no way to generalize threshold value (T) from one image for all types of fabrics. Notice this phenomenon in histograms illustrated in Fig. 3 (The identified threshold value T, should be greater then 120 and less than 170) and Fig. 5 (The identified threshold value T, should be greater then 155 and less then 200). A local threshold was used based on decision tree, which was constricted using set of 200 image histograms of fabric data. Illustration of the decision tree is provided in Fig. 6.
After restoration local thresholding technique (decision tree processing) is used in order to convert grayscale image into binary image (right in Fig. 4). Finally, this binary image is used to calculate the following attributes.

- The area of the faulty portion: calculates the total defected area of an image.
- Number of objects: uses image segmentation to calculate the number of labels in an image.

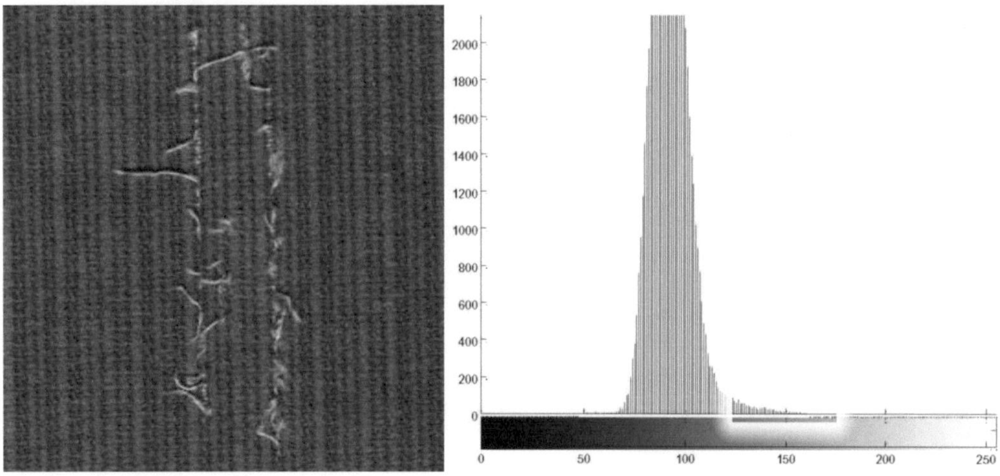


Fig. 3. Original faulty scratch fabric image and histogram representation

- Shape factor: distinguishes a circular image form a noncircular image. Shape factor uses the area of a circle to identify the circular portions of the fault.

These attributes are used as input sets to adapt the neural network through training set in order to recognize expected defects. An example of neural network input set is presented in Table 1.

| Area | Number of Objects | Shape Factor |
|---|---|---|
| 76700 | 1 | 0.77389 |

Table 1. Neural network input set

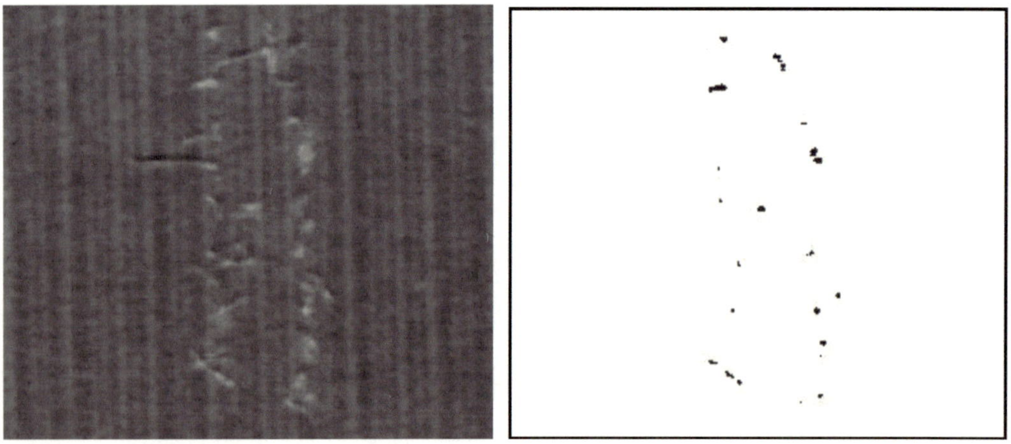

Fig. 4. Faulty scratch grayscale (left) and binary (right) fabric images

Fig. 5. Original faulty hole fabric image and the histogram representation

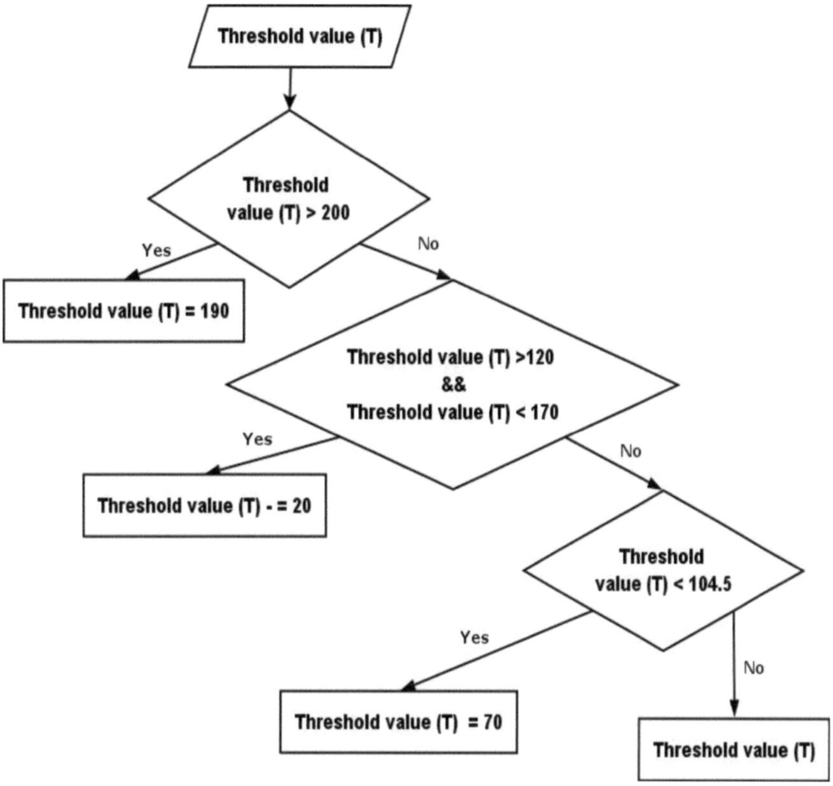


Fig. 6. Decision Tree for Threshold Value (T) to convert from gray to binary

### 3.1.2 Suitable neural network

In search of a fully connected multi-layer neural network that will sort out the defected textiles, we start with a two layer neural network (Fig. 7). Our neural network contains one hidden of 44 neurons and one output layer of 4 neurons.

The neurons in the output layer is delegated as 1st neuron of the output layer is to Hole type fault, 2nd neuron of the output layer is to Scratch type fault, 3rd neuron of the output layer is to Other type of fault and 4th neuron of the output layer is for No fault (not defected fabric). The output range of the each neuron is in the range of [0 ~ 1] as we use log-sigmoid threshold function to calculate the final out put of the neurons. Although during the training we try to reach the following for the target output [{1 0 0 0}, {0 1 0 0}, {0 0 1 0}, {0 0 0 1}] consecutively for Hole type defects, Scratch type defects, Other type defects and No defects, the final output from the output layer is determined using the winner- take-all method.

To determine the number of optimal neurons in the hidden layer was the tricky part, we start with 20 neurons in the hidden layer and test the performance of the neural network on the basis of a fixed test set, and then we increase the number of neurons one by one and till 60, the number of neurons in the hidden layer is chosen based on the best performance. The error curve is illustrated in Fig. 8.

The parameters used in the neural network can be summarized as:

- Training data set contains 200 images; 50 from each class.
- Test data set contains 20 images; 5 from each class

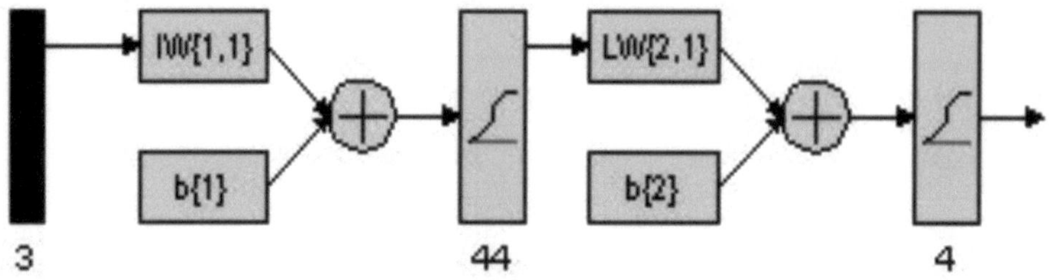


Fig. 7. Design of Feed Forward Back propagation Neural Network

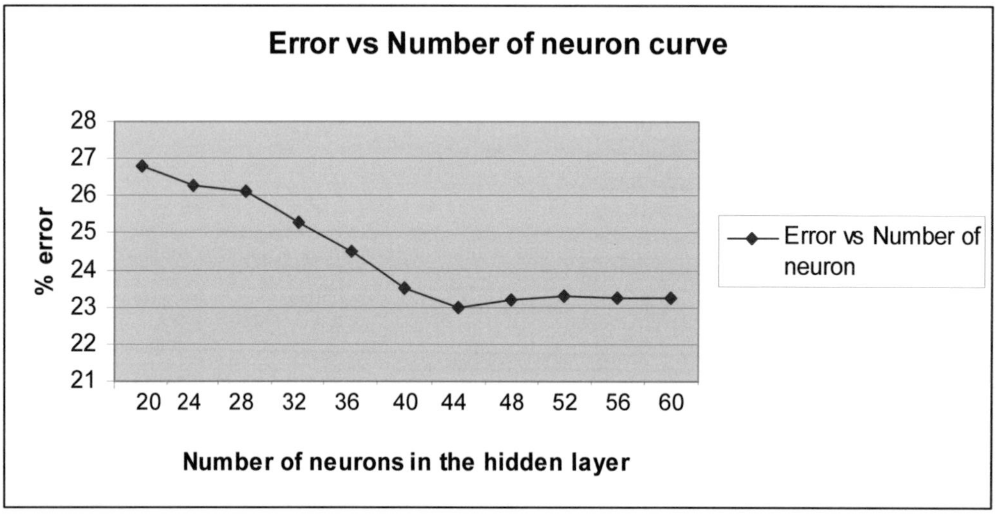


Fig. 8. Performance (in % error) carve on the neuron number in the hidden layer

- The transfer function is Log Sigmoid.
- Performance function used is mean square error
- Widrow-Hoff algorithm is used as learning function (Hagan et al., 2002) with a learning rate of 0.01.
- To train the network resilient back propagation algorithm (Riedmiller and Braun, 1993), (Neural Network Toolbox, 2004) is used. Weights and biases are randomly initialized. Initial delta is set to 0.05 and the maximum value for delta is set to 50, the decay in delta is set to 0.2.
- Training time or total iteration allowed for the neural networks to train is set to infinity, as we know it is a conversable problem. And we have the next parameter to work as stopping criterion

Disparity or maximum error in the actual output and network output is set to $10^{-5}$. After calculating input set, neural network simulates the input set and recognizes defect of image as an actual output. From the resultant output, the software system can release final result by the help of decision logic. So, the software system is a simple engine based on computer vision methodology and neural networks in textile industries sector. Efficiency is one of the key points of this system as a result all the algorithms applied on the system is aggressively tested by time and space complexity. The system will successfully minimize inspection time than other manual or automated inspection based system.

### 3.2 The hardware system

The hardware system is capable to detect the upper offset and the lower offset of the faulty portion. The upper offset and the lower offset implies the 2 inches left and 2 inches right offset of faulty portion and needs to be extracted from the fabric roll. After cutting the desired portions of fabric, the detector resumes its operation.

**Microcontroller Implementation:** In order to program the microcontroller, PICProg is used to burn the program into the PIC16F84A. It is pic basic program, which uses the serial port of the computer and a simple circuit. The code for the PIC was written and saves as *.asm file. Then PicBasic Pro 2.45 was used to convert it into an *.hex file and after that using PICProg the hex file was written into the PIC. The outlet of the microcontroller is exposed in Fig.9 and Fig. 10.

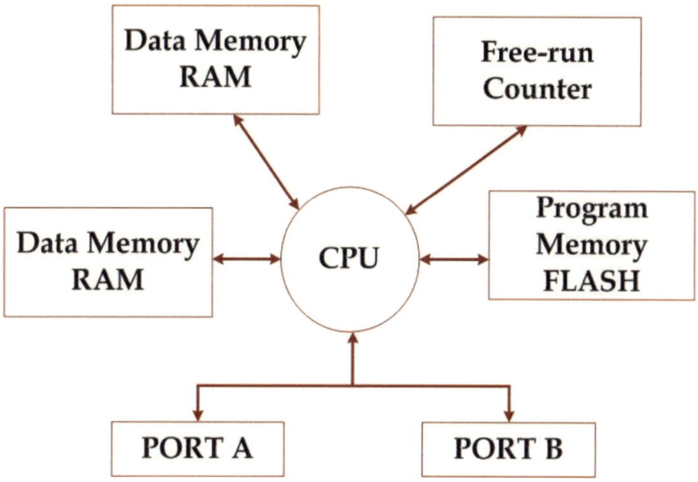


Fig. 9. PIC 16F84A Microcontroller outline

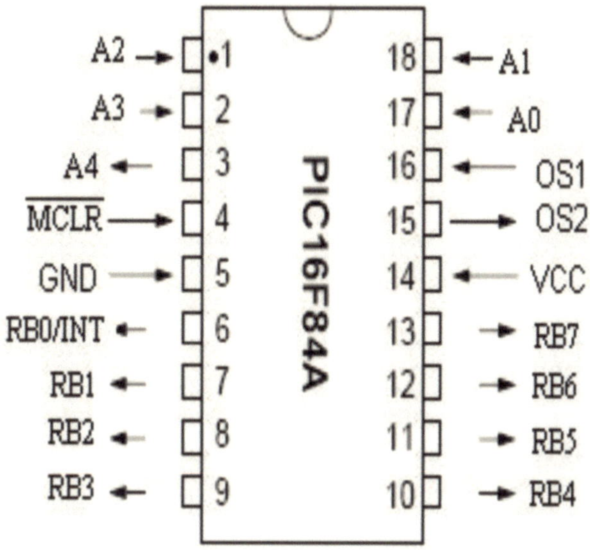


Fig. 10. PIC16F84A

The main circuit contains the following three parts:

- Implementation of 12-Volt DC power supply: Two diodes, one transformer or (24 v peak to peak) one capacitor of 470 µF and one resistor are required to implement the circuit. Here, the centre tap rectifier converts the AC into DC. The capacitor is used in parallel to the load to stable the output at a fixed voltage. A 470 µF is connected to the circuit to get a fixed 12 V voltage.
- Arrangement of Microcontroller: 12V DC is applied to steeper motor voltage terminal and as an input of a Voltage Regulator 7805 which provides 5V DC. After burnt the Microcontroller, these 5V supplied to the Vdd and MCLR and Vss connected with ground. OSC1 is connected with 5V DC through 4.7K resistances. Port A0, A1, A2 is used in a switch to control Stepper motor speed and direction.
- Implementation of switching circuit to control a stepper motor: Here four Transistors have been used (BD135), which Bases (B) is connected to the Microcontroller port $B_0$, $B_1$, $B_2$ and $B_3$ through 1K resistances. Transistor's Emitters (E) are shorted and connected with ground. Collectors (C) are connected to the motor windings in sequentially. The pulse width is passing from port $B_0$, $B_1$, $B_2$ and $B_3$ to the stepper motor windings according to the code.

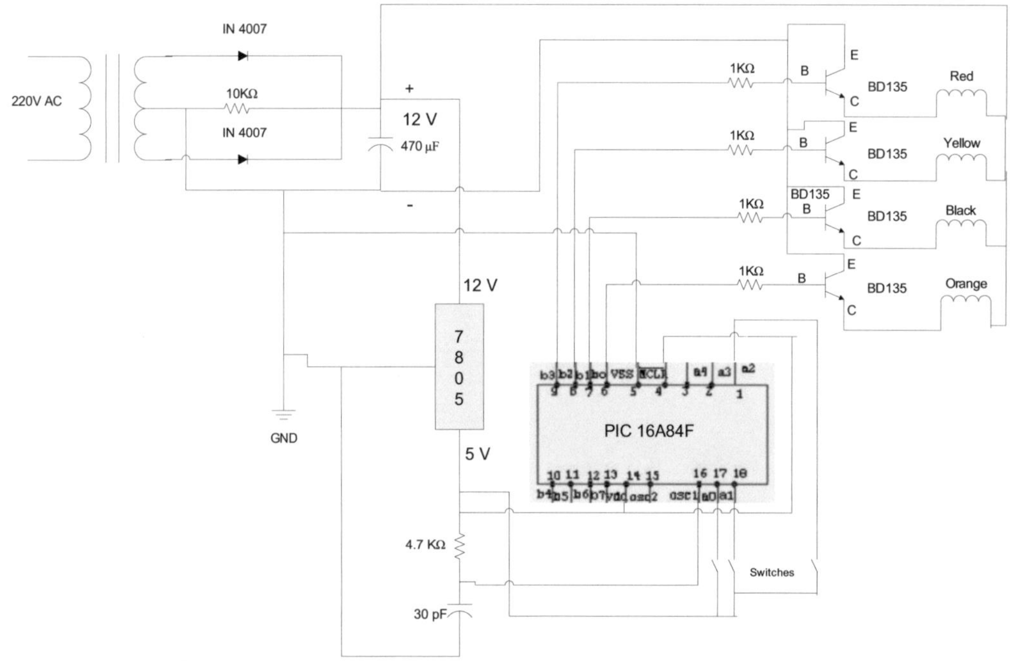


Fig. 11. Complete circuit diagram

As depicted in Fig. 11, the circuit consists of four TIP122 power transistors (T1, T2,T3 & T4), 330 ohm resistors (R1, R2,R3 & R4), 3.3k ohm (R5,R6,R7 & R8), IN4007 freewheeling diodes (D1,D2,D3 & D4) and one inverter IC 7407, which is used as buffer chip (IC1). The 7407 buffer used here is a hex-type open-collector high-voltage buffer. The 3.3k ohm resistors are the pull up resistors for the open-collector buffer. The input for this buffer comes from the parallel port. The output of the buffer is of higher current capacity than the parallel port output, which is necessary for triggering the transistor; it also isolates the circuit from the

PC parallel port and hence provides extra protection against potentially dangerous feedback voltages that may occur if the circuit fails. The diode connected across the power supply and the collector is used as a freewheeling diode and also to protect the transistor from the back EMF of the motor inductance. The motor used in this experiment is two STM 901 from Srijan Control Drives. The common of four parallel ports are connected with the power supply (VCC) of 5V and head of four parallel is connected to the respective of printer port pin no 2, 3, 4 & 5 and pin no 25 is connected with common point of ground of the circuits.

During normal operation, the output pattern from the PC drives the buffer, and corresponding transistors are switched on. This leads to the conduction of current through these coils of the stepper motor which are connected to the energized transistor. This makes the motor move one step forward. The next pulse will trigger a new combination of transistors, and hence a new set of coils, leading to the motor moving another step. The scheme of excitation that we have used here has already been shown above. In this construction, 50V- 470 μF capacitor is used for filtering or discharging voltage while converting to pure DC from AC power supply. Regulator IC 7812 is used for voltage transferring down from 24V to 5V. Then a positive voltage (+ve) is supplied from the board to one of the motors (red) and the other wire point is used for grounding (maroon). LED is used for examining the proper voltage supply to the circuit. Capacitor is used for discharging so that no charge is hold. Regulator IC 7805 is used for transferring down voltage from 12V to 5V. Resistance of 330ohm, 10k ohm is used to guard the LED from impairment. For getting pure DC voltage from supplied AC voltage, diode IN 4007 is used. From this circuit, a positive voltage is supplied to the other motor of our experiment just like the other transformer board and the point is grounded.

## 4. Experimental results

The performance of the Textile Defect Detector is determined based on the cross validation method. The average result is provided in Fig. 12. Here, notice that the recognizer can

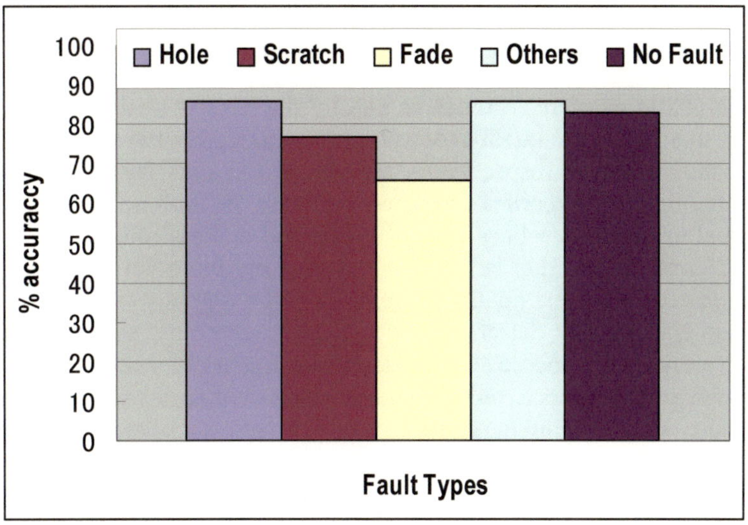


Fig. 12. The bar chart for the performance accuracy of the system

Fig. 13. The real test-bed implementation

successfully identifying Hole type faults with 86% accuracy, 77% of Scratch type faults, 86% of the Other type faults and 83% No faults. Later, the neural network is updated to detect the fade type faults also and the accuracy is 66%. Thus, the average performance of the system determining the defects in textile industry is 74.33% and the overall all performance of the system is 76.5%.

## 5. Conclusion

In most of the textile garment factories of LDC(s) the defects of the fabrics are detected manually. The manual textile quality control usually goes over the human eye inspection. Notoriously, human visual inspection is tedious, tiring and fatiguing task, involving observation, attention and experience to detect correctly the fault occurrence. The accuracy of human visual inspection declines with dull jobs and endless routines. Sometimes slow, expensive and erratic inspection is the result. Therefore, the automatic visual inspection protects both: the man and the quality. Here, it has been demonstrated that Textile Defect Detector System is capable of detecting fabrics' defects with more accuratly and efficiency. In the research arena, the proposed system tried to use the local threshold technique without the decision tree process. Since, our recognizer deals with different types of faults and fabrics, therefore the recognition system cannot access a general approach for local thresholding technique.

The image processing system works very well except the quality of the web camera. Because of which sometimes the perfect fabric is also found as faulty part. However, this problem is easily defeatable by using a good quality camera. Additionally, the proposed research

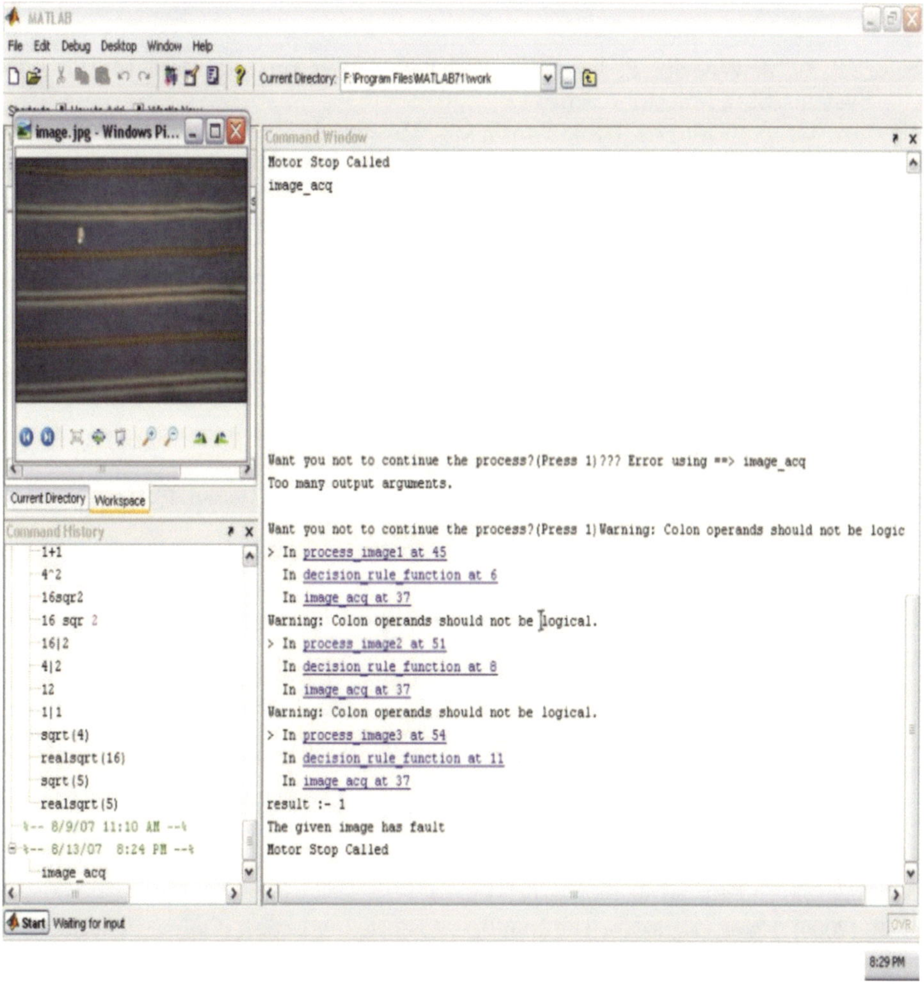


Fig. 14. The MATLAB software interface

observes that there are a large percentage of misclassifications using Widrow-Hoff learning algorithm and Resilient back propagation training algorithm to recognize the defects or non-defects of fabrics for the variations of area of faulty portion, number of objects and sharp factor. As a result, a variation of performance is noticed, in identifying other faults than hole and scratch faults. The Textile Defect Detector can detect few amounts of multi-colored defect fabrics. There have many types of defects, which are not within the scope of the above recognition system. Thus, the system performs quite well except some of false negative classification problems, where it fails to classify the good fabric as good and marks it as faulty fabric; the future versions of the system will try to notice this problem more precisely.

## 6. Acknowledgement

The Authors, thank M.A. Islam, F.Z. Eishita and A.R. Islam for their support with experiments on the Textile Defect Detector system. They also acknowledge their appreciation for Dr. M. A. Amin.

## 7. References


Batchelor, B. G. & Whelan, P. F. (1994). Selected Papers on Industrial Machine Vision Systems, SPIE Milestone Series.

Ciamberlini, C.; Francini, F.; Longobardi, G.; Sansoni, P. & Tiribilli, B. (1996). Defect detection in textured materials by optical filtering with structured detectors and selfadaptable masks, *Opt. Eng.*,35(3), 838-844

Dockery, A. (2001). Automatic fabric inspection: assessing the current state of the art, [Online document], [cited 29 Apr. 2005], Available HTTP:

Escofet, J.; Navarro, R.; Millán, M.S. & Pladellorens, J. (1996). Detection of local defects in textile webs using Gabor filters in vision systems: new image processing techniques, *Ph. Réfrégier, ed. Proceedings SPIE*, Vol. 2785, 163-170

Escofet, J.; Navarro, R.; Millán, M.S. & Pladellorens, J. (1998). Detection of local defects in textile webs using Gabor filters, *Opt. Eng.*, 37(8) 2297-2307

Gonzalez, R. C.; Woods, R. E. & Eddins, S. L. (2005). *Digital Image Processing using MATLAB*, ISBN 81-297-0515-X, pp. 76-104,142-166,404-407

Hagan, M. T.; Demuth, H. B. & Beale, M. (2002). *Neural Network Design*, ISBN 981-240-376-0, part 2.5, 10.8

Jasper, W.J.; Garnier, S.J., & Potlapalli, H. (1996). Texture characterization and defect detection using adaptive wavelets, *Opt. Eng.*, 35(11), 3140-3149

Jasper, W.J. & Potlapalli, H. (1995). Image analysis of mispicks in woven fabric, *Text. Res.J.*, 65(1), 683-692

Ji, Y.; Chang, K.H. & Hung, C.C. (2004). Efficient edge detection and object segmentation using Gabor filters, *ACMSE*, USA

Kang, T.J. et al. (1999). Automatic recognition of fabric weave patterns by digital image analysis, *Textile Res. J.*, 69(2), 77-83

Kang, T.J. et al. (2001). Automatic structure analysis and objective evaluation of woven fabric using image analysis, *Textile Res. J.*, 71(3), 261-270

Martin, T.; Jones, M.; Edmison, J., Sheikh, T. & Nakad, Z. (2004). Modeling and simulating electronic textile applications, *LCTES*, USA

Meier, R. (2005). Uster Fabriscan, The Intelligent Fabric Inspection,[Online document], cited 20 Apr. 2005], Available HTTP:
http://www.kotonline.com/english_pages/ana_basliklar/uster.asp

Millán, M.S. & Escofet, J. (1996). Fourier domain based angular correlation for quasiperiodic pattern recognition. Applications to web inspection, *Appl. Opt.*, 35(31), 6253-6260

Neural Network Toolbox (2004). MATLAB -The Language of Technical Conputing, [CD Document], Version 7.0.0.19920(R14)

Newman, T. S. & Jain, A. K. (1995). A Survey of Automated Visual Inspection, *Computer Vision and Image Understanding*, Vol. 61, pp. 231–262.

Ralló, M.; Millán, M. S. & Escofet, J. (2003).Wavelet based techniques for textile inspection, *Opt. Eng.* 26(2), 838-844

Riedmiller, M. & Braun, H. (1993). A direct adaptive method for faster backpropagation learning: The RPROP algorithm, *Proceedings of the IEEE International Conference on Neural Networks*

Stojanovic, R.; Mitropulos, P.; Koulamas, C.; Karayiannis, Y. A.; Koubias, S. & Papadopoulos, G. (2001). Real-time Vision based System for Textile Fabric Inspection, *Real-Time Imaging*, Vol. 7, No. 6, pp. 507–518.

Zhang, H.; Guan, J. & Sun, G. C. (1992). Artificial Neural Network-Based Image Pattern Recognition, *ACM 30th Annual Southeast Conference*

# 2

# Wear Simulation

Sören Andersson
*Professor Emeritus in Machine Elements*
*Royal Institute of Technology (KTH), Stockholm, Sweden*

## 1. Introduction

### 1.1 Can the wear process be modelled and simulated?

The wear process can be modelled and simulated, with some restrictions. If we know the operating wear process, or how to model the wear process, we can also simulate and predict wear. In this presentation I will first outline how to use simplified estimations in machine design, and thereafter indicate how to perform more detailed wear simulations.

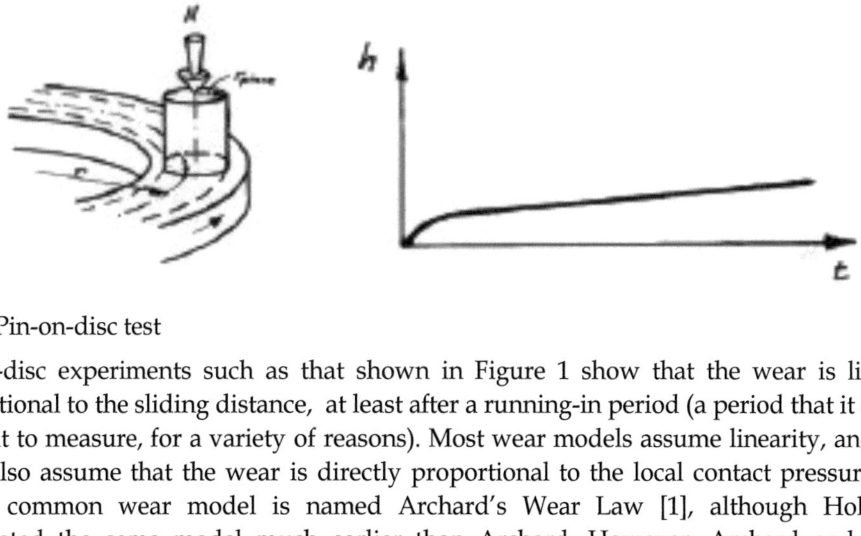


Fig. 1. Pin-on-disc test

Pin-on-disc experiments such as that shown in Figure 1 show that the wear is linearly proportional to the sliding distance, at least after a running-in period (a period that it can be difficult to measure, for a variety of reasons). Most wear models assume linearity, and they often also assume that the wear is directly proportional to the local contact pressure. The most common wear model is named Archard's Wear Law [1], although Holm [2] formulated the same model much earlier than Archard. However, Archard and Holm interpreted the model differently. The model has the following general form;

$$V = K \cdot \frac{F_N}{H} \cdot s \,, \tag{1}$$

where $V$ is the wear volume, $K$ is the dimensionless wear coefficient $F_N$, is the normal load, $H$ is the hardness of the softer contact surface and $s$ is the sliding distance. Equation (1) is often reformulated by dividing both sides by the apparent contact area $A$ and by replacing $K/H$ with $k$:

$$h = k \cdot p \cdot s \tag{2}$$

where $h$ is the wear depth in m, $k$ is the dimensional wear coefficient in $m^2/N$, $p$ is the contact pressure in Pa and $s$ is the sliding distance in m, as before. This wear model is widely used.

The wear coefficient is influenced by many factors, including whether the contact is mixed or boundary lubricated. Figure 2 shows how the dimensional wear coefficient depends on the lubricating conditions at the contact if the lubricant is clean. In many cases, however, the lubricant includes abrasive particles, which mean that even if the contact surfaces are well lubricated, they may become worn, as shown in figure 3. In such cases it is difficult to estimate the contact pressure, and so the wear assumption for abrasive contacts is often changed to state only that wear is proportional to sliding distance. The wear models in Figure. 3 are formulated as initial value wear models, as described later.

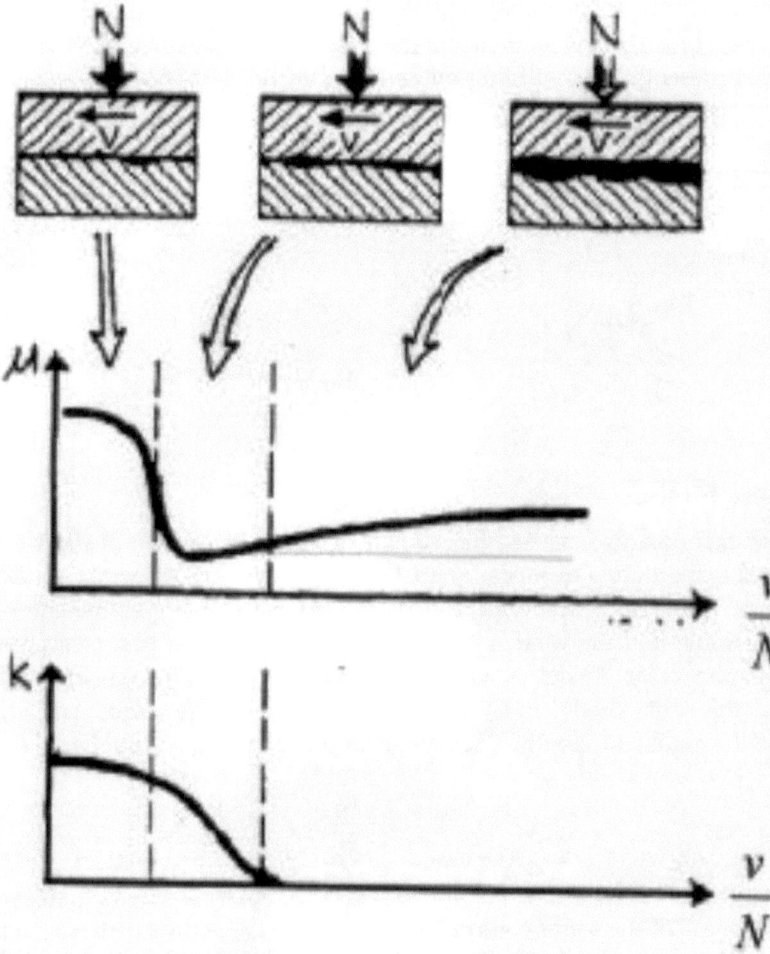


Fig. 2. The influence on the k-value of the lubrication conditions.

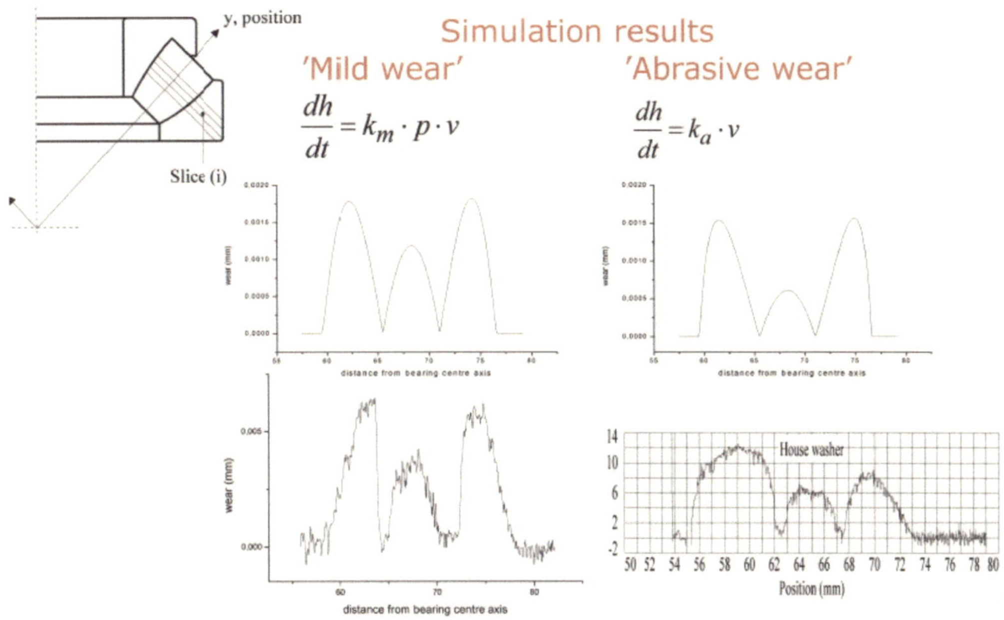


Fig. 3. Abrasive wear compared with mild sliding wear

The easiest and perhaps the most useful part of wear prediction is determining a good *k* value for a particular design. You can perform tests to determine this value, and compare the results with the estimated value. These estimates are based on the simple linear relation in equation (2) and involve a number of simplifications that vary from case to case. We also consult engineering handbooks and papers in international journals. Another way to approach this is by building up your own expert knowledge about typical *k* values based on previous estimates and experiments. This is what I have done for more than 10 years in industry. I have found that the best *k* value for dry contacts is about $1 \cdot 10^{-16}$ m²/N. This values applies to a very smooth hard surface against a dry, filled Teflon liner. It is often necessary to lubricate contacts in order to obtain a reasonable operating life. For boundary-lubricated case hardening contact surfaces running under mild conditions, the value may be $1 \cdot 10^{-18}$ m²/N. However, it is easy to get severe conditions in lubricated contacts, in which case the wear will increase about 100 times. In order to maintain mild conditions (i.e. to prevent transition to a severe situation), different types of nitrated surfaces are often used.

How can you ensure that the estimated *k* values are achieved in practice? Let's look at the example of a sliding journal bearing. You can perform a simple calculation of the *k* value needed to achieve a reasonably long operating life. If the value you calculate is between $1 \cdot 10^{-16}$ m²/N and $1 \cdot 10^{-18}$ m²/N, you know that wear conditions must be mild, and that you need to lubricate the contact with a clean lubricant to keep them that way. If the answer is less than $1 \cdot 10^{-18}$ m²/N, your task is challenging and you will need a separating film (full film lubrication) and a clean lubricant in order to be successful.

The approach I have just presented is a common way to predict whether a wear problem can be solved at the design stage, and is thus a very useful application of predictions or simulations. You can also carry out laboratory experiments to check your findings. However you should bear in mind that researchers often compare different materials and coatings

under harsh conditions, because mild wear takes too long to show. Consequently the results obtained are not very useful as a guide to wear under mild sliding conditions.
The above example shows you how it is possible to estimate wear during product development. This knowledge can be used to anticipate problems or design around them.
An expert in this field can usually suggest solutions to wear problems by doing simulations or estimations.
In the rest of this chapter, I will discuss more complex simulations and predictions of wear in high-performance machine elements.

## 2. Wear models and simulation methods

Wear can be defined as the removal of material from solid surfaces by mechanical action. Wear can appear in many ways, depending on the material of the interacting contact surfaces, the operating environment, and the running conditions. In engineering terms, wear is often classified as either mild or severe. Engineers strive for *mild wear*, which can be obtained by creating contact surfaces of appropriate form and topography. Choosing adequate materials and lubrication is necessary in order to obtain mild wear conditions. However, in order to get mild wear you often have to harden and lubricate the contacts in some way. Lubrication will often reduce wear, and give low friction. Mild wear results in smooth surfaces. *Severe wear* may occur sometimes, producing rough or scored surfaces which often will generate a rougher surface than the original surface. Severe wear can either be acceptable although rather extensive, but it can also be catastrophic which always is unacceptable. For example, severe wear may be found at the rail edges in curves on railways.
Mild and severe wear are distinguished in terms of the operating conditions, but different types of wear can be distinguished in terms of the fundamental wear mechanisms involved, such as. adhesive wear, abrasive wear, corrosive wear, and surface fatigue wear.
*Adhesive wear* occurs due to adhesive interactions between rubbing surfaces. It can also be referred to as scuffing, scoring, seizure, and galling, due to the appearance of the worn surfaces. Adhesive wear is often associated with severe wear, but is probably also involved in mild wear.
*Abrasive wear* occurs when a hard surface or hard particles plough a series of grooves in a softer surface. The wear particles generated by adhesive or corrosive mechanisms are often hard and will act as abrasive particles, wearing the contact surfaces as they move through the contact.
*Corrosive wear* occurs when the contact surfaces chemically react with the environment and form reaction layers on their surfaces, layers that will be worn off by the mechanical action of the interacting contact surfaces. The mild wear of metals is often thought to be of the corrosive type. Another corrosive type of wear is fretting, which is due to small oscillating motions in contacts. Corrosive wear generates small sometimes flake-like wear particles, which may be hard and abrasive.
*Surface fatigue wear,* which can be found in rolling contacts, appears as pits or flakes on the contact surfaces; in such wear, the surfaces become fatigued due to repeated high contact stresses.

### 2.1 Wear models

Wear simulations normally exclude surface fatigue and only deal with sliding wear, even if it seems unlikely that the sliding component is the only active mechanism. Yet rolling and sliding contacts are common in high performance machines. Thus the Machine Elements Department at KTH began to investigate whether sliding is actually the main source of wear in rolling and sliding contacts. We first studied this question in relation to gears, but have also simulated other contacts. In a rolling and sliding contact in a gear, the sliding distance per mesh is fairly short. The sliding distance of a contact point on a gear flank against the opposite flank is geometrically related to the different gear wheels and the load. In the first paper we published about wear in gears, we introduced what we called the 'single point observation method' [3] (explained in Fig. 5). We later found that this method is generally applicable, and have used it since then. You will now find the same principle being used under different names in other well-known papers, but we have chosen to stay with our original term.

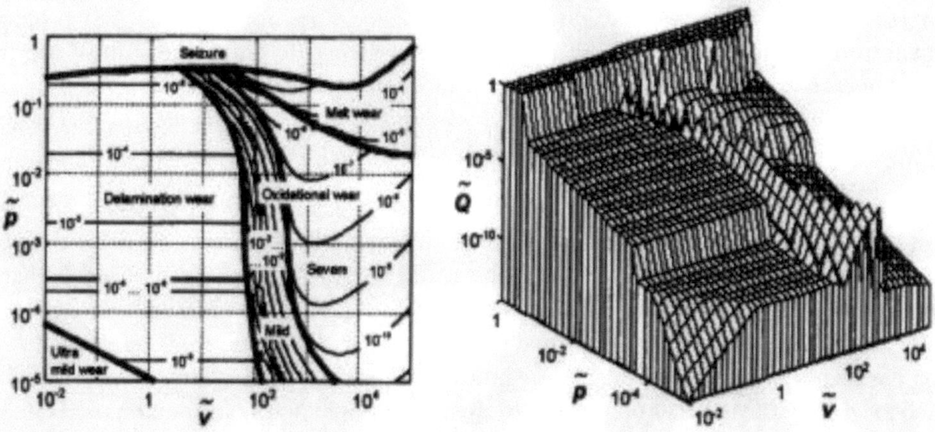


Fig. 4. a) Wear map according to Lim and Ashby [5] b) The same wear map according to Podra [20]

The possibility of predicting wear is often thought to be limited. Even so, many wear models [4] are found in the literature. These models are often simple ones describing a single friction and wear mechanism from a fundamental point of view, or empirical relationships fitted to particular test results. Most of them represent a mean value. The random characteristics of both friction and wear are seldom considered. In this chapter we present some of the models most used in simulations of wear in high performance machine elements.

Surfaces may wear if they rub against each other and are not completely separated by a clean oil film; they may also wear if the oil film separating them contains abrasive particles. The amount of wear is dependent on the properties of the surfaces, surface topography, and lubrication and running conditions. The best-known wear model is

$$\frac{V}{s} = K\frac{F_N}{H} \tag{3}$$

where $V$ is the wear volume, $s$ is the sliding distance, $K$ is the dimensionless wear coefficient, $H$ is the hardness of the softer contact surface, and $F_N$ is the normal load. This model is often referred to as Archard's Wear Law [1].

By dividing both sides of equation (3) by the apparent contact area, $A$, and by replacing $K/H$ with a dimensional wear coefficient, $k$, we get the following wear model:

$$\frac{h}{s} = k \cdot p \tag{4}$$

where $h$ is the wear depth and $p$ is the contact pressure.

Some scientists have tried to analyse the validity of the wear model according to equations (3) and (4), and one result of their work are wear maps or transition diagrams. The wear map of Lim and Ashby [5] (Fig. 4), shows two wear mechanisms: delamination wear and mild oxidational wear. Both these mechanisms are considered mild in engineering terms, and both produce thin, plate-like wear debris. Delamination wear theory, as developed by Suh [6], sets out to explain flake debris generation. Suh based his theory on the fact that there is a high density of dislocations beneath the contact surfaces. During sliding interactions between the contact surfaces, these dislocations form cracks that propagate parallel to the surfaces. The total wear volume is assumed to equal the sum of the wear volume of each contact surface. The basic wear model developed by Suh is:

$$V = N_1 \cdot \left(s/s_{01}\right) \cdot A_1 \cdot h_1 + N_2 \cdot \left(s/s_{02}\right) \cdot A_2 \cdot h_2 \tag{5}$$

where $V$ is the wear volume, $N_i$ is the number of wear sheets from surface $i$, $A_i$ is the average area of each sheet, $h_i$ is the thickness of the delaminated sheet, $s_{0i}$ is the necessary sliding distance to generate sheets and $s$ is the actual sliding distance. It is noticeable that the wear volume from each contact surface adds up the total wear volume, which was not clearly formulated before. Suh also stated that a certain sliding distance is required before a wear particle is formed. However, the sliding distance in his equation is equal for both surfaces, which indicates that he was not aware of the single point observation method.

Another interesting sliding wear mechanism is the oxidative wear mechanism proposed by Quinn [7], who stated that the interacting contact surfaces oxidize. The oxide layer will gradually grow until the thickness of the oxide film reaches a critical value, at which stage it will separate from the surface as wear debris. Even in this case a certain sliding distance is required before wear debris will be formed. Depending on whether the oxide growth is linear or parabolic, the wear is directly proportional to the sliding distance or to the power of the sliding distance. Experimental observations indicate that the wear is nearly directly proportional to the sliding distance under steady-state mild conditions.

Although Suh did not observe that the sliding distance points on the contact surfaces are different, the single point observation method has been found to be a very useful general method for understanding and modelling many friction and wear processes. This method was developed and successfully used in many projects at KTH Machine Design in Stockholm. The theoretical application of the method was based on formulas for the sliding distances in gears developed by Andersson [8]. He found that the distance traversed by a point on a gear flank against the opposing gear flank in one contact event varies depending on the position on the flank, the gear ratio, the size of the gears, and the loads applied to the gear tooth flanks. This finding about the sliding distance means that gear contacts cannot generally be replicated by rolling and sliding rollers. Simulations of the wear on gear flanks, based on sliding distance among other factors, has been validated by empirical measurements from gear tests. That observation and many years of pin-on-disc tests have inspired me and others to simulate friction and wear in rolling and sliding contacts of different types, and the results have been verified by experiments. This work has also improved our understanding of what occurs in contacts.

The single point observation method can be illustrated by the type of pin-on-disc experiment shown in Figure 1. A point on the pin contact surface is in contact all the time, but a contact point on the disc is only in contact with the pin when the pin passes that point. Even if the two contact surfaces have the same wear resistance, the pin will wear much more than the disc. Another illustration of the method is the two disc example shown in Fig. 5. The contact surfaces move with peripheral speeds of $v_1$ and $v_2$, with $v_1 > v_2$. We observe a point on surface 1, $P_1$, which has just entered the contact, and follow that point through the contact. We also note a point on surface 2, $P_2$ that is opposite the first observed point $P_1$ on surface 1 when it enters the contact. As $P_1$ moves through the contact, the interacting opposite surface will not move as fast as surface 1, since $v_1 > v_2$. A virtual distance $\Delta\delta_v = x \cdot (v_1 - v_2)/v_1$ in the tangential direction will occur between $P_1$, the observed point, and a point $P_2$. That distance is first compensated for by tangential elastic deformations of the contact surfaces $\Delta\delta_{el,1} + \Delta\delta_{el,2}$, but when that is no longer possible, the observed point will slide against the opposite surface for a distance $\Delta\delta_s$ equal to:

$$\Delta\delta_s = \Delta\delta_v - \Delta\delta_{el,1} - \Delta\delta_{el,2} \tag{5}$$

The frictional shear stress in the contact depends on the process, which means that at first it will be dependent mainly on elastic deformations. At higher torques or higher slip, the frictional shear stress will depend mainly on the sliding between the surfaces. Since these phenomena are always active in rolling and sliding contacts, it is interesting to analyse to what extent the stick zone, represented by the elastic deformation, influences the friction and wear in a contact. The results show that in many cases the effect of elastic deformation on friction and wear can be neglected.

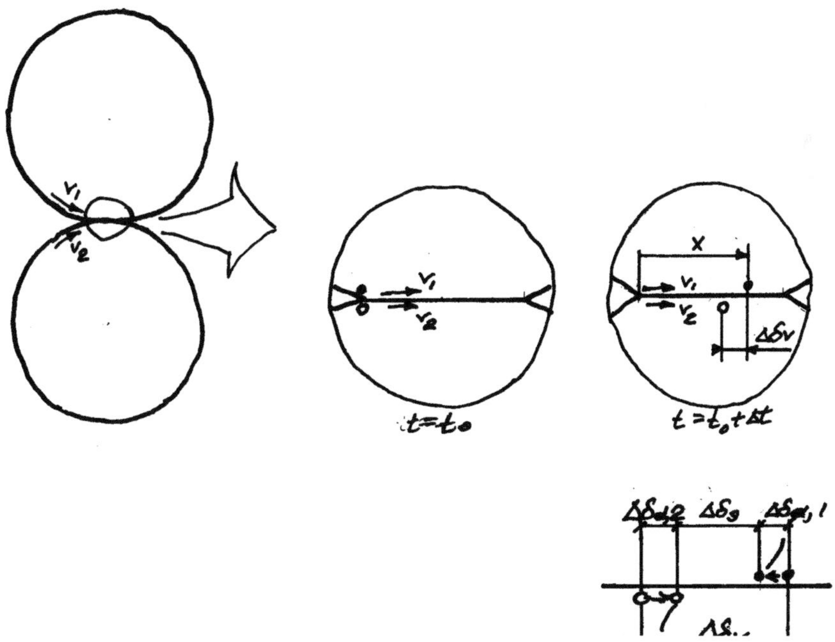


Fig. 5. Two discs: The basic principle for determining the sliding distance in a rolling and sliding contact

## 2.2 Wear maps and transition diagrams

As mentioned in the introduction, friction and wear can be of different types. It is thus helpful to know what types of friction and wear we can expect in a particular contact and when and why the transitions between different types occur. Some interesting research on that subject has been done, and continues to be done. I will briefly present some results from work on the transitions between different friction and wear modes. The relevant diagrams are often named wear maps or transition diagrams. The most referenced paper about wear maps is that by Lim and Ashby [5], (Fig. 4), who classified different wear mechanisms and corresponding wear models for dry sliding contacts. They studied the results of a large number of dry pin-on-disc experiments and developed a wear map, based on the parameters: $\tilde{Q} = \frac{V}{As}$, $\tilde{p} = \frac{F_N}{AH}$, and $\tilde{v} = \frac{vr_0}{a_0}$, where $V$ is the wear volume, $A$ is the apparent contact area, $F_N$ is the normal load, $H$ the hardness of the softer material in the contact, $v$ the sliding velocity, $r_0$ the radius of the pin, and $a_0$ is the thermal diffusivity of the material.

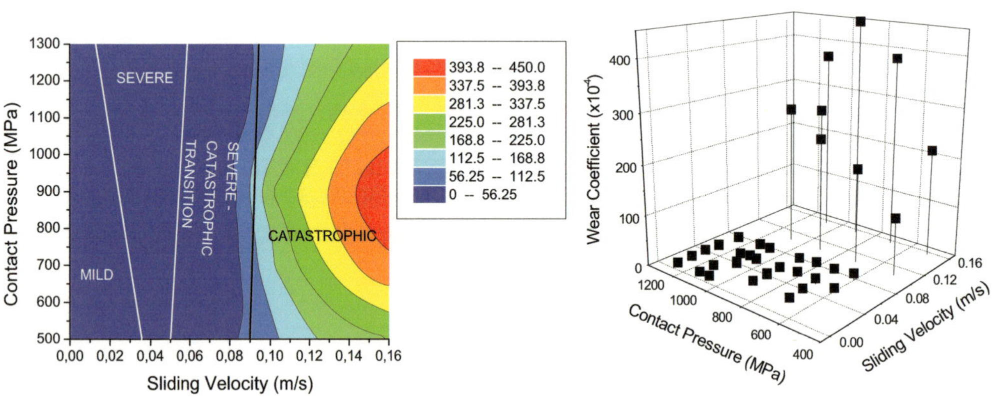


Fig. 6. Wear coefficient map according to Lewis and Olofsson [9].

Lewis and Olofsson [9] performed a similar investigation of contacts between railway wheels and tracks, Their goal was 'to produce tools in the form of maps of rail material wear data for identifying and displaying wear regimes and transitions'. They collected wear data from both laboratory and field tests, but found that data are often lacking for rail gauge and wheel flange contacts. They also collected available data and structured the data in different ways. Figure 6 shows an example of a wear coefficient map developed by Lewis and Olofsson [9]. The wear coefficient they used was determined using Archard's Wear Law.

Sundh [10] has also done considerable work on transitions in wheel/rail contacts. His goal is to construct wear maps that include the contact between rail gauge and wheel flange. An additional goal is to study how the transitions from mild to severe wear depend on different types of lubricants, surface coatings and topographies. He studies both dry and lubricated contacts.

For lubricated contacts, the degree to which a lubricant separates the surfaces very strongly influences both the friction and the wear. The degree of separation is often divided into boundary lubrication, mixed lubrication, and full-film lubrication (Fig. 2).

*Boundary lubrication* refers to lubrication in which the load is supported by the interacting surface asperities and the lubrication effect is mainly determined by the boundary properties of the lubricant between the interacting asperities. In *mixed lubrication,* the lubricant film itself supports some of the load in the contact, though the boundary properties of the lubricant are still important. In this case, the hydrodynamic and elastohydrodynamic effects are also important. Mixed lubrication is therefore sometimes referred to as partial lubrication or partial elastohydrodynamic lubrication (EHL). In *full-film lubrication,* the interacting contact surfaces are fully separated by a fluid film. In the literature, full-film lubrication is sometimes referred to as elastohydrodynamic lubrication, since the film-formation mechanism of high-performance contacts and local asperity contacts is probably elastohydrodynamic.

As mentioned in the introduction, transitioning from a desired mild situation to a severe situation should be avoided. Research has been performed to determine when and under what conditions transitions from one kind of friction and wear to another may occur in lubricated contacts. One such study developed what is called an IRG transition diagram [11] on which one can identify different lubrication regimes: a mixed or partial elastohydrodynamic lubrication regime, a boundary lubrication regime, and a failure regime. The last regime is sometimes called the scuffed or unlubricated regime and is a severe condition. The other regimes are mild.

The transition from a desired mild regime to a severe regime has also been studied by Andersson and Salas-Russo [12]. They used the track appearance as the transition criterion. When a significant part of the track is scored, seized or strongly plasticized, severe conditions are in effect. They found that for bearing steels the surface topography has a stronger influence on the mild to severe transition level than does the viscosity of the lubricant (Fig. 7). That was later confirmed by Dizdar [13].

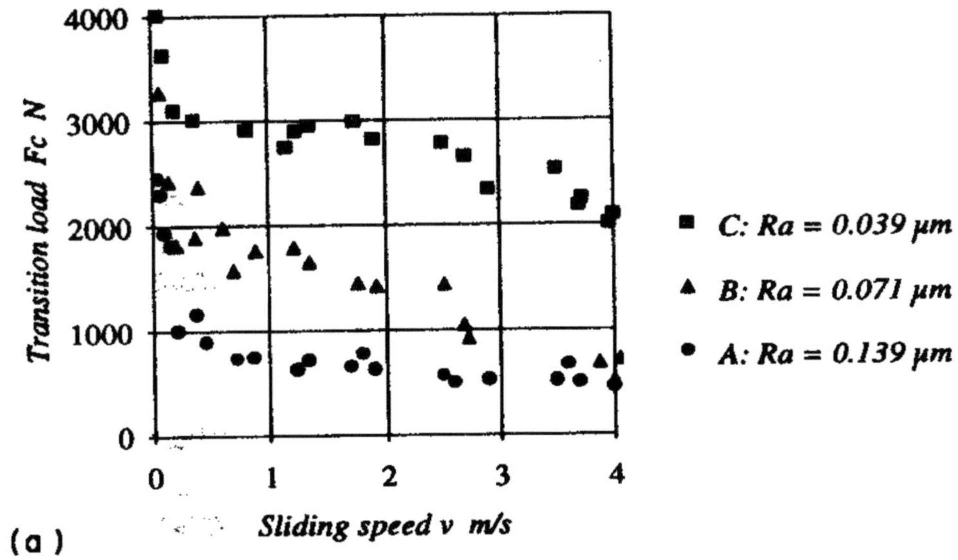


Fig. 7. The influence of surface roughness on the transition load of a lubricated sliding steel contact. Ball (d=10 mm) and disc material: SAE52100, $H_{v,ball}$ = 8000-8500 MPa, $H_{v,disc}$ = 5800-6300 MPa, $R_{a,ball}$ = 0.008$\mu$m . Lubricant: ISO VG 46 mineral oil. [12]

The Machine Elements Groups at KTH in Stockholm and at the Luleå Technical University in Luleå, along with a number of Swedish companies, have pursued a research program named INTERFACE. The goal of the program was to develop relevant friction and wear models for simulations in industry of different types of mechanical devices. The program was based on previous work by Sellgren [14], who developed general principles for modelling systems. His approach was modular, and laid down strict guidelines for behavioural models of machine elements, modules, and interfaces. Sellgren defined an interface as an attachment relation between two mating faces. That definition was elaborated on by Andersson and Sellgren [15] in terms of an interaction relation between two functional surfaces. A functional surface is a carrier of a function.

**2.3 Sliding wear in a rolling and sliding contact**

Predicting the amount of wear is generally thought to be rather difficult and uncertain. This section however addresses this task, outlining some possibilities for predicting wear in rolling and sliding contacts, and thus in the general case, the wear in most type of contacts. If the rolling and sliding contacts are running under boundary or mixed conditions, the wear of the contact surfaces is often low. If the surfaces are contaminated with particles, however, wear may be extensive. Different environmental contaminants may reduce or increase friction and wear, but they always have a strong influence on both.

In a rolling and sliding contact, the two interacting surfaces characteristically move at different speeds in a tangential direction. The Tribology Group at KTH Machine Design has performed simulations of friction and wear in rolling and sliding contacts for a long time. The modelling principles the group has successfully used are based on 1) the single-point observation method and 2) treating wear as an initial-value process.

Wear in rolling and sliding contacts can be of different types. If a surface is subject to high, repeated dynamic loading, surface fatigue may occur, and pits may form on the surface. Here, however, we will not deal with surface fatigue; instead, we will focus our attention on sliding wear. To illustrate the wear process, a typical wear curve obtained in a pin-on-disc testing machine using a flat-ended cylindrical pin rubbing against a disc under any condition is shown in Figure 8.

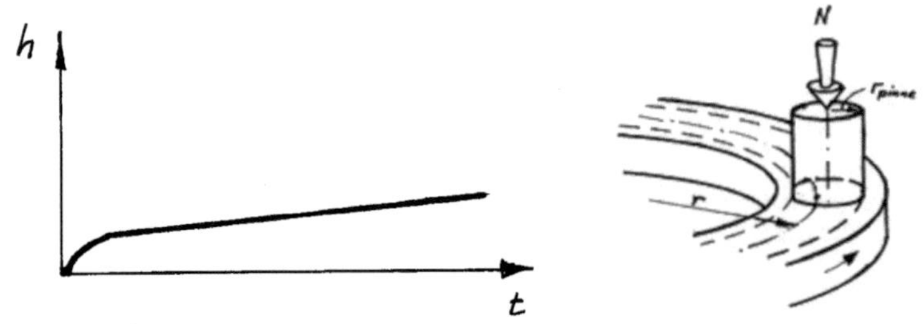


Fig. 8. A schematic wear curve from a pin-on-disc test with a flat ended cylindrical pin

A typical wear process always starts with a short running-in period during which the highest asperities and the contact surfaces in general are plastically deformed and worn; this is followed by a steady-state period in which the wear depth is directly proportional to the sliding distance. The initial running-in period is rather brief but not very well understood.

The general appearance of a wear curve seems to be similar for dry, boundary and mixed lubricated contacts, as well as for contacts with lubricants contaminated with abrasive particles. Aside from ease of testing, the pin-on-disc configuration is a popular testing geometry because most of the wear is on the pin. The distance a point on the pin's contact surface slides against the disc is much longer than the corresponding distance a contact point on the disc slides against the pin during a single revolution of the disc.

Simple pin-on-disc test results indicate that sliding distance is an important parameter determining sliding wear. For rolling and sliding contacts, the sliding part of the surface interactions, although not obvious, is therefore of interest. Some researchers maintain that the effect of sliding is negligible in most rolling and sliding contacts. Various investigations have demonstrated, however, that the distances the contacts slide against the opposite interacting surfaces during a mesh are sufficient to form wear debris in most rolling and sliding contacts. For this reason, we will show how much a point on a contact surface slides against an opposite contact surface during a mesh.

Consider two discs that are pressed together and run at different peripheral velocities (see Fig. 5 above). This is a typical situation in tractive rolling contacts. The absolute value of the sliding distance is $s_i$, with $i = 1$ a point on the contact surface of body 1 and $i = 2$ a point on the contact surface of body 2. The sliding distance, $s_i$, during one mesh at a point on one of the contact surfaces sliding against the opposite interacting surface is equal to

$$s_i = 2a \cdot \left| \frac{v_1 - v_2}{v_i} \right| \tag{6}$$

where $a$ is the half width of the contact, $v_1$ is the peripheral velocity of surface 1, and $v_2$ is the peripheral velocity of surface 2. The sliding distances in rolling and sliding contact according to Equation (6) apply to rollers.

For contacts between other bodies, such as gears and railway wheels and rails, determining the sliding distances may be more complicated. The principle, however, is the same, namely, to study the distance a point on a contact surface slides against the opposite surface during a single mesh.

In the examples shown, the elastic deformations of the contact surfaces in the tangential direction are ignored; those displacements would reduce the sliding distance a little, but micro-displacements normally have very little effect on the contact conditions.

### 2.4 Wear simulation

The single point observation method was initially found to be very useful during our work on simulating friction and wear of boundary-lubricated spur gears [3] as previously mentioned (Fig. 9). The distance a point on a gear flank slides against an opposite flank during one mesh varies depending on the position on the flank, the gear ratio, the size of the gears, and the loads applied on the gear tooth flanks. The principle for determining these sliding distances is shown in Fig. 9. In this figure the sliding distance is referred to as $g$, although $s$ is used elsewhere in this paper.

Test results obtained indicate that the amount of wear on the gear flanks seems to correlate with the sliding distances recorded. That observation and many years of pin-on-disc tests have inspired us to try to simulate sliding wear in rolling and sliding contacts. Our first effort was a simulation of the mild wear of gear tooth flanks under boundary-lubricated conditions [3] (Fig. 10). The first wear simulation was based on the wear model shown in Equation (4). The simulation was simplified by assuming that the wear coefficient was constant throughout the process, and the initial running-in period was not considered. The contact pressure between the flanks was assumed to be constant (i.e., the mean contact

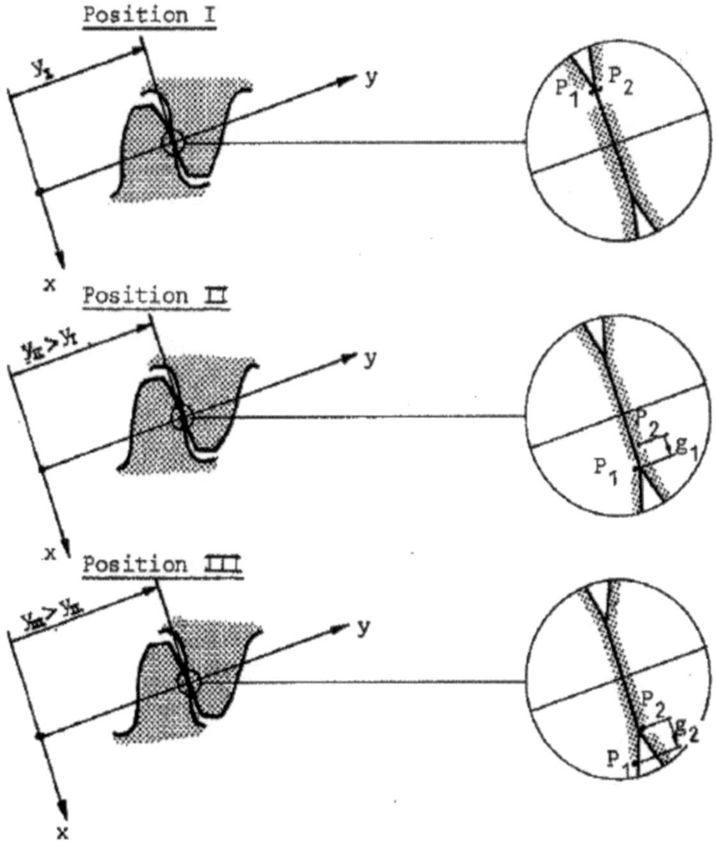


Fig. 9. The distance, $g_1$, point $P_1$ on the pinion flank and the distance, $g_2$, point $P_2$ on the gear flank slide during one mesh; position I corresponds to the moment in time when $P_1$ and $P_2$ come into contact with each other, while positions II and III correspond to the moments in time when $P_1$ and $P_2$ disengage, respectively. [8]

pressure was determined and used). This assumption is acceptable as long as the wear model is linear. Using these simplifications and the sliding distances determined according to derived equations, it was possible to simulate the wear depth at a particular point on a gear flank (the wear simulation was run as a simple spreadsheet program). The wear distribution and estimated wear coefficient were found to be in reasonably good agreement with the experimental observations. Our awareness of the risk that the basic principle and simplifications used in the model might only be relevant to this particular case motivated us to continue our research into simulating wear in rolling and sliding contacts. Further studies were successfully conducted to determine how generally applicable the principle and the simplifications are.

The principle when modelling the process is to start with the wear model, which is best formulated as a first order differential equation with respect to time, as shown below. If we use Euler's method to numerically integrate the equation, we have to determine the parameters for sliding speed and local contact pressure for all points on the contact surfaces at each time step. Determining the parameters is often rather time-consuming, and thus the integration and simulation also take time.

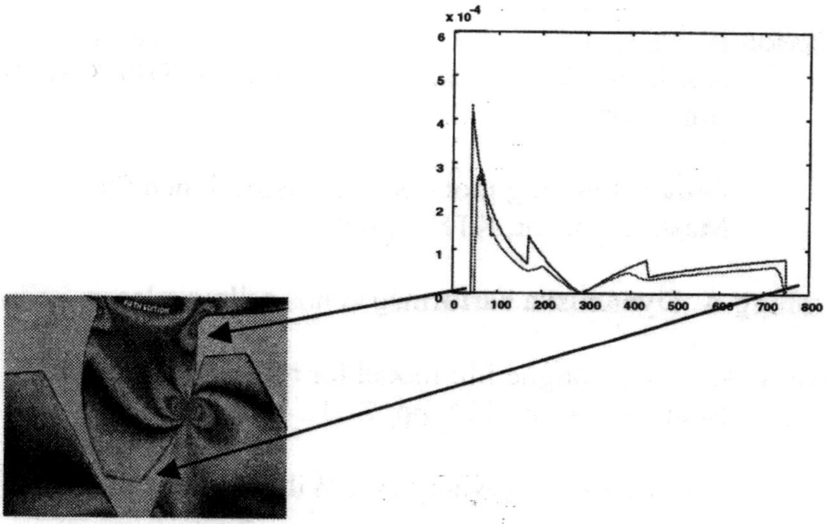


Fig. 10. Results of two simulations of a spur pinion. The sharp curves are from Anderssson and Eriksson [3] and the other is from Flodin [18].

### 2.5 Wear as an initial-value process

Wear is seldom a steady-state process, even if steady-state conditions are desirable and often predominate in the wear process. Normally, the running-in wear is greater than the ensuing wear. The forms of the contact surfaces are often such that the wear depth will vary with time. Moreover, mild wear of the contact surfaces causes geometric changes that initiate other wear processes. Olofsson [16], for example, found that mild wear of the contact surfaces of spherical thrust roller bearings increases the contact pressure at the pure rolling points. The increased contact pressure means that surface fatigue wear at the pure rolling points begins much earlier than expected.

As a direct result of that finding, and because wear simulations often contain many simplifications, we started to investigate wear simulations from a mathematical-numerical point of view. We found that simulations of wear processes can be regarded as initial-value problems [17]. We know the initial conditions and properties of the contacts fairly well, and if we can also formulate how the surfaces change, it should be possible to predict the states of the surfaces at any time during operation. The wear rate may then be formulated according to the following model:

$$\frac{dh}{dt} = f\left(\text{material,topography,lubricant,load,velocity,temperature, ........}\right) \tag{7}$$

where $h$ is the wear depth at a particular point on an interacting surface and $t$ is time. This formulation is in agreement with the dynamic behaviour of mechanical systems and can easily be numerically integrated. A model often used in many wear simulations is

$$\frac{dh}{dt} = k \cdot p \cdot v_s \tag{8}$$

where $v_s$ is the sliding velocity. The wear model in Equation (8) may be regarded as a generalization of Archard's wear law (see Eq. (3) and (4)).
Equation (8) is often reformulated as:

$$\frac{dh}{ds} = k \cdot p \tag{9}$$

since $ds = v_s dt$ is often true.

**2.6 Determination of the pressure distribution**

When working with the linear relation between wear, pressure and sliding distance, the determination of the contact pressure at a particular point is often the trickiest and most time-consuming part of the simulation. The deformation at a particular point is dependent on the deformation of all other points around the observed point, which implies a rather complex process for accurately calculating the pressure distribution. Today, there are several different approaches to determining the contact pressure.

Finite element (FE) calculation is becoming increasingly popular as computer power increases and FE programs improve. The main drawback of the FE method is that determining the pressure distribution often entails considering a great many small elements on the surfaces. This is often difficult to do, since the combination with the body models often leads to a huge number of elements and a very long calculation time. The FE method will probably be used more in the future for interface-related problems than it is today.

Boundary element (BE) methods are commonly used to determine the micro-topography in the contact zone. BE programs are often based on the same assumptions that Hertz used when he derived his equations. As a result, most BE programs cannot be used for all applications. The BE method becomes a numerical process that is solved in different ways in order to obtain a reasonably accurate result as quickly as possible [20,21]. Some smart combinations of BE and FE methods will probably be used in future.

Machine Elements in Luleå are using another very promising method to determine the contact deformation and the pressure distribution.

A common way to simplify the determination of local pressure is to use a Winkler surface model in which the surfaces are replaced by a set of elastic bars, the shear between the bars is neglected, and the contact pressure at a point depends only on the deformation at that point according to

$$p = K_N \cdot u_z \tag{10}$$

where $u_z$ is the deformation of the elastic rod. The spring constant, $K_N$, can be determined by

$$K_N = C_w \cdot \frac{E^{'}}{b} \tag{11}$$

where $C_w \approx 1$, $E'$ is the combined elastic modulus of the contact surfaces, and $b$ is approximately the width of the elastic half space according to Hertz. The Brush model is an extension of the Winkler model to take tangential deformations into account. The Brush model is often used for simulating friction in complex contacts.

The Winkler method cannot be used for local phenomena, but some reasonable results can be obtained for complete contacts.

### 2.7 Numerical integration of a wear model

Equation (8) is a commonly used in wear simulation. Numerically integrating a wear model entails discretising geometry and time. The simplest numerical integration method is the Euler method. The wear depth at a chosen point on a contact surface is determined by

$$h_{i,new} = h_{i,old} + k_i \cdot p_i \cdot |v_1 - v_2| \cdot \Delta t \tag{12}$$

where $h_{i,new}$ is the obtained wear depth on surface $i$, $h_{i,old}$ is the wear depth on $i$ in the previous simulation loop, $k_i$ is the dimensional wear coefficient multiplied by the number of meshes or revolutions before geometry is changed, $p_i$ is the local pressure at $i$ when the actual time step starts, and $\Delta t$ is the time step. Other numerical integration methods can, of course, be used in similar fashion, as different schemes are used in behavioural simulations of dynamic technical systems.

After a simulation, one must always check its accuracy. Common tests for doing so are the k and $\Delta t$ checks. However, if the values chosen for these are too large, the results may not be correct. A common way to handle this is to check whether the same results are obtained using half the values of k or $\Delta t$.

One of the most difficult and time-consuming parts of a simulation is determining the pressure at a particular point in each simulation loop because pressure at any point depends on the pressure at all other points in the contact.

## 3. Typical results and their applicability (KTH)

At the start of this chapter, I demonstrated a simple method of estimating wear for a new designs, and I have also dealt with the typical $k$ values for dry and boundary lubricated journal bearings. It is very important that anyone working in the field of tribology be able to make such estimates and understand their implications for the engineering design process.

At this point I will present some results of more accurate simulations of wear and their applicability. As previously mentioned, simulation of wear at KTH began with the simulation of mild wear in gears [3]. The process was programmed using a spreadsheet, since many simplifications were used. Later more accurate simulations of wear in gears were conducted by Flodin [18]. Figure 10 shows a comparison of the results obtained using the two methods to analyse wear in spur gears. Flodin also conducted experiments to correlate theoretical results with experimental results.

Not long after the initial gear wear simulation, a very difficult simulation of wear at the contact between a cam and a follower was performed by Hugnell et al. [19]. The contact is a rolling and sliding contact between the cam and the follower, which is rotating at the same time as it is moving. The result of a simulation is shown in Fig. 11.

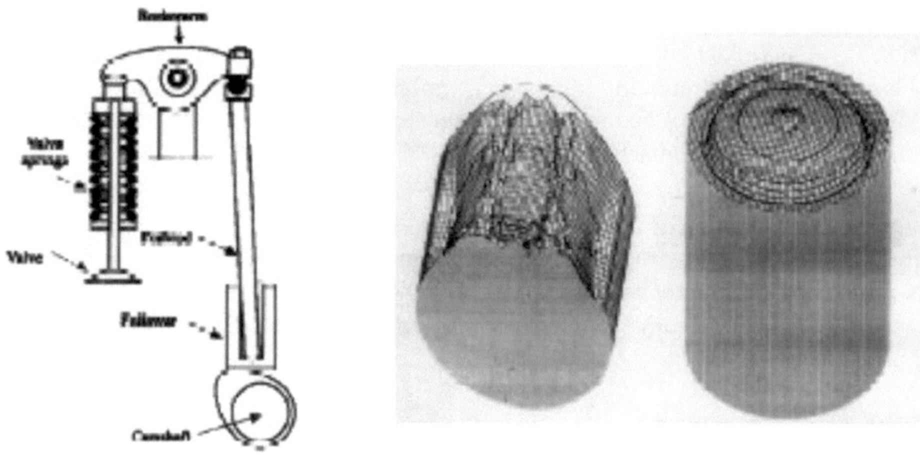

Fig. 11. Result of a wear simulation by Hugnell et al. [19]

### 3.1 Determining the wear of interacting rollers

We consider two cylindrical rollers both of radius $R$. The rollers are pressed together by force $F_N$ and rotate at angular velocities $\omega_1$ and $\omega_2$, respectively. The peripheral velocities of the contact surfaces are $v_1 = \omega_1 \cdot R$ and $v_2 = \omega_2 \cdot R$. The wear of the contact surfaces is assumed to be properly described by the following wear model:

$$\frac{dh_i}{dt} = k_i \cdot p \cdot v_{i,s}$$

where $i = 1$ for roller 1 and $i = 2$ for roller 2; $h_i$ is the wear depth at a point on surface $i$ when it rubs against the opposite contact surface, $k_i$ is the wear coefficient for a point on surface $i$ when it rubs against the opposite contact surface, $p$ is the local contact pressure, and $v_{s,i}$ is the sliding velocity at a point on surface $i$ sliding against the opposite interacting surface. The sliding velocity, $v_{s,i}$, for points on both contact surfaces equals

$$v_{s,i} = |v_1 - v_2|$$

We assume that the rollers are subject to a constant load and that the angular velocities are constant. The wear model will then have the following form after integration:

$$\int_0^{h_i} dh_i = k_i \cdot |v_1 - v_2| \int_0^t p dt$$

$$h_i = k_i \cdot |v_1 - v_2| \cdot \int_0^t p dt$$

If we study complete meshes, the contact pressure, $p$, can be replaced by the mean contact pressure, $p_m$. The wear depth is small compared with the radius of the rollers; $p_m$ can thus be determined once and used for all simulated revolutions. The integral equation can thus be reformulated according as follows:

$$h_{inew} = h_{iold} + k_i \cdot p_m \cdot |v_1 - v_2| \cdot \Delta t$$

If $\Delta t$ is very small, so that only one point on each of the contact surfaces passes the contact once, then the wear of each surface per mesh will be

$$h_{1/mesh} = k_1 \cdot p_m \cdot \frac{|v_1 - v_2|}{v_1} \cdot 2a$$

and

$$h_{2/mesh} = k_2 \cdot p_m \cdot \frac{|v_1 - v_2|}{v_2} \cdot 2a$$

respectively.

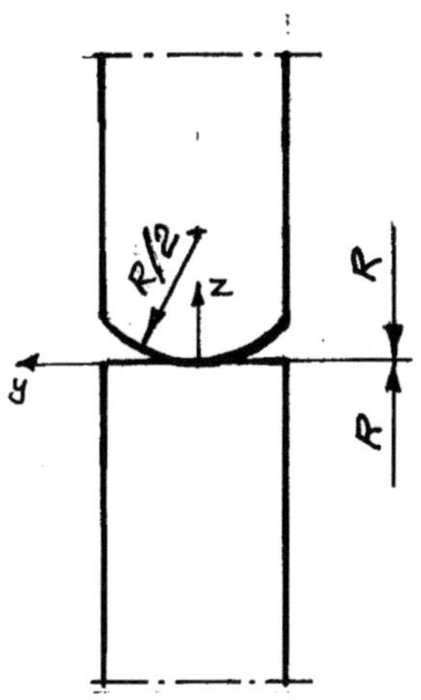


Fig. 12. Interacting modified roller and cylindrical roller

If surface 1 is moving faster than surface 2, in the long run points on surface 1 will be in contact more often than points on surface 2. Consequently, the wear of the two surfaces will only differ in relation to the wear coefficients. This can be demonstrated by the following relationships: Assume that the mechanism has been running for a fairly long time and that roller 1 has rotated $n_1$ revolutions. Roller 2 has then rotated $n_2 = n_1 \cdot (\omega_2/\omega_1)$ revolutions. The wear of the rollers will then be as follows:

$$h_{1/longtime} = k_1 \cdot p_m \cdot \frac{|v_1 - v_2|}{v_1} \cdot 2a \cdot n_1$$

$$h_{2/longtime} = k_2 \cdot p_m \cdot \frac{|v_1 - v_2|}{v_2} \cdot 2a \cdot n_2 = k_2 \cdot p_m \cdot \frac{|v_1 - v_2|}{v_2} \cdot 2a \cdot \frac{\omega_2}{\omega_1} \cdot n_1 = k_2 \cdot p_m \cdot \frac{|v_1 - v_2|}{v_1} \cdot 2a \cdot n_1$$

since $v_1 = \omega_1 \cdot R$ and $v_2 = \omega_2 \cdot R$.
From an experimental point of view, it is advantageous to change the form of roller 1 so that the contact surface will have a radius of R/2 perpendicular to the direction of motion of the

contact surface (Fig. 12). The contact will then be a point contact instead of a line contact as in the previous example. This change improves the experimental set-up, but unfortunately it makes the wear simulation more difficult. The assumption that the wear coefficients for points on each surface are constant throughout the whole process is, however, relevant even in this case. The sliding velocity can also be assumed to be constant. As in the previous example, the contact pressure variation at a point on a surface during a mesh can be replaced by a mean pressure. An important difference, however, is that the mean pressure does not remain constant throughout the whole wear process, since the wear of the contact surfaces will change the pressure distribution in the contact. We assume that the same wear model as in the previous example is valid in this case as well. The resulting equation, after considering the simplifications, will be as follows:

$$h_{i,new} - h_{i,old} = k_i \cdot p_m \cdot |v_1 - v_2| \cdot (t_{new} - t_{old})$$

When the contact surfaces wear, the forms of the surfaces will change and thus also the pressure distribution in the contact. This means that we cannot assume that the pressure is constant, so we cannot, as in the previous example, run a large number of revolutions in one simulation loop. Thus there are two questions in this case: determining the local pressure at a point in every simulation loop, and deciding on the duration of each loop before a new local pressure determination must be made.

In this case, we do not have a standard Hertzian contact case, so we make $b$ equal to the radius of a contact cylinder between the sphere of radius R/2 against a plane. A Winkler surface model of rod stiffness $K_N$ is used to simulate the wear process of a modified roller interacting with a cylindrical roller. The contact surfaces are divided into a number of slices of width $\Delta y = b/10$ perpendicular to the sliding direction (Fig. 13). We assume that we can simplify the wear simulation by determining the wear for each slice in the same way as before. The penetration, $d$, of the modified upper roller against the lower cylindrical roller is determined so that the sum of the load of each slice support equals the applied force, $F_N$. The local wear can now be determined and the geometry of the contact surfaces modified. Thereafter, a new penetration, $d$, is determined, and so on. Figure 14 presents some simulation results for a modified upper roller interacting with a cylindrical roller. The rollers will wear while running. The wear of the discs will increase in both depth and width with time (see Fig. 14).

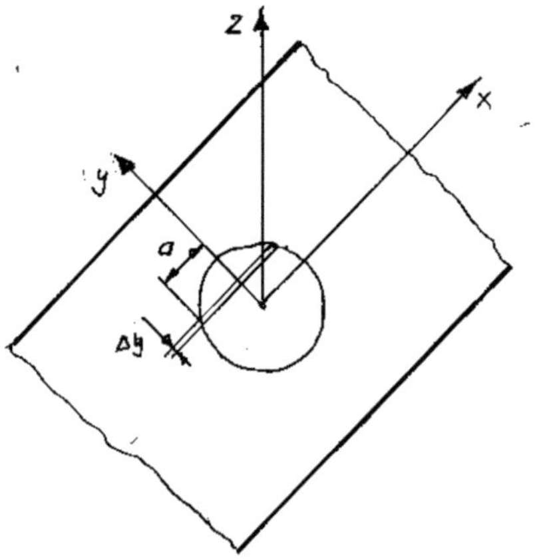


Fig. 13. Contact point and coordinate system, sliced contact

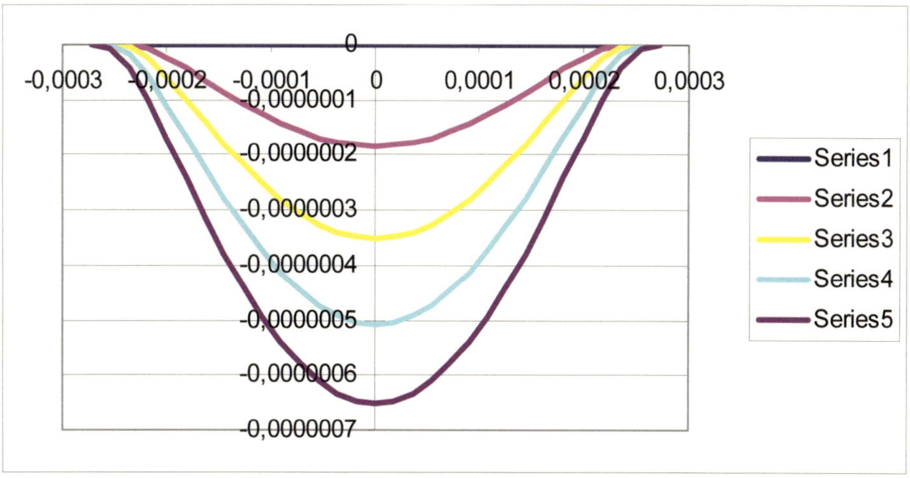


Fig. 14. Simulated wear of an ellipsoidal roller 1 interacting with a cylindrical roller 2. $R_{1x}$ = $25{\cdot}10^{-3}$ m, $R_{1y}$=$12.5{\cdot}10^{-3}$m, $R_{2x}$= $25{\cdot}10^{-3}$m, $F_N$=100N, $v_1$=1.25 m/ s, $v_1 - v_2$= 0.06 m/ s. Series 1 is at t=0, Series 2 is after n revolutions, Series 3 is after 2n rev. , Series 4 is after $3n$ rev. and series 5 is after $4n$ rev.. The figure shows the change in shape of the contact surface of the rollers during running.

### 3.2 Concluding remarks

The wear of rolling and sliding contacts can be simulated. The basic principles to be remembered are 1) use the single point observation method and 2) treat the wear process as an initial-value problem. Using these principles, nearly any practical case can be simulated if you have a relevant wear model that can imitate the behaviour of a particular case. The most common wear model is the one known as Archard's generalized wear model:

$$\frac{dh}{dt} = k \cdot p \cdot v_s$$

How well that model describes the wear process is still being investigated. In many cases, however, simulated wear distributions agree fairly well with experimental observations. Wear simulations are quite often done stepwise, with repeated determinations of pressure, sliding velocities, etc. Determining the pressure distribution in the contact is often considered the most difficult and time-consuming task, and thus much effort is put into the task. Most simulations are done numerically, so choosing the appropriate surface element size and time step is critical. Too long a time step may produce incorrect results or an unstable simulation, while too short a time step, on the other hand, may result in excessive computation time. I believe that the main research tasks in the near future will be to develop relevant wear models accommodating transitions and choice of time step size, and the determination of pressure distributions.

### 3.3 Some examples from KTH

The three examples shown previously are results from the author and Hugnell et al. [19]. Flodin [18] results from the author, Hugnell et.al. [19] and Flodin [18]. Figure 15 shows some of the results obtained by Flodin [18]. Figure 15 shows some of the results obtained.

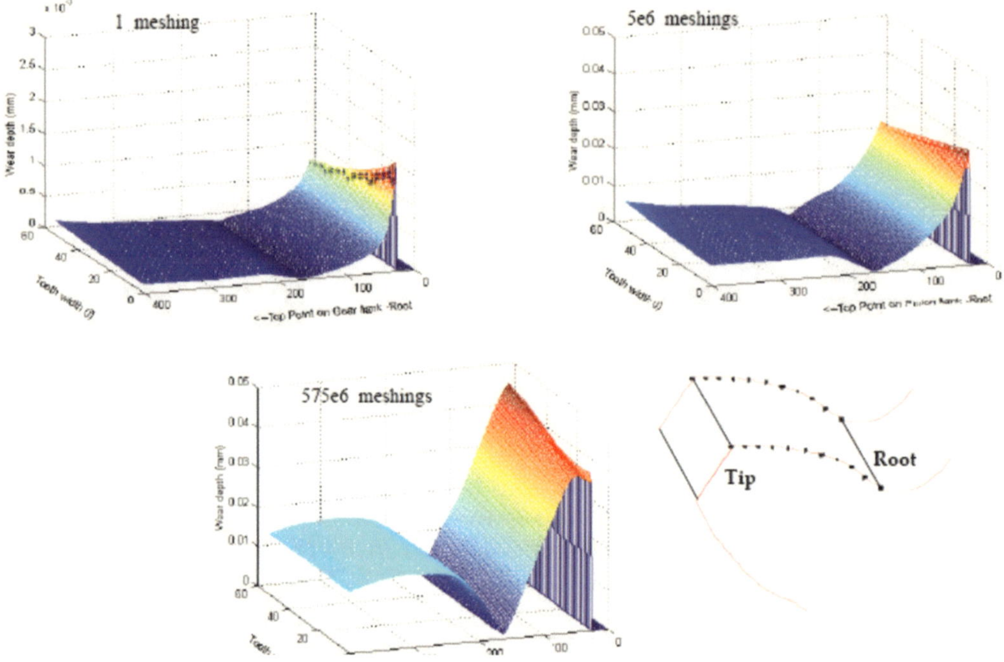


Fig. 15. Wear simulation results obtained by Flodin [18]

The programs Flodin developed were used by MacAldener [21] in his investigation of the influence of wear on judgements of the manufacturing robustness of gears.

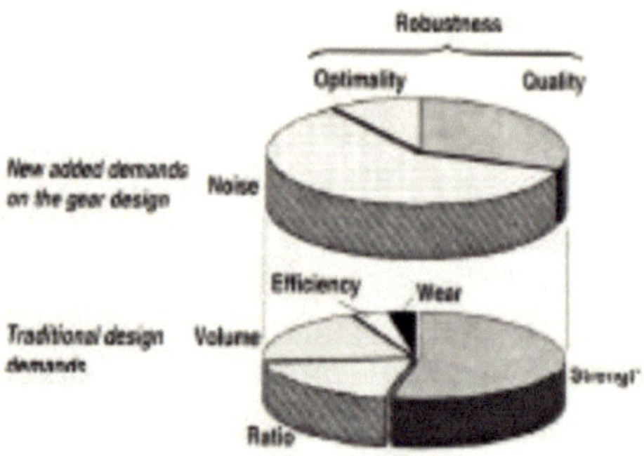


Fig. 16. The demands on a new gear developer and manufacturer [21]

Spiegelberg [23] performed some wear simulations of a rolling and sliding contact in an engine mechanism. His results can be used in different ways depending on the running conditions in the contact.

Another interesting application of work done at KTH is that of Åkerblom [22] who used the knowledge developed within the INTERFACE project. He found that the preset loading of bearings strongly influences noise excitation from a gearbox. The influence seems to be stronger than the effect of transmission error.

Podra [20] performed the first FE wear simulation. Söderberg [24] recently simulated wear in disc brakes using FE.

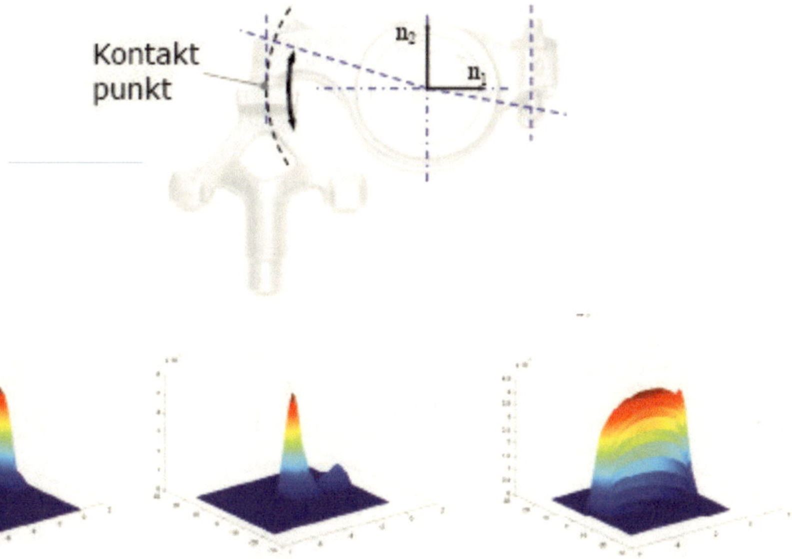


Fig. 17. Some wear simulation results obtained by Spiegelberg [23]

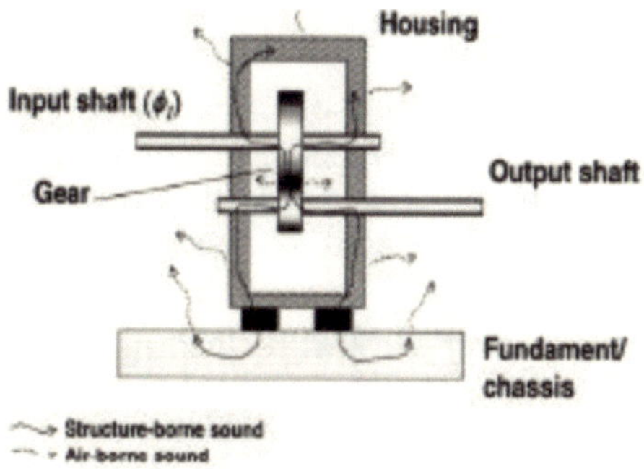


Fig. 18. Noise excitation from a gearbox [22]

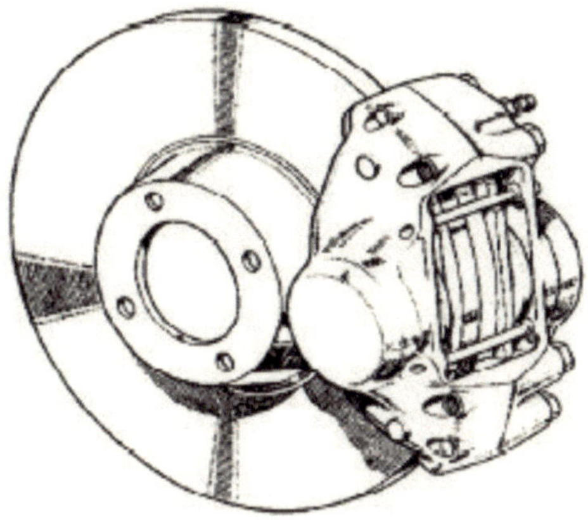

Fig. 19. The disc brake subjected to wear simulations by Söderberg [24]

## 4. References


[1] Archard, J.F. (1980) Wear theory and mechanisms. In: M.B. Peterson, W.O. Winer (eds.). *Wear Control Handbook*. ASME.

[2] Holm, R. (1946) *Electric Contacts*. Almqvist & Wiksells Boktryckeri AB, Uppsala.

[3] Andersson, S. and Eriksson, B. (1990) Prediction of the sliding wear of spur gears. *Nordtrib'90*, Hirtshals, Denmark.

[4] Meng, H.-C. (1994) Wear modeling: Evaluation and categorization of wear. Dissertation, University of Michigan.

[5] Lim, S.C. and Ashby, M.F. (1987) Wear mechanism maps. *Acta Metal.*, 35(1), pp. 1–24.

[6] Suh, N.P. (1973) The delamination theory of wear, *Wear*, 25, pp. 111–124.

[7] Quinn, T.F.J. (1962) Role of oxidation in the mild wear of steel. *British Journal of Applied Physics*, 13, pp. 33–37.

[8] Andersson, S. (1975) Partial EHD theory and initial wear of gears. Doctoral thesis, Department of Machine Elements, KTH, Stockholm, Sweden.

[9] Lewis R. and Olofsson, U. (2004) Mapping rail wear regimes and transitions. *Wear*, 257, pp. 721-729.

[10] Sundh, J. (2009) On wear transformations in the wheel-rail contact. Doctoral thesis, Dept. of Machine Design, KTH.

[11] Begelinger, A. and DeGee, A.W.J. (1981) Failure of thin film lubrication. *ASME J. Lubrication Techn.*, 103.

[12] Andersson, S. and Salas-Russo, E. (1994) The influence of surface roughness and oil viscosity on the transition in mixed lubricated sliding contacts. *Wear*, 174, pp. 71–79.

[13] Dizdar, S. (1999) Formation and failure of chemireacted boundary layers in lubricated steel contacts. Doctoral thesis. Dept. of Machine Design, KTH.

[14] Sellgren, U. (2003). Architecting models of technical systems for non-routine simulations. International Conference on Engineering Design, ICED 03, Stockholm, August 19-21.

[15] Andersson, S. and Sellgren, U. (2004) Representation and use of functional surfaces. 7$^{th}$ Workshop on Product Structuring-Product Platform Development, Chalmers University of Technology, Gothenburg, March 24-25.

[16] Olofsson, U. (1997) Characterisation of wear in boundary lubricated spherical roller thrust bearings, *Wear*, 208, pp. 194–203.

[17] Strang, G. (1986) *Introduction to Applied Mathematics*. Wellesley-Cambridge Press. ISBN 0-9614088-0-4.

[18] Flodin, A. (2000) Wear of spur and helical gears. Doctoral thesis, Dept of Machine Design, KTH.

[19] Hugnell, A., Björklund, S. and Andersson, S. (1996) Simulation of the mild wear in a cam-follower contact with follower rotation. *Wear*, 199, pp. 202-210.

[20] Podra, P. (1997) FE wear simulation of sliding contacts. Doctoral thesis, Dept. of Machine Design, KTH.

[21] MacAldener, M. (2001) Tooth interior fatigue fracture and robustness of gears. Doctoral thesis, Dept. of Machine Design, KTH.

[22] Åkerblom, M. (2008) Gearbox noise. Doctoral thesis, Dept. of Machine Design, KTH.

[23] Spiegelberg, C. (2005) Friction and wear in rolling and sliding contacts. Doctoral thesis, Dept. of Machine Design, KTH.

[24] Söderberg, A. (2009) Interface modelling: friction and wear. Doctoral thesis, Dept. of Machine Design, KTH.

3

# On-line Optodynamic Monitoring of Laser Materials Processing

Janez Diaci and Janez Možina
*University of Ljubljana, Faculty of Mechanical Engineering*
*Slovenia*

## 1. Introduction

A new term "optodynamics" has been introduced to describe a wide range of optically induced dynamic phenomena (Možina & Hrovatin, 1996). A laser pulse is considered not only as a tool in laser material processing but also as a generator of information about the material transformation. The information is retained and conveyed by different kinds of optically induced mechanical waves generated during laser material interaction. Several generation/detection schemes have been developed to extract this information especially in the field of non-destructive material evaluation (laser ultrasonics). In a wider aspect these techniques can be used for optodynamic monitoring and characterization of laser cutting, drilling, welding and other laser material processing methods.

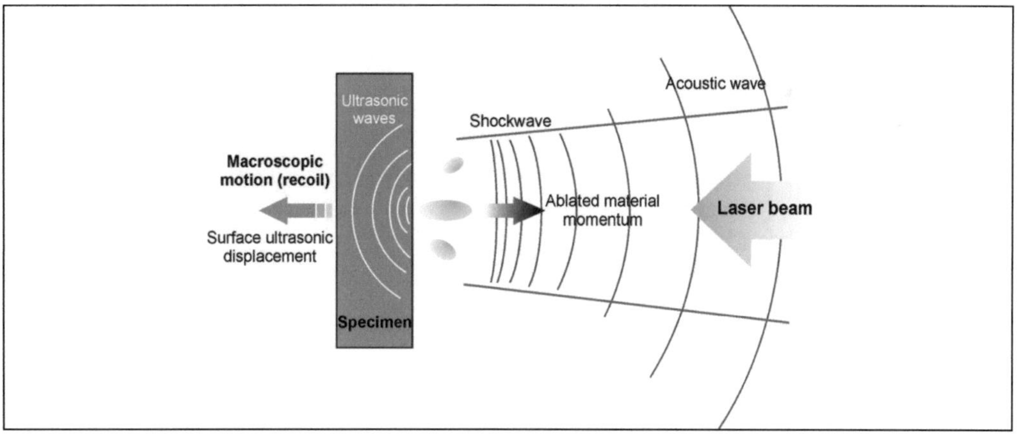


Fig. 1. Optodynamic phenomena during laser material interaction

Fig. 1 shows a schematic of optodynamic (OD) phenomena that occur during pulsed laser - material interaction. Material irradiated by short laser pulses becomes rapidly locally overheated. Its temperature may exceed vaporization temperature, the mixture of vapor and surrounding gas may become ionized forming a plasma cloud above the irradiated surface. This local thermal nonequilibrium relaxes through emission of light, heat conduction and various forms of macroscopic material motion, e.g. mechanical waves that propagate through the workpiece and the surrounding gas. Blast and acoustic waves, which propagate in air surrounding the workpiece, have been studied using microphone detection as well as various set-ups of the laser beam deflection probe (LBDP). These techniques provide time resolved information at certain points in space. Various fast imaging techniques have been used on the other hand to acquire spatially resolved information at certain points in time. Ultrasonic waves propagating through the workpiece have been studied using piezoelectric transducers and laser interferometers.

In the first part of this chapter we present various OD detection methods which have been developed during our research work in this field in recent years. In the subsequent part we discuss applications of these methods in particular laser processing applications focusing on the ones that exhibit the potential for on-line process monitoring.

## 2. Optodynamic detection

### 2.1 OD waves in air

Suitable detection methods represent one of the foundations of on-line process monitoring methods. When it comes to detection of sonic waves in air, the microphone comes forward as an almost obvious choice. It is widely available, the technology is mature and well understood, it has high sensitivity, it is simple to set-up and use, all of which are important advantages from the viewpoint of a potential application. It does, however, suffer from serious drawbacks in terms of detection bandwidth and dynamic range which are needed when very short acoustic and blast waves of high amplitude are to be detected, a quite common requirement in pulsed laser process monitoring.

The LBDP is a newer technique that allows non-contact, high bandwidth detection of high amplitude waves close to the processing spot. We hypothesize that the signal detected in that region contains more information about the process than the signals detected in the far-field region. Fig. 2 shows a schematic of a typical LBDP set-up employed to study OD phenomena during pulsed laser processing (Diaci & Možina, 1994).

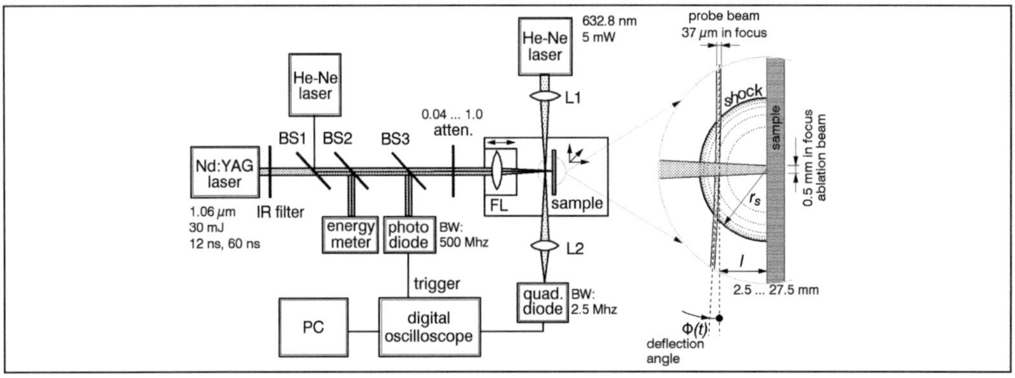


Fig. 2. A typical LBDP set-up

We ablate the samples by a Q-switched Nd:YAG laser with the beam focused to a spot of 0.5 mm in diameter on the ablated surface (Fig. 2). The sample assembly and the focusing lens are mounted together on a mechanical translator allowing precise setting of the distance $r_s$ while maintaining constant focusation of the ablation beam. Nearly spherical blast waves are generated by the ablation laser pulse and propagated in air. A He-Ne laser is used as a source of the probe beam, aligned parallel to the irradiated surface and perpendicular to the ablation beam. Refractive index gradients that exist within the region encompassed by the blast wave due to density gradients cause transient deflection of the probe beam. We detect this deflection by means of a quadrant photodetector with a 2.5 MHz bandwidth. Alternative detection method by a knife edge and a photodiode can also be used (Diaci & Možina, 1992), especially if a high-speed quadrant photodetector is not available.

The two discussed OD detection methods (microphone and LBDP) have their own strengths and weaknesses. To examine them in a quantitative way we conducted a comparative study of the two detection systems (Diaci & Možina, 1992). We have examined blast waves generated in air during laser ablation of absorbing samples with Nd:YAG laser pulses. Blast waves were detected simultaneously by a wideband microphone and a LBDP set-up. In order to explain the experimental data we employed the weak shock solution of the point explosion model. The blast energy of each signal was determined, using measured wavefront transition times and the theoretical shock trajectory. Comparing detected signals with the corresponding theoretical pressure waveforms in the time and frequency domain, we found good agreement on several waveform evolution features. A further proof of the adequacy of the adopted model was obtained by examination of response functions, determined by applying deconvolution to measured signals and the corresponding theoretical pressure waveforms. With both detection systems we found that response functions, obtained from quite different signals, matched very well. In addition, the microphone transfer function agreed with the calibration data supplied by the manufacturer.

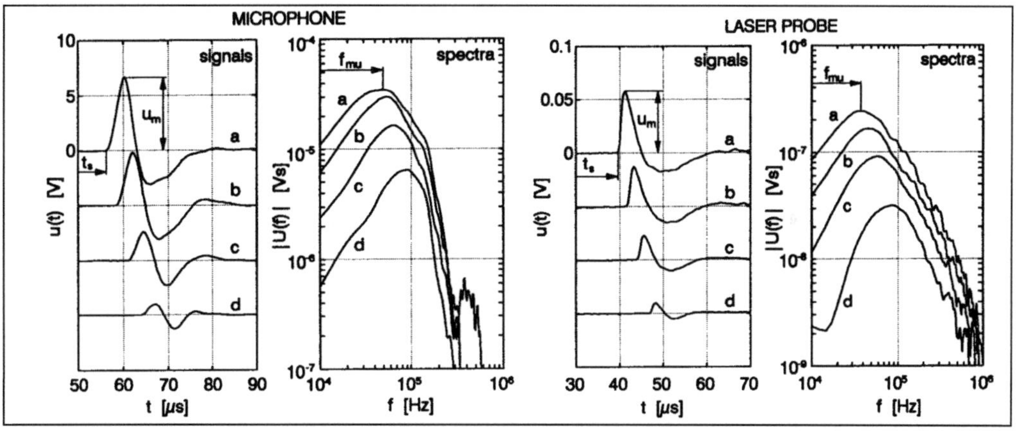


Fig. 3. A comparison of microphone (left) and LBDP (right) OD signals and their spectra. Reprinted from (Diaci & Možina, 1992) with kind permission from Springer Science+Business Media

We find the microphone somewhat easier to use, but the performance of the laser probe could be improved in this respect by building it as a compact instrument. With the laser probe, all the important performance parameters (bandwidth, dynamic range, sensitivity) can be changed and adapted optimally to a particular experimental situation, while with the microphone they are fixed. We therefore consider the laser probe as a more versatile tool for studying laser generated blast waves.

Most beam deflection studies employ a relatively simple arrangement where the probe beam interacts with the wave only once. Much more information about the wave field, however, can be gained by using an arrangement where the beam interacts with the wave field several times. For this purpose we have developed a novel "multiple-pass" LBDP arrangement for detection of acoustic and weak shock waves in fluids (Diaci & Možina, 1995). The probe beam is folded by two parallel plane mirrors in such a way that the probe beam passes the wave propagation region several times before it reaches the deflection-detecting photodetector (Fig. 4 - left). In this way the probed wave interacts with several segments of the probing beam in sequence. A single oscilloscope trace of the photodetector output thus opens the possibility to study the evolution of the probed wave at several distances from the source. A large number (40 at present) of reflections is possible which can be altered easily by changing the angle of incidence. To demonstrate the potentials of the arrangement we present waveforms of spherical blast waves detected in air during laser ablation of solid samples (Fig. 4 - right). Two variants of the folded arrangement were examined. The one with the probe beam traveling from the laser to the detector in a zigzag path in the same direction as the acoustic wave we call the "co-directional" arrangement while the other one where the two directions are opposite we label the "counter-directional" one. We have developed a theoretical model that qualitatively explains the most characteristic features of both arrangements. The counter-directional arrangement exhibits low sensitivity for strong signals and high sensitivity for weak signals, a property which is very convenient in many cases. Measurement of time delays between successive pulses, for example, is much easier and more precise when the successive pulses have equal amplitudes. The other advantage is a clear visualization of the evolution of wave forms.

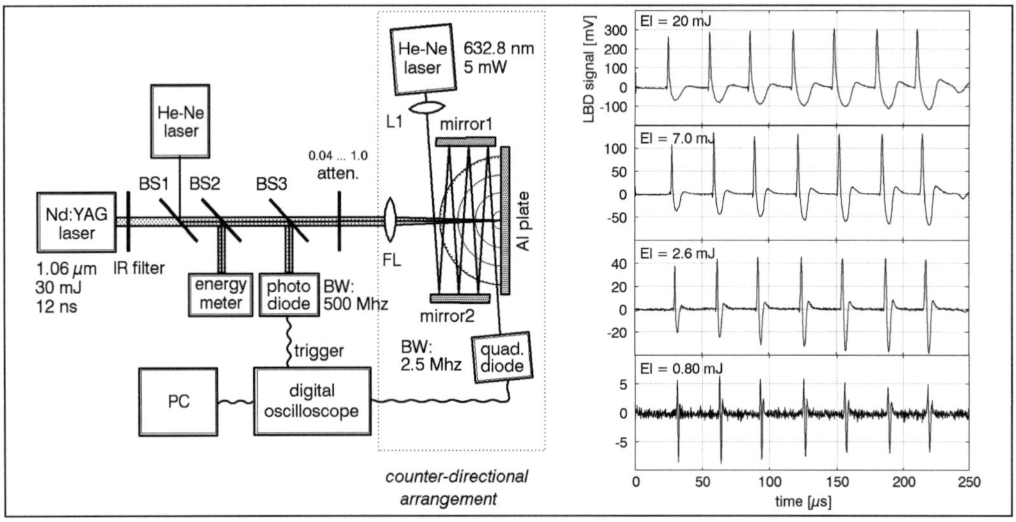


Fig. 4. Multiple-pass LBDP in a counter-directional arrangement (left) and the corresponding detected signals (right). Reprinted from (Diaci & Možina, 1995) with kind permission from American Institute of Physics

While microphone and LBDP provide time resolved information at certain points in space, various fast imaging techniques have been developed to acquire spatially resolved information at certain points in time. As these two approaches are single-pointed in one domain, a problem arises if the space-time evolution of the event needs to be assessed. With the techniques referred to above it is still possible to average by repeating the measurement and varying the single-pointed parameter. However, to obtain meaningful results in such a case, the phenomenon under study has to be reasonably reproducible. We have developed a

set-up employing two complementary techniques that allows monitoring the spatial and temporal evolution of non-reproducible optodynamic events (Diaci et al., 1996). A high-speed cineholography system provides a sequence of spatially resolved information (8 holograms separated by 28 ns) while a beam deflection probe provides temporally resolved information at 6 discrete spatial points over a 4.5 mm distance above the target.
A schematic of the key part of the combined system is shown in Fig. 5. The holographic recording beams (Fig. 5 – top view) were generated by a high-power frequency-doubled Q-switched Nd:YAG laser. Its output beam was directed into a phase-front-preserving optical delay line. A specially made step-graded beam splitter allowed light to exit the cell in the form of 8 beams of equal energy. Each output beam from the delay line was split into object and reference beams. The object beams were arranged so that lay on a plane parallel to the ablated surface and that each interrogated the test volume at a slightly different angle. The object beams were then combined with the corresponding reference beams at the film plane. As a result of the beam diameter at the film plate and the angular separation between beams, the holographic images were spatially and angularly multiplexed. The second technique was a multiple-pass LBPD, similar to the one described above. A He-Ne probe beam was directed into the test volume where it passed six times between two parallel silver mirrors, separated by 20 mm, in a plane perpendicular to the ablated surface (Fig. 1 – side view). A long focal length lens was used to focus the probe beam to a 0.3 mm waist located within the test volume. In this way the segments of the beam that interacted with the shock lay in the Rayleigh range of the beam.

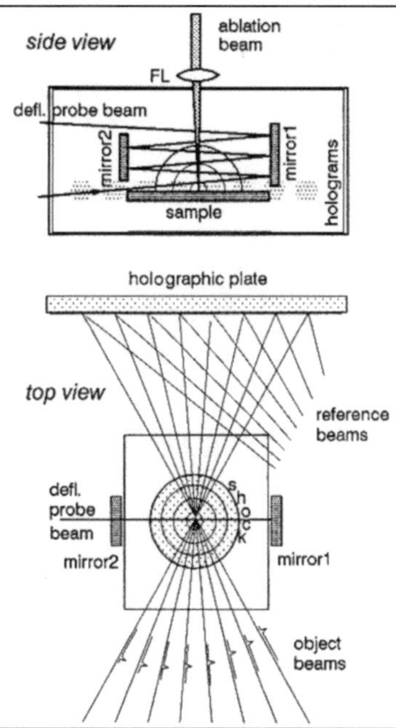


Fig. 5. A set-up for simultaneous detection of shock waves by a high-speed cineholography system and a multiple-pass LBDP. Reprinted from (Diaci et al., 1996) with kind permission from Elsevier

These techniques have been applied to investigate the shock dynamics resulting from the laser ablation of metallic samples. With the holographic set-up we examined the early period of shock evolution (the strong shock region) and with the beam deflection probe the subsequent transition through the intermediate into the weak shock range. By combining the two techniques we were able to examine a fairly broad range of the shock lifetime in time and space domain.

The described holographic set-up is rather complex and difficult to set-up. We have subsequently developed a much simpler method which can provide quite similar results (Perhavec & Diaci, 2010). A novel double-exposure shadowgraph method allows visualization of an expanding shock wave in two time instances on a single image. The shock wave is illuminated by pulsed green laser light coupled into two optical fibers (Fig. 6) of different lengths to establish two illumination flashes separated by a fixed time delay. An image of the shock wave region, acquired by a digital still camera, exhibits two well separated shock wavefronts. The optical set-up was analyzed using a paraxial ray model to explain the observed eccentricity of the two acquired wavefronts and provide guidelines for assembling the set-up. The method has been developed to study shock waves generated in air during interaction of Er:YAG laser light with water and biological tissues.

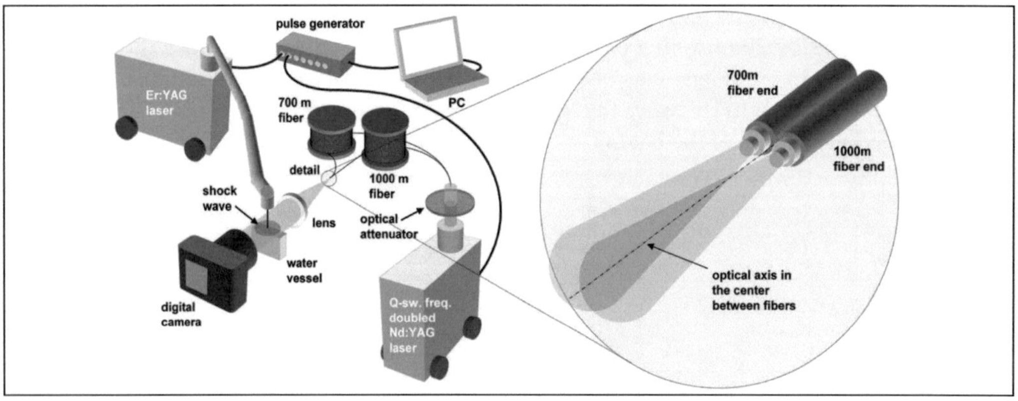


Fig. 6. A novel double-exposure shadowgraph set-up. Reprinted from (Perhavec & Diaci, 2010) with kind permission from Strojniški vestnik – Journal of Mechanical Engineering

### 2.2 OD waves in the workpiece

OD waves propagating through the workpiece have been studied using piezoelectric transducers and laser interferometers.

A arm compensated Michelson interferometer has been developed to study the laser ablation process from a novel, optodynamic aspect (Hrovatin & Možina, 1995). Fig. 7 shows the schematic of the set-up. The beam from a He-Ne laser is split into the reference and measurement arm. The reference beam is reflected from a mirror mounted on a piezoelectric device driven by a low frequency stabilizer circuit to maintain the optimum optical path difference. The detected signals are amplified and digitized by a sampling oscilloscope. The interferometer detects normal ultrasonic displacements with bandwidth between 150 kHz and 60 MHz, governed by the amplifier. The sensitivity in the linear part of the characteristics is $S = 4\pi V_0/\lambda$, where $V_0$ is the peak output voltage when a long displacement is observed by the unstabilized interferometer and $\lambda$ is the laser wavelength.

Simultaneous detection of OD waves in air and workpiece using a LBDP/microphone and interferometer, respectively was used to characterize the ablation dynamics. In this way the

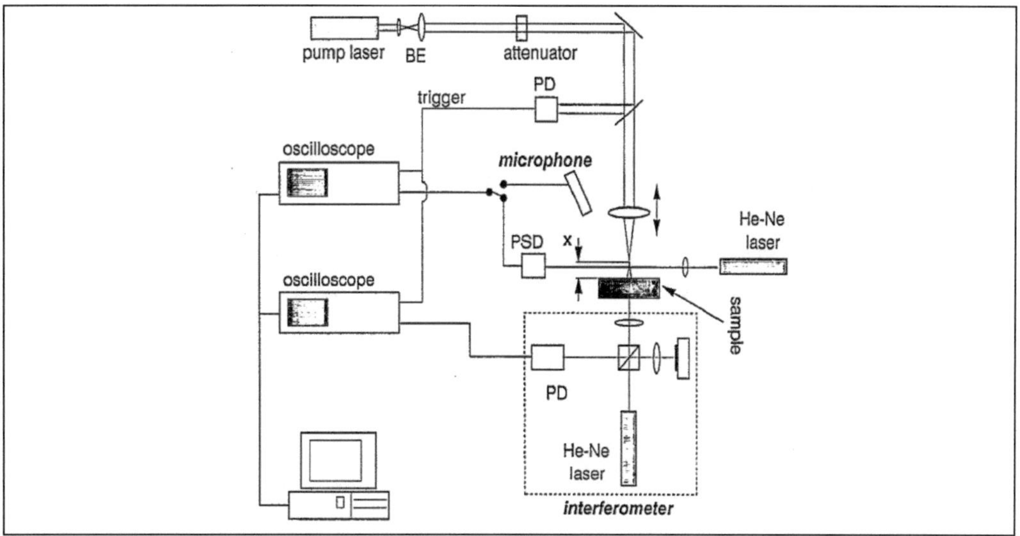


Fig. 7. A set-up for simultaneous detection of OD wave is air and in the workpiece. Reprinted from (Hrovatin & Možina, 1995) with kind permission from Elsevier

influence of the laser pulse parameters and of the interacting material on the ablation process was assessed. By the analysis of the laser drilling process of thin layered samples the material influence was demonstrated. Besides the ultrasonic evaluation of the laser pulse power density the plasma shielding for 10 ns laser pulses was analyzed by the same method.

A practical optodynamic study was performed to determine the usability of different lengths of laser pulses for the generation of ultrasonic transients in a solid material (Hrovatin et al., 2006). The aim of the study was to evaluate the possibility of a dual use for a laser pulse - for laser material processing on the one hand, and for the ultrasonic wave generation on the other - with both processes being combined on the same production line. The ultrasonic transients generated by 'classical' nanosecond laser pulses were compared with the transients generated by industrial laser pulses with duration of a few tenths of a microsecond. The experimental results were compared with the results of a time-of-flight analysis that also involved part of a mode-conversion analysis for both regimes in a layered material structure. The differences between the two waveforms were assessed in terms of their visibility, wavelength and resolution. The possibility of using an industrial marking laser for laser ultrasound generation was thus demonstrated.

Recently, a homodyne quadrature laser interferometer (HQLI) has been developed as a powerful tool to study OD motion with high temporal resolution on longer time scales (Gregorčič et al., 2009). A schematic of the HQLI set-up is presented in Fig. 8. The light from a stabilized He-Ne laser is polarized at a 45° angle in the $xy$ plane. The beam splitter (BS) splits the beam into reference and measurement arms. A $\lambda/8$ wave plate (OWP) is placed in the reference arm. Two transitions (back and forth) through the OWP in the reference arm, gives rise to the $\lambda/4$ phase difference between the orthogonal polarizations. The orthogonal polarizations in the measurement arm experience an equal phase shift due to the displacement of the target mirror. The polarizing beam splitter (PBS) transmits the $x$-polarization and reflects the y-polarization. Two interfering beams with polarizations in the $x$-plane, one from the reference arm and the other from the measurement arm, reach the photodiode PDx. Similarly, the perpendicular polarizations coming from both arms illuminate the photodiode PDy.

Ideally, the interference signals on the photodiodes are shifted by $\lambda/4$, which can be achieved with a properly rotated OWP. Two signals in quadrature (sin-cos) are thus obtained which allow measuring of a few hundred micrometer displacements with nanometer resolution. Band-pass filters (BFP) are placed in front of photodiodes to attenuate the scattered light. The high reflectivity (HR) mirror of the reference arm is driven by a piezoelectric transducer (PZT) which provides harmonic vibration that aids the system setting-up. The sample with a mirror-polished rear surface is placed in the measurement arm. The ultrasonic displacement ($u(t)$) is caused by the laser ablation of the front surface.

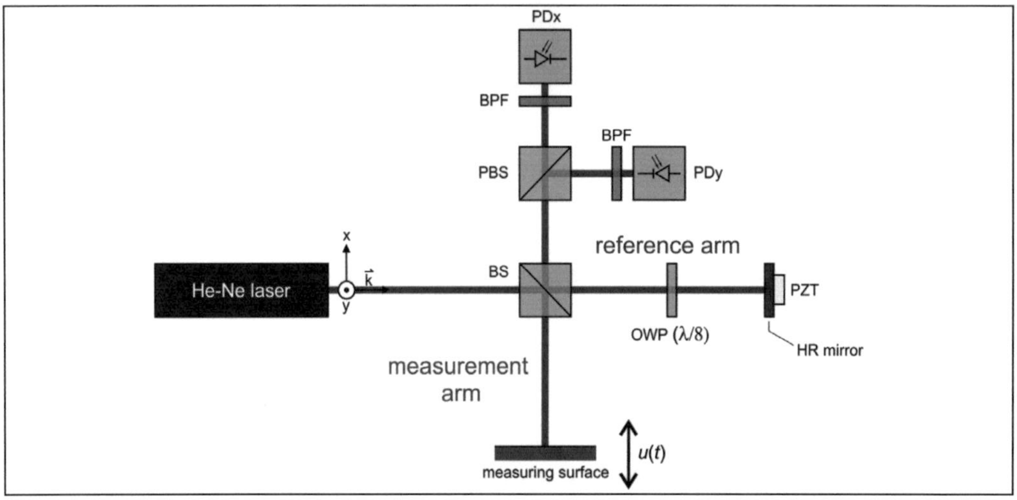


Fig. 8. Top view of a homodyne quadrature laser interferometer (HQLI)

The influence of quadrature phase shift on the measured displacement error was experimentally investigated using a HQLI (Gregorčič et al., 2009). Common nonlinearities, including the phase-shift error, were determined and effectively corrected by a robust data-processing algorithm. The measured phase-shift error perfectly agrees with the theoretically determined phase-shift error region. This error is systematic, periodic and severely asymmetrical around the nominal displacement value.

We performed a single-shot, contactless measurement of ultrasonic waves on a laser-propelled rod with a HQLI during the entire duration of its motion (Požar et al., 2009). This is the first such experimental demonstration of a laser-induced, elastic-body motion, where all the most important mechanisms that reveal the nature of its motion are presented and explained from a single-shot measurement. Furthermore, these measurements quantitatively demonstrate that the HQLI is an appropriate tool for monitoring high-amplitude (>1 μm) and high-frequency (up to 200 MHz) ultrasonic waves on moving objects. It has a constant sensitivity and can measure a total displacement of ~1mm with a resolution and accuracy of 1 nm, i.e., it covers a dynamic range of $10^6$.

## 3. Applications

### 3.1 Laser drilling

Laser drilling is used to machine very small holes, unusual-shaped holes, blind holes, precisely tapered holes, holes at steep angles, holes with small diameter and high aspect ratio, etc. It makes possible to drill holes into difficult-to-machine materials. Current industrial laser drilling stations employ monitoring and control systems that rely parameters such as the laser power, pulse duration, energy, beam quality, the distance between the workpiece and the focusing lens etc. More refined systems would allow monitoring the result of the process on-line. A promising approach to developing such monitoring systems is based on the acquisition and analysis of OD signals, generated during the process. We have conducted several studies to develop and refine OD monitoring methods in laser drilling using a variety of lasers and materials.

We studied laser drilling of different woods using a free-running pulsed Er:YAG laser (Grad & Možina, 1998). Very long and narrow holes with depth-to-diameter ratio above 100 could be achieved which is an indication of the occurrence of laser beam trapping within the hole. The process has been investigated as a typical optodynamic process. Optoacoustic waves in air above the irradiate surface were detected by microphone and analyzed to monitor the hole depth produced by consecutive laser pulse exposure of the same spot. Measurements of laser drilling rate were performed. Fig. 9shows a typical result that illustrates the potential of OD detection for process monitoring. The macro photography in the upper part shows a high-aspect-ratio hole running horizontally from left to right and the growth rings running diagonally through the image. The diameter of the entry hole is 1 mm.

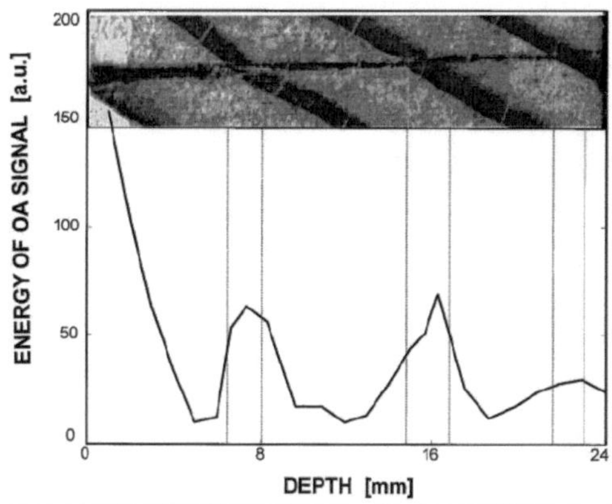


Fig. 9. Energy of optoacoustic signals vs. wood density profile. Reprinted from (Grad & Možina, 1998) with kind permission from Elsevier

Below the image is a diagram, which relates energy $E_{OA}$

$$E_{OA} = \int_{t_1}^{t_2} y^2(t)dt \quad (1)$$

of the microphone signal $y(t)$ with the depth $H$ of the hole, which has been determined from the number $N$ of successive laser pulses. The relation between $H$ and $N$ had been established by another experiment where several holes were drilled in the wood sample using different number $N$ of laser pulses. The sample was subsequently ground in a parallel plane to the holes' axis to determine the hole depth $H$ corresponding to a particular $N$. As evident from Fig. 1, local peaks of $E_{OA}$ correspond to local areas of increased wood density. Information on inner density profile of the wood can be obtained through these measurements.

Pulsed laser drilling of laminated aluminum with a Q-switched Nd:YAG laser was studied to explore the possibility of on-line monitoring of the hole depth growth (Strgar, et al., 2000).

The optodynamic responses were acquired by means of a single LBDP which detected shock waves generated in surrounding air during the drilling process. Detected signals were processed and analyzed to extract the optodynamic characteristics of the drilling process. The characteristics were correlated with geometric properties of the holes. A simple and reliable method for determining the depth of holes was developed. Specimens were produced by firmly pressing together a stack of thin sheets of uniform and equal thickness. After the processing the sheets were separated. The resulting hole depth was estimated from the number of sheets pierced. Experiments were performed to examine how the LBDP signal characteristics, hole depth, and material removal rate change with the number of consecutive laser pulses. A strong correlation between the depth of the laser-drilled hole and an optodynamic response was found and examined. It was found, however, that supersonic propagation of the shock wavefront introduces a systematic error into the OD depth measurement.

To evaluate this phenomenon more closely we employed simultaneous detection of OD waves in air and in the workpiece by means of a LBDP and a piezoelectric transducer, respectively (Strgar & Možina, 2002a). Fig. 10 shows the set-up.

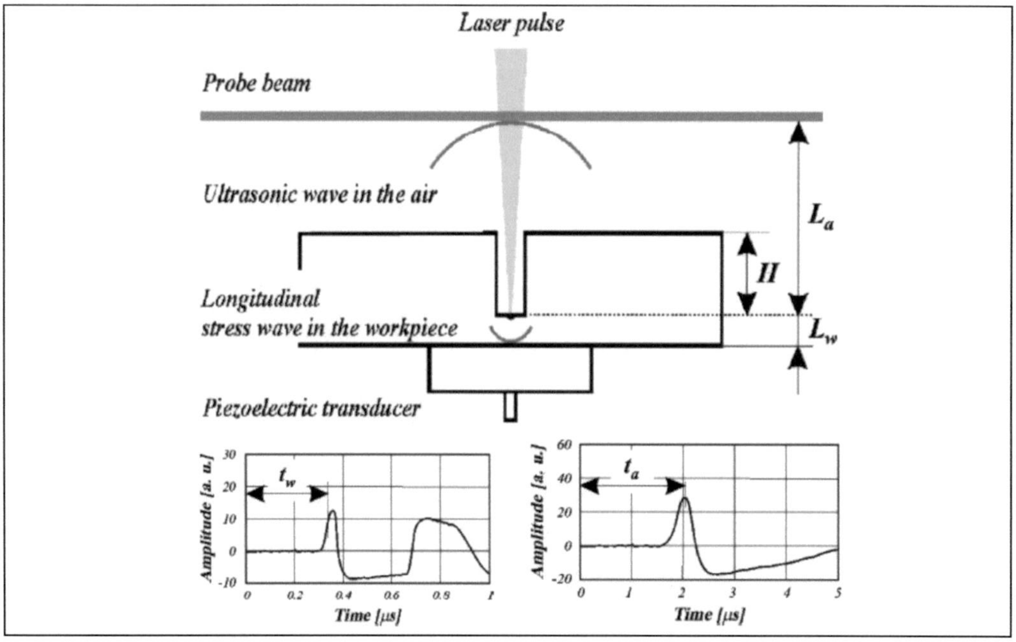


Fig. 10. A schematic of the set-up for simultaneous detection of OD signals by a LBDP and a piezoelectric transducer (top). Typical detected signals by the piezoelectric transducer (bottom-left) and LPDP (bottom-right). Reprinted from (Strgar & Možina, 2002a) with kind permission from Elsevier

The increasing depth $H$ of the hole and its maximum extent were estimated from changes in the propagation time ($t_w$ and $t_a$) of the ultrasonic waves traveling from the bottom of the hole to both detectors. Measurements of the maximum hole depth were compared with the predictions of a theoretical model and they were found to be in a good agreement.

A further study (Strgar & Možina, 2002b) in this area concentrated on the relationship between the propagation time of the longitudinal stress wave in workpiece and the number of consecutive laser pulses. The aim was to develop a method for determining the depth of laser-drilled holes in real time. Piezoelectric detection was used. Fig. 11 shows a typical obtained result.

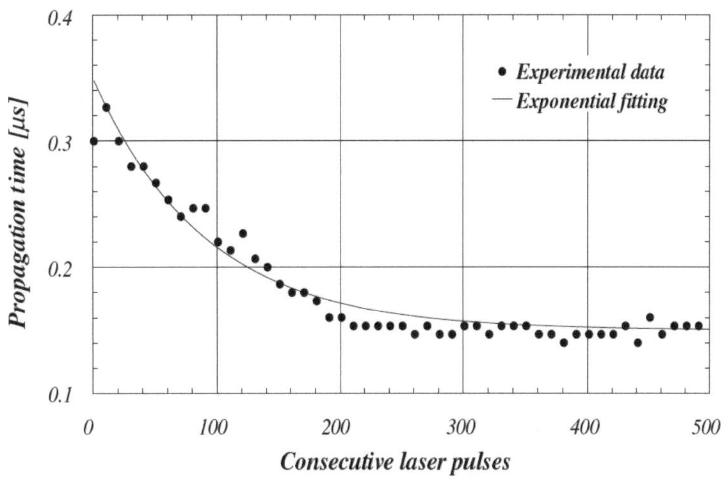


Fig. 11. Propagation time of the longitudinal stress waves vs. the number of consecutive laser pulses during laser drilling of a 1.2-mm thick stainless-steel sample. Experimental data are fitted with an exponential curve. Reprinted from (Strgar & Možina, 2002b) with kind permission from Springer Science+Business Media

We found that during laser drilling of a blind hole the propagation time $t_m(N)$ of the longitudinal stress waves in material decreases with the number of consecutive laser pulses $N$ in a way which could be approximated by an exponential function:

$$t_m(N) = t_{mf}+(t_{mi}-t_{mf})\cdot\exp(-N/N_0) \quad (2)$$

where $t_{mi}$ and $t_{mf}$ are the initial and the final propagation times, respectively, and $N_0$ is the characteristic laser pulse number. The initial and final propagation times were measured while the characteristic laser pulse number was determined from a comparison of the calculated values and the experimental data. We have verified that the final depth $H_f$ of the hole can be determined from:

$$H_f = c_m\,(t_{mi}-t_{mf}) \quad (3)$$

where $c_m$ is the propagation velocity of the longitudinal stress wave through the material. Building on these observations, a further study was conducted aimed at analyzing pulsed laser micro-drilling of different metals (Petkovšek et al., 2006). The OD waves were detected by using the arm compensated Michelson interferometer. Monitoring of the main parameters of the micro drilling such as material ablation rate and efficiency was realized by analysis of the optodynamic signals. The process is characterized by decreasing ablation rate that leads to the finite hole depth. In order to describe decreasing ablation rate a theoretical model based on the energy balance has been proposed. It considers the energy/heat transfer from the laser beam to the material and predicts a decreasing drilling rate with an increasing number of successive laser pulses. According to the proposed model, the finite depth of the hole appears as a consequence of the increasing surface area through which the energy of the laser beam is conducted away to the material around the processed area. Decreasing ablation rate and the finite hole depth predicted by model were in good agreement with the experimental results as shown in Fig. 12.

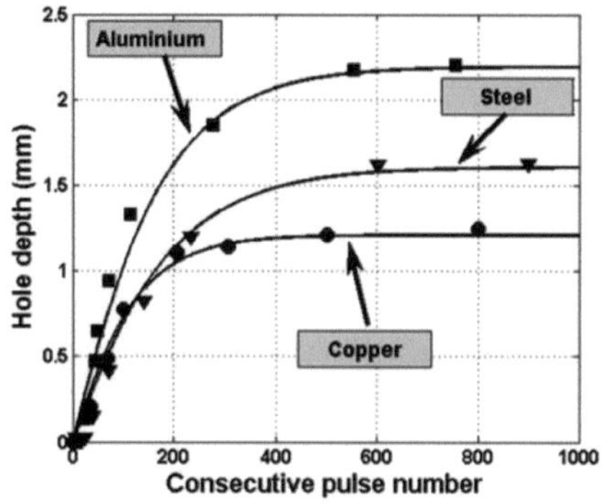


Fig. 12. Hole depth vs. consecutive laser pulse number for three metals. The markers represent the measured data, while the solid lines represent the predictions of the theory. Reprinted from (Petkovšek et al., 2006) with kind permission from Elsevier

Another research direction in this area was focused on developing a reliable method for drilling specified micro-holes into glass ampoules and vials (Petkovšek et al., 2006). Test ampoules with holes are used in pharmaceutical production lines for the adjustment of the high-voltage leak-detection devices. Our set-up is built around a XeCl excimer laser that provided the processing beam (Fig. 13).

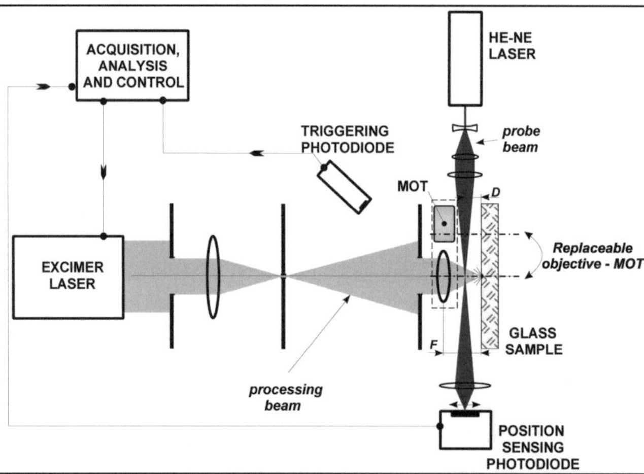


Fig. 13. The set-up for laser drilling of specified micro-holes into ampoules

The beam is lead through a circular orifice and focused through a pinhole and a focusing lens onto the sample front side. The focal diameter of the beam is 100 μm and the focal fluence of the processing beam is in the range from 7 to 13 J/cm$^2$. The samples are clamped by a holder in such a way that the processed surface is perpendicular to the processing beam. The holder is mounted on a translation stage to enable fine adjustment of the focus to surface distance F. A mechano-optical triangulation (MOT) sensor has been developed to achieve precise and repeatable sample positioning relative to the focal plane of the processing beam.

The key novelty of the developed solution is an accurate and reliable method for the detection of perforation of the ampoule wall during the processing. The method is based on the detection of shock waves generated in the air during the drilling process using a LBDP. An analysis of the detected optodynamic signals gives important information about the progress of the drilling process, and we employed this as the basis for the presented online process-monitoring method. A significant change in the signal's amplitude is observed when the wall of a liquid-filled ampoule is perforated and the exit process point is in contact with the liquid. This signal change can serve as an indicator of wall perforation. We have verified this optodynamic method by examining the processed holes using optical and electron microscopy as well as with a non-destructive gas-leakage test method. Holes with a diameter of less than 10 μm were produced in the walls of 0.5 mm thick glass ampoules. The test ampoules are successfully applied in the pharmaceutical production.

In a further development (Petkovšek et al., 2008) of the described microdrilling method we augmented the experimental set-up by means of a digital micrographic system (Fig. 14) which enables the acquisition of images of the plasma plume and of the hole cross-section during a drilling sequence.

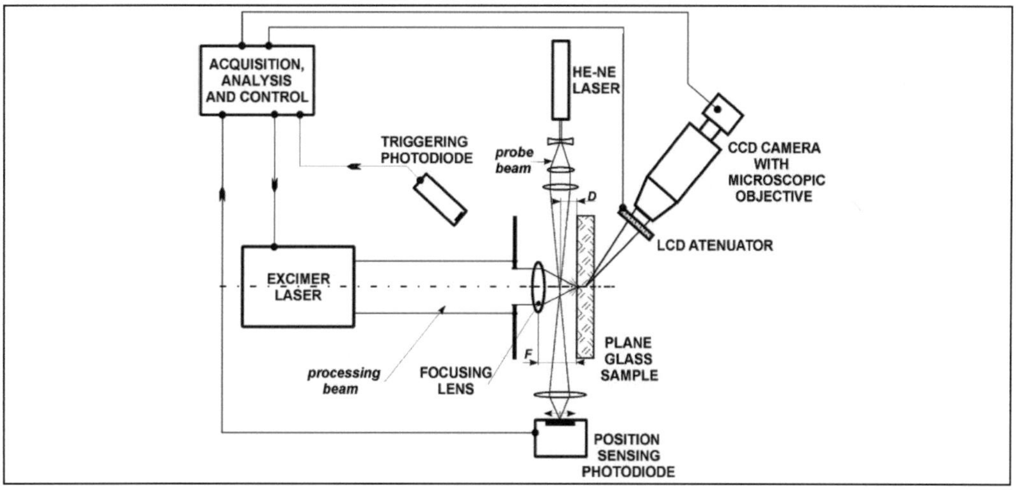


Fig. 14. The set-up for laser drilling of specified micro-holes into ampoules. Reprinted from (Petkovšek et al., 2008) with kind permission from Springer Science+Business Media

The first processing phase, called "incubation," is characterized by 3D plasma plume expansion (Fig. 15b, image a). The initial hole has a shape close to a half-sphere with radius related to the processing beam radius. The nonuniformity of the process at this phase manifests itself in the LBDP amplitude variation greater than ±10% (Fig. 15a).

During the second phase ("the deep hole ablation"), a self-focusing effect appears leading to the recessing hole diameter that is more prominent at lower processing beam fluences. Recession also depends on numerical aperture and focus adjustment of the processing beam. One-dimensional expansion of the plasma plume (Fig. 15b, images b and c) leads to a strong attenuation of the processing beam and consecutively to a strong (approximately exponential) decrease of the LBDP signal amplitude (Fig. 15a). By comparing the hole cross-section and plasma plume images we see that in this phase the plasma plume originates and expands in the hole. LBDP signal amplitude exhibits less variation in this phase than during the previous one. The hole is crack-free.

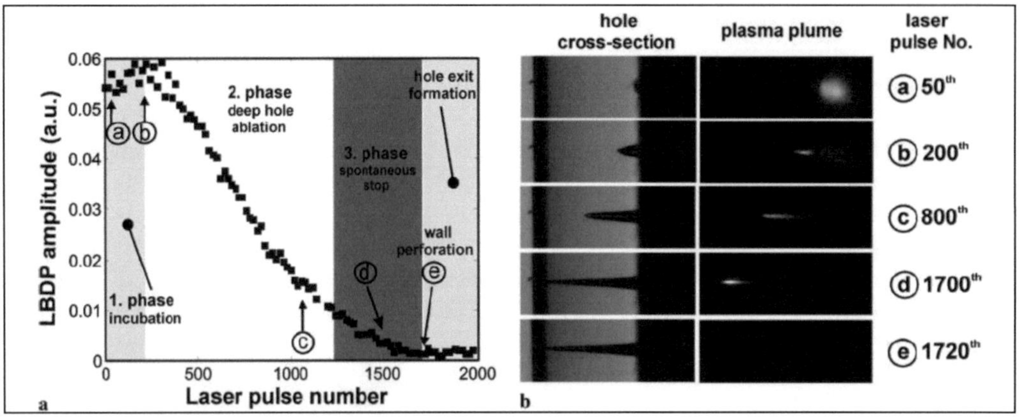


Fig. 15. Phases of the micro-drilling process evident in (a) LBDP signal amplitude diagram and (b) characteristic micrograph images of the hole cross-section and the corresponding plasma plume. Reprinted from (Petkovšek et al., 2008) with kind permission from Springer Science+Business Media

The third phase occurs when ablation tends to stop due to the predominant absorption by the side walls in a deep hole. Plasma energy and consequently its visibility decrease (Fig. 15b, image d), and consequently the LBDP signal amplitude decreases below the noise level (Fig. 15a). At the moment of sample perforation, the plasma plume vanishes (Fig. 15b, image e). During this phase, the hole apex can exhibit an unpredictable form (branched hole apex). A further study in this area (Petkovšek & Možina, 2007) has been devoted to developing a theoretical model, which serves as a basis for understanding the physical background of the developed method for pulsed-laser microdrilling of glass using nanosecond pulses. The model considers plasma formation and shockwave propagation (Fig. 16).

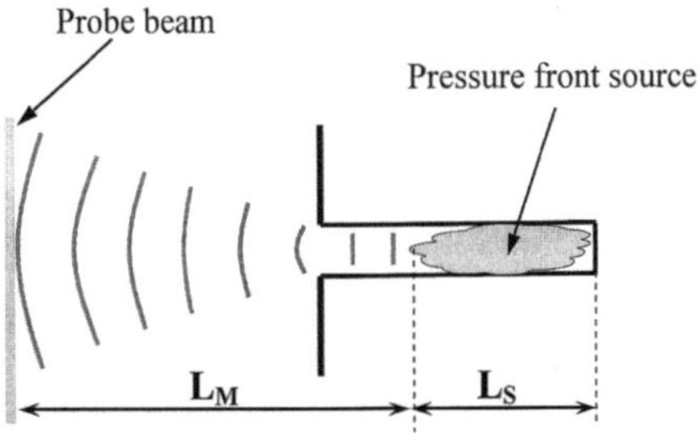


Fig. 16. Plasma formation and shock wave propagation during laser micr-drilling. Reprinted from (Petkovšek & Možina, 2007) with kind permission from American Institute of Physics

### 3.2 Laser engraving

We have examined OD signals detected by a microphone and a laser beam deflection probe during laser engraving of printed circuits (Gorkič et al., 2009). The experimental set-up (Fig. 17) has been built around a diode pumped pulsed Nd:$YVO_4$ engraving laser (1) with average output power up to 15W, pulse repetition frequency up to 100 kHz, and pulse duration of 20-60 ns. The processing laser beam was translated over the workpiece (2) using a scanner head (3). The workpiece was mounted on a clamping device which had two electrodes for measuring engraved gap conductance (4). OD waves, propagated in the air above the processed surface, were detected by a condenser microphone (5) and a laser beam deflection probe (LBDP). A LBDP beam from a He-Ne laser (6) was aligned parallel to the line engraving and intersecting the processing beam at the right angle. Deflection of the probe beam by the transition of the OD transient wave was detected by a fast photodiode with a preamplifier (7) (40 MHz bandwidth). According to the manufacturer specification the microphone had a 100 kHz bandwidth. Another fast photodiode (8) was used to detect stray processing laser light, reflected from the workpiece, in order to acquire the time history of the processing beam and to trigger the oscilloscope (9).

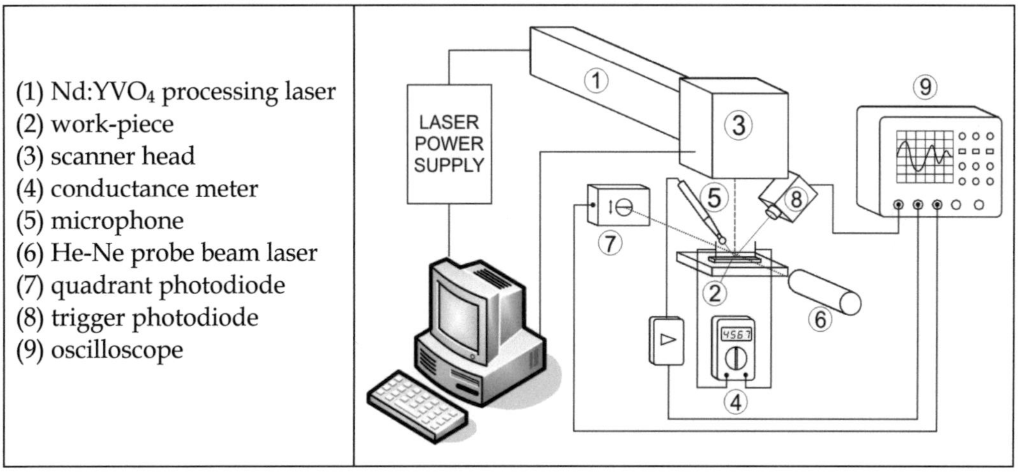


Fig. 17. Experimental set-up for OD analysis of laser engraving. Reprinted from (Gorkič et al., 2009) with kind permission from Springer Science+Business Media

Different process regimes were studied varying laser power, pulse repetition frequency and beam translation speed. The detected OD signals had the form of a train of well separated pulses. Comparing microphone and LBDP signal pulses we found the latter to be shorter as expected due to the higher detecting bandwidth of the LBDP. We observed that during the process both kinds of OD signals exhibited characteristic amplitude variations which could be related to the process outcome. An efficient windowed peak-to-peak signal processing algorithm for amplitude extraction was developed to process the signals and examine their relation to the engraving quality. The results of signal analysis were compared to the engraving surface topography, measured by means of optical microscopy with extended depth of field digital photography. We have found that microphone and LBDP signal amplitude was larger in the cases of optimal engravings than in the cases of shallow and overburnt engravings (Fig. 18). The results show that the signals could be applied to on-line monitoring of the process of laser engraving PCBs.

We examined different combinations of processing parameters, which would uniquely describe different processing regimes: shallow, good and obverburnt engraving. We found that the parameter, defined as

$$E_s = P_L / v_L \tag{4}$$

where $P_L$ and $v_L$ are laser power and beam translation speed, respectively, suited well for this purpose. $E_S$ [J/m] represents incident pulse energy, averaged over a pulse repetition period, per unit length of an engraving. We have found in our case that using parameters that gave $E_S < 77$ J/m we obtained shallow engravings. Using parameter combinations that gave $E_S > 90$ J/m we observed excessive substrate burn.

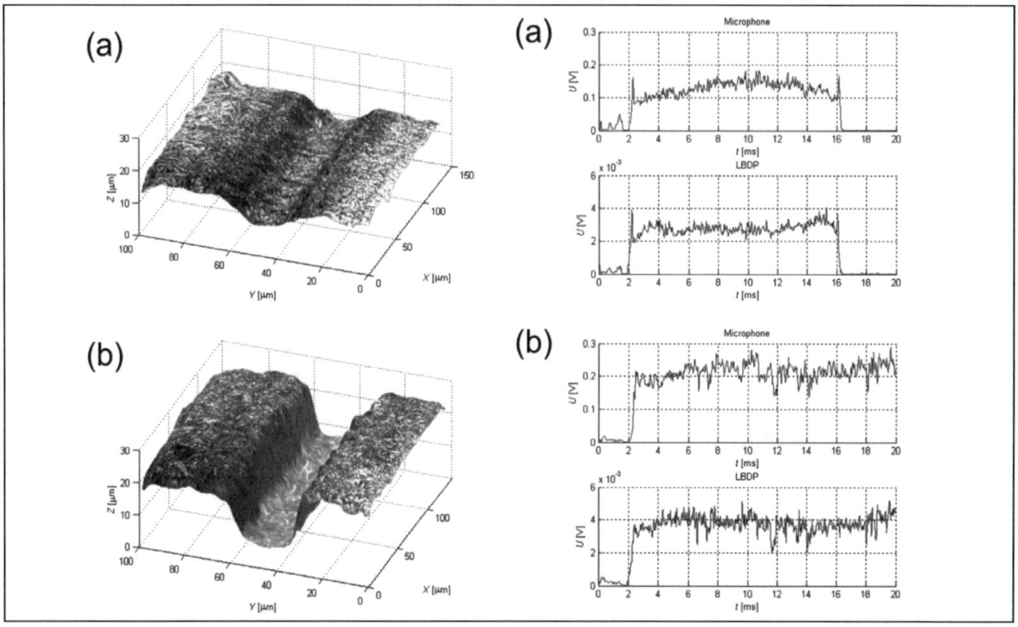


Fig. 18. 3D scans (left) and amplitudes of OD signals (right) of a shallow (a) and good (b) engraving. Reprinted from (Gorkič et al., 2009) with kind permission from Springer Science+Business Media

### 3.3 Laser cleaning

We have investigated laser cleaning as an optodynamic process in which the optically induced removal of a liquid or a solid contaminant from a substrate is accompanied by an optodynamic wave in the surrounding air (Bregar & Možina, 2002). In our experiments we used both dry and steam laser-cleaning techniques for various samples. OD waves, produced by the abrupt heating and detachment of the contaminants, were detected with a laser beam deflection probe. Analyzing the acquired signals we observed supersonic propagation velocities, density profiles matching the shock-wave profile, and reasonable agreement between the shock-wave theory and measured data. Two characteristic parameters of the optodynamic wave: the amplitude and the time-of-flight of the wavefront were examined as possible indicators of the contaminant removal. Analysis of the OD signals has indicated possible sound generating mechanisms. During a sequence of successive cleaning laser pulses we have observed a decrease of the amplitude and the propagating velocity of the detected OD waves. When both parameters reached constant values, the cleaning process ceased (Bregar & Možina, 2003). Fig. 19 presents times of flight (TOFs) measured during the cleaning of two samples with different surface contaminant particle densities. As expected, the higher density and consequently the higher particle removal rate correlates with a significantly larger change in both OD parameters; for the first few pulses stronger and faster shockwaves are generated, with the propagation velocities up to 470 m/s. By OD signal detection and analysis the progress of the cleaning process could be monitored on-line.

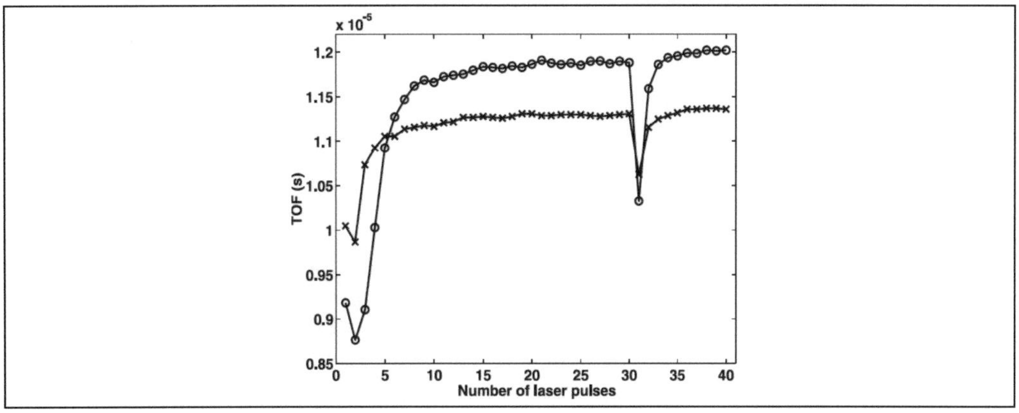


Fig. 19. Times of flight of the OD signals detected during the laser cleaning of a stainless-steel surface with low (×) and high (◦) surface contaminant particle density. Reprinted from (Bregar & Možina, 2003) with kind permission from Springer Science+Business Media

We have studied the removal of paint layers from metal surfaces using excimer and pulsed Nd:YAG lasers (Jezeršek et al., 2004). The effects of each individual laser pulse were monitored by a three-probe system (Fig. 20). Ultrasonic signals from the rear surface of the substrate were obtained using an arm compensated Michelson interferometer (ACMI), the OD waves in the surrounding air were detected using a LBDP and the 3D shape of the growing crater was measured using a laser anamorph profilometer.

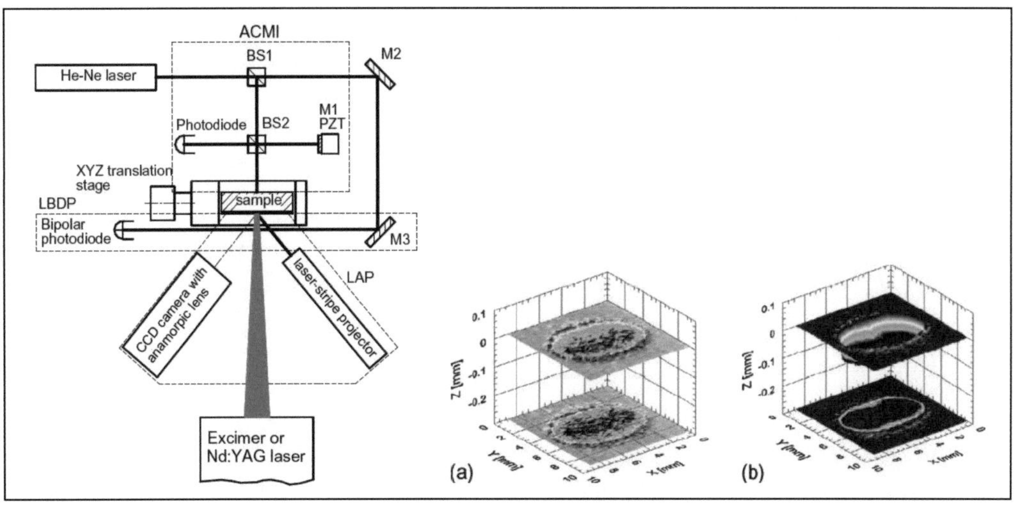


Fig. 20. Experimental set-up used for monitoring the laser-based decoating (left). The shape of the ablated area after (a) the first and (b) the tenth Nd:YAG laser pulse measured by the laser anamorph profilometer (right). Reprinted from (Jezeršek et al., 2004) with kind permission from Elsevier

The Nd:YAG laser proved to be more efficient in terms of decoating rate. When using ACMI the integral of the ultrasonic signal was found to be a representative parameter that has a linear correlation with the decoating rate (Fig. 21). In a similar way, the amplitude and the time-of-flight are appropriate parameters when using the LBDP, but they have an exponential relation versus decoating rate. From a process-control point of view the above measurement techniques make it possible to monitor the laser-based decoating process in real-time.

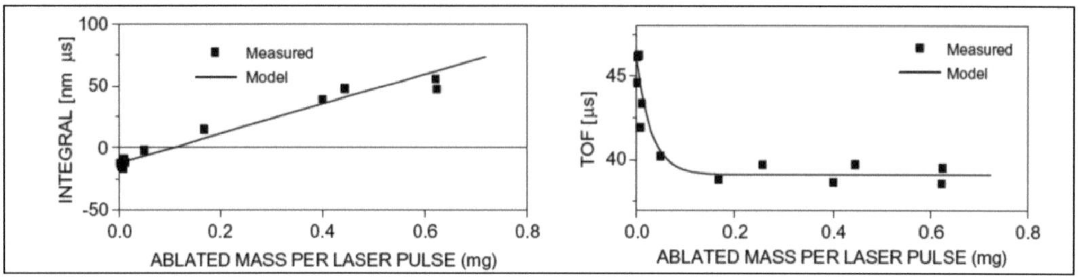


Fig. 21. The correlation between the ablated mass per laser pulse and (a) the interferometric integral and (b) the TOF. Reprinted from (Jezeršek et al., 2004) with kind permission from Elsevier

### 3.4 Laser writing

We have investigated the direct laser writing of graduation lines in Cr thin films on glass substrates (Kopač et al., 1996a; 1996b). A Nd-YAG laser and an astigmatic optical system have been used to write rectangular holes in the Cr film. The optimal writing parameters: the laser pulse energy, the Cr layer thickness and the substrate-objective distance were determined using the probe beam deflection method to detect the evaporation of the material. We have shown that evaporation was the essential process in the laser writing of graduation lines. The rims formed by the surface tension gradient at the hole edges have indicated that the laser writing of graduation lines is a typical two-phase removal process. Based on this assumption the process was analyzed experimentally and theoretically. The transmitted portion of the incoming laser pulse and the optodynamic wave amplitude have been detected and used in monitoring the line opening dynamics in real time.

Fig. 22 shows AFM images of the graduation lines for different writing parameters. The region of the removed material is located in the middle of the AFM image, while the rims of resolidified Cr can be seen at the edges of these regions.

Fig. 23 shows the variations of OD amplitudes for the sequentially written graduation lines while the writing parameters were changing. For the first 50 written lines, the pulse energy was varied from 150 to 315 μJ; for the next 75 lines the refocus was simulated.

The next 50 lines were written with the system set to the optimal writing parameters and the last lines were written in the Cr layer with the inhomogeneous adhesion. All the experiments were performed on the 40 nm thick Cr layer with the laser beam impacting through the glass substrate. Comparing these results with OM, SEM and AFM analysis of the same graduation pattern, one can conclude that the OD signal amplitude is a good measuring parameter for the on-line evaluation of the quality of the graduation pattern, since the graduation lines written in the OD amplitude range between 130 and 160 mV satisfy the quality requirements.

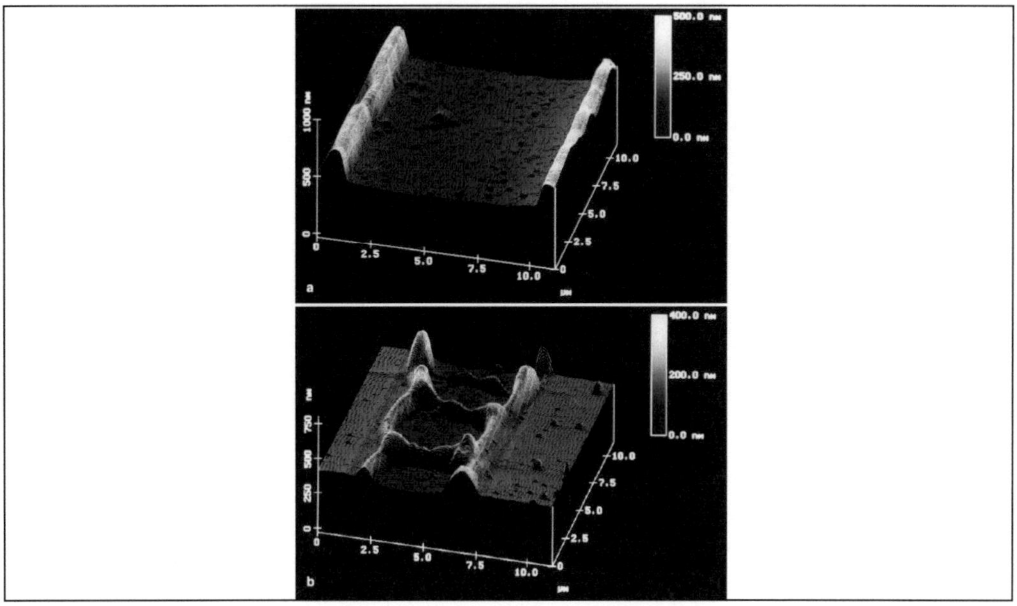

Fig. 22. AFM images of graduation lines for different writing parameters (size 11×11 μm). Reprinted from (Kopač et al., 1996a) with kind permission from Springer Science+Business Media

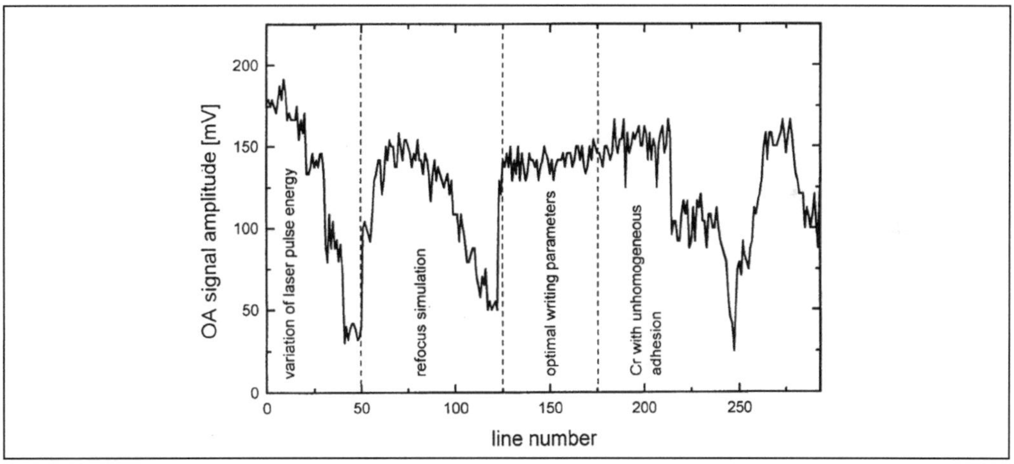


Fig. 23. On-line OD monitoring of the graduation lines quality. Reprinted from (Kopač et al., 1996b) with kind permission from Elsevier

### 3.5 Laser ablation

The LBDP has been employed to study ablation of metallic surfaces by sequences of 1.06 μm Nd:YAG laser pulses separated by less than 1 μs (Diaci & Možina, 1993). A fluence threshold has been found, below which the effects of individual pulses can be resolved by the laser probe. Above that, the deflection signal has a similar form as if the surface were irradiated with a single pulse. Analysis of the signal in terms of the spherical blast wave theory shows that a pulse sequence generates a weaker blast wave than a single pulse of equal total energy. Inspection of the irradiated surfaces shows a monotonous increase of the etch depth with pulse energy in all cases, confirming that no appreciable plasma shielding takes place. The amplitude of the LBD signal, which also increases monotonically with pulse energy, could therefore be used for the on-line monitoring of the etch depth. In the case of multiple pulse irradiation, however, the amplitude changes so drastically when the consecutive shocks merge that an integral parameter, like mean square value of the signal, should be more appropriate for monitoring the total etch depth. For the same total energy, the multiple pulse irradiation produces a higher etch depth than the single pulse, but it also yields a larger heat affected zone, more irregular shape of the crater with larger remnants of melted and resolidified material (Fig. 24).

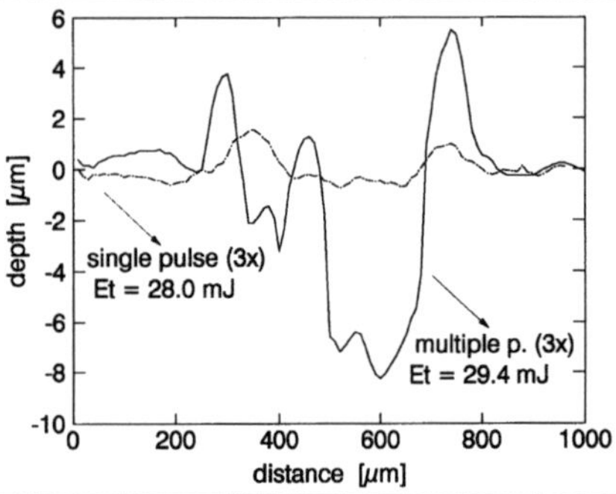


Fig. 24. Profiles of craters ablated into a stainless steel surface using single pulses (the dash-dot line) and multiple pulses (the solid line) with similar total energy. Reprinted from (Diaci & Možina, 1993) with kind permission from Elsevier

We have applied the multiple-pass LBDP to investigate spherical shocks generated during laser ablation of metallic targets in air (Diaci & Možina, 1996). For each ablation event we determine shock transit times at several points in space and fit the data to the theoretical shock trajectory in order to determine the blast energy $E_h$ released in the shock wave. This multiple-point procedure improves the accuracy and reliability of blast energy measurement. As an illustration of the result we show in Fig. 25 the ratio $E_h/E_l$, which we call the energy conversion efficiency, as a function of incident laser energy $E_l$. The efficiency increases with incident energy: quite rapidly at low $E_l$ and only gradually at high $E_l$. In the low $E_l$ range we also find that pulse-to-pulse variations of blast energy are much higher than the variations of $E_l$ while in the high $E_l$ range they are comparable.

Several processing parameters, like the ablation rate, the shape and size of the ablation crater, are considerably affected by the conditions of focusing of the laser beam, i.e. by the focal distance of the focusing lens system and by the distance $l$ between the irradiated surface and the focal plane of the lens system (waist—surface distance). In order to control and optimize the ablation process, a monitoring method of the ablation beam focusing is required. We have examined the possibility of employing the optodynamic detection to control and optimize the ablation process (Grad et al., 1993a). We have studied OD signals acquired during laser ablation of aluminum and brass samples using two detection techniques: a resonant piezoelectric (PZT) transducer mounted on the opposite side of the irradiated surface detecting the OD waves in the sample and a wideband microphone detecting the OD waves in the surrounding air. Simultaneous detection is used to evaluate the potentials of both detection techniques for monitoring the laser beam focusing.

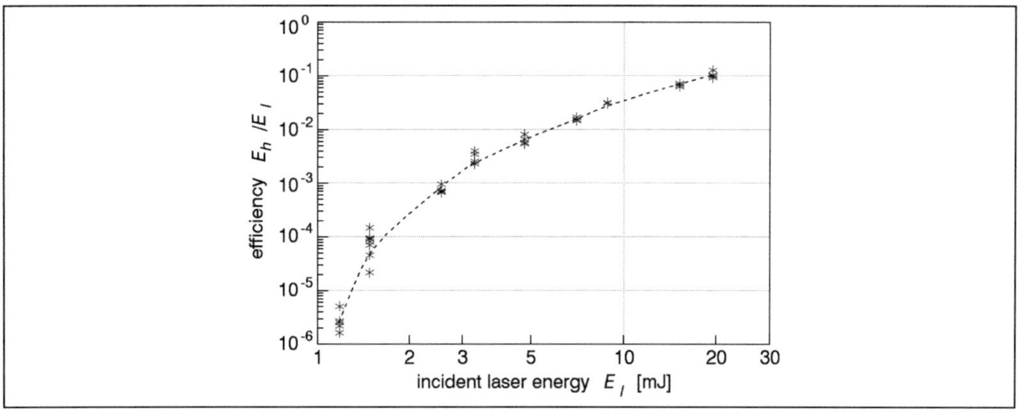


Fig. 25. Conversion efficiency vs. incident laser energy during laser ablation metallic targets. Reprinted from (Diaci & Možina, 1996) with kind permission from Elsevier

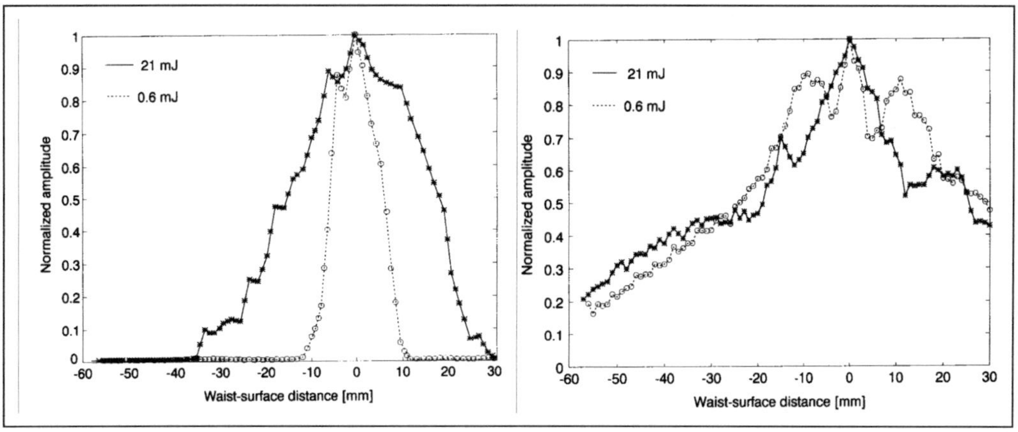


Fig. 26. Normalized amplitude dependence of the microphone (left) and piezoelectric (right) signals on the waist–surface distance at two different laser pulse energies.

With all samples we find that both signals have maximum amplitudes when the target surface is in the focal plane of the ablation beam ($l = 0$ in Fig. 26). The peaks associated with the longitudinal wavefront arrivals are used for the comparison of the PZT signals. The curves, normalized with their focal values, exhibit more complex shapes than those from the microphone signals. In all cases the curves narrow when the incident laser energy $E_l$ decreases. The results indicate that it is possible to use the OD signal amplitudes to determine the position of the ablation beam focus and to detect displacements of the sample surface from the focus.

The same simultaneous detection technique was applied to study excimer laser ablation of ceramic samples at different laser pulse energies and laser beam spot sizes (Grad & Možina, 1993b; Grad & Možina, 1995). Several techniques of OD signal analysis were used to study the correlation between OD signal parameters and the ablation rate. Combining the parameters of the microphone and PZT signals an ablation parameter was defined whose dependence on the ablated mass was found to be linear. The investigations have shown that the ablation rate changes with the increasing number of the laser pulses applied.

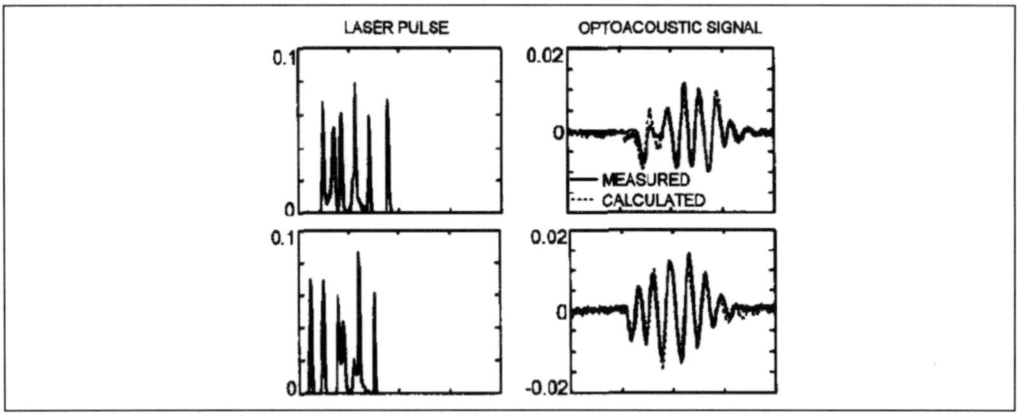


Fig. 27. Comparison between the measured and the calculated microphone signals. Reprinted from (Grad & Možina, 1996) with kind permission from Elsevier

Er:YAG laser ablation of dental tissue has been investigated as the typical optodynamic process (Grad & Možina, 1996). An experimental method was developed which enables evaluation of a laser pulse temporal profile influence on the ablation process of hard dental tissue. The OD signals were detected by a microphone and analyzed within the frame of linear systems theory to monitor laser induced microexplosions. Statistical distribution of the optodynamic efficiency was performed in terms of partial weights of the OD system response function. Fig. 27 shows a comparison of measured and calculated microphone signals. The calculated signals were determined by convolution of the laser pulse signal with the experimentally determined impulse response of the OD system. The results indicate that the laser spikes shorter than 2 μs are more efficient in ablative mechanism regime.

## 4. Conclusion

The chapter presents a synthesis of the results of original research in the area of pulsed laser materials processing. Within this framework, special emphasis has been given to the optodynamic (OD) aspects of interaction, which include the links between the laser material removal and the resulting material motion. The chapter examines several methods that have been employed to study optodynamic aspects of laser processing and reports several applications of the developed methods in laser processing.

## 5. References

Bregar, V. & Možina, J. (2002). Optoacoustic analysis of the laser-cleaning process. *Appl. Surf. Sci.*, Vol. 185, No. 3-4, 277-288, ISSN 0169-4332

Bregar, V. & Možina, J. (2003). Shock-wave generation during dry laser cleaning of particles. *Applied Physics A (Materials Science Processing)*, Vol. A77, No. 5, 633-639, ISSN 0947-8396

Diaci, J. & Možina, J. (1992). A study of blast waveforms detected simultaneously by a microphone and a laser probe during laser ablation. *Applied Physics A (Solids and Surfaces)*, Vol. A55, No. 4, 352-3588, ISSN 0721-7250

Diaci, J. & Možina, J. (1993). Laser-beam deflection monitoring of Nd-YAG laser ablation - pulse shape and repetition rate effects. *Appl. Surf. Sci.*, Vol. 69, No. 1-4, 321-325, ISSN 0169-4332

Diaci, J. & Možina, J. (1994). Study of energy conversion during Nd:YAG laser ablation of metal surfaces in air by means of a laser beam deflection probe. *Journal de Physique* IV, Vol. 4, No. 7, 737-740, ISSN 1155-4339

Diaci, J. & Možina, J. (1995). Multiple-pass laser beam deflection probe for detection of acoustic and weak shock waves in fluids. *Rev. Sci. Instrum.*, Vol. 66, No. 9, 4644-4648, ISSN 0034-6748

Diaci, J. & Možina, J., (1996). Measurement of energy conversion efficiency during laser ablation by a multiple laser beam deflection probe. *Ultrasonics*, Vo. 34, No. 2-5, 523-525, ISSN 0041-624X

Diaci, J. et al., (1996). Simultaneous monitoring of ablative shocks in air by high-speed cineholography and multiple-pass beam deflection probe. *Appl. Surf. Sci.*, Vol. 96-98, 154-158, ISSN 0169-4332

Jezeršek, M. et al., (2004). Real-time optodynamic monitoring of pulsed laser decoating rate. *Ultrasonics*, Vol. 42, 37-41, ISSN 0041-624X

Jezeršek, M., Gruden, V. & Možina, J. (2004). High-speed measurements of steel-plate deformations during laser surface processing. *Opt. Express*, Vol. 12, No. 20, 4905–4911, ISSN 1094-4087

Gorkič, A., Kovačič, D. & Diaci, J. (2009). Analysis of sonic waves generated during laser engraving of printed circuits. *Int. J. Adv. Manuf. Technol.*, Vol. 42, No. 1-2, 138-144, ISSN 1433-3015

Grad, L. & Možina, J. (1993a). Optoacoustic monitoring of laser beam focusing. *Lasers in Engineering*, Vol. 1, No. 4, 275-282, ISSN 0898-1507

Grad, L. & Možina, J. (1993b). Acoustic insitu monitoring of excimer-laser ablation of different ceramics. *Appl. Surf. Sci.*, Vol. 69, No. 1-4, 370-375, ISSN 0169-4332

Grad, L. & Možina, J. (1995). Optodynamic monitoring of excimer-laser drilling of ceramics. *Lasers in Engineering*, Vol. 4, No. 4, 255-262, ISSN 0898-1507

Grad, L. & Možina, J. (1996). Optodynamic studies of Er:YAG laser induced microexplosions in dentin. *Appl. Surf. Sci.*, Vol. 96-8, 591-595, ISSN 0169-4332

Grad, L. & Možina, J. (1998). Optodynamic studies of Er : YAG laser interaction with wood. *Appl. Surf. Sci.*, Vol. 127, 973-976, ISSN 0169-4332

Gregorčič, P., Požar, T. & Možina, J. (2009). Quadrature phase-shift error analysis using a homodyne laser interferometer. *Opt. Express*, Vol. 17, No. 18, 16322–16331, ISSN 1094-4087

Hrovatin, R. & Možina, J. (1995). Optodynamic aspect of a pulsed laser ablation process. *Appl. Surf. Sci.*, Vol. 86, No. 1-4, 213-218, ISSN 0169-4332

Hrovatin, R. et al., (2006). The applicability of a material-treatment laser pulse in non-destructive evaluations. *Ultrasonics*, Vol. 44, 1199-1202, ISSN 0041-624X

Kopač, S., Pirš, J. & Možina, J. (1996a). Optodynamic analysis of direct laser writing of graduation lines. *Applied Physics A (Materials Science Processing)*, Vol. A62, No. 1, 77-82, ISSN 0947-8396

Kopač, S., Pirš, J. & Možina, J. (1996b). Optodynamics of laser ablation of graduation lines in chromium thin film on glass. *Appl. Surf. Sci.*, Vol. 96-8, 420-424, ISSN 0169-4332

Možina, J. & Hrovatin, R. (1996). Optodynamics - a synthesis of optoacoustics and laser processing, *Progress Nat. Sci.*, Vol. 6, S709-S714, ISSN 1002-0071

Perhavec, T. & Diaci, J. (2010). A novel double-exposure shadowgraph method for observation of optodynamic shock waves using fiber-optic illumination. Stroj. vestn. - J. Mech. Eng., accepted for publication, ISSN 0039-2480

Petkovšek, R. et al. (2006). Optodynamic study of multiple pulses micro drilling. *Ultrasonics,* Vol. 44, 1191-1194, ISSN 0041-624X

Petkovšek, R., Babnik, A. & Diaci, J. (2006). Optodynamic monitoring of the laser drilling of through-holes in glass ampoules. *Meas. Sci. & Technol.*, Vol. 17, No. 10, 2828-2834, ISSN 0957-0233

Petkovšek, R., Možina, J. (2007). Monitoring of the laser microdrilling of glass by the optodynamic method. *J. Appl. Phys.*, Vol. 102, no. 4, pp. 44905-44909, ISSN 0034-6748

Petkovšek, R. et al. (2008). Optodynamic monitoring of laser micro-drilling of glass by using a laser probe. *Applied Physics A (Materials Science Processing)*, Vol. A93, No. 1, 141-145, ISSN 0947-8396

Požar, T., Gregorčič, P. & Možina, J. (2009). Optical measurements of the laser-induced ultrasonic waves on moving objects. *Opt. Express,* Vol. 17, No. 25, 22906–22911, ISSN 1094-4087

Strgar, S., Diaci, J. & Možina, J. (2000). Optodynamic measurements of Q-switched Nd: YAG laser drilling of laminated aluminium. *Lasers in Engineering*, Vol. 10, No. 4, 243-253, ISSN 0898-1507

Strgar, S. & Možina, J. (2002a). An optodynamic determination of the depth of laser-drilled holes by the simultaneous detection of ultrasonic waves in the air and in the workpiece. *Ultrasonics*, Vol. 40, No. 1-8, 791-795, ISSN 0041-624X

Strgar, S. & Možina, J. (2002b). An optodynamic method for the real-time determination of the depth of a laser-drilled hole. *Applied Physics A (Materials Science Processing)*, Vol. A74, No. 2, 321-323, ISSN 0947-8396

4

# Properties of Hard Carbon Coatings Manufactured on Magnesium Alloys by PACVD Method

Marcin Golabczak
*Technical University of Lodz, Department of Production Engineering*
*Poland*

## 1. Introduction

Magnesium alloys found a plethora of applications in various branches of industry where reduction in weight is of importance (Gray & Luan, 2002). These alloys are used in aerospace, automobile and electronic industries, for manufacturing of sporting goods etc. Advantages of magnesium alloys include: the high strength: weight ratio, high thermal conductivity, small heat extensibility, good welding characteristics and high functional integrity, which allow to produce near-net-shape elements as well as good machinability (Hawkins, 1993). However, magnesium alloys have also certain disadvantages. The most troublesome of them is the high susceptibility to corrosion, which contributes to dwindling of their size and reduces mechanical durability. Other disadvantages of magnesium alloys comprise their weak wear resistance, a drop in durability at high temperature and interference of electromagnetic field. The aforementioned faults considerably reduce the area of application of this material.
Presented studies aimed at elimination of the listed drawbacks by means of covering of magnesium alloy AZ31 with special hard carbon coatings to form a protective barrier with decorative appearance. Plasma Activated Chemical Vapor Deposition (PACVD) method was used for this purpose. Optimum conditions of this process were determined and the material properties of the coatings were characterized.

## 2. Experimental apparatus and procedure

Hard carbon films were deposited on magnesium alloys AZ31 by PACVD method, which relied on decomposition of methane in electric field with high frequency of 13.56 MHz, obtained at the pressure of approximately 12 Pa in a working chamber (Golabczak, 2005). Processes of PACVD were realized in the stand presented in figure 1. It consisted of the chamber of water cooled plasma reactor, the high frequency electrode fixed to the plate of the base and connected through the condenser (the latter provided the negative potential of self-polarization), generator of high frequency (facilitated production of plasma with high density and maintained the frequency at the constant level), vacuum system and systems of measurement and control.
Hard carbon coatings were deposited on magnesium alloy AZ31 in two steps comprising the process of ionic digestion of their surface followed by the process of synthesis of these coatings. Parameters of these steps are shown in table 1.

Fig. 1. The scheme of the system used for deposition of hard carbon coatings by PACVD method

| Parameter | Ionic digestion of the surface | Process of coating deposition |
|---|---|---|
| Feed gas | $CH_4$ | $CH_4$ |
| Pressure in a working chamber | 8 ÷ 10 Pa | 12 Pa |
| Time of process - t | 4 min | 5 ÷ 9 min |
| Gas flow rate - V | 5 $cm^3$/min | 20÷60 $cm^3$/min |

Table 1. Parameters of PACVD process

## 3. Results and discussion

The experiments included optimization of technological parameters of PACVD process of deposition of carbon films and characterization of their material properties. To determine the optimum condition of PACVD process a series of test specimens was produced according to the fractional experimental $2^{n-1}$ design (Golabczak, 2005). The studies of material properties of carbon coatings deposited on magnesium alloy AZ31 comprised determination of morphology of these coatings, measurements of their nanohardness and thickness (Golabczak & Konstantynowicz, 2010), tribologic tests and determination of their corrosion resistance.

### 3.1 Determination of morphology of hard carbon coatings deposited on a surface of magnesium alloy

Morphology of hard carbon coatings deposited on the surface of magnesium alloy AZ31 was determined on the basis of their Raman spectra (Golabczak, 2005). For this purpose, the mathematical modeling of fitting of gaussian peaks of the identified carbon phases to the Raman spectra was performed (Golabczak, 2005). The contents of the identified carbon phases in the deposited carbon coatings were determined on the basis of the relative index - $E_i$, described by the following equation (1):

$$E_i = \frac{A_{p_i}}{A_s} = \frac{\int p_i(x)dx}{\sum \int p_i(x)dx} \quad (1)$$

where: $A_{pi}$ - surface area between the baseline and the curve of fitting to the plot for the carbon phases identified in the coating, calculated by the method of numerical integration; $A_s$ - the summary surface area between the baseline and the curve of fitting to Raman spectrum, calculated by the method of numerical integration (Golabczak, 2005).
Results of computing of the relative index $E_i$, obtained for each specimen prepared within the scope of the planned experiment, are shown in figure 2.

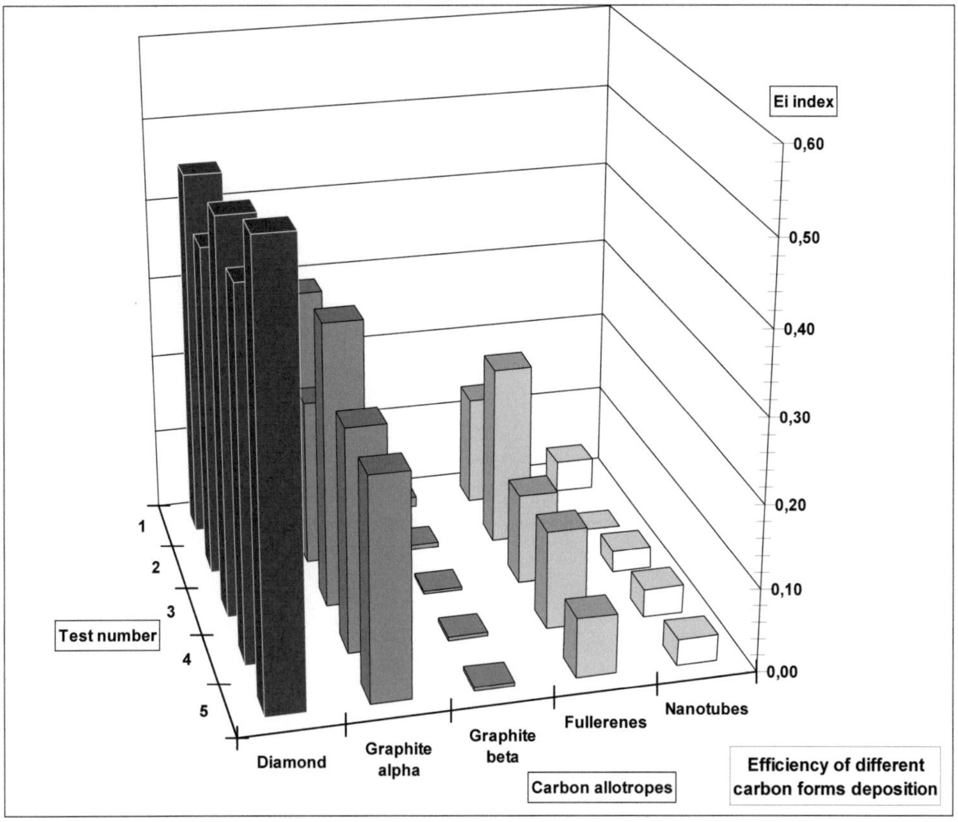


Fig. 2. Comparison of values of the relative index $E_i$ for carbon phases identified in hard carbon coatings deposited on magnesium alloy specimens obtained within the scope of the planned experiments of PACVD process

Analysis of results obtained for individual specimens produced within the scope of the planned experiment (specimens 1÷4), revealed that the diamond phase ($E_i$=0.40÷0.48) and alfa-graphite phase ($E_i$=0.20÷0.35) dominated in the deposited coatings. Also other carbon phases were identified, such as beta-graphite- ($E_i$=0.003÷0.013), fullerens ($E_i$=0.11÷0.22), nanotubes ($E_i$ of approximately 0.034) and other, including some unidentified forms ($E_i$=0.006÷0.068), rings ($E_i$ of approximately 0.008), and chains ($E_i$=0.018÷0.12), but their contents were minor. Optimization of deposition conditions (specimen 5) showed that the rise in contents of diamond phase (to $E_i$=0.54) in the coatings was achievable. The latter content of diamond phase in the coating was reached under the following PACVD process conditions: U=900V, t=8min, and V=60cm³/min.

### 3.2 Measurements of nanohardness of hard carbon coatings deposited on magnesium alloy AZ31

Nanohardness of hard carbon coatings was measured using Nano Test 600 meter (Micro Materials Ltd., Great Britain) equipped with a diamond pyramidal penetrator (Golabczak, 2005). The measurements of nanohardness were conducted at the penetrating force (F) of 0.1–0.6 mN (extorted by the penetrator) and the rate of F increase (dF/dt) of 0.02 mN/s. Values of nanohardness of hard carbon coatings, measured by using the pyramidal penetrator, were calculated as follows (2):

$$H_n = \frac{F}{24{,}5h_p^{\ 2}} \qquad (2)$$

where: $H_n$ - nanohardness of the outer layer [GPa], F - the penetrating force [N], $h_p$ - indentation made by the penetrator [m].

Representative results of nanohardness measurements of the examined hard carbon coatings deposited on magnesium alloy AZ31 are shown in figure 3.

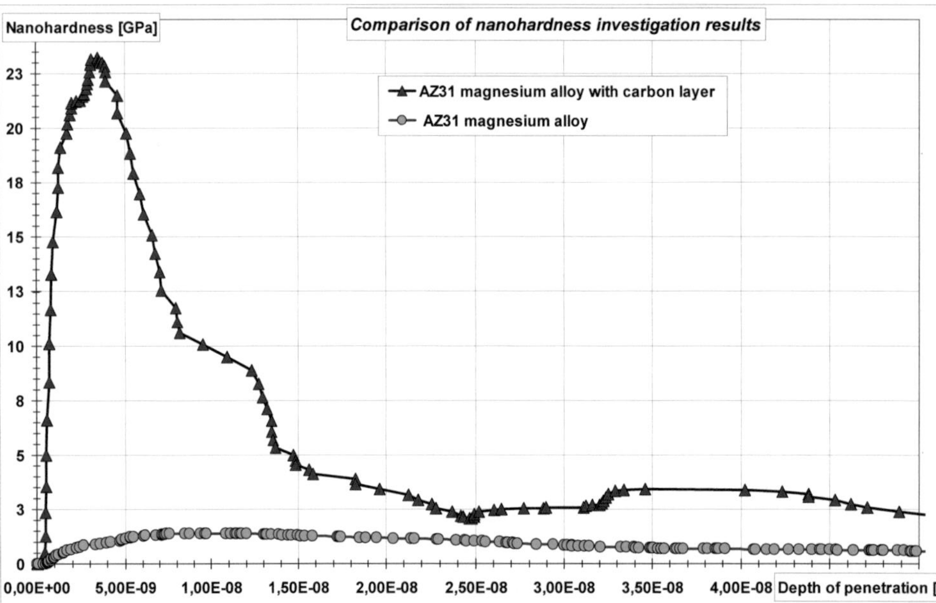


Fig. 3. Comparison of the nanohardness of magnesium alloy AZ31 protected by the carbon coating deposited under optimum conditions of PACVD process and the specimen without this coating

The latter presents the difference between the nanohardness of magnesium alloy AZ31 protected by the hard carbon coating deposited under optimum conditions of PACVD process and the alloy without this coating. These results provide evidence that the nanohardness of magnesium alloy AZ31 protected by the hard carbon coating deposited by the PACVD method was considerably higher (24 GPa) than that of the alloy without the coating (0.8 GPa).

### 3.3 Determination of the thickness of hard carbon coating

The thickness of hard carbon coatings was determined by the method of direct profilography using the highly precise Taylor Hobson profilographometer (Golabczak, 2005, 2010). To achieve the accurate results of measurements, the carbon coatings were deposited only on selected fragments of the examined samples of magnesium alloy. Therefore, some parts of their surface were protected by quartz plates during synthesis of the coatings (Fig. 4). Thus the examined surfaces of magnesium alloy contained the fragments coated by the carbon layer and free from the latter. Results of these measurements are collected in figure 5. The mean value (from 5 distinct measurements) of the thickness of a carbon coating was approximately 220 nm.

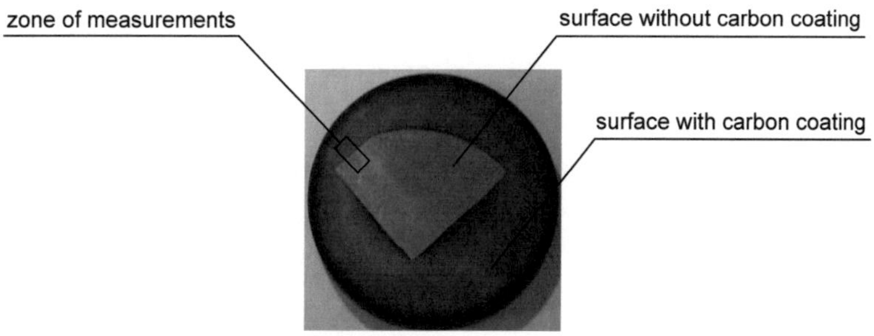


Fig. 4. The image of the surface of a specimen of magnesium alloy AZ31 prepared for the measurements of hard carbon coating thickness and the zone of measurements carried out by profilography method

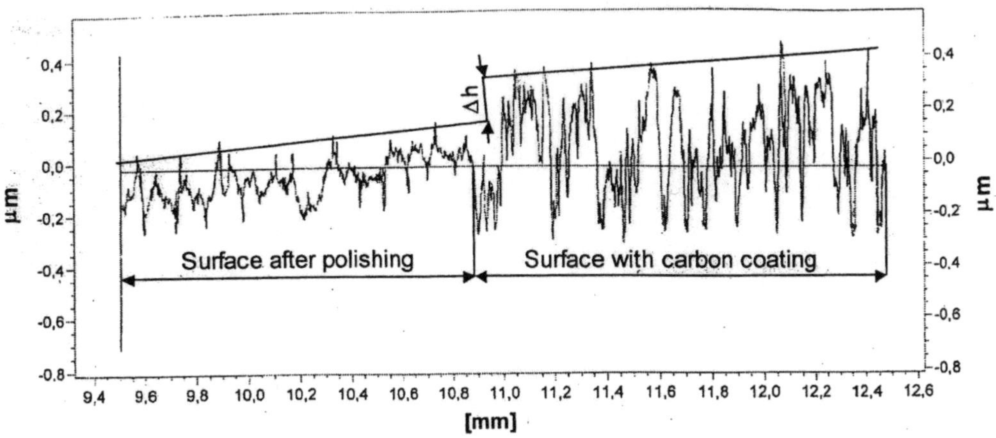


Fig. 5. Results of measurements of the thickness of hard carbon coating deposited on magnesium alloy AZ31 carried out by the method of direct profilography; the thickness of hard carbon coating (Δh) is equal to 220 nm

### 3.4 Tribologic measurements of hard carbon coatings

Tribologic measurements relied on tests of rubbing interaction between rectangular specimens of magnesium alloy AZ31 covered by the carbon coating and deprived of this layer with the cylindrical rubbers (Golabczak, 2005). The rubbers were prepared from three different materials such as hydrogenated rubber butadiene-acrylonitrile - HNBR, poly(methylmetacrylate) - PMMA (plexsiglass), and poly(tetrafluoroethylene) - PTFE (teflon). Dimensions of rectangular specimens of magnesium alloy were 10x4x5mm. The cylindrical rubbers had the diameter of 35mm and width of 10mm. Tribologic tests were conducted using Tribometer T-05 under the following conditions: normal load of the rubber - 6N, the rubbing speed - 3.67 cm/s, time of test duration - 2h, frequency of recording of measurements - 2E+14, and ambient temperature (T) of 20.7°C. Representative results of tribologic measurements are shown in figure 6-7. They present differences in the total friction energy and volumetric wear of the examined specimens during the test. The displayed results provide evidence that the carbon coatings deposited on magnesium alloy considerably improve its properties. They both reduce the total energy of friction and enhance their resistance to wear. Our experiments revealed that the total energy of friction of the listed above specimens with carbon coatings, was considerably lower and reached: 44% for the rubber one, 130% for the plexiglass rubber and 440% for that made of teflon. Carbon coatings also significantly decreased the total volumetric wear of the examined samples of magnesium alloy. The relative increase in wear resistance was: 660% - in case of the rubber rubber, 540% - for the plexiglass rubber and 800% - for the teflon one.

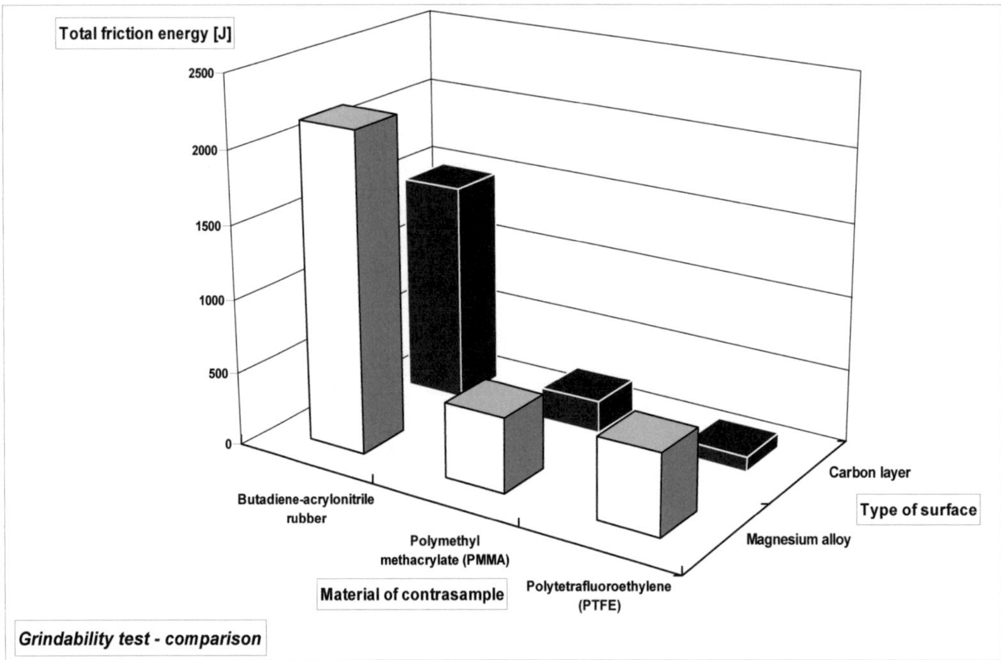


Fig. 6. Comparison of values of the total energy of friction determined by tribologic measurements for specimens of magnesium alloy AZ31 protected by the hard carbon coating and without the latter

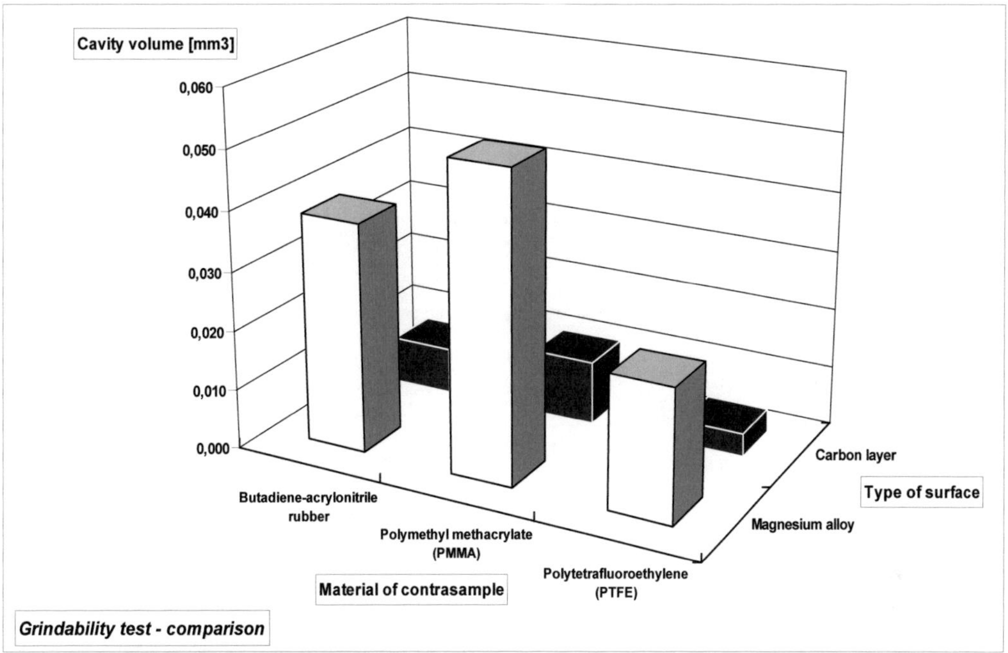


Fig. 7. Comparison of volumetric wear of the specimens of magnesium alloy AZ31 (one covered by the hard carbon coating and the second – without this coating) determined by tribologic measurements

### 3.5 Determination of corrosion resistance of hard carbon coatings in the salt spray chamber

Corrosion resistance tests of hard carbon coatings were conducted in SIGMA DIESEL salt chamber (BOSCH) (Golabczak, 2005). The examined specimens of magnesium alloy AZ31 were either protected with the carbon coating or not. Test conditions are displayed in table 3. The samples without the carbon coating were exposed to sodium chloride solution for 5h while the samples protected by this coating were exposed for 200h.

| Test parameters | Value |
|---|---|
| Time of test duration | 5h and 200 h |
| Temperature in the chamber | 35°C ± 1°C |
| Humidity in the chamber | 85% - 90% |
| Intensity of spraying (the sprayed surface area of 80 $cm^2$) | 2ml ± 1ml / h |
| Air pressure | 1.0 bar ± 0.2 bar |
| NaCl concentration in the solution | 5% (w/v) |

Table 2. Parameters of corrosion test carried out in a salt spray chamber

To estimate results of the corrosion test, images of the surface of specimens, which were subjected to this test were recorded using two microscopes, i.e. metallographic and SEM. Representative images of the surface of examined specimens are shown in figure 8 and 9.

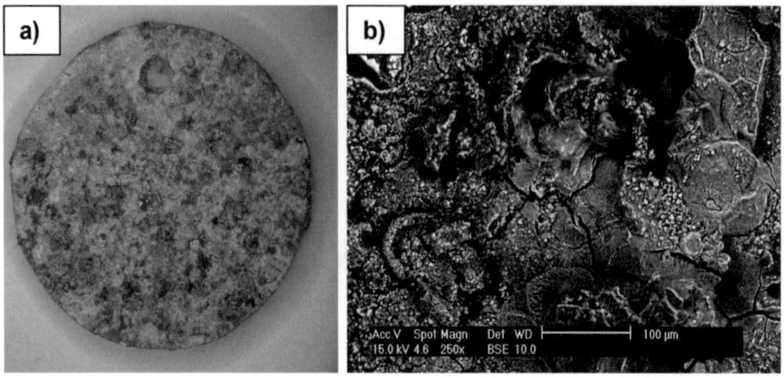


Fig. 8. Microscopic images of AZ31 magnesium alloy specimens without the hard carbon layer after 5h exposition in a salt spray chamber: a) magnification 3x, b) magnification 250x

Fig. 9. Microscopic images of AZ31 magnesium alloy specimens with deposited hard carbon layer after 200h exposition in a salt spray chamber: a) magnification 3x, b) magnification 250x

Comparison of the images of surface of specimens of magnesium alloy AZ31 exposed to the corroding environment in a salt chamber showed that the samples, which were not protected by the carbon coating were strongly corroded after the relatively short time of exposition (5h). In contrast, the specimens coated by the carbon film contained only small pits of corrosion after 200h of treatment under the same conditions. Results of these experiments demonstrate that carbon coatings explicitly protect magnesium alloy from corrosion.

### 3.6 Determination of corrosion resistance of hard carbon coatings using electrochemical method

The accelerated electrochemical method consisted in repeated potentiostatic measurements carried out by using Volta Master 1 set comprising a potentiostat Radiometr-Copenhagen PGP 201. The examined samples were immersed in Tyrod's electrolyte (its chemical composition is shown in table 3) at the temperature of 20°C.

| NaCl [g/dm³] | $CaCl_2$ [g/dm³] | KCl [g/dm³] | $NaH_2PO_4$ [g/dm³] | $MgCl_26H_2O$ [g/dm³] | NaHCO [g/dm³] | pH |
|---|---|---|---|---|---|---|
| 8.00 | 0.20 | 0.20 | 0.05 | 0.10 | 1.00 | 6.9 |

Table 3. Chemical composition of Tyrod's electrolyte

Modeling of phenomena occurring at the contact interface between the conductor (metal) and the electrolyte was based on the standard Butler-Volmer equation (Golabczak, 2008). It is a half-empirical equation and characterizes the rate of electric charge transfer through the interface of phases: metal-electrolyte. This rate depends, first of all, on the difference of potentials and its sign (positive or negative) at this interface. The analysis of current flow through the medium which is far from the state of equilibrium cannot be done without the model of Butler-Volmer. The model based on an electric nonlinear circuit was proposed to determine the flow of current in the wide range of potential values. This circuit contains some elements responsible for individual physical phenomena that take place during potentiostatic measurements. The scheme of this substitute circuit is shown in figure 10.

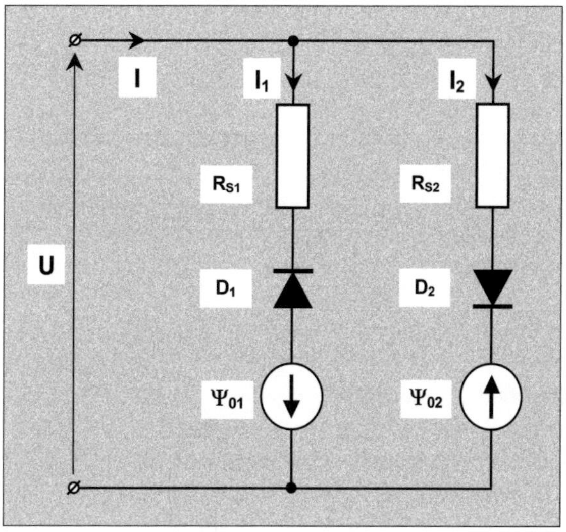


Fig. 10. The structure of proposed model in the form of the nonlinear electric circuit with lumped constants

The proposed model consists of two branches characterizing anodic and cathodic currents. Relationships between the elements of the model shown in figure 10 and phenomena occurring at the interface conductor-electrolyte are as follows:

- diodes $D_1$ and $D_2$ that are fundamental elements of the proposed model correspond to the exponential components of Butler-Volmer equation that are responsible for diffusion ,
- resistors $R_{S1}$ and $R_{S2}$ are responsible for the transfer of electric charge carriers and are particularly important at higher values of voltage U,
- voltage generators $\Psi_{01}$ and $\Psi_{02}$ are responsible for the difference in potentials at the contact interface for anodic and cathodic parts of the characteristics.

Equations describing the substitute electric circuit (Fig. 10) are as follows:

- for the anodic branch (left parts of descending curves in figure 11 and 12):

$$j_1 = -j_{01}\left(e^{-\frac{q \cdot m_1}{k \cdot T} \cdot U_{D1}} - 1\right) \qquad (3)$$

- for the cathodic branch (right parts in ascending curves in figure 11 and 12):

$$j_2 = j_{02}\left(e^{\frac{q \cdot m_2}{k \cdot T} \cdot U_{D2}} - 1\right) \qquad (5)$$

The total current flowing through the interface is the sum of anodic current and cathodic current:

$$j = j_1 + j_2 \qquad (7)$$

where: q- the elementary charge of an electron, expressed in [C] [A·s], $q=1.6022 \cdot 10^{-19}$ C;
k- Boltzman constant, expressed in [J/K] [kg·s²/m²·K], $k=1.3807 \cdot 10^{-23}$ J/K;
T- the temperature of the contact interface [K];
$j_{01}$, $j_{02}$ – the density of saturation currents, expressed in [mA/cm²];
$R_{S1}$, $R_{S2}$ - resistances representing the phenomenon of electron transfer, expressed in [Ω];
$m_1$, $m_2$ - coefficients dependent on division of currents and valences of ions in the electrolyte, dimensionless quantities.

Electric parameters of this model for individual potentiostatic curves (Tafel curves) were identified by means of the least square method and by resolving the system of nonlinear equations by the gradient method. The obtained parameters are effective estimators of the true model parameters. Results of potentiostatic measurements were plotted in figure 11 and 12. Intercepts of curves presenting the voltage on diodes with OX axis correspond to potentials on the interface metal-solution. The values of electric parameters that were calculated for the assumed models are presented in table 4 and 5. On completion of potentiostatic measurements the surface of the examined samples was subjected to SEM analysis. Examples of the recorded images are shown in figure 13 and 14. Analysis of results of electrochemical studies revealed that deposition of the hard carbon coating on the surface of AZ31 magnesium alloy significantly dislocated and increased the difference in potentials (corrosion potential increased) at the interface between the metal and solution (Fig. 12) as compared to the reference sample without the coating (Fig. 11). It provides evidence of the beneficial effect of hard carbon coating deposited on this alloy because the barrier protecting the latter from electrochemical corrosion was increased.

| Model parameters | $J_0$ | $\Psi_0$ | m | $R_S$ |
|---|---|---|---|---|
| | mA/cm² | V | - | Ω |
| Diode I | 0.009145 | -1.6622 | 0.4276 | 1092.46 |
| Diode II | 0.000100 | -1.6482 | 0.9607 | 643.96 |
| Fitting error | | 4.027E-03 | | |
| Deviation 3σ | | 5.280E-02 | | mA/cm² |

Table 4. Electric parameters of the potentiostatic curve of electrochemical corrosion for sample made of AZ31 magnesium alloy free of carbon coating

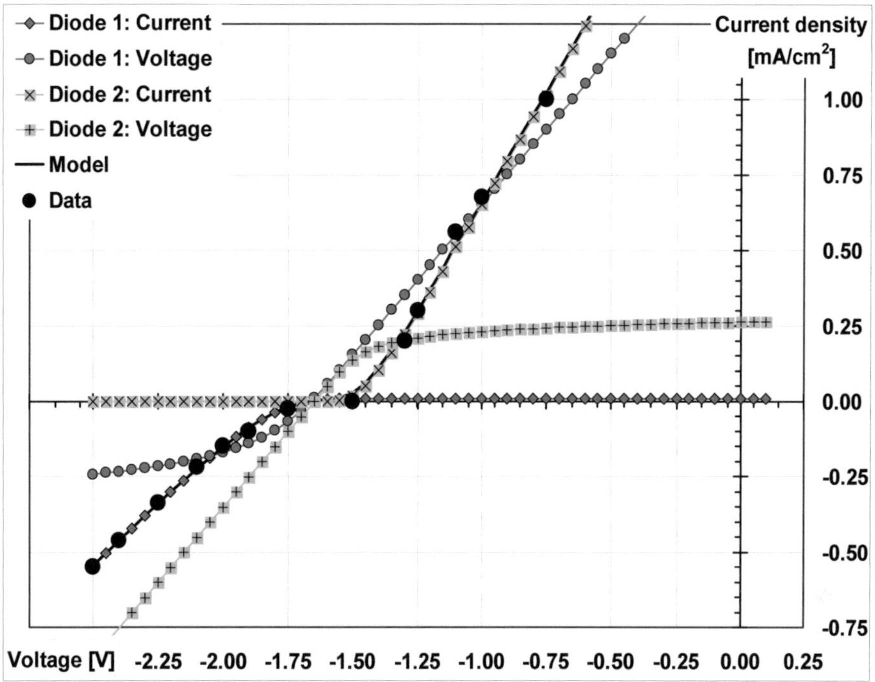


Fig. 11. Potentiostatic curve of electrochemical corrosion for AZ31 magnesium alloy free of hard carbon coating

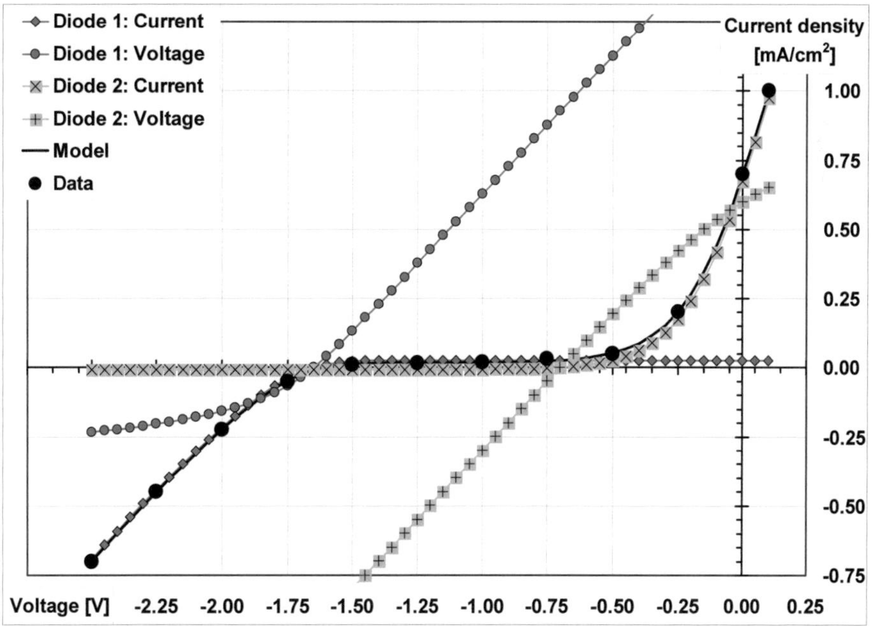


Fig. 12. Potentiostatic curve of electrochemical corrosion for AZ31 magnesium alloy protected by hard carbon coating

| Model parameters | $J_0$ | $\Psi_0$ | m | $R_S$ |
|---|---|---|---|---|
| | mA/cm$^2$ | V | - | Ω |
| Diode I | 0.026058 | -1.6501 | 0.3588 | 892.26 |
| Diode II | 0.008067 | -0.7000 | 0.1867 | 152.36 |
| Fitting error | | 7.947E-05 | | |
| Deviation 3σ | | 7.720E-03 | | mA/cm$^2$ |

Table 5. Electric parameters of the potentiostatic curve of electrochemical corrosion for sample made of AZ31 magnesium alloy bearing the carbon coating

Also SEM analysis of the surface of the examined samples confirmed this desirable impact (Fig. 13 - 14). Only single dark spots (probably very small corrosion pits) were visible at the surface of the samples bearing hard carbon coating (Fig. 13) whereas harmful results of electrochemical corrosion were visible on the whole surface of unprotected AZ31 magnesium alloy (Fig. 14).

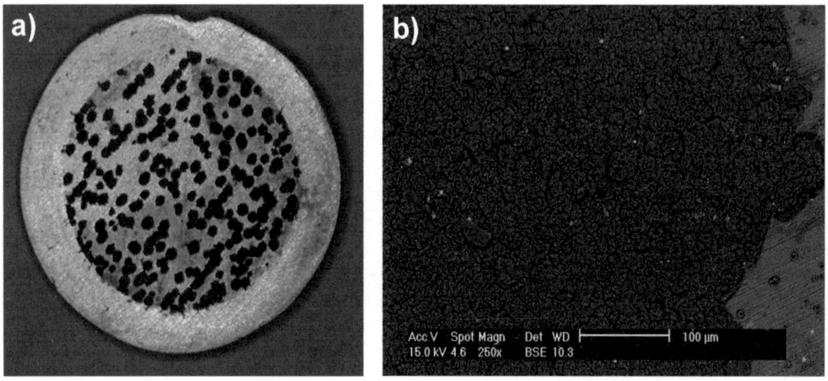


Fig. 13. SEM image of AZ31 magnesium alloy surface on completion of the potentiostatic corrosion test; test duration-1h: a) magnification 3x, b) magnification 250x

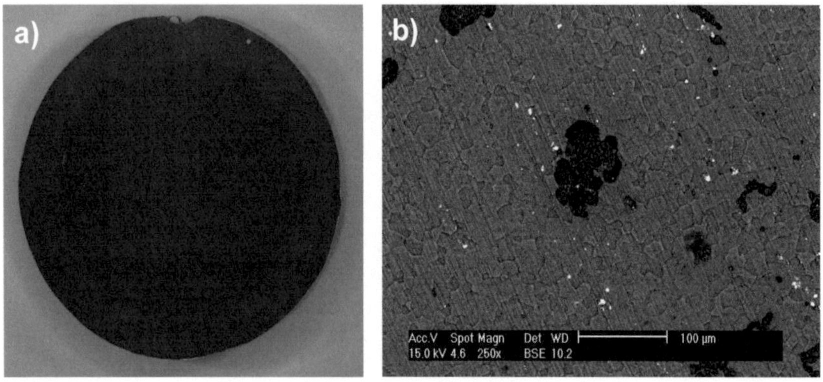


Fig. 14. SEM image of the surface of AZ31 magnesium alloy protected by hard carbon coating on completion of the potentiostatic corrosion test; test duration 1h: a) magnification 3x, b) magnification 250x

## 4. Raman spectra evaluation of the hard carbon layers

Raman effect has been widely used for carbon layers analysis from years for qualitative analysis of samples as well as quantitative. Two main lines of attitude to the quantitative analysis of the Raman spectra have been developed. The first one is applied mainly in forensic investigations when one have prepared comparative sample consist of known substances with known concentration which is the base for comparison of spectra from unknown sample. A tool used in these investigations is Voigt profile based on Faddeeva function, allowing a very precise comparison of spectra with elimination of individuality of measurement equipment. This attitude seems not to be the best solution when one has not comparative samples and sample under test is unique - the situations often meet in scientific investigation. Using Voigt profiles may cause a lost of information carried with spectrum, especially related with small quantities of nanotubes or fullerenes generated in the process of imposing diamond layers in plasma arc. Another function for approximation shape of the Raman peak based on Breit-Figner-Fano curve is frequently used but difficulties arise when identifying physical meaning of parameters and subtracting idle pedestal from the experimental spectrum. A different attitude based on simple Gaussian peak approximation has been discussed leading to the conclusion, that engaging more advanced and sophisticated methods does not provide automatically better results. Especially for coatings used in health care very careful evaluation of the experimental data have to be performed (Golabczak & Konstantynowicz, 2009). In this paper we would like to deal more deeply with Voigt profile matching to the Raman spectrum taking into account the measurement equipment characteristics, i.e. filtering efficiency of the Fabry-Pérot interferometer. Accordingly the figure 15 mutual relationship between wave of the wave number $k_S$ being anti-stokes scattered and detected with Fabry-Pérot interferometer and incident laser wave of the wave number $k_L$ is given by the so called Raman shift denoted $k_R$:

$$k_S - k_L = k_R \tag{8}$$

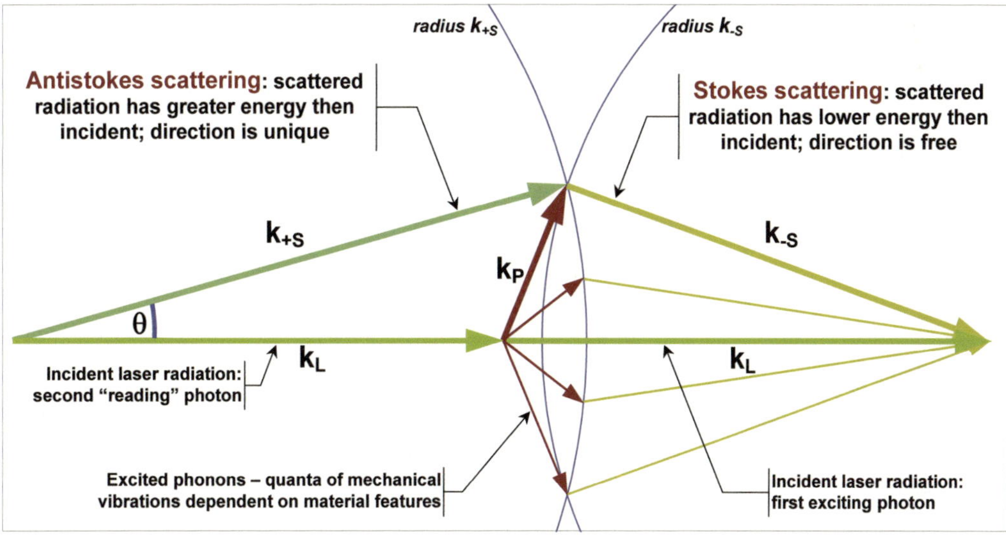


Fig. 15. A schematic diagram of the Raman scattering mechanism (multi-photon/fonon interaction)

Passing to the wavelength domain gives:

$$\frac{2\pi}{\lambda_S} - \frac{2\pi}{\lambda_L} = k_R \quad (9)$$

Finally we obtain relationship used further:

$$\lambda_S = \frac{\lambda_L}{1 + \lambda_L \cdot \frac{k_R}{2\pi}} \quad (10)$$

Obviously, all of the length units in the equation (10) have to be the same. It is worth of memory, that wavelength of the laser emitted beam is usually given in [nm] ($10^{-9}$ m) and Raman shift wave number is given in [$cm^{-1}$] ($10^{-2}$ m) as a rule. The relationship (10) allows us to draw the Raman spectrum from an experiment in the wavelength domain, which is dependent on the laser beam wavelength. Following, it allows comparison of the Raman spectrum with the Fabry-Pérot interferometer characteristics evaluated traditionally in the wavelength domain (Golabczak & Konstantynowicz, 2009). Accordingly this rule Raman spectrum has been drawn in the figure 19 showing the simulated Fabry-Pérot interferometer characteristics interaction with the Raman spectrum from an experiment. In this paper we have been used Raman spectrum investigation for determining both layer composition and quantitative determination of the diamond-like structure participation in the layer. Examination of the layer imposing procedure shows, that different carbon allotropes or compounds could be expected in the layer, not only diamond-like (Golabczak & Konstantynowicz, 2009). Although efforts have been made to enhance content of the diamond-like structures is not possible to obtain a pure one. In our further works related with optimization of the layer content, especially assuring proper balance between diamond and graphite structures, we will need especially precise tools for quantitative examination of the layer, presumably more precise then tools based on the standard Raman spectrum profile matching for recognition purpose only.

### 4.1 The Voigt profile basics

In the paper we have examined use of different functions modeling shapes of the Raman spectrogram for different purposes. Here we like to deal in details with Voigt profile use and computational problems. Voigt profile is a specific convolution function, with two parameters, which covers features of the Raman spectrum generated by the investigated material features as well as the influence of the Fabry-Pérot interferometer used as the detector:

$$V(x,\sigma,\gamma) = \int_{-\infty}^{+\infty} G(t,\sigma)C(x-t,\gamma)dt \quad (11)$$

where: $G(x,\sigma)$ - central Gaussian (with zero mean value) distribution modeling features of the investigated material, given as the probability distribution function with one parameter $\sigma$ determining its width:

$$G(x,\sigma) = \frac{1}{\sigma\sqrt{2\pi}} e^{-\frac{x^2}{2\sigma^2}} \quad (12)$$

$C(x,\gamma)$ - central Cauchy distribution modeling influence of the Fabry-Pérot interferometer, called also "Lorentz distribution", given as the probability distribution function with one parameter $\gamma$ determining its width:

$$C(x,\gamma)=\frac{\gamma}{\pi\left(x^2+\gamma^2\right)} \tag{13}$$

In closed form, after performing integration in convolution, Voigt profile can be expressed as:

$$V(x,\sigma,\gamma)=\frac{\mathrm{Re}[F(z)]}{\sigma\sqrt{2\pi}} \tag{14}$$

where complex $z$ variable is of the form:

$$z=\frac{x+j\gamma}{\sigma\sqrt{2}} \tag{15}$$

where in turn $F(z)$ is complex complementary error function called also Faddeeva function.

$$F(z)=e^{-z^2}erfc(-jz) \tag{16}$$

where in turn:

$$erfc(z)=1-erf(z) \tag{17}$$

is the complementary error function of the complex variable expressed as (non-analytical!) integral:

$$erfc(x)=\frac{2}{\sqrt{\pi}}\int_x^{\infty}e^{-t^2}dt \tag{18}$$

Effective computation of the *erfc* function i.e. fast and precise even for relatively big $|z|$, and the following computation Faddeeva function, establish a real problem. A number of methods is known, sometimes assuming very specific use in spectrum recognition, eq. (Estevez-Rams et al., 2005). They are all based on different approximations of the $F(z)$ function (power series expansions) easy (relatively!) for computation (Di Rocco et al., 2004; Ida et al., 2000). Sometimes these approximations are very specific and not usable beside rare programming environments or operating systems.

A universal and effective computation of the complex error function at the given point can be also performed traditionally by expansion in the Taylor power series (Abramowitz et al., 1968), which seems to be more practical then basing upon the very special functions one can meet only in a few types of processors or programming languages:

$$erf(z)=\frac{2}{\sqrt{\pi}}\sum_{n=0}^{\infty}\frac{(-1)^n z^{2n+1}}{n!(2n+1)} \tag{19}$$

from (13), (14) and (16) we obtain:

$$F(z)=e^{-z^2}\left(1-\frac{2}{\sqrt{\pi}}\sum_{n=0}^{\infty}\frac{(-1)^n z^{2n+1}}{n!(2n+1)}\right) \tag{20}$$

Computing of the series (17) can be speed up with using two goals:

- iteratively counting each next summand from previous - it is so called conversion into multiplicative form of the (16) expression;
- performing full complex multiplication in algebraic form, not passing to trigonometrical functions which computation is the most long-lasting elementary operation.

Preserving of the about 30 terms in power series allows to compute complex error function with relative error less than $10^{-10}$ in the neighborhood of center which is enough for most of the purposes. Increasing the number of terms to about 250 allows to compute function with the precision of $10^{-15}$ even at the radius of $|z|$ at the level of 5. This has been computationally proven in our practice.

Plots of the described functions are depicted on the figure 16 and 17., where comparison has been made among peaks for different $\gamma$ parameter related with Fabry-Pérot interferometer used in an experiment.

### 4.2 The Fabry-Pérot interferometer

The Fabry-Pérot interferometer was developed in 1899 as a device for the very precise measurement of the length with using visible light wave as a "ruler". This is also the origin of its other name - an "etalon". Because of its excellent abilities in electromagnetic waves filtering in very narrow bands it has soon became a valuable tool in spectrometry. It is comprised of the two parallel surfaces reflecting light or electromagnetic wave from the other range eq. infrared or ultraviolet. Light is reflected and transmitted through the interferometer plate and reflected internally many times. Incident beam interfere with internally reflected, which gives an effect of selective passing the electromagnetic wave through the plate in the very narrow bands - transmission windows. This process is depicted schematically on the figure 18 where one of the possible configurations is considered. More sophisticated constructions based on two wedged plates are in use as well as the three plates assemblies, however this simply scheme covers the scope of our investigations with sufficient precision (Flowles, 1989). Preserving of the paralellnes of the surfaces is essential for the precision of the interferometer both in making the transmission window as narrow as possible and assuring that it is set in the prescribed point of the whole spectrum (Hernandez, 1986). This precision is in the scope of our special attention and will be practically identified from Raman spectrograms. We have been considered also with the tuning mechanisms of the Fabry-Pérot interferometers, but at this stage of investigations we have found them neglectable.

Spatial phase difference between two consecutive beams internally reflected - see figure 18 is given by the equation, setting up base relationship in the Fabry-Pérot interferometer analysis:

$$\delta=\frac{2\pi}{\lambda}\cdot 2\cdot n(\lambda)\cdot d\cdot\cos(\theta) \tag{21}$$

where: $\lambda$ - wavelength of the incident electromagnetic radiation, [m];

$n(\lambda)$ - refraction index of the material between reflecting surfaces, variable along the wavelength of the radiation, [-];

$d$ - distance between reflecting surfaces, normally is the thickness of the plate, eq. made of quartz crystal or quartz glass, which surfaces are silvered, [m];

$\theta$ - angle between normal to the plate surface and incident beam of radiation, [rad].

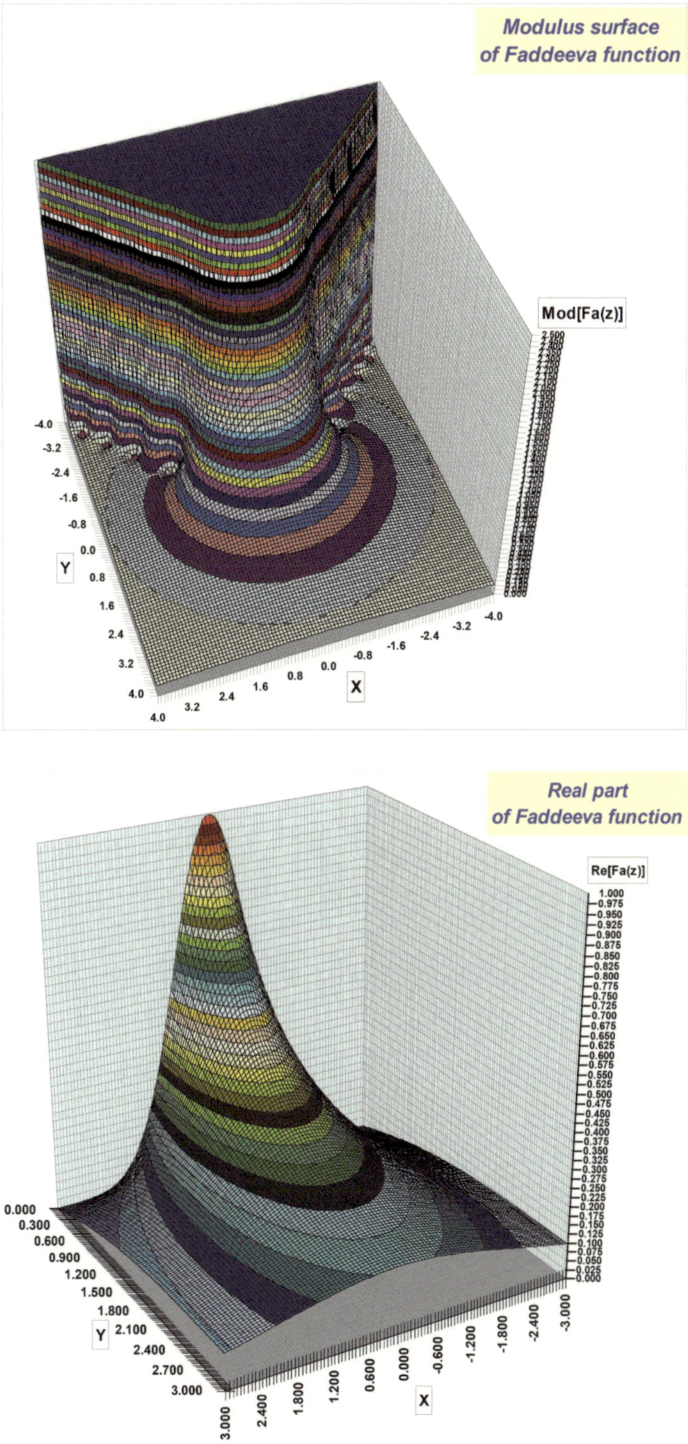


Fig. 16. Complex error function (Faddeeva function): modulus surface and real part surface

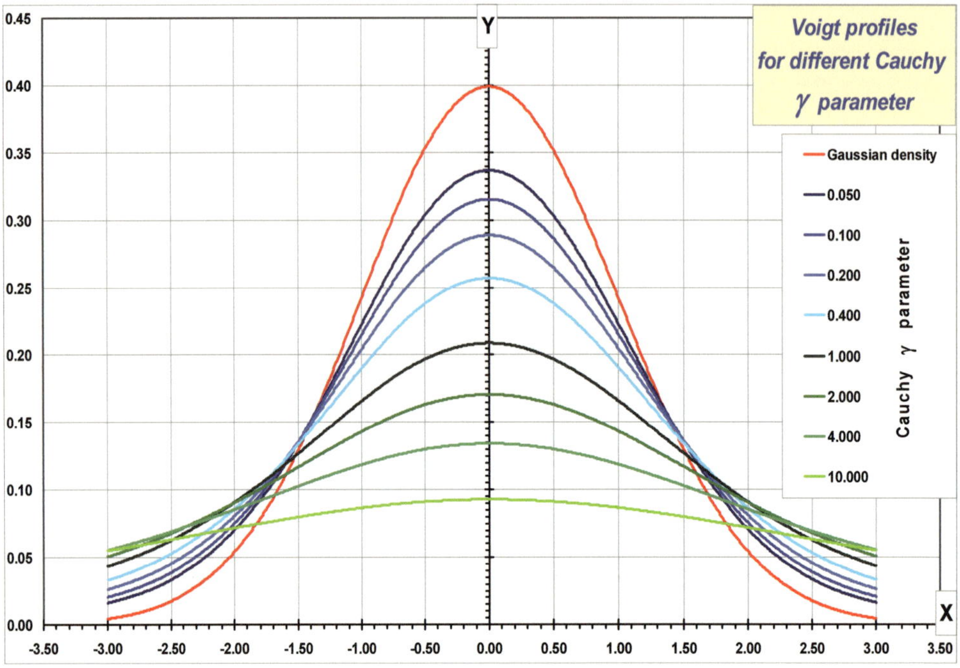


Fig. 17. Comparison of the Voigt profiles made of the normalized Gaussian density and the Cauchy densities of different width parameters γ

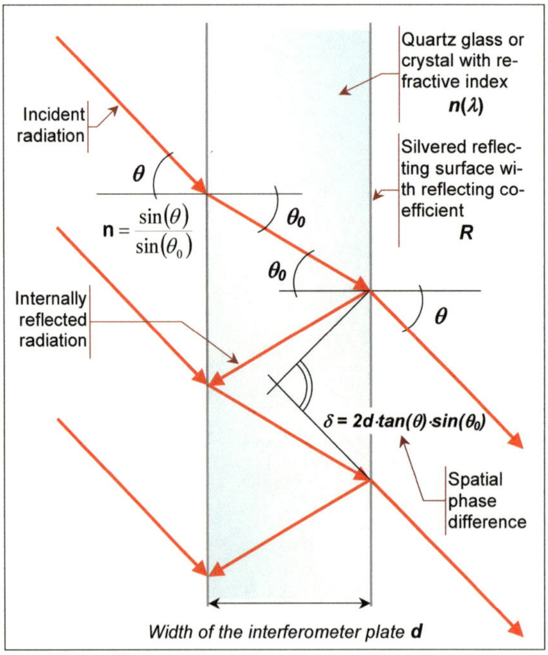


Fig. 18. Schematic diagram of the simply Fabry-Pérot interferometer and subsequent reflections of the interfering light beams.

Infinite summation of the series of reflections gives well-known Airy formula for transmission coefficient $T_E$ of the interferometer as the function of its construction parameters, wavelength of the radiation and direction of the radiation toward interferometer plate:

$$T_E = \frac{(1-R)^2}{1+R^2-R\cdot\cos(\delta)} = \frac{1}{1+F\cdot\sin^2\left(\frac{\delta}{2}\right)} \quad (22)$$

where: $R$ - coefficient of the reflection assumed the same for both surfaces, [-];
$F$ - finesse coefficient of the Fabry-Pérot interferometer:

$$F = \frac{4R}{(1-R)^2} \quad (23)$$

Coefficient of the maximal reflection of the interferometer plate - between spectral windows is given by:

$$R_{\max} = \frac{4\cdot R}{(1-R)^2} \quad (24)$$

Distance between consecutive spectral windows i.e. peaks of the interferometer characteristics - see figure 19, so called FSR - *Free Spectral Range* of the interferometer, which describes the range of unambiguous measurements, is given by the equation:

$$FSR = \Delta\lambda = \frac{\lambda_0^2}{\lambda_0 + 2\cdot n(\lambda_0)\cdot d\cdot\cos(\theta)} \quad (25)$$

where: $\lambda_0$ - wavelength of the peak to whom the FSR is associated when the plate is set appropriately to pass this peak through, [m];

- the rest of variables as in the previous equations.

Shape determination of the peak (transmission window) of the Fabry-Pérot interferometer have to be done at the fixed $\theta$, i.e. for the fixed value of wavelength $\lambda_0$ in the center of the peak with corresponding wave number $k_0 = 2\pi / \lambda_0$ and for the current variable $k = k_S - k_0$ as:

$$\frac{\delta}{2} = (k_S - k_0)\cdot n\cdot d\cdot\cos(\theta) = (k_S - k_0)\cdot c_F \quad (26)$$

where: $c_F$ - coefficient, constant in the contiguity of the peak, [m]:

$$c_F = n(\lambda_0)\cdot d\cdot\cos(\theta_0) \quad (27)$$

The relationship between $T_E$ and wave number of the incident radiation should be determined in the nearest vicinity of the peak's center, for the very small values of the $\delta$ angle when one can use the approximation $sin(x) \approx x$:

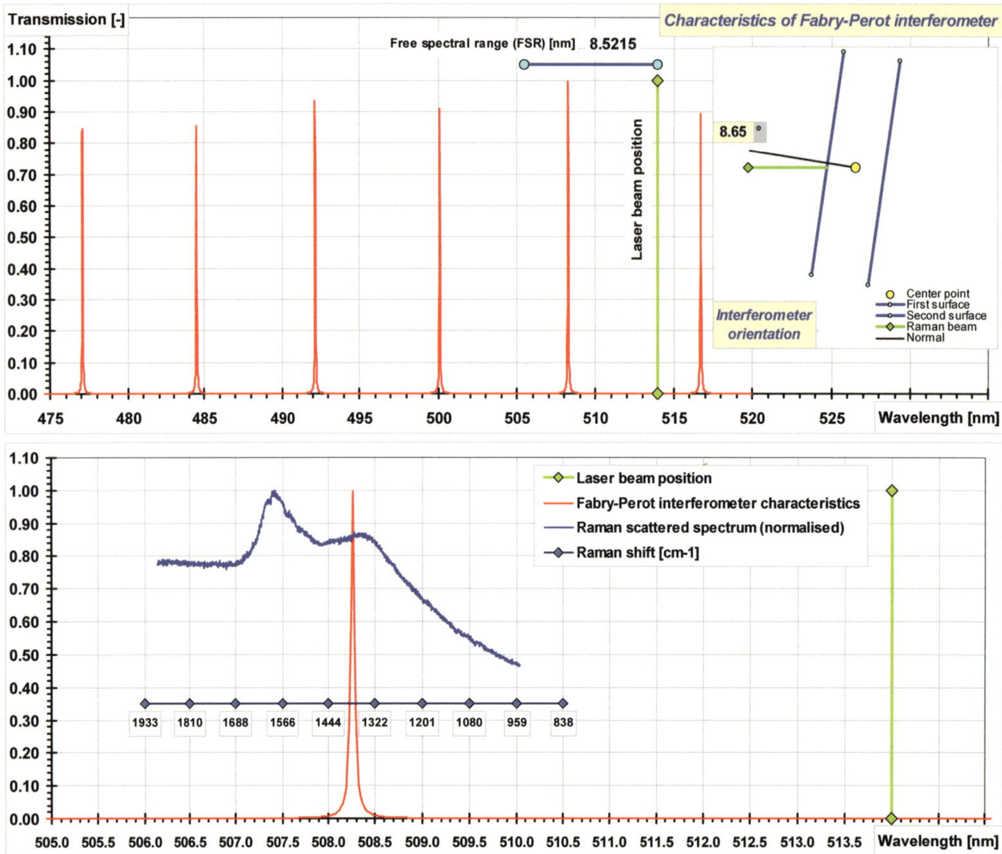


Fig. 19. Simulated characteristics of the Fabry-Pérot interferometer used in the Raman spectrum analyzer. Parameter γ of the interferometer has been extracted from the Voigt profile matched to the Raman spectrum from an experiment, which has been exposed in the background of the lower diagram. The lower diagram is to scale!

$$T_E = \frac{1}{1 + F \cdot \sin^2\left(\left(k_S - k_0\right) \cdot c_F\right)} \cong \frac{\dfrac{1}{F \cdot c_F^2}}{\dfrac{1}{F \cdot c_F^2} + \left(k_S - k_0\right)^2} \tag{28}$$

It follows from the equation (25) that the spectral peak placed at the wave number $k_0$ has the shape described by the curve of the type (10), i.e. Cauchy/Lorentz, where:

$$\gamma = \frac{1}{c_F \cdot \sqrt{F}} \tag{29}$$

The equation (26) allows relating constant $\gamma$ derived during matching the Voigt profile based function to the Raman spectrum, with technical parameters of the Fabry-Pérot interferometer used as the detector of the scattered radiation. Let make this evaluation for the interferometer which characteristics is depicted on figure 19. We have assumed the following construction parameters (realistic!):

- Wavelength of the laser radiation: $\lambda_L$ = 514 nm (green-yellowish light);
- Material of the interferometer plate: quartz glass;
- Refraction coefficient of the plate material at laser wavelength: $n$ = 1.461582;
- Plate thickness (after tuning of course): $d$ = 10.5503 μm = 10550.3 nm;
- Reflection coefficient of the silvered surface: $R$ = 0.982900;
- Finesse of the interferometer: $F$ = 13445.5;
- Order of the used peak: $m$ = 30;
- Free spectral range: $FSR$ = 8.5295 nm;
- Parameter $\gamma$ describing peak shape from equation (19): $\gamma = 5.66\ cm^{-1}$;
- Extraction of the γ parameter of the Fabry-Pérot interferometer from the Voigt profile matched to the real Raman spectrum from an experiment - investigation of the hard carbon layer imposed with PACVD method on the magnesium alloy, has gave mean value for the all peaks and spectra: $\gamma \approx 5.66\ cm^{-1}$

It could be easily seen that matching of the Voigt profile based function has provided us with the very realistic evaluation of the γ parameter. What more this parameter has happen to be at the same level for all the peaks and all the matched spectra. A sample matching result is depicted on the figure 20 showing plenty of different carbon forms, which one can expect in the layer. The spread of the γ parameter for all the five matching spectra is exhibited on the figure 21.

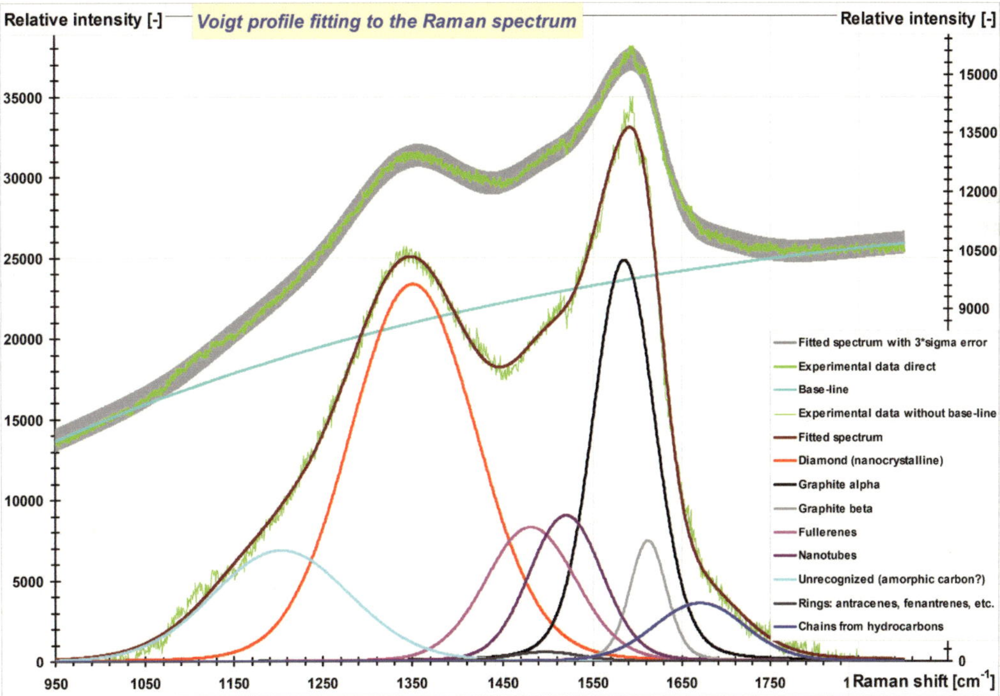


Fig. 20. Matching of the Voigt profile based function to the Raman spectrum of the DLC layer imposed on the light alloy

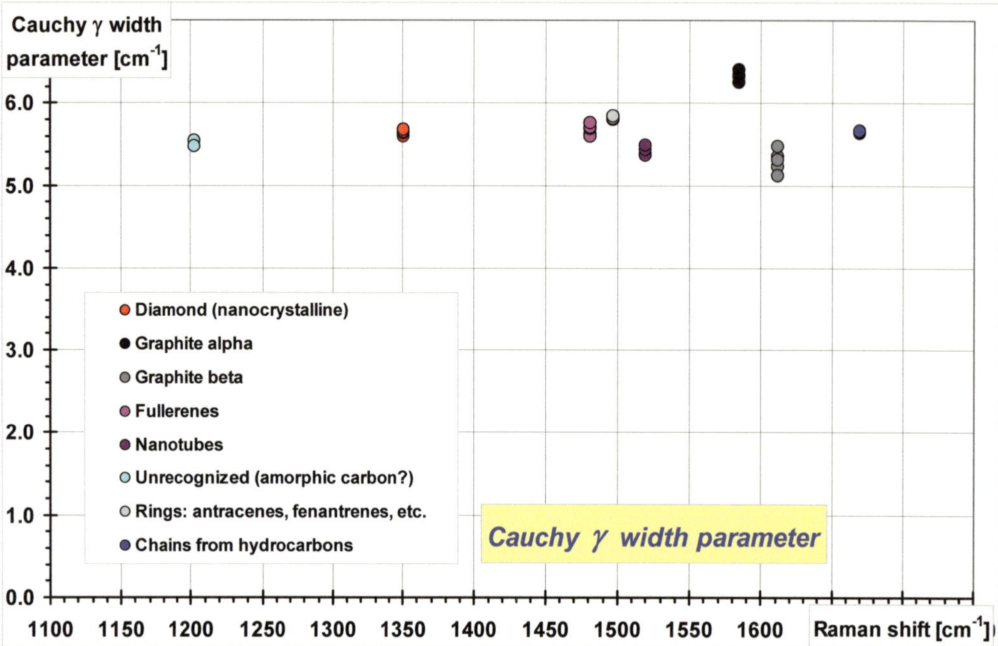


Fig. 21. Distribution of the γ parameter for all the analyzed peaks in the five Raman spectra of the hard carbon layers

### 4.3 The Voigt profile matching to the Raman spectra

The profile formulas, which could be matched to the Raman spectra, were discussed in details from metrological point of view in this paper (Golabczak & Konstantynowicz, 2009). Here we have used Voigt profile based function:

$$I_V(k) = \sum_{n=1}^{N} I_{0_n} \cdot V\left(k - k_{0_n}, \sigma_n, \gamma_n\right) + \\ + \left(I_{B_{MAX}} - I_{B_{MIN}}\right) \cdot \left(1 - \exp\left(-S_B \cdot k\right)\right) + I_{B_{MIN}} \tag{30}$$

where: $k_{0n}$ - wave number of the $n$-th peak, [m$^{-1}$];
$I_{0n}$ - maximal value of the $n$-th peak, [-];
$\sigma_n$ - width of the Gaussian component in the Voigt profile, [m$^{-1}$];
$\gamma_n$ - width of the Cauchy component in the Voigt profile, [m$^{-1}$].

The proper construction of the base function is a very complicated problem if one would like to relay it upon detailed deliberation about the whole spectrum of the radiation scattered when the laser beam impact sample under test. Here we have made use of a rather simple model, functional not structural, giving baseline of the spectrum (pedestal of the spectrum) as a very "flat" exponential function with three free parameters:

$$I_B(k) = \left(I_{B_{MAX}} - I_{B_{MIN}}\right) \cdot \left(1 - \exp\left(-S_B \cdot k\right)\right) + I_{B_{MIN}} \tag{31}$$

A sight at figure 18 with mutual placing of the Raman spectrum and the laser beam allows one to get additional, "visual" justification of the choose expressed in equation (31). Admitting three parameters for baseline function gives sufficient number of degrees of freedom during matching Voigt profile based function (30) to the Raman spectrum. In our case the coefficient SB was at the level about 0.0009 for all of the analyzed spectra.
All of the computations related with matching function (30) to the experimental data we have conducted in the calculation diagram built in the *Excel* spreadsheet with application the *Solver* tool. Solver seeks for the maximum or minimum of the user-prescribed function in the space of the user-prescribed variables. We have applied the following set-up to the *Solver* tool: searching for a minimum with using Newton method; scaling at each stage (iteration), square approximation of the function in the minimum vicinity, limit for searching only positive values. The number of variables was in our case as follows:

- 8 peaks with 4 parameters = 32 variables,
- baseline function: 3 parameters = 3 variables,
- total: 35 variables.

Results exhibited on figure 21 are highly reproducible from peak to peak in the given spectrum and among the Raman spectra obtained from the same spectrometer. It gives an assumption that they truly reflect quality of Fabry-Pérot interferometer and its tuning mode.

## 5. Conclusions

Presented studies provide evidence that PACVD method facilitates deposition of hard carbon coatings on magnesium alloy and the content of diamond phase in these coatings is high. Hard carbon coatings deposited by this method display very attractive material properties such as high nanohardness, resistance to wear, resistance to corrosion and reduced friction coefficient. Continuation of these studies aimed at the development of the devised technology of hard carbon films deposition on magnesium alloys is undoubtedly purposeful. Further research will focus on covering of items with more complicated shapes and on protecting of the inside surfaces.
Accuracy of matching the given Raman spectrum model as Voigt profile with experimental data could be improved basing on some additional information related with Raman spectrometer construction: Fabry-Pérot interferometer quality and its tuning through wavelengths expected in the Raman shift of investigated hard carbon layers manufactured on magnesium alloy. When performing Raman spectroscopy permanently with the same instrument one can include data related with this instrument, gathered from the previous spectra, in matching process of the current spectrum with Voigt profile.
Data about Fabry-Pérot interferometer gathered in our five spectrograms proved to be very homogenous. What more, some light tendency of peak broadening for higher Raman shift expressed in $\gamma$ parameter decrease, correspond well with natural tendency of the Fabry-Pérot interferometer of spectral window broadening due to interferometer tuning.
Investigations described in this paper allow making some assumptions for further research: deconvolution of Raman spectra with Cauchy-type Fabry-Pérot interferometer characteristics. This should give peaks narrowing effect and then, substantial improvement in Raman spectrum recognition due to the material components detection and improvement in quantitative determination of its content.

## 6. References

Abramowitz, M. & Stegun, I.A. (1968). *Handbook of Mathematical Functions,* Dover Publications, New York.

Di Rocco H.O. & Aguirre Téllez M. (2004). *Acta Physica Polonica,* Vol. 106, No 6, pp. 36-48.

Estevez-Rams, E.; Penton, A.; Martinez-Garcia, J. & Fuess, H. (2005). *Crystal Research and Technology,* Vol. 40, pp. 166-176.

Flowes, G.R. (1989). *Introduction to Modern Optics,* Dover Publications, New York.

Golabczak M. (2005). *Manufacturing of Carbon Coatings on Magnesium Alloys by PACVD Method,* Technical University of Lodz, Poland.

Golabczak, M. (2008). *Mechanics and Mechanical Engineering,* Vol. 12, No 2, pp. 157-164.

Golabczak, M. & Konstantynowicz, A. (2009). *Journal of Achievements in Materials and Manufacturing Engineering,* Vol. 37, pp. 270-276.

Golabczak, M. & Konstantynowicz, A. (2010). *Defect and Diffusion Forum,* Vols. 297-301, pp. 641-649.

Gray, J.E. & Luan, B. (2002). *Journal of Alloys and Compounds,* No 336, pp. 88-113.

Hawkins, J.H. (1993). *Global View Magnesium: Yesterday, Today, Tomorrow,* International Magnesium Association, pp. 46-54.

Hernandez, G. (1986). *Fabry–Pérot Interferometers,* Cambridge University Press, Cambridge.

Ida T.; Ando M. & Toraya H. (2000). *Journal of Applied Crystallography,* Vol. 33, pp. 1311-1316.

# 5

# Simulation of Cold Formability for Cold Forming Processes

Kivivuori, Seppo Onni Juhani
*Aalto University, School of Science and Technology*
*Finland*

## 1. Introduction

Massive metal forming processes include several manufacturing methods like drawing, extrusion, forging, coining and rolling. As manufacturing processes, these methods offer good mechanical properties to the products, a short production time, high productivity and optimal material utilization. These advantages are normally achieved with rather large production quantities because of the high cost of tooling and long set-up times of the production lines. However, potential savings in energy and material can be expected when medium and large production quantities are produced. (Kivivuori, 1987 b).
Normally massive metal forming processes are carried out using cold, warm or hot working conditions. The forgeability of deformed material or the limitations due to the deformation process used are the limiting factors when these massive metal forming processes are used.
The cold forgeability of a material can be measured by using upsetting, tensile or torsion tests. The upsetting test based either the measuring of critical reduction in height or the critical strain values measured from the free surface of the upset specimen are the methods most used for predicting the formability of the material during a massive cold forming process.

## 2. Forgeability of materials

Formability (Workability, Forgeability) is the ability of a material to deform plastically without the occurrence of any defect in a forming process (Dodd, 1996). A defect occurs when the properties of a component do not conform to the design specifications, making it unsuitable for the purpose for which it was designed. The occurrence of the defect depends on the geometry of the tooling, forming conditions and the properties of the work piece material. (ICFG document 11/01, 2001)

### 2.1 Ductility of materials

Cold forming is limited either by the high deformation force or the ductile fracture. It has been generally accepted that ductile fracture results when voids are formed around inclusions and other heterogeneities from the early stage of forming. If the deformation is continued, the voids grow and coalescence into a microcrack which further grows and becomes visible when it reaches the specimen surface (Kivivuori, 1978).

The stress and strain relations as well as alloying, microstructure and strain history also have a great influence on the ductile fracturing. Very important factor affecting the cold forgeability is the inclusion properties of the steel. The inclusion properties include the size, shape and volume fraction of inclusion and their distribution as well as chemical composition.

Alloying of steel normally reduces the ductility. Lamellar carbides as in pearlite, increase flow stress and strain hardening thus reducing ductility more than spheroidical carbides.

For practical purposes the effects of metallurgical variables or forgeability and machinability are roughly summarized in Table 1 (ICFG document 11/01, 2001).

| METALLURGICAL PARAMETER | | COLD FORGEABILITY | | | | TOOL WEAR IN MACHINING | |
|---|---|---|---|---|---|---|---|
| | | FLOW STRESS | | DUCTILITY | | | |
| | | Yield stress | Rate of strain hardening | Fracture strain in RD | Critical height reduction | HSS tool | Carbide tool |
| Chemical composition | C | ↑↑ | ↑ | ↓ | ↓↓ | ↑↑ | ↑↑ |
| | Si | ↑↑ | ↑↑ | ↓ | ↓↓ | ↑ | ↑ |
| | Mn | ↑ | ↑ | ↓ | ↓ | ↑ | ↑ |
| | P | ↑ | ↑ | ↓ | ↓ | → | → |
| | S | ↓ | ↓ | → | ↓↓ | ↓↓ | ↓ |
| | Cr | ↓ | ↑ | ↑ | ↑ | → | → |
| | Ni | ↑ | ↑ | ↓ | ↓ | ↑ | ↑ |
| | Mo | ↑ | ↑ | ↓ | ↓ | ↑ | ↑ |
| | Al | → | → | → | → | → | ↑↑ |
| | V | ↑ | U | ↓ | ↓ | ↑ | ↑ |
| | Nb | ↑ | U | ↓ | ↓ | ↑ | ↑ |
| | Ti | ↑ | U | ↓ | ↓ | ↑ | ↑↑ |
| | N | ↑↑ | ↑↑ | ↓ | ↓ | ↑ | ↑ |
| | B | → | → | → | → | → | → |
| | Metallic residuals | ↑ | ↑ | ↓ | ↓ | → | → |
| | Ca | → | → | → | → | ↓ | ↓↓ |
| Microstructure | Small grain size | ↑ | ↑ | → | → | ↑ | ↑ |
| | Lamellar carbides | ↑ | ↑ | ↓ | ↓ | ↓ | ↓ |
| | Segregations | → | → | ↓ | ↓ | ↑ | ↑ |

↑ Increase ↓ Decrease → Not effective

↑↑ Strong increase ↓↓ Strong decrease U Unknown

Table 1. The effect of chemical composition and microstructure on cold forgeability and tool wear in machining (ICFG document 11/01, 2001).

## 2.2 Defects in cold forging

When considering formability the type of the defect must be specified. The same material may show good formability, eg. with respect to ductile fracture, or very poor formability with respect to galling (ICFG document 11/01, 2001). The influence of the material properties on the different types of defects can be seen in Fig. 1.

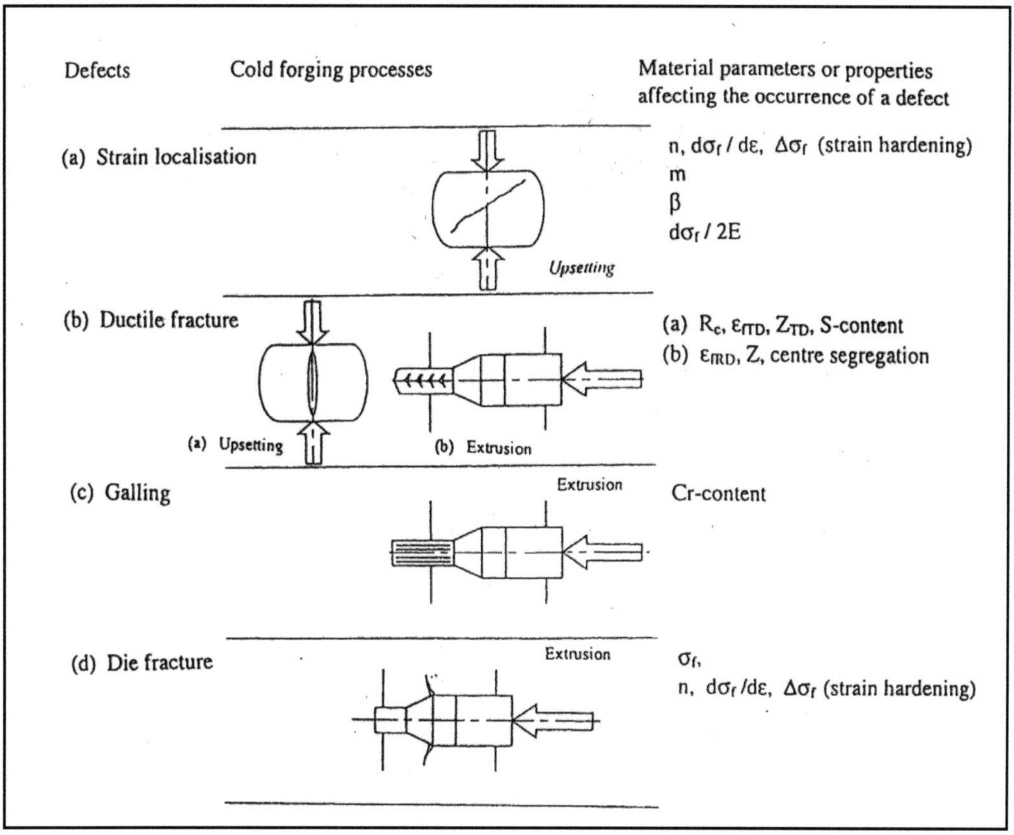


Fig. 1. Examples of defects in massive forming processes and their relation to material parameters (ICFG document 11/01, 2001).

## 3. Cold forgeability testing

Because of the complex nature of cold forgeability, there are no single test that can be used to evaluate it (ICFG document 11/01, 2001). Several testing methods to measure material forgeability have been developed.

Compression tests are normally used to measure material forgeability in massive metal forming processes (Kudo, 1967). On the other hand, for assessing the material formability upsetting tests based on measuring the critical reduction or forming limit diagram are often used. Therefore, for cold forgeability testing, firstly, compression tests for flow stress and upsetting tests for ductility and forming limit testing are recommended (ICFG document 11/01, 2001).

### 3.1 Compression testing

Flow stress testing is normally carried out by using compression tests under uniaxial stress state. To achieve this condition and to reduce the frictional forces between tool and specimen either conical compression tests or Rastegaev compression tests must be used. In fig. 2 the test specimens normally used for uniaxial compression testing has been shown.

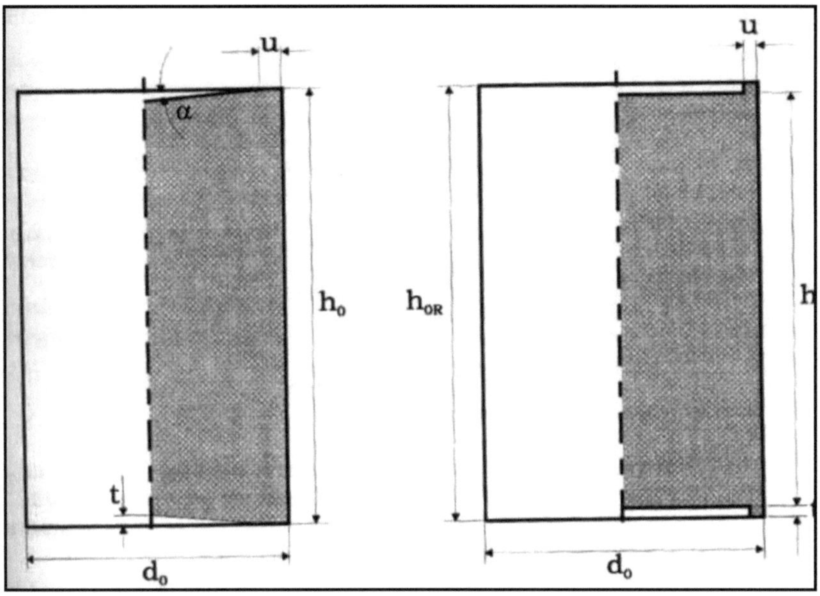


Fig. 2. Test specimens of compression test (ICFG document 11/01, 2001).
Left: Conical compression test
Right: Rastegaev compression test.

The dependence of the flow stress ($\sigma$) on strain ($\varepsilon$), strain rate ($\dot{\varepsilon}$) and temperature (T) can be expressed by

$$\sigma = \sigma\,(\varepsilon, \dot{\varepsilon}, T). \qquad (1)$$

This equation cannot be expressed generally, but rather for a particular material and a limited strain, strain rate and temperature range. The most widely used equation for steel and aluminum is the Hollomon type, which for isothermal conditions can be written in the form

$$\sigma_{iso} = K\,(\varepsilon/\varepsilon_o)^n\,(\dot{\varepsilon}/\dot{\varepsilon}_o)^m \qquad (2)$$

where $\varepsilon_o$, $\dot{\varepsilon}_o$, K, n and m are material constants. Assuming that $\varepsilon_o = 1$ and $\dot{\varepsilon}_o = 1\ s^{-1}$ eqn. (2) takes the form

$$\sigma_{iso} = K\,\varepsilon^n\,\dot{\varepsilon}^m \qquad (3)$$

The constants are determined from experimental stress-strain data. The strain-hardening exponent, n, is a measure of the ability of the material to harden as a result of deformation. the strain-rate hardening exponent, m, gives the response of a material to the strain rate. At ambient temperatures the strain-rate hardening is negligible since the m value for most metals is small.

In rapid forming, the temperature of the material being deformed can increase owing to deformation heating. The temperature dependence of the flow stress can be expressed by

$$\sigma = \sigma_{iso}\,(1 + \beta\,\Delta T) \qquad (4)$$

where $\beta$ is an experimentally determined constant and $\Delta T$ is the temperature difference from the isothermal condition.

### 3.2 Upset testing

When measuring ductility of the material upsetting test based on measuring of the critical reduction can be used. A collective round-robin study of a standardized cold upsettability test with a cylindrical test specimen compressed between grooved dies (fig. 3) was carried out by CIRP (Kudo, 1975).

To prevent effect of surface defects the test specimens must be machined out from the bars with sharp edged tool. Specimens are incrementally upset with the reduction increase of 2.5% until fracturing. The fracture of the specimen has detected after each increment and upsetting has continued until the fracture has observed by naked eyes.

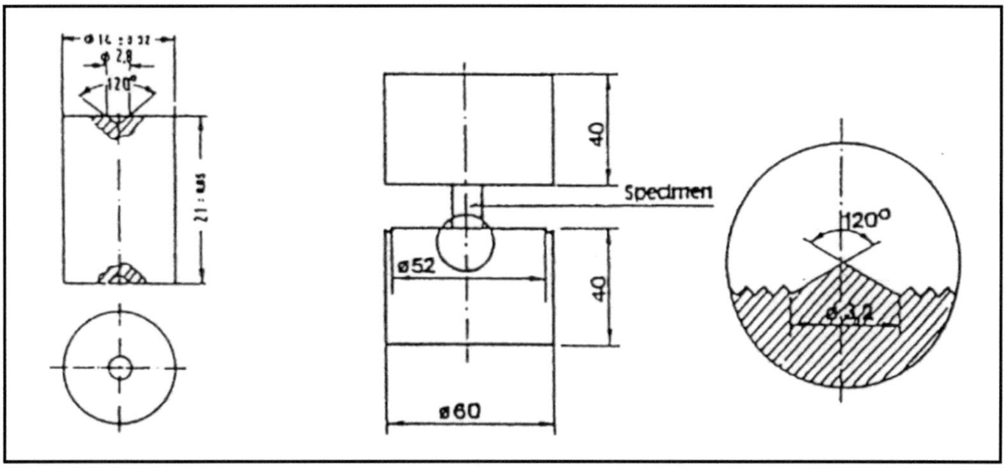


Fig. 3. Test specimens and grooved dies used in standardized upsetting testing (Kudo, 1975).

Collecting all fracture data of the testing serie containing normally 20 test pieces the critical reduction value can be calculated. The critical reduction value is obtained when 50 % of all fractures observed during testing have reached. The critical reduction values of several test materials can be seen in fig. 4.

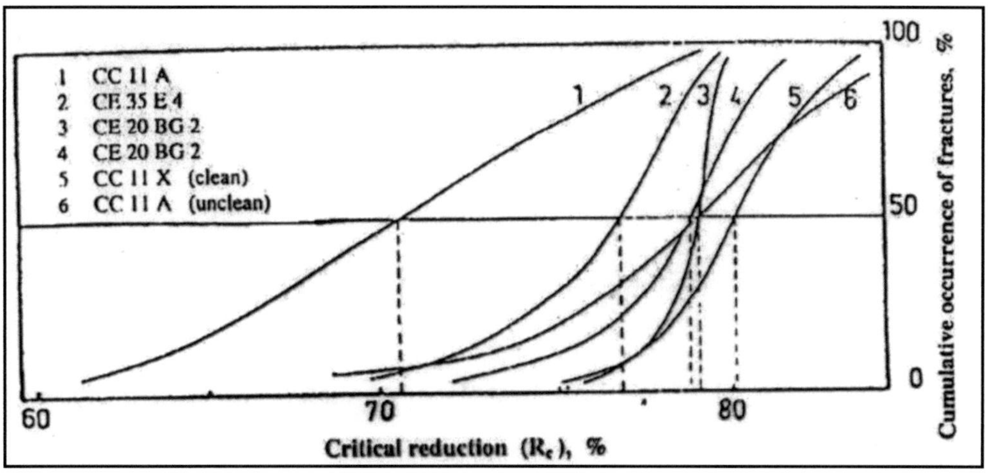


Fig. 4. The critical reduction of several materials tested in upsetting testing (ICFG document 11/01, 2001).

The pre-drawing has a considerable effect on the values of the critical reduction. The increased values of critical reduction have a maximum point at the pre-drawing reduction about 30 %, as can be seen in fig. 5. However, if the specimens are pulled in the tension testing machine without drawing tool, no increasing tendency have been noticed, but the value of critical reduction decreased according to fig. 5. It is significant that the specimen tensioned to the point of plastic instability could still be upset 75 % without cracking (Kivivuori, 1987 a)).

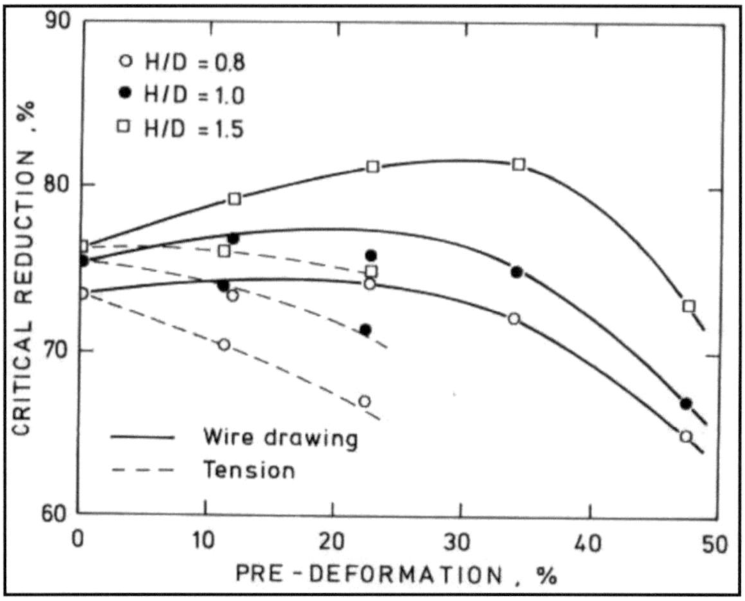


Fig. 5. The effect of pre-drawing on the critical reduction when specimens with H/D ratios of 0.8, 1.0 and 1.5 are upset in sticking friction conditions (Kivivuori, 1987 a)).

### 3.3 Formability testing

For the determination of the formability diagrams, a grid of 2 mm diameter circles was electrochemically etched on the surface of the specimens. Coordinate axes corresponding to the cylindrical symmetry used in the determination of fracture strains of the specimens, are presented in fig. 6.

When the cylindrical specimen is compressed the external surface barrels, fig. 6, developing tensile stresses at the free surface. In the case of severe barreling even the axial surface stress may become tensile which favors fracturing (Kivivuori, 1978). The surface strain values can be calculated using the following equations

$$\varepsilon_z = \ln (h/h_o) \tag{5}$$

$$\varepsilon_\theta = \ln (w/w_o) \tag{6}$$

$$\varepsilon_r = -(\varepsilon_z + \varepsilon_\theta) \tag{7}$$

where $h_o$ and $w_o$ are the original and h and w the current dimensions of grid marks on the surface of the specimens (see fig. 6).

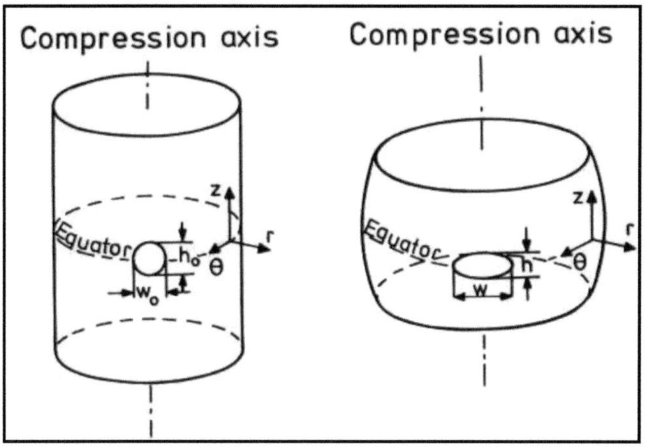


Fig. 6. Coordinate axis of the cylindrical symmetry on the surface of original and upset specimen (Kivivuori, 1987 a)).

Specimens will be compressed incrementally and the surface strain values will be measured after each compression step. Compression steps will be added incrementally until the specimen fractures. The strain values at fracturing are measured and plotted on the $\varepsilon_z$ - $\varepsilon_\theta$ coordination axis. Formability limits can be presented as a forming limit diagram (FLD) consisting of straight line having slopes between -0.33 and -0.7 (fig. 7). In the case of steel CC 35, the FLD consists of two lines as seen in fig. 7. One of these has roughly the direction of homogeneous deformation while the other is placed at higher strain values and limits the total strain in the circumferential direction.

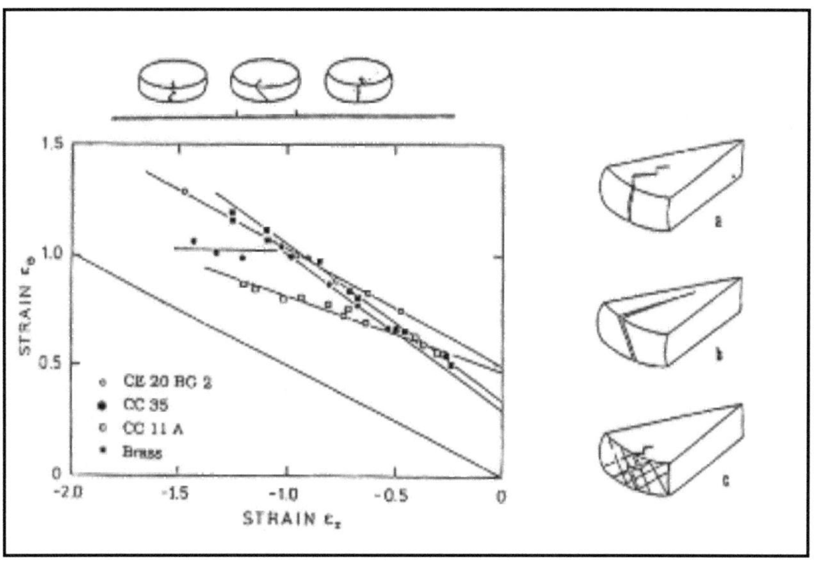


Fig. 7. Formability diagrams for several materials. Cracking modes and their occurrence in the forming limit diagrams (ICFG document 11/01, 2001).
a) longitudinal cracking at low strain values
b) oblique cracking at medium strains
c) shear cracking at large strain values.

To examine the validity of the formability limit diagram, two series of bolt heading tests were carried out using H/D ratios of 1.7 and 1.8. The results of these industrial bolt heading tests are given in fig. 8. It can be seen that the strain values in the heading process are quite far from the critical values measured with compression testing. This result agree well with the practical observations.

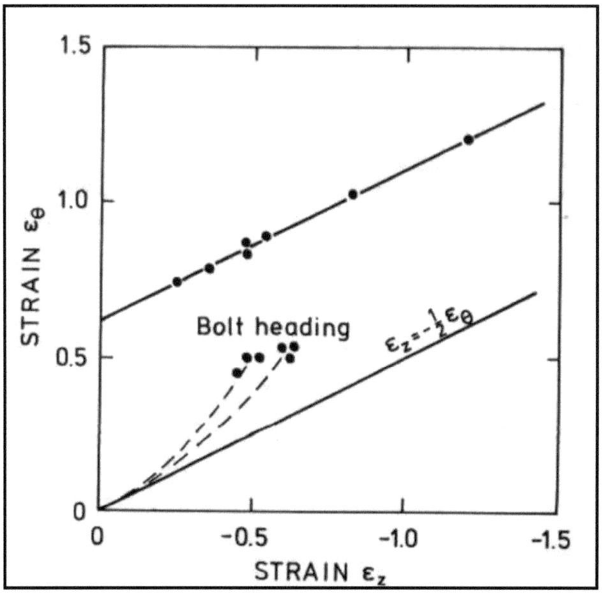


Fig. 8. Strain values in the cold heading of a bolt compared to the forming limit diagram of the material (Kivivuori, 1987 a)).

### 3.4 Other testing methods

The uniaxial tensile test is probably the most common used mechanical material testing method giving information on the flow stress level and ductility. However, there are serious limitations when using tensile testing to examine cold forgeability parameters.

To evaluate ductility, the reduction of area in the tensile test, Z, or fracture strain, $\varepsilon_f$, may be used. The fracture strain measured with tensile test specimens taken in rolling direction, $\varepsilon_{RD}$, can be utilized to asses forgeability in such cold forming methods, as bending, expanding, drawing and forward extrusion (ICFG document 11/01, 2001). On the other hand, in upsetting operations $\varepsilon_{RD}$ is not relevant but fracture strain measured in the transverse direction, $\varepsilon_{TD}$, can be employed to predict the critical reduction as seen in fig. 9.

The torsion testing is sometimes used to assess forgeability. To avoid the variation of shear stress across the wall thickness thin walled tubes may be used to obtain stress-strain curves to high strain and strain rates. Torsion test has the advantage of allowing very large strains to be generated (ICFG document 11/01, 2001).

Plane strain compression test is used to estimate accurately flow stress at very large strains and high strain rates. The barreling occurring in normal compression testing at high values of friction is avoided using plane-strain compression. The test specimen is in the form of thin strip which is compressed across its width by narrow plates.

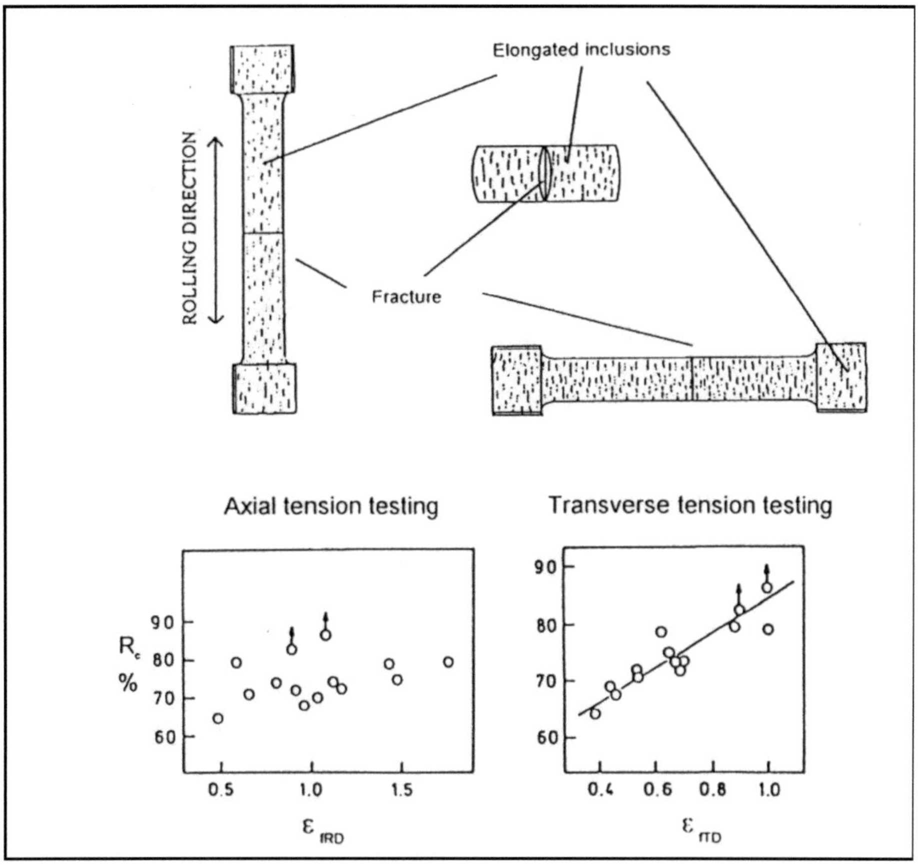


Fig. 9. The critical height reduction in cold upsetting against axial and transverse fracture strains, $\varepsilon_{RD}$ and $\varepsilon_{TD}$, respectively, measured in a uniaxial tensile testing (ICFG document 11/01, 2001).

## 4. Conclusions

The cold forgeability of the materials can be measured using several testing methods. Flow stress testing is normally carried out by using tensile or compression tests under uniaxial stress state. Other testing methods used are torsion and plane strain testing methods.

The formability of materials was determined by testing small cylindrical specimens under uniaxial compression. Using upsetting testing the critical reduction values of the materials can be measured. The forming limit diagrams can be measured by using compression testing at different frictional and geometrical conditions.

The effect of wire drawing on the cold forgeability was studied by using the upsetting test. The pre-drawing has a considerable effect on the values of the critical reduction. The increased values of critical reduction have a maximum point at the pre-drawing reduction about 30 %.

The critical reductions have been measured and compared with the values of reduction of area measured using uniaxial tensile testing. It was found that the reduction in area measured by tensile testing does not describe the cold upsettability of a material if the axial tensile testing was used. Therefore, the transverse tension testing must be employed to predict the value of critical reduction of the material.

## 5. References

Dodd, B. (1996). Defects in Cold Forging, In: *ICFG Final Report*, 12 p., Unpublished

ICFG document No 11/01; (2001). *Steels for Cold Forging - their behaviour and selection*, Meisenbach Verlag, ISBN 3-87525-148-2, Bamberg, Germany

Kivivuori, S.; Sulonen, M. (1978). Formability Limits and Fracturing Modes of Uniaxial Compression Specimens. *Annals of the CIRP*, Vol. 27, No. 1, 141-145

Kivivuori, S. (1987) a). Assessing cold forgeability by the upsetting test. *Scandinavian Journal of Metallurgy*, Vol. 16, 98-11

Kivivuori, S.; (1987) b). *Designing Extrusion and Forging Dies Taking into Account the Limitations due to Metal Flow and Formability*, Helsinki University of Technology, D.Tech. Thesis, Helsinki

Kudo, H. ; Aoi, K. (1967). Effect of compression test condition upon fracturing of a medium carbon steel., *J. Japan Soc. Tech. of Plasticity*, vol. 8, pp. 17-27

Kudo, H. (1975) The International collective calibration test program of cold upsettability test. Unpublished.

# 6

# Investigation and Comparison of Aluminium Foams Manufactured by Different Techniques

Rossella Surace[1] and Luigi A.C. De Filippis[2]
[1]*Institute of Industrial Technology and Automation, National Research Council,*
[2]*Politecnico di Bari,*
*Italy*

## 1. Introduction

Cellular metals offer a large potential for industrial application. Nevertheless, besides the costs, there are a lot of technical improvements necessary in order to gain more widespread use. The reasons for the lack of applications, since now, are multiple and they depend from the physical properties of foams that are still not good enough and not completely experienced, and from the insufficient spreading of research results to designers.

To fulfill parts of these requirements, this work investigates in detail three foam production processes, studies the effect of modifications to standard manufacturing methods, clarifies the influence of process parameters on the structure of foams, characterises relevant properties, and finally discusses the difference between powder or melt routes. During experimentation hundreds of samples were realised to reach these objectives. Moreover mechanical, physical, and microstructural properties of the produced foams have been studied using various techniques including compression testing, scanning electron microscopy, visual inspection, and software measurement tool. The three methods for manufacturing aluminium foams, applied in this investigation, are named $TiH_2$, SDP and MGI. Two of them ($TiH_2$ and SDP) start from powdered aluminium as row material, while MGI starts from melt aluminium. Moreover $TiH_2$ and MGI methods let the production of closed cells foam while SDP of open cells foam named, more correctly, metal sponge.

The term "foam" was firstly reserved for a dispersion of gas bubbles in a liquid. The morphology of this type of foams can be preserved by letting the liquid solidify, thus obtaining what is called a "solid foam". When speaking of "metallic foams" one generally means a solid foam. The liquid metallic foam is a stage that occurs during the fabrication of the material. For metallic systems it is possible to define the following classification according with Babcsan et al. (2003):

- cellular metals are materials with a high volume fraction of voids made up of an interconnected network of walls and membranes;
- porous metals have isolated spherical pores and a porosity level of usually less than about 70%;
- metal foams are a soubgroup of cellular metals usually having a polyhedral cells with closed or open cells (even if there are no membranes across the faces and the voids are inteconnected, the better definition is metal sponges).

## 2. Manufacturing methods

Considerable progress has been made recently in the production of metallic and in particular aluminium foam. Scale up has progressed so far that widespread commercial use has now become a reality. Methods to produce metal foams are already known since the fifties but their use has not spread so far since now for the difficulties to control the process parameters and high costs. Due to the progress of the last decade with the respect to the production techniques gave new birth to the foam (Surace & De Filippis, 2010).
There are different ways to manufacture cellular metallic materials but some of them methods will always be restricted to specialised applications where cost is not a parameter of paramount importance. The various methods can be classified according to the state the metal is processed in. This defines four group of processes each one corresponding to one state of matter (Banhart, 2001):

- liquid metal;
- solid metal (usually in powdered form);
- metal vapour;
- metal ion solution.

The three methods studied in this work will be now briefly presented.
The "$TiH_2$" method consists of mixing aluminium or aluminium alloys powders with an appropriate blowing agent, usually titanium hydride ($TiH_2$) for aluminium and its alloys: in particular AlSi7 e AlSi12 show an excellent foamability due to their low melting point. The mixture is then compacted to a dense product called "foamable precursors materials" with different methodologies ensuring the embedding of blowing agent in the matrix without residual porosity: in IFAM process (Fraunhofer Institute in Bremen - IFAM) by uniaxial compression, CIP, powder rolling or extrusion, the Mepura process uses a continuous extrusion technology (Baumgartner & Gers, 1999). The following step is the heat treatment up to the melting point of the matrix and above the decomposition temperature of the blowing agent that release hydrogen gas. The gas leads to an expansion of the material resulting in a porous structure with closed cells. By cooling under the melting point the foaming is stopped. Fig. 1 shows a sketch of the process. The time needed for full expansion depends on temperature and on size of the precursor, and ranges from a few seconds to several minutes. Fig. 2 shows the expansion of an $AlSi12/TiH_2$ powder compact: the pictures were taken interrupting the foaming by quenching (ex situ measurements of foam expansion). By varying the time span from start to quenching, a series of samples was obtained reflecting various stages of foam evolution. The expanding foam is shown as a function of the furnace holding time; foaming started after about 10 min and was completed after 11 min and 15 s (in this way the best structure was obtained). Beyond this time the foam collapses for two reason: drainage (i.e. the flow of the molten metal, driven by gravity) and coalescence (i.e. merging to form a larger cells).
For attaining by this route near net shape foam parts, it is necessary to insert the precursor material into a hollow mould but also hollow profiles (es. tubes or columns) that can be filled with foam (Fig. 3).
The second studied method is the Sintering and Dissolution Process (SDP). Generally, foams can be obtained by using a leachable material (e.g. salt) together with metal. Following this principle there are two different techniques starting from melt metal or powders. The first method, called Replication Technique, consists of three basic steps: by packing a soluble salt in a mould to have a pattern, casting melt metal around these granules and finally removing

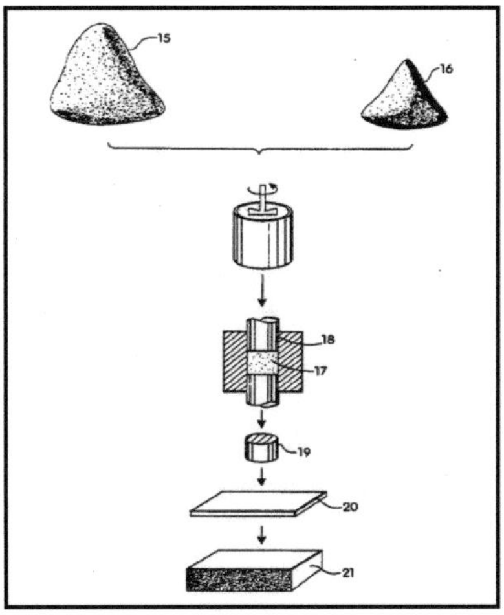


Fig. 1. Sintering of metal powders (US Patent 5,151,246)

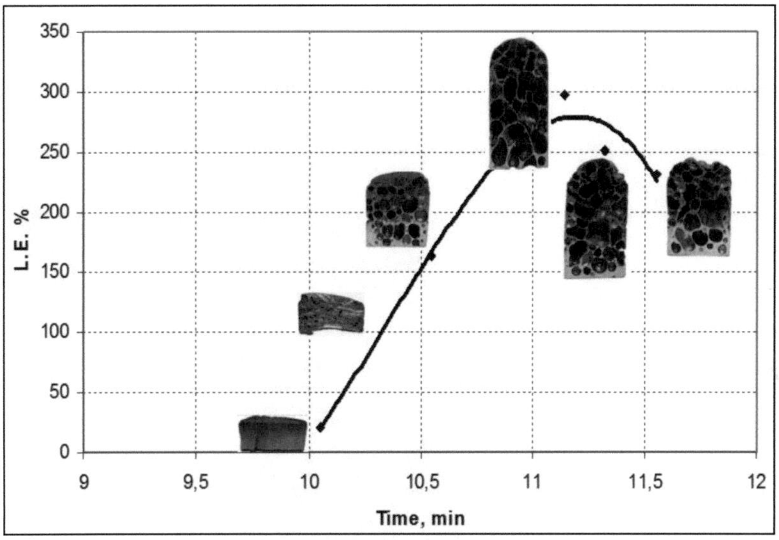


Fig. 2. Foam samples presenting different expansions at different foaming stages

Fig. 3. Hollow tube filled with foam (courtesy of Valerio Mussi - MUSP)

the pattern. Reference technique was first applied in 1966 (Kuchek, 1966) and similar processes have been developed in recent years (San Marchi et al., 2000; Li et al., 2003; Gaillard et al., 2004) . A more advanced version of this process uses a hot-wall pressure infiltration process: the salt preform is held under vacuum while a block of aluminium is melted over it and an inert gas at high pressure is applied during the subsequent infiltration step. In the second method, called Sintering and Dissolution Process (SDP), the powders have been used to produce a dense two-phase precursor where one phase is water soluble. The powders (usually Al and NaCl) are mixed and compacted, forming double-connected structures of both phases. After furnace sintering (Fig 4 a-b), by dissolving the leachable phase, a foam of the other phase is produced (Fig. 4 c). This process, studied at Liverpool University (Zhao et al., 2004; Sun & Zhao, 2002; Zhao & Sun, 2001; Sun & Zhao, 2005), belongs to the processes defined "space holder techniques" giving structure of a great uniformity (Ashby et al, 2000). A recent study compares the sintering of Al–NaCl compact by traditional electric furnace sintering and by spark plasma sintering that allows the increase of plateau stress (Wen et al, 2003). Moreover Zhao developed Lost Carbonate Sintering process (LCS) to manufacture copper foam using potassium carbonate ($K_2CO_3$) as leachable salt with the same reference technique of SDP (Zhao et al., 2005). Fig. 5 shows a cross section of a sample.

(a) (b) (c)

Fig. 4. Sample after sintering (a), machining (b) and leaching (c) (40 wt% Al, 3 h, 650 MPa)

Fig. 5. SDP sample cross section

By far the cheapest type of process is melt-route processing (the Alcan/Norsk Hydro process) called Melt Gas Injection - MGI (Wood, 1997 and Asholt, 1999). According to this process, silicon carbide, aluminium oxide or magnesium oxide particles are used to enhance the viscosity of the melt metal; their volume fraction ranges from 10% to 20% and the mean size from 5 to 20μm. The ceramic particles trap gas bubbles owing to the favorable interface energy and serve as stabilizer of the cell walls and delay their coalescence. They also reduce the velocity of the rising bubbles by increasing the viscosity of the melt (Ip et al., 1999;

Kaptay, 2003; Hur et al., 2003). Therefore, the first step requires the preparation of a melt bath containing these substances. A variety of aluminium alloys is used, e.g. the casting alloy AlSi10 Mg (A359) or wrought alloys such as 1060, 3003, 6016, or 6061. The liquid Metal Matrix Composites (MMC) is then foamed in a second step by injecting gas (air, nitrogen or argon) into it, using specially designed rotating propellers or vibrating nozzles as depicted in schematic form in Fig. 6. The function of the propellers or nozzles is to create very fine gas bubbles in the melt and distribute them uniformly. This is an important requirement because only if sufficiently fine bubbles are created, a foam of a satisfactory quality can be obtained. The floating foam is then continuously pulled of from the surface of the melt with different techniques (for example by means of conveyor belt to obtain sheets).

The MGI for processing closed-cell metal foams is very actractive since this approach allows economic handling of large quantities of material. Melt route processes are also well suited to the use of scrap as feedstock. Although cheap and relatively simple, consistently obtaining a cell structure with a reasonably high quality is difficult, which has given rise to various adaptations to control the cells more closely. Fig. 6 shows a sample of foam obtained by MGI process.

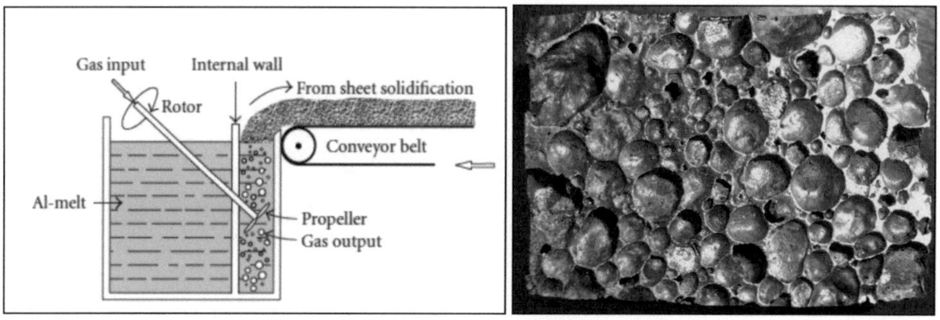


Fig. 6. Apparatus for MGI and example of foam obtained by MGI

Moreover, with this method, it is possible to produce 3D-shaped parts with complicated shape or configuration, with a modification of original process (Fig. 7) (Surace et al., 2009). These parts are expected to be utilized as filling material and for encasing in components without machining. Casting aluminum around a foam can create components where a low density foam core is completely surrounded by a massive outer shell. Potential applications for this kind of foam core castings are space frame nodes, knukles, control arms, cross-members, and stiffness providing structural components.

(a) (b) (c)

Fig. 7. MGI foam cores attached by mechanical bonding (front and lateral view (a-b) and foam part with parallelepiped shape (c)

## 3. Processes comparison

In this section will be discussed the advantages and disadvantges of each of three presented processes. The first advantage of $TiH_2$ process is that complex-shaped metal foam parts can be easily manufactured by expanding the foam inside a confined mould. The light weight solution based on aluminium foam can replaces traditional cast aluminium parts saving 30% weight because composite structures of aluminium foam and bulk metal parts can be made without using adhesives. For making such composites the foamable precursors material is first bonded to the solid section or sheet by co-extrusion or roll-cladding, after which the foamable core layer is expanded by heat treatment. Others advantages of the powder-compact route are listed in Table 1 reported from Banhart & Baumgartner, 2002. Besides the first two features already mentioned, the flexibility arising from the preparation of the precursor from powders is important because different alloys composition can be made simply by mixing elementary powders. No ceramic additives are needed to stabilize the foam, in contrast to some of the melt-route foaming processes in which silicon carbide has to be added. However, if required, ceramic powders or fibers can be added for a special applications such as for reinforcement ot to increase wear resistance.
Naturally, there are also some disadvantages inherent to the process. Metal powders are more expansive than bulk metal and they require efforts for compaction. This rules out applications that require very cheap materials. Moreover, the size of aluminum foam parts that can be manufactured is limited by the size of the backing processes.
Differently, the liquid-metal route allows for making panel 15 m in length (Cymat Corporation, 2002) and 100 cm thickness (Miyoshi et al., 1999). However, as reported from Banhart & Baumgartner (2002), these processes cannot be used for near-net-shape production and only permit very simple geometries but Surace et al., 2009 have demonstrated the possibility of production of shaped parts with MGI-mould process.
In $TiH_2$ process, it is of critical importance to reach the right compaction of the precursors so that blowing agent results tightly embedded into the metal matrix. Foam formation, indeed, happens during the heating process when the metal matrix is near the melting point and sufficient liquid phase is formed so that the gas released by the foaming agent can bubbles in it. The more the two phenomena, liquid metal formation and gas development, will overlap, as easier will be the foam formation (Matijašević-Lux, 2006; Speed, 1976). Decomposition of $TiH_2$ begins at a temperature around 350 °C at amosferic pressure, and continues up to 600 °C. However fot the hydride embedded in the metal matrix, the gas release is shifted to higher temperatures because of the increase in partial hydrogen pressure that counteracts further $TiH_2$ decomposition. In principle, the compaction can be done by any technique that ensures that the blowing agent is embedded into the metal matrix without any notable residual open porosity. From this point of view, a higher compaction helps to match the main hydride decomposition with the metal melting temperature. Examples of compaction methods are hot uniaxial or isostatic compression, rod extrusion or powder rolling. However, extrusion seems to be the most economical method at the moment and is therefore the most used way (Banhart, 2001).
In this investigation powder compaction was performed by cold compaction by uniaxial pressing. This is a fair simplification of the process respect to others methods. Even if cold uniaxial compaction can not reach densification values like that obtained by hot processing and residual porosity in the green is higher, using appropriate process parameters combination it is possible to foam aluminium with a cell structure comparable with the

foam made by the usual method (Fig. 8). The middle column of Table1 lists some of the problems that are still encountered when foaming aluminium with the powder-compact method.

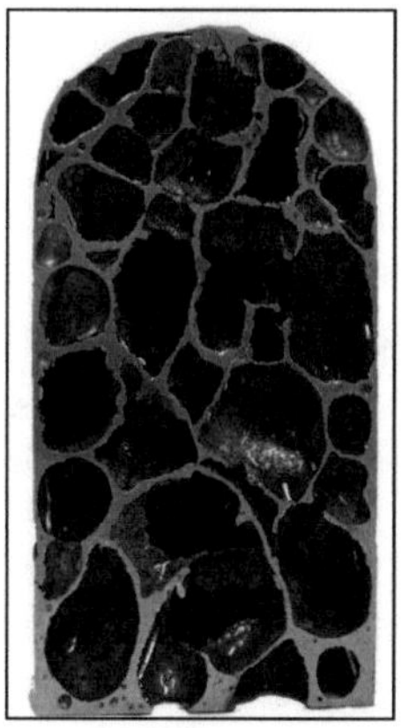

Fig. 8. $TiH_2$ foam sample obtained by cold uniaxial pressure

| ADVANTAGE | PROBLEM | DISADVANTAGE |
|---|---|---|
| Net-shape foaming possible | Uniformity of pore structure still not satisfactory | Cost of powders |
| Composites can be manufactured | Process control must be improved | Very large volume parts difficult to make |
| Parts are covered by metal skin | Permeable (holes) | Coating process requires sealing |
| Graded porosity can be achieved | Difficult to control | |
| Flexibility in alloy choice | | |
| No stabilising particles have to be added | | |
| Ceramics and fibers can be added | | |

Table 1. Characteristic of powder compact foaming method

Advantages of SDP process comprise considerable control of the pore size, and thus density, the capacity for near-net shape component production, and the potential for production of components that are part dense and part porous. Also, the open-porosity that is intrinsic to metal sponge can be put to advantage in several applications that require fluid flow through the porous metal, such as filters and heat-exchangers.

The structure or architecture of metal sponge produced by replication is flexible and determined by the pattern: porosity as high as 98% (Wagner et al., 2000) and as low as 55% (Banhart, 2000) for different pattern materials have been reported and pore sizes as small as 10 μm have been achieved (San Marchi et al., 2000). In addition, metal sponge can be produced from virtually any alloy that can be cast or powdered including aluminium alloys, magnesium alloys, and iron and nickel alloys. Sodium chloride (NaCl) has been employed most extensively as a leachable pattern, because it is inexpensive and easy to handle. Salt patterns are limited by their melting point; NaCl, for example, is limited to aluminum and lower-melting alloys, while NaF could potentially be used at temperatures greater than 900°C. Additionally, highly concentrated saline solutions are generated during dissolution and can cause significant corrosion in some alloys.

The main disadvantage of the powder metallurgy techniques are their relatively high cost, due mainly to the handle fine metal powders. But differently from each powder technique, SDP does not require a powder foaming agent but only a culinary salt with saving of money and precautions. Material chosen as space holder for the production of SDP foams must fulfill a main requirements: it must be chemically compatible with the foam material. For the production of foams with materials that are processed at temperature around 650-750 °C, sodium chloride is a well suited space holder. It is inexpensive, chemically inert in contact with molten aluminium and many other materials, leaches easily since it is highly soluble in water, and creates essentially no environmental or healt hazards (Conde et al., 2006).

In some cases, leachable patterns can also be machined to complex geometries prior to leaching and without damaging the architecture of the sponge. In the case of salt, removal of the pattern is by immersion in water causing dissolution of the salt. Dissolution is primarily a diffusive process, as the dissolved salt ions diffuse from their place-holding position into the water bath through the narrow channels in the sponge and the rate and total time of dissolution depend strongly on the size of the specimen. Salt is more difficult to remove from small pores, particularly if gas is entrapped in the pores; this is the so-called "gas-lock" phenomenon, which can block the penetration of fluid into the porous network. Corrosion of metal sponge during leaching of the pattern can be a problem due to the large surface area of the porous network, thus the salt concentration and the immersion must be minimised (San Marchi & Mortensen, 2002). Summarizing the advantages of this process are:

- Low cost: space holders are cheap.
- Environmentally friendly: removal of space holders does not lead to harmful emissions. However, if polymers are used, care must be taken to condense and collect the extracted polymers.
- Recyclable: used components can be recycled in the same way as normal cast components.
- Composite structures: sponge and non-porous metal parts can be bonded during casting.
- Near-net-shape manufacturing of components is possible.

The melt route MGI for processing closed-cell metal foams is very actractive since this approach allows economic handling of large quantities of material. Melt route processes are also well suited to the use of scrap as feedstock. For the production of homogeneous foams some prerequisites have to be fulfilled. One important step is to increase the viscosity of the melt to prevent gas escape with particles added that increase the melt viscosity and stabilise the cell walls. But if ceramic particles are used for stabilising the liquid foam, the excessive wear on the machine tools has to be taken in account during machining, especially if SiC particles are present. It should also be noted that the preparation of the composite material requieres relatively long time steerring processes to achieve the proper homogeneous distribution of the particles in the melt. The production facility setup by Cymat is capable of casting foam panel in continuous length at an average rate of 900 kg/h up to 1.5 m wide with a thickness range of 25-150 mm (Korner & Singer, 2002). This shows that the process is relatively strightforward and economical.

The foam, obtained by MGI, usually presents a gradient in density and pores elongation as a natural consequence of the gravitationally induced drainage and the shearing forces of the conveyor belt that lead to distorted cells in the final product. This obviously has a pronounced effect on the mechanical properties which become anisotropic (Beals & Thompson, 1997). The situation could be improved by pulling off the foam vertically (Sang et al., 1994). Moreover, obtaining shaped parts by this process is very difficult for the ceramic particles that make difficult the cutting. Attempts for making shaped parts have been undertaken by casting the semiliquid foam into moulds or by shaping the emerging foam with rolls, thus trying to eliminate this disadvantage (Kenny & Thomas, 1994, Kleinheyer & Bilz, 1995; Nichol, 2006). Surace et al. (2009) proposed a new method, called MGI-mould process, that makes possible to produce 3D-shaped parts with complicated shape or configuration using some moulds obtained by traditional investment casting process. The MGI-mould process was capable of producing the near net shape aluminum foam parts with length of about 200 mm and different shapes with skin surface and good internal quality especially for the core of automotive articles.

Foam parts prepared by expansion in a mould show a closed surface skin with a thickness comparable to the cell-wall thickness of about 200 µm (Fig. 9). Casting aluminum around a foam can create components where a low density foam core is completely surrounded by a massive outer shell. The shell can be designed in such a way that additional functions besides its load carrying can be fulfilled. As only one processing step is required to produce such a foam core component, production is expected to be very economical (Degischer & Kottar, 1999). A further difficulty results from the fact that methods have to be developed for fixing the cores. A prerequisite for encasing by casting is a dense foam surface.

A suitable core attachment system has to perform two functions: first it has to keep the core in place in the die when the die is open and during the movement of die closing. The more important second function is to maintain the desired distance between the foam core and the die wall during the casting process because this distance determines the wall thickness of the castings. One method to realise a suitable attachment of the core is by creating elongated wedge-shaped spacers during the foaming process of the cores (Fig. 9). These spacers have to be long enough to transfer the acting forces to the foam core without damage. It is very important to place the spacers corresponding to the melt flow to avoid flow barriers resulting in "dead zones".

Generally, no bonding develops between the core and the shell during castings because of the continuous aluminium oxide layer that prevents the core surface from reaction with the molten metal (Simancik & Schoerghuber, 1998). There are two possible ways to improve the bonding:

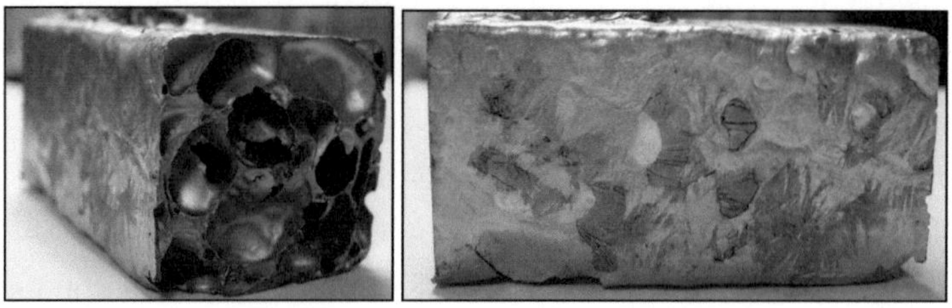

Fig. 9. Shaped MGI part with dense skin

Fig. 10. MGI foam core insert with spacers

- mechanical bonding by flow of liquid metal into the outer foam structure supported by intentional weakening of the surface skin, e.g., by sand-blasting. Disadvantages are that the weight of the casting increases and the bonding occurs only locally and is difficult to control (Fig. 11).
- Metallurgical bonding by coating the cores with various agents supporting diffusion through the aluminium oxide layer. With a suitable metallic coating a metallurgical bonding can be achieved. On this point, however, further research is necessary.

Stress bonding, which is caused by shrinkage of the casting during solidification or the fixing of the core due to its geometry, leads to a solid joining of the core insert in the casting (Kretz & Wolfsgruber, 2003).

Fig. 11. MGI foam cores attached by mechanical bonding (front and lateral view)

The recyclability of metal a benefit, enabling ecologically sustainable product life cycles. Cellular metals can be shredded too and treated as normal scrap. It might be of interest to recycle the MMC matrix of the foam without significant reduction of the particle content. Any reuse of MMC saves the effort necessary to bond the two components together during processing. Originally, this type of foam was a spin-off of particulate-reinforced aluminum processing, consequently it has been proposed to reuse particle-reinforced aluminum alloys in the production of aluminum foam (Gergely et al., 2000). For SDP could be difficult the recycling due to trapped salt that can contaminate the melt. Recycling of $TiH_2$ seems to be the most simple.

## 4. Experimental

The aim of the experimental part is to evaluate the properties and to optimize the process parameters of the three mentioned techniques by means of a statistical approach. During the experimental work many samples have been made following the principles of the design of experiments (DOE) and the final evaluation of the most important features (morphology and compression strength) was carried out.

### 4.1 $TiH_2$ process

In this process the selection of the aluminium powders was a very difficult task. In fact, during the initial screening, four types of Al powders from different suppliers were tested. The problems were associated with the size of the powders: too small particles are not suitable to obtain foam. The content of the blowing agent ($TiH_2$) was in the range of 0.5-2 wt%. This wide range (different from that reported by Duarte & Banhart, 2000) was chosen due to the mentioned problems with fine Al powder (causing hydrogen loss during precursors heating). Moreover, in order to improve the stability of metal foams, usually ceramic particles were added. Literature data report that ceramic particles inhibit melt flow, after increasing the viscosity, thus decreasing the rate of cell coarsening and drainage of liquid through the structures (Ip et al., 1999). The tested amount of SiC was in the range of 0-10 wt%.

The mixing was the second process step carried out through mixing of the metal powders with the blowing agent in glass mixer to ensure the homogenization of components. After the powder compaction may be performed using different techniques (hot pressing, cold isostatic pressing, extrusion) (Baumgartner & Gers, 1999). In our experiments, powder compaction was performed adding about 15 g of the mixture (depending on the composition) in a 32 mm diameter steel die, followed by cold compaction by uniaxial pressing. This is a fair simplification of the process in comparison to others methods. Compaction in the range of 100-700 MPa was obtained with a MATEST E157 hydraulic motorized press. Finally foaming was carried out in a pre-heated electric furnace at different emperatures in the range of 620-950°C. Foaming operation took place in normal atmosphere and the mould was opened only at the top. In the furnace, the mould was placed on a ceramic plate, excluding temperature gradient in vertical direction as suggested from Arnold et al., 2003. Careful control of heating conditions during foaming is essential to obtain quality foams. The difficulty is that the liquid foam is thermodynamically unstable and conditions change constantly during foaming (Baumgartner et al., 2000). Due to that, when the mould is filled with foam, it must be suddenly cooled down below its melting point to stabilize the structure. Air quenching leads to foam collapse, therefore water was preferred for cooling. Moreover, in air-cooled samples the foam structure shows pronounced cracking of cell walls that is not the case by water quenching (Lehmus & Banhart, 2003). In the present work, foaming was stopped at a moment, which depended mainly on the furnace temperature.

Variables, influencing the foaming process, are the $TiH_2$ and SiC content, mixing time, compaction tool, pressure, sintering temperature and time, mould features and the cooling procedure. Each variable influences the output foam quality. In the initial screening, a large number of samples was tested by changing parameters in wide ranges. As a result it was found that although many control factors influence the process, the output quality depends mainly on three primary control factors: SiC fraction, compaction pressure and sintering temperature. Influence of these reference factors on the cells area, cell wall thickness, linear expansion, relative density and plateau stress was investigated. A standard approach of DOE is to use the full factorial method that requires a total of 27 experimental runs if there are 3 factors to be investigated and each consists of 3 different levels (high, medium and low). Table 2 shows the levels of factors in this systematic investigation. For each combination of the parameters, three replications have been carried out. The quantity of Al was fixed at 15 g and $TiH_2$ at 1 wt%. After screening, different samples were made in the second experimental step, following the principles of DOE to study mechanical properties and the evolution of the foam in time.

| Factors | Levels | | |
|---|---|---|---|
| SiC content, wt% | 0 | 2.5 | 5 |
| Pressure, MPa | 310 | 370 | 430 |
| Temperature, °C | 750 | 800 | 850 |

Table 2. Experimental factors and levels for $TiH_2$ process

**4.2 SDP process**

Two types of Al atomised elemental powders from different suppliers (Baker and Riedel-de-Haen) have been tested and final experimentation Riedel-de-Haen aluminium powder has been used. The NaCl particles have been obtained by commonly culinary salt particles with different sizes. In order to control the cell sizes of the resulting foam, the commercial salt has been sieved into three groups with different particle diameters: <3, 3-4, and >4 mm. Large particles (70 wt%) have been mixed with medium size particles (30 wt%) in order to increasing porosity and to create an interconnected structures and because Li et al., 2003, found that the stiffness and the strength of foams increase with multi size cells with identical relative density. Before mixing, NaCl powder was dried in two steps: at 110 °C for 1 h in a heater and at 400 °C for 45 min in an electrical furnace as suggested in the literature (Sun & Zhao, 2005).

Magnesium addition in the mixture is due to oxidation problems. In fact the sintering of aluminium has always been considered problematic due to the oxide film present on the surface of powder particles. Trace additions of magnesium react with the oxide to form spinel. This breaks up the oxide, which facilitates sintering (Shaffer et al., 2001).The tested amount of Mg is 0.15 wt% of Al-NaCl compact.

The mixing is the second process step carried out: firstly through mixing of the Al with Mg powders to ensure the homogenization of metal components, and secondly with NaCl particles. Because of the need to ensure a continuous network of Al,a n upper limit to NaCl fraction is necessary in the compact. Similarly there should be a lowest obtainable porosity to avoid trapped NaCl in the final structure which could lead to corrosion of the foams. A quantification of the content of NaCl has been carried out in the range 30-70 wt%.The powder compaction may be performed using different techniques (i.e. hot pressing, cold isostatic pressing). In these experiments powder compaction has been performed adding about 15 g of mixture (depending on composition) in a 25 or 32 mm diameter steel die followed by uniaxial cold pressing. A compaction in the range 100-600 MPa has been realised with a hydraulic motorised press. This wide range (different from literature data) is due to the mentioned problems associated with Al oxide films that have to be disrupted by mechanical deformation.

The sintering has been carried out in a pre-heated electric furnace at different temperatures in the range 650-700 °C (Al melting point is 660 °C). The sintering takes place in liquid state so the metal viscosity is enough to fill the spaces between NaCl particles. If the sintering temperature is too low, the sintering can take too long time causing severe oxidation. If it is excessively high, some molten Al often oozes out from the surface of the compact to form globules. The same considerations involve the sintering time. The experiments have been carried out in the range 2–20 h. Moreover NaCl has a much lower thermal conductivity than Al, so the sintering time should be increased in presence of great salt amount. The sintering takes place at normal atmosphere and both ends of the mould are sealed in order to protect the compact from air effects. In the furnace the mould is positioned on a ceramic plate guaranteeing no temperature gradient along vertical direction as suggested by Arnold et al., 2003. Careful control of heating conditions during foaming is essential to obtain "quality" foams. After required time the samples have been cooled by air.

The salt dissolution takes place into two steps. Firstly, the sintered specimens have been placed into a running hot water bath to leach out the most of embedded NaCl particles. Secondly, samples have been immerged in an ultrasonic washer to ensure the complete removing of salt. The dissolution of the NaCl is a significant rate-limiting step: in large samples, the tortuosity of the foam structure means that it takes a long time to dissolve all the salt. Finally the samples have been washed by ethanol and dried. After screening the experimental full factorial plan reported in Table 3 have been carried out.

| Factors | Levels | | |
|---|---|---|---|
| Al fraction, wt% | 30 | 40 | 50 |
| Pressure, MPa | 550 | 600 | 650 |
| Time, h | 2 | 3 | 4 |

Table 3. Experimental factors and levels for SDP process

### 4.3 MGI process

The aluminium liquid foam has been produced by melting aluminium ingots in a graphite crucible by an induction furnace. The applied foaming equipment has been specifically designed for these experiments. It is formed by a rotating system that allows to distribute the bubbles in the melt aluminium. The experimental apparatus is constituted by a drill, a shaft, a propeller, a panel of stainless steel, and a pipe for the gas injection. This system is designed, in a proper way that allows the gas coming out from the pipe, and diffusing homogenously in the bath by the propeller (connected to the drill by the shaft). The presence of the stainless steel panel is of paramount importance for the success of the experiment reducing turbulences and vortex formations in the bath (Cingi, 1992). The process control for aluminium foam is regarded to be difficult due to its multivariability and invisibility. There is a close similarity of behaviour of bubbles in water and in melt aluminium, and such similarity is very useful. The bubbles generation and their rise to surface can be investigated much more easily in water and, then, the results can be applied to metal. In fact Reynolds number for both water and aluminium, within the turbulent regime, are close enough so that very similar properties of bubbles should be expected in these liquids. Therefore, to simulate bubble generation in foamed aluminium, a screening has been carried out also by means of this physical modelling (Oak et al., 2002).

Duralcan metal matrix composite (A356/SiC/20p) with a particle size of approximately 12 μm have been used. Aluminium 356 has the following composition: Al 90.1-93.3 wt%, Si 6.5-7.5 wt%, Mg 0.2-0.45 wt%, Cu max 0.25%, Fe max 0.6%, Mn max 0.35%. Nitrogen is injected as foaming medium and temperature usually has been kept around 700 °C. After a

screening test using different combinations of parameters, the selected factors for deep observations have been: flow rate (Q), spin speed of the propeller (N), and silicon carbide particles content, because they shown the high influence on foam properties (mechanical and morphological).
The authors assumed these three reference main factors and verified their effects on cells area, cells wall thickness, relative density and plateau stress. The adopted standard approach for Design Of Experiments (DOE) has been the use of a full factorial method. Moreover, two replications of each combination were realised. Table 4 shows the levels of factors in this systematic investigation.

| Factors | Levels | | |
|---|---|---|---|
| Gas flow rate, l/min | 2 | 4 | 8 |
| Spin speed, RPM | 300 | 700 | 900 |
| SiC content, wt% | 10 | 15 | 20 |

Table 4. Experimental factors and levels for MGI process

## 5. Results discussion and comparisons

### 5.1 Morphological characterization

In the following section the results about morphological charcterization will be compared and discussed. In this investigation the foams have been cut by a diamond saw ($TiH_2$ and SDP) a by a metallographic saw (MGI). The major problems have been encountered with MGI foams due to the high level of SiC particles fraction; in fact, for 5 parameters combinations of experimental plan, were not possible to cut specimens and some of them were damaged during cutting. For TiH2 and SDP this problem was not so critical. The morphological parameters have been measured in 2D cross section by an images software tool and cell walls have been observed by a Scanning Electron Microscope Philips XL 20.
The most important parameters that influence the structure-sensitive properties of cellular metals are (order by their importance):

1. intrinsic properties (properties of cell wall material);
2. relative density;
3. type of cellular structure (open or closed cells) ;
4. in a closed-cell foam, the fraction of the solid contained in the cell nodes, edges of the cell faces;
5. irregularity or gradients in mass distribution;
6. the cell size and size distribution (including exceptional sizes) ;
7. shape of the cells and the anisotropy of cells (including exceptional shapes) ;
8. connectivity of cell edges;
9. defects, by which we mean buckled or broken cell walls.

Table 5 (Kriszt et al, 2002) defines a list of 20 structural parameters for describing the geometrical structure and microstructure of cellular materials. They were studied and measured for each foam types obtained with the $TiH_2$, SDP and MGI methods and Table 6 gives here a summary to compare the results.
The significant differences in the structures of the $TiH_2$, SDP and MGI foams are function of the manufacturing process. The $TiH_2$ foams realised in this investigation have a variety of little defects including: cracks, voids, shared cells and the pore area range is wide (Fig. 1a).

| **Geometric structure** | **Pores** | **Cell skeleton** | **Microstructure** |
|---|---|---|---|
| open or close cells | Volume fraction | Thickness and length of cell walls | Dendritic structure |
| Arrangement of cells | Shape factor | Number/area of nodes | Grains |
| Neighborship relation | Aspect ratio | Curvature/corrugation of cell walls | Chemical inhomogeneity |
| Stochastical models | Orientation | | Micropores |
| Chemical composition | Size | | Inclusions |
| | | | Precipitates |
| | | | Dislocations |

Table 5. List of parameters for describing structure of metallic foam

| **Property** | **$TiH_2$** | **SDP** | **MGI** |
|---|---|---|---|
| Alloy | Al, AlSi12 | Al | A356/SiC/20p (AlSi7) |
| Density range, $g/cm^3$ | 0.63-1.07 (0.77) | 0.69-1.51 (0.99) | 0.18-0.91 (0.51) |
| Equivalent diameter, mm | 0.53-6.40 (1.85) | 0.53-4.85 (1.54) | 1.65-6.19 (2.81) |
| Pore area range, $mm^2$ | 0.22-32 (3.77) | 2-35 (4.92) | 2.13-30.13 (6.89) |
| Cell wall thickness, mm | 0.10-1.82 (0.63) | 0.05-0.4 (0.21) | 0.10-1.3 (0.40) |
| Circularity parameter | 0.33-0.91 (0.62) | 0.13-0.85 (0.46) | 0.35-0.98 (0.81) |

Table 6. Obtained properties of the three families of investigated aluminium foams

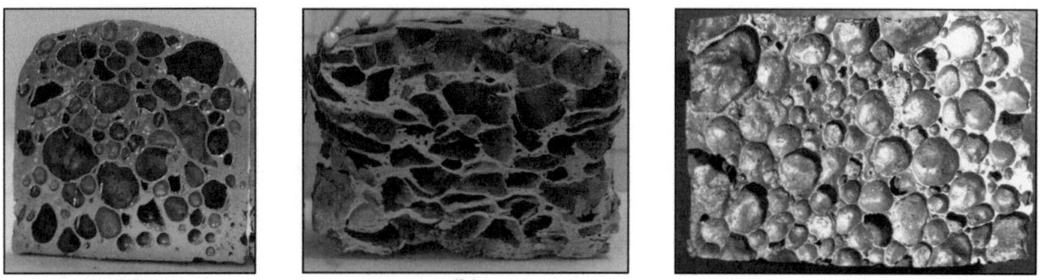

(a) (b) (c)

Fig. 13. Foam samples: a) $TiH_2$ b) SDP and c) MGI

In particular oversized pores as well mass concentrations can be observed and they can cause degradation if specific properties. Presence of microvoids has been observed also in open cell SDP foams but no cell edge curvature (Fig. 1b). Microstructural observation of the MGI foams has identified a number of irregularities. Many of the cell walls have some initial

curvature as well as small voids within them. There are local regions of higher density where the cell walls are thicker at the nodes. The shape and orientation of the cells in the lower density MGI foams vary throughout the thickness. In particular there is a density gradient throughout the thickness of the lower density MGI foams realised with moulds due to drainage of the liquid before solidification (Fig. 1c). Observations of cells of MGI foams indicate that they are slightly oriented due to the direction of rotation of the impeller during foaming. Also SDP foam has been found with elongated cells due to the compaction pressure. Only $TiH_2$ foams have roughly equiaxed cells. The cells area of the three types of foam is comparable. The foams, obtained by the processes $TiH_2$ and SDP, have a solid skin on the outer surfaces, which was removed before testing. Instead traditionally MGI foams does not have the skin; the implemented version, realised by mould, shows the presence of external skin originated by the contact with the ceramic moulds.
Obviously the structural performance of the three foams can be improved by reducing the occurrence of defects in the cell walls (curvature, porous inclusions, corrugations). Cell wall defects can cause drastic decreases in the mechanical properties of cellular materials. Cell wall curvature and porous inclusions within cell walls can be prevented by reducing the size distribution of cells and controlling better the foaming conditions in order to minimize convection etc. The face wrinkling in the cell walls of the MGI foams can be avoided by reducing the stresses applied to the foam immediately after solidifcation and by reducing the rate of cooling.
The major encountered problem has been the lack of standard test method: in particular achitectural quality criteria should be better developed and nondestructive test method has to be well established and standardized. Moreover the determination of pore size, area, cell wall thickness and of all architectural features request intensive labor and it is time consuming. This can be a problem for future quality control in industrial environment.
Fig. 14 shows a diagram taken from Wadley (2002) reporting the range of cell size against relative density for different metal foam manufacturing methods. Red, orange and green lines represent the mean values of foams obtained in this investigation. The diagram does not show reference about SDP foam. $TiH_2$ foams enter in the expected range while MGI foams show better behaviour because for equal density they present lower cell size figures. Table 7 reports numerical figures showed in the diagram.

### 5.2 Mechanical characterization

After checking foam morphology, mechanical tests were carried out on the samples. Compressive strength has been chosen as evaluation criterion because it is relevant in the context of energy absorption of foam.. The tests were carried out using a machine model 5869 from Instron in quasi static condition, following the statements of the italian standard UNI 558 and of the standard test method for compressive properties of metal foam (Cymat Corporation, 2002) prepared by Cymat Company taking into account ASTM and DIN

| Process | Average relative density | Average cell area ($mm^2$) | Average cell size (mm) |
|---|---|---|---|
| $TiH_2$ | 0.286 | 3.77 | 2.19 |
| SDP | 0.368 | 4.92 | 2.50 |
| MGI | 0.165 | 6.89 | 2.96 |

Table 7. Cell size and relative density

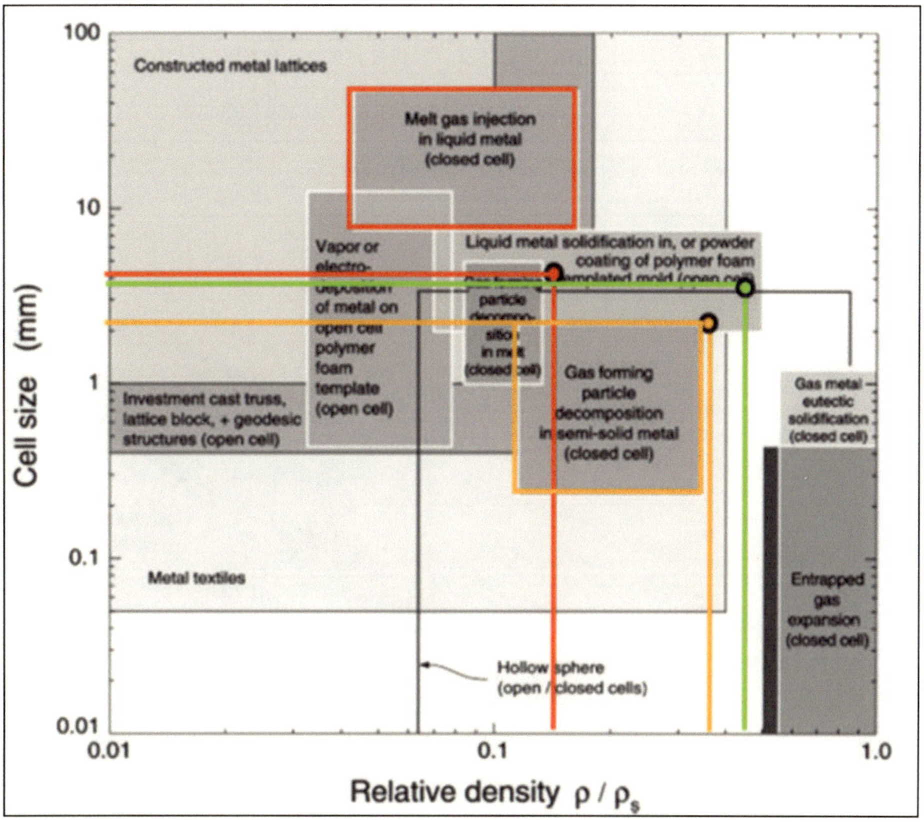


Fig. 14. The range of cell size and relative density for the different metal foam manufacturing methods (Wadley, 2002)

standards. In all mechanical testing, load and displacement were recorded using a National Instruments data acquisition unit and a personal computer. Stress was evaluated as the load per total area of the specimen, including porosity as suggested from Fusheng & Zhengang (1999). Likewise, strain, defined as a nominal value for the foam structure, is not the real strain experienced by the cell walls.

The compressive strenght of foams have been measured in a number of studies and the results of several of these studies are summarized in Fig. 15 which plot the stregth normalized by that of the solid cell wall material against the foam density normalized by the solid density (Wadley, 2002). In the figure with coloured lines and in Table 8 are reported the numerical figures founded in this investigation. There is an essential difference between oper-cell and closed-cell structures. Open-cell foams are represented by a network of connected struts. The main deformation mechanism is bending of the cell edges and, at higher relative foam densities, $\rho_r$>0.1, additional extension and compression of the edges. In closed-cell foams the cell walls between the cell edges and the membrane stresses in the cell walls also play a major role on the deformation mechanisms. Owing to the higher constraints, arising from the existence of cell walls, in closed-cell structures the Young's modulus is theoretically higher by several magnitudes compared with open-cell structures of the same relative density.

| Process | Relative density | Relative compressive strength |
|---|---|---|
| $TiH_2$ | 0.286 | 0.148 |
| SDP | 0.368 | 0.119 |
| MGI | 0.165 | 0.026 |

Table 8. Relative density and relative compressive strenth

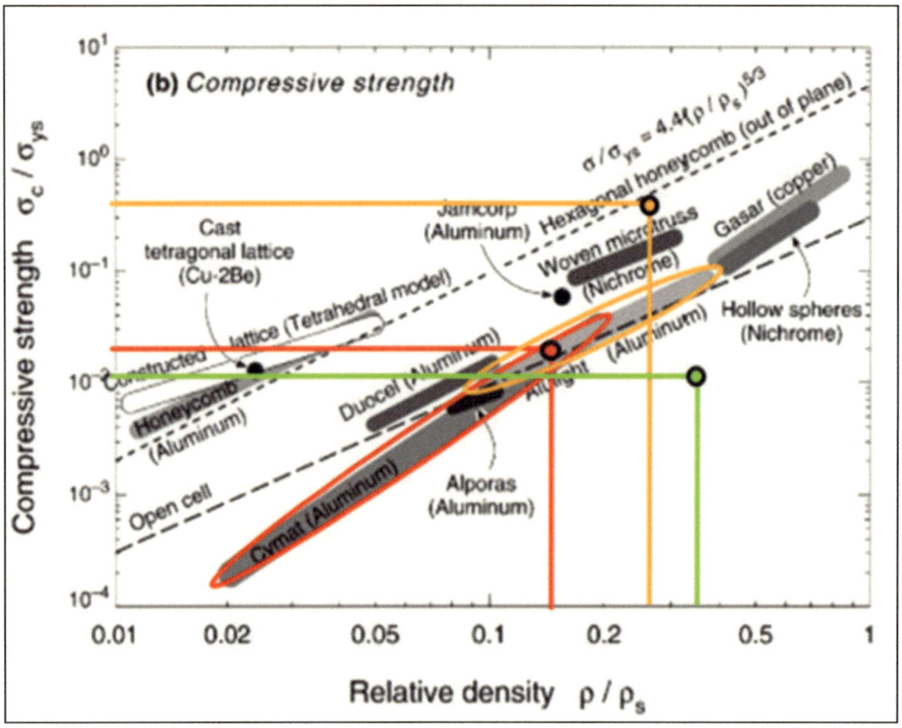


Fig. 15. A comparison of the mechanical properties of cellular metals: relative compressive strength plotted against relative density (Wadley, 2002)

The stress plateau for MGI foam is serrated (red lines Figs. 4-5), as a typical of a brittle foam: the serration correspond to fracture of cell walls. The initial yield point of MGI foam corresponds to debondign between the SiC particles and the aluminium matrix, which is then followed by ductile tearing of the matrix. Once number of cells have yielded, a deformation bands forms and subsequent cell collapse is by membrane tearing and the growth of interfacial cracks. The deformation of MGI foams under compressive loads is not spatially uniform deformation first occurs in the weakest region and propagated in this region until it is completely crushed or becomes fully densified. Then a second weakest band begins to deform until it is densified. This process is repeated in subsequent bands. Final densification occurs at 70% (relative density 0.25 - Fig. 16 a) and at 80% (relative density 0.31 - Fig. 16 b) of the strain.

The Plateau stress for the $TiH_2$ and SDP are gradually increases with strain until the densification occurs. But the $TiH_2$ foam shows a gently rising stress-strain curve in compression, and with no evidence of the formation of discrete crush bands (orange lines

Fig. 16). In contrast, the SDP foams crush by the sequential formation of crush bands at random sections of the foam. The foams are ductile in compression: they can undergo much larger strains than the tensile ductility of a fully dense aluminium alloy. This suggests that the cell edges deform mainly in bending, with the bending strains in the cells much less than the macroscopic uniaxial strain. For SDP foams final densification occurs at 40% of the strain while for $TiH_2$ foams at 50% of the strains.

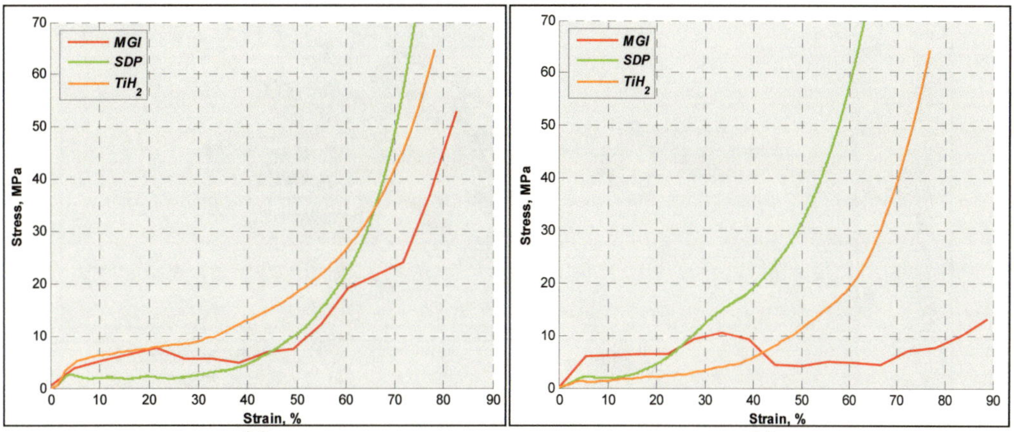


(a) (b)

Fig. 16. Stress-strain diagram for 3 samples: a) relative density of 0.25 ($TiH_2$ 370-750-5, SDP 30-2-550, MGI 300-8-20), b) relative density of 0.31 ($TiH_2$ 310-850-0, SDP 30-3-600, MGI 300-2-15)

Ideal energy absorbers have a long flat stress-strain curve. The absorbers collapses plastically at a constant at a constant nominal stress, called the Plateau stress up to a limiting nominal strain (50% in this investigation). Energy absorbers for packaging and protection are chosen so that the plateau stress is just below that which will cause damage to the packaged object; the best choice is then the one which has the longest plateau, and therefore absorbs the most energy before reaching $\varepsilon_D$. The area under the curve, roughly $\sigma_{pl}\varepsilon_D$, measures the energy the foam can absorb, per unit initial volume, up to the end of the plateau. Foams which have a stress-strain curve like that shown in figure perform well in this function. Fig. 17 shows a plot of absorbed energy plotted against Plateau stress for some available metal foams. Foams retain the advantage that they are isotropic, absorbing energy equally well for any direction of impact. In the plot no reference point is presents for SDP or other similar processes. Mean values of Plateau stress and absorbed energy for $TiH_2$ and MGI foams show a behaviour slightly worst.

| Method | Plateau stress (MPa) | Absorbed energy (MJ/m$^3$) | Absorbed energy (J/g) |
|---|---|---|---|
| $TiH_2$ | 16.0 | 3.56 | 4.61 |
| SDP | 26.0 | 5.69 | 5.72 |
| MGI | 5.85 | 2.16 | 4.76 |

Table 9. Plateau stress and absorbed energy

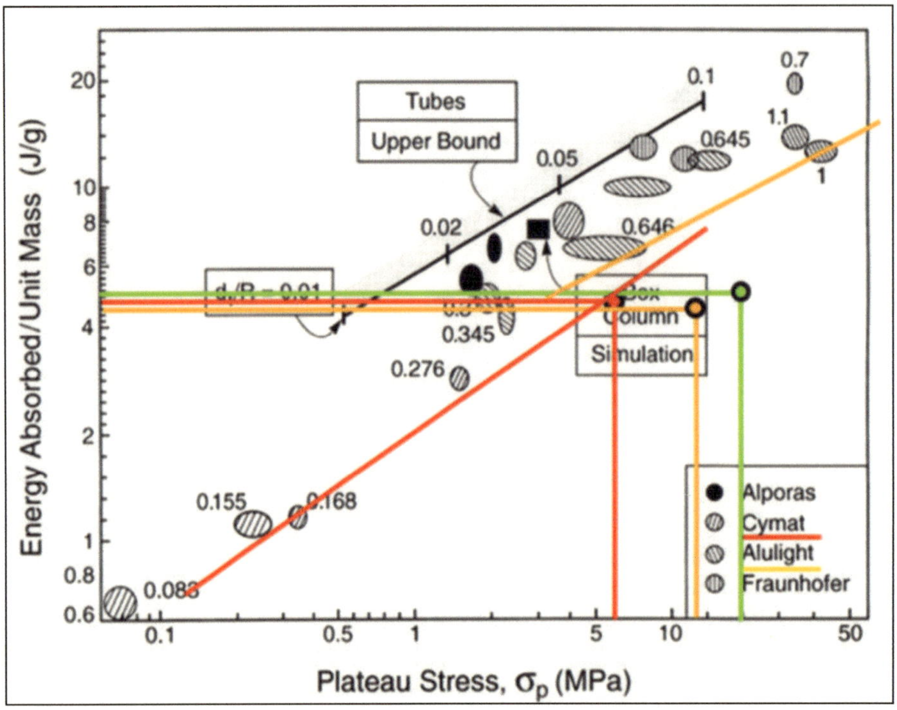


Fig. 17. Energy per unit mass against plateau stress for cellular Al alloys. Also shown is a comparison of the energy absorption per unit mass for Al tubes (Evans et al., 1999)

## 6. References


Arnold, M.; Korner, C. & Singer, R. F. (2003). PM aluminium foams: stabilizing mechanism and optimisation. In Cellular Metals: Manufacture, Properties, Application, pp. 71-76 Banhart, J., Fleck, N. A. and Mortensen, A. (eds.) Verlag MIT Publishing, Berlin

Ashby, M.F.; Evans, A.G.; Fleck, N.A.; Gibson, L.J.; Hutchinson, J.W. & Wadley, H.N.G. (2000). *Metal foams: a design guide*. USA: Butterworth-Heinemann

Asholt, P. (1999). Aluminium foam produced by the melt foaming route process, properties and applications, *in Proc. of Int. Conf. on Metal Foam and Porous Metal Structures*, pp. 133-140, June 1999, MIT Publishing, Bremen - Germany, Editors J. Banhart, M.F. Ashby, N.A. Fleck

Babcsan, N.; Banhart, J. & Leitlmeier, D. (2003). Metal foams - Manufacture and physics of foaming, *Proceedings of the International Conference Advanced Metallic Materials* 2003, pp. 5-15, Bratislava, November 2003, Jerz J. Editor, Slovakia

Banhart, J. (2000). Properties and applications of cast aluminum sponge, *Advanced Engineering Materials*, 2, No. 4, pp. 188-191

Banhart, J. (2001). Manufacture, characterisation and application of cellular metals and metal foams, *Progress in Material Science*, 46, pp. 559-632

Banhart, J. & Baumgartner, F. (2002), Industrilizationn of Powder-Compact Foaming Technique. In: *Handbook of Cellular Metals: Production, Processing, Applications*, Degischer H.P. & Kriszt B. (Eds), <pp. 14-21, Wiley-VCH Verlag GmbH &Co. KGaA, ISBN 3-527-30339-1

Baumgartner, F. & Gers, H. (1999). Industrialisation of P/M foaming process, *Proceedings of International Conference of Metal Foams and Porous Metal Structures 1999*, pp. 73-78, Bremen, 1999, J. Banhart, M.F. Ashby and N.A. Fleck Editors, Verlag MIT Publishing

Baumgartner, F.; Duarte, I. & Banhart, J. (2000). Industrialization of powder compact foaming process. *Advanced Engineegring Materials*, 4, pp. 168–174

Beals, J.T. & Thompson, M.S. (1997). Density gradient effects on aluminium foam compression behaviour, Journal of Materials Science, vol. 32, no. 13, pp. 3595–3600

Cingi, C. (1992). Degassing of aluminum melts and rotary impeller degassing, *Licentiate's Thesis*, Helsinki University of Technology

Conde, Y.; Despois, J.F.; Goodall, R.; Marmottant, A.; Salvo, L.; San Marchi, C. & Mortensen A. (2006). Replication (a.k.a. Space holder) processing of highly porous materials, In: *Proc. of 4th Int. Conf. on Porous Metals and Metal Foaming Technology*, pp. 199-206, September 2005, Editors H. Nakajima and N. Kanetake, The Japan Institute of Metals

Cymat Corporation. (2002), *Technical manual for stabilized aluminum foam*, http://www.cymat.com Ontario-Canada

Degischer, H.P. & Kottar, A.(1999). On the non-destructive testing of metal foams, in: *Proc. of Int. Conf. on Metal Foam and Porous Metal Structures*, pp. 213-220, Editors J. Banhart, M.F. Ashby, N.A. Fleck, Jun 1999, MIT Publishing, Bremen - Germany, ISBN 3-9805748-7-3

Duarte, I. & Banhart, J. (2000). A study of aluminium foam formation - kinetics and microstructure. *Acta Materialia*, 48, pp. 2349–2362

Evans, A.G.; Hutchinson, J.W. & Ashby M.F. (1999). Multifunctionality of cellular metal system, Progress in Materials Science, 43, pp. 171-221

Fusheng, H. & Zhengang, Z. (1999). The mechanical behaviour of foamed aluminum, *Journal of Material Science*, 34, pp. 291-299

Gaillard, C.; Despois, J.F. & Mortensen, A. (2004). Processing of NaCl powders of controlled size and shape for the microstructural tailoring of aluminium foams. *Materials Science & Engineering A*, 374, pp. 250–62

Gergely, V.; Degischer, H.P. & Clyne, T.W. (2000). Recycling of MMC and production of metallic foams, in: *Comprehensive Composite Materials*, pp. 797-820, Vol. 3, T.W. Clyne et al. Editors, Elsevier, London

Hur, B.Y.; Park, S.H. & Hiroshi, A. (2003). Viscosity and surface tension of Al and effects of additional element. Materials Science Forum, vol. 439, pp. 51–56

Ip, S.W.; Wang, Y. & J Toguri, J.M. (1999). Aluminum foam stabilization by solid particles. Canadian Metallurgical Quarterly, vol. 38, no. 1, pp. 81–92

Kaptay, G. (2003). Interfacial criteria for stabilization of liquid foams by solid particles. Colloids and Surfaces A, vol. 230, no. 1–3, pp. 67–80

Kenny L.D. & Thomas, M. (1994). Process for shape casting of particle stabilized metal foam," *US patent no. 5281251*

Kleinheyer, S. & Bilz, G. (1995). Process and apparatus for manufacturing formed (shaped, moulded) parts from metal foam, *German patent no. DE4326982*

Korner, C. & Singer, R.F. (2002) Foaming Processes for Al, In: *Handbook of Cellular Metals: Production, Processing, Applications*, Degischer H.P. & Kriszt B. (Eds), pp. 8-14, Wiley-VCH Verlag GmbH &Co. KGaA, ISBN 3-527-30339-1

Kretz, R. & Wolfsgruber, E. (2003). Development of aluminium castings with permanent aluminium cores, in: *Proc. of Int. Conf. on Cellular Metals: manufacture, properties, applications*, pp. 181-186, Editors J. Banhart, N.A. Fleck and A. Mortensen, Jun 2003, Verlag MIT Publishing, Bremen - Germany

Kriszt, B.; martin, U. & Mosler, U. (2002) Characterization of Cellular and Foamed Metals, In: *Handbook of Cellular Metals: Production, Processing, Applications*, Degischer H.P. & Kriszt B. (Eds), pp. 130-145, Wiley-VCH Verlag GmbH &Co. KGaA, ISBN 3-527-30339-1

Kuchek, H.A. (1966). Method of making porous metallic article. US Patent 3,236,706

Lehmus, D. & Banhart, J. (2003). Properties of heat treated aluminium foams. *Materials Science & Engineering A*, 349, pp. 98–110.

Li, J.R.; Cheng, H.F.; Yu, J.L. & Han, F.S. (2003). Effect of dual-size cell mix on the stiffness and strength of open-cell aluminum foams. Materials Science & Eng A, pp. 240–8.

Matijašević-Lux, B. (2006). Characterisation and optimisation of blowing agent for making improved metal foams, *Doctor Eng. Science thesis*, Technical University of Berlin

Miyoshi, T.; Itoh, M.; Akiyama, S. & Kitahara, A. (1999). Aluminium foam, "Alporas": the production process, properties and applications. In: *Proc. of Int. Conf. on Metal Foam and Porous Metal Structures*, pp. 125-132, Jun 1999, Editors J. Banhart, M.F. Ashby, N.A. Fleck MIT Publishing, Bremen - Germany

Nichol, S. (2006). Metal foam casting apparatus and method, *US patent no. 6998535*

Oak, S.M.; Kim, B.J.; Kim, W.T.; Chun, M.S. & Moon, Y.H., (2002) Physical modeling of bubble generation in foamed-aluminum, *Journal of Materials Processing Technology*, 130-131, pp. 304-309

Sang, H.; Kenny, L.D. & Jin, I. (1994). Process for producing shaped slabs of particle stabilized foamed metal,*US patent no. 5334236*

San Marchi, C.; Despois, J.F. & Mortensen, A. (2000). Fabrication and compressive response of open-cell aluminum foams with sub-millimeter pores, In: *Metal matrix composites and metallic foams*, Proc. of Euromat '99, pp. 34-39, edited by T.W. Clyne and F. Simancik, 2000, Weinheim, Wiley-VCH

San Marchi, C. & Mortensen, A. (2001). Deformation of open-cell aluminium foam. Acta Materialia, 49, pp. 3959–69

San Marchi, C. & Mortensen, A. (2002). Infiltration and the Replication Process for producing metal sponges. In: *Handbook of Cellular Metals: Production, Processing, Applications*, Degischer H.P. & Kriszt B. (Eds), pp. 43-55, Wiley-VCH Verlag GmbH &Co. KGaA, ISBN 3-527-30339-1

Schaffer, G.B.; Sercombe, T.B. & Lumley, R.N. (2001). Liquid phase sintering of aluminium alloys. *Materials Chemistry Physics*, pp. 85–91

Simancik, F. & Schoerghuber, F. (1998). Complex foamed aluminum parts as permanent cores in aluminum castings, in: *MRS Symposium Proceedings*, pp. 151-156, Ed. by D.S. Schwartz, D.S. Shih, A.G. Evans and H.N.G. Wadley, Vol. 521, Materials Research Society, Warrendale-Pennsylvania

Speed, S.E. (1976). Foaming of metals by the catalized and controlled decomposition of zyrconium hydride and titanium hydride, *US Patent 3,981,720*

Sun, D.X. & Zhao, Y.Y. (2002). Static and dynamic absorption of Al foams produced by sintering and dissolution process. *Metallurgical Materials Transactions B*, 34, pp. 69.

Sun, D.X. % Zhao, Y.Y. (2005). Phase changes in sintering of Al/Mg/NaCl compacts for manufacturing Al foams by the sintering and dissolution process. *Materials Letters*, 59, pp. 6–10

Surace, R.; De Filippis, L.A.C.; Niini, E.; Ludovico, A.D. & Orkas, J. (2009). Morphological Investigation of Foamed Aluminum Parts Produced by Melt Gas Injection, *Advances in Materials Science and Engineering*, Volume 2009, Article ID 506024, 9 pages doi:10.1155/2009/506024

Surace, R. & De Filippis L.A.C. (2010). Scale-up of Aluminium Foam Production, In: *Scale up in Metallurgy*, Maximilian Lackner (Ed.), ProcessEng Engineering GmbH (Publisher), ISBN: 978-3-902655-10-3

UNI 558 (1985). Prove meccaniche dei materiali metallici, prova di compressione a temperatura ambiente, Norma Italiana

Wadley, H.N.G. (2002). Cellular metals manufacturing, *Advanced Engineering Materials*, 4, No. 10, pp. 726-733

Wagner. I.; Hintz, C. & Sahm R., (2000) Precision cast near net shape components based on cellular metals materials, In: *Metal matrix composites and metallic foams*, Proc. of Euromat '99, pp. 40-45, edited by T.W. Clyne and F. Simancik, Weinheim, Wiley-VCH

Wen, C.E.; Mabuchi, M.; Yamada, Y.; Shimojima, K.; Chino, Y. & Hosokawa, H. (2003) Processing of fine-grained aluminum foam by spark plasma sintering. *Journal of Materials Science Letters*, 22, pp. 1407–9

Wood, J.T. (1997). Production and applications of continuosly cast, foamed aluminum, in *Proc. of Fraunhofer USA Metal Foam Symposium*, pp. 31-35, Delaware, October 1997, editors J. Bahart and H. Eifert.

Zhao, Y.Y. & Sun, D.X. (2001). A novel sintering-dissolution process for manufacturing Al foams. *Scripta Materialia*, 44, pp. 105–10

Zhao, Y.Y.; Han, F.& Fung, T. (2004). Optimisation of compaction and liquid-state sintering in sintering and dissolution process for manufacturing Al foams. *Materials Science Engineering A*, 364, pp. 117–25

Zhao, Y.Y.; Fung, T.; Zhang, L.P & Zhang, F.L. (2005). Lost carbonate sintering process for manufacturing metal foams. *Scripta Materialia*, 52, pp. 295–8

# 7

# Application of Fractal Dimension for Estimation of the Type of Passenger Car Driver

Andrzej Augustynowicz, Assoc. Prof. Dr. Eng.[1],
Hanna Sciegosz Dr. Eng.[2] and Sebastian Brol, Dr. Eng.[1]
[1]*Chair of Road and Agricultural Vehicles, Faculty of Mechanical Engineering, Opole University of Technology*
[2]*Institute of Mathematics, Physics and Chemistry - Division of Mathematics, Opole University of Technology*
*Poland*

## 1. Introduction

Chaos theory can be used for quantitative dynamics of uncertainty and finding order in its perturbances. Chaos theory is largely a colloquial notion and is referred to as an analysis of non-linear dynamical systems. The studies devoted to linear dynamical systems and theories of complexity involve studies of turbulence, or, more precisely, the transfer from stability to turbulence. The dynamical system by its nature does not follow long-term forecasts. There are two reasons for the unpredictability. Dynamical systems involve both feedback and critical levels. To paraphrase, one can say that a dynamical system forms a system of non-linear feedback. The most important properties of the system include: sensitivity to the change of the initial conditions, occurrence of critical points and a fractal dimension. Non-linear dynamical systems tend to have more than one solution. The case often is that the number of solutions is huge or even infinite. A visual representation of the data forms a finite space called the phase space of the system. The number of dimensions in the space is determined by the number of variable presents in the system. If there are two or three variables, it is possible to visually examine the data. In case of a larger number of dimensions, the data are examined with the use of mathematical data. Another term used in non-linear dynamical systems is the attractor. This is an area of a equilibrium of non-linear system within a time series. A system which aims to achieve an equilibrium in the form of a single value has a point attractor. Besides, there are phase attractors, which form periodic cycles or orbits in space forming a limit cycle. An attractor, in which none of the points in the space overlaps and whose orbits do not cross but both originate in the same area of phase space, is called strange attractor. Such attractors in contrast to point attractors are non-periodic and predominantly have a fractal dimension [10,11].

## 2. Fractal dimension in a time series

The fractal dimension forms an important piece of information regarding the system. This is the number which quantitatively describes the way in which an object occupies the surrounding space. The lowest total number higher than the fractal dimension informs of the minimum number of dynamic variables needed for the development of a dynamic model for a system. Concurrently, fractal dimension determines the lowest number of the possible degrees of freedom. The practical measure used to determine fractal dimension is with the aid of the method developed by Grassberger and Procaccio in 1983 [5]. It involves the determination of a correlation dimension, which forms an approximation of a fractal dimension using correlation integral C(R). This integral determines the probability of finding a pair of points in attractor whose distance from each other is R. The correlation integral is calculated from the following formula

$$C(R)=\frac{1}{N}\cdot\sum_{\substack{i,j=1\\ i\neq j}}^{N} H\left(R-\left|x_i-x_j\right|\right)$$

where:

$$H(x)=1 \quad dla \quad R-\left|x_i-x_j\right|\geq 0,$$
$$H(x)=0 \quad dla \quad R-\left|x_i-x_j\right|<0,$$

N - number of measurement points,
R - distance.
H(x) takes the form of the Heaviside step function, which assumes the value of 1, when the distance between $x_i$ and $x_j$ is lower than R or 0 when the distance is larger. The correlation integral expresses the probability that randomly selected points are within the distance of less than R units. Along with an increase of the value of R, C(R) should increase at the rate of $R^D$, where D is the fractal dimension. This hence gives the following relations:

$$C(R)\sim R^D$$
$$\log\left(C(R)\right)=D\log(R)+const$$

For a given capacity dimension we calculate C(R) by increasing the value of R and setting the inclination of the function log(C(R)) relative to log(R). With the use of linear regression we can determine correlation dimension *D*. Along with an increase of the dimensions of embedding space d, the correlation dimension *D* will approach its actual value. Prior to the calculation of the correlation integral for a time series it is necessary to process the data in order to reconstruct the phase space and in particular in order to determine the capacity dimension and delay [12].

## 3. Reconstruction of phase space for a time series for a defined capacity dimension and time delay

The object of non-linear analysis is to establish an appropriate state for a given signal s(t) and, in particular, the reconstruction of the dynamic state of the system. In the classical approach the co-ordinates of a state space include displacement and speed. However, in practice it is very difficult to measure them in addition to the lack of information regarding the original state space dimensions. The up-to-date methods of signal analysis based on the theory of deterministic chaos render it possible to reconstruct the state space equivalent to the original without the necessity of a reference to the derivatives (speed) and dimensions of the original space. It involves the embedding of a time series with the aid of the method of time delay embedding. The procedure involves the identification of a space which is formally equivalent to the original space of the system state, while the identification applies the co-ordinates developed from the observed variables and their delays. The specific duration of the delay time $\tau$ can be found as the first occurrence of the zero point crossing of the autocorrelation function for a $K(\tau)$ signal. The selection of an appropriate delay time $\tau$ has an important impact on the entire dynamic process. The selection of an insufficient value of $\tau$ results in an insufficiently short duration of the evolution process for the exploration of the entire state space. The reconstructed attractor will be focused along the main diagonal or along the identical line of the embedded space. The selection of a limited value can lead to the distribution of co-ordinates so far away that they will no longer be correlated. As a result of the internal instability of chaotic system the extended delay time, the relation between the measurement of s(n) and s(n+T) will be equivalent to a random process [1,4,8]. The autocorrelation function can take the form

$$K(\tau) = \sum \left[ S_n - \bar{S} \right] \left[ S_{n+T} - \bar{S} \right],$$

$$\textit{where} \quad \bar{S} = \frac{1}{N} \sum_{n=1}^{N} S_n$$

Given a delay time $\tau$ the dimension of a state space is estimated, in which the dynamic state is reproduced. For this purpose the dynamic state is reproduced in the subsequent state spaces with gradually increasing dimension with the aid of the false nearest neighbor method. The final number of dimensions is determined by an answer to the question regarding the time when the geometric structure generated within the subsequent two-, three- and more dimensional will be unfolded; that is, when the closeness of the points will come as a result of only dynamic state z not mapping in the space with a smaller dimension. The smallest dimension, which unfolds the attractor, due to which the overlapping is discontinued is called the global dimension of embedding $d_G$. Every measurement signal constitutes a different combination of original dynamic variables and is capable of generating various global mappings of the original space on the reconstructed space in the $d_G$ dimension. Moreover, $d_G$ is a global dimension and can differ from the local dimensions for a given dynamic state. In order to identify the adequate dimension one can refer to the false nearest neighbor method, which reflects the unfolding of an attractor. It is necessary to take into consideration the following dimensions d=1,2,3,.., and check the successive data vectors and their neighbors for whether the closeness comes as a consequence of mapping or maybe is due to the dynamic characteristics of the system. The neighboring points, which turn out to be the result of mapping are denoted with the term false neighbors. Whether a neighbor is false can be checked by evolution and observation whether the distance between the vectors increases, remains constant or decreases. Given an appropriate dimension and delay time it is possible to develop vectors to reconstruct the dimension of a state space and its dynamic characteristics. The further course of action may involve an analysis of a trajectory and testing the value of the fractal dimension.

## 4. Road test

An issue, which has attracted a lot of attention recently, is associated with the modeling of the driver's characteristics. The complexity of driver's behavior and a large number of external parameters affecting it are the major causes why the extensive use of the driver's model can be forecasted as a distant target. Hence the issue of modeling is often limited to a selected aspect of the model, which accounts for the most important characteristics, e.g. style of driving. An appropriate analysis of signals, which reflect the driver's intention, offers the possibility of identification of driver type and interpretation of the driver's behaviors in various situations on the road. On the basis of this information the control system will be capable of selecting an optimum control algorithm and parameters of the engine and powertrain thus adapting to the behavior and expectations of the driver [2,3,6,7].

This paper contains a proposal of the application of non-linear analysis of signal generated on the accelerator pedal by the drive. The classification of the driving style is based on the Grassberger-Procaccio correlation dimension [5].

The test object was the middle class car with a 1.6 $dm^3$ engine and a manual transmission. An optical Datron LS3 sensor has been installed in the car for the measurement of kinematic parameters with a contact free method. The measurement range of the sensor is (0.5÷400) km/h, by generating around 400 impulses per second. Beside the speed and distance the following parameters wee also taken: instantaneous displacement of acceleration pedal and longitudinal acceleration of the car. Data received from the Daqbook measuring interface were subsequently processed with the use of a PC under the supervision of the operator in the passenger seat. This system was used for the registration of the measured parameters with the frequency of 33 per second. Experimental studies involved 76 road tests with the car under various conditions specific to urban traffic, with the length of the road stretch of around 7 kilometers. Selected drivers covered the distance two times, trying to cover the distance in a style which were considerably different in each attempt. Each of the drives was subsequently classified as mild or active. In order to secure a similarity of the measurement conditions the distance was covered at a time of the day when the traffic was the smallest. Fig. 1 illustrates the curves representing the speed of the displacement of the accelerator pedal during car acceleration. The interpretation of the curves indicates that the driver preferring active driving test tend to press the pedal deeper and more intensively in comparison to drivers whose driving style is named mild.

An initial assessment of the results makes it possible to assume with a high degree of probability that it is possible to assess driving style on the basis of the realized speed profile as well as on the basis of analysis of a signal generated by the driver over the accelerator pedal. From the point of view of the control theory this value plays the role of an input signal for the dynamic object, i.e. the car, whereas the speed and car acceleration represent variables of the state and are correlated with this input value. Fig. 2 contains curves representing the changes in the displacement of the accelerator pedal in the function of the speed of the displacement. The presented curves for an active driver display the highest extent of changes both regarding the displacement and speed of the speed of accelerator pedal displacement.

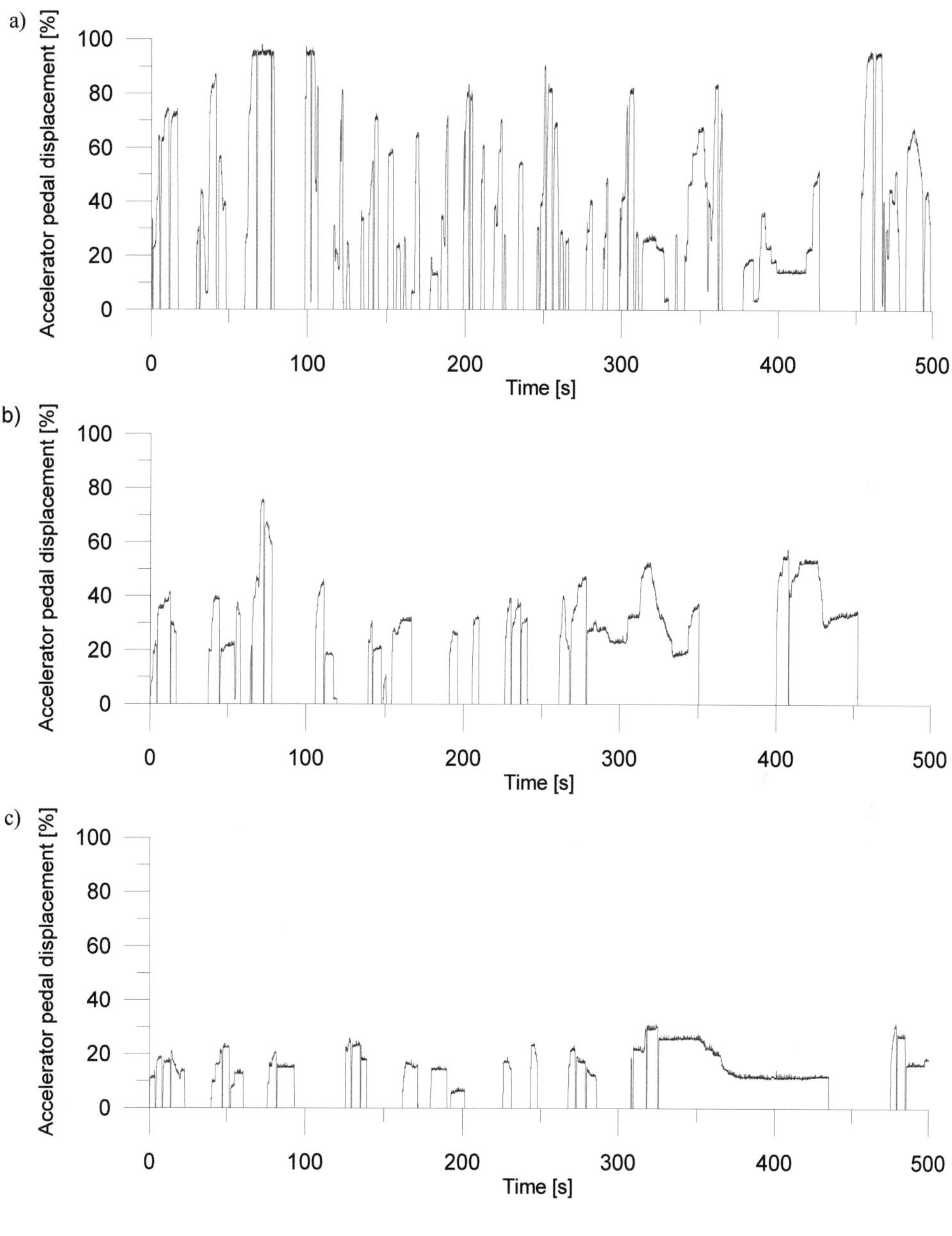


Fig. 1. Displacement of accelerator pedal for the case of a) „active", b) „neutral" and c) „mild" driver.

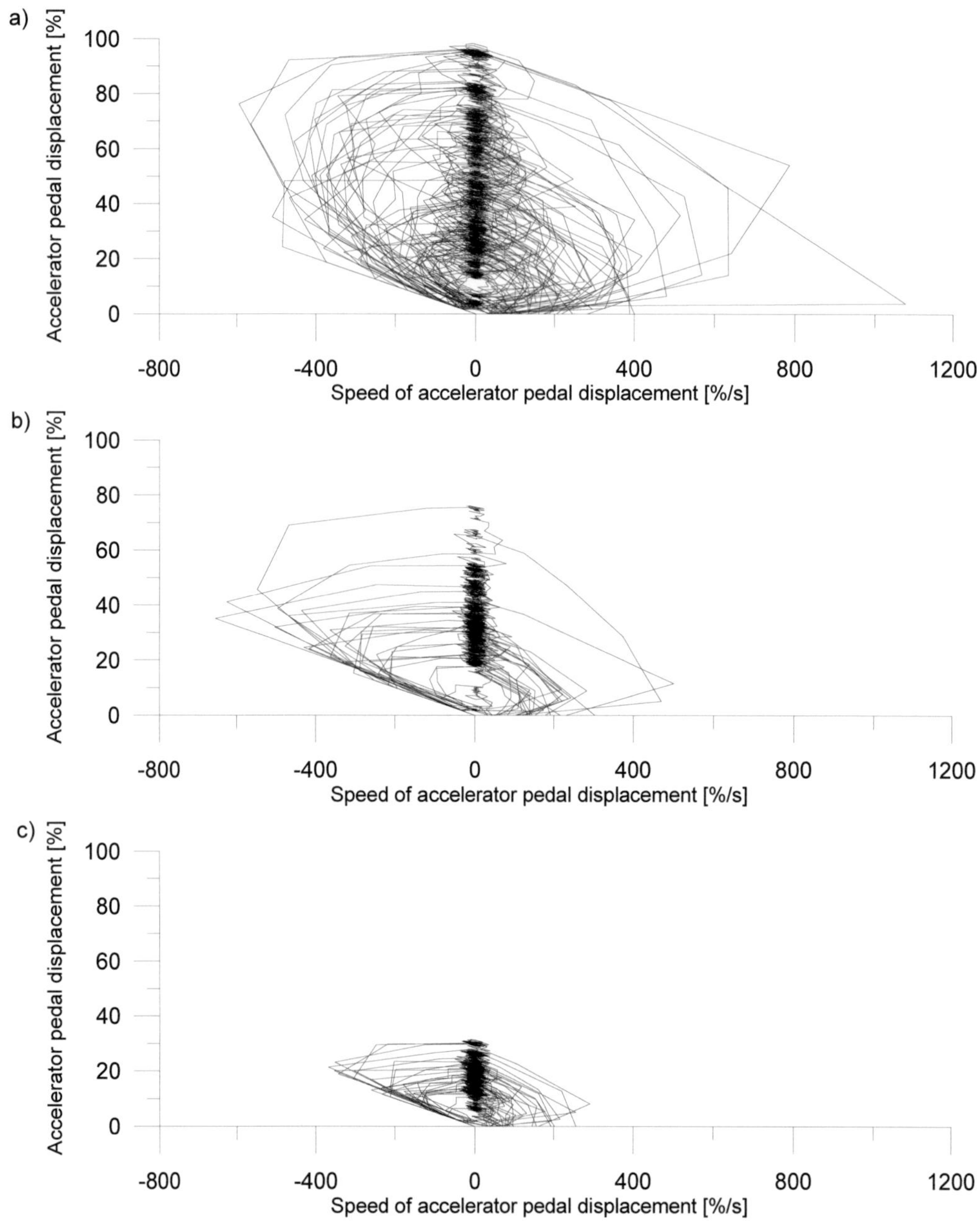


Fig. 2. Speed of accelerator pedal displacement in the function of changes in its speed for the case of a) „active", b) „neutral" and c) „mild" driver

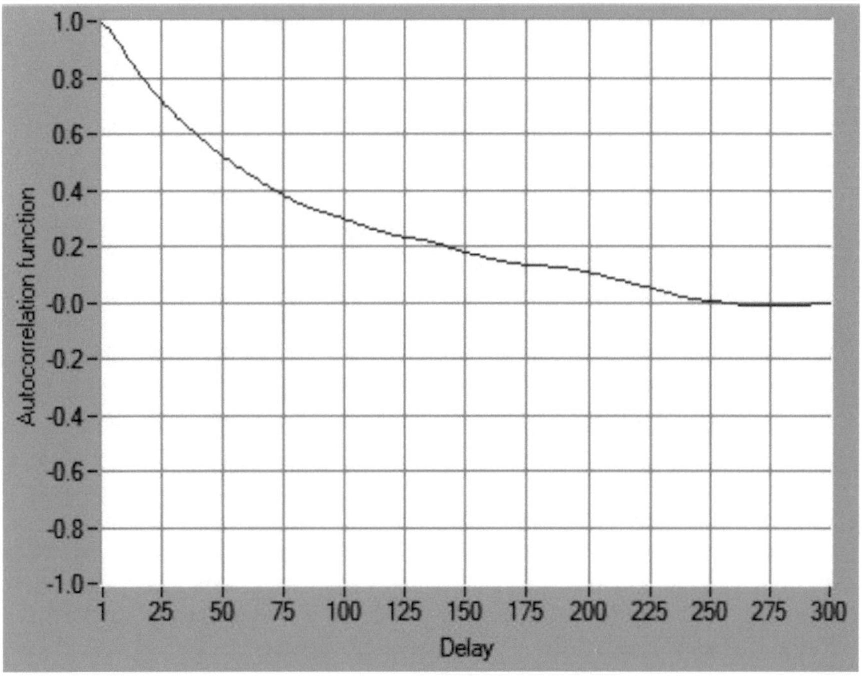


a)

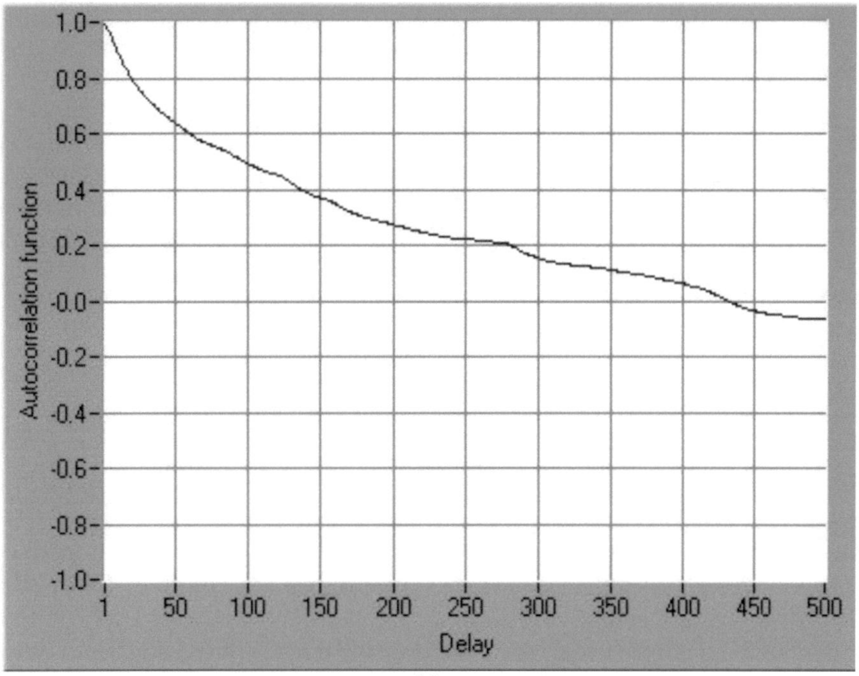


b)

Fig. 3. Delays determined from time histories of autocorrelation function $K(\tau)$
a) active driver $\tau = 255$, b) mild driver $\tau = 432$

## 5. Correlation dimension of accelerator pedal signal

The signals recorded during road test (measurements of accelerator pedal displacement) were subjected to non-linear analysis with the aim of determination of the correlation dimension with the use of NDT (Nonlinear Dynamics Toolbox) software [9] available online. The object of the testing was the search for a method of estimation of the driver type on the basis of an assumption that it is possible to apply correlation dimension as the estimator of the driver type. In order to do this, time curves of signals generated by accelerator pedal by the drivers were subjected to non-linear analysis. By reference to the results in a rank list presented in paper [2], in which drivers were classified from the least to the most active, the relation between the driver type and correlation dimension was established. In the former part of this paper it was indicated that in order for the calculation of correlation dimension t was necessary to determine the values of the delay time $\tau$ and dimensions of the embedded space d. The two data formed an input for further calculations. The delay time $\tau$ was calculated as the first zero crossing in the history of autocorrelation function $K(\tau)$.The correspondence between driver type and delay $\tau$ was not found. Fig. 3 presents the zero crossing places for two types of drivers.

At the same time the embedding dimension d was determined with the use of the false nearest neighbor method. For this purpose an analysis of the charts presenting the relations between dimension d and per cent of false neighbors was undertaken. The charts tend to be monotonically decreasing and did not pose any problems during calculations. The embedding dimension was assumed to be the value of d at which the per cent of the false friends reached zero. It can be concluded that the value of zero was gained for considerably distinct values of embedding dimension d. In the case of this parameter the correspondence between the type of driver was found to be irrelevant. Fig. 4 presents the dimensions of embedding space d for two extreme driver types.

In summary, it was concluded that for all examined signals from the accelerator pedal based on 76 drivers the values of $\tau$ and d were diverse. The delay time $\tau$ was in the range between 146÷1171, whereas embedding dimension d between 7÷20. The above results were used for the calculations of correlation dimension. The chart representing the relation between log(C(R)) and log(R) displays a characteristic slope. Only the linear section of the chart was used for the assessment of the correlation dimension D. This results from D being the coefficient of the sloping in this section. The correlation dimensions gained for 76 drivers were grouped into 3 sets. They are presented in Table 1.

| Correlation dimension | Number of drivers | Driver types |
|---|---|---|
| $2<D$ | 4 (5.3%) | „most active" group |
| $1 \le D \le 2$ | 66 (86.8%) | remaining group |
| $D<1$ | 6 (7.9%) | „mildest" group |

Table 1. Results of calculated correlation dimension

The charts with the relations between function log(C(R)) and log(R) for various driver types are illustrated in Figs. 5, 6 and 7.

In conclusion of the conducted analysis, it can be stated that the proposed chaotic estimator in the form of correlative Grassberger-Procaccio based on the analysis of the signal generated by the driver with the accelerator pedal makes it possible to identify the driver's style. The disadvantage of this method is that it is capable of identifying only the extreme driving types, and hence does not offer graded classification of intermediate types of drivers.

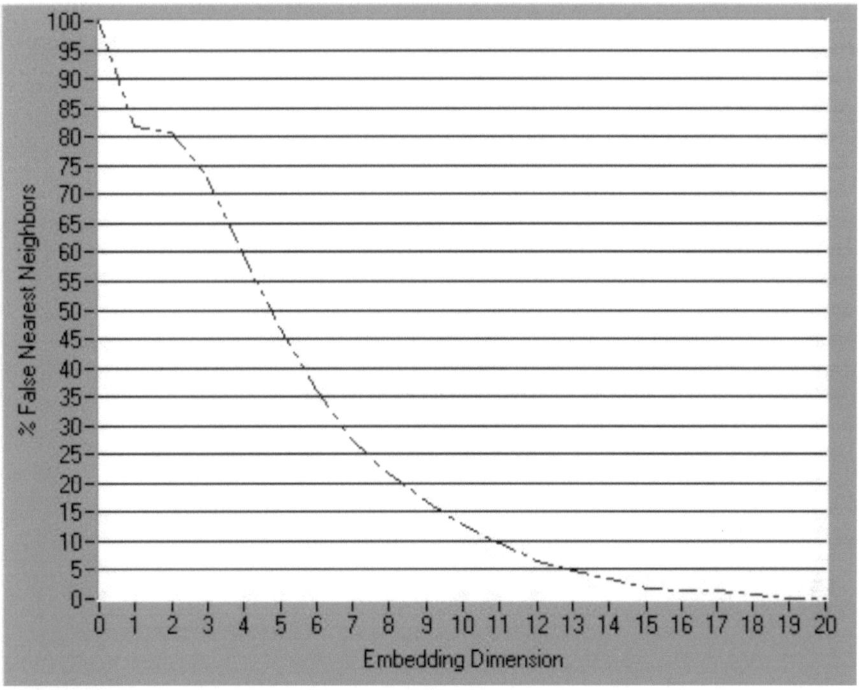


a)

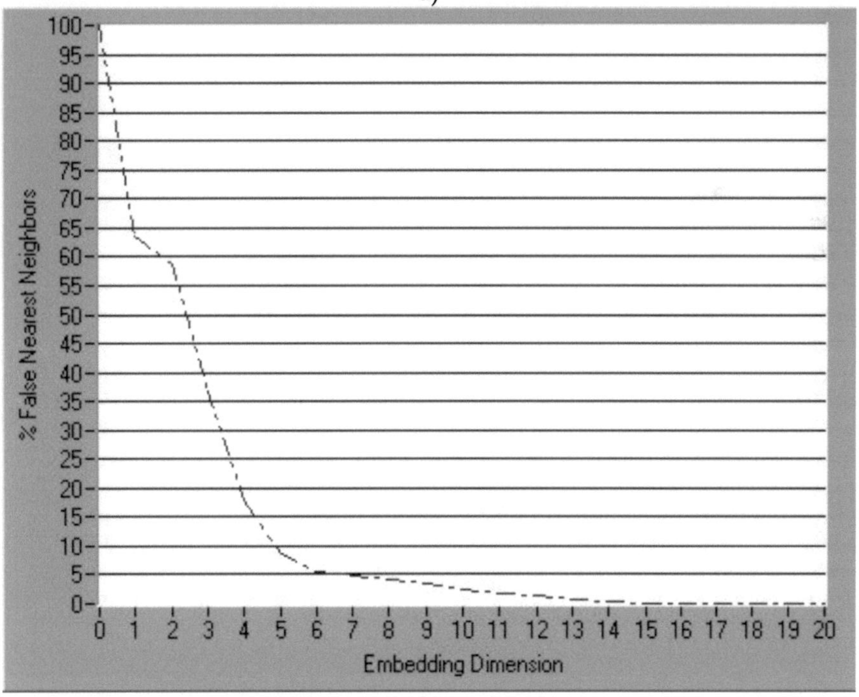


b)

Fig. 4. Embedding dimensions d determined with false nearest neighbor
a) for an active driver d = 19, b) for a mild driver d = 15

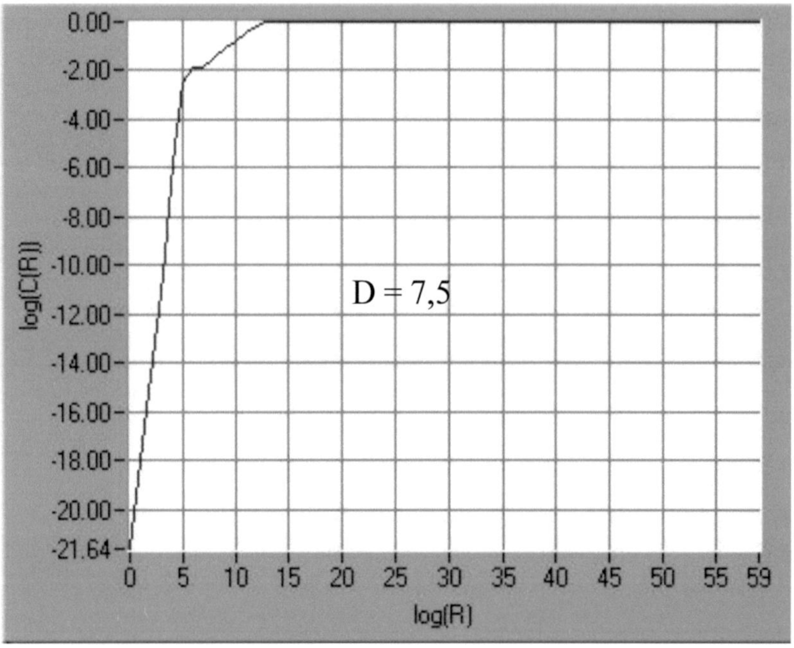


Fig. 5. Relation between function log(C(R)) and log(R) for active driver type

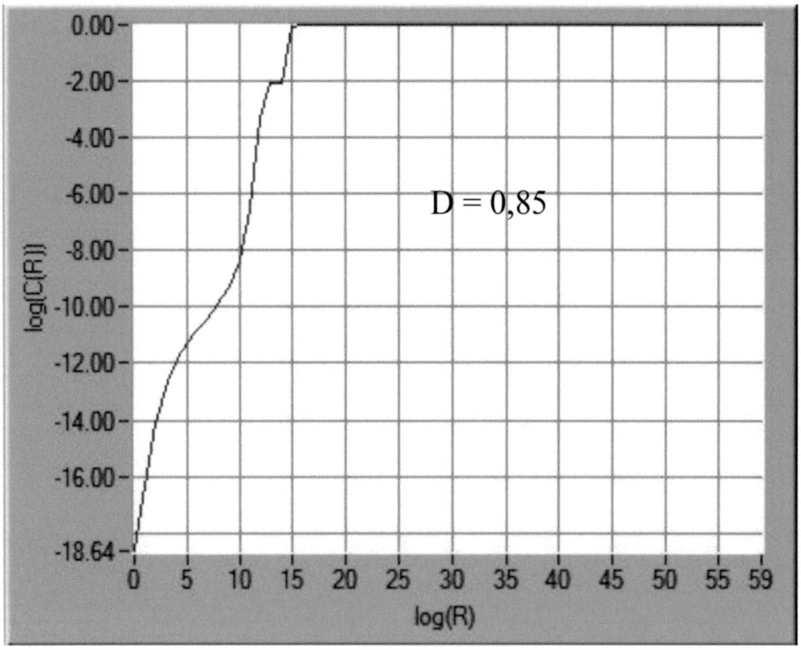


Fig. 6. Relation between function log(C(R)) and log(R) for mild driver type

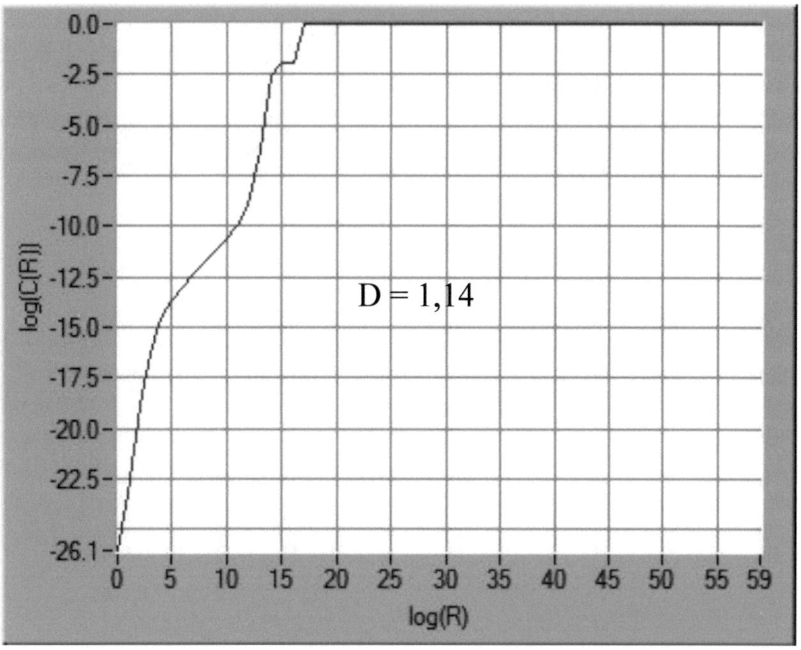


Fig. 7. Relation between function log(C(R)) and log(R) for neutral driver type

## 6. References


[1] AKAY M.(Ed.): Nonlinear Biomedical Signal Processing, Vol. 2: Dynamic Analysis and Modeling. John Wiley & Sons 2001.

[2] AUGUSTYNOWICZ A.: Preliminary classification of driving style with object rank method, International Journal of Automotive Technology, Vol. 10, No. 5, pp. 607−610 (2009)

[3] AUGUSTYNOWICZ A.,BARTECKI K.: Estimation of driving characteristics by the application of Elman's recurrent neural network. The Archives of Transport. Vol.XVIII, no. 4. pp.5-13

[4] BOGUŚ P., MERKISZ J., GRZESZCZYK R., MAZUREK S.. Nonlinear Analysis of Combustion Engine Vibroaccoustic Signals for Misfire Detection. SAE Technical Paper Series 2003-01-0354.

[5] GRASSBERGER P., PROCACCIA I.: Characterization of Strange Attractors. Physical Review Letters 50, 346-349, 1983.

[6] GUO K., CHENG Y., DING H.: Analytical Method for Modeling Driver in Vehicle Directional Control, Vehicle System Dynamics Supplement 41/2004.

[7] HAYAKAWA K., OSAWA M., et al.: Real Time Estimation of Driver's Intention and Environment Based on Operational Signals. FISITA World Automotive Congress, Paris 1998, nr F98S204.

[8] KANTZ H., SCHREIBER T.: Nonlinear time series analysis. Cambridge University Press 1997

[9] NDT Nonlinear Dynamics Toolbox. Version 0.9.1. Created by Josh Reiss. School of Physics. Atlanta - Georgia. USA. 1999.

[10] OTT E.: Chaos In Dynamical Systems, Cambridge University Press 1993
[11] PETERS E.E.: Chaos and Order in the Capital Markets: A New View of Cycles, Prices, and Market Volatility. John Wiley and Sons, Inc, 1996
[12] POKRZYWNICKI S., SCIEGOSZ H.: The Saddle-Node and Hopf Bifurcation Systems with the External Forcing", The 8-th Experimental Chaos Conference, Florence, Italy, 14-17 June 2004, p. 99.

# 8

# Advanced Technologies in Biomechanics Investigations for the Analysis of Human Behaviour in Working Activities

Mihaela Ioana Baritz and Diana Cotoros
*Transilvania University from Brasov*
*Romania*

## 1. Introduction

The analysis of the human behavior during performing working activities represents at this moment a huge importance domain in obtaining performances and assuring occupational comfort.

Thus the behavioral analyses are oriented towards determinations upon the bipodal posture, normal gait with or without weights carried by the human subject and not last upon the human body motions required for performing different handlings or actions in working activities.

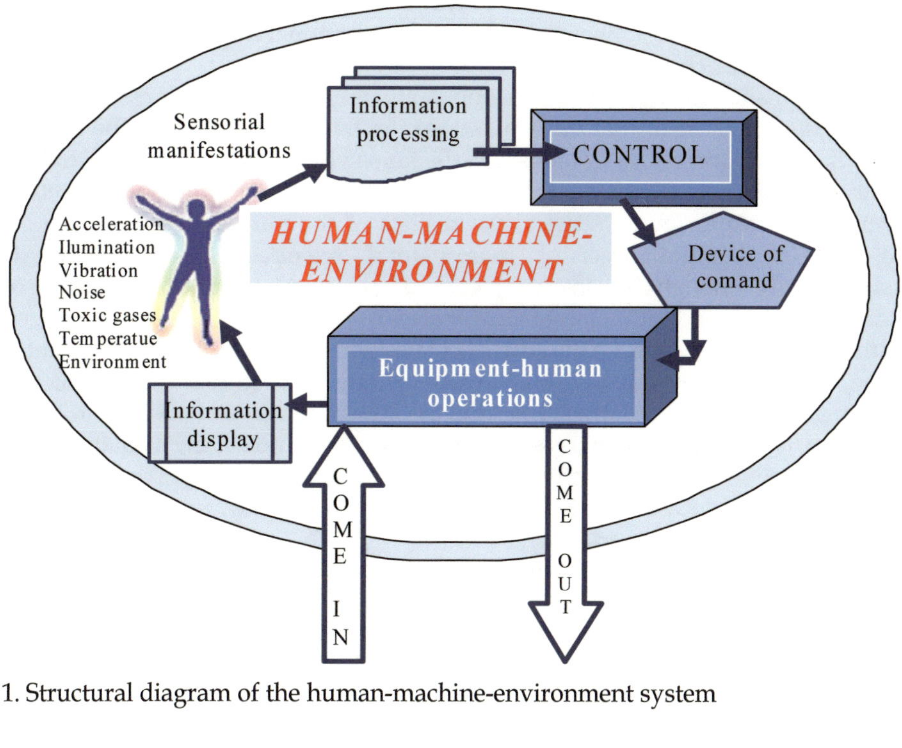


Fig. 1. Structural diagram of the human-machine-environment system

In these behavioral analyses we adopted the concept of human-machine-environment to be used in a unitary way and to be able to consider all the aspects connected to the sources of influence, ways of interaction and obtaining sensorial and decisional responses.
At the same time it is obvious there are three subsystems among which there are interactions, their resultant influencing the quality and quantity of human performed work.
*The human subsystem* is described by the information receiving and processing functions, decision making and the action function for directly acting upon the machine.
*The machine subsystem* consists of the following elements: display and signal devices, control devices; between these the machine performs a series of operations.
*The environment subsystem* influences the system operation by its components given by: noise, temperature, humidity, toxic pollutants, illumination, etc.
In order to reduce the design effort and time we assumed that the working environment is designed and used in virtual conditions, at the same time considering the economical aspects, to eliminate the costs associated with the physical prototypes production, but the workers' safety and work quality remain in the foreground.
For example in 2006, the Bureau of Labor Statistics - BLS in France reported that during production activities occurs the highest number of non-lethal occupational diseases, an average of 6 incidents for 100 workers yearly, so this is why the necessity of virtual modeling occurred, also operation simulation for some equipments especially when the human factor is involved. Digital human models (DHM), possible to be used in such analyses are virtual representations of the human body and allow the products and processes interacting to the human individual, to be virtually "brought" near him, forming together and also with the geometry of the "working cell", a computer designed system, analyzed and optimized by help of the software mechanisms.
A high range of models were developed, their main feature being that the human subjects involved in working activities will be able to choose the postures allowing the human body joints to develop the highest moments and forces, in an optimal self-adjusting manner of the motion and stability mechanisms.
Seitz et al. (2005) and Rothaug (2000) developed a model based on the optimization of the predictive posture, which in its turn is based on the human posture and the information related to the strains and forces developed in the human body's segments. The strains were used in these models as constraints that come closer to the "more natural" aspects of the human biomechanics to improve the visual realism of the posture prediction (Liu, 2003, Zhao et al., 2005). But the aspects of "more natural" regarded as subjective criteria are necessary but not enough for the validation of ergonomic analyses and for solving optimization and efficiency of biomechanical analyses.
Also in the works of Seitz et al. (2005) who calculates with a lot of accuracy the postures in a "plausible" way, there is no comparison between the present posture and the predictive one for the human factor. In a similar way, we find the same modality of approach in Liu (2003) and Zhao et al. (2005) works, who develop models capable of predicting a "natural" form as an opposite situation to the predictive posture but observe that the natural aspect is not enough for a quantity measurement and for the prediction process used for comparison to the present posture of the workers.
Many researches suggested that the working postures should be predictive by optimization of some factors such as potential energy, deviation towards the neutral location of the joint involved by the motion, discomfort and tension. The general approach is to select form a multitude of postures, that are cinematically connected to the constraints, the one that minimizes (or maximizes) an objective function.

For example Marler et al. (2005) suggests three solutions "keys" (the tendency of moving in sequences different body segments, preferably forward with respect to the neutral comfort position, the discomfort of motion near the limits of the joint motion range) that hypothetically are related to the human behavior in the chosen posture.

The human body posture or motion prediction can be completed by the set of information related to motion or stability (Park et al. 2004), and in order to define a precision process, then the fundamental data set should include those characteristics that are similar to those to be modeled, including the forces directions and magnitudes (e.g., Dufour et al., 2001).

Extensive researches conducted in different international centres examined the evolution of the bipedal human gait (Vaughan, 2003), have measured two broad types of gait - the pathological and the normal one (Oberg et al., 1993; Macellari et al., 1999; Perry, 1999 etc.), examined the aging effects (Grieve et al., 1966; Dahlstedt, 1978; Owings et al., 2004; Richardson et al., 2005; DeMott et al., 2007), or investigated the effects of variability in stepping, sliding, going up or down the stairs, jumping or side stepping (Stolze et al., 2000; Danion et al., 2003; Beauchet et al., 2005; Hausdorff, 2005).

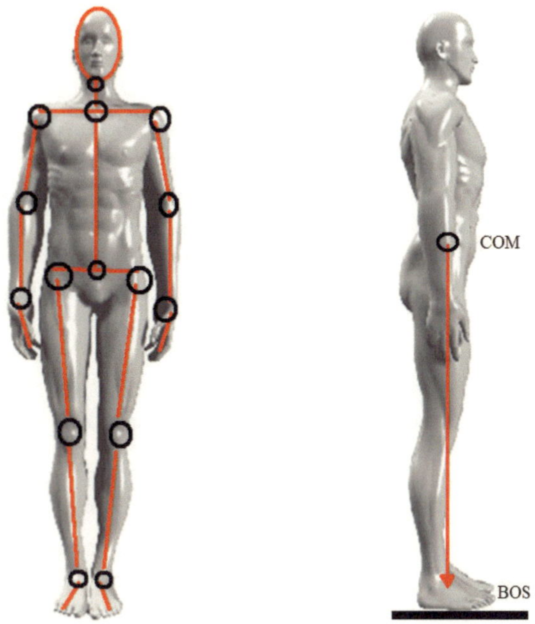


Fig. 2. Human body structure

The analyses of the postures and muscles activity set (Breniere & Do, 1981; Breniere & Do, 1986; Winter, 1995), gait cycles or stability characterization (Nissan et al., 1990; Breniere et al., 1991), were analyzed, studied and conceptualized (Winter 1995), in order to obtain multiple information for the management of ergonomic posture issues, for lucrative activity and way of life (Sparrow et al., 2005).

Thus we define the vertical-bipedal position of the human body as a mutual relationship between all the body segments and its vertical orientation as being determined by the gravitational field, the segments shape and size. In order to sample and configure the modular structure of the morpho-functional elements and for defining the bio-behavioral performances, the international anthropometric databases are to be accessed.

The anthropometric databases are created by the national and international agencies respecting the same acquisition, analysis, storing and creating principles of an interactive configuration for representative samples of population from different parts of the world. The variables of the human body are divided in standard modules and are defined by a unique anthropometric dimensional parameter.
The average anthropometric dimension which is selected - percentile 50 - allows the estimation of the standard deviation with respect to the other percentiles.
Because the human body is a multi segment architecture joined by links with different actions, this aspect may determine the occurrence of a certain postural instability which is controlled by the human organism in its whole by *feed-back* type reactions.
For the general definition of the postural stability of the human body we use a unitary parameter named **centre of mass (COM)** whose positions and displacements about the basis of support are recorded along different durations, in controlled environmental conditions, correlated by using several biomechanical investigation technologies (video, mechanical, electromagnetic, optical or mechatronic).
In static postures such as standing, sitting or laying, the human body and its segments are aligned and maintained in a certain position unlike the dynamic posture when these are in relative motion one about the other and the entire body about the environment. In this respect the study of a certain posture includes the kinetic and kinematical analyses for all the human body segments.
Especially in the static analyses, it is important to identify the **base of support (BOS)** defined as the area between the heels line in the back and the line of the sole tips in the front. This quantity may determine certain stability manifestations when the human body is subjected to some stimuli (audio, light, vibrations, shocks, temperature, etc.).
Even if the base of support is small and the centre of mass is higher on the human body, maintaining the stability in static postures requires a low quantity of energy consumption and only for keeping the muscle contraction.
Also the bones, joints and ligaments are systems capable to assure the necessary torques, the energy quantity being used to counteract gravitation and body's positions change induced by the circulatory and digestive system.
An important aspect in the action and maintaining postural stability is represented by its control, be it static or dynamic, manifested by the ability of the human subject to maintain the balance between the external forces and the organism response to their effect.
The feature of maintaining balance is "taught" by the **central nervous system** (CNS) using information captured from the sensorial system, passive biomechanic elements and from muscles.
Also CNS should be capable of detecting and predicting the future instability of the organism in bipodal posture and must react to all input signals by responses at the system output in the form of balance maintaining reactions of the human body. For this, the entire body with the component segments must present a **range of motions** (ROM) which corresponds with the kinematical and kinetic requirements and also is capable to respond fast by applying the necessary forces and velocities.
The postural stability as well as the initial orientation of the human body position may be altered if the inputs or outputs of the system are distorted, absent or incomplete, forcing thus the CNS to respond suitably by indicating a compromise of the action.
In case of organism normal operation, CNS selects the necessary muscles and joints combination to accomplish the stability or motion requirements of the human body. The

external forces that may intervene upon the human body system are: the forces of inertia and the forces of reaction, while the internal ones are developed by muscular activities and tensions in ligaments, tendons, joints or other tissues structures.

The effect of each category of forces, external and internal is in balance and the sum of all forces and moments acting in the human body is equal to zero for this body being in equilibrium.

In order to maintain the equilibrium in bipodal posture using minimum energy it is important that the body's centre of mass is kept above the base of support and the head position and orientation must allow the gaze direction to orient properly.

That is why only an active control of the 3D position of the body's centre of mass may determine the system to remain stable in the psycho-physiological limits and the body's centre of mass is controlled by non linear control mechanisms. The bipodal position of the human body determines an anisotropic structure, which is in equilibrium as long as there are no external stimuli, of any kind acting upon it (light, audio, mechanical or thermo dynamical).

Unlike the stability state of the human body that is considered a statically balanced state and for which the imposed initial conditions are kept in time, changing only when it is subjected to external stimuli, human gait is a dynamic stability state for which the forces, moments, velocities and accelerations of the entire body and of the component segments are balancing each other in real time by the controlled mechanism of the neuro-muscular system.

Additionally, the human gait represents also a repetitive motion with an energetic consumption divided along all the cycle stages in order to obtain a unitary displacement of the human body segments to overcome the forces of inertia, friction and resistance from the action environment.

In a lot of researches from the biomechanical area (Baritz M. et al. 2008) they consider that the mechanical parameters of the human body affect the gait type, the duration of the gait cycle or the way of reaction to the interaction with the environment, thus resulting a passive dynamics that affects its quality.

The structural analysis of the human body gait model performances uses especially the modeling by inverse dynamics and the model of the double pendulum because the segments mass distribution simplifies the mechanical and mathematical approach.

In this respect, at first the introduction of the system reference points is important both about the environment and about the support surface.

Between these points there is always a set of one-sided or multilateral connections depending on the modules, segments or component junctions that are involved in the stability, gait or specific segments motion processes.

These reference points are: (according to Vukobratovic & Juricic 1969; Vukobratovic & Stepanenko 1973; Takanishi et al. 1985; Yamaguchi et al., 1993; Hirai 1997; Hirai et al. 1998) **the zero moment point (ZMP), foot rotation index (FRP)**-a reference point that assures the connection between the base and the angular acceleration of the foot in the gait initial phase when only one foot is positioned on the support surface.

Another important point is the **centre of the rotation moment (CRM)** which determines also the connection of the human body to the support surface (Herr et al., 2003; Hofmann, 2003; Goswami & Kallem 2004; Popovic et al., 2004).

Another point as important as the centre of mass but may be used for measuring and assessing both the static and the dynamic stability is the **centre of pressure (COP).** This represents the point where the resultant of the ground reaction forces about the human body weight acts. During the measurements performed in bipedal position - stability - the centre of pressure is generally located in the centre of the plantar surface, the small oscillations of the human body being recorded as an oscillation diagram around an initial position.

The displacement (oscillation area) which is performed by the centre of pressure in order to assure the bipedal stability is engaged in the plantar surface and in its turn is determined by the human subject posture type (strained, relaxed), hands position (in front, sideways, along the body, upwards), base of support size (small, big, normal), position of spine (bent in front, upright, bent to the back, bent sideways), sensors operation conditions (visual - open eyes, closed eyes, acoustic) and not last the environmental conditions (temperature, pressure, humidity, vibrations, noises, light stimuli).

In the system assuring the bipedal posture of the human body, a whole series of elastic and damping properties of the muscles, joints and segments are manifesting, being coordinated and controlled also by *feed-back* type reactions.

This is why the COM displacements correlated to the COP oscillations during the bipedal position assess and measure the chaotic motions (Myklebust et al. 1995) of the stability using non-linear dynamics methods and chaos theories (Schuster 1988).

By applying these theories of adjusting the dynamic mechanism of balance and stability we may develop and introduce specific strategies for preventing and treating postural instabilities due to some previously identified malfunctions.

## 2. Theoretical aspects of human body modeling process

### 2.1 Gait cycle and postural analysis

Gait defined as alternative bipedalism is characterized by the unit gait cycle (double step) represented by the distance between the contact point with the ground (heel) for one foot and the immediately following contact point of the same foot. By composing two simple successive steps we get a double step. From functional point of view, the gait cycle is divided in two main stages: the support stage and the balance stage.

Support is the period concerning the contact between the foot and the ground and takes 60% of the gait cycle duration. Balance is the period when the same foot is no more in contact with the ground but is balanced in order to prepare the next contact with the ground. The balance duration is approx. 40% of the gait cycle duration.

In the beginning and at the end of the support stage, there is the double support period (24% of the gait cycle) when both feet are in contact with the ground, allowing thus the body weight transfer from one foot to the other.

The gait cycle is divided into 8 phases, five of them taking place during the support period and the other three during the balance period. These phases are the ones connecting the foot motion to the beginning of this motion within these periods. Thus the 5 phases defining the support period are: **initial contact, load, middle of support, final support and ground separation.**

Within the initial contact the body centre of mass is in the lowest position, thus the inferior limb being maximum extended will determine the pelvis to perform a horizontal adduction motion on the attack part relative to the support limb. This action represents a percent between 0 and 25% from the gait cycle duration.

Load, representing 25-35% of the gait cycle occurs when the plane surface of the foot touches the ground. The contact is achieved in the beginning only by the heel, then on the entire sole, the subject being in monopod equilibrium so that the maximum length of the inferior limb is limited subjecting the centre of mass to a very important vertical acceleration.

A percent of 35-40% of the gait cycle representing the middle of support phase is happening when the balance foot overpasses the support foot, thus the body passes in a very short time through this position, being supported by a single foot. At this moment the human body has maximum height and the centre of mass is slightly moved to the side towards the support foot for maintaining equilibrium.

Then, a percent of up to 45% of the gait cycle is represented by the period when the heel loses the contact with the ground and the pushing is performed by the *triceps surae* muscles which drive the ankle bending. At the same time with the heel raising the toes still keep contact with the ground, the ankle being in the most upper position.

The end of the support period represents a 53% percent and is called ground separation, occurring when the foot leaves the ground.

In case of the balance stage, the three phases are: acceleration, middle of the balance and deceleration.

The acceleration starts at the moment when the foot leaves the ground, activating thus the hip muscles in order to accelerate the foot forward. At this stage the inferior limb reaches its minimum length, the hip and knee joint is bending, the ankle joint is mobilized to lead the foot in flexion action so that the human subject body weight is entirely supported by the opposed inferior limb.

The positioning action in the middle of the balance takes place when the foot is moving exactly under the body and concurs with the moment the other foot reaches the half support phases. Deceleration describes the action of the muscles that slow down and stabilize the foot expecting the next contact between the heel and the ground. The pelvis is in maximum rotation towards the part the heel will attack and the hip is in flexion.

The closed kinematical chain formed by the locomotion system components acts for maintaining and supporting the body in orthostatic position, for propulsion motions or for damping motions during a fall (on the feet).

The inferior limb acts like an open kinematical chain in the different variants of adduction and abduction motions, external and internal rotation, kicking, pushing and not least in accomplishing the gait cycle, all these actions being included in a system of coordinates.

The stability stance as well as the integral balance around the equilibrium position are determined by the health level of the entire human body and may constitute clear informational sources for the human behavior evaluation in any situation.

The small deviations of the human body posture around the vertical direction determine the occurrence of a torsion moment, which acts upon the entire structure and may unbalance the human body or may create a vibration state.

However, this process of corrective torque generation is not fully understood and controversy remains regarding the organization of sensory and motor systems contributing to the postural stability of the entire human body.

Balanced state of postural sway is controlled by central nervous system, and the upright stance cannot be sustained without this control. It is widely accepted that the corrective torque is generated through the action of feedback control system; the input sources include visual, proprioceptive and vestibular system.

In fig. 3 it is showing the block diagram of the postural sway feedback control and also a simplified pelvic structural model during static upright stance. A, B are the masses of legs, C is the mass of pelvis and D is the mass of upper trunk.

Because the lumbar-sacral always sways in inverse direction of the ankle joint with the same value of θ, the upper trunk is kept perpendicular to the horizontal (the human body symbolic represented is for a subject with leg impairment). Location of COM remains fixed as long as the body does NOT change shape.
In order to locate the center of mass it is necessary to establish some main principles:

- its precise location depending on individual's anatomical structure;
- habitual standing posture;
- current position;
- external support;
- location in human body;
- variations with body build, posture, age, and gender
- infant > child > adult (in % of body height from the floor);
- generally accepted that it is located at ~57% of standing height in males, and ~ 55% of standing height in females;

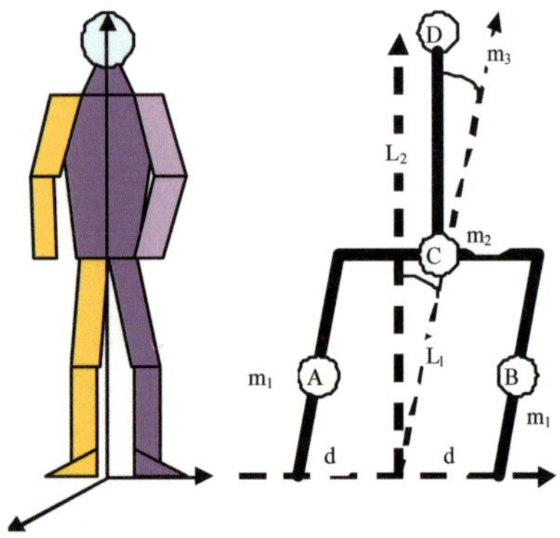


Fig. 3. Bipodal posture diagram

The maintenance of equilibrium in standing position is one of the most important activities for two main reasons: firstly, the center of mass must be located in the support area; secondly, for a major period of the standing action, the body is supported first by two legs and after a short time by a single limb with the center of mass inside the base of support but with the tendency of going outside it.
In elder people especially, up to 70% falls occur during standing and of course, locomotion action or stepping (Baritz M. et al, 2008)
By **the static stability margin** is meant a distance of the GCOM from the edge of the support polygon, measured along a current vector of motion of the gravity center, where:

$$x_{GCOM} = \frac{\sum_{i=1}^{n} M_{xi}}{\sum_{i=1}^{n} F_{xi}} = \frac{\sum_{i=1}^{n} m_i x_{ci}}{\sum_{i=1}^{n} m_i} \tag{1}$$

$$y_{GCOM} = \frac{\sum_{i=1}^{n} M_{yi}}{\sum_{i=1}^{n} F_{yi}} = \frac{\sum_{i=1}^{n} m_i y_{ci}}{\sum_{i=1}^{n} m_i} \tag{2}$$

and $m_i$ is mass of the $i$-th body, whereas $x_{ci}$, $y_{ci}$ denotes location of the center of mass of the $i$-th body.

With respect to analyses upon the human body static stability, human gait is a motor ability by means of which the displacements are usually performed using the alternative and constant motions mechanisms of the two inferior limbs, as support and as propellant.

As a follow, the motions of the human body are performed by a series of muscles groups, which form a harmonious assembly of muscular-kinematic chains, created according to the motion particularities under the control of the cerebral cortex. The motions performed by the human body have spatial directional characteristics of the motion and of the trajectory length traveled by the body or the body segments. They may be continuous, interrupted or combined according to a certain succession. The ratio between the spatial and temporal characteristics that establish the velocity and also acceleration parameters of the motion and all these characteristics as a whole, represent the kinematic particularities of the motion: where, how much and how is the body and its segments moving, along which trajectories described by the body segments and which controlled way is the complex motion of the human body performed.

All these aspects are important to be known when we analyze the disfunctionalities of the human body locomotion system.

The motions that can be performed by the human body are translations and rotations, complex and in 3D. The locomotion motions may be also cyclic or non cyclic (when the disfunctionalities occur).

### 2.1 Human body static and dynamic behavior modeling

The computer analysis of the human motions emphasizes a series of features of the gait cycle concerning the forces developed at the contact support, the duration, the forces developed in the joints, velocities, displacements or spatial positioning of different parts of the human body.

Humans possess a unique physical structure that enables them to stand up against the pull of gravity.

To build a model of interaction of human body it is necessary to understand its component parts, the biggest part of the human body is the trunk; comprising on the average 43% of total body weight. Head and neck account for 7% and upper limbs 13% of the human body by weight. The thighs, lower legs, and feet constitute the remaining 37% of the total body weight. There are 206 bones in the human body and almost all bones are facilitators of movement and protect the soft tissues of the body.

The frame of the human body is a tree of bones that are linked together by ligaments in joints called articulations. Skeletal muscles act on bones using them as levers to lift weights or produce motion.

In the human body each long bone is a lever and an associated joint is a fulcrum, acting like a lever which can alter the direction of an applied force, the strength of a force, and the speed of movement produced by a force in moving.

The walking model includes three body parts: an upper link, a lower link, and a foot.

Two joints are represented by the hip and the ankle, the lower and upper links represent the leg and the upper body of the human, respectively and the sources of movements are joint torques and thrust force.

This model was used to simulate human walking in the sagittal plane during the weight acceptance phase, that is, the time duration from heel contact to the middle of the single leg

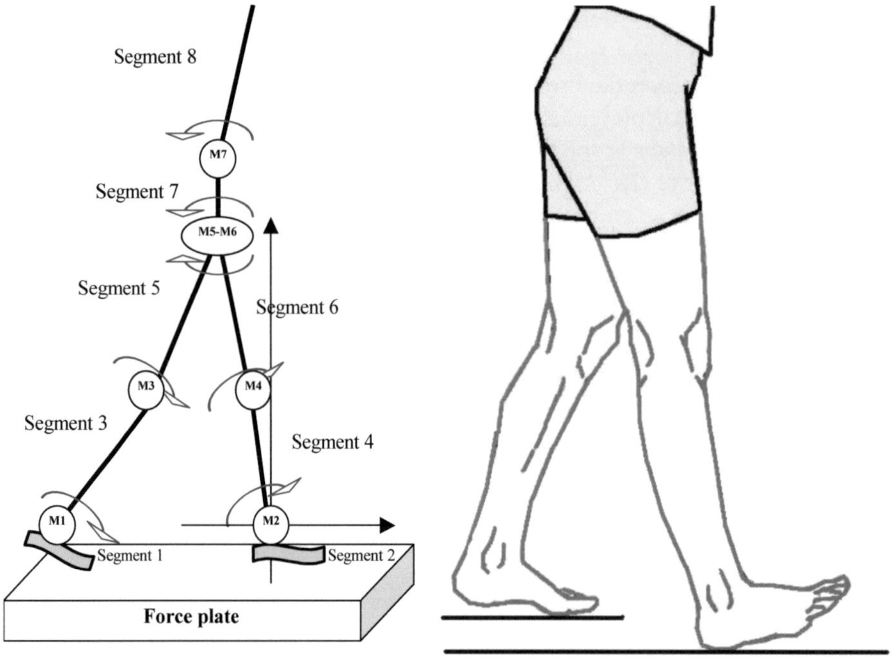


Fig. 4. Locomotion system model

support phase. The equation of motion of the model consists of two parts: the rotational dynamic of the two links and the moving dynamic of the foot. The equation of motion of the links is expressed as follows:

$$[M]\ddot{\theta} = [N]\dot{\theta}^2 + [G] + \tau + F_{TH} \tag{3}$$

where [M] is the mass and inertia matrix; [N] is the Coriolis and centrifugal force matrix; [G] is the gravitational force; τ is the matrix of torques angles and $F_{TH}$ is the thrust force.

Starting from a pre-defined skeleton module and considering the anthropometrical database NASA-STD-3000 we build the shape of the human inferior locomotion system with direct contact to the walking support.

For modeling human gait we considered a series of data connected to motion, trajectory, velocity or acceleration but at the same time we introduced the boundary values of the gait type (normal, malfunction of the right or left foot, jumps or steps, slips or sliding on plane surfaces etc.).

The modeling stages aim at introducing data both for the normal mode and for the one used to model a certain gait type in order to simultaneously visualize these differences.

In fig.5 a block diagram is presenting the steps in which these methodology of human gait and standing stability modeling are fitting the marker configuration, analyze and calculate kinematics, calculate kinetics, study control strategies and simulate human walking or standing stability using experimental data and the model created.

Thus, for a complete analysis of the way the human body acts and reacts in stability position or in gait cycle we approached the inverse pendulum model (IPM) for the lower locomotion system and then we establish the motion or stability equations.

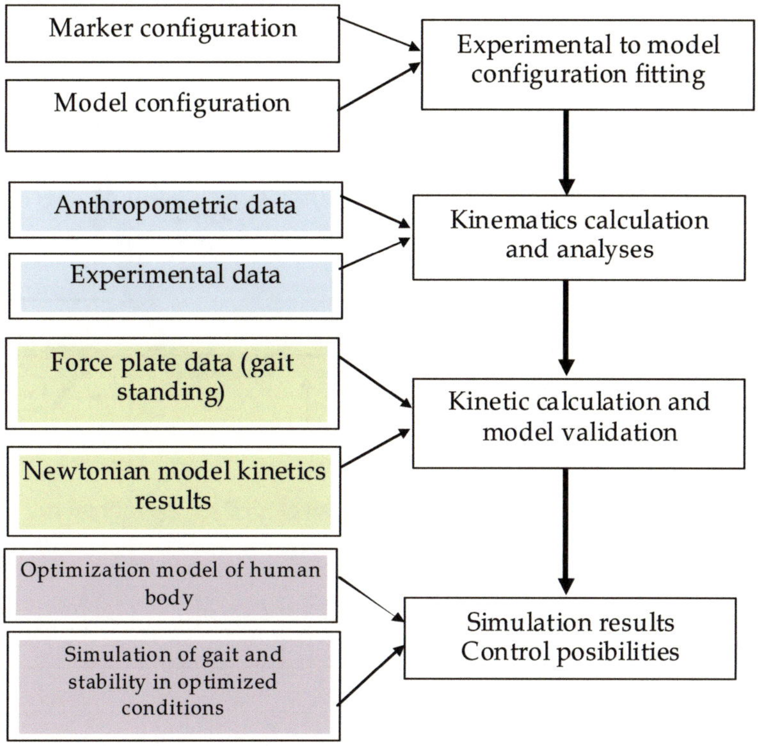


Fig. 5. Block diagram of biomechanic modeling for human bio-behavior

Applying the Newtonian Mechanics we may write the following equations:

$$\begin{cases} m\ddot{y} = F_y \\ m\ddot{z} = F_z \\ I\ddot{\theta} = mgL\sin\theta - N \\ N = uF_z + \varsigma F_y \end{cases} \tag{4}$$

where $I$ represents the moment of inertia of the body considering the ankle segments joints; $m$ represents the body mass; $g$ represents the gravitational acceleration; $L$ is the distance from the ankle joint to the centre of gravity (COG); $F_y$ and $F_z$ are the components of the reaction force from the support surface relative to $N$-torque produced at plantar level by the muscle system that counterbalances the gravitational moment $mgy$.

From the above equations we may determine in certain conditions of approximation the coordinate $u$ anterior/posterior (A/P) of COP that changes according to the muscles activity.

In case of the human body dynamic action we may define the laws of motion for the inferior limbs as follows: the two coupled second-order differential equations of motion are given below for the swing phase of the motion, where $\beta = m/M$ and $\theta$; $\phi$ are functions of time $t$.

These equations represent angular momentum balance about the foot (for the whole mechanism) and about the hip (for the swing leg), respectively.

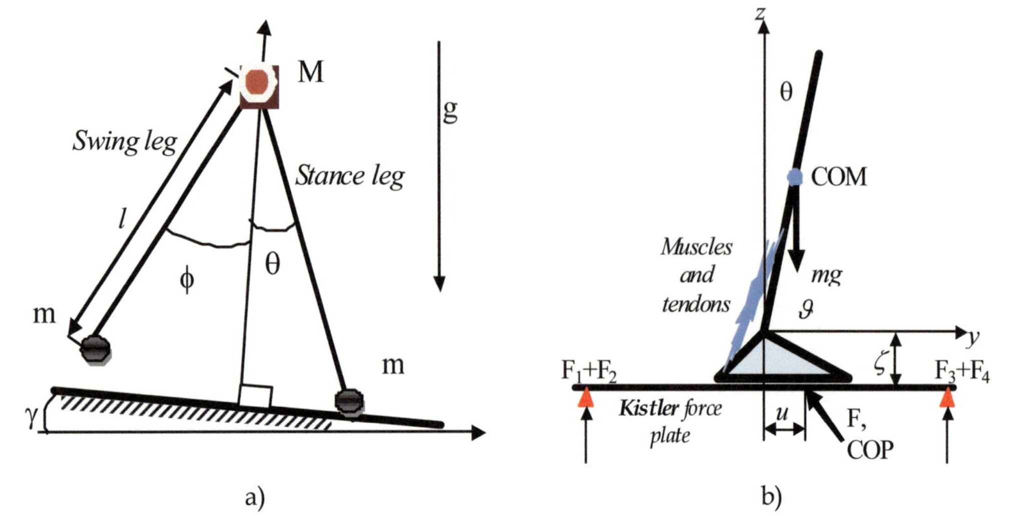


Fig. 6. Typical diagram of a step (a) and the forces developed by the foot on the force plate (b) (Borg F. 2005)

$$\begin{bmatrix} 1+2\beta(1-\cos\phi) & -\beta(1-\cos\phi) \\ \beta(1-\cos\phi) & -\beta \end{bmatrix}\begin{bmatrix} \ddot{\theta} \\ \ddot{\phi} \end{bmatrix}+\begin{bmatrix} \beta\sin\varphi\left(\dot{\phi}^2-2\dot{\theta}\dot{\phi}\right) \\ \beta\dot{\theta}^2\sin\phi \end{bmatrix}+ \\ +\begin{bmatrix} \left(\frac{\beta g}{l}\right)\left[\sin(\theta-\phi-\gamma)-\sin(\theta-\gamma)\right]-\frac{g}{l}\sin(\theta-\gamma) \\ \left(\frac{\beta g}{l}\right)\sin(\theta-\phi-\gamma) \end{bmatrix}=\begin{bmatrix} 0 \\ 0 \end{bmatrix} \tag{5}$$

These are the equations of motion for a simple double pendulum (Garcia M, et al., 1998). In this situation we assume that the foot mass is smaller than the entire human body mass and we adopt the value $\beta=0$ in the next equations.

$$\ddot{\theta}(t)-\sin\left[\theta(t)-\gamma\right]=0 \tag{6}$$

$$\ddot{\theta}(t)-\ddot{\phi}(t)+\dot{\theta}^2(t)\sin\phi(t)-\cos\left[\theta(t)-\gamma\right]\sin\phi(t)=0 \tag{7}$$

Equation (6) represents thus a simple inversed pendulum (the stance leg) that is not affected by the motion of the other foot and the equation (7) represents the swing leg like a simple pendulum moving on a circular arc.

The variation parameter in these equations is $\gamma$, the base inclination angle.

For the modeling and determination of the gait cycle parameters we integrate the above equations by applying a transition law between the support leg towards the swing leg and the activation of the contact conditions with the support surface.

Another model for the human gait study is represented by the model that assumes the central nervous system becomes a super system (SCNS) and is connected to the mobility control system, together they will coordinate the locomotion and the gait cycle.

Thus applying the fractals and multifractals theory upon the recorded data during the investigations there is the possibility of estimating the Holder correlation coefficients defined for wavelet transformations.
By estimating the Holder exponents and their spectra using a wavelet transform, it can be possible to show that the stride-interval time series is weakly multifractal with a main fractality close to that of $1/f$ noise. The time series is sometimes non-stationary and its fractal variability changes in the different gait mode regimes (normal, with disabilities, without complete locomotion system etc.)

### 2.3 Analysis techniques of the human body behavior

Maintaining a competitiveness level of the systems, increasing their performances as well as highlighting their weak points, the aspects requiring improvements based on the system analysis need at first data provision for the system "diagnosis".
Due to the importance presented in analysis, the collection of data should provide the necessary information in time, these information being based on real data.
Obtaining the data concerning the activities developed within the system and reflecting upon the studied problem is based on various investigation techniques.
According to the conditions upon the activities of the persons that are to be observed, the systems investigation techniques are divided in controlled and non-controlled techniques.
**The controlled techniques** are characterized by the fact that the information are directly collected from the persons that perform the activities upon which the study is focused.
The observation takes place in-situ or in a controllable environment used for the simulation of various tasks (laboratory observation).
**Activity analysis.** This technique aims at the observation of an activity by help of those working on it, human subjects that have to be carefully selected.
This way we aim at the identification of working level, errors occurring during the activity performance and thus the factors that influence in a negative way the obtained bio-behavioral performances.
We identify in this respect, the execution frequency, the materials and information required by the execution, the encountered difficulties, connections to other activities, connections and interactions with adjacent systems.
In order to establish a correct result, the "acquirer" training, executant's selection and accomplishing a valid observation schedule with experimental data validation possibility are very important.
An activity data acquisition system may be the computer, in this case it is necessary to know the accomplishment parameters of the observed events.
This way we assure a fast analysis, very little influenced by errors, by the human factor bias, things that compensate to a smaller or larger extent their inflexibility towards some initially unforeseen elements.
**Protocol analysis.** This technique is based on the observer-participant status of the operator of a certain activity and aims at the identification of the conscious bio-behavior of the person performing the activity in order to assess the performance level.
The time of performing this investigation is represented by the period when the desired action takes place, thus we can survey the decisions made by the operator, his options, causes of the occurred errors and not last the observer attitude towards the performed activity.

**Direct observation techniques** are influenced by a series of factors such as:
- effects due to the observer manifested both upon the system operation and upon the operator;
- sampling effects due to the inadequate size of the human subjects number whose activity is investigated and the choice of a time period with a small relevance to the covered objective;
- observation limiting effect occurred in case of selecting human subjects unable to offer the necessary data for analysis.

The main reason for this is the wrong choice of the observation-assessment scheme, increased time pressure, leading to the ignorance of some important aspects of the investigated activities.
**Non-controlled techniques.** These investigation methods of a system may be classified according to the observation subject.
Thus, we can distinguish between the individual, group and informational techniques.
**Individual investigation techniques.** Their use assumes the collection of data for each human subject, concerning his anthropometric dimensions, environmental conditions and the performed activities.
Within them we can distinguish several classes according to the existence or absence of an analysis system at the time of data collection or according to the temporal position of the data collection time with respect to the analyzed activity.
**Individual interview technique.** The individual interview represents a personal investigation technique, physiological history type that may be developed in real time but also retrospectively. This requires several stages.
The first step would be the investigation, a process that aims at the conception of a set of questions in the form of a questionnaire with a control key.
The content of these questions should be relevant for the objective targeted by the system analysis and should also cover the entire studied problem.
The obtained information will be collected and recorded in the next stage, representation, their validity will be later assessed within interpretation.
All these represent the preoccupations agenda and also an important part in obtaining the necessary information for analysis because it highlights the aspects to be monitored in the investigation activity.
Sample determination should be done according to the requirements connected to representativeness and considers also the problem complexity, its content and research objectives.
Starting from these, we will determine the human subjects' sample that will be investigated so that all those included are able to provide the necessary response and are aware of the data that the researcher is trying to collect in the interviewing process.

## 3. Experimental setup for investigation

### 3.1 Setting the investigation configuration

In order to perform the analyses upon the human factor that develops various working activities, we accomplish an analysis configuration consisting of a series of device modules dedicated to these biomechanical measurements and also the analysis modules (anthropometric, gait cycle, stability in different conditions). This configuration is presented in fig.7. (Rogozea L. 2009)

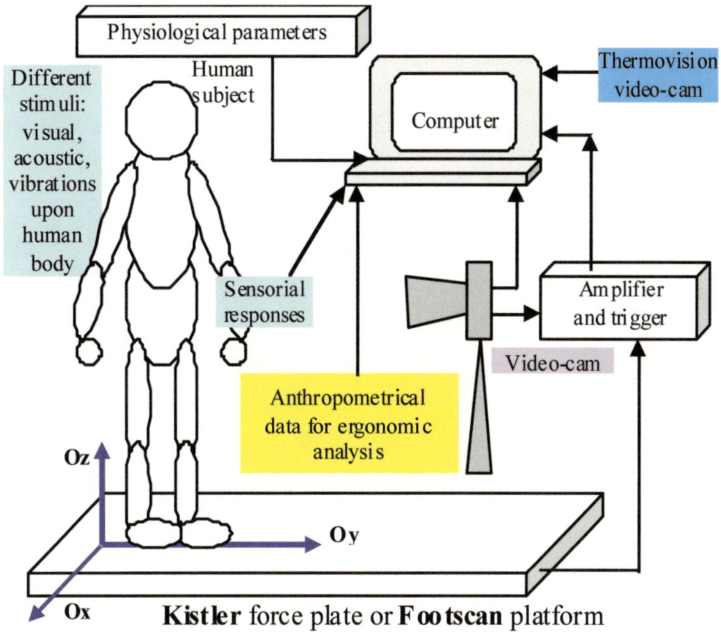


Fig. 7. Recording configuration of the human behavior along the working activities

Using this modular equipment structure we performed some analyses and recordings in order to correlate the information concerning the human bio-behavior in different working activities. The equipments structure consists of: a Kistler type force plate for measuring forces and moments developed by the human body during the stability and gait cycle evaluation along the three (Ox, Oy and Oz); a set of anthropometric devices for measuring the locomotion system quantities; a set of devices used for recording the physiological parameters of the subjects involved in the experiment; an evaluation and goniometric measurements of the relative positions of the human body segments; a high speed video cam for recording the successive positions of the human body along the gait cycle duration; a "sensor glove" type system for assessing the handling performances along the working activities; computer and modeling software compatible to the above mentioned equipments.
The analysis performed upon the subjects started by establishing an investigation protocol, which aimed at a large range of measuring the bipedal stability (big support base with different polygons, small support base trapeze shaped, open eyes and arms along the body, in three moments of the day - morning, afternoon and evening) and walking inside.
The corresponding soft for the values acquisition is **Bioware**, which allows the recording of the forces and moments values, measured along the three directions by help of some piezzo-electric sensors of the force plate. We also aimed at the fact that the bipedal position of each subject is centered on the plate, with no high heels shoes, arms relaxed along the body, open eyes and the eyes oriented straight ahead.

### 3.2 Data recording

In first stage of the experiments we established and kept the parameters of the laboratory environment. Temperature into laboratory was 22$^{0}$C, air humidity 80% and atmospheric pressure 755 mmHg. [4]

In the second stage we measured the physiological parameters of the human subjects (weight, height, age, blood pressure, temperature, pulse, visual and audio acuity, lactic and glucose parameters) in relaxed stance, without any general health problems and with a good metabolism (example: blood pressure 155/82 mmHg, pulse 78-88, face temperature 36,7$^0$C, height 170-185 cm, weight from 50-95 kg).

Fig. 8. Acquiring and creating the physiological database for the analyzed subjects

All these parameters are necessary to establish a common modeling base to measure and to evaluate the human body bio-behavior in working activities. It is very important to keep these initial conditions in all investigations procedures to have the same initial line of human behavior analysis.

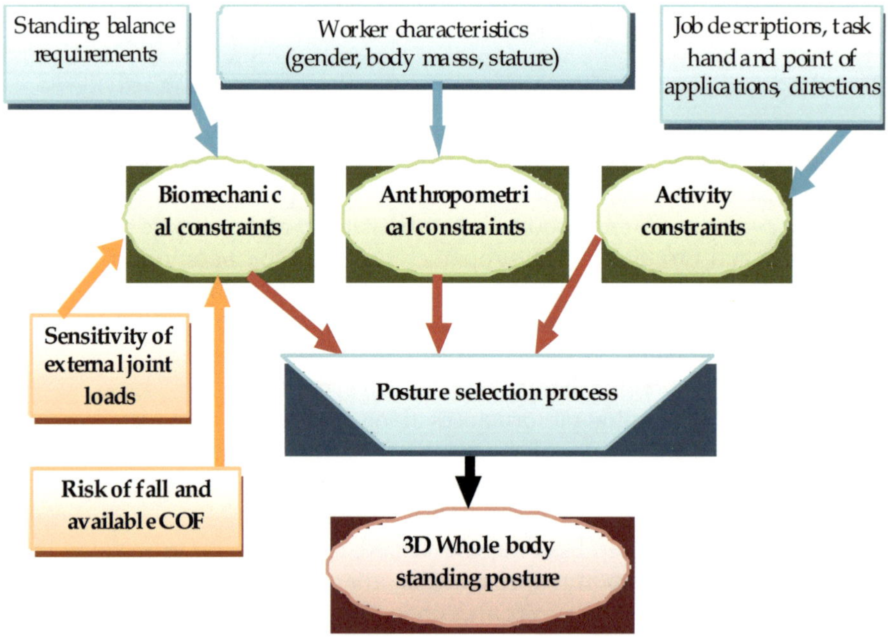


Fig. 9. Postural analyses subjected to anthropometric, biomechanic and activity constraints

The initial analysis posture was determined by the vertical position, hands along the body, big/small base of support, open eyes, gaze straight ahead.

About this position considered as initial, we established a series of different postures, considering both the orthostatic changes (fig.10) and the hands position relative to the body or the head and respective the eyes position (fig.11.) also the use of some perturbing stimuli (audio, visual) that may affect the postural stability.

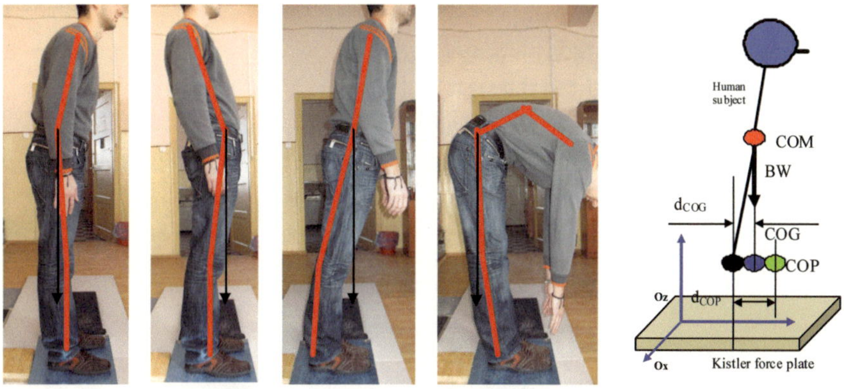


Fig. 10. Selection of orthostatic position for bipodal equilibrium

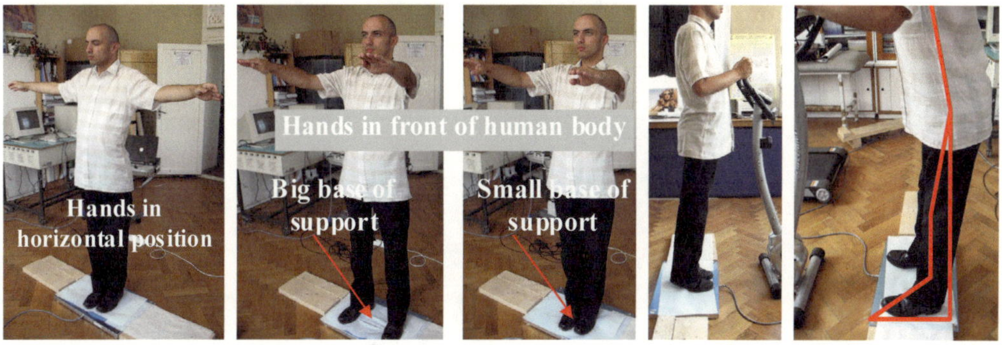


a. b. c. d. e.

Fig. 11. Relative position of hands and head, and eyes respectively during recordings

Thus, we chose the following recording variants of the human subject's behavior in analyzing the postural stability, taking into account as many bipodal postures as possible to be encountered in the subjects' working activities:

- Vertical position, small/big base of support, hands along the body, open eyes, gaze straight ahead;
- Vertical position, small/big base of support, hands along the body, closed eyes;
- Vertical position, small/big base of support, hands in horizontal position sideways, open eyes, gaze straight ahead;
- Vertical position, small/big base of support, hands in horizontal position sideways, closed eyes (fig.11.a.);
- Vertical position, small/big base of support, hands in front of the body, open eyes, gaze straight ahead (fig.11.b. and c.);
- Vertical position, small/big base of support, hands in front of the body, closed eyes;
- Vertical position, small/big base of support, hands along the body, closed eyes and use of different external stimuli (audio, visual)
- Vertical position, small/big base of support, hands on a vertical support, open eyes (fig.11.d. and e.)

For the analyses along a gait cycle (fig.12.) we considered the following situations:

- normal gait starting with the right/left foot;
- added steps gait, starting with the right/left foot;

- dragged gait, starting with the right/left foot;
- normal gait holding a weight with both hands;
- normal gait holding a weight in the right/left hand;
- stepping on stairs, up/down with the right/left foot (fig.13.)

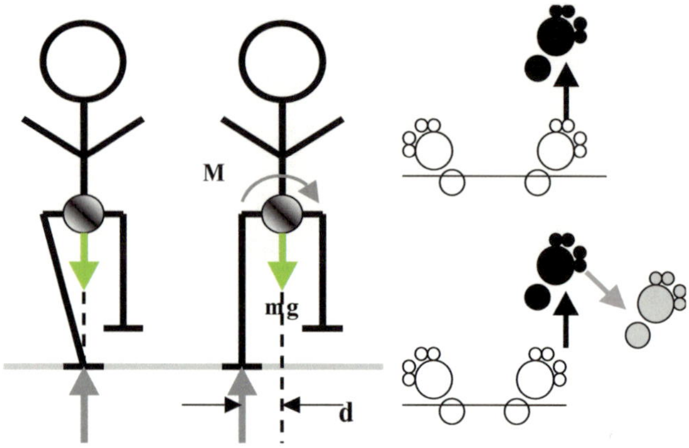


Fig. 12. Changing the stability on gait cycle

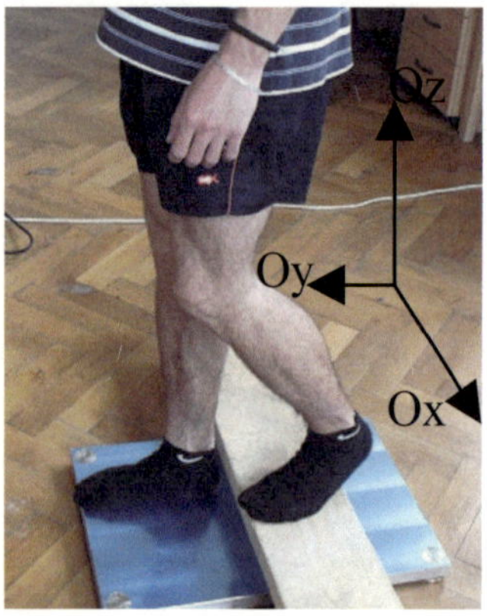


Fig. 13. Up/down the stair

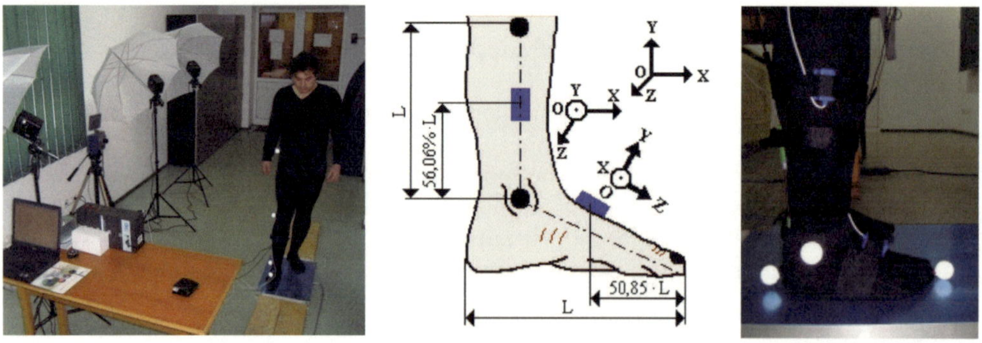


Fig. 14. Acquiring and measuring system, Biopac type, for the foot and lower leg linear accelerations

In order to perform the correlated analyses upon the subjects locomotion system behavior, we used a system for measuring linear accelerations of the foot and lower leg along the displacement directions, respectively on a perpendicular direction during the ground support phases of the foot (Radu C. 2007)
The experiment was developed in two stages, as follows: the initial setting of the used system, Biopac type and respectively acquiring the values of the linear accelerations specific to the foot and lower leg (fig.14.)
At the same time it was necessary to use a high speed video cam (500 frames/sec) to record and draw, by software means, the joints trajectories during the displacement in a gait cycle. Finally, all these recordings are correlated by means of the *LifeMod* software for developing a virtual model for the human subject analysis, subjected to different actions, in various conditions of environment and activity.

## 4. Results and conclusions

### 4.1 Bipodal posture stability

The analyses performed using this experimental structure and advanced investigation technologies have the final goal of highlighting some correlations between the different measured quantities, on various types of subjects involved in the same types of recordings.
Thus, one of the most important recordings performed by this experimental structure was the one that manifested the changes in the stability areas with respect to the subjects' posture, hands position, eyes and respectively the effort level developed by the organism.
In the example below we analyze the evolution of this area (measured along Ox and Oy) for a subject with the following features: female, height 1,68m, age 53, no general health problems but with a knee impairment, weight 80kg, for which we analyzed the stability area and the force evolution along Oz axis, in three moments of the day (morning, afternoon, evening) without any source of additional *effort induced to the body*…(use of ergometric bicycle), with hands near body and open eyes.
As we can notice from the diagrams analysis in fig.15, the evolution of the stability area in this case presents a compact and symmetrical surface for the first time in the morning, a smaller and more concentrated area for the afternoon and a substantial change of balance - slightly shifted along Ox for the evening recording.
This manifestation can be found in all the analyses performed on the selected subjects allowing a unitary evaluation of the stability area.
As far as the recorded force on Oz is concerned, these results are presented in fig.16 (morning, afternoon, evening).
The recording time was each time the same - 16 sec and the data set was stored in the measurements database used for evaluation.
In the case of force evolution analysis we observe the same type of manifestation for the recording performed in the evening, emphasized by an increase of the variation limits of the force along Oz, but also by a higher frequency of their occurrence, values that indicate an increased instability of the human body and a fatigue state at the inferior limbs level.
In this situation and correlating with the age and the influence of the poor sensorial system we may confirm that the installation of the fatigue state as a follow of a normal daily activity takes place in the second part of the day determining a motor activity deficit and the diminishing of the orientation perception.

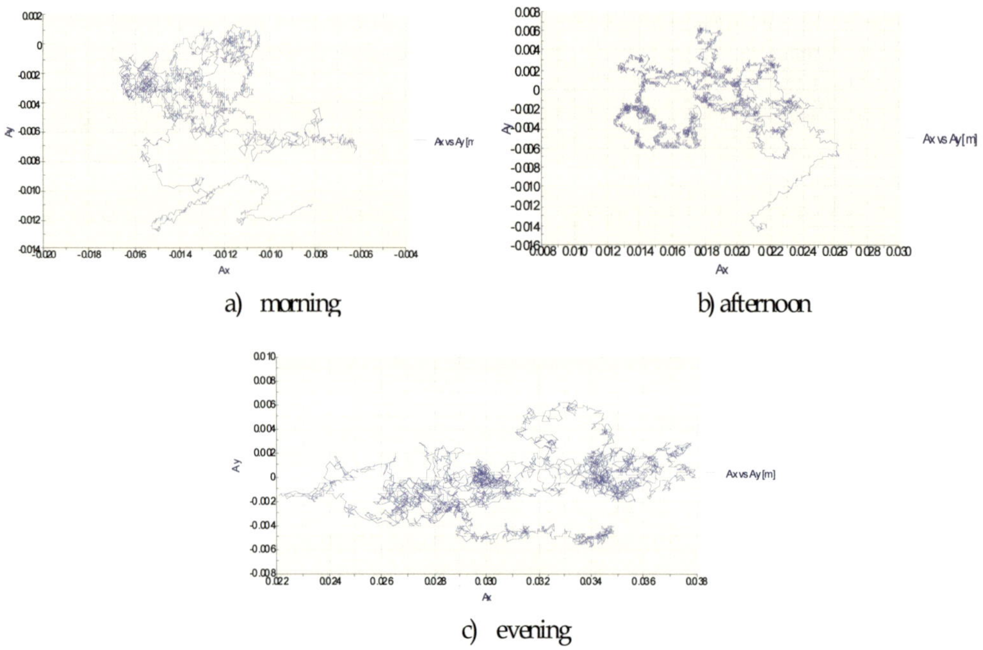


Fig. 15. Example of results for subject stability recordings

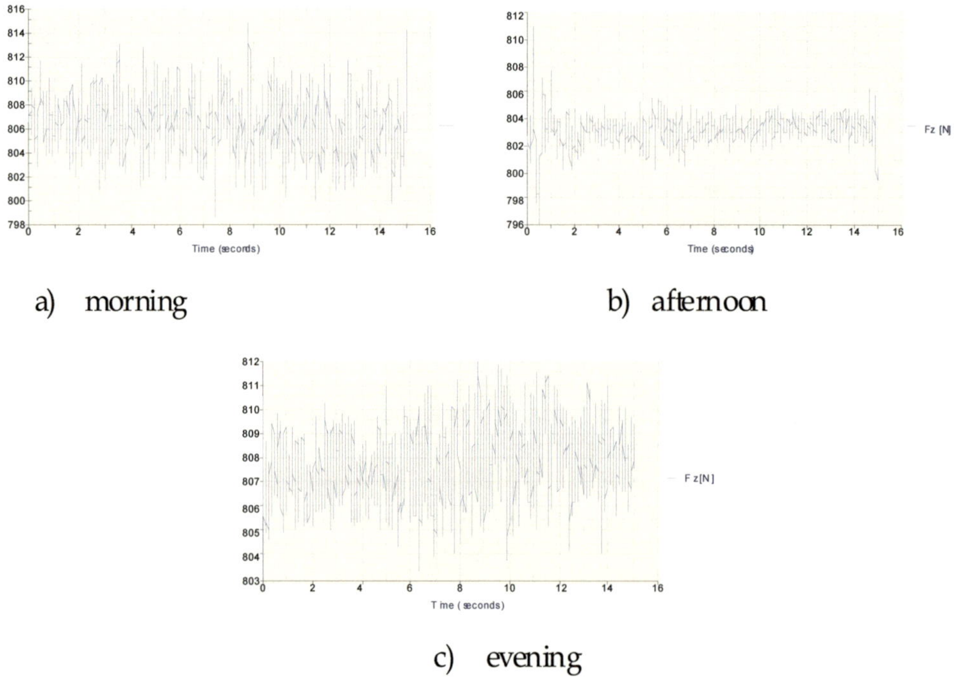


Fig. 16. Manifestation of the Fz force change, acting along Oz, for the same subject

In the case of a male subject age 34, no health problems, not wearing glasses, weight 97kg and height 1,75m, the evolution of stability area in the three moments indicates a more compact and symmetrical shape around the theoretical equilibrium position as we can observe in fig.17. and the forces variation diagram is changing towards the diminishing of the oscillations number for the recordings situation related to those in the morning.
This fact establishes a more equilibrated behavior for which the fatigue due to daily activity does not influence the motor capacity and also does not reduce the resistance to effort.

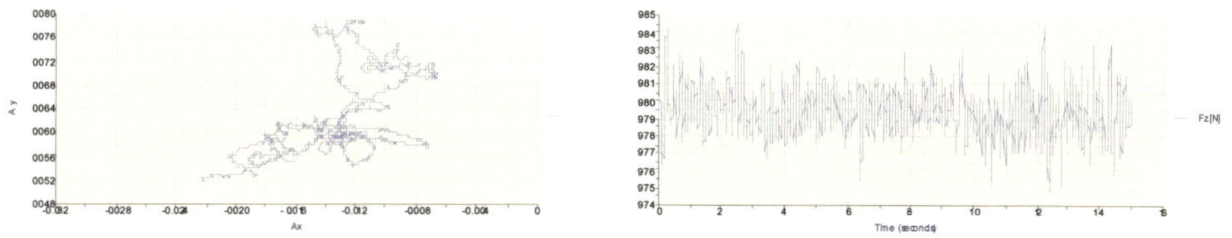


Stability area and force Fz variation in morning time

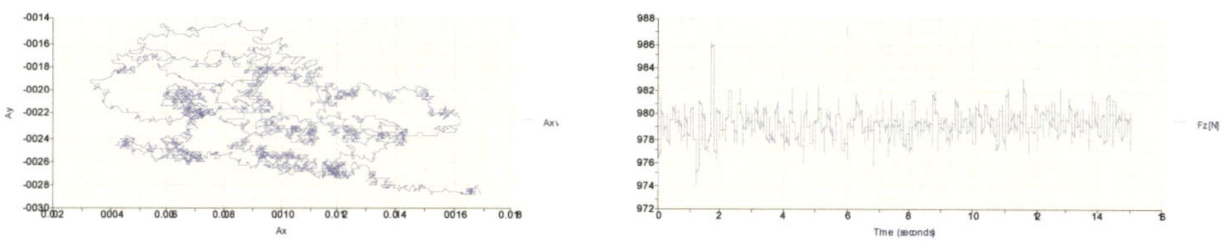


Stability area and force Fz variation in afternoon time

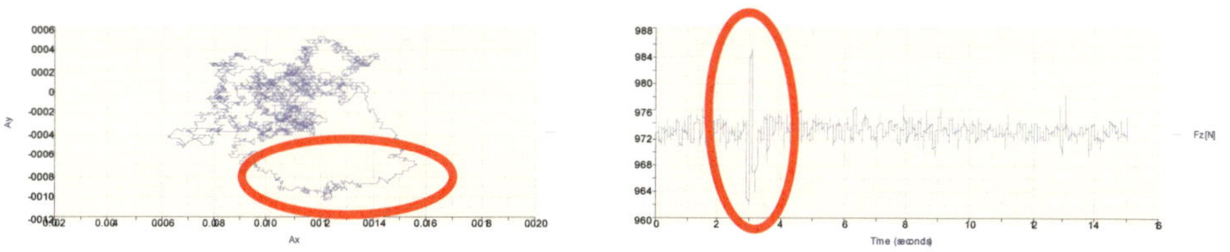


Stability area and force Fz variation in evening time

Fig. 17. Stability area and Fz force variation, along Oz, for the 34 years old subject

When the human subject is subjected to the action of external stimuli, the response of the subjects' behavior is manifested by the changes of the Fz force variation, especially if in the same conditions we change the subject's base of support. As we may notice in the normal posture version the Fz force variation is uniform along the entire recording, without reaching extremely high values or changes along extended durations. In this respect we observe that when the person is subjected to a visual stimulus (controlled) he reacts firstly by a short duration variation of the force, and then the variation returns and presents a peak proving that the body is trying to come back to the previously determined stability position.
Another sort of experiments and recordings are made with the person using an external support to observe the behavior of the human body in balance from the front of the leg to the back, taking in account some external stimulus, like environmental and working activities (fig.11.d, e). In these experiments we record the forces variations, the stability area, the force and moment in the same direction in different situations - with big (test no.1.) or small (test no.2) support base, but with open eyes in the time of recordings.

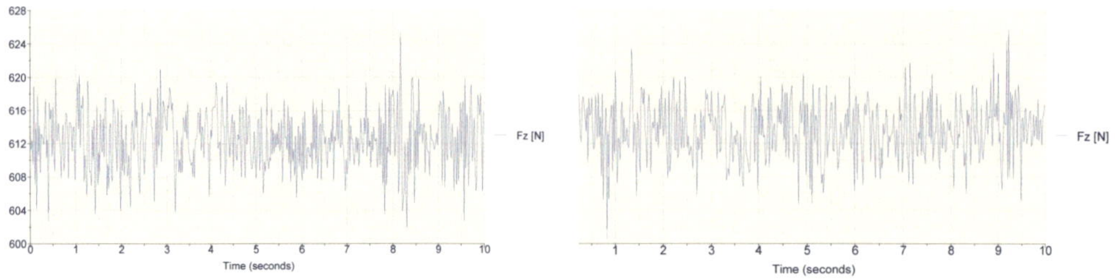


Fig. 18. Force recording on Oz axis without any stimulus and on a big base support

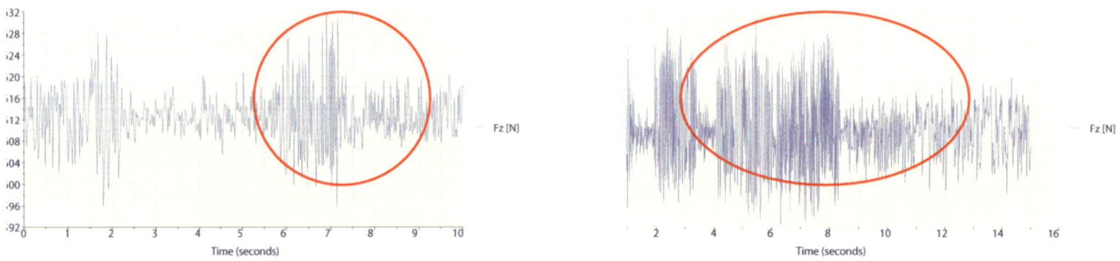


Fig. 19. Force recording on Oz axis with visual stimulus and on a big base support

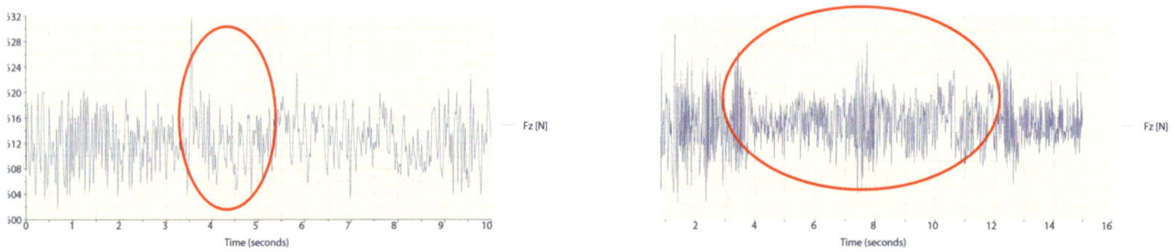


Fig. 20. Force recording on Oz axis without any stimulus and on a small base support

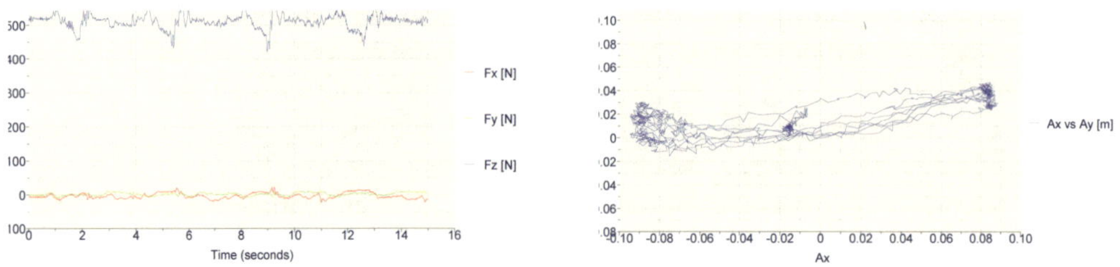


Fig. 21. The forces graph for all directions (x, y, z) and the stability area for the test no.1

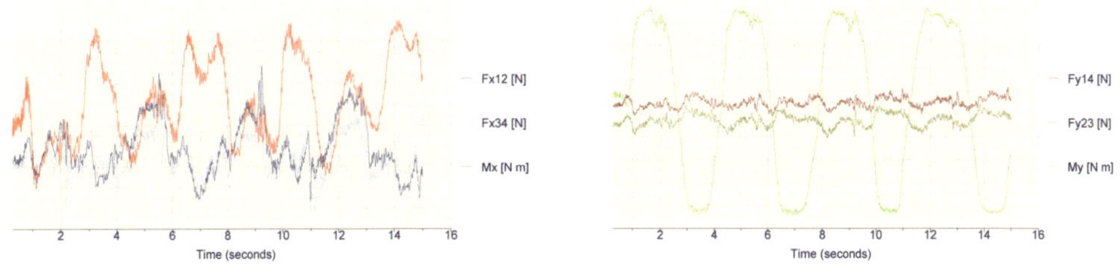


Fig. 22. The force and the moment for Ox direction, also for Oy direction in the test no.1

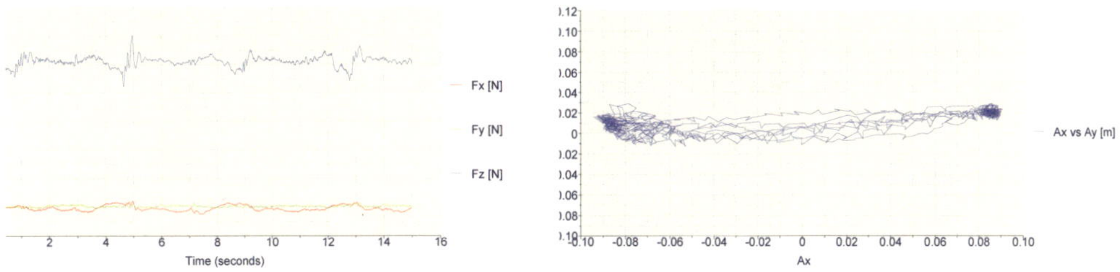


Fig. 23. The forces graph and stability area for all directions (x, y, z) (test no.2.)

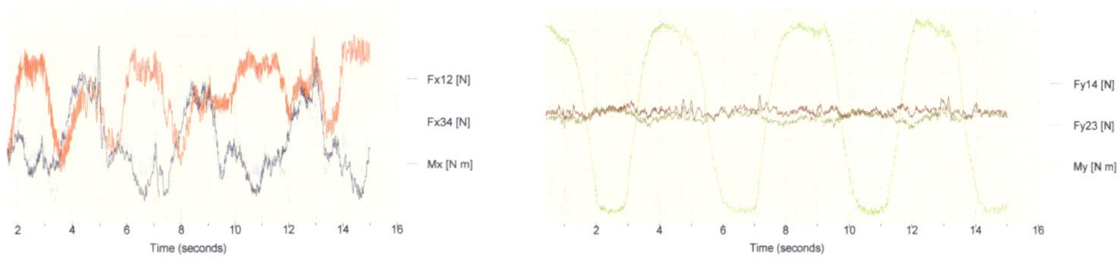


Fig. 24. The force and the moment for Ox direction, also for Oy direction in the test no.2

From these recordings and in according with the initial conditions and the demands of the researches we can observe:

- changes in foot position have been found to affect measurements of standing balance, the location of the line of gravity and the postural sway;
- under normal conditions the size of the base support is a primary determiner of stability;
- the height of the CG relative to the base of support can also affect stability;
- the most important values of the forces are the force components from direction Oz because they can establish the amplitude of the balance in other two directions Ox and Oy;
- changing the size of the support base from small to big one it can observe that the stability areas are different like shape, but almost the same like values;
- the influence of the visual stimuli in the eyes positions are also the most important because the instability will be bigger in the open eyes position than the closed eyes position. This situation is due of the visual or audio external stimuli from environmental space or other kind of stimuli, controlled or not.

### 4.2 Gait cycle analysis

The gait cycle analysis for the subjects in the used sample considered the same recording procedure as far as the environment conditions are concerned and also the subjects' state. Besides the recordings performed by help of the Kistler force plate and Bioware software, we recorded at the same time the responses of the accelerations measurement system for the lower leg and foot centre of gravity in order to correlate these values. For example in fig.25 and fig.26 we represent the graphical variation of the foot and lower leg centre of gravity accelerations and velocity along the two directions Ox and Oy, for a human subject, 28 years old, having 89,7 kg weight and 1,76 m height in normal effort and environmental conditions.

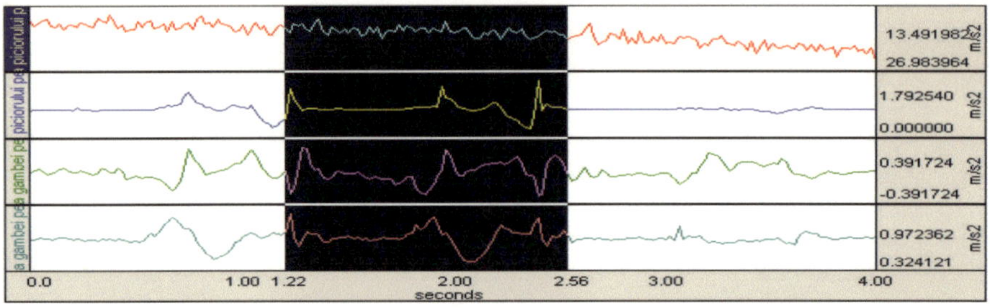


Fig. 25. Variation of the foot/lower leg centre of gravity acceleration on Ox and Oy

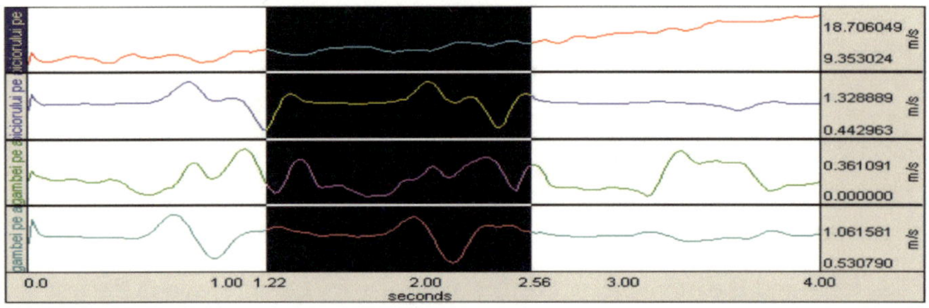


Fig. 26. Variation of the foot/lower leg centre of gravity velocity on Ox and Oy

In the following graphs we present the recordings made with the same subject, in the same conditions (position of hands, day time-morning after a relaxed period, the same environment physical conditions etc.) but in different situations, simulating the influence of the biomechanical effort in the human body.

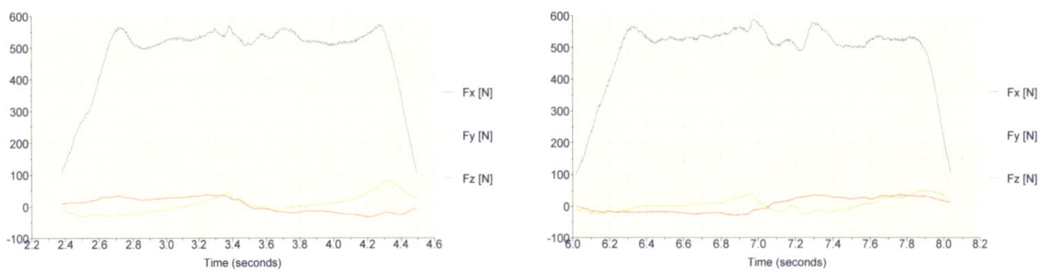


Fig. 27. Recordings of the forces measurements in normal gait before controlled effort

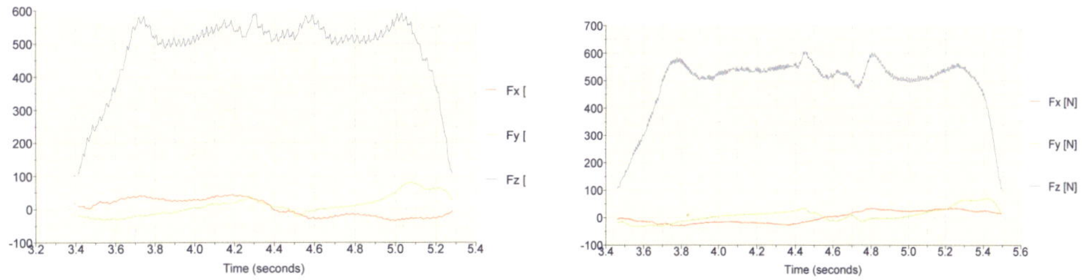


Fig. 28. Recordings of the forces measurements in normal gait after controlled effort

Following these multiple analyses, an evaluation structure was created, based on advanced techniques and focused on the study and characterization of the bio-behavioral performances for the locomotion system by configuring the system in relation to the visual, acoustic and thermal stimuli, with a future development towards a complementary analysis that takes into account also the upper part of the human body.

This system is completed by an investigation technique with computerized correlated systems for obtaining results in real time and setting proper sequences for each subjects sample selected for different assessment procedures.

In the same context and by this proposed investigation structure we establish also that the human subjects are analyzed and compared to the corresponding virtual models of the stability or walking measurements simulations in order to correlate all the influence factors from environmental space (Cotoros D. et al., 2009)

From these recordings and according to the initial conditions and the demands of the researches we can conclude: that the most important force values are the components on the direction **Oz** because they can establish the amplitude of the balance (moments) in other two directions Ox and Oy.

Also the changes in foot position have been found to affect measurements of standing balance, force and stability surface and in normal conditions the size of the support is a primary determiner of stability.

Other influences were the light stimuli on the visual system because they are the most important stimuli inducing the instability that will be bigger in the open and fixed oriented eyes position than free gaze even if the optical stimulus was the same.

This situation is due to the unknown visual external stimuli reactions and concentration on the automatic activities.

Other applications of these modeling and simulation structures represent the subject of a more extended research, which allows the developing of an investigation-assessment-rehabilitation protocol for the hip implant patients or for the patients with different walking impairments or for disabilities developed into working activities or for analyzing the ergonomy of a working place (Hausdorff M.J. 2005).

Thus, for a quick response in the analysis of the gait type and forces developed in the subject locomotion system or stability, the created methodology can estimate and correlate data at different recording times and respectively for different anthropometrical dimensions or mobility restrictions to improve by advanced techniques the ergonomy and capabilities of working places.

## 5. Acknowledgment

These researches are part of the Grant PNII-IDEI 722 and 744 with CNCSIS Romania and we've developed the investigations with apparatus from Research Project "CAPACITATI" in Mechatronic Researches Department from University Transilvania of Brasov

## 6. References

Baritz M., Cristea L., Cotoros D., Balcu I., (2008) Interconnections between optometry and biomechanics for ergonomics studies, *Buletinul Institutului Politehnic din Iasi, Tomul LIV (LVIII), Fasc. X, 2008*

Baritz M., Cristea L., Cotoros D., Repanovici A., *Analyze of postural stability in stepping action for person wearing composite progresive lens*, 2nd International Conference "Advanced Composite Materials Engineering " COMAT, Brasov, Romania, 2008

Baritz M., Cotoros D., Cristea L., Rogozea L. Analyze of human body bipedal stability for neuromotors disabilities, *BICS'2008, Tg.Mures, Nov.6-7, 2008,* ISSN 2065-0418

Borg F., An inverted pendulum with a springy control as a model of human standing, *arXiv:physics/0512122v1 [physics.bio-ph] 14 Dec 2005*

Blaszczyk J., Klonowsk W. (2001). Postural stability and fractal Dynamics, *Acta Neurobiol. Exp. 2001, 61: 105-112*

Cotoros D., Baritz M., Albu A., Cristea L., Modeling the human gait and standing stability by *LifeMode* software, *The 3rd International Conference on International Conference "Computational Mechanics and Virtual Engineering"COMEC Brasov, Romania, 2009*

Garcia M., Chatterjee A., Ruina A., Coleman M. (1998). The Simplest Walking Model: Stability, Complexity, and Scaling, *ASME Journal of Biomechanical Engineering 1998;*

Hausdorff M. Jeffrey and Alexander B. Neil, *Gait Disorders Evaluation and Management*, Taylor & Francis Group, LLC, 2005, ISBN 978-0-8247-2393-4

Jiang Y., Nagasaki S., You M., Zhou J., Dynamic studies on human body sway by using a simple model with special concerns on pelvic and muscles roles, *Asian Journal of Control, Vol. 8, No. 3, pp. 297-306, September 2006;*

Katiyar R., (2010). Clinical gait data analysis based on Spatio-Temporal features *(IJCSIS) International Journal of Computer Science and Information Security,* Vol. VII, No. II, February, 2010, ISSN 1947-5500

Mrozowski J., Awrejcewicz J., ZMP and GCOM criteria as a base of assessment of the human gait stability, *Department of Automatics and Biomechanics, Technical University of Łódź,*

Radu C., Determinarea fortelor de reactiune in articulatia gleznei in conditii dinamice, *ANNALS of the ORADEA UNIVERSITY. Fascicle of Management and Technological Engineering, 2007;*

Rogozea L.; Sechel G; Fleancu A - Ethical Aspects in Bioengineering Research, 8th WSEAS Conference, May 20-22, 2009, China Jiliang, Univ. Hangzhou pg: 139-143

Tozeren A., *Human Body Dynamics: Classical mechanics and Human Movement*, 2000 Springer-Verlag New York, Inc.ISBN 0-387-98801-7

# 9

# Polar Sport Tester for Cattle Heart Rate Measurements

Marjan Janzekovic, Peter Vindis, Denis Stajnko and Maksimiljan Brus
*University of Maribor, Faculty of Agriculture and Life Sciences*
*Slovenia*

## 1. Introduction

Well-being and health status of the animal in relations to achieving optimal production, become a standard when grading intensive livestock systems. Heart rate and body temperature have traditionally been used as parameters for different animal species health assessment, since they can indicate a problem with the animal. Also, interest for stress-related research increased in the last decades, resulting in many available techniques, but as stated by (Janczarek, 2009) the simplicity and practical applicability for the average user should be taken into account. According to (Hopster, 1998; Janzekovic, 2005; Aerts et al., 2008) the change of heart rate can be a relevant parameter, when studying the response of the animal to stress. This is in correlation with findings in the humane medicine that variability of the heart rate serves as an important mechanism of the adaptation capability.

Reaction of heart is viewed as an objective way of representing the autonomous responses of the nervous system to psychological stressors, associating increased and decreased heart rates with the predominant influence of sympathetic or parasympathetic nervous systems. Challenges of the environment activate both branches of the autonomous nervous system. This induces changes in the frequency of the heart rate, which is viewed as the index of the psychological influence of outside events (Herd, 1991). Recent findings also demonstrated direct hard-wired linkage between control of cardiac function and animal response (Lefcourt et al., 1999).

Most important stimuli for variations in heart rate generally are excitement, stress, exercise, or some kind of altered physical homeostasis. Because of this, focus in research has always been to investigate and monitor changes in the mentioned parameters, aiming to get a strong correlation with health status. This resulted in invention of special devices which rely on heart rate as certainly the most practical means for judging animal's status.

Heart rate monitors have been developed for purpose of fitness in human and equine athletes, but have evolved into modern health status measuring devices. This equipment became recommended and highly advocated tool in illness, disease, or stress diagnostics. Because of accuracy of measurements with Polar Sport Tester (best accuracy in comparison with ECG) (Macfarlane et al., 1989; Hopster & Blokhuis, 1994; Lefcourt et al., 1999) the said finding was taken into account to a greater extent in the analysis of the data of our test.

### 1.1 Heart rate as indicator of stress state of cattle

Measurement of heart rate is one of most common used non-invasive methods for gathering physiological parameters of stress. From the point of animal welfare it has major advantage over traditionally used blood sample test techniques (Janzekovic et al., 2006). Heart frequency, implying the number of heart contractions per minute (bpm) is mainly measured, as it has a good correlation as indicator for impending problems in the animal. This advocates resting heart rate which represents measurement in relaxed condition when animal is calm, but attention must be taken since sometimes this is very hard and can mask elevated values meaning also masking the potential health problem. Depending from environment, the heart frequency is different and varies from animal to animal. Monitoring of the heart rate and its variability is, from the technical side, very complicated and impractical to measure in situations like milking, transport, or calving. Likewise in barns with the free housing system of breeding of milking cows (Janzekovic et al., 2005) it is impossible with meters and/or devices to be put onto animals. In our preliminary test that was found out already during the time of habituation of animals to wearing adapted measuring devices. The cows, freely moving about, mutually took off or tore from the body the elastic straps, simulating the girth belt with transmitter, already during the first seconds of wearing. In the milking parlour they had not enough time to focus on straps and it took only a short time until they have accustomed themselves to them with the use of a simulated girth belt (Janzekovic et al.,2005). (Hopster, 1998) also noticed a similar effect during the period of accustoming to wearing the measuring equipment. On animals in groups it is possible to measure the heart rate for a longer time only by means of implants with transmitter under the skin. For this reason use of the electrocardiography pill for cattle was investigated by (Warren et al., 2008), to provide veterinarians with data to assess cattle state without the need to physically restrain it. Nevertheless much work is still to be done concerning its practical applicability.

With the introduction of automatic milking systems the interest for reliable and practical measuring of stressful situations, implicating health status and production of the animal, increased (Gygax et al., 2008). As stress is mainly expressed by plasma cortisol concentrations and heart rate variation (Schmidt et al., 2010), the decision to use non-invasive measuring technique of heart rate (HR) on cows in tandem milking parlour was made based on this and results presented in many studies describing methods of heart rate measure on different categories of animals. Tests dealt with telemetric recording of surface electrocardiograms (Kovalcik et al., 1988; Lay et al., 1992; Royle et al., 1992.), and most of the research has been done in the field of equine exercise physiology by means of Polar heart rate monitors like »Horse Tester« and »Polar Equine« (Evans et al., 1986; Oldruitenbourgh-OOsterbaan et al.,1988, Art et al., 1993; Gygax et al., 2008; Kedzierski & Janczarek, 2009; Leleu et al., 2005). New solutions include complete wireless HR equipment systems, and findings show that these devices play an important role in diagnostics, and sometimes even enable health problem prevention and certainly on time intervention and clinical checking for further treatment from responsible personnel. It should be taken into account that not all values (like recovery heart rate) can be used and compared with research in human athletes, since differences between species exist. Elevation of heart beats without any notable environmental challenge can only be marked as internal health problem or even lameness like seen in horses (Foreman & Lawrence, 1991).

(Karvonen et al., 1984) report that telemetric devices for measuring the heart rate on humans during the sports activity are also suitable for transmitting the signal from animals, freely moving about or tied. Researchers (Seaward et al., 1990; Royle et al., 1998; Knierim & Waran, 1993; Hopster, 1998) also measured the heart rate on milking cows and other categories of cattle with various types of adapted telemetric devices from the heart rate meter sets of the Finnish maker Polar Electro Oy, which have also been used as measuring equipment in our research.

## 2. Modification of measuring device

Methods for checking heart rate have undergone a significant change with advancement in the latest technology. For many years, simple palpation of the artery was used, but it always had a potential subjective error. This was also the case for stethoscope, besides better accuracy in determining normal and higher heart rates, but still not enough practical when monitoring maximal heart rate and minimizing human handling and restrain stress on the mentioned. Recently all of those began to be replaced with electronic heart rate monitors which measure electrical pulses of the heart, and which were widely tested during exercise in horses. Since it boosted better performance and training techniques in equine sports, practical applicability was also investigated in other farm and wild animals, like cows, pigs and reindeers (Hopster & Blokhuis, 1994; Seo et al., 1998; Eloranta et al., 2002).

For measuring the heart rate special apparatuses, used by top sportsman during training, were tested. This was, particularly, the heart rate meter "Polar Sport Tester-Profi" (PST) made by the Finnish maker of equipment Polar Electro Oy. The meter is equipped with a transmitter and elastic belt with movable holder and with an intermediate unit for connection to the computer "Polar Interface". Taking into account the 70 cm length of the elastic belt the mentioned device could be located only on sucking and weaned calves of up to 180 kg body mass. With the lengthened belt, into which simply the transmitter was inserted, periodical response was obtained during testing on the animals of up 280 kg body mass only, if the electrolyte was added between the animal's skin and the sensor. The response was slightly better after the hairs have been removed from the skin at the place where the electrodes were located. On animals weighing more than 280 kg the desired response was not reached. By further modifications of the Polar device the distance between the two electrodes was increased and, thus, the response was achieved also on adult cattle (Janzekovic et al., 2006; Ploj et al., 2006; Mursec & Cus, 2003).

The elastic belt with transmitter was located round the animals' thorax. The used type of the transmitter has two electrodes of 20.7 $cm^2$ size installed in a tightly closed frame. The two electrodes are 9 cm long so that the ECG signal can be reliably recognized. That design ensures complete water-tightness. It has ribbed surface for better contact with the skin. The two electrodes are 9 cm distant from each other. On the calf the first electrode was located on the left side between the shoulder-blade and back areas and at 3 to 4 cm below the control back line. The second electrode was located in the area of the sternum. If the two electrodes and the two places of their locating on the skin were wetted with ordinary water, better conductivity between the skin and the two electrodes was reached. The heart beat signal was telemetrically transmitted to the hand receiver which was worn on the hand and later on fixed to the girth belt. The receiver calculated the heart beats on the basis of the time average algorithm between two consecutive heart beats and counted in 5, 15 or 60s intervals (Seaward et al., 1990). For measurements the apparatuses were set to the 5 second interval. The first read off value was calculated from the first 4 values of the heart beat (Hopster, 1998). With the use of the maker's computer programme (programme package Polar HR Analysis, version 4.10) the data were electronically transferred to the personal computer (Mursec et al., 2000; Mursec et al., 2006; Janzekovic et al., 2005; Janzekovic et al., 2005; Cus & Mursec, 2004; ).

Fig. 1. The alteration on girth belt with Polar Sport Tester transmitter adjusted by the author

By increasing the distance between the two electrodes it was, thus, possible to obtain continuous signal also on adult animals. Care must be taken to place them on the chest of the animal below and above the heart, taking care that the negative one is placed below, but all the time priority must be to put them as far as possible from each other. Usually sweat provides sufficient contact, but since its production depends on environmental factors and sometimes can be unpredictable, water or special electrolyte mixture between skin and electrodes advisable to secure the conductivity. Instead of the incorporated Polar transmitter from the Sport Tester-Profi set the transmitter with two separated electrodes Polar Sport Tester was used. The two electrodes were connected with two wires and connecting buttons. On a specially made elastic belt for fixing of electrodes it was possible to change the distance between the two electrodes according to the size of the animal (Figure 1).

### 2.1 The possibility of heart rate measurements in cattle with the updated equipment

The measurements are possible also with Polar Equine RS800CX G3 (Figure 2) horse training system (Polar Electro Oy, Kempele, Finland) on the cattle. At the moment some measurements are investigated on different categories of cattle. The electrical heart signals that in-struct the heart to beat and create contraction can be measured on the skin by means of two electrodes of the Polar Equine T56 W.I.N.D. transmitter. This coded, wire-less textile transmitter has ECG accuracy and sends data even over 5m distance to the receiver for further analyses or storage. Electrodes are placed on the chest of the horse below and above the heart, taking care that the negative one is placed below, but all the time caution must be taken to put them as far as possible from each other. Usually sweat provides sufficient contact, although water or special electrolyte mixture has been used to secure the conductivity. The set also included Polar G3 GPS Sensor which tracks the route on mapping software, like Google Earth. It enables record of altitude, speed and distance, likewise with the software provided color change was possible on the route trajectory when heart rate intensity and workload was altered. This makes it the most complete heart-rate based training solution for horses, which accents its importance in the era of GPS introduction and usage in biomedicine (Aerts el al., 2008; Hebenbrock et al., 2005).

Fig. 2. State of art equipment for heart rate measurements Polar Equine RS800CX G3 horse training system, including receiver, transmitter, GPS sensor, and software

### 2.2 Test measurements

In our test the cows' heart rate depended on various influences: farm (A and B), individual cow, consecutive lactation (2, 3 and 4), consecutive measurements (M = 1, 2, 3), morning and evening milking (M = 1; E = 2). As an example, Figures 3 and 4 show the processes of the HR on milking cows No. 3 (3 consecutive lactation) and No. 4 (2 consecutive lactation) from the herd on the farm A.

Taking into account the differences in the process of the heart rate it can be concluded that the influence on the HR is conditional upon the individual responsiveness of the cow. The average HR of six units of measurements (Table 1) was 75.05 beats per minute on the cow

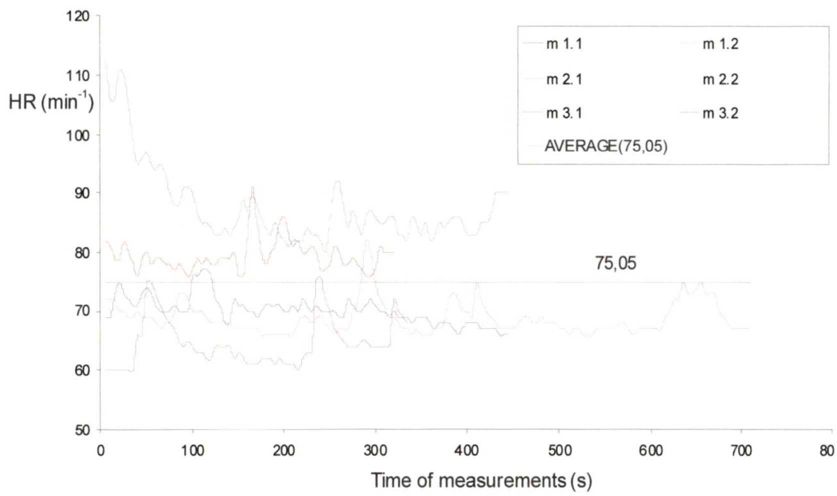


Fig. 3. Measured heart rates of milking cow No. 3 and average of measurements

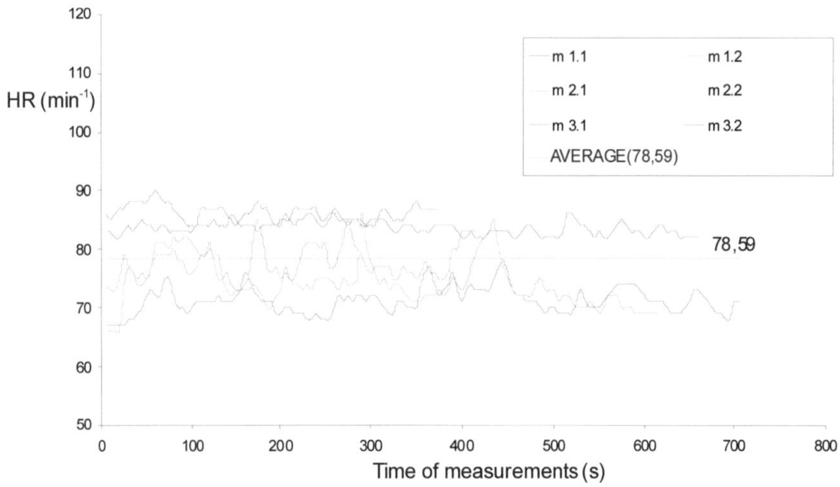


Fig. 4. Measured heart rates of milking cow No. 4 and average of measurements

| | Cow 3 | Cow 4 |
|---|---|---|
| Total number of measurements | 513 | 622 |
| Average of heart rate (min$^{-1}$) | 75.05 | 78.59 |
| SD | 9.27 | 6.27 |
| CV (%) | 12.35 | 7.98 |
| SEM | 0.41 | 0.25 |

Table 1. Basic statistics of the heart rate on cow No. 3 and No. 4 taking all measurements into account

No. 3 (SD = 9.27; SEM = 0.41) and 78.59 beats per minute on the cow No. 4 (SD = 6.27; SEM = 0.25). In spite of high variability of the HR during each measurement, which was 12.35 %, on the cow No. 3 and 7.98 %, on the cow No. 4, the two average values are comparable.
Research on comparing telemetric and ECG data showed essentially identical heart rates, differing only less than 5 bpm, which were mainly the result of depending how average heart rate was calculated (Lefcourt et al., 1999). Nevertheless, changes can happen momentarily, and attention is required in interpretation results in the means of delay time between computed PST values and rapid heart rate alteration. This is in correlation with present study and even more signifies the importance of HR monitors, likewise advantage of averaging responses.
Among the milking cows there were also differences in the quantity of the milk produced and its composition on the day of measurements as shown in Table 2.
The cow No. 4, during three consecutive measurements (M1, M2, M3) produced 31.2 kg of milk daily on the average (FCM = 27.79 kg; ECM = 23.77 kg), which is 5.3 kg more than the cow No. 3 that, on the average, produced 25.9 kg of milk daily at the time of three consecutive measurements (FCM = 30.73 kg; ECM = 29.31 kg). Higher daily milk production relies on greater need for nutritive substances from the feed ration. In the same time, intensive digestion and metabolism take place in the animal's organism, which, consequentially, can influence the heart rate. In relations to this, research by (Seo et al., 1998) shows that tongue-playing caused as developing stereotype in calves, has a de-arousal function to reduce sympathetic nervous activity especially after feeding and consequent metabolic processes, and by that way also influence heart rate.

| Measured property | Cow 3 | | | | Cow 4 | | | |
|---|---|---|---|---|---|---|---|---|
| | M1 | M2 | M3 | Average | M1 | M2 | M3 | Average |
| Milk (kg/day) | 23.8 | 28.0 | 26.0 | 25.9 | 32.0 | 32.6 | 29.0 | 31.2 |
| Milk fat (%) | 4.96 | 4.47 | 4.46 | 4.63 | 4.20 | 3.64 | 3.86 | 3.90 |
| FCM (kg/day) | 27.23 | 29.97 | 27.79 | 28.33 | 32.96 | 30.84 | 28.39 | 30.73 |
| Milk protein (%) | 3.08 | 3.14 | 3.00 | 3.07 | 3.24 | 3.13 | 3.03 | 3.13 |
| ECM (kg/day) | 21.86 | 26.34 | 23.11 | 23.77 | 31.29 | 30.55 | 26.10 | 29.31 |
| Milk sugar (%) | 4.42 | 4.40 | 4.60 | 4.47 | 4.62 | 4.36 | 4.58 | 4.52 |

FCM = fat corrected milk to 4 % of milk fat
ECM = protein corrected milk to 3.3 % of milk proteins
Table 2. Properties of milk production during complete measurements on cows 3 and 4

On the cow No. 3 the fat content in milk during the average of three consecutive measurements was higher for 0.73 percental point in comparison with the milking cow No. 4, whereas, conversely, the protein content was greater on the milking cow No. 4 (3.13 %). Both milk sugar contents were lower than the average contents (4.7 %) started in technical literature. Variations of the average lactose contents are not in accordance with the expected values depending on the process of lactation itself. Generally in mammals heart frequency increases or decreases for 4.5 beats per minute with respect to each breathing motion independently of the body mass. The body mass of cows can have an effect on the heart frequency through breathing frequency which can amount to 15 to 30 breathing motions per minute on the cow in lactation. Numbers of heart beats are also influenced by cows' reactions, in the first place by previous milking experience. With every consecutive parity and increasing age, pressure is on higher milk yield, putting greater physiological demand on the animal. Because of this, likewise possible accumulation of negative milking experience, and changes in immune status (somatic cell counts), potential effect could be in metabolism.
On the first successful insemination the cow No. 4 was 58 days younger than the cow No. 3 and 88 kg lighter (Table 3). The difference compels us to think that lighter and younger cows with the first calf are maybe more stressed during their later productive period and, therefore, have higher heart rate.

| Established values | Cow 3 | Cow 4 |
|---|---|---|
| First successful insemination (days) | 542 | 484 |
| Height of withers* | 136 | 128 |
| Height of the back* | 138 | 131 |
| Length of trunk* | 140 | 130 |
| Thorax circumference* | 202 | 184 |
| Calculated body mass (kg) | 566 | 478 |

*- measured in cm on cows with first calf
Table 3. Age of cows 3 and 4 on the first successful insemination and body dimensions of cows with the first calf

During the evening milkings average heart rate on the milking cow No. 3 and No. 4 was higher than during the morning milking. The heart rate of milking cows was measured during three followed up morning milkings: 74.23 beats per minute on the milking cow No.

3 and 77.34 beats per minute on the milking cow No. 4. During three evening milkings the milking cow No. 3 had 77.60 measured beats per minute, whereas the milking cow No. 4 had 81.87 beats per minute. According to one of the interpretations the found out measurement results can be attributed to fluctuations in the warmth production and, consequently, in the milking cow body temperature (Purwanto et al., 1990) depending, particularly, on the age of the animal, sex, season, ambient temperature, muscular activity, feed consuming, digestion and drinking of water. The normal rectal temperature of the milking cows amounts to 38.6 °C with 38.0 to 39.3 °C range. On the Holstein cows the rectal temperature starts to increase already at 21 °C ambient temperature, which is associated with the decrease in appetite and milk production. Intensively fed animals have somewhat higher temperature than the cows fed more poorly (Purwanto et al., 1990). According to the digestion increases the body temperature for 0.2 to 1 °C, followed by an increase in heart frequency (Rozman et al., 2006). Also from the measured heart rates of cow No. 3 and No. 4 it can be concluded that higher HR during the evening milking is partly a consequence of more active metabolism and/or higher ambient temperature during the afternoon time. Also as shown in study by (Gygax et al., 2008) all milking systems result in higher HR values during milking than during resting, and more specifically vagal tone (related to temperament and stress vulnerability; strongly reflects short-term, high-frequency components of heart rate variability) is lower in cows with higher milk production. Since milking process is stressful itself, should be expected to have higher values during it, and decreased vagal tone and elevated heart rates are remarked during milking as compared to resting.

## 3. Adapted PST apparatuses in milking parlour

As previously mentioned there is influence of milking systems on various physiological parameters. Even cow handling (in the means of free or guided traffic) has some influence on the heart rate values (Gygax et al., 2008). During milking in the milking parlour surprising results were achieved in measuring the HR by modified Polar Sport Tester apparatuses in production conditions with 27 cows (Table 4).
The reached data were processed in the statistical package SAS/STAT 1996 (Cary, 1996).

| Property | N | Average | SD | KV (%) |
|---|---|---|---|---|
| Milk production (kg/milking) | 162 | 13.03 | 3.46 | 26.55 |
| Duration of milking (s) | 162 | 407.8 | 65.24 | 16.00 |
| Speed of consuming (g/min) | 162 | 249.7 | 59.12 | 23.68 |
| Consumed DM (kg/milking) | 162 | 2.14 | 0.85 | 39.72 |
| HR ($min^{-1}$) average per milking | 161 | 82.38 | 11.55 | 13.85 |
| HR ($min^{-1}$) 1 - 30 s | 161 | 84.70 | 13.16 | 15.54 |
| HR ($min^{-1}$) middle of milking | 156 | 82.18 | 11.99 | 14.59 |
| HR ($min^{-1}$) last 30 s | 111 | 82.20 | 11.23 | 13.66 |

HR = heart rate; DM = dry meal; SD = standard deviation; KV = coefficient of variability;
N = number of measurements

Table 4. Statistical parameters for milk production, duration of milking and consumption of concentrate; mean value, standard deviation and coefficient of variability for heart rate during milking

New technologies in dairy industry, in the first place use of automatic milking systems, affected research in relevant scientific fields. This is also accounted for welfare of the animal, and study by (Gigaw et al., 2008) comparing these two figures concluded that there is no serious impairment of the welfare when milking cows in automatic milking systems.

### 3.1 Relations between the average HR process and the variability coefficient

During the first two minutes of milking the process of variability of the average HR (Figure 5) was followed up with the variability coefficient. The average HR during milking increased during the first 20 seconds when it reached the highest value 85.14 ± 1.10 beats per minute (r = 0.9859; P = 0.0141), SD 13.92 beats per minute; then during the next 15 seconds it dropped to the average value 83.63 ± 0.98 (r = -0.8387; P = 0.0184), SD 12.41 beats per minute; afterwards it becomes slightly stable until the 50th second when from the value 83.53 beats per minute it drops until the 95 second to the lowest value 82.24 ± 0.93 beats per minute (r = -0.9642; P < 0.0001), SD 11.86 beats per minute. between 95 and 110 seconds it is possible to see a slight increase in the HR to 82.71 ± 0.97 beats per minute (r = -0.9283; P < 0.0001), SD 12.28 beats per minute. From the 111th second onwards again dropping until the 120th second is noticed in case of 159 measurements performed. During this duration of milking the average HR amounted to 82.47 ± 0.98 beats per minute (r = -0.9127; P < 0.0001), SD 12.35 beats per minute.

After the first 5 seconds (t = 5 s) of measuring and/or duration of milking the value KV = 16.47 %, which is a higher value than KV = 11.30 % calculated from the value in case of the normal range of the HR of adult cattle, which, according to amounts to 60 to 80 beats per minute. Since in the same time we have to do also with increased average value of the HR it can be concluded that parallel factors influence these two properties. After 10 seconds a tendency towards reduction of variability for 0.26 % is noticeable; afterwards during 15 seconds of milking it stabilizes itself again to the initial value (KV = 16.47 %).

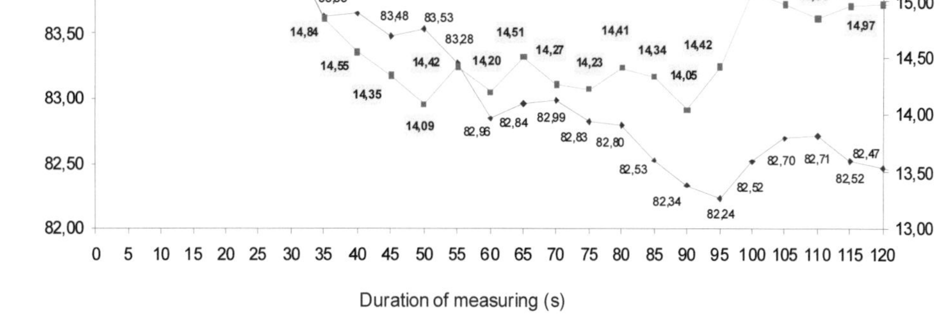


Fig. 5. Process of HR and variability coefficient during the first 120 seconds of milking

That drop of the value of the variability coefficient could indicate the events before the start of milking (prestimulation of udder, secretion of oxytocin, consuming the offered feed concentrate), which, consequentially, still influenced the process of value of the HR (increasing during the first 20 seconds) and the variability coefficient in the beginning of milking. Due to differently long prestimulation time probably also a delay in responsiveness of the value of the variability coefficient occurred, when the actual transition into the steep drop of the variability coefficient took place prior to the drop of the average HR value. The tendency towards the drop of variability did not stop at the 35 second level, where the HR value calmed down, but that happened only in case of 50 seconds with the value 14.09 %. At that time the drop of the variability coefficient amounted to 0.07 % per second on the average. The HR value in the beginning of the calming down level during the 35th second amounted to 83.65 beats per minute and the drop during the time between the 20th and 35th second amounted to 0.02 %, i.e., 1.51 beat per minute. From the 35th to 50th second the HR calmed down at the value 83.53 beats per minute followed by a rather steep drop within 10 seconds to the value 82.96 beats per minute. From the 60th to the 80th second of milking the HR was near the value 82.90 beats per minute; afterwards it decreased again and, at the 90th second, it reached the value 82.24 beats per minute. The motion of the variability coefficient up to the 90th second is in dynamic variation within the values 14.51 to 14.05 %, which is the lowest calculated value of the KV. From the 90th second of milking onwards the variability coefficient steeply increases again for about 1 %, followed with 5 second delay by gradual increase of the HR to the value 82.70 beats per minute at the 105th second, where it remains at the same value level until the repeated drop at the 110th second, which practically follows the previous drop of the KV with 10 second delay.

From the described process of the HR and KV it can be presumed that the greater decrease or increase of the KV value (over the 1 %) with shorter or longer delay was followed by an increase or decrease in the average HR value. In our case, the beginning of the change of the curve progress (drop or rise) is a matter of variability as clearly shown in Figure 5 here below, whereas reaching the calming down level is a matter of the HR.

### 3.2 Comparison and testing of differences in correlation values of HR process with milking time and variability coefficient

Figure 6 shows the relations between the process of the average HR values and the time of milking and progress of coefficients of correlations between the HR, KV of the heart frequency and the time of milking.

After the first 20 seconds of milking the time of milking and the HR frequency are highly positively related ($r = 0.986$; $P = 0.0141$), whereas during the same time interval the statistically significant degrees of relatedness between the time of milking and the heart rate KV were not found ($r = -0.107$; $P = 0.893$). Herebelow the tendency towards repeated increase of high negative relatedness of the heart frequency as well as the KV with the time of milking is indicated.

Highly significant relatedness between the heart frequency and the time of milking can, then, be traced up to the 120th second, although gradual constant exchanging of the increase and decrease of relatedness up to its maximum value in the 95th second of milking ($r = -0.964$; $P < 0.0001$) is followed by a turning point indicating the process of the increase of the average value of the HR between the 95th and 110th second. After the 120th second the relatedness of the heart frequency to the time of milking is still always significantly negative ($r = -0.916$; $P < 0.0001$). After 35 seconds the KV is significantly highly negatively related

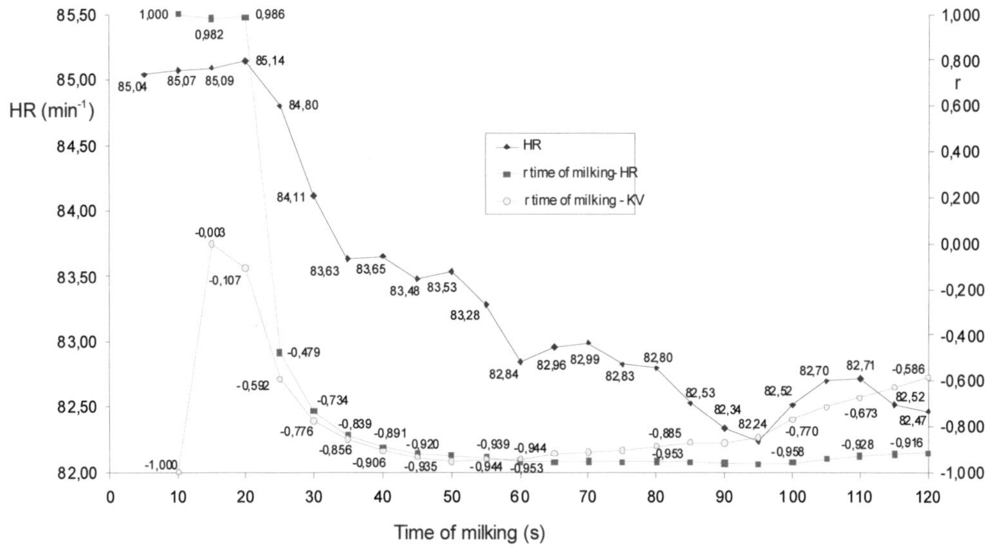


Fig. 6. Process of average HR value during the first 120 seconds of milking, coefficient of correlation (r) between HR, heart rate KV and time of milking

with the duration of milking (r = - 0.856; P = 0.014) up to the 50th second of milking when it reaches the maximum relatedness (r = - 0.952; P < 0.0001) near the relation of the time of milking to the HR. Between the 50th and 60th second the parallelism of the process of both coefficients of correlations with the time of milking is interrupted, the negative relatedness between the time of milking and the KV decreases (the KV increases again) and at the 120th second of milking it reaches only one half or so of the greatest relatedness (r = - 0.586; P = 0.003. the degree of relatedness of the KV of the heart frequency only approaches zero, the positive relatedness with the time of milking can be traced only on sections where the negative relatedness decreases.

Figure 7 shows the process of the correlation coefficient and the coefficient of partial correlation between the average value of the HR and its variability (KV) during milking. During the initial 20 seconds of milking the actual relatedness of the HR and its variability is negative and insignificant (r = - 0.663; P = 0.368); it is possible to trace the transition into positive relatedness between the 20th and 25th second, which coincides with the change of the process of the heart frequency and its variability (see Figure 4). The highest relatedness was noticed after the 35th second of milking (r = 0.952; P = 0.0016), then it decreases and after the 65th second it reaches the lowest value after the turning point (r = 0.709; P = 0.0059). Then up to the 120th second of milking the heart frequency and its variability have the tendency towards the positive relatedness (r = 0.903; P < 0.0001).

As the heart dynamics is usually monitored by the nervous system (Peng et al., 1993) and also by hormonal influences, this would imply that the sound heart as an example of arousable medium incorporates a mechanism responsible for prevention of the extremes of the heart rhythm. The change of the dynamics of the heart frequency is probably also a consequence of the changed hormonal status in the organism, when the udder stimulation during the time prior to milking is transmitted through nervous stimuli over the hypothalamus into the hypophysis where the hormone oxytocin is secreted from the neurohypophysis into blood; its secretion is additionally stimulated by consumption of the

feed concentrates through gastrointestinal hormones. According to these authors the increased concentrations of the injected oxytocin have an effect on the heart rate blood pressure and minute volume; this was reflected in our test in such a way that from the 60th second onwards during milking the HR values were no longer normally distributed.
Also the non-planned fall of a cow into the milking canal confirmed that the HR can be one of important indicators of stress state of the animals. Upon the fall the average HR of 205 beats per minute was measured, which represents 218 % of the average of the same cow during other evening milkings. Here, a considerable deviation from the preceding state of the heart rate frequency was concerned, which, however, cannot be a parameter for establishing the influence of stress in case of apparently healthy animals, when in answer to occurrence of metabolic trouble, i.e. acidosis, the sympathic nervous system, acting on the haemodynamic variables, is activated: the contractability of the heart muscle, the heart rate and the minute volume are increased.

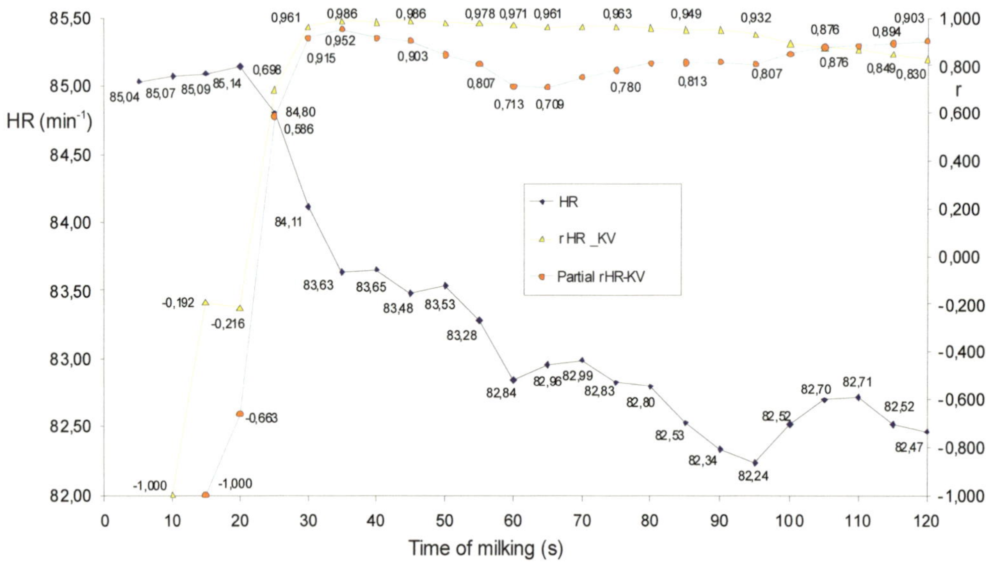


Fig. 7. Process of average heart rate value during the 120 seconds of milking, correlation coefficient (r) and coefficient of partial correlation (partial r) between HR and KV of HR during milking

## 4. Conclusion

The use of measuring of the heart frequency as an indicator of stress in the course of feeding milking cows with concentrates in the milking parlour is recommendable only conditionally, namely for the cases when the healthy animals have available balanced basic ration and a sufficient quantity of feed concentrates. The used methods of following up the process of milking, e.g., measuring of the electric activity of the oxytosynergic nervous cells, changes in intramammary pressure, concentration of oxytocin in blood and recording of the milk flow characteristics, could be complemented by a more non-invasive method, e.g., measuring of heart frequency so that more precise and, particularly, faster following up of the events before and during milking would be introduced, based on good familiarization

with the changes of the heart rhythm features and correct evaluation of influences on their change.
Variability of the HR can indicate individual response to the stress and vulnerability due to stress. The study shows that the PST values importantly reflect the HR frequency and its variability; therefore, we have concluded that the PST is adequate for measuring the heart rate and the variability of the HR on milking cows.
The process of the correlation coefficients shows that in our case, up to 25th second of milking, a dynamic turning point of relatedness between the HR, KV and partial relatedness of the HR and KV with the milking process are in question. Another obvious change took place during that time between the 55th and 65th second of milking. In our test, during the first two minutes of milking, the average value of the heart frequency was more related with the time of milking than its variability.
According to our findings, the measured properties of the HR during the first 5 and 120 seconds of milking had the smallest variability on the cows in the fourth consecutive lactation; the highest variability was recorded on cows in the third consecutive lactation, producing the greatest average quantity of milk during each milking, with the highest fat content and the lowest content of proteins and lactose.
In consideration of the mentioned relationship between the amount of concentrate and HR, our assumption is that cows could not consume all available concentrate and for that reason the HR was elevated. The analysis of the data with D' Agostino - Pearson test of normality suggests that distribution of the heart rate was changed between 60 and 65 second of milking and was continually persistent up to 120 second of milking. The nondirectional alternative hypotesis supported at 0.001 level cleary suggests that the data sets of heart rate were not derived from a normally distributed population between 60 and 65 second and furthermore, between 95 and 100 second of milking. The assessment of heart rate measurement provides several advantages over blood measurements as the measuring procedure is non-invasive and stress-free, making it ideal for use on healthy animals like a physiological indicator of stress and in psychoneuroendocrinological research.

## 5. References


Aerts, J.M. ; Gebruers, F. ; Van Camp, E. ; Berckmans, D. (2008). Controlling horse heart rate as a basis for training improvement, *Computers and electronics in Agriculture*, 64, 78-84

Art, T. & Lekeux, P. (1993). Training-induced modifications in cardiorespiratory and ventilatory measurements in thoroughbred horses, Equine Veterinary Journal, 25 532-536.

Cus, F. & Mursec, B. (2004). Databases for technological information systems, *Journal of Materials Processing Technology*, 157/158, 75-81

Eloranta, E. ; Norberg, H. ; Nilsson, A. ; Pudas, T. ; Sakkinen, H. (2002). Individually Coded Telemetry : a Tool for Studying Heart Rate and Behavious in Reindeer Calves, *Acta veterinaria scandinavica*, 43, 135-144

Evans, D.L. & Rose, R.J. (1986). Method of investigation of the accuracy of four digitally-displaying heart rate meters suitable for use in the exercising horse, *Equine Veterinary Journal*, 18, 129-132

Foreman, J.H. & Lawrence, L. (1991). Lameness and heart rate elevation in the exercising horse, *Journal of equine veterinary science*, 11, 353-356

Gygax, L. ; Neuffer, I. ; Kaufmann, C. ; Hauser, R. ; Wechsler, B. (2008). Restlessness behaviour, heart rate and heart-rate variability of dairy cows milked in two types of automatic milking systems and auto-tandem milking parlours, *Apllied Animal Behaviour Science*, 109, 167-179

Hebenbrock, M.; Due, M.; Holzhausen, H.; Sass, A.; Stadler, P.; Ellendorff, F. (2005). A new tool to monitor training and performance of sport horses using Global Positioning System (GPS) with integrated GSM capabilities, *Dtsch. Tierarztl. Wschr.*, 112, 241 - 280

Herd J.A. (1991). Cardiovascular response to stress, *Physiological Reviews*, 71, 305-330

Hopster, H. (1998). Coping strategies in dairy cows, Dissertation Thesis, Agricultural University Wageningen, Wageningen, 152

Hopster, H. & Blokhuis, H.J. (1994). Validation of a heart-rate monitor for measuring a stress response in dairy cows, *Canadian Journal of Animal Science*, 74, 465-474

Janczarek, I. (2009). Connections between the heart rate and selected motor and biometric parameters in young half-bred stallions, *Annales Universitatis Mariae Curie-Sklodowska*, Section EE, Vol. XXVII (1), pp 27-36

Janzekovic, M. (2005). Measuring heart rate of cows in milking parlour, *Agricultura*, 3, 21-25

Janzekovic, M. ; Mursec, B. & Janzekovic, I. (2005). Development of noninvasive method of measuring of heart rate in cattle, *Proceedings of the 4th DAAAM International Conference on Advanced Technologies for Developing Countries*, Vienna DAAAM International, pp 523-528, Mechanical Engineering Faculty, Slavonski Brod, Croatia

Janzekovic, M. ; Janzekovic, I. & Mursec, B. (2005). Researches and applicability of noninvasive method of measuring of heart rate in cattle, *Annals of DAAAM for 2005 & proceedings of the 16th International DAAAM symposium*, Vienna DAAAM International, pp 173-174, University of Rijeka, Opatija, Croatia

Janzekovic, M. ; Mursec, B. & Janzekovic, I. (2006). Techniques of measuring heart rate in cattle, *Technical Gazete*, 13, 31-37

Janzekovic, M. ; Mursec, B. ; Cus, F. ; Ploj, A. ; Janzekovic, I. ; Zuperl, U. (2005). Use of machines for liquid manure aerating and mixing, *Journal of Materials Processing Technology*, 162-163, 744-750

Janzekovic, M. ; Janzekovic, I. & Mursec, B. (2005). Following up heart rate in cattle by noninvasive method, *DAAAM International scientific book 2005*, pp 291-298, DAAAM International Vienna, Austria

Karvonen, J. ; Chwalbinska-Moneta, J. & Saynajakangas, S. (1984). Comparison of heart rates measured by ECG and microcomputer, *Physician and Sportsmedicine*, 12, 65-69

Kedzierski, W. & Janczarek, I. (2009). Sex-related effect of early training on stress in young trotters as expressed by heart rate, *Animal Science and Reports*, vol 27, no 1, 23-32

Knierim, U. & Waran, N.K. (1993). The influence of the human-animal interaction in the milking parlour on the behaviour, heart-rate and milk yield of dairy cows, *Proceedings of the international congress on applied ethology*, Humboldt University, Berlin, 169-173

Kovalcik, K. ; Kovalcikova, M. & Broucek, J. (1988). Interbreed differences in the responses of first-calvers to artificially induced stress conditions, *Scientia Agriculturae Bohemoslovaca*, 20, 203-209

Lay, D.C. Jr. ; Friend, T.H. ; Grissom, K.K. ; Hale, R.L. ; Bowers, C.L. (1992). Novel breeding box has variable effects on heart rate and cortisol response of cattle, *Applied Animal Behaviour Science*, 35, 1-10

Lefcourt, A. ; Erez, B. ; Varner, M.A. ; Barfield, R. ; Tasch, U. (1999). A Nonivasive Radiotelemetry System to Monitor Heart Rate for Assessing Stress Responses of Bovines, *Journal of Dairy Science*, 82, 1179-1187

Leleu, C. ; Cotrel, C. & Courouce-Malblanc, A. (2005). Relationships between physiological variables and race performace in French standardbred trotters, *Veterinary Record*, 156, 339-342

Macfarlane, D.J. ; Fogarty, B.A. & Hopkins, W.G. (1989). The accuracy and variability of commercially available heart rate monitors, *The New Zealand Journal of Sports Medicine*, 17, 51-53

Mavrin, D. & Ostir, S. (2002). *Technology of milk and milk products*, Technical publishing company of Slovenia, Ljubljana, 27-51

Mursec, B. & Cus, F. (2003). Integral model of selection of optimal cutting conditions from different databases of tool makers, *Journal of Materials Processing Technology*, 133, 158-165

Mursec, B. Cus & F. Balic, J. (2000). Organization of tool supply and determination of cutting conditions, *Journal of Materials Processing Technology*, 100, 241-249

Mursec, B. ; Janzekovic, M. ; Cus, F. ; Zuperl, U. (2006). Comparison of rollers after sowing of buckwheat, *Journal of achievements in materials and manufacturing engineering*, 17, 269-272

Peng, C.K. ; Mietus, J. ; Hausdorff, J.M. ; Havlin, S. ; Stanley, H.E. ; Goldberger, A.L. (1993). Long-range anticorrelations and non-gaussian behavior of the heartbeat, *Physical Review Letters*, 70, 1343-1346

Ploj, A. ; Mursec, B. ; Cus, F. ; Zuperl, U. (2006). Characterization of machines for processing of waste materials, *Journal of Materials Processing Technology*, 175, 338-343

Purwanto, B.P. ; Abo, Y. ; Sakamoto, R. ; Furumoto, F. ; Yamamoto, S. (1990). Diurnal patterns of heat production and heart rate under thermoneutral conditions in Holstein Friesian cows differing in milk production, *Journal of Agricultural Science*, 114, 139-142

Rietmann, T.R. ; Stuart, A.E.A. ; Bernasconi, P. ; Stauffacher, M. ; Auer, J.A. ; Weishaupt, M.A. (2004). Assessment of mental stress in warmblood horses : heart rate variability in comparison to heart rate and selected behavioural parameters, *Applied Animal Behaviour Science*, 88, 121-136

Royle, C. ; Garnsworthy, P.C. ; McArthur, A.J. ; Mepham, T.B. (1992) Heart rate changes in dairy cows associated with milking, *Journal of Physiology*, 446-575

Rozman, C. ; Pazek, K. ; Bavec, M. ; Bavec, F. ; Turk, J. ; Majkovic, D. (2006). The Multi-criteria analysis of spelt food processing alternatives on small organic farms, *Journal of sustainable agriculture*, 28, 159-179

SAS/STAT 1996. *Users Guide*, Cary, SAS Institute

Seaward, B.L. ; Steamaker, R.H. ; McAuliffe, T. ; Clapp, J.F. (1990). The precision and accuracy of a portable heart rate monitor, *Biomedical Instrumentation and Technology*, 24, 37-41

Seo, T. ; Sato, S. ; Kosaka, K. ; Sakamoto, N. ; Tokumoto, K. (1998). Tongue-playing and heart rate in calves, *Apllied Animal Behaviour Science*, 58, 179-182

Schmidt, A. ; Mostl, E. ; Wehnert, C. ; Aurich, J. ; Muller, J. ; Aurich, C. (2010). Cortisol release and heart rate variabilities in horses during road transport, *Hormones and Behavior*, 57, 209-215

van Oldruitenborgh-Oosterbaan, M.M.S. ; Hoven, R. & Breukink, H.J. (1988). The accuracy of the different heart rate meters used for studies in the exercising horse, *Journal of Veterinary Medicine*, 35, 665-672

Visser, E.K. ; van Reenen, C.G. ; van der Werf, J.T.N. ; Schilder, M.B.H. ; Knaap J.H. ; Barneveld A. ; Blokhuis H.J. (2002). Heart rate and heart rate variability during a novel object test and handling test in young horses, *Physiology & Behavior*, 76, 289-296

Warren, S. ; Martinez, A. ; Sobering, T. ; Andresen, D. (2008). Electrocardiographic Pill for Cattle Heart Rate Determination, *30th Annual International IEEE EMBS Conference*

# 10

# Realization of a Control IC for PMLSM Drive Based on FPGA Technology

Ying-Shieh Kung[1] and Chung-Chun Huang[2]
[1]Department of Electrical Engineering, Southern Taiwan University
[2]Green Energy and Environment Research Laboratory, Industrial Technology Research Institute
Taiwan

## 1. Introduction

The advantages of superior power density, high-performance motion control with fast speed and better accuracy, are such that PMLSM (Permanent Magnet Linear Synchronous Motor) are being increasingly used in many automation control fields as actuators (McLean, 1988; Gieras & Piech, 2000; Budig, 2000;), including computer-controlled machining tools, X-Y driving devices, robots, semiconductor manufacturing equipment, etc. However, the PMLSM does not use conventional gears or ball screws, so the payload upon the mover greatly affects the positioning performance (Liu et al., 2004). To cope with this problem, many advanced control techniques (Qingding et al., 2002; Lin et al., 2007; Wai & Chu, 2007), such as fuzzy control, neural networks control and robust control have been developed and applied to the position control of the PMLSM drive to obtain high operating performance. However, the execution of a neural network or fuzzy controller requires many computations, so implementing these highly complex control algorithms depend on the PC systems in most studies before (Qingding et al., 2002; Liu et al., 2004). In recent years, the fixed-point DSP (Digital Signal Processor) and the FPGA (Field Programmable Gate Array) provide a possible solution in this issue (Lin et al., 2005; Kung, 2008). Comparing with FPGA, although the intelligent control technique using DSP provides a flexible skill, it suffers from a long period of development and exhausts many resources of the CPU.
Nowadays, the FPGA has brought more attention before. The advantages of the FPGA includes their programmable hard-wired feature, fast time-to-market, shorter design cycle, embedding processor, low power consumption and higher density for the implementation of the digital system (Cho, et al., 2009; Monmasson & Cirstea, 2007; Naouar et al., 2007; Kung & Tsai, 2007; Jung & Kim, 2007; Huang & Tsai, 2009; Kung, et al., 2009). FPGA provides a compromise between the special-purpose ASIC (application specified integrated circuit) hardware and general-purpose processors (Wei et al., 2005). Recently, Li et al. (2003) utilized an FPGA to implement autonomous fuzzy behavior control on mobile robot. Lin et al., (2005) presented a fuzzy sliding-mode control for a linear induction motor drive based on FPGA. But, due to the fuzzy inference mechanism module adopts parallel processing circuits, it consumes much more FPGA resources; therefore limited fuzzy rules are used in their proposed method.
To solve the aforementioned problem, this work firstly proposed to use an FPGA and an embedded NiosII processor to develop a control IC for PMLSM. The control IC has two modules. One module performs the functions of the PTP motion trajectory for PMLSM. The

other module performs the functions of position/speed/current controllers of PMLSM drive. The former is implemented by software using Nios II embedded processor and the latter included by an AFC circuit, QEP (Quadrature Encoder Pulse) capture circuits, SVPWM (Space Vector Pulse Width Modulation) circuits, ADC interface circuit and current vector control circuit are implemented by hardware in FPGA. Secondly, to reduce the usage of FPGA resource, an FSM (Finite-State Machine) joined by a multiplier, an adder, a lookup table, and some comparators and registers is presented to model the circuits of AFC, SVPWM and current vector control. And VHDL (VHSIC hardware description language) is adopted to describe the circuits of the FSM (Hsu et al., 1996). Therefore, the hardware/software co-design technology can make the controller of PMLSM more compact, flexible, better performance and less cost. The FPGA chip employed herein is an Altera Stratix II EP2S60F672C5 (Altera, 2008) with 48,352 ALUTs, maximum 492 user I/O pins, 36 DSP blocks, 2,544,192 bits of RAM, and a Nios II embedded processor. Finally, an experimental system including an FPGA experimental board, an inverter and a PMLSM, is set up to verify the correctness and effectiveness of the proposed method.

The core idea and some results of this work have been published in the IEEE ICIT2006 conference (Kung, et al., 2006). This work exposes more clearly technical description in control IC design of PMLSM. The organization of this chapter is that the first section is the introduction, the second session describes the mathematical model of PMLSM, current vector control and position AFC design, the third session presents the control IC design, the fourth session shows the experimental system and results, and the final session is the conclusion.

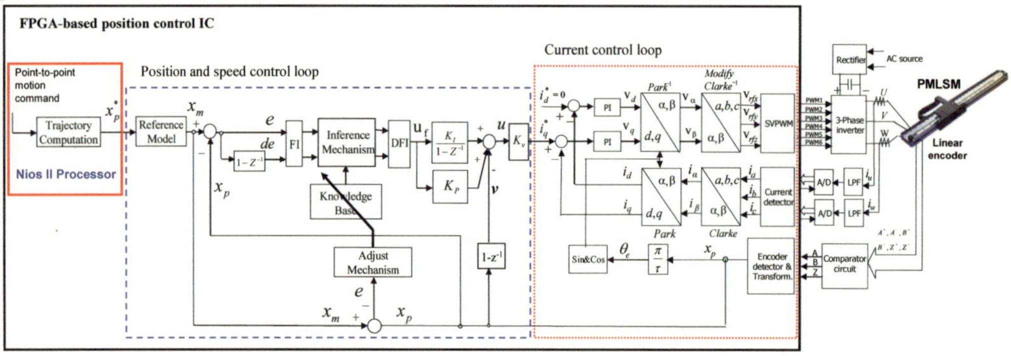


Fig. 1. The architecture of the FPGA-based position control IC for PMLSM drive system

## 2. System description of PMLSM drive and AFC design

The internal architecture of the proposed FPGA-based controller system for a PMLSM drive is shown in Fig. 1. A PTP motion trajectory, an AFC in the position loop, a P controller in the speed loop and a current vector control scheme for PMLSM are all realized in one FPGA.

### 2.1 Mathematical model of the PMLSM drive

The dynamic model of a typical PMLSM can be described in the synchronous rotating reference frame, as follows

$$\frac{di_d}{dt} = -\frac{R_s}{L_d} i_d + \frac{\pi}{\tau}\frac{L_q}{L_d} \dot{x}_p i_q + \frac{1}{L_d} v_d \tag{1}$$

$$\frac{di_q}{dt} = -\frac{\pi}{\tau}\frac{L_d}{L_q}\dot{x}_p i_d - \frac{R_s}{L_q} i_q - \frac{\pi}{\tau}\frac{\lambda_f}{L_q}\dot{x}_p + \frac{1}{L_q} v_q \tag{2}$$

where $v_d$, $v_q$ are the d and q axis voltages; $i_d$, $i_q$, are the d and q axis currents, $R_s$ is the phase winding resistance; $L_d$, $L_q$ are the d and q axis inductance; $\dot{x}_p$ is the translator speed; $\lambda_f$ is the permanent magnet flux linkage; $\tau$ is the pole pitch. The developed electromagnetic thrust force is given by

$$F_e = \frac{3\pi}{2\tau}((L_d - L_q)i_d + \lambda_f)i_q \tag{3}$$

The current control of a PMLSM drive is based on a vector control approach. That is, if we control $i_d$ to 0 in Fig.1, the PMLSM will be decoupled, so that control a PMLSM will become easy as to control a DC linear motor. After simplification and considering the mechanical load, the model of a PMLSM can be written as the following equations,

$$F_e = \frac{3}{2}\frac{\pi}{\tau}\lambda_f i_q \triangleq K_t i_q \tag{4}$$

with

$$K_t = \frac{3}{2}\frac{\pi}{\tau}\lambda_f \tag{5}$$

and the mechanical dynamic equation of PMLSM is

$$F_e - F_L = M_m \frac{d^2 x_p}{dt^2} + B_m \frac{dx_p}{dt} \tag{6}$$

where $F_e$, $K_t$, $M_m$, $B_m$ and $F_L$ represent the motor thrust force, the force constant, the total mass of the moving element, the viscous friction coefficient and the external force, respectively.

The current loop of the PMLSM drive in Fig.1 includes PI controller, coordinate transformations of Clark, Modified inverse Clark, Park, inverse Park, SVPWM (Space Vector Pulse Width Muldulation), pulse signal detection of the encoder etc. The coordination transformation of the PMLSM in Fig. 1 can be described in synchronous rotating reference frame. Figure 2 is the coordination system in rotating motor which includes stationary *a-b-c* frame, stationary α-β frame and synchronously rotating *d-q* frame. Further, the formulations among three coordination systems are presented as follows.

1. *Clarke*: stationary *a-b-c* frame to stationary α-β frame.

$$\begin{bmatrix} i_\alpha \\ i_\beta \end{bmatrix} = \begin{bmatrix} \frac{2}{3} & \frac{-1}{3} & \frac{-1}{3} \\ 0 & \frac{1}{\sqrt{3}} & \frac{-1}{\sqrt{3}} \end{bmatrix} \begin{bmatrix} i_a \\ i_b \\ i_c \end{bmatrix} \tag{7}$$

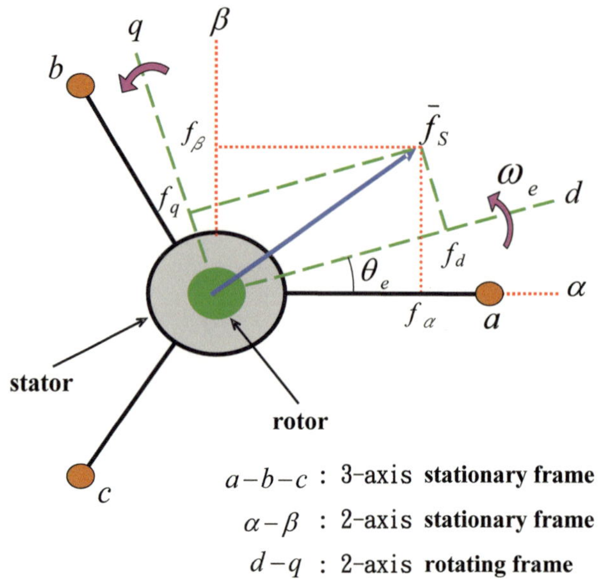


Fig. 2. Transformation between stationary axes and rotating axes

2. Modified *Clarke*$^{-1}$: stationary α-β frame to stationary *a-b-c* frame.

$$\begin{bmatrix} v_a \\ v_b \\ v_c \end{bmatrix} = \begin{bmatrix} 1 & 0 \\ \frac{-1}{2} & \frac{\sqrt{3}}{2} \\ \frac{-1}{2} & \frac{-\sqrt{3}}{2} \end{bmatrix} \begin{bmatrix} v_\beta \\ v_\alpha \end{bmatrix} \tag{8}$$

3. *Park*: stationary α-β frame to rotating *d-q* frame.

$$\begin{bmatrix} i_d \\ i_q \end{bmatrix} = \begin{bmatrix} \cos\theta_e & \sin\theta_e \\ -\sin\theta_e & \cos\theta_e \end{bmatrix} \begin{bmatrix} i_\alpha \\ i_\beta \end{bmatrix} \tag{9}$$

4. *Park*$^{-1}$: rotating *d-q* frame to stationary α-β frame.

$$\begin{bmatrix} v_\alpha \\ v_\beta \end{bmatrix} = \begin{bmatrix} \cos\theta_e & -\sin\theta_e \\ \sin\theta_e & \cos\theta_e \end{bmatrix} \begin{bmatrix} v_d \\ v_q \end{bmatrix} \tag{10}$$

where $\theta_e$ is the electrical angle.

In Fig. 1, two digital *PI* controllers are presented in the current loop of PMSM. For the example in *d* frame, the formulation is shown as follows.

$$e_d(k) = i_d^*(k) - i_d(k) \tag{11}$$

$$v_{p\_d}(k) = k_{p\_d}\, e_d(k) \tag{12}$$

$$v_{i\_d}(k) = v_{i\_d}(k-1) + k_{i\_d}\, e_d(k-1) \tag{13}$$

$$v_d(k) = v_{p\_d}(k) + v_{i\_d}(k) \tag{14}$$

the $e_d$ is the error between current command and measured current. The $k_{p\_d}, k_{i\_d}$ are *P* controller gain and *I* controller gain, respectively. The $v_{p\_d}(k)$, $v_{i\_d}(k)$, $v_d(k)$ are the output of *P* controller only, *I* controller only and the *PI* controller, respectively. Similarity, the formulation of *PI* controller in *q* frame is the same.

### 2.2 Design scheme of Space Vector Pulse Width Modulation (SVPWM)

SVPWM is a special switching scheme of a 3-phase power converter with the six power transistors. The typical structure of 3-phase power converter is shown in Fig. 3. According to the ON/OFF switching of upper transistors in Fig. 3, there have eight possible combinations. The eight vectors are called basic space vectors and they are denoted by $U_0$, $U_{60}$, $U_{120}$, $U_{180}$, $U_{240}$, $U_{300}$, $O_{000}$ and $O_{111}$, which are shown in Fig. 4. Using the *Clarke* transformation, the project values in α-β axis for six basic space vectors can be obtained and are also shown in Fig. 4. The SVPWM technique is applied to approximate the reference voltage $U_{out}$, and it combines of the switching pattern with the basic space vectors. Therefore, the motor-voltage vector $U_{out}$ will be located at one of the six sectors (S3, S1, S5, S4, S6, S2) at any given time. Thus, for any PWM period, it can be approximated by the vector sum of two vector components lying on the two adjacent basic vectors, as the following:

$$U_{out} = \frac{T_1}{T}U_X + \frac{T_2}{T}U_{X+60} + \frac{T_0(O_{000}\ or\ O_{111})}{T}, \tag{15}$$

where $T_0 = T - T_1 - T_2$ and $T$ is half of PWM carrier period. The detailed design scheme is described as following steps:

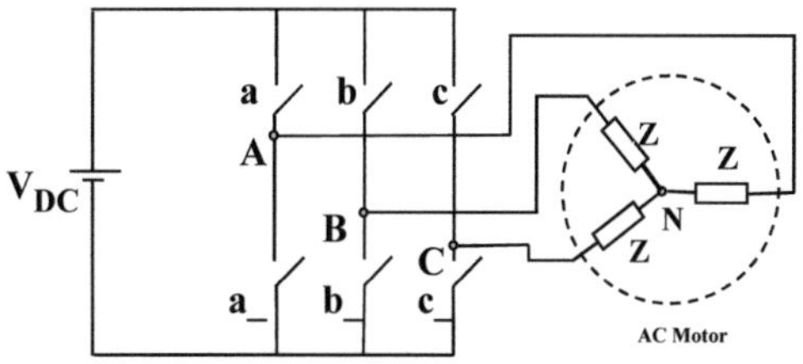


Fig. 3. Typical 3-phase power converter and AC motor

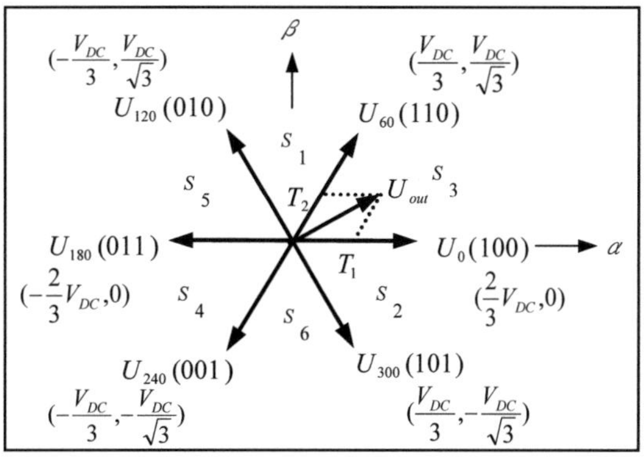


Fig. 4. Basic vector space and switching patterns

1. *Calculation of $T_1$ and $T_2$:* Any output voltage can be projected into each adjacent basic vector in SVPWM strategy. For example, the output voltage vector $U_{out}$ in the sector $S_3$ can be the combination of $U_0$ and $U_{60}$ shown in Fig. 4. Therefore, the calculation of $T_1$ and $T_2$ can be shown as,

$$U_0 = \frac{2}{3} V_{DC}\vec{\alpha} \tag{16}$$

$$U_{60} = \frac{1}{3} V_{DC}\vec{\alpha} + \frac{1}{\sqrt{3}} V_{DC}\vec{\beta} \tag{17}$$

If we substitute (16)~(17) into (15), we obtain

$$\begin{aligned} U_{out} &= \frac{T_1}{T} U_0 + \frac{T_2}{T} U_{60} = \frac{T_1}{T}\left(\frac{2}{3} V_{DC}\vec{\alpha}\right) + \frac{T_2}{T}\left(\frac{V_{DC}}{3}\vec{\alpha} + \frac{V_{DC}}{\sqrt{3}}\vec{\beta}\right) \\ &\underline{\underline{\Delta}}\ V_\alpha \vec{\alpha} + V_\beta \vec{\beta} \end{aligned} \tag{18}$$

and compare the coefficient in (18), thus

$$T_1 = \frac{T}{2V_{DC}}(3V_\alpha - \sqrt{3}V_\beta) \tag{19}$$

$$T_2 = \sqrt{3}\frac{T}{V_{DC}} V_\beta \tag{20}$$

In the similar way, the $T_1$ and $T_2$ in other sector can be derived and be rearranged in Table 1, which $T_X$, $T_Y$ and $T_Z$ are represented as the followings:

$$T_X = \sqrt{3}\frac{T}{V_{DC}} V_\beta \tag{21}$$

$$T_Y = \frac{T}{2V_{DC}}(3V_\alpha + \sqrt{3}V_\beta) \tag{22}$$

$$T_Z = \frac{T}{2V_{DC}}(-3V_\alpha + \sqrt{3}V_\beta) \tag{23}$$

If it is at the saturation condition $T_1 + T_2 > T$, the $T_1$ and $T_2$ should be modified as:

$$T_{1SAT} = T_1 \frac{T}{T_1 + T_2} \tag{24}$$

$$T_{2SAT} = T_2 \frac{T}{T_1 + T_2} \tag{25}$$

2. *Determination of the duty cycles and CMPx:* After the calculation of $T_1$ and $T_2$, it has to re-transfer it to the duty cycles and *CMPx* values to generate the PWM output signals for controlling the power transistor switching time in Fig. 3. First, the duty cycles are defined as $Ta_{on}$, $Tb_{on}$ and $Tc_{on}$ which are calculated as the follows:

$$Ta_{\text{on}} = (T - T_1 - T_2)/2 = T_0/2 \tag{26}$$

$$Tb_{\text{on}} = Ta_{\text{on}} + T_1 \tag{27}$$

$$Tc_{\text{on}} = Tb_{\text{on}} + T_2 \tag{28}$$

Then, the *CMP1~CMP3* values can be obtained in Table 2, depend on the sector number. For example in S3 sector, its output waveforms PWM1~PWM3 are depicted in Fig. 5 with the duty time at $U_0$ (100), $U_{60}$ (110) and zero vector ($O_0$ and $O_{111}$) be $T_1$, $T_2$, $T_0$, respectively.

3. *Determination of the sector:* To determine the sector, we first modified the *Clarke*$^{-1}$ transformation as follows,

$$\begin{bmatrix} V_{rfx} \\ V_{rfy} \\ V_{rfz} \end{bmatrix} = \begin{bmatrix} 1 & 0 \\ \frac{-1}{2} & \frac{\sqrt{3}}{2} \\ \frac{-1}{2} & \frac{-\sqrt{3}}{2} \end{bmatrix} \begin{bmatrix} V_\beta \\ V_\alpha \end{bmatrix} \tag{29}$$

then, the output waveforms of $V_{rfx}$, $V_{rfy}$ and $V_{rfz}$ for sinusoid wave inputs ($V_\alpha, V_\beta$) can be calculated and shown in Fig. 6. They can determine the sector according to the following rules:

$$\begin{aligned} &\text{If } V_{rfx} > 0 \text{ then a} = 1 \text{ else a} = 0 \\ &\text{If } V_{rfy} > 0 \text{ then b} = 1 \text{ else b} = 0 \\ &\text{If } V_{rfz} > 0 \text{ then c} = 1 \text{ else c} = 0 \\ &\text{Sector} = \text{a} + 2\text{b} + 4\text{c} \end{aligned} \tag{30}$$

From equations (21)~(23) and (29), we have.

$$\begin{bmatrix} T_x \\ T_y \\ T_Z \end{bmatrix} = \frac{\sqrt{3}T}{V_{DC}} \begin{bmatrix} V_{rfx} \\ -V_{rfz} \\ -V_{rfy} \end{bmatrix}. \tag{31}$$

$T_x$, $T_y$ and $T_z$ can be derived directly from $V_{rfx}$, $V_{rfy}$ and $V_{rfz}$.

| | $S_3$ | $S_1$ | $S_5$ | $S_4$ | $S_6$ | $S_2$ |
|---|---|---|---|---|---|---|
| $T_1$ | $-T_Z$ | $T_Z$ | $T_X$ | $-T_X$ | $-T_Y$ | $T_Y$ |
| $T_2$ | $T_X$ | $T_Y$ | $-T_Y$ | $T_Z$ | $-T_Z$ | $-T_X$ |

Table 1. $T_1$ and $T_2$ in all specific sectors

| Sector | $S_3$ | $S_1$ | $S_5$ | $S_4$ | $S_6$ | $S_2$ |
|---|---|---|---|---|---|---|
| *CMP1* | $Ta_{\text{on}}$ | $Tb_{\text{on}}$ | $Tc_{\text{on}}$ | $Tc_{\text{on}}$ | $Tb_{\text{on}}$ | $Ta_{\text{on}}$ |
| *CMP2* | $Tb_{\text{on}}$ | $Ta_{\text{on}}$ | $Ta_{\text{on}}$ | $Tb_{\text{on}}$ | $Tc_{\text{on}}$ | $Tc_{\text{on}}$ |
| *CMP3* | $Tc_{\text{on}}$ | $Tc_{\text{on}}$ | $Tb_{\text{on}}$ | $Ta_{\text{on}}$ | $Ta_{\text{on}}$ | $Tb_{\text{on}}$ |

Table 2. Assigning duty cycle to *CMPx* in any sector

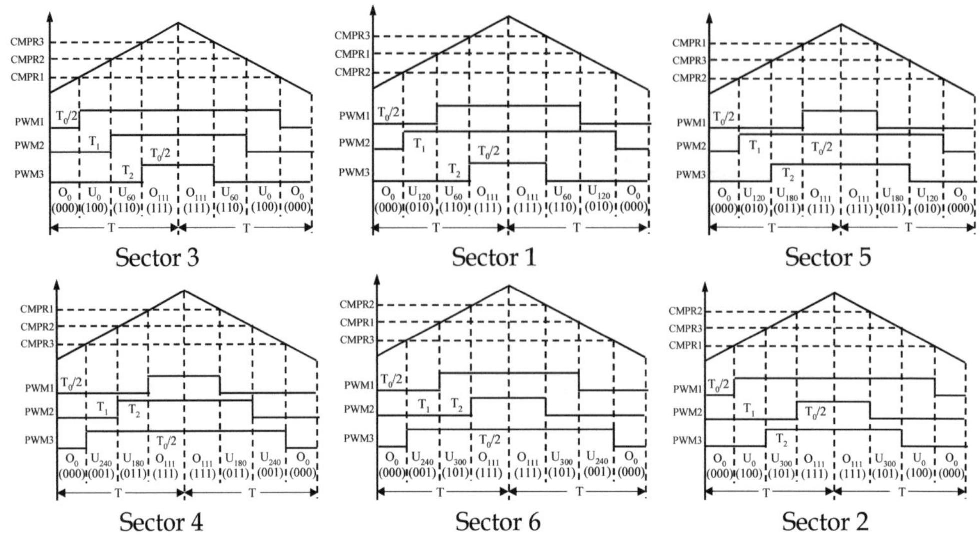


Fig. 5. PWM patterns and duty cycle operating at all sectors

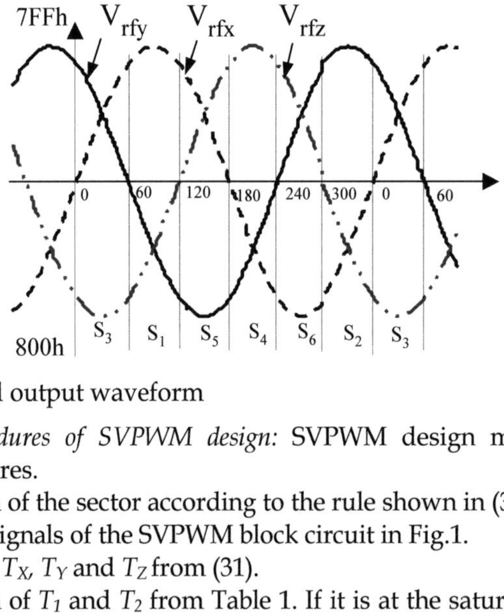


Fig. 6. 3-phase sinusoid output waveform

4. *Computation procedures of SVPWM design:* SVPWM design method is summary as following procedures.

**Step 1.** Determination of the sector according to the rule shown in (30), where $V_{rfx}$, $V_{rfy}$, $V_{rfz}$ are the input signals of the SVPWM block circuit in Fig.1.

**Step 2.** Calculation of $T_X$, $T_Y$ and $T_Z$ from (31).

**Step 3.** Determination of $T_1$ and $T_2$ from Table 1. If it is at the saturation condition, we can use (24) and (25) to modify the $T_1$ and $T_2$.

**Step 4.** Determination of the duty cycle $Ta_{on}$, $Tb_{on}$, $Tc_{on}$ from (26)~(28).

**Step 5.** Assignment of the duty cycles to *CMP1*, *CMP2* and *CMP3* from Table 2.

### 2.3 Adaptive fuzzy controller (AFC) in position control loop

The blue dash rectangular area in Fig. 1 presents the architecture of an AFC for the PMLSM drive. It consists of a fuzzy controller, a reference model and a parameter adjusting mechanism. Detailed description of these is as follows.

1. *Fuzzy controller (FC):*
In Fig.1, the tracking error and the change of the error, *e*, *de* are defined as

$$e(k) = x_m(k) - x_p(k) \tag{32}$$

$$de(k) = e(k) - e(k-1) \tag{33}$$

and *e*, *de* and $u_f$ are input and output variables of FC, respectively. The fuzzifier gains $K_e$, $K_{de}$ and defuzzifier gain $K_u$ are used in the normalization and denormalization condition. The design procedure of the FC is as follows:

a. Take the *e* and *de* as the input variables of the FC, and define their linguist variables as *E* and *dE*. The linguist value of *E* and *dE* are $\{A_0, A_1, A_2, A_3, A_4, A_5, A_6\}$ and $\{B_0, B_1, B_2, B_3, B_4, B_5, B_6\}$, respectively. Each linguist value of *E* and *dE* is based on the symmetrical triangular membership function which is shown in Fig.7. The symmetrical triangular membership function are determined uniquely by three real numbers $\xi_1 \le \xi_2 \le \xi_3$, if one fixes $f(\xi_1) = f(\xi_3) = 0$ and $f(\xi_2) = 1$. With respect to the universe of discourse of [-6.6], the numbers for these linguistic values are selected as follows:

$$\begin{aligned} &A_0 = B_0 : \{-6,-6,-4\},\ A_1 = B_1 : \{-6,-4,-2\},\ A_2 = B_2 : \{-4,-2,0\},\ A_3 = \\ &= B_3 : \{-2,0,2\}, A_4 = B_4 : \{0,2,4\},\ A_5 = B_5 : \{2,4,6\},\ A_6 = B_6 : \{4,6,6\} \end{aligned} \tag{34}$$

b. Compute the membership degree of the *e* and *de*. Figure 7 shows that the only two linguistic values are excited (resulting in a non-zero membership) in any input value, and the membership degree is obtained by

$$\mu_{A_i}(e) = \frac{e_{i+1} - e}{2} \quad \text{and} \quad \mu_{A_{i+1}}(e) = 1 - \mu_{A_i}(e) \tag{35}$$

where $e_{i+1} \triangleq -6 + 2*(i+1)$. Similar results can be obtained in computing the membership degree $\mu_{B_j}(de)$.

c. Select the initial fuzzy control rules, such as,

$$\text{IF } e \text{ is } \mathrm{A_i} \text{ and } \Delta\mathrm{e} \text{ is } \mathrm{B_j} \text{ THEN } u_f \text{ is } \mathrm{c_{j,i}} \tag{36}$$

where *i and j* = 0~6, $A_i$ and $B_j$ are fuzzy number, and $c_{j,i}$ is a real number. The graph of the fuzzy rule table and the fuzzification are shown in Fig. 7.

d. Construct the output of the fuzzy system $u_f(e,de)$ by using the singleton fuzzifier, product-inference rule, and central average defuzzifier method. Although there are total 49 fuzzy rules in Fig. 7 will be inferred, actually only 4 fuzzy rules can be effectively excited to generate a non-zero output. Therefore, if an error *e* is located between $e_i$ and $e_{i+1}$, and an error change *de* is located between $de_j$ and $de_{j+1}$, only four linguistic values $A_i$, $A_{i+1}$, $B_j$, $B_{j+1}$ and corresponding consequent values $c_{j,i}$, $c_{j+1,i}$, $c_{j,i+1}$, $c_{j+1,i+1}$ can be excited, and the output of the fuzzy system can be inferred by the following expression:

$$u_f(e,de)=\frac{\sum_{n=i}^{i+1}\sum_{m=j}^{j+1} c_{m,n}[\mu_{A_n}(e)*\mu_{B_m}(de)]}{\sum_{n=i}^{i+1}\sum_{m=j}^{j+1}\mu_{A_n}(e)*\mu_{B_m}(de)} \triangleq \sum_{n=i}^{i+1}\sum_{m=j}^{j+1} c_{m,n}*d_{n,m} \tag{37}$$

where $d_{n,m} \triangleq \mu_{A_n}(e)*\mu_{B_m}(de)$. And those $c_{i,j}$ are adjustable parameters. In addition, by using (35), it is straightforward to obtain $\sum_{n=i}^{i+1}\sum_{m=j}^{j+1} d_{n,m} = 1$ in (37).

2. *Reference model (RM)*:
Second order system is usually as the RM in the adaptive control system. Therefore, the transfer function of the RM in Fig.1 can be expressed as

$$\frac{x_m(s)}{x_p^*(s)}=\frac{\omega_n^2}{s^2+2\varsigma\omega_n s+\omega_n^2} \tag{38}$$

where $\omega_n$ is natural frequency and $\varsigma$ is damping ratio. Furthermore, because the characteristics of no overshoot, fast response and zero steady-state error are the important factors in the design of a PMLSM servo system; therefore, it can be considered as the selective criterion of $\omega_n$ and $\varsigma$. The design methodology is described as follows: Firstly, the (38) matches the requirement of a zero steady-state error condition. Secondly, if we choose $\varsigma \geq 1$, it can guarantee no overshoot condition. Especially, the critical damp value $\varsigma = 1$ has a fastest step response. Hence, the relation between the rising time $t_r$ and the natural frequency $\omega_n$ for a step input response in (38) can be derived and shown as follows.

$$(1+\omega_n t_r)e^{-\omega_n t_r}=0.1 \tag{39}$$

Once the $t_r$ is chosen, the natural frequency $\omega_n$ can be obtained. Furthermore, applying the bilinear transformation, (38) can be transformed to a discrete model by

$$\frac{x_m(z^{-1})}{x_p^*(z^{-1})}=\frac{a_0+a_1z^{-1}+a_2z^{-2}}{1+b_1z^{-1}+b_2z^{-2}} \tag{40}$$

and the difference equation is written as.

$$x_m(k)=-b_1x_m(k-1)-b_2x_m(k-2)+a_0x_p^*(k)+a_1x_p^*(k-1)+a_2x_p^*(k-2) \tag{41}$$

3. *Parameter adjusting mechanism*:
The gradient descent method is used to derive the AFC control law in Fig. 1. The objective of the parameters adjustment in FC is to minimize the square error between the mover position and the output of the RM. The instantaneous cost function is defined by

$$J(k+1)=\frac{1}{2}e_m(k+1)^2=\frac{1}{2}\left[x_m(k+1)-x_p(k+1)\right]^2 \tag{42}$$

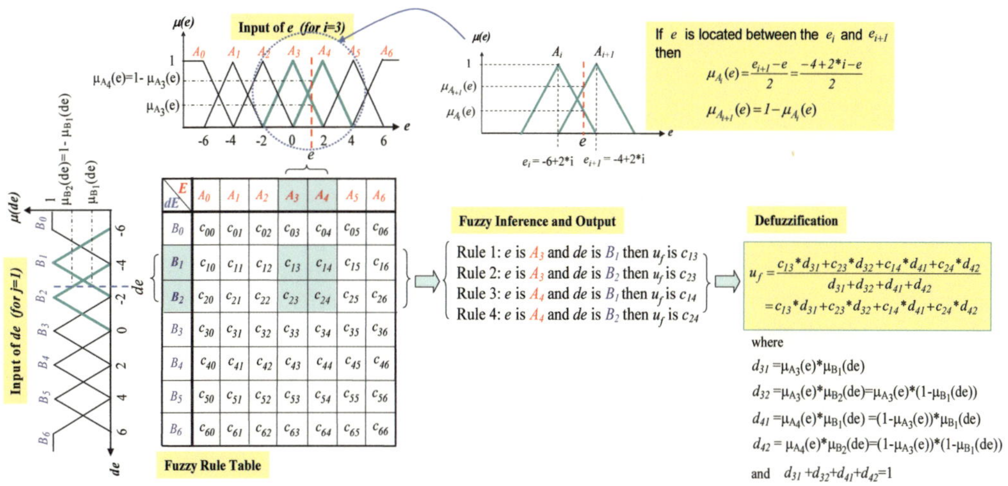

Fig. 7. The symmetrical triangular membership function of *e* and *de*, fuzzy rule table, fuzzy inference and fuzzification

and the four defuzzifier parameters of $c_{j,i}$, $c_{j+1,i}$, $c_{j,i+1}$, $c_{j+1,i+1}$ are adjusted according to

$$\Delta c_{m,n}(k+1) \propto -\frac{\partial J(k+1)}{\partial c_{m,n}(k)} = -\alpha \frac{\partial J(k+1)}{\partial c_{m,n}(k)} \tag{43}$$

with $m = j,\ j+1$, $n = i,i+1$ and where $\alpha$ represents learning rate. However, following the similar derivation with (Kung & Tsai, 2007), the $\Delta c_{m,n}$ can be obtained as

$$\Delta c_{m,n}(k) = \alpha(K_p + K_i)\Psi K_v e(k) d_{n,m} \approx \alpha(K_p + K_i) Sign(\Psi) K_v e(k) d_{n,m} \tag{44}$$

with $m = j, j+1$ and $n = i,i+1$. Because the motor parameter $\Psi$ is not easily to determined, so the $sign(\Psi)$ is used in (44). The sign (.) represents the sign operator.

4. *Point-to-point (PTP) Motion Trajectory*

The PTP trajectory is considered to evaluate the motion performance in PMLSM. For smoothing the move of the PMLSM at the start and stop condition, the motion trajectory is designed with the trapezoidal velocity profile and its formulation is shown as follows.

$$s(t) = \begin{cases} \frac{1}{2}At^2 + s_0 & 0 \le t \le t_a \\ v_m(t-t_a) + s(t_a) & t_a \le t \le t_d \\ -\frac{1}{2}A(t-t_d)^2 + v_m(t-t_d) + s(t_d) & t_d \le t \le t_s \end{cases} \tag{45}$$

Where $0<t<t_a$ is at the acceleration region, $t_a<t<t_d$ is at the constant velocity region, and $t_d<t<t_s$ is at the deceleration region. The $S$ represents the position command; $A$ is the acceleration/deceleration value; $s_0$ is the initial position; $v_m$ is the maximum velocity; $t_a$, $t_d$ and $t_s$ represents the end time of the acceleration region, the start time of the deceleration region and the end time of the trapezoidal motion, respectively.

## 3. The design of a motion control IC for PMLSM drive

Figure 8 illustrates the internal architecture of the proposed FPGA implementation of a PTP motion trajectory, an AFC and a current vector controller for PMLSM drive system. The internal circuit comprises a Nios II embedded processor IP (Intelligent Properties) and a position control IP. The Nios II processor is depicted to perform the function of the PTP motion trajectory, generate the position command, collect the response data and communicate with external device. All programs in Nios II processor are coded in the C language. The position control IP includes mainly a circuit of the position AFC and speed P controller, a circuit for current controllers and coordinate transformation (CCCT), a QEP circuit, a SVPWM circuit and an ADC interface circuit. The sampling frequency of the position control loop is designed with 2kHz. The frequency divider generates 50 Mhz (Clk), 25 Mhz (Clk-step), 12 kHz (Clk-cur), and 2 kHz (Clk-sp) clock to supply all circuits in Fig. 8. The internal circuit of CCCT performs the function of two PI controllers, table look-up for *sin/cos* function and the coordinate transformation for Clark, Park, inverse Park, modified inverse Clarke. The CCCT circuit designed by FSM is shown in Fig. 9, which uses one adder, one multiplier, an one-bit left shifter, a look-up-table and manipulates 24 steps machine to carry out the overall computation. The data type is 12-bit length with Q11 format and 2's complement operation. In Fig. 9, steps s0~s1 is for the look-up *sin/cos* table; steps s2~s5 and s5~s8 are for the transformation of Clarke and Park, respectively; steps s9~s14 is for the computation of d-axis and q-axis PI controller; and steps s15~s19 and s20~s23 represent the transformation of the inverse Park and the modified inverse Clarke, respectively. The

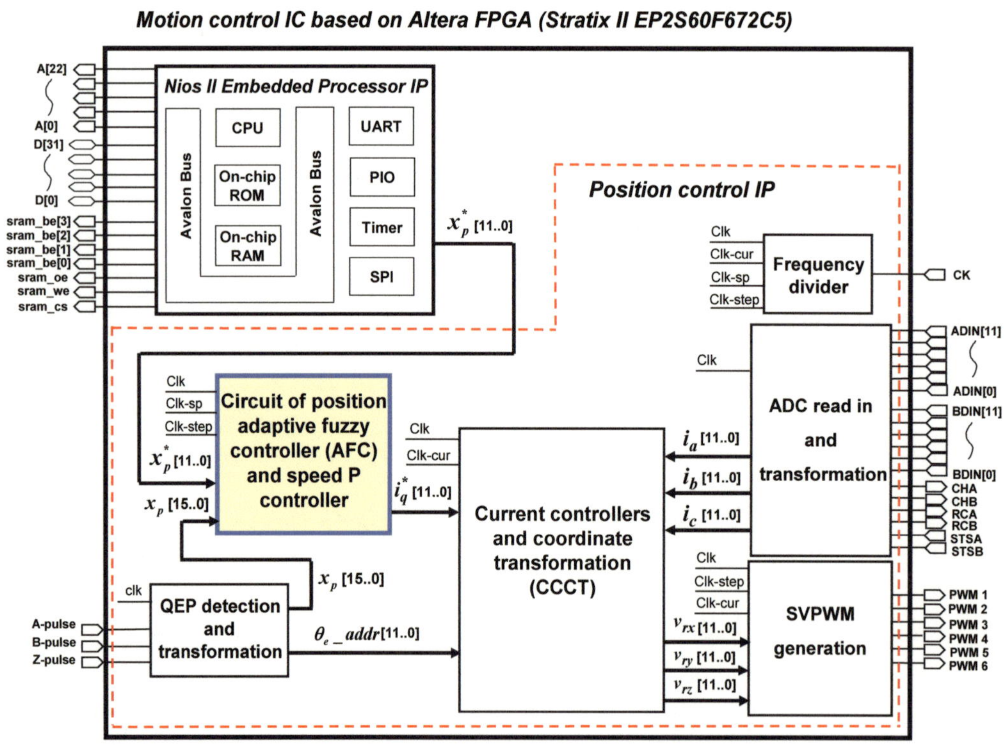


Fig. 8. Internal architecture of a motion control IC for PMLSM in FPGA

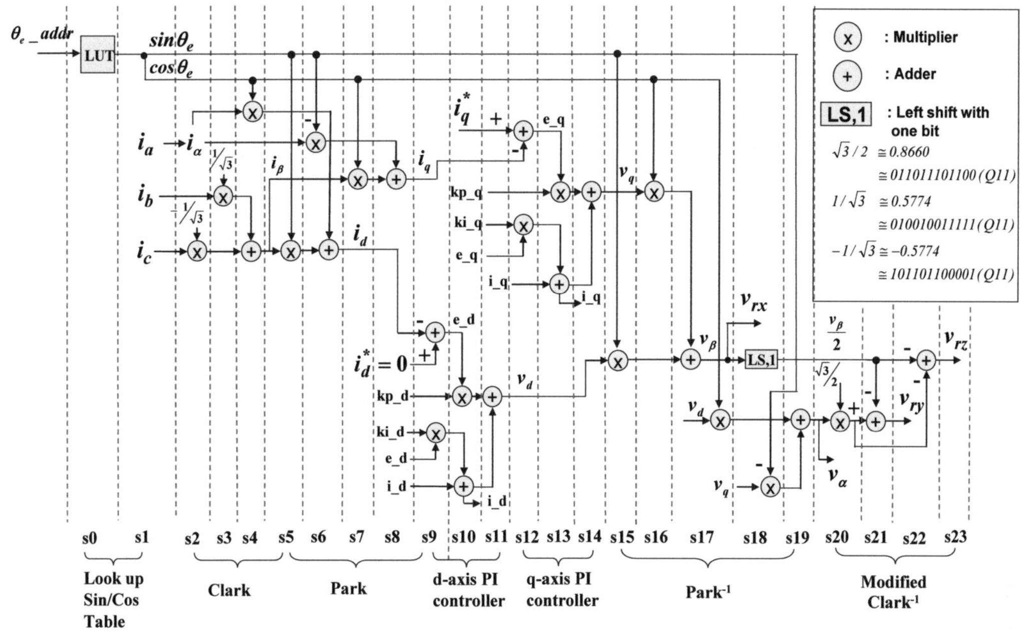


Fig. 9. Designed CCCT circuit in Fig. 8

operation of each step in FPGA can be completed within 40ns (25 MHz clock); therefore total 24 steps need 0.96 μs operation time. Although the FSM method needs more operation time than the parallel processing method in executing CCCT circuit, it doesn't loss any control performance in overall system because the 0.96 μs operation time is much less than the designed sampling interval, 62.5 μs (16 kHz) of current control loop in Fig. 1. To prevent numerical overflow and alleviate windup phenomenon, the output values of I controller and PI controller are both limited within a specific range.

An FSM is also employed to model the AFC of the position loop and P controller of the speed loop in PMLSM and shown in Fig. 10, which uses one adder, one multiplier, a look-up table, comparators, registers, etc. and manipulates 35 steps machine to carry out the overall computation. With exception of the data type in reference model are 24-bits, others data type are designed with 12-bits length, 2's complement and Q11 format. Although the algorithm of AFC is highly complexity, the FSM can give a very adequate modeling and easily be described by VHDL. Furthermore, steps $s_0$~$s_6$ execute the computation of reference model output; steps $s_6$~$s_9$ are for the computation of mover velocity, position error and error change; steps $s_9$~$s_{12}$ execute the function of the fuzzification; $s_{13}$ describe the look-up table and $s_{14}$~$s_{22}$ defuzzification; and steps $s_{23}$~$s_{34}$ execute the computation of velocity and current command output, and the tuning of fuzzy rule parameters. The SD is the section determination of *e* and *de* and the RS,1 represents the right shift function with one bit. The operation of each step in Fig.10 can be completed within 40ns (25 MHz clock) in FPGA; therefore total 35 steps need a 1.4μs operation time. It doesn't loss any control performance for the overall system because the operation time with 1.4μs is much less than the sampling interval, 500 μs (2 kHz), of the position control loop in Fig.1. In Fig. 8, the SVPWM circuit and QEP circuit are presented in Fig. 11(a) and Fig. 11(b). The SVPWM circuit in Fig.11(a) herein is designed to be 16 kHz frequency and 1μs dead-band, respectively. The algorithm

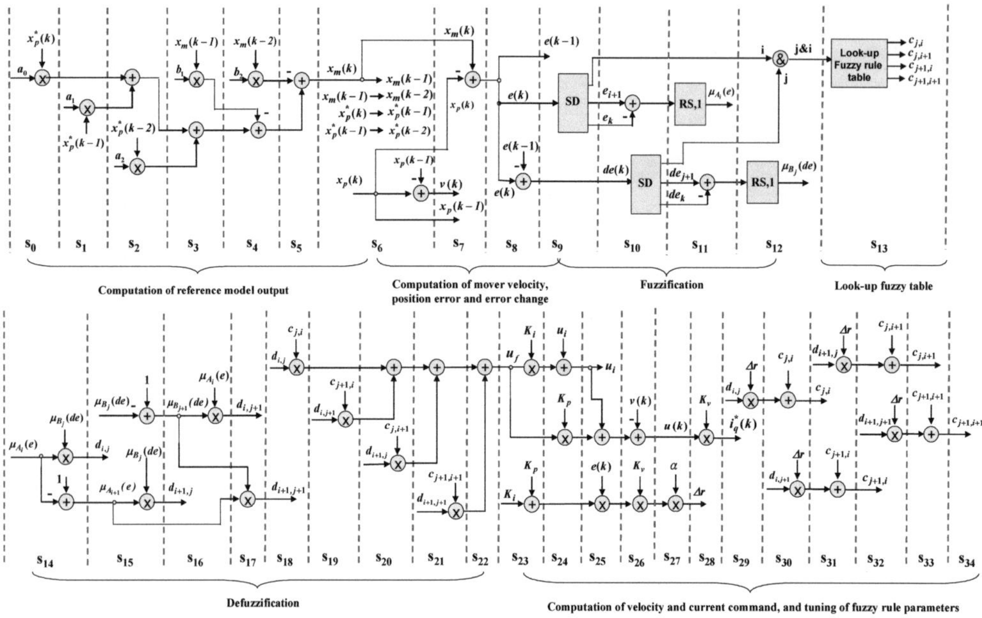


Fig. 10. State diagram of an FSM for describing the AFC in position loop and P controller in speed loop

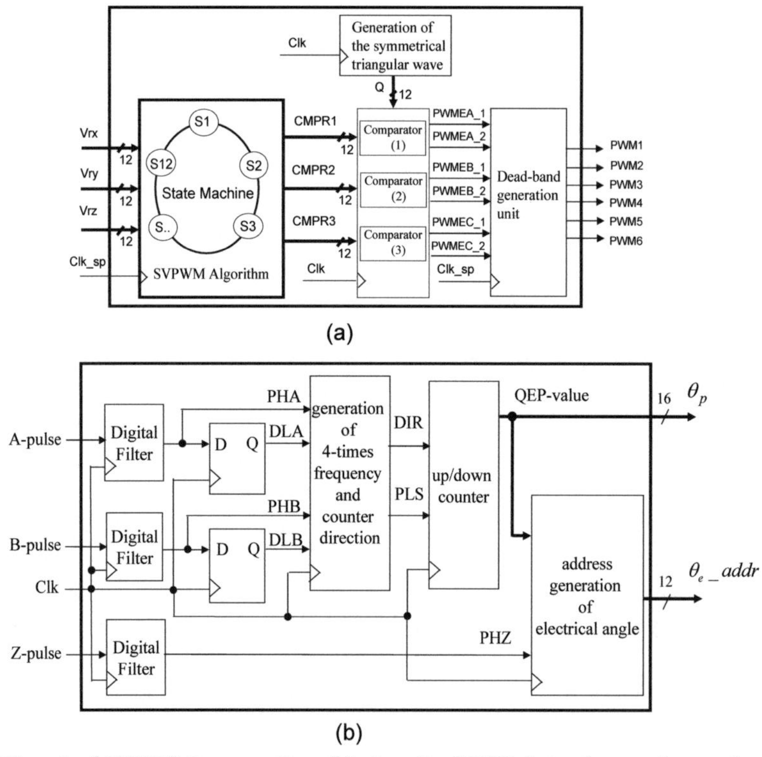


Fig. 11. (a) Circuit of SVPWM generation (b) circuit of QEP detection and transformation

of SVPWM refers to Section 2.2. The circuit of the *QEP* module is shown in Fig.11(b), which consists of two digital filters, a decoder and an up-down counter. The filter is used for reducing the noise effect of the input signals *PA* and *PB*. The pulse count signal *PLS* and the rotating direction signal *DIR* are obtained using the filtered signals through the decoder circuit. The *PLS* signal is a four times frequency pulses of the input signals *PA* or *PB*. The *Qep* value can be obtained using *PLS* and *DIR* signals through a directional up-down counter. The overall resource usage of the AFC circuit needs 8,055 ALUTs, the Nios II embedded processor IP needs 8,275 ALUTs and 46,848 RAM bits and the position control IP needs 12,269 ALUTs and 297,984 RAM bits in FPGA. Therefore, the motion control IC uses 42.4% ALUTs resource and 13.6% RAM resource of Stratix II EP2S60.

## 4. Experimental results

The overall experimental system depicted in Fig.1 includes an FPGA (Stratix II EP2S60F672C5), a voltage source IGBT inverter and a PMLSM. The PMLSM was manufactured by the BALDOR electric company; and it is a single-axis stage with a cog-free linear motor and a stroke length with 600mm. The parameters of the motor are: $R_s = 27\,\Omega$, $L_d = L_q = 23.3$ mH, $K_t = 79.9$N/A. The input voltage, continuous current, peak current (10% duty) and continuous power of the PMLSM are 220V, 1.6A, 4.8A and 54W, respectively. The maximum speed and acceleration are 4m/s and 4 g but depend on external load. The moving mass is 2.5Kg, the maximum payload is 22.5Kg and the maximum thrust force is 73N under continuous operating conditions. A linear encoder with a resolution of 5μm is mounted on the PMLSM as the position sensor, and the pole pitch is 30.5mm (about 6100 pulses). The inverter has three sets of IGBT power transistors. The collector-emitter voltage of the IGBT is rated 600V; the gate-emitter voltage is rated ±20V, and the DC collector current is rated 25A and in short time (1ms) is 50A. The photo-IC, Toshiba TLP250, is used in the gate driving circuit of IGBT. Input signals of the inverter are PWM signals from the FPGA device.

For validating the effectiveness of the current vector control in Fig. 1, the input current command, $(i_d^*, i_q^*) = (0A,\ 1A)$ is set, and the measured currents of $i_d$, $i_q$ are shown in Fig. 12(a), the corresponding currents in *a-b-c* axes and in $\alpha - \beta$ axes are shown in Fig. 12(b) and Fig. 12(c), respectively. In Fig. 12, as a result of the EMI effect in the motor driver board, the ripple in measured current has a little high. Nevertheless, the experiment result is still presented that the measured current could tracks the current command. Furthermore, it not merely validates the function of the current vector control, but also could make the PMLSM decouple.

Have confirmed the effectiveness of the current loop vector control in the PMLSM drive in loop, the realization of position controller based on the FPGA in Fig.1 is further evaluated. The control sampling frequency of the current, speed and position loops are designed as 16kHz, 2kHz and 2kHz, respectively. In the proposed motion control IC, the current controller, the speed controller and the adaptive fuzzy position controller are all realized by hardware in FPGA, and the PTP motion trajectory algorithm is implemented by software using the Nios II embedded processor. The speed controller adopts a P controller with gain $K_v$=1.4.The AFC is used in the position loop, the membership function and the initial fuzzy rule table are designed as Fig.13(a), and the PI gains are chosen by $K_p$=2.5, $K_i$=0.08. The transfer function of the reference model is selected by a second order system with the natural frequency of 40 rad/s and damping ratio of 1. The step response is first tested to evaluate the performance of the proposed controller. Figure 14 shows the position step responses of the mover under a payload of 0 Kg and 11 Kg using the FC (learning rate=0) when the position command is a 4/3Hz square wave signal with a 10mm amplitude. The parameters $c_{i,j}$ of the fuzzy rule table are adequately selected in Fig. 13(a) at the 0kg payload condition, and the step response shows a good dynamic response with a rising time of 0.1s, no overshoot and a near-zero steady state in Fig. 14(a). However, when a 11 kg load is

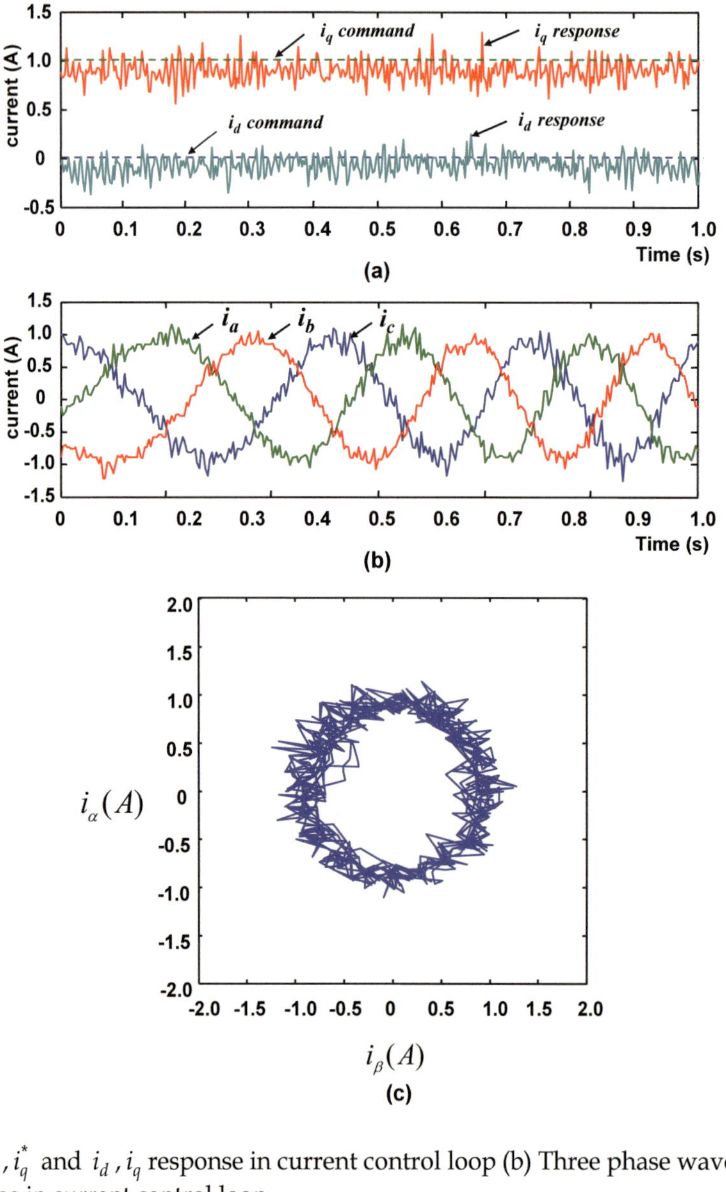


Fig. 12. (a) $i_d^*, i_q^*$ and $i_d, i_q$ response in current control loop (b) Three phase waveforms (c) $i_\alpha, i_\beta$ response in current control loop

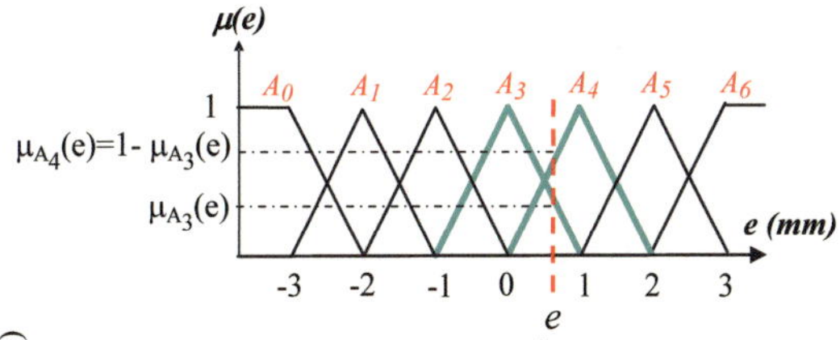


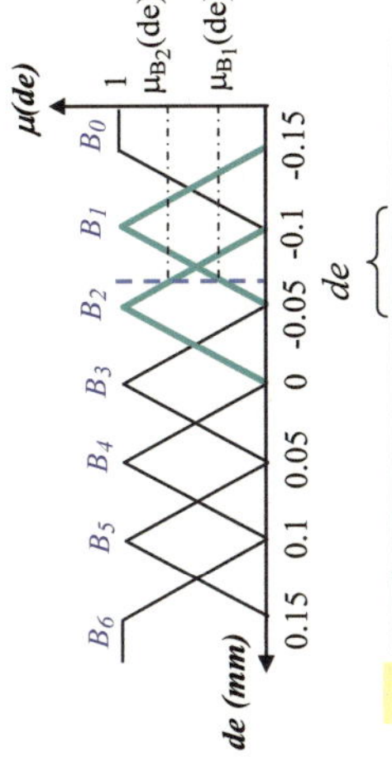


| E / dE | $A_0$ | $A_1$ | $A_2$ | $A_3$ | $A_4$ | $A_5$ | $A_6$ |
|---|---|---|---|---|---|---|---|
| $B_0$ | -1.0 | -1.0 | -0.65 | -0.65 | -0.3 | -0.3 | 0 |
| $B_1$ | -1.0 | -0.65 | -0.65 | -0.3 | -0.3 | 0 | 0.3 |
| $B_2$ | -0.65 | -0.65 | -0.3 | -0.3 | 0 | 0.3 | 0.3 |
| $B_3$ | -0.65 | -0.3 | -0.3 | 0 | 0.3 | 0.3 | 0.65 |
| $B_4$ | -0.3 | -0.3 | 0 | 0.3 | 0.3 | 0.65 | 0.65 |
| $B_5$ | -0.3 | 0 | 0.3 | 0.3 | 0.65 | 0.65 | 1.0 |
| $B_6$ | 0 | 0.3 | 0.3 | 0.65 | 0.65 | 1.0 | 1.0 |

**Fuzzy Rule Table** $C_{i,j}$ *is Q11 format*

(a)

| E / dE | $A_0$ | $A_1$ | $A_2$ | $A_3$ | $A_4$ | $A_5$ | $A_6$ |
|---|---|---|---|---|---|---|---|
| $B_0$ | -1.0 | -1.0 | -0.65 | -0.65 | -0.3 | -0.3 | 0 |
| $B_1$ | -1.0 | -0.70 | -0.86 | -0.36 | -0.17 | 0 | 0.3 |
| $B_2$ | -1.0 | -1.0 | -1.0 | -1.0 | 0 | 1.0 | 1.0 |
| $B_3$ | -1.0 | -1.0 | -1.0 | 0 | 1.0 | 1.0 | 1.0 |
| $B_4$ | -0.93 | -1.0 | 0 | 0.16 | 1.0 | 1.0 | 1.0 |
| $B_5$ | -0.3 | 0 | 0.1 | 0.21 | 0.80 | 0.74 | 1.0 |
| $B_6$ | 0 | 0.30 | 0.30 | 0.65 | 0.65 | 1.0 | 1.0 |

(b)

Fig. 13. Fuzzy membership function and (a) the initial fuzzy rule table in experiment (b) the tuned fuzzy rule table at 4th second

added upon the mover and the same fuzzy control rule table and controller parameters are used, the position dynamic response worsens and exhibits a 14.2% overshoot in Fig. 14(b). It reveals that the dynamic performance of the PMLSM is affected by the payload on the mover. Accordingly, an AFC is adopted in Fig.1 to solve this problem. When the proposed AFC is used with learning rate being 0.1, the tracking results are highly improved and presented in Fig. 15. Initially, the mover of the PMLSM tracks the output of the reference model with oscillation. After five square wave commands, the $c_{i,j}$ parameters are tuned to adequate values which is shown in Fig. 13(b), and the mover can closely follow the output of the reference model. Simultaneously, in Fig. 15(c), the peak of the instantaneous cost function is gradually decayed to a constant value. Secondly, the frequency response is considered to evaluate the performance of the proposed controller. A tested input signal of a sinusoid wave with 10mm amplitude and the frequency variation from initial 2 Hz to final 6 Hz is provided. In this design, the frequency tracking response and the tracking error of the PMLSM without and with adaptation under 11kg payload are shown in Fig. 16 and Fig.17. Figure 17 reveals that the position tracking error by using the AFC (learning rate=0.1) is only 0.35~0.7 times of that obtained by using the FC in Fig.16. However, Fig.16 reveals the phase lag phenomenon using the FC is more serious than using the AFC in Fig.17. Finally, to test the tracking performance of a PTP motion trajectory, a repeated go-and-return displacement motion command with a trapezoidal velocity profile under 11kg payload is provided, and the overall displacement, the maximum velocity and the acceleration/ deceleration are designed to be 400 mm, 1m/s and 3.6m/s$^2$, respectively. The tracking results concerning the displacement trajectory and its velocity profile corresponding to the aforementioned input commands using the FC and the AFC are shown in Fig. 18 and Fig. 19, respectively. The experimental results reveal that both in position and velocity response are well tracked, but the position tracking error by using the AFC is less than the one by using the FC. Therefore, the experimental results in Figs. 12 to 19 demonstrate that the proposed FPGA-based AFC and PTP motion trajectory for the PMLSM drive is effective and robust.

## 5. Conclusion

A motion control IC for a PMLSM drive based on the FPGA technology is successfully demonstrated in this chapter. The conclusions herein are summarized as follows. Firstly, an FSM joined by one multiplier, one adder, one LUT, some comparators and registers has been employed to model the overall AFC algorithm for the PMLSM, such that it not only is easily implemented by VHDL but also can reduce the FPGA resources usage. Secondly, the functionalities required to build a fully digital motion controller of the PMLSM, such as a PTP motion trajectory, an AFC in the position loop, a P controller in the speed loop and a current vector controller are all realized within one FPGA. Thirdly, the PTP motion trajectory scheme is implemented in software by using Nios II embedded processor and the AFC and the current vector controller algorithm are implemented in hardware by FPGA. The software/hardware co-design technology with the parallel processing can make the system performance increased. Finally, the experimental results by step response, frequency response and PTP motion tracking have been revealed well performance in the proposed FPGA-based PMLSM motion control system.

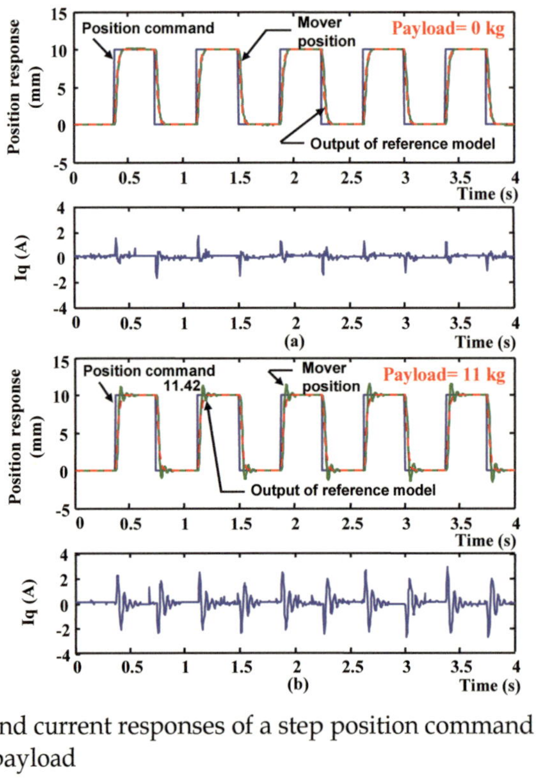


Fig. 14. The position and current responses of a step position command using the FC under (a) 0kg and (b) 11 kg payload

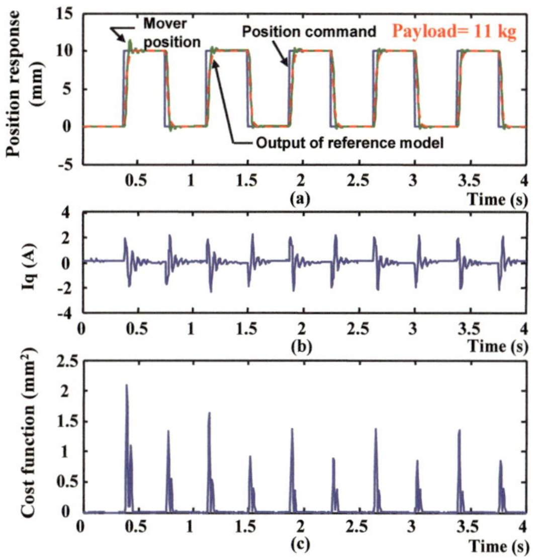


Fig. 15. The (a) position (b) current and (c) cost function responses of a step position command using the AFC under 11 kg payload

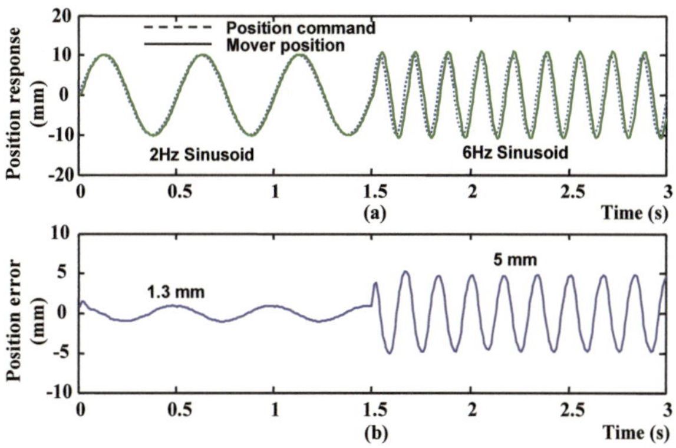


Fig. 16. (a) The frequency and (b) the position error responses of a 2Hz to 6Hz sinusoid input signal using the FC under 11 kg payload

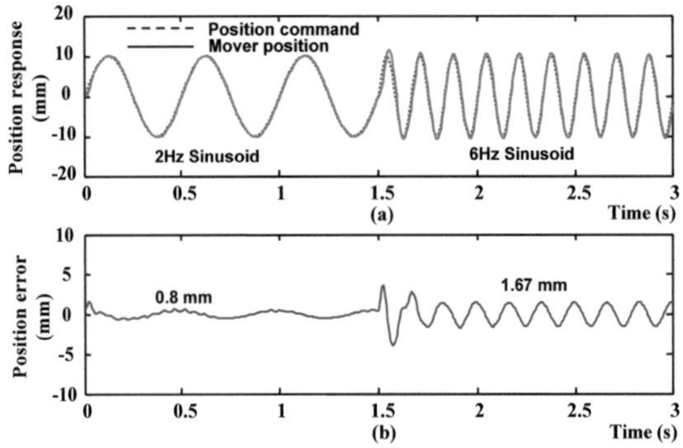


Fig. 17. (a) The frequency and (b) the position error responses of a 2Hz to 6Hz sinusoid input signal using the AFC under 11 kg payload

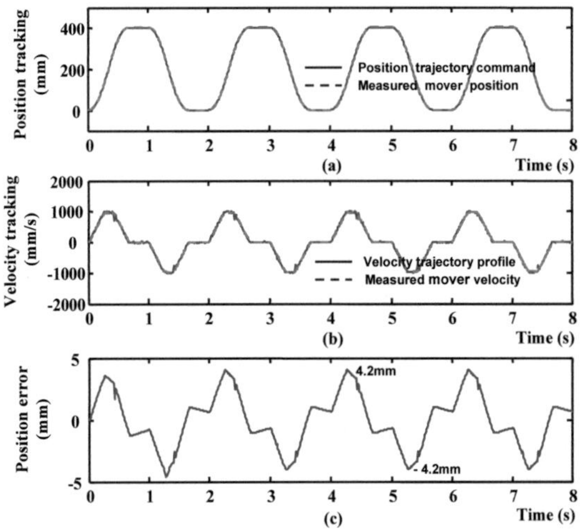


Fig. 18. The PTP motion trajectory experiment using the FC under a maximum velocity of 1m/s, acceleration/deceleration of 3.6m/s$^2$ and with 11kg payload and its (a) displacement tracking (b) velocity tracking (c) displacement tracking error responses

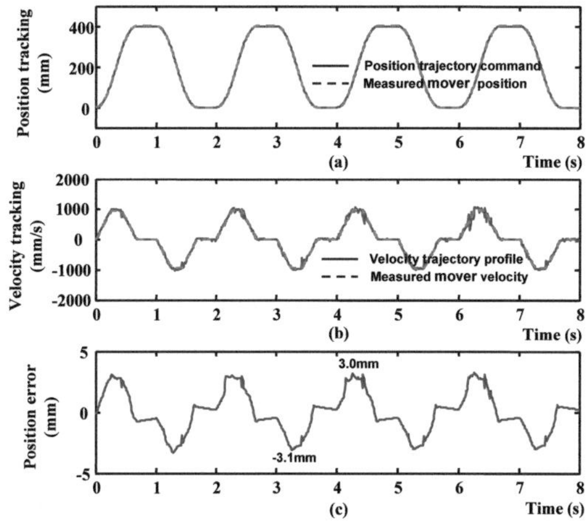


Fig. 19. The PTP motion trajectory experiment using the AFC under a maximum velocity of 1m/s, acceleration/deceleration of 3.6m/s$^2$ and with 11kg payload and its (a) displacement tracking (b) velocity tracking (c) displacement tracking error responses

## 6. References

Altera (2008): www.altera.com.

Budig, P.K. (2000). The application of linear motors, *Proceedings of PIEMC 2000*. vol. 3, pp.1336-1340.

Cho, J. U.; Le, Q. N. & Jeon, J. W. (2009) An FPGA-based multiple-axis motion control chip, *IEEE Trans. Ind. Electron.*, vol. 56, no.3, pp.856-870.

Gieras, F. & Piech, Z.J. (2000). *Linear synchronous motors – transportation and automation systems*, CRC Press.

Hsu, Y.C.; Tsai, K.F.; Liu, J.T. & Lin, E.S. (1996) *VHDL modeling for digital design synthesis*, KLUWER ACADEMIC PUBLISHERS, TOPPAN COMPANY (S) PTE LTD.

Huang, H.C. & Tsai, C.C. (2009) FPGA Implementation of an embedded robust adaptive controller for autonomous omnidirectional mobile platform, *IEEE Trans. Ind. Electron.*, vol. 56, no. 5, pp. 1604-1616.

Jung, S. & Kim, S.S. (2007). Hardware implementation of a real-time neural network controller with a DSP and an FPGA for nonlinear systems, *IEEE Trans. Ind. Electron.*, vol. 54, no. 1, pp. 265-271.

Kung, Y.S.; Tseng K.H. & Tai T.Y. (2006) FPGA-based servo control IC for X-Y table, *Proceedings of the IEEE International Conference on Industrial Technology (ICIT'06)*, pp. 2913-2918.

Kung, Y.S. & Tsai, M.H. (2007). FPGA-based speed control IC for PMSM drive with adaptive fuzzy control, *IEEE Trans. on Power Electronics*, vol. 22, no. 6, pp. 2476-2486.

Kung, Y.S. (2008) Design and implementation of a high-performance PMLSM drives using DSP chip, *IEEE Trans. on Ind. Electron.*, vol. 55, no. 3, pp. 1341-1351.

Kung, Y.S.; Fung, R.F. & Tai, T.Y.(2009) Realization of a motion control IC for X-Y Table based on novel FPGA technology, *IEEE Trans. Ind. Electron.*, vol. 56, no. 1, pp. 43-53.

Li, T.S.; Chang S.J. & Chen, Y.X. (2003). Implementation of human-like driving skills by autonomous fuzzy behavior control on an FPGA-based car-like mobile robot, *IEEE Trans. Ind. Electro.*, vol. 50, no.5, pp. 867-880.

Lin, F.J.; Wang, D.H. & Huang, P.K. (2005) FPGA-based fuzzy sliding mode control for a linear induction motor drive, *IEE Proc.- Electr. Power Application*, vol. 152, no.5, pp. 1137-1148.

Lin, F. J.; Huang, P. K. & Chou, W. D. (2007). Recurrent fuzzy neural network controlled linear induction motor servo drive using genetic algorithm, *IEEE Trans. Ind. Electron.*, vol. 54, no. 3, pp. 1449-1461.

Liu, T.H.; Lee Y.C. & Chang, Y.H. (2004). Adaptive controller design for a linear motor control system," *IEEE Trans. on Aerospace and Electronics System*, vol. 40, no.2, pp. 601-613.

Qingding, G.; Qingtao H. & Yanli, Q. (2002). Neural network real-time IP position controller on-line design for permanent magnetic linear synchronous motor, *Proceedings of the International on Advanced Motion Control*, pp. 386-389.

McLean, G.W. (1988) Review of recent progress in linear motors, *IEE Proc., Part B*, vol. 135, no. 6, pp. 380-416, November 1988.

Monmasson, E. & Cirstea, M.N. (2007). FPGA design methodology for industrial control systems - a review, *IEEE Trans. on Ind. Electron.*, Vol. 54, No. 4, pp.1824-1842.

Naouar, M.W.; Monmasson, E.; Naassani, A.A.; Slama-Belkhodja, I. & Patin, N. (2007). FPGA-based current controllers for AC machine drives - a review, *IEEE Trans. Ind. Electron.*, vol. 54, no.4, pp.1907-1925.

Wai, R.J. & Chu, C.C. (2007). Motion control of linear induction motor via petri fuzzy neural network, *IEEE Trans. Ind. Electron.*, vol.54, no. 1, pp. 281-295.

Wei, R.; Gao, X.H.; Jin, M.H.; Liu, Y.W.; Liu, H.; Seitz, N.; Gruber, R. & Hirzinger, G. (2005). FPGA based hardware architecture for HIT/DLR hand, *Proceeding of the IEEE/RSJ International Conference on Intelligent Robots and System*, pp. 523~528.

# 11

# Adaptive Control for Power System Stability Improvement

Jožef Ritonja
*University of Maribor, Faculty of Electrical Engineering and Computer Science*
*Slovenia*

## 1. Introduction

The basic function of an excitation system is to provide a direct current to the synchronous generator field winding. In addition, the excitation system performs control and enables protective functions essential for the satisfactory operation of the power system by controlling the field voltage and thereby the field current. The control functions include the control of voltage and reactive power flow, and the enhancement of system stability. Because of the generator stator voltage control loop, the excitation system essentially changes the synchronous generator dynamics. Under certain loading conditions the entire system becomes unstable. Therefore, subsystem, which is called 'power system stabilizer (PSS)', is used to improve the dynamics of the complete system. The basic function of the PSS is to add damping to the rotor oscillations by controlling its excitation using an auxiliary stabilizing signal.
Linear control theory is still commonly used for the design of a conventional power system stabilizer with fixed parameters (CONV PSS) (Demello & Concordia, 1969; Anderson & Fouad, 1977; Bergen, 1986; Kundur, 1994; Machowsky et al., 2008). The necessary mathematical representation of a synchronous generator is given by a simplified linear model (SLM), which satisfactorily describes the behaviour of the machine in the vicinity of the operating point (Heffron & Phillips, 1952). A CONV PSS is simple to realize, but its application shows non-optimal damping through the entire operating range - by varying the loading, also the synchronous generator dynamic characteristics vary; the fact due to which the stabilizer determined in the nominal operating point does not assure the optimal damping in the entire operating range (Ritonja et al., 2000).
The stabilization of the synchronous generator has represented an attractive problem for testing different concepts of the modern control theory. The majority of the contributions have presented the application of adaptive control, robust control (Chow et al., 1990), variable structure control (Subbarao & Iyer, 1993), fuzzy control (Hassan & Malik, 1993), artificial neural network (Zhang et al., 1993), feedback linearization (Mielcszarski & Zajaczkowski, 1994), and internal model control (Law et al., 1994). The presented research has been focused to the study of adaptive stabilization methods.
The adaptive control has been used in order to assure the optimal damping through the entire generator operating range. The use of the adaptive control is possible because the loading variations and consequently the variations of the synchronous generator dynamic characteristics are, in most cases, essentially slower than the adaptation mechanism.

The simplest, the oldest and the most tested adaptive approach is gain scheduling. In this case, the gain of the stabilizer is set with respect to the selected operating point. The main disadvantage of such approach is a rather time-consuming determination of the adequate loading schedule for the complete operating range. The gain scheduling represents an introductory step to real adaptive systems because of the gain setting being performed in open-loop fashion.

The first real adaptive approach to the stabilization of a synchronous generator is the self tuning control (STC). In this case, the calculation of parameters of the adequate discrete controller is based on the identified parameters of the SLM obtained by one of the parametric identification methods. The beginning of the self tuning PSS go back in 1979 (Ledwich, 1979). The combination of the recursive least square identification method and the pole shifting controller proved to be the most successful (Cheng et al., 1986). A disadvantage of such indirect approach is inconsistency in assuring the stability of the complete adaptive system. The stability of self tuning adaptive systems is assured only in case of simpler, less applicable, controller synthesis methods. Additional difficulties are caused by disturbances and non-modelled dynamics.

Direct model reference adaptive methods (direct MRAC) do not show these disadvantages; their design and the design of the belonging adaptation mechanism is based on assuring the stability of a complete adaptive system. Unfortunately, the synchronous generator with its specific nonlinear behavior does not allow a simple application of adaptation mechanisms of direct model reference systems.

Almost all MRAC methods are developed from one of the following approaches (Kaufman et al., 1993):

- adaptive control based on the full-state access method, which requires that all the state variables of the controlled plant are measurable (MRAC-FSA) (Landau, 1979) ,
- adaptive control based on the input-output description of a controlled plant, which can be divided into:
  - adaptive control where an adaptive observer is incorporated into the controller to overcome the inability to access the entire state space vector (MRAC-AO) (Narendra & Annaswamy, 1989) and
  - adaptive control for almost strictly positive real plants (MRAC-ASPR), called also command generator tracker concept (CGT) (Kaufman et al., 1993).

For the needs of PSS, the MRAC-FSA algorithms have proved to be less adequate. Reference (Irving et al., 1979) represents one of the first papers where the MRAC-FSA approach is used for stabilization. Difficulties in applying this concept are found especially in the unmeasurability of the necessary state space variables, which results in the unfulfillment of the Erzberger's perfect model following conditions (Landau, 1979). Not all state space variables of a synchronous generator are measurable, therefore a simplified linearised model, whose state variables can be measured, is used for the design. When using a model which considers the exciter dynamics, Erzberger's conditions are not fullfiled, i.e. perfect model following control cannot be obtained.

For the MRAC-AO implementation one should also be familiar with the structure of the controlled plant. The assumptions, which are required to assure the existence of an asymptotic stable solution, are found in (Narendra & Annaswamy, 1989). CONV PSS control structures cannot be directly extended to the MRAC-AO PSS because a controlled plant does not fulfil the required assumptions. Modifications in the structure of the power system stabiliser, as well as changes in adaptive law, were needed for a complete solution.

One of the implementations of MRAC-AO methods for the stabilisation of a synchronous generator is presented in (Ritonja et al, 1995).

MRAC-ASPR (or CGT) is more recent than the previously mentioned adaptive approaches. This approach is an output feedback method, which requires neither full state feedback nor adaptive observers. Other important properties of this class of algorithms are given as follows:

- they are applicable to non minimum phase systems and to multiple input and output systems,
- the order of the controlled plant needs not be known to select the reference model and the adaptation mechanism,
- the adaptation mechanism is computational undemanding

In this chapter, by studying the effects of the machine loading on the model dynamics, the reasons for the adaptive PSS are shown and the development and validation of the PSS based on MRAC-ASPR is described.

## 2. Mathematical model of the synchronous generator

The synchronous generator connected to an infinite bus is a multivariable nonlinear dynamic system described with the 7$^{th}$ order nonlinear state-space model. For the analysis and design of the control systems for synchronous machines, a simplified linearized third order model, which is called also Heffron-Phillips model, is the most popular. The model is described with equations (1) to (4):

$$T'_{d0}\dot{E}'_{q\Delta} = E_{FD\Delta} - K_4\delta_\Delta - \frac{1}{K_3}E'_{q\Delta} \tag{1}$$

$$T_{e\Delta} = K_1\delta_\Delta + K_2E'_{q\Delta} \tag{2}$$

$$V_{t\Delta} = K_5\delta_\Delta + K_6E'_{q\Delta} \tag{3}$$

$$\frac{2\mathrm{H}}{\omega_r}\ddot{\delta}_\Delta = T_{m\Delta} - T_{e\Delta} - \mathrm{D}\omega_\Delta \tag{4}$$

where $T_m$ represents the mechanical torque [pu], $T_e$ represents the electrical torque [pu], $\omega$ is the rotor speed [pu], $\delta$ is the rotor angle [rad], $E_q'$ is the voltage behind transient reactance [pu], $E_{fd}$ is the field excitation voltage [pu], $V_t$ is the terminal voltage [pu], H is the inertia constant [s], D is the damping coefficient representing the total lumped damping effects from the damper windings [pu], $\omega_r$ is the synchronous speed [rad s$^{-1}$], $T_{do}'$ is the direct axis transient open circuit time constant [s], $K_1$ ... $K_6$ are the linearization parameters, s is the Laplace variable and the subscript $_\Delta$ denotes the small signal incremental quantities.

Fig. 1 shows the block diagram of the Heffron-Phillips model.

### 2.1 Synchronous generator without voltage control

By varying the operating point, the parameter values $K_1$ through $K_6$ also vary. For the stability analysis the parameters $K_1$ to $K_6$ are not sufficiently transparent. The Heffron Phillips model is a 3$^{rd}$ order linear model whose characteristic polynomial has 2 complex

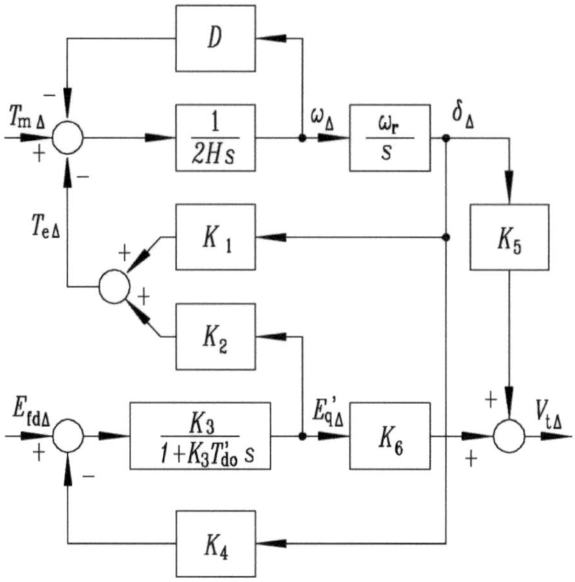


Fig. 1. Simplified linearized model of the synchronous generator connected to an infinite bus

conjugate roots and 1 real root. The influence of the machine loading on the synchronous generator dynamic characteristics can be evaluated by eigenvalue loci analysis. The dominant complex conjugate eigenvalues are especially interesting for the dynamic stability analysis. They are directly related to the period and damping ratio of the rotor angle oscillation. The results of the numerical eigenvalue analysis of a typical 160 MVA turbogenerator are presented. The turbogenerator has following parameters:

| | | | |
|---|---|---|---|
| $S_n$=160 MVA | $U_n$=15 kV | cos $\varphi_n$=0.85 | $T'_{d0}$=5.9 s |
| $x_d$=1.7 [pu] | $x_d'$=0.245 [pu] | $x_q$=1.64 [pu] | |
| $R_e$=0.02 [pu] | $X_e$=0.02 [pu] | D=2 [pu] | H=3.96 s |

Table 1. Data for 160 MVA turbogenerator

where $S_n$ is the nominal power, $U_n$ the nominal stator voltage, cos $\varphi_n$ the nominal power factor, $x_d$ the direct axis reactance of the generator, $x_q$ the quadrature axis reactance, $x_d'$ the direct axis transient reactance, $R_e$, $X_e$ the resistance and the reactance of the transmission line.

Fig. 2 shows the dominant complex conjugate eigenvalue loci of a turbogenerator as the function of the loading. The individual curves correspond to the constant reactive power. The active power P has varied in the range from 0.0 to 1.2 [pu] at the reactive power Q values from 0.0 to 1.2 [pu] in steps of 0.1 [pu]. The inductive generator load has been presumed. From Fig. 2 it is evident:

- by the increase of the active power the oscillation damping also increases,
- by the increase of the reactive power the natural frequency also increases.

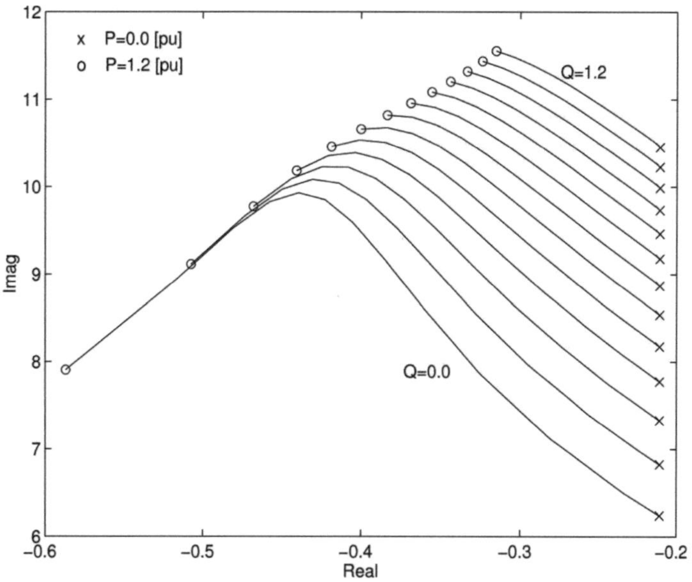


Fig. 2. Conjugate eigenvalue loci as a function of loading, turbogenerator, 160 MVA

### 2.2 Synchronous generator with voltage control

Automatic voltage regulator (AVR) with voltage control loop essentially changes the synchronous generator dynamics. The simplest model of the AVR with exciter is a first order lag, described with the transfer function:

$$\frac{E_{FD\Delta}(s)}{V_{t\Delta ref}(s)-V_{t\Delta}(s)}=\frac{\mathrm{k}_{AVR}}{s\mathrm{T}_{AVR}+1}, \tag{5}$$

where $V_{t\Delta ref}$ represents the reference terminal voltage [pu], $k_{AVR}$ represents the exciter and the voltage controller gain and $T_{AVR}$ represents the exciter time constant [s]. The time constant $T_{AVR}$ depends on the selected exciter while the gain $k_{AVR}$ is selected so that the nonequation $k_{AVR} < T_{d0}/(2\ T_{AVR})$ is fulfilled. In this way the sufficient damping of the voltage control loop is assured. Fig. 3 shows the voltage control system.

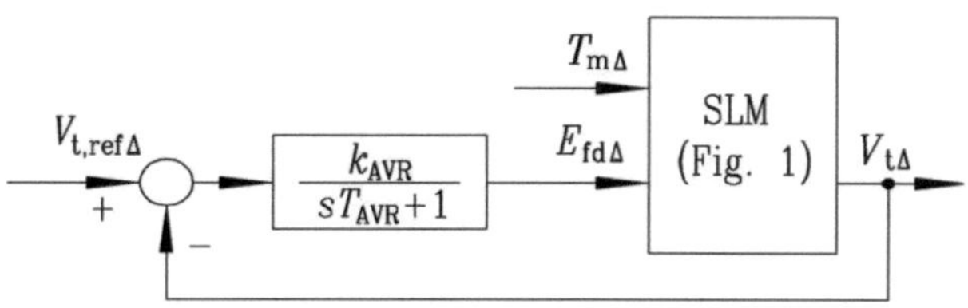


Fig. 3. Block diagram of SLM with voltage control

The linearized model of a synchronous generator with the voltage control system has four eigenvalues. The dominant complex conjugate eigenvalues are especially interesting. The results of the numerical eigenvalue analysis of a typical 160 MVA turbogenerator with adequate voltage control system are presented. Fig. 4 shows the dominant complex conjugate eigenvalue loci of a turbogenerator with the voltage control system as the function of the loading. The individual curves correspond to the constant reactive power. The loading variation is the same as in case of an uncontrolled generator (Fig. 2). The selected exciter has had the time constant $T_{AVR}$ = 0.05 s. The corresponding controller gain has been calculated according to the equation $k_{AVR} = 0.9\, T_{d0}/(2\, T_{AVR})$.

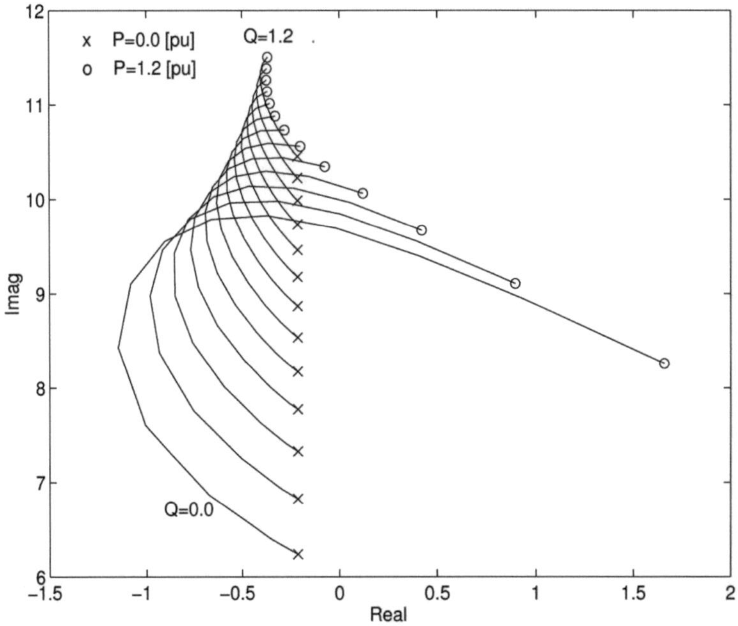


Fig. 4. Conjugate eigenvalue loci as a function of loading, turbogenerator with voltage control system, 160 MVA

In Fig. 4. the convexity of the constant Q-curves, which is characteristic of turbogenerators, is clearly evident. The convexity of curves increases with the decrease of the reactive power. Fig. 5 shows the dominant complex conjugate eigenvalue loci of a hydrogenerator as the function of the loading. The hydrogenerator has following parameters:

| | | | |
|---|---|---|---|
| $S_n$=158 MVA | $U_n$=13.8 kV | cos $\varphi_n$=0.90 | $T'_{d0}$=5.2 s |
| $x_d$=0.92 [pu] | $x_d'$=0.3 [pu] | $x_q$=0.51 [pu] | |
| $R_e$=0.02 [pu] | $X_e$=0.02 [pu] | D=2 [pu] | H=3.18 s s |

Table 2. Data for 158 MVA hydrogenerator

The loading variation, exciter and the voltage controller calculation is the same as in case of the analysed turbogenerator (Fig. 4).

After the numerical analysis of many typical turbo- and hydrogenerators of the nominal power between 9 MVA and 911 MVA, the region borders of the dominant complex conjugate eigenvalues has been caluclated. The angle $\psi$ denotes the deviation from the negative real axis and it is related to oscillations damping, whereas the natural frequency $\omega_0$

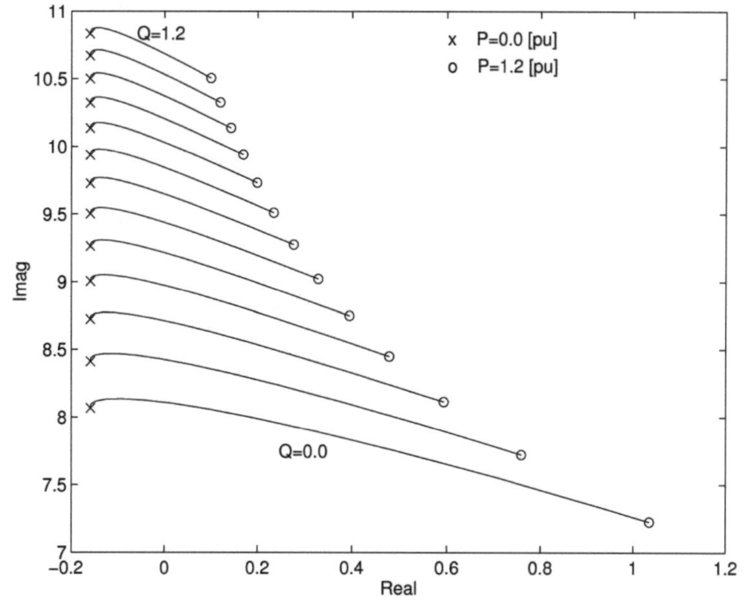


Fig. 5. Conjugate eigenvalue loci as a function of loading, hydrogenerator with voltage control system, 158 MVA

represents the distance from the origin and it is directly related to the oscillation frequency. Tables 3 and 4 show the region borders of dominant eigenvalues of the studied synchronous generators without and with the voltage control, respectively. It is evident that the voltage control loop with automatic voltage regulator greatly reduces oscillations damping.

| | $\psi_{min}(^o)$ | $\psi_{max}(^o)$ | $\omega_{0,min}(s^{-1})$ | $\omega_{0,max}(s^{-1})$ |
|---|---|---|---|---|
| turbogenerators | 79.9 | 89.6 | 3.8 | 17.3 |
| hydrogeneratos | 85.3 | 89.6 | 3.7 | 18.3 |

Table 3. The damping ratio and the natural frequency of complex conjugate eigenmodes of synchronous generators without voltage control loop

| | $\psi_{min}(^o)$ | $\psi_{max}(^o)$ | $\omega_{0,min}(s^{-1})$ | $\omega_{0,max}(s^{-1})$ |
|---|---|---|---|---|
| turbogenerators | 83.5 | 90.9 | 4.6 | 17.3 |
| hydrogeneratos | 88.6 | 92.4 | 4.6 | 18.3 |

Table 4. The damping ratio and the natural frequency of complex conjugate eigenmodes of synchronous generators with voltage control loop

From the analysis of the effect of different loadings on the synchronous generator dynamic characteristics can be concluded that the variations in the machine dynamics are considerable and therefore, an implementation of the adaptive power system stabilizer is meaningful.

## 3. MRAC based on command generator tracker theory

For the stabilization of the synchronous generator, the direct adaptive control (DAC) is used. The applied DAC procedure represents a simplified version of the MRAC based on command generator tracker theory (MRAC-CGT) (Kaufman et al., 1993).
The MRAC-CGT is considered for the controlled plant, which is described by

$$\dot{\mathbf{x}}_p(t) = \mathbf{A}_p\mathbf{x}_p(t) + \mathbf{B}_p\mathbf{u}_p(t) \tag{6}$$

$$\mathbf{y}_p(t) = \mathbf{C}_p\mathbf{x}_p(t) \tag{7}$$

where $\mathbf{x}_p(t)$ is the plant state vector, $\mathbf{u}_p(t)$ is the control vector, $\mathbf{y}_p(t)$ is the plant output vector, and $\mathbf{A}_p$, $\mathbf{B}_p$ and $\mathbf{C}_p$ are matrices of appropriate dimensions.
It is assumed that:

- the range of the plant matrices parameters is bounded,
- all possible pairs $\mathbf{A}_p$ and $\mathbf{B}_p$ are controllable and output stabilizable,
- all possible pairs $\mathbf{A}_p$ and $\mathbf{C}_p$ are observable.

The reference model is described by

$$\dot{\mathbf{x}}_m(t) = \mathbf{A}_m\mathbf{x}_m(t) + \mathbf{B}_m\mathbf{u}_m(t) \tag{8}$$

$$\mathbf{y}_m(t) = \mathbf{C}_m\mathbf{x}_m(t) \tag{9}$$

where $\mathbf{x}_m(t)$ is the model state vector, $\mathbf{u}_m(t)$ is the model command vector, $\mathbf{y}_m(t)$ is the model output vector and $\mathbf{A}_m$, $\mathbf{B}_m$ and $\mathbf{C}_m$ are matrices of appropriate dimensions. The model is assumed to be stable. The dimension of the model state may be less than the dimension of the plant state.
The output tracking error is defined as

$$\mathbf{e}_y(t) = \mathbf{y}_m(t) - \mathbf{y}_p(t) \tag{10}$$

The control $\mathbf{u}_p(t)$ for the plant output vector $\mathbf{y}_p(t)$ to approximate "reasonably well" the output of the reference model $\mathbf{y}_m(t)$ without explicit knowledge of $\mathbf{A}_p$, $\mathbf{B}_p$ and $\mathbf{C}_p$ is generated by the adaptive algorithm

$$\mathbf{u}_p(t) = \mathbf{K}_e(t)\mathbf{e}_y(t) + \mathbf{K}_x(t)\mathbf{x}_m(t) + \mathbf{K}_u(t)\mathbf{u}_m(t) \tag{11}$$

$$\mathbf{u}_p(t) = \mathbf{K}(t)\mathbf{r}(t) \tag{12}$$

where

$$\mathbf{K}(t) = [\mathbf{K}_e(t), \mathbf{K}_x(t), \mathbf{K}_u(t)] \tag{13}$$

$$\mathbf{r}^T(t) = [\mathbf{e}_y^T(t), \mathbf{x}_m^T(t), \mathbf{u}_m^T(t)] \tag{14}$$

The adaptive gains $\mathbf{K}(t)$ are obtained as a combination of the "proportional" and "integral" terms

$$\mathbf{K}(t) = \mathbf{K}_P(t) + \mathbf{K}_I(t) \tag{15}$$

$$\mathbf{K}_P(t) = \mathbf{e}_y(t)\mathbf{r}^T(t)\mathbf{T} \tag{16}$$

$$\dot{\mathbf{K}}_I(t) = \mathbf{e}_y(t)\mathbf{r}^T(t)\overline{\mathbf{T}} - \sigma\mathbf{K}_I(t) \tag{17}$$

where σ-term is introduced in order to avoid divergence of the integral gains in the presence of disturbance, **T** and $\overline{\mathbf{T}}$ are positive definite and positive semi-definite adaptation coefficient matrices, respectively. The necessary condition for asymptotic tracking when $u_m$(t) is a step command is

- the existence of a solution to the MRAC-CGT equation and
- the existence of the feedback gain $\mathbf{K}_e$ (not needed for implementation) so that

$$\mathbf{H}(s) = \mathbf{C}_p(s\mathbf{I} - \mathbf{A}_p + \mathbf{B}_p\mathbf{K}_e\mathbf{C}_p)^{-1}\mathbf{B}_p \tag{18}$$

is strictly positive real. In this case the controlled plant is said to be almost strictly positive real (ASPR).

When the number of inputs is greater than or equal to the number of outputs, the solutions of MRAC-CGT equation almost always eqists.

If the controlled plant is not ASPR, the augmenting of the plant with parallel dynamics such that the augmented plant is ASPR is suggested. In this case the previously described adaptive controller may be utilized.

For the non-ASPR plant described by the transfer matrix

$$\mathbf{G}_p(s) = \mathbf{C}_p(s\mathbf{I} - \mathbf{A}_p)^{-1}\mathbf{B}_p \tag{19}$$

the feedforward compensation is defined by the strictly proper transfer function matrix $\mathbf{R}_p$(s) with the realization:

$$\dot{\mathbf{s}}_p(t) = \mathbf{A}_s\mathbf{s}_p(t) + \mathbf{B}_s\mathbf{u}_p(t) \tag{20}$$

$$\mathbf{r}_p(t) = \mathbf{D}_s\mathbf{s}_p(t) \tag{21}$$

Instead of the plant output $\mathbf{y}_p$(t) augmented output $\mathbf{z}_p$(t) is to be controlled:

$$\mathbf{z}_p(t) = \mathbf{y}_p(t) + \mathbf{r}_p(t) \tag{22}$$

The augmented system is defined as

$$\mathbf{G}_a(s) = \mathbf{G}_p(s) + \mathbf{R}_p(s) \tag{23}$$

The feedforward compensator $\mathbf{R}_p$(s) is an inverse of a (fictious) stabilising controller for the plant, and must be selected such that the resulting relative degree of the augmented plant $\mathbf{G}_a$(s) is indeed 1: For example, if a plant $\mathbf{G}_p$(s) is stabilisable by PD controller, one can use its inverse that is just a simple first-order low-pass filter.

## 4. PSS based on direct adaptive control

The block diagram of the excitation system with the DAC stabilizer and inner automatic voltage regulation (AVR) loop is shown in Figure 6.

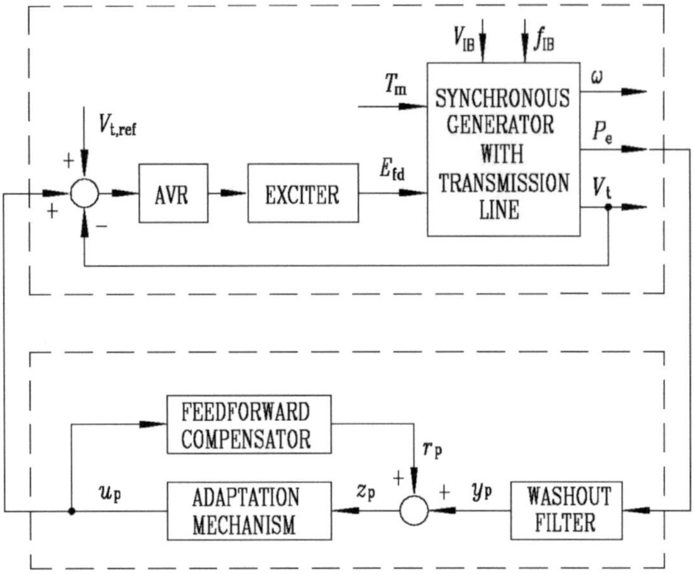


Fig. 6. Block diagram of the DAC-PSS structure

The benefit of the control diagram shown in Fig. 6 if compared to other adaptive structures is a very simple realization of the adaptation mechanism. The presented DAC-PSS is essentially simplified; because of the constant (zero) command signal, a reference model is namely not required.

The reference terminal voltage $V_{t,ref}$ and the mechanical torque $T_m$ represent the main disturbances which affect the synchronous generator dynamics. The variations of the synchronous generator loading can be treated as a controlled plant parameters perturbations. The washout filter is a part of the controlled plant. Such controlled plant does not satisfy the necessary ASPR conditions, therefore the augmenting of the controlled plant with the parallel feedforward compensator must be carried out. Adaptation mechanism is described by equations 11 to 17.

## 5. Simulation results

For the analysis and design of the power system stabilizer the simplified linear model of the synchronous generator is used.

Simulation results given on the basis of the simplified linear model, show the applicability of the DAC-PSS for small-signal disturbances and parameters perturbations rejections. But the simplified linear model does not include the effects of the synchronous generator, which could be restrictive for the usage of the adaptive control, basically designed for linear plants. In order to examine the influence of

- non-modeled dynamics and
- nonlinearities

the proposed DAC-PSS is tested with a non-linear seventh order model of a synchronous generator (Machowsky et al., 2008).

The typical 160 MVA synchronous generator is considered. Dynamics of the system inputs are the same in all cases. Their traces for the nominal operating point are shown in Fig. 7. As it can be seen in Fig. 8, the response of the generator without PSS is poorly damped; hence it is inevitable to use the PSS.

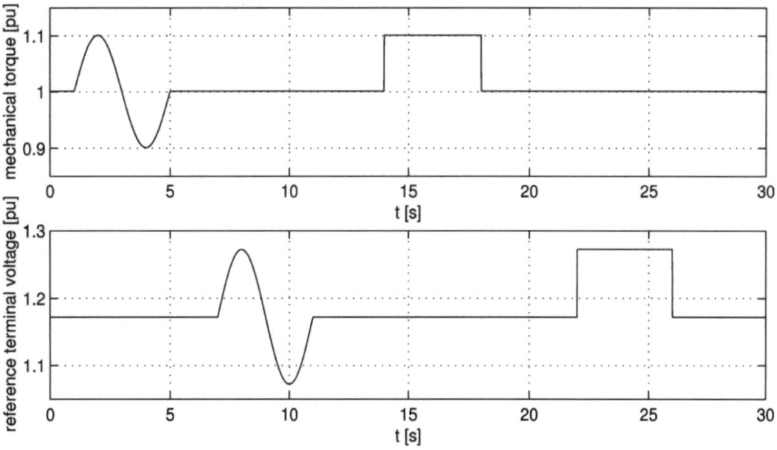


Fig. 7. Mechanical torque $T_m$ and reference terminal voltage $V_{t,ref}$

The adaptive controller consists of feedforward compensator, adaptation mechanism and washout filter.

The feed forward augmentation was defined as

$$\frac{r_p(s)}{u_p(s)} = \frac{k_{ff}}{sT_{ff}+1}, \tag{24}$$

and $k_p$ and $k_i$ denote proportional and integral gain,

$$k_p = T, \quad k_i = \bar{T}, \tag{25}$$

The parameters of the control system are shown in the Table 5:

| | | | |
|---|---|---|---|
| Feedforward compensator: | $k_{ff}$=1 | $T_{ff}$=0.1 s | |
| Washout filter time constant: | $T_w$=10 s | | |
| Adaptation mechanism coefficients: | $k_p$=1 | $k$i=100 | σ=0.1 |

Table 5. Control system data

The control system parameters $k_{ff}$, $T_{ff}$, $k_p$, $k_i$ and $\sigma$ were obtained using systematic analysis.

Fig. 9 and Fig. 10 show the synchronous generator behavior under small-signal disturbances:

- with DAC-PSS in the nominal operating point P=1.0 [pu], cos φ = 0.85, which corresponds to the dominant eigenvalues $p_{1,2}$=-0.49 ± j 10.67,
- with DAC-PSS in the operating point P=1.25 [pu], cos φ = 0.95, which corresponds to the dominant eigenvalues $p_{1,2}$=+0.0.033 ± j 10.30 (unstable)

The proposed DAC-PSS assures the damping improvement in the complete operating range.

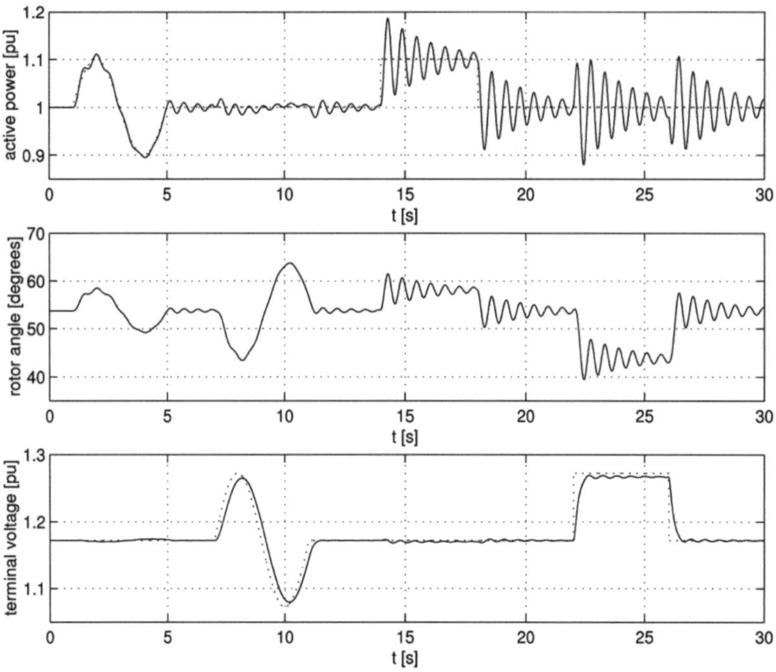


Fig. 8. Generator active power $P_e$, rotor angle $\delta$ and terminal voltage $V_t$ in the nominal operating point without PSS

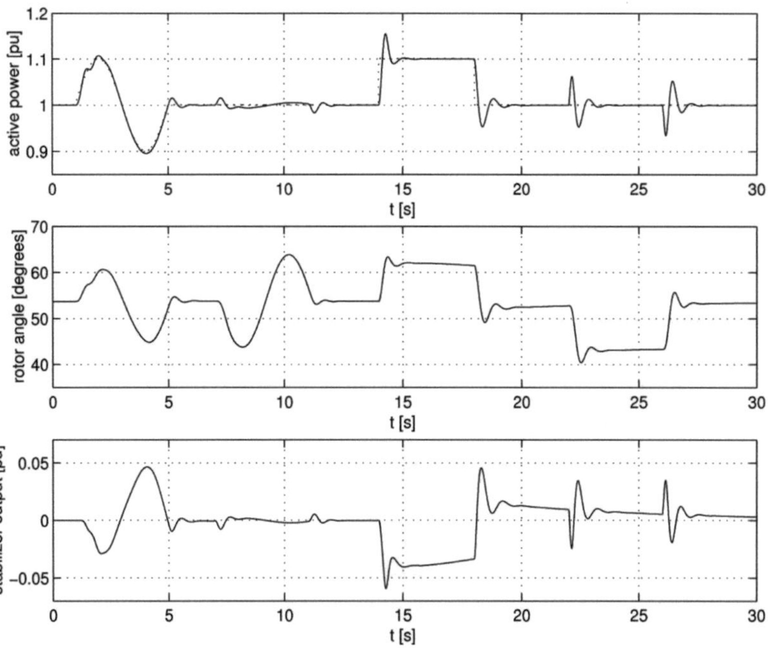


Fig. 9. Generator active power $P_e$, rotor angle $\delta$ and stabilizer output $u_p$ in the nominal operating point with DAC-PSS

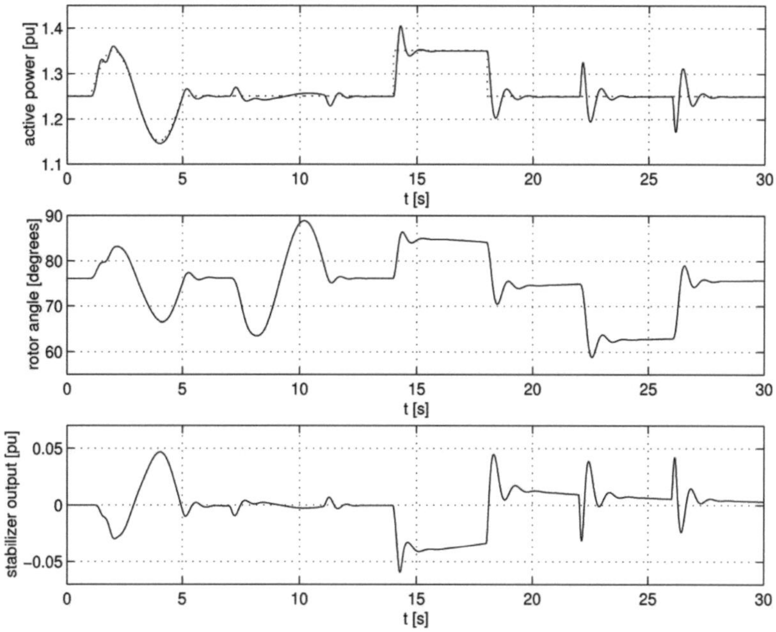


Fig. 10. Generator active power $P_e$, rotor angle $\delta$ and stabilizer output $u_P$ in the unstable operating point $P$=1.25 [pu], cos $\varphi$ = 0.95 with DAC-PSS

The bursting phenomenon is notable from the simulation. In the case when the unstable controlled plant (operating point $P$=1.25 [pu], cos $\varphi$ =0.95 has no disturbances during a long period of time, the system ends with oscillations of the active power and of the adaptive gain. The oscillations begin approximately at 1200 s after the last disturbance. To avoid the bursting phenomenon, **K**(t), obtained from equations (15) to (17) and used in equation (12), can be replaced by **K**(t), calculated from:

$$\mathbf{K}_{bf}(t) = \mathbf{K}(t) + \mathbf{K}_0 \tag{26}$$

where $\mathbf{K}_0$ is any constant output feedback gain that stabilizes the controlled plant ($\mathbf{K}_0 \geq \mathbf{K}_{min}$). The bursting phenomenon is shown in Fig. 11.

## 6. Experimental results

The presented DAC-PSS is implemented on a lab size testing system, composed of a 35 kW DC motor with current control as prime mover, a 28 kVA synchronous generator, connected to the infinite bus, 3-phase 6-pulse thyristor exciter, active power and terminal voltage measuring units, necessary analog low pass filters and an PC with AD/DA peripherie card used for implementing AVR and PSS scheme. Disturbances are created by altering DC motor mechanical torque. Generator active power responses during the disturbances are recorded by PC.

Results show again that the DAC-PSS provides more effective and reliable damping. Diagram of the testing system is shown in Fig. 12, with measured testing results shown in Fig. 13.

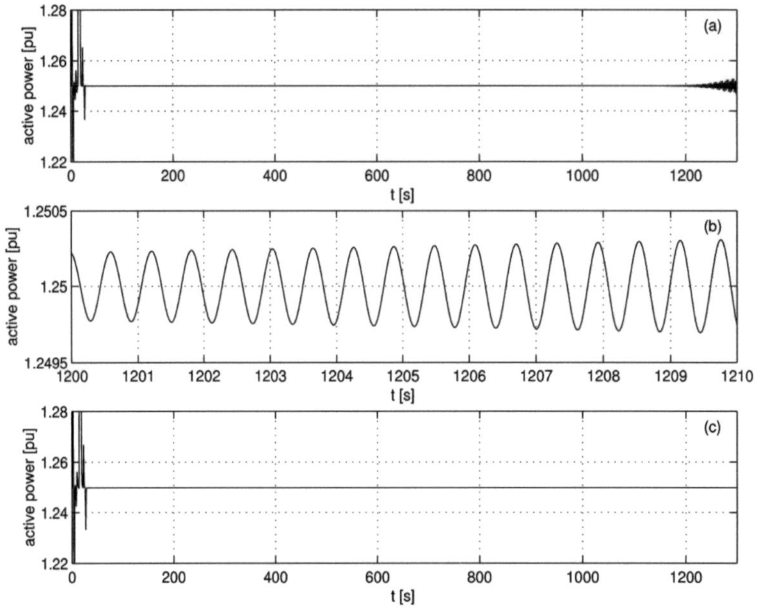


Fig. 11. Bursting phenomenon - generator active power $P_e$ in the nominal operating point with DAC-PSS: a) $\mathbf{K}_0$=0, b) $\mathbf{K}_0$=0 (zoom) and c) $\mathbf{K}_0$=0.5

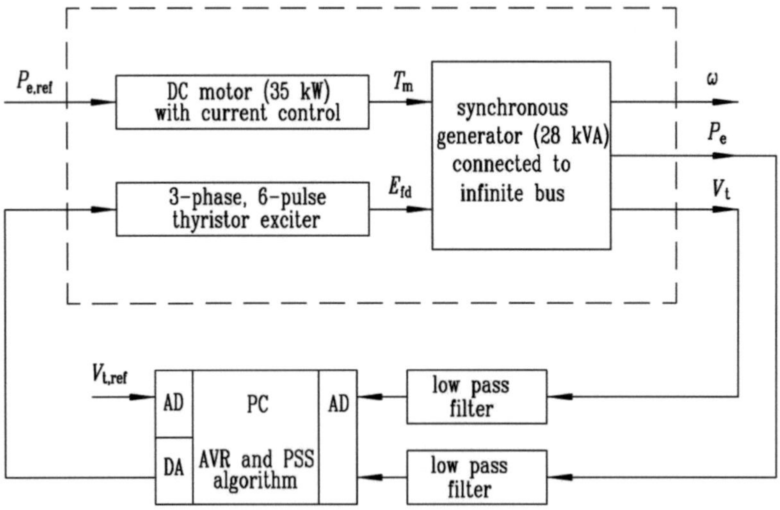


Fig. 12. Testing system block diagram

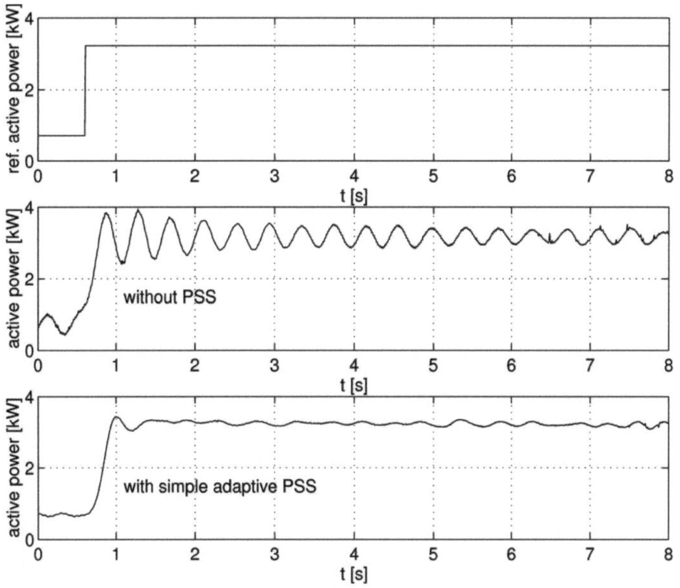


Fig. 13. Experimental results: the variation of the reference active power $P_{e,ref}$ and the generator active power $P_e$ responses without PSS and with DAC-PSS

## 7. Conclusion

This chapter examines the synchronous generator stability and the implementation of the adaptive stabilizer based on direct adaptive control. The simplified linearised model eigenvalue analysis for the synchronous generator without and with voltage control loop show the insufficiency of the conventional stabilizer. The use of the developed adaptive stabilizer is recommended. The advantage of the presented concept is unsophisticated realization and optimal damping in entire operating range. The results of simulations and experiments show essential improvement of stability.

## 8. References

Anderson, P. M. and Fouad, A. A. (1977), *Power system control and stability,* The Iowa State University Press, Ames, Iowa.

Bergen, A. R. (1986), *Power system analysis,* Prentice Hall Inc., Englewood Cliffs, New Jersey.

Cheng, S. and Chow, Y. S. and Malik, O. P. and Hope, G. S. (1986), An adaptive synchronous machine stabilizer, *IEEE Transactions on Power Systems,* vol. 1, no. 3 , pp. 101-107.

Chow, J. H. and Harris, L. P. and Kale, M. A. and Othman, H. A. and Sanchez-Gasca, J. J. (1990), "Robust control design of power system stabilizers using multivariable frequency domain techniques", *Proc. of the 29th Conference on Decision and Control, Honolulu Hawai,* pp. 2067-73.

Demello, F. P. and Concordia, C. (1969), Concepts of synchronous machine stability as affected by excitation control", *IEEE Tran. Power Appar. Syst.,* vol. 88, no. 4 , pp. 316-29.

Hassan, M. A. M. and Malik, O. P. (1993), Implementation and laboratory test results for a fuzzy logic based self tuned power system stabilizer, *IEEE Transactions on Energy Conversion*, vol. 8, no. 2 , pp. 221-228.

Heffron, W. G. and Phillips, R. A. (1952), Effect of modern amplidyne voltage regulator on underexcited operation of large turbine generators, *AIEE Transactions*, vol. 71, pp. 692-97.

Irving, E. and Barret, J. P. and Charcossey, C. and Monville, J. P. (1979), Improving power network stability and unit stress with adaptive generator control, *Automatica*, vol. 15, pp. 31-46.

Kaufman, H. and Bar-Khana, I. and Sobel, K. (1993), *Direct adaptive control algorithms*, Springer Verlag, New York.

Kundur, P. (1994), *Power system stability and control*, McGraw-Hill Inc. New York.

Landau, Y. D. (1979), *Adaptive control*, Marcel Dekker Inc., New York.

Law, K. T. and Hill, D. J. and Godfrey, N. R. (1994), Robust controller structure for coordinated power system voltage regulator and stabilizer design, *IEEE Transactions on Control System Technology*, no. 3 , pp. 220-232.

Ledwich, G. (1979), Adaptive excitation control, *Proc. IEE*, vol. 126, no. 3 , pp. 249-253.

Machowsky, J. and Bialek, J. W. and Bumby, J. R. (2008), *Power system dynamics, stability and control*, John Wiley and Sons, Ltd., West Susex, United Kingdom.

Mielcszarski, W. and Zajaczkowski, A. M., (1994), Nonlinear field voltage control of a synchronous generator using feedback linearization, *Automatica*, vol. 30, no. 10 , pp. 1625-1630.

Narendra, K. S. and Annaswamy, A. M. (1989), *Stable adaptive systems*, Prentice Hall Inc., Englewood Cliffs, New Jersey.

Ritonja, J. and Dolinar, D. and Grčar, B. (1995), Combined conventional-adaptive power system stabilizer, *IEEE/KTH Stockholm Power Tech Conference*, pp. 441-446.

Ritonja, J. and Dolinar, D. and Grčar, B. (2000), Simple adaptive control for a power system stabiliser, *IEE Proc.-Control Theory Appl.*, vol. 147, no. 4 , pp. 373-380.

Subbarao, G. V. and Iyer, A. (1993), "Nonlinear excitation and governor control using variable structures", Int. Journal of Control, vol. 57, no. 6 , pp. 1325-1342.

Zhang, Y. and Chen, G. P. and Malik, O. P. and Hope, G. S. (1993), "An artificial neural network based adaptive power system stabilizer ", IEEE Transactions on Energy Conversion., vol. 8, no. 1 , pp. 71-77.

# 12

# General Theory and Practice of Basic Models in the Building of Hydroacoustical Antennas

Zvonimir Milošić
*Institute for Research and Development of Defence Systems - MoD, HR 10000 Zagreb, Croatia*

## 1. Introduction

The general form of a model of electromechanical vibration system with concentrated parameters, presented in Fig. 1.1., is a good example for the input in the analysis of transmit and receive sensitivity of hydroacoustical transducer. A well known model of electromechanical elements transformed in electrical substitute components of hydroacoustic transducer, presents a widely known procedure for de-embedding its different characteristics which are necessary in producing of antenna. This procedure has been derived on an idealized model of block scheme of hydroacoustic transducer on the level of electrical analogy of all electric and mechanical parameters. In a hydroacoustical system with one piezoelectric element (hydrophone), different values of a phase angle at electric clamps come from phase relations of mechanical force and vibration velocity in a mechanical vibration system.

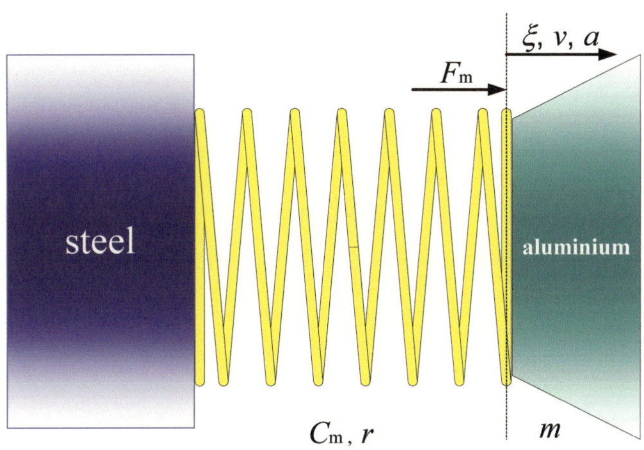


Fig. 1.1. Model of illustration of general mechanical system with potential mechanical force, vibrating spring and concentrated parameters of mass

This general form of a mechanical model of vibration of medium with concentrated mechanical parameters presented as a starting point of analysis of receive sensitivity of hydroacoustical transducers on the basis of well known differential equations (Aronov &

Matveev 1953) and with Laplace transformation has very complex mathematical solves which in the domain of the complex variable have a special usability and meaning.
On the level of mathematical solves in the domain of the complex variable harmonic motions are characterised by the values as follows,
$F$(N)=$F_m$(N)-the amplitude of mechanical force on the elastic system of motion and vibration is at the same time an active generator of mechanically forced vibrations/oscillations. The mechanical force brings piezoelectric system in interaction with piezoelectric effect of electrical force with mechanical mass of the system. In that case, $F(t)$ as mechanical force in dependence of time $t$, is given in a general form as follows

$$F(t)=F_m e^{j\omega t}= F e^{j\omega t} \tag{1.1}$$

The amplitude of harmonic motion, elongation-$\xi_m$(m), or the highest displacement of material point of elastic medium to the central position of motion, and $\xi(t)$ as displacement of material point of elastic medium to the point at the beginning as a function of time $t$ in general form, can be in the phase of moving to the mechanical force and it can be written in mathematical form as follows

$$\xi(t)=\xi_m e^{j(\omega t-\psi)} \tag{1.2}$$

where is
$T$(s)-time as a period of one vibration of material point of mass,
$\omega$(rad/s)-angular velocity as frequency of mechanical oscillator or number of vibrations in 2π seconds,
$t$(s)-time,
$\psi$(rad)-phase angle of phase shift of deviation of material point in given time $t$ in the reference to mechanical force $F$ damped with mass $m$
$v$(m/s)-velocity as value of velocity of projection of material point on axes which is parallel to elongation, this is explained as the change of distance in time

$$v(t)=\frac{\partial \xi}{\partial t} \tag{1.3}$$

or simpler in a symbolic form, when we have

$$v=v(t)= \xi' \tag{1.4}$$

As the first derivation of moving in time, the velocity of material point in elastic medium is

$$v=j\omega \cdot \xi_m \cdot e^{j(\omega t-\psi}$$

$$v=v_m \cdot e^{j(\omega t-\psi+\pi/2)} \tag{1.5}$$

with amplitude of this velocity $v_m= \omega \cdot \xi_m$.
Furthermore, the acceleration of a particle in harmonic motion $a(t)$ in a mathematical form is equal

$$a(t)=\frac{\partial v}{\partial t}=\frac{\partial^2 \xi}{\partial t^2} \tag{1.6}$$

or simpler, in a symbolic form we can write

$$a = \xi'' \tag{1.7}$$

After a double derivation of displacement $\xi(t)$ as a variable in time $t$ we have a symbolic form as follows

$$\xi'' = -\omega^2 \cdot \xi \cdot e^{j(\omega t - \psi)} = -\omega^2 \cdot \xi(t) \tag{1.8}$$

Using the known meaning of parameters in mechanics, we can arrive to the known differential equation as follows

$C$(m/N)-constant of mechanical elasticity of the vibration system of concentrated parameters,

$m$(kg)-mass of material point,

$r$(Ns/m)-resistance of friction and mechanical losses in the vibration system

$\delta$(1/s)-factor of suppressing of mechanical vibration defined by $r$ and $m$ in mathematical relation as follows

$$\delta = \frac{r}{2m} \tag{1.9}$$

By introducing partial expressions for all forms of energies contained in different forces, we have the force of elastic system $F_e$ as follows

$$F_e = \frac{\xi(t)}{C_m} = \frac{\xi}{C_m} \tag{1.10}$$

The force of acceleration $F_a$ of mass $m$ in moving is

$$F_a = m \cdot a(t) = m \cdot \xi'' \tag{1.11}$$

The force of resistance of friction and mechanical losses in the vibration system is

$$F_t = r \cdot v(t) = r \cdot \xi' \tag{1.12}$$

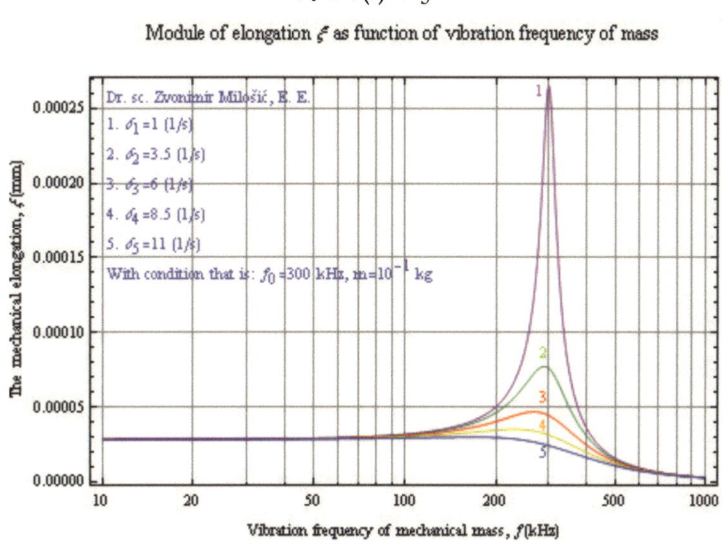


Fig. 1.2 Dependence of module of elongation of mass $\xi(f)$ with concentrated parameters on working frequency $f$

The balance of energy is made by the balance of all forces in a harmonic vibration system and then we get a differential equation as follows

$$m\cdot\xi''+r\cdot\xi'+\xi/C_m=F\cdot e^{j\omega t} \tag{1.13}$$

By using mathematical expression for $\omega_0$ as a parameter in conditions of mechanical resonance, we have

$$\omega_0^2=\frac{1}{m\cdot C_m} \tag{1.14}$$

and with a factor of choking and damping of mechanical vibration $\delta$ in (1.9) we have a symbolic form of differential equation as follows

$$\xi''+2\delta\cdot\xi'+\omega_0^2\cdot\xi=\frac{F}{m}\cdot e^{j\omega t} \tag{1.15}$$

To solve this differential equation we need to determine the beginning conditions of displacement of a material point of the vibration system in $t$=0. By using differential solves of stationer state we can get Fig. 1.2 as a model of physical state of the matter. We have two important fields in the frequency domain of hydroacoustic transducer sensitivity: constant value of displacement of material point in medium and the field of resonance.

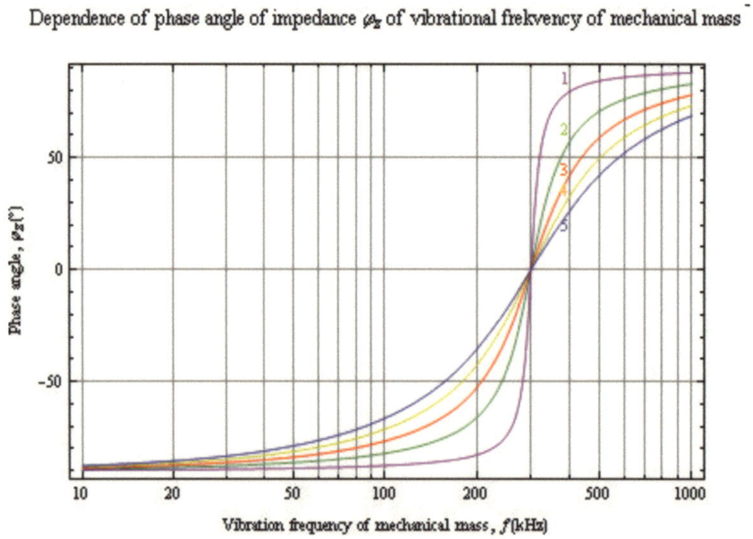


Fig. 1.3 Dependence of phase angle of working frequency $f$ of elongation of mass $\xi(f)$ with concentrated parameters as function on vibration frequency

On the other hand, according to Fig. 1.3, the values of phase angles with too high dispersion of different parameters at a receive multi-element antenna can have negative influences on the parameters which are very important for detection, in the resolution and in the less of great ranges of sonars and medicine ultrasound scanners, too. Accordingly, with the analysis of the behaviour of mathematical functions of sensitivity and sources of wide dispersion of phase angles of antenna elements at hydroacoustical and ultrasound transducers, we can choose the best model for an optimal range in the given system.

## 2. The accordance of a model of mechanical vibration system with concentrated parameters and composed hydroacoustical transducer

On the basis of their mathematical solutions we analyze the frequency characteristic of receive sensitivity of hydrophone. In a hydroacoustical antenna system with one piezoelectric element (hydrophone) the values of phase angles on electrical clamps come from phase relations of mechanical vibrations in an electromechanical vibration system of single elements.

The value of a phase angle is not of great importance and influence on other parameters of single elements. On the other hand, the values of a phase angle with too wide dispersion of different parameters of single element at receive multi-elemental antenna, can have negative influence on parameters, which is very important for great ranges of sonars and medicine ultrasound scanners, too. Accordingly, with the analysis of the behavior of mathematical functions of sensitivity and sources of wide dispersion of phase angles of antenna elements at hydroacoustical and ultrasound transducers, we can choose the best model for optimal range in the given system.

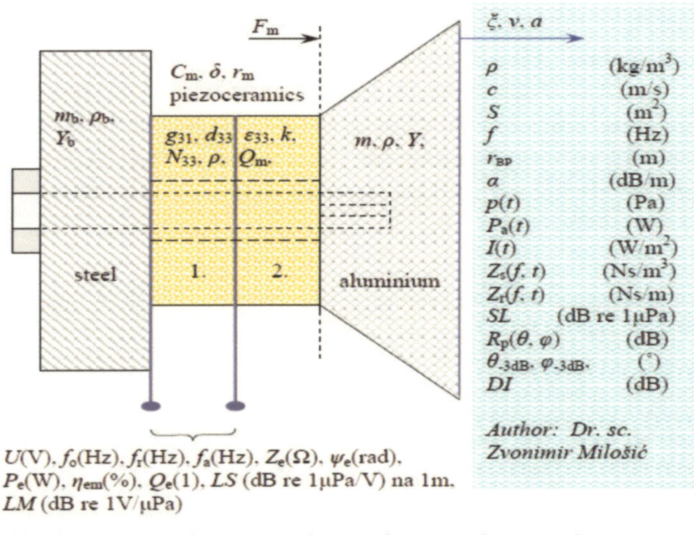


Fig.2.1 Model of hydroacoustical composed transducer with general positions of all parameters, ones on the side of water and others on the side of electrical ends and inside their mechanical body, (Milošić 2004)

### 2.1 Theory of hydroacoustical composed transducer in the form of two-port network(6pt)

In this chapter is presented the procedure of calculating some characteristics of hydroacoustical antenna. The procedure is derived on an idealized model of a electromechanical block scheme of hydroacoustical transducer, (Masson 1950, Beranek 1954, Kinsler&Frey 1962, Caruthers 1977, Sverdlin 1976, 1980, Bogorodskii&All 1983, Wilson 1998).

We analyze the complex behavior of mechanical vibration system of hydroacoustic transducer analyzing at electrical analogy of electric impedance on its electrical ends in specific conditions. We more often use the block scheme of hydroacoustical transducer in Fig. 2.1.1 as electromechanical two-port network devices in theory and practice of the system than in the construction analyses of the transducer.

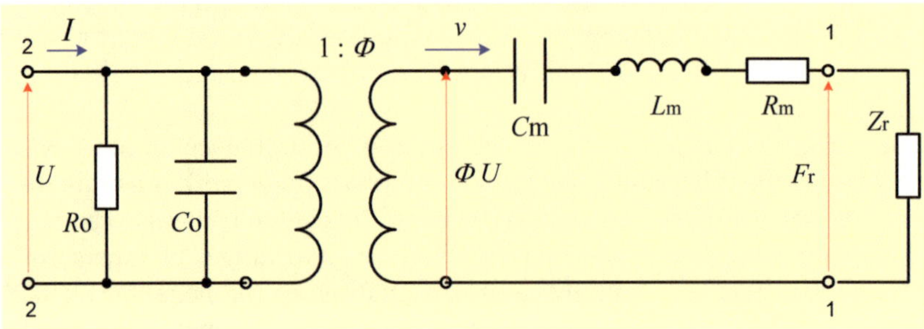


Fig. 2.1.1 Model of electromechanical block scheme of hydroacoustical composed transducer in the form of two-port network devices for determining electrical frequency characteristic of sensitivity

Mutual dependence of mechanical and electrical components of parameters is defined by coefficient of mechanical transformation $\Phi$ (N/V). The balance of electromechanical vibration system must be realized at all lines of spreading of the sound, from source of electric energy to impedance of radiation of acoustical energy and reversely.

By using the model of electromechanical block scheme Fig. 2.1.1 of hydroacoustical transducer on the left electrical circuit, we can write that is

$$I=UY_0+\Phi v \tag{2.1.1}$$

Mechanical vibration system in the second circuit on the right is in balance with equation (2.1.2) also, and then yield

$$F=\Phi U+vZ_m \tag{2.1.2}$$

But, on the other hand, we can introduce mechanical force $F$ and vibration of velocity of the transducer face of effective surface in equation (2.1.3), as

$$v=-\frac{F}{Z_r} \tag{2.1.3}$$

In this case, we have three equations as starting points for different directions with solves of different important parameters of hydroacoustic transducer.

## 2.2 The de-embedding of electric input impedance of hydroacoustical transducers

By using three equations (2.1.1), (2.1.2) and (2.1.3) we can get electric input impedance at port 2-2 in general form as in equation (2.2.1) which is in accordance with equation (2.14) at reference (Caruthers 1977). Electric form of block scheme is given in Fig. 2.2.1.

$$Z_{in}=R_{in}+jx_{in} \tag{2.2.1}$$

In accordance with equations above, we have a general form of real and imaginary part of impedance, then yield

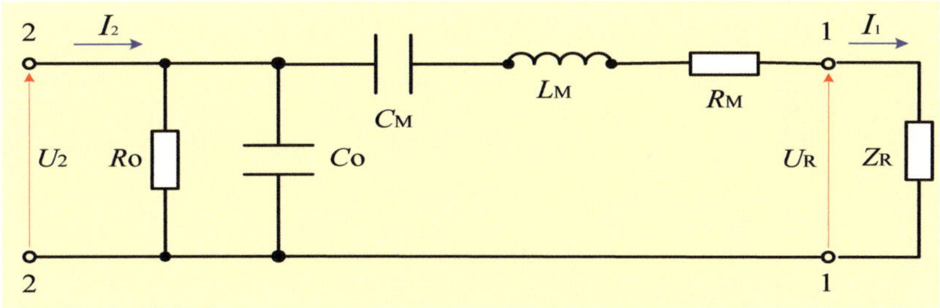


Fig. 2.2.1 Electric block scheme is given in a general form of equation of electric parameters on the input and electric analogy of mechanical parameters of vibration system

$$R_{\text{in}} = R_{\text{t}} = \frac{R_0 x_0 (R_{\text{MR}}{}^2 + x_{\text{M}}{}^2)(R_0 R_{\text{MR}} x_0 + R_{\text{MR}}{}^2 x_0 + x_0 x_{\text{M}}{}^2)}{(R_0 R_{\text{MR}} x_0 + R_{\text{MR}}{}^2 x_0 + x_0 x_{\text{M}}{}^2)^2 + (R_0 x_0 x_M + R_0 R_{\text{MR}}{}^2 + R_0 x_M{}^2)^2} \quad (2.2.2)$$

$$x_{\text{in}} = x_{\text{t}} = \frac{R_0 x_0 (R_{\text{MR}}{}^2 + x_{\text{M}}{}^2)(R_0 x_{\text{M}} x_0 + R_{\text{MR}}{}^2 R_0 + R_0 x_{\text{M}}{}^2)}{(R_0 R_{\text{MR}} x_0 + R_{\text{MR}}{}^2 x_0 + x_0 x_{\text{M}}{}^2)^2 + (R_0 x_0 x_M + R_0 R_{\text{MR}}{}^2 + R_0 x_M{}^2)^2} \quad (2.2.3)$$

where is

$\Phi$(N/V)-factor of electro-mechanical transformation of electrical parameters in associated mechanic parameters and reverse (electric voltage $U$(V) in mechanical force $F$(N)),

$R_0$(Ω)-resistor of electrical losses in piezoelectric material, can be measured with electrical tools at input electric clamps of transducer,

$C_0$(F)-electrical capacity of condenser of piezoelectric material at input clamp of electromechanical transducer, can be calculated from catalogue data and mechanical dimensions or measured with electrical tools at input electric clamps of transducer,

$Z_0$(Ω)-the clamped electric impedance as reciprocity value of electric admittance $Y_0$ calculated from data of parallel connection of $R_0$ and $C_0$ to Fig. 2.2.1,

$C_M$(F)-electrical capacity as analogous of mechanical system as mechanical capacitance defined as $C_m$. It can be calculated from catalogue data and data of special measured tools of transducer,

$$C_M = \Phi^2 C_m \quad (2.2.4)$$

$L_M$(H)-electric inductivity as analogous of elasticity of mechanical system defined as $L_m$. It can be calculated from catalogue data and data of measured tools of transducer,

$$L_M = L_m / \Phi^2 \quad (2.2.5)$$

$R_M$(Ω)-electric resistor as analogous of mechanical resistance of mechanical system defined as $R_m$. It can be calculated from catalogue data and data of measured tools of transducer,

$$R_M = R_m / \Phi^2 \quad (2.2.6)$$

$Z_M$(Ω)-electric impedance as analogous of mechanical impedance of mechanical system defined as $Z_m$. We calculate it from calculated and measured data as follows,

$$Z_M = R_M + jx_M = R_M + j(x_L + x_C) = R_M + j(\omega L_M - 1/\omega C_M) = Z_m/\Phi^2 \quad (2.2.7)$$

$R_R$(Ω)-electric resistor as analogous of acoustical resistance of acoustical effective radiated surface of system defined as $R_r$ which presents the resistance of radiation of value of sound energy, can be calculated from catalogue data and data of measured tools of transducer,

$$R_R = R_r / \Phi^2 = \rho c A K_R / \Phi^2 \qquad (2.2.8)$$

$x_R(\Omega)$-electric reactive resistor as analogous of acoustical reactance of acoustical effective radiated surface of system defined as $x_r$ which presents the reactance of radiation system of sound energy, can be calculated from catalogue data and data of measured tools of transducer. In fact we make it to be zero or to obtain to zero ($x_R \rightarrow 0$),

$$x_R = x_r / \Phi^2 = \rho c A K_x / \Phi^2 \qquad (2.2.9)$$

$A(m^2)$-effective aperture, effective surface of radiated face of transducer,
$\rho(kg/m^3)$-specific mass of water as medium of spreading of sound,
$c(m/s)$-velocity of sound in water or people's body. Velocity in the sea is complex function of a lot of parameters, but approximately, we can take that $c \approx 1500$ m/s
$Z_R(\Omega)$-electrical value of acoustic radiation impedance $Z_r$ presents the value and character of radiated acoustic energy in space. We calculate it from data of $R_R$ and $x_R$ as follows

$$Z_R = R_R + jx_R = Z_r / \Phi^2 = \rho c A (K_R + K_x) / \Phi^2 \qquad (2.2.10)$$

$K_R(1)$-coefficient of acoustic resistance $R_r$ as real part of acoustical radiated impedance. By using Bessel and Struve special functions we can calculate it at piston model of transducer (Caruthers 1977) and it is shown in Fig. 2.2.2, but mainly using cylindrical model of transducer, we can calculate it with equation by using special Hankel functions (Rževkin 1960, Smarišev 1973) or we take data in Fig. 2.2.3.
$K_x(1)$-coefficient of acoustic reactance $x_r$ as imaginary part of acoustically radiated impedance at mentioned figures,

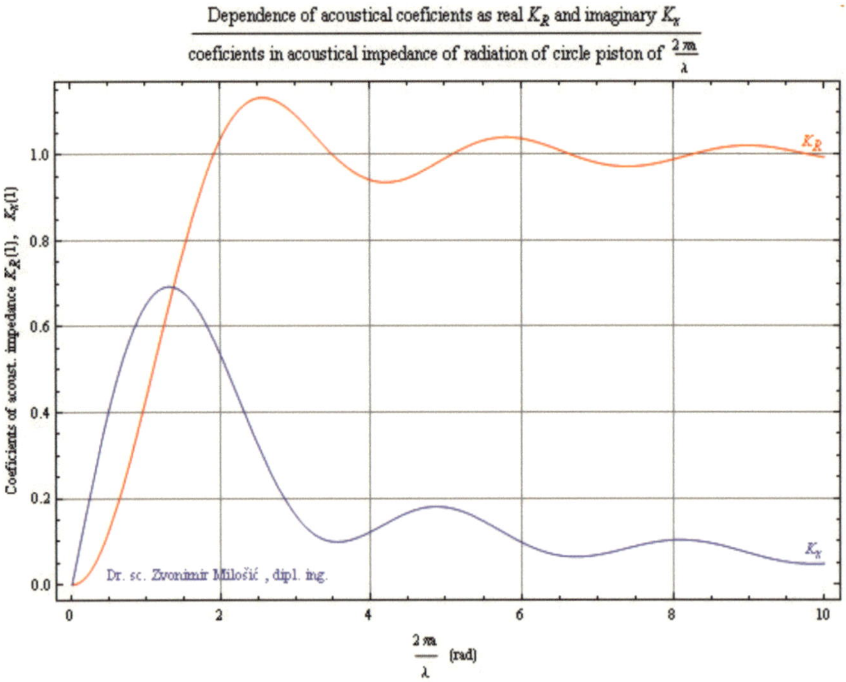


Fig. 2.2.2 Graphic presentation of data for $K_R$ and $K_x$ at circle piston model of transducer

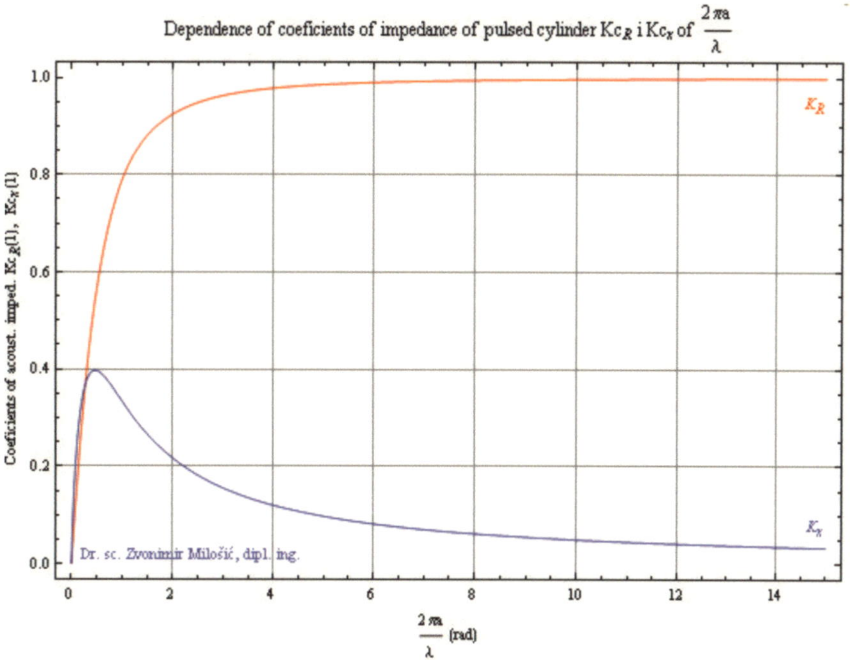


Fig. 2.2.3 Graphic presentation of data for $K_R$ and $K_x$ at cylindrical model of transducer

In fact, according to the graph in Fig. 2.2.3, we can choose a transducer with cylindrical radiated face as a great advantage because in an equal volume cylinder, in relation to the piston transducer or to the composed transducer, it has a higher voltage sensitivity and lower reactive radiated impedance. Keeping in line with this logic, using transducers with cylindrical radiated face at circle (barrel) antennas systems in receive is very often.

If we assume that $R_0$ is infinite or increase to infinite, we have good conditions for special impedance analysis in frequency domain. By using mathematical operator 'limes' at expressions (2.2.2) and (2.2.3) with $R_0 \to 0$ we have shorter equations as follows

$$R_{in} = R_t = \frac{R_{MR} x_0^2 (R_{MR}^2 + x_M^2)}{R_{MR}^2 x_0^2 + (R_{MR}^2 + x_0 x_M + x_M^2)^2} \tag{2.2.11}$$

$$x_{in} = x_t = \frac{x_0 (R_{MR}^2 + x_M^2)(R_{MR}^2 + x_M x_0 + x_M^2)}{R_{MR}^2 x_0^2 + (R_{MR}^2 + x_0 x_M + x_M^2)^2} \tag{2.2.12}$$

By using different conditions of maximal and of minimal value of module of electric impedance $Z_t$ and admittance $Y_t$ and on condition that $x_t = x_{in} = 0$ if it is possible, we can de-embed the important series of frequencies as follows: $f_m < f_s < f_r < f_a < f_p < f_n$. Four of them: serial frequency $f_s$, resonance frequency $f_r$, anti-resonance frequency $f_a$ and frequency of parallel resonance of system $f_p$ in given conditions can be calculated to expressions as follows

$$f_s = \lim_{R_{MR} \to 0} f_r = \frac{1}{2\pi\sqrt{L_M C_M}} \tag{2.2.13}$$

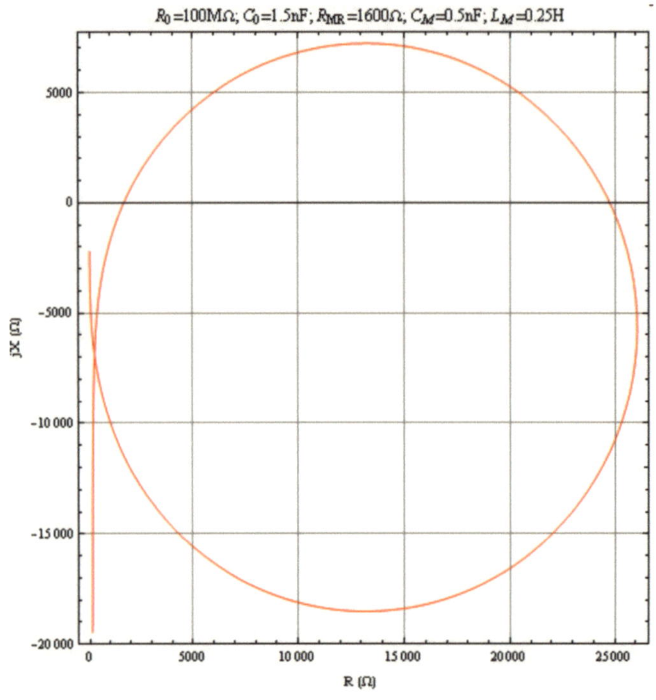


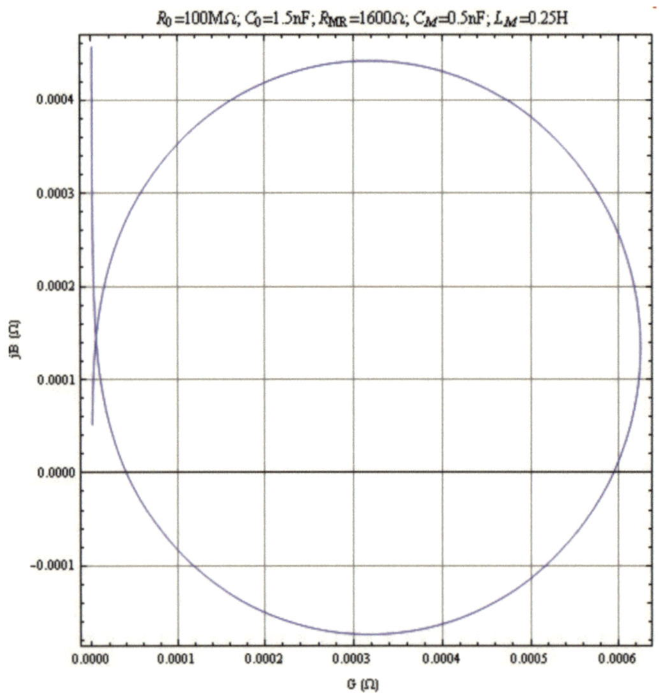


Fig. 2.2.4 Circle diagrams of input electric impedance and admittance of piezoelectric transducer at $R_{MR}$=1600Ω, $L_M$=0.25H, $C_M$=0.5nF i $C_0$=1.5nF, $R_c$=50Ω

$$f_{\mathrm{r}}=\frac{1}{2\pi}\cdot\sqrt{\frac{1}{2L_{\mathrm{M}}C_0}+\frac{1}{L_{\mathrm{M}}C_{\mathrm{M}}}-\frac{R_{\mathrm{MR}}{}^2}{2L_{\mathrm{M}}{}^2}-\sqrt{\frac{R_{\mathrm{MR}}{}^4}{4L_{\mathrm{M}}{}^4}+\frac{1}{4L_{\mathrm{M}}{}^2C_0{}^2}-\frac{R_{\mathrm{MR}}{}^2}{L_{\mathrm{M}}{}^3C_{\mathrm{M}}}-\frac{R_{\mathrm{MR}}{}^2}{2L_{\mathrm{M}}{}^3C_0}}} \tag{2.2.14}$$

$$f_{\mathrm{a}}=\frac{1}{2\pi}\cdot\sqrt{\frac{1}{2L_{\mathrm{M}}C_0}+\frac{1}{L_{\mathrm{M}}C_{\mathrm{M}}}-\frac{R_{\mathrm{MR}}{}^2}{2L_{\mathrm{M}}{}^2}+\sqrt{\frac{R_{\mathrm{MR}}{}^4}{4L_{\mathrm{M}}{}^4}+\frac{1}{4L_{\mathrm{M}}{}^2C_0{}^2}-\frac{R_{\mathrm{MR}}{}^2}{L_{\mathrm{M}}{}^3C_{\mathrm{M}}}-\frac{R_{\mathrm{MR}}{}^2}{2L_{\mathrm{M}}{}^3C_0}}} \tag{2.2.15}$$

$$f_{\mathrm{p}}=\lim_{R_{\mathrm{MR}}\to 0} f_{\mathrm{a}}=\frac{1}{2\pi}\sqrt{\frac{C_{\mathrm{M}}+C_0}{L_{\mathrm{M}}C_{\mathrm{M}}C_0}} \tag{2.2.16}$$

We de-embed two of the frequencies: $f_{\mathrm{m}}$ in relation to the minimum of module of electric impedance $Z_{\mathrm{t}}$ and $f_{\mathrm{n}}$ as frequency to the minimal value of admittance $Y_{\mathrm{t}}$ at circle impedance and admittance diagrams respectively. Yield at example, Fig. 2.2.4.

### 2.3 The matching of electric impedance of hydroacoustical transducers

In accordance with maximal efficiency and maximal transmission of electric energy and maximal relations of signal/noise, we can calculate parameters of matching with electric transformer to Fig. 2.3.1 or with *LC* transformer to Fig. 2.3.3 (Milošić 1978, 2004, 2010). On the other hand, in accordance with maximal efficiency for noise factor we need to make the matching of electric impedance in conditions for the lowest noise (Jelaković 1973).
The most suitable using of electric transformer is in active systems of transmitter with narrow band pass and stable transmitting frequency.
General forms of original equations for matching in the system with electric transformers are taken over from the mentioned literature (Milošić 2010) and we have as follows

$$w_{\mathrm{s}}=\sqrt{\frac{|Z_{\mathrm{tc}}|}{\omega A_L\cdot|\sin\psi_{\mathrm{tc}}|}}=\sqrt{\frac{|Z_{\mathrm{tc}}|}{2\pi f A_L}\cdot\frac{\sqrt{1+\tan^2\psi_{\mathrm{tc}}}}{|\tan\psi_{\mathrm{tc}}|}} \tag{2.3.1}$$

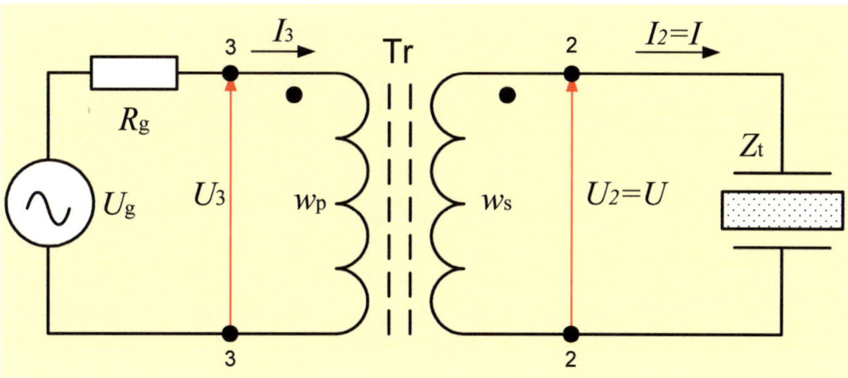


Fig. 2.3.1 Electric block scheme is given for general form of equation of electric parameters of electric transformer on input impedance of transducer $Z_{\mathrm{t}}$ (Milošić 1976, 2004, 2010)

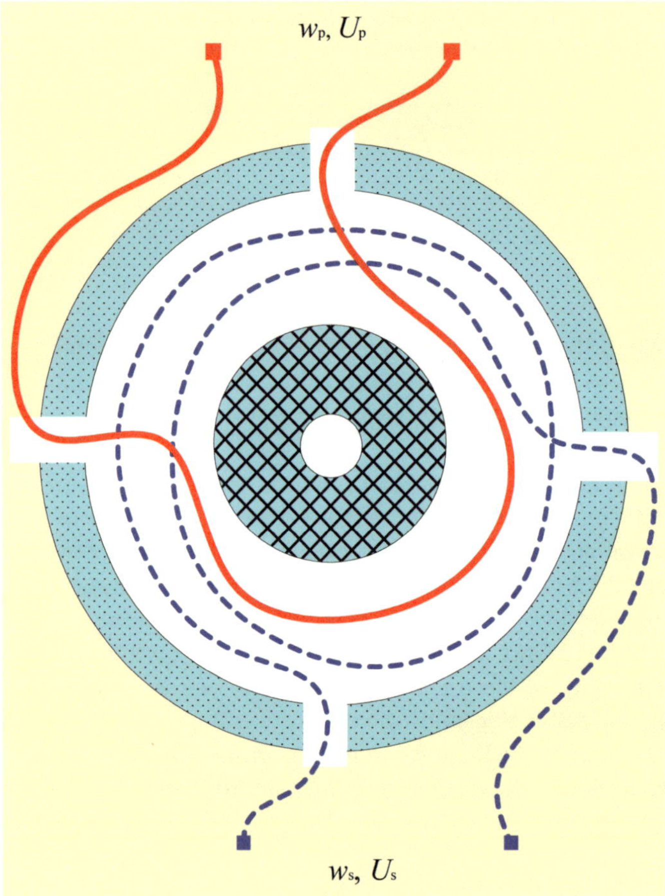


Fig. 2.3.2 The illustration of the turn spacing with the coiling conduct and the decimal value of the turn on the four-slot ferrite core, $w_p$=0.75 turn and $w_s$=1.75 of the turns in theory and in practice (Milošić 1978, 2010)

$$w_p = \sqrt{\frac{R_0}{A_L\omega \cdot |\tan\psi_{tc}|}} = \sqrt{\frac{R_0}{2\pi f A_L \cdot |\tan\psi_{tc}|}} \tag{2.3.2}$$

$$\left(\frac{w_s}{w_p}\right)^2 = \frac{R_t}{R_0} \cdot \frac{1}{\cos^2\psi_t} \tag{2.3.3}$$

On the other hand, *LC* electric transformer is good in wide band sonar systems in receiving of signals and at physically very composed systems of antenna. Given parameters of LC transformers can be calculated very fast and precisely to (2.3.4), (2.3.5) and (2.3.6).

$$C_{tr} = \frac{R_t - R_0}{2\pi f \cdot |Z_t| \cdot (-R_0 \sin\psi_t + \sqrt{R_0 R_t - R_0{}^2 \cos^2\psi_t})} \tag{2.3.4}$$

$$L_{tr} = \frac{1}{2\pi f} \cdot \frac{|Z_t|^2 x_C - x_C^2 |Z_t| \cdot \sin\psi_t}{|Z_t|^2 + x_C^2 - 2x_C |Z_t| \cdot \sin\psi_t} \tag{2.3.5}$$

$$\tan\psi_{in} = \tan\psi_t + \frac{R_t}{2\pi f A_L w_s^2} \cdot \frac{1}{\cos^2\psi_t} \tag{2.3.6}$$

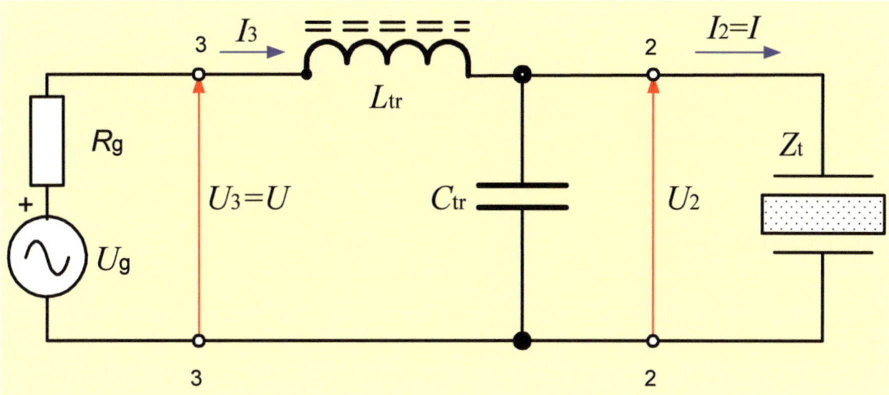


Fig. 2.3.3 Electric block scheme is given for general form of equation of electric parameters of *LC* transformer on input impedance of transducer $Z_t$ to reference (Milošić 1978, 2010)

## 3. The de-embedding of the level of transmitting voltage sensitivity of transducers – *LS* (dB re 1µPa/V at 1m)

Keeping in line with the de-embedding of the level of transmitting voltage sensitivity of transducer we need to eliminate the vibration velocity and with substituting equation (3.3) in (3.2) yield

$$F = \Phi U + vZ_m = \Phi U - FZ_m / Z_r \tag{3.1}$$

$$F\left(1 + \frac{Z_m}{Z_r}\right) = U\Phi \tag{3.2}$$

$$F = U\Phi \frac{Z_r}{Z_r + Z_m} = U\Phi \frac{Z_R \cdot \Phi^2}{Z_R \cdot \Phi^2 + Z_M \cdot \Phi^2} = U\Phi \frac{Z_R}{Z_R + Z_M} \quad \text{(N)} \tag{3.3}$$

On the other hand we have

$$F = pA \tag{3.4}$$

If we substitute (3.4) in (3.3) we have

$$pA = U\Phi \frac{Z_R}{Z_R + Z_M} \Big/ : UA$$

$$\frac{p}{U} = \frac{\Phi}{A} \frac{Z_R}{Z_R + Z_M} \tag{3.5}$$

and in accordance with the definition of transmitting voltage sensitivity $S$(Pa/V//1m) we have

$$S = \frac{p}{U} = \frac{\Phi}{A} \frac{Z_R}{Z_R + Z_M} \tag{3.6}$$

So we have that the level of transmitting voltage sensitivity - $LS$ is

$$LS = 20 \log |S| \quad \text{(dB re 1Pa/V//1m)} \quad \text{or} \tag{3.7}$$

$$LS = 20 \log |S| + 120 \quad \text{(dB re 1μPa/V//1m)} \tag{3.8}$$

By using (3.6) in the form of module value, we have that is

$$LS = 20 \cdot \log \left| \frac{\Phi}{A} \frac{Z_R}{Z_R + Z_M} \right| + 120 \quad \text{(dB re 1μPa/V//1m)} \tag{3.9}$$

Also, if we substitute the complex value of electric impedance $Z_R$ and $Z_M$ in equation (3.9) we get real and imaginary part of transmitting voltage sensitivity $S_{Re}$ and imaginary $S_{Im}$ as follows

$$S_{Re} = \frac{\Phi}{A} \frac{R_R (R_R + R_M)}{(R_R + R_M)^2 + x_M^2} \quad \text{(dB re 1μPa/V//1m)} \tag{3.10}$$

$$S_{Im} = \frac{\Phi}{A} \frac{R_R x_M}{(R_R + R_M)^2 + x_M^2} \quad \text{(dB re 1μPa/V//1m)} \tag{3.11}$$

If the module of transmitting voltage sensitivity $|S|$ is given to (3.12)

$$|S| = \sqrt{S_{Re}^2 + S_{Im}^2} \quad \text{(dB re 1μPa/V//1m)} \tag{3.12}$$

then in the end we have the level of transmitting voltage sensitivity as follows

$$LS = 20 \cdot \log |S| + 120 \quad \text{(dB re 1μPa/V//1m)} \tag{3.13}$$

where is
$S$(Pa/V)-transmitting voltage sensitivity $S=S_{Re}+S_{Im}$ of hydroacoustical transducer
$|S|$(Pa/V)-module of transmitting voltage sensitivity of hydroacoustical transducer
$LS$(dB re 1μPa/V)-level of transmitting voltage sensitivity of hydroacoustical transducer with references of pressure in water of $p_0$=1μPa and voltage of 1V,
In accordance with equation (3.13) we can show given solves in a practical example as follows in Fig. 3.1.

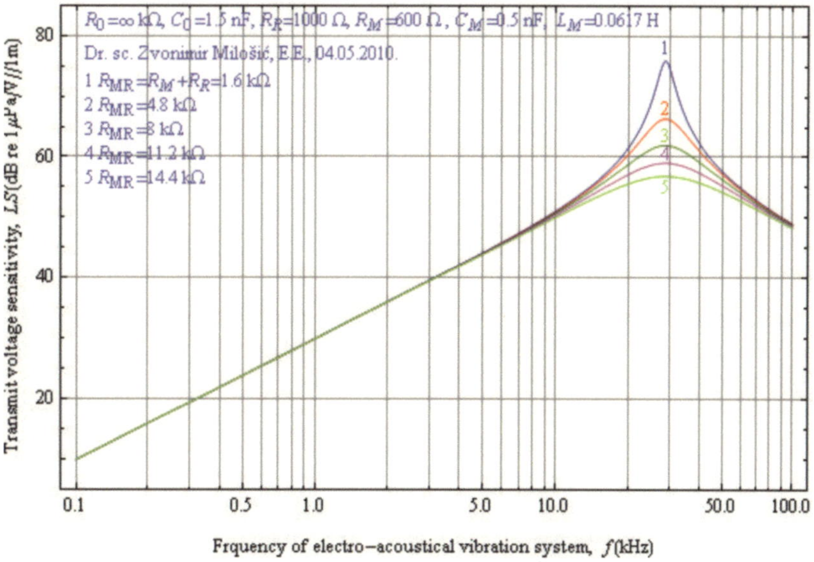


Fig. 3.1 Level of transmitting voltage sensitivity of piezoelectric transducer - *LS*

## 4. The de-embedding of the level of the receive voltage sensitivity of transducers – *LM* (dB re 1V/μPa)

By using equations (2.1.1), (2.1.2), (2.1.3) and (3.4) to Fig. 4.1 in the system with equivalent electric elements and *LC* transformer we have that partial receive voltage sensitivity $M_{22}$ at port 2 and at clamps 2-2 is defined by real and imaginary parts of impedances as follows.

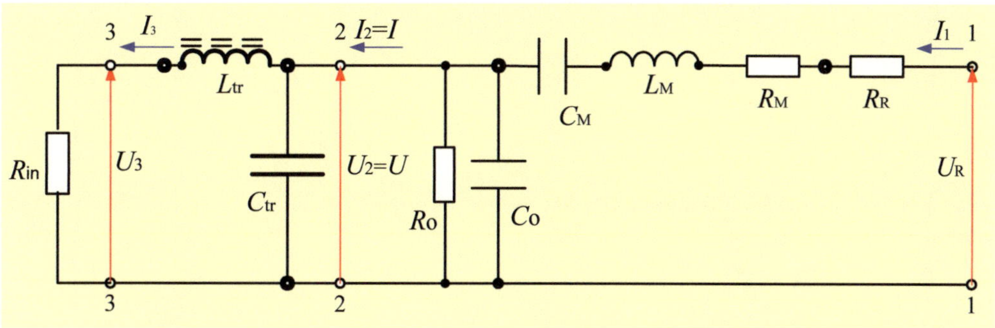


Fig. 4.1 Electric block scheme for general form of equation of electric parameters on input and electric analogies of mechanical parameters of vibration system with *LC* transformer

$$M_{r22} = \frac{A}{\Phi} \frac{R_0 X_0 \left[ R_{MR} X_0 + R_0 (X_0 + X_M) \right]}{\left[ R_{MR} X_0 + R_0 (X_0 + X_M) \right]^2 + (X_0 X_M - R_{MR} R_0)^2} \quad \text{(V/Pa)} \qquad (4.1)$$

$$M_{i22} = \frac{A}{\Phi} \frac{R_0 X_0 (R_0 X_M - R_{MR} X_0)}{\left[ R_{MR} X_0 + R_0 (X_0 + X_M) \right]^2 + (X_0 X_M - R_{MR} R_0)^2} \quad \text{(V/Pa)} \qquad (4.2)$$

These solves of receive voltage sensitivity have special solves with special values of resistor of losses $R_0$. If we divide (at real $M_{r22}$ and imaginary $M_{i22}$) the numerator and denominator with the product of $R_0X_0$ and for $R_0$>>, we can apply 'limes' with $R_0\to\infty$, yields

$$\lim_{R_0\to\infty} M_{r22} = \frac{A}{\Phi}\cdot\frac{X_0(X_0+X_M)}{{R_{MR}}^2+(X_0+X_M)^2} \quad (\mathrm{V/Pa}) \tag{4.3}$$

$$\lim_{R_0\to\infty} M_{i22} = \frac{A}{\Phi}\cdot\frac{R_{MR}X_0}{{R_{MR}}^2+(X_0+X_M)^2} \quad (\mathrm{V/Pa}) \tag{4.4}$$

By using real and imaginary part of receive voltage sensitivity in the de-embedding and plotting of characteristics of level of receive voltage sensitivity in the complex form of presentation, yields that the module of complex value is

$$M_{22} = \sqrt{{M_{r22}}^2+{M_{i22}}^2} \quad (\mathrm{V/Pa}) \tag{4.5}$$

In accordance with the general definition for level of receive voltage sensitivity $LM_{22}$ at clamps 2-2, at valid reference of $p_0$=1 μPa in hydroacoustics, we have

$$LM_{22} = 20\log M_{22} - 120 \quad (\mathrm{dB\ re\ 1V/\mu Pa}) \tag{4.6}$$

Also, in accordance with equation (4.6) we have graphic presentation for analysis of parameters and conditions for next steps. Fig. 4.2 shows us the functional dependence of the receive sensitivity of frequency with high impact of values of acoustic resistors in the character of form and of colored functions.

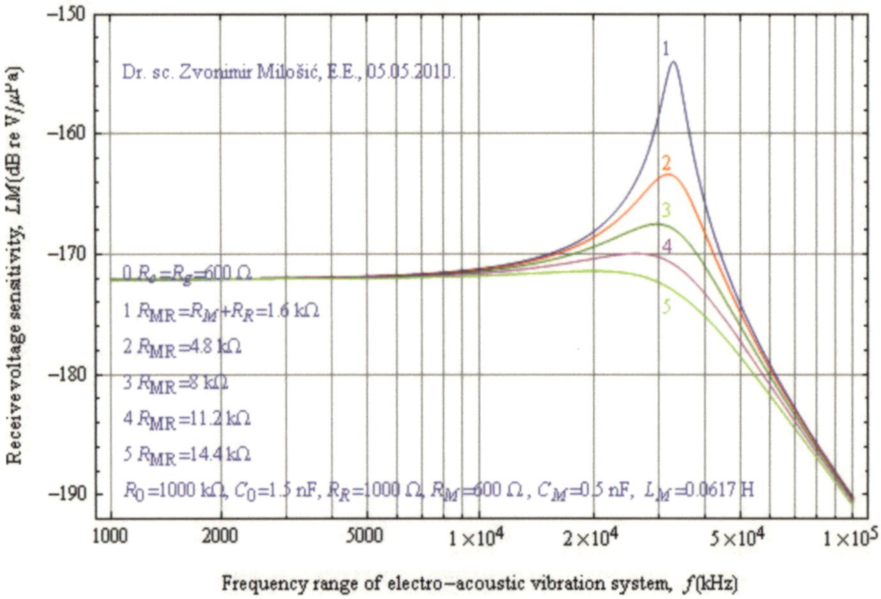


Fig. 4.2 Functional dependence of the level of the receive voltage sensitivity on frequency at different parameters contained in mechanical, electric and acoustical part of transducer body calculated with given numerical values inside figure

In this part of the analysis we can also see the characteristic of the functional dependence of receive voltage sensitivity of different values of capacity at clamps 2-2 given in the form of $C_0$ and shown in Fig. 4.3.

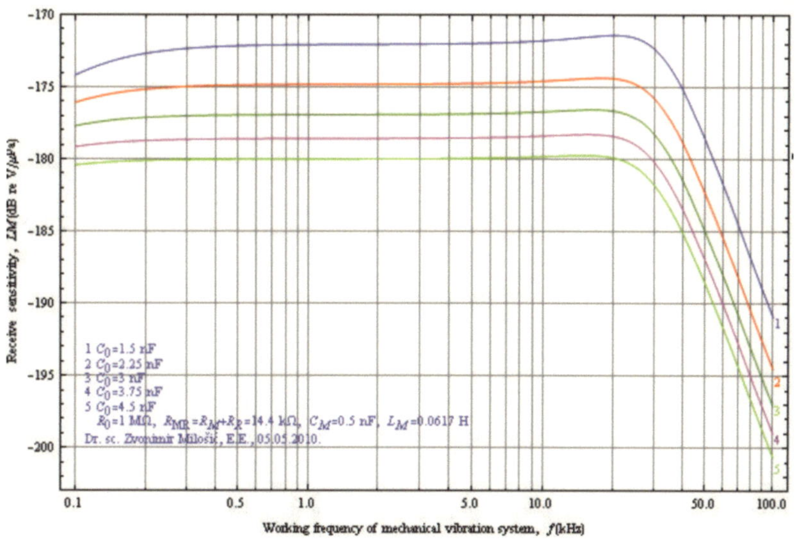


Fig. 4.3 Functional dependence of the level of the receive voltage sensitivity on the frequency at different parameters contained in mechanical, electric and acoustical part of transducer body calculated with given different numerical values of $C_0$ noticed inside figure

By using Fig. 4.1 we can write equations for the next step, the step of matching electric impedance of hydroacoustical transducer as a hydrophone. Then we have

$$I_3 = \frac{U}{R_c + jX_{Ltr}} \tag{4.7}$$

$$U_3 = I_3 R_c \tag{4.8}$$

$$U_3 = U\frac{R_c}{R_c + jX_{Ltr}} \tag{4.9}$$

$$U = U_c\left(1 + j\frac{X_{Ltr}}{R_c}\right) \tag{4.10}$$

$$U_3 = U_2\frac{R_c}{R_c + jX_{Ltr}} = U\left[\frac{R_c^{\,2}}{R_c^{\,2} + X_{Ltr}^{\,2}} - j\frac{R_c X_{Ltr}}{R_c^{\,2} + X_{Ltr}^{\,2}}\right] \Big/ : p \tag{4.11}$$

$$\frac{U_3}{p} = \frac{U}{p}\left[\frac{R_c^{\,2}}{R_c^{\,2} + X_{Ltr}^{\,2}} - j\frac{R_c X_{Ltr}}{R_c^{\,2} + X_{Ltr}^{\,2}}\right] \tag{4.12}$$

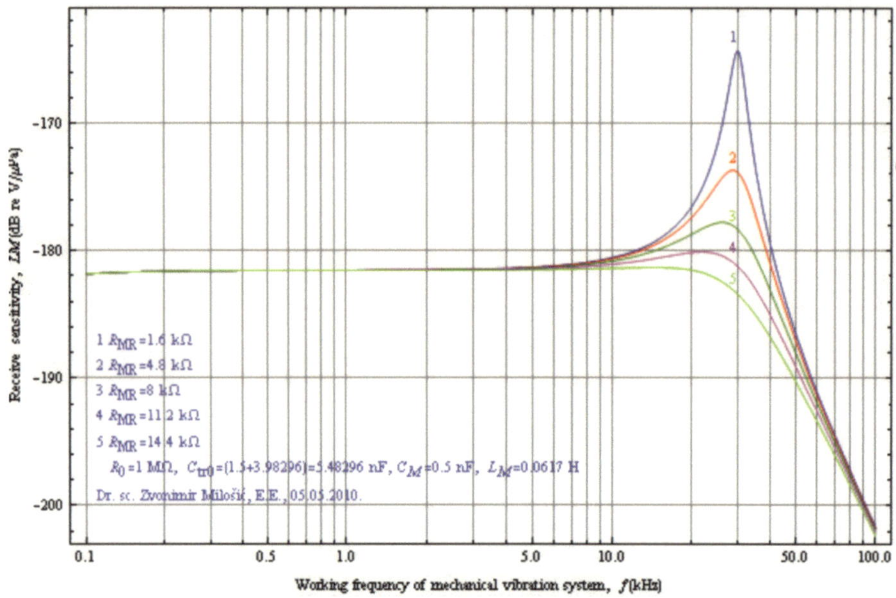


Fig. 4.4 Function of the level of the receive voltage sensitivity of hydrophone with *LC* transformer of inner impedance $Z_g$ of hydrophone as a generator of electric signal

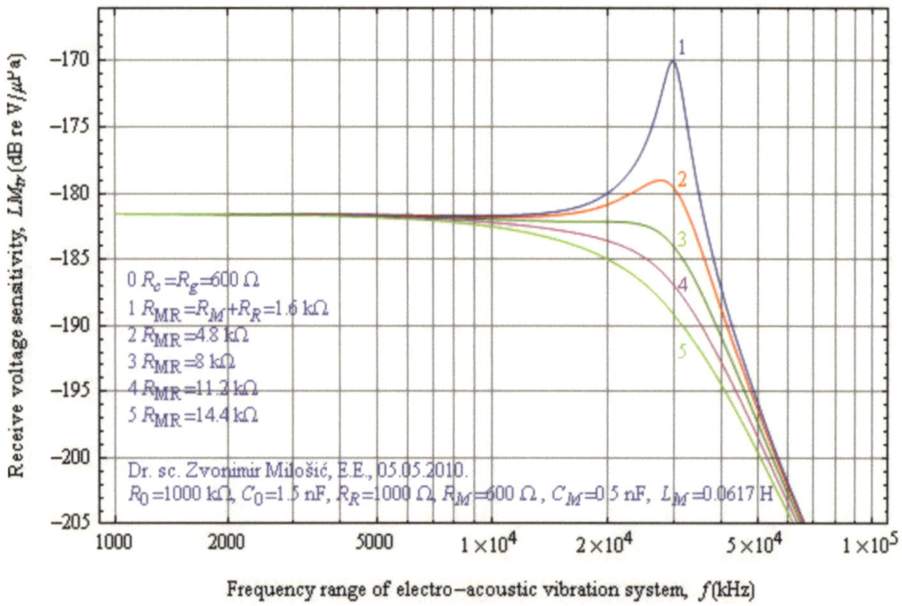


Fig. 4.5 Function of the level of the receive voltage sensitivity of hydrophone with *LC* transformer of inner impedance depending on the frequency at different parameters contained in mechanical, electric and acoustic part of transducer body calculated with given different numerical values of resistance $R_{MR}$ and resistance of electric cable $R_c$ noticed inside figure

At this moment we have two new receive voltage sensitivities: new virtual $M_{vir}$(V/Pa) and new receive voltage sensitivity $M_{tr}$ (V/Pa) with $LC$ transformer. So, in the end, we must know that they are defined to (4.13) and (4.14)

$$M_{tr} = \frac{U_3}{p} \quad \text{(V/Pa)} \tag{4.13}$$

$$M_{vir} = \frac{U}{p} \quad \text{(V/Pa)} \tag{4.14}$$

Both of them can be calculated to given equations, which can also be measured in the hydroacoustical tank separately.
In accordance with the given equations we can calculate virtual receive voltage sensitivity to equation (4.5) with intervention in the new value of $X_{CtrCo}$ as a parallel connection of value $C_{tr}$ and $C_0$ or to equation (4.15) directly.

$$LM_{22vir} = LM_{22} - 20\log\left(\frac{C_{tr}^{'} + C_0}{C_0}\right) \quad \text{(V/Pa)} \tag{4.15}$$

$$M_{tr} = M_{vir}\left[\frac{R_c^{\,2}}{R_c^{\,2} + X_{Ltr}^{\;2}} - j\frac{R_c X_{Ltr}}{R_c^{\,2} + X_{Ltr}^{\;2}}\right] = M_{vir}\cdot(\alpha - j\beta)$$

$$M_{tr}=(M_{rvir}+jM_{ivir})(a-j\beta)=(aM_{rvir}+\beta M_{ivir})_{retr}+j(aM_{ivir}-\beta M_{rvir})_{imtr}= M_{retr}+ M_{imtr} \tag{4.16}$$

And now, the module of receive voltage sensitivity of hydroacoustical transducer is given to

$$\left|M_{tr}\right| = \sqrt{M_{retr}^{\;2} + M_{imtr}^{\;2}} \quad \text{(V/Pa)} \tag{4.17}$$

In the end, we have the level of voltage receive sensitivity of transducer, as follows

$$LM_{tr}=20 \log \left|M_{tr}\right| -120 \quad \text{(dB re 1V/µPa)} \tag{4.18}$$

It is good to say that in accordance with mentioned equations we will get a new function as follows in Fig. 4.5, where is voltage sensitivity approximately 11 dB less then at the beginning.

## 5. The de-embedding of directivity pattern characteristic $R_p(\lambda, \theta, \varphi, LoSoS)$ of antenna

In accordance with the previous matter, we also have directivity pattern as one of important parameters of acoustical transducers. Directivity pattern of one hydroacoustical transducer, and directivity pattern in array of antenna are fundamental roots of all analyses in the systems where they are installed. The de-embedding of all parameters of systems begins with main parameters of hydroacoustical directivity pattern characteristic of composite transducers separately or transducers in antenna array.
By using this model of coordinate system to show and define the beginning conditions for de-embedding or the measurement of different functions of directivity pattern

characteristics of antennas at frequency from infrasound to ultrasound range, we can make correct analyses of all parameters in the system without restricted parameters of producers and data of technology owner.

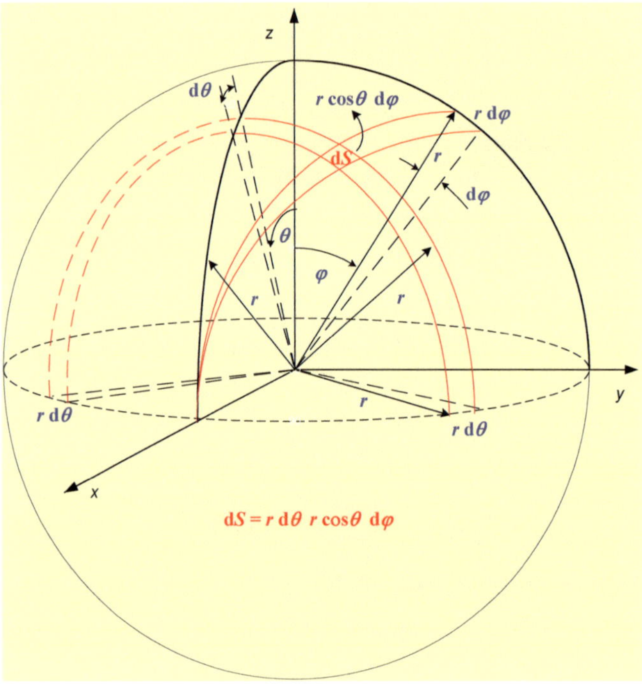


Fig. 5.1 Coordinate system to show and define the beginning conditions in all derivations and analyses of contemporary systems of monitoring with special review on underwater technology, $dS=r^2\cos\theta d\theta d\varphi$

Keeping in line with this intention, we can talk about a composite cylindrical barrel antenna, mainly installed in the bulb at bow of great tankers for monitoring of possibly forthcoming dangerous rocks, crags and shallows in the sea, or not less simple composed antenna array of ultrasound scanners in medicine. It is contained in equations taken over from literature (Evtjutov & Mitko 1981, Sverdlin 1980, Milošić 1996) in short explanation as follows

By using equation (5.1) (Evtjutov & Mitko 1981) we can get directivity pattern characteristics for different model of contemporary sonar horn antenna as follows

$$Rp = 20\log\left\{\frac{D_2^2}{\left(D_2^2 - D_1^2\right)}\cdot\left\{\frac{2J_1\left(\frac{\pi\cdot D_2}{\lambda}\cdot\sin\theta\right)}{\frac{\pi\cdot D_2}{\lambda}\cdot\sin\theta} - \left(\frac{D_1}{D_2}\right)^2\cdot\frac{2J_1\left(\frac{\pi\cdot D_1}{\lambda}\cdot\sin\theta\right)}{\frac{\pi\cdot D_1}{\lambda}\cdot\sin\theta}\right\}\right\} \quad \text{(dB)} \quad (5.1)$$

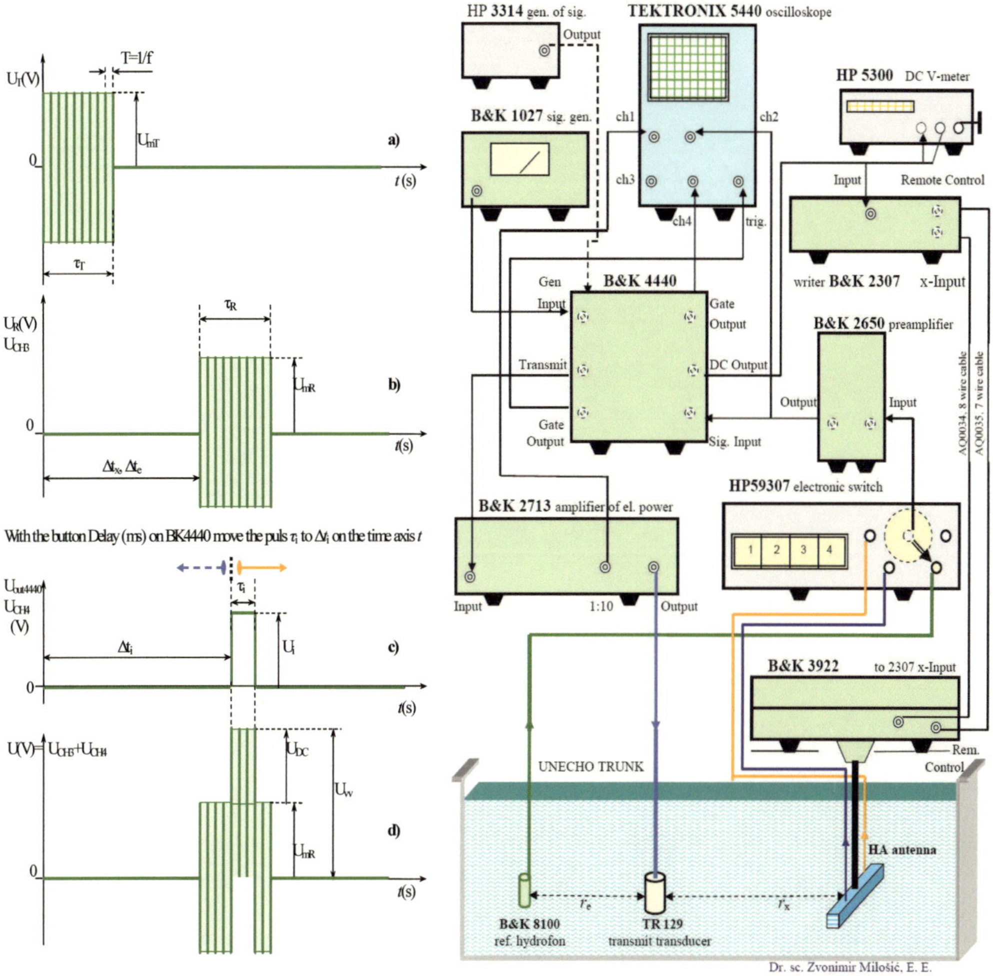


Fig. 5.2 Model of block scheme of impulse method for measurement of receive voltage sensitivity characteristics and directivity pattern characteristics of antenna showing electric pulses in the real time domain in the process of calibration (BI, Zagreb)

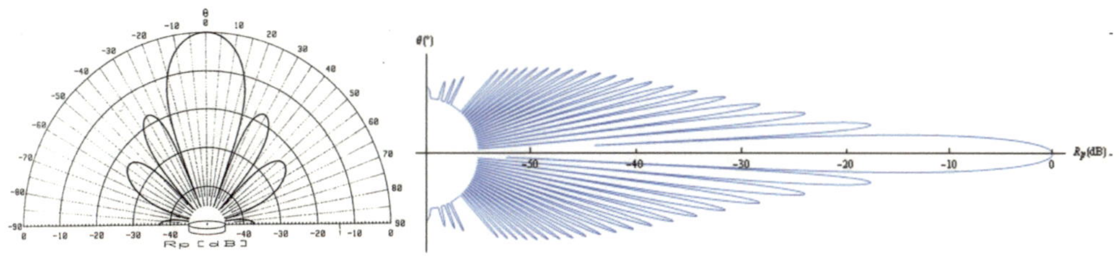

Fig. 5.3 Two different directivity pattern characteristics of baffled circle piston (Milošić 1988/2010 to equations of Evtjutov&Mitko 1981, Smarišev 1973, Sverdlin 1976)

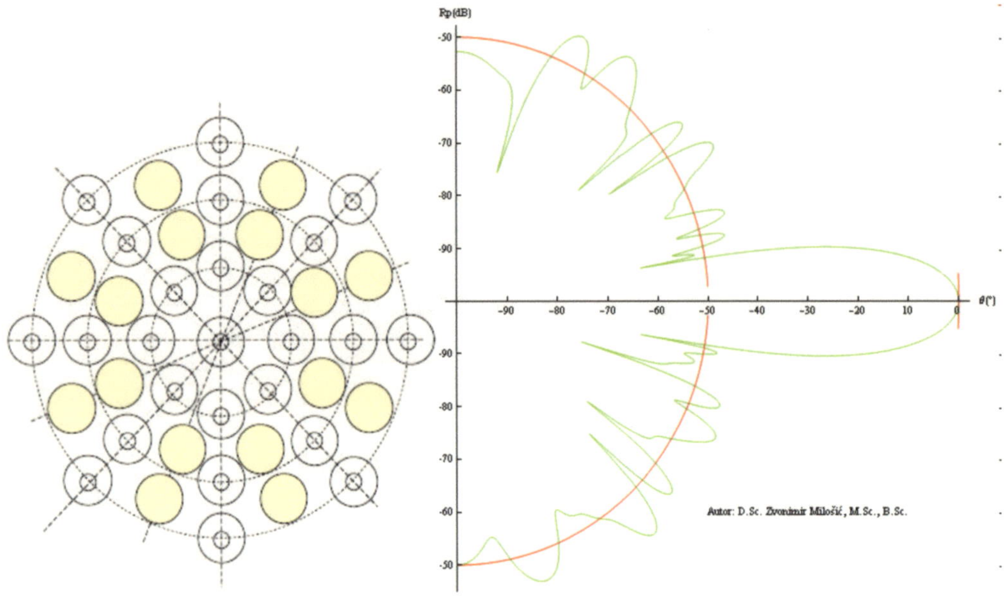


Fig. 5.4 Physical contain of forty transducers in specific form of circle series in symmetric positions with belonging function of directivity pattern characteristic of antenna (Milošić 2008)

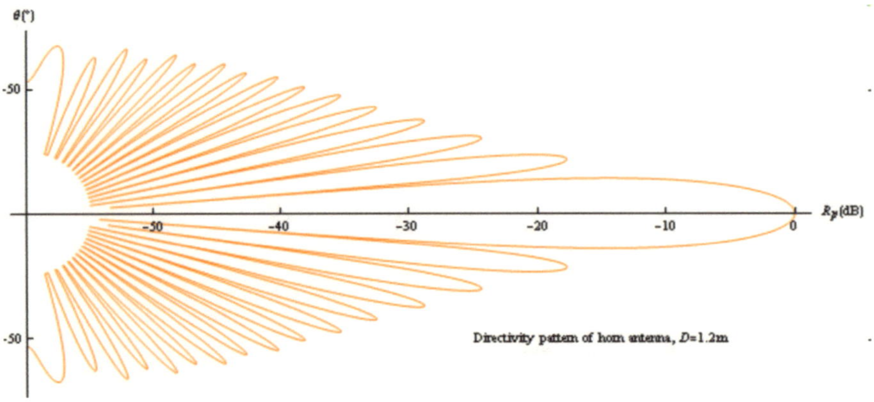


Fig. 5.5 Directivity pattern characteristic of contemporary horn antenna at relations of outside diameter and wave length $D_2/\lambda$=16 to (5.1)

## 6. The new impact of directivity pattern characteristic $R_p(\lambda, \theta, \varphi, LoSoS)$ on directivity index and effective aperture $A_{eff}(\lambda, \theta, \varphi, LoSoS)$, of antenna

Depending on a model of antenna (linear array, circle array, barrel array or spherical array), of working frequency $f$(Hz), of their transmitting power $P$(W), of efficiency of antenna in receive or in transmitting $\eta(1)$, to general known definition, we can have three forms of directivity index in receive $DI_R$(dB) or in transmit $DI_T$(dB) and effective aperture of antenna in receive $A_{effR}$ or in transmit $A_{effT}$ as follows: at rectangle cross section - $CS_r$ of main beam of pattern, at circle cross section - $CS_c$ and at elliptical cross section of main lobe of pattern characteristic - $CS_e$. In accordance with three models of cross sections of main lobe of pattern characteristic of antenna, mentioned above, we have five different new equations for *Directivity Index-DI* and five new functions for *Effective Aperture-*$A_{eff}$ in antenna theory (Milošić 2004, 2005, 2007 and 2008). On the other hand, we have graphical presentation in two and three dimensions of both mentioned parameters for different conclusions, for practice. In accordance with equation (6.1) at the beginning, we have fundamental definition (Urick 1967, 1975, 1998, Smarišev 1973, Sverdlin 1976, Burdic 1984,)[1] as the most suitable at new equations (Milošić 2004, AAAA2005, Acoustics'08 Paris) for rectangle, circle and ellipse CS (cross section) of main lobe with parameter *LoSoS* (Level of Suppression of Side lobes as negative value) in all equations to Fig. 5.1 and to 'general definitions'[2], as follows

$$AG = DI = 10 \cdot \log \frac{\int_{4\pi} d\Omega}{\int_{4\pi} R_I(\theta,\varphi) d\Omega} = 10 \cdot \log \frac{4\pi}{\int_0^{2\pi} \int_{-\pi/2}^{+\pi/2} R_I(\theta,\varphi) \cdot \cos\theta \cdot d\theta \cdot d\varphi} \quad \text{(dB)} \qquad (6.1)$$

$$DI = 10 \cdot \log D_f\,(\lambda, \theta, \varphi, LoSoS) \quad \text{(dB)} \qquad (6.2)$$

$$A_{eff} = \frac{\lambda^2}{4\pi} D_f(\lambda, \theta, \varphi, LoSoS) \quad (\text{m}^2) \qquad (6.3)$$

Also, we have equations for effective aperture $A_{eff}$ as new function with parameter *LoSoS*.

### 6.1 New function for directivity index $DI_{r\text{-}cs}$ on the basis of theory at rectangle cross section $CS_r$ of main lobe of receive or transmit directivity pattern characteristic

In accordance with the mentioned condition in Fig. 5.1 we have correct values of *DI* at idealized directivity pattern characteristics in Fig. 6.1.1.

Equation (6.1.1) is absolutely correct at given condition of rectangle CS of main lattice

$$DI_{\text{rectangle\_CS}} = 10\log \frac{2\pi}{\left(1\text{-}10^{\frac{LoSoS}{10}}\right) \cdot \varphi_{-3dB} \sin\left(\frac{\theta_{-3dB}}{2}\right) + 2\pi \cdot 10^{\frac{LoSoS}{10}}} \quad \text{(dB) (Milošić 2004)} \qquad (6.1.1)$$

---

[1] Before about 1948, directivity index was regarded as negative instead of a positive quantity (Urick R. J., Peninsula Publishing, California, Los Altos, 3rd edition, page 42).

[2] By using the mathematical coordinate system (by all authors), at $dS = r^2 \sin\theta d\theta d\varphi$ as differential surface, they had a big problem to make a join of suppression of side lobes and directivity index in one function at contemporary sonar systems. It is important to point out Russian scientist Grigorii M. Sverdlin as one of the first authors who introduced so called '*rectangle approximation*' in directivity pattern characteristic in Fig. 3.28 in the de-embedding of directivity index, at wrong equation 3.76, published in the book from 1976.

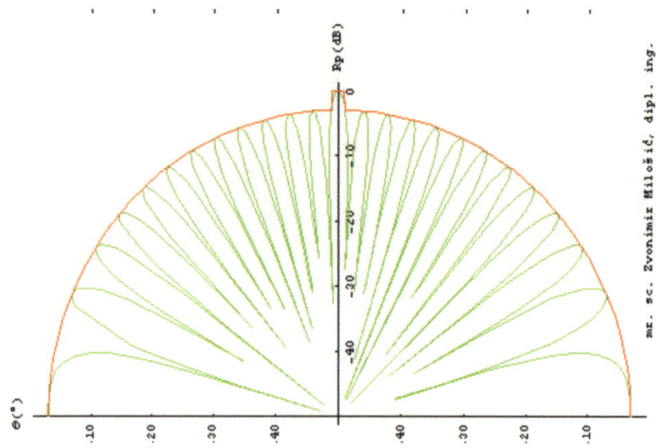


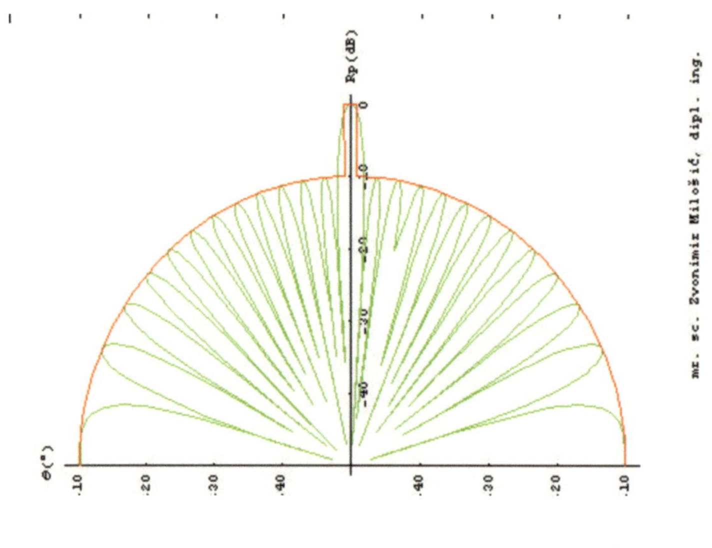


Fig. 6.1.1 Directivity patterns of the theoretical sonar antenna at azimuth angle $\theta_{-3dB}$=1° and elevation angle $\varphi_{-3dB}$=15° and with *LoSoS*=-3 dB we have *DI*=3 dB, and also in the second example in azimuth of $\theta_{-3dB}$=1° and elevation angle $\varphi_{-3dB}$=15° and with *LoSoS*=-10 dB and in that case we have that is *DI*=10 dB

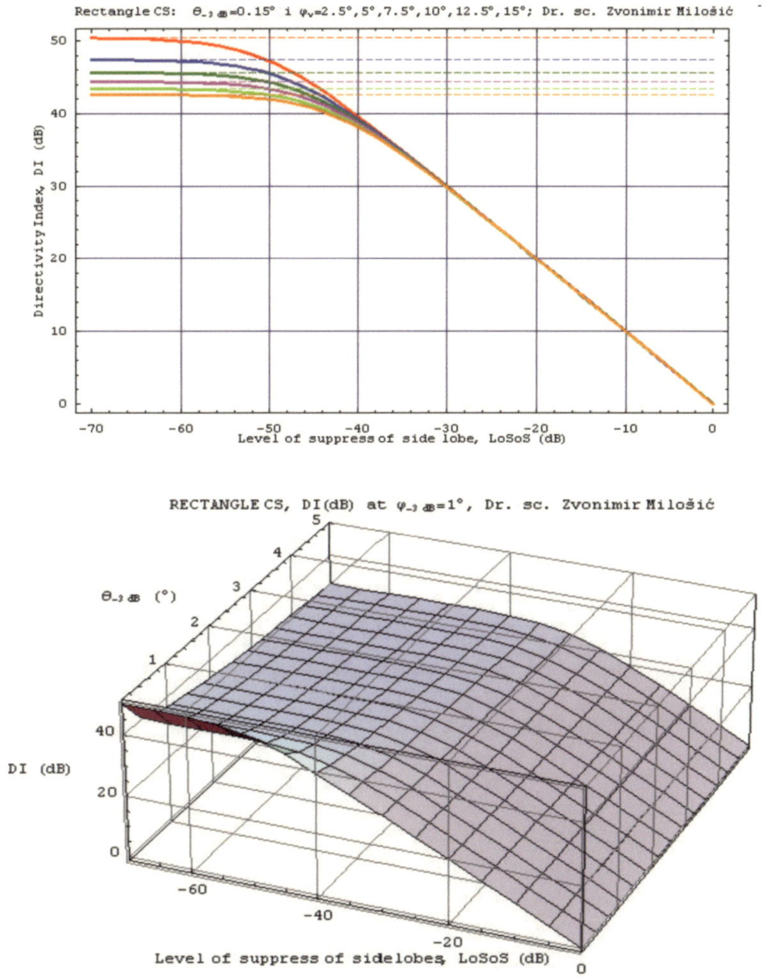


Fig. 6.1.2 Directivity index shown in two and three dimensions to (6.1.1) as correct function for theory and practice in dependence of *LoSoS* (dB) (Milošić 2004, 2005, 2007)

Directivity index of ideal mathematical case to (6.1.2) is mainly in use in theory and in practice as a beginning point in analysis. But, this value is mainly one of the largest wishes, which produces approximate error of directivity index to 20 dB. Taking the product of ideal directivity factor $D_f(1)$ and efficiency factor $\eta(1)$ of antenna as final value of array gain or directivity index is additionally wrong. Efficiency factor and directivity factor are absolutely different parameters in the root (Caruthers page 27). Absolutely all solves of directivity index, effective aperture or array gain of antenna are contained in equations (6.1.1), (6.2.1) and (6.3.1) or in contemporary figures Fig. 6.1.2 to Fig. 6.3.5, (Milošić 2004, 2005, 2007, 2008).

$$DI_{\text{rectangla\_CS}} = 10 \cdot \log D_f = 10 \cdot \log \frac{41253}{\varphi_{-3\text{dB}}(^\circ)\theta_{-3\text{dB}}(^\circ)} \text{ (dB)} \qquad (6.1.2)$$

**6.2 New function for directivity index $DI_{c\text{-}cs}$ on the basis of theory at circle cross section $CS_c$ of main lobe of receive or transmit directivity pattern characteristic**

Both equations, (6.2.1) when used in practice and (6.2.2) as mathematical ideal function are new in theory and practice for circle CS of main lattice given and explained in the paper at Acoustics'08 (Milošić 2008).

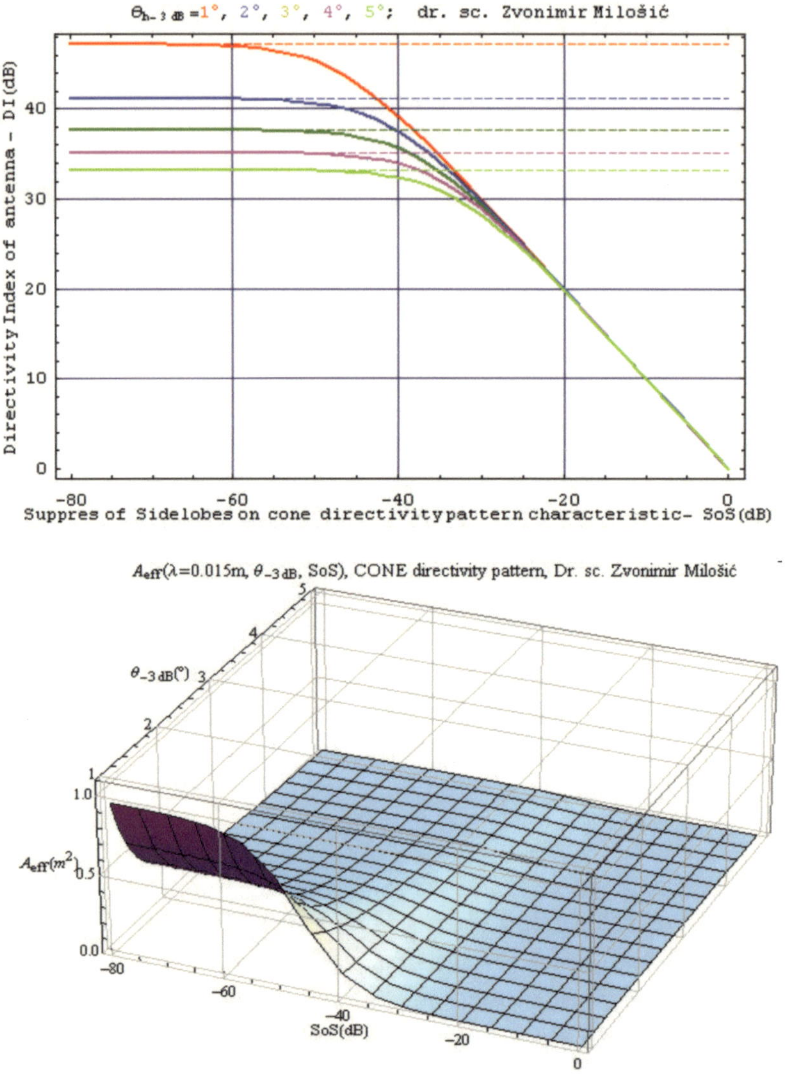


Fig. 6.2.1 Directivity index and effective aperture of antenna at cone directivity pattern characteristic in condition of circle CS of main lobe (Milošić 2008)

$$DI_{\text{circle\_CS}} = 10\log\frac{1}{\left(1-10^{\frac{LoSoS}{10}}\right)\cdot\sin^2\left(\frac{\theta_{-3\text{dB}}}{4}\right)+10^{\frac{LoSoS}{10}}}\ \text{(dB)}\quad \text{(Milošić Acoustics'08)}\quad (6.2.1)$$

$$DI_{\text{circle\_CS}} = 10 \cdot \log \frac{52525}{\theta^2_{-3\text{dB}}(°)} \text{ (dB) (Milošić 2008, Acoustics'08)} \quad (6.2.2)$$

In accordance with mentioned equations (6.2.1) and (6.2.2) for circle CS of the main lobe of pattern characteristic of antenna, we have graphic presentation in Fig. 6.2.1 for *DI* in two dimensions and for $A_{\text{eff}}$ in three dimensions.

### 6.3 New function for directivity index $DI_{e\text{-}cs}$ on the basis of theory at ellipse cross section $CS_c$ of main lobe of receive or transmit directivity pattern characteristic

In absolute accordance with the mentioned conditions of rectangle and circle cross section in this case, we have the best general function for the presentation of important parameters of antennas in the systems of monitoring, in the underwater or in the air.

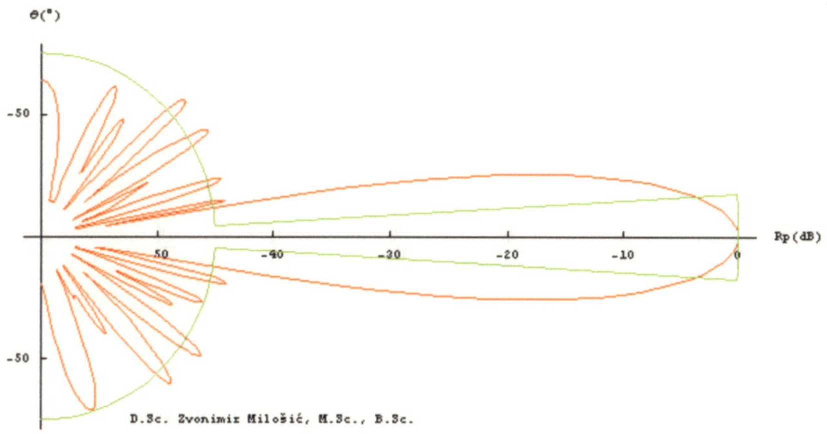


Fig. 6.3.1 Directivity patterns of sonar antenna at elliptic CS of the main lobe, if we have azimuth angle $\theta_{-3dB}$=4.8° and the value of given elevation angle $\varphi_{-3dB}$=15° then with the level of suppression of minor lobes of characteristic *LoSoS*= −45 dB we have that is *DI*=28.5 dB

$$DI_{\text{ellipse\_CS}} = 10 \cdot \log \frac{8}{\left(1\text{-}10^{\frac{LoSoS}{10}}\right) \cdot \varphi_{-3\text{dB}} \sin\left(\frac{\theta_{-3\text{dB}}}{2}\right) + 8 \cdot 10^{\frac{LoSoS}{10}}} \text{ (dB) (Milošić 2007)} \quad (6.3.1)$$

$$DI_{\text{ellipse\_CS}} = 10 \cdot \log \frac{52525}{\varphi_{-3\text{dB}}(°)\theta_{-3\text{dB}}(°)} \text{ (dB) (Milošić 2007)} \quad (6.3.2)$$

That is a general equation (6.3.1) (Milošić Workbench 2007 in Germany published & recessional unrealized OCEANS'09 & recessional unrealized in 158th ASA meeting 2009 & recessional unrealized Euronoise09 & recessional unrealized at ECUA2010) for using in theory and practice at all conditions of environmental influence and new equation (6.3.2), mainly as very high and unattainable value.

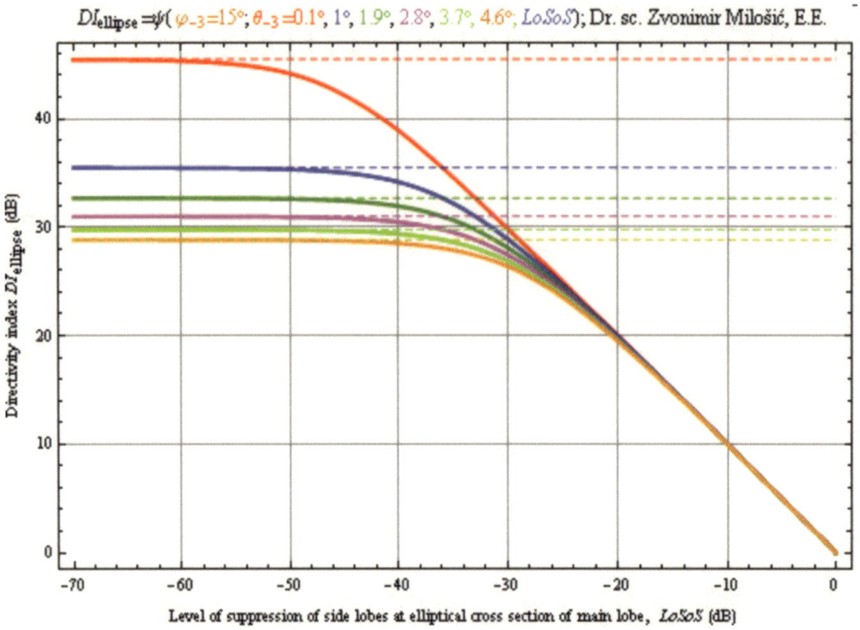


Fig. 6.3.2 Graphic presentation of *DI* as function of angles of sensitivity $\theta_{-3dB}$ in azimuth and $\varphi_{-3dB}$ in elevation and the level of suppression of side lobes *LoSoS* of the sonar antenna (Milošić 2007, 2008)

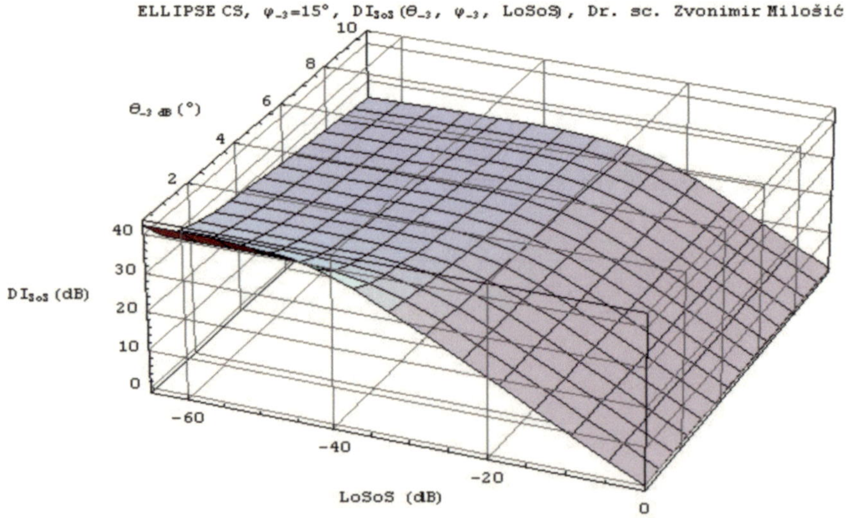


Fig. 6.3.3 Graphic presentation of $DI(\theta_{-3dB},\varphi_{-3dB},LoSoS)$ in three dimensions have a special meaning by comparison of different sonar systems (Milošić 2007, 2008)

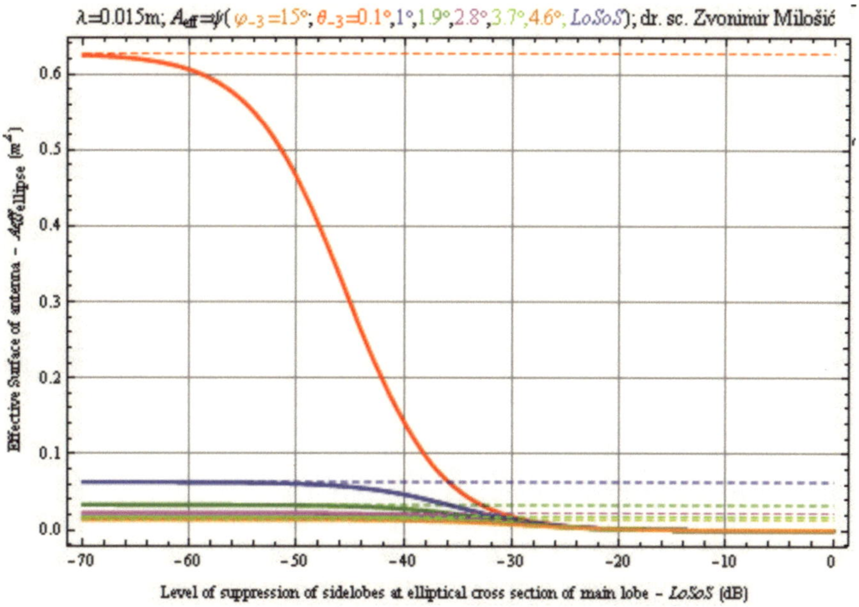


Fig. 6.3.4 Graphic presentation of an effective aperture of antenna $A_{eff}(\theta_{-3dB}, \varphi_{-3dB}, LoSoS)$ in two dimensions at the model with elliptical cross section (CS) (Milošić 2007, 2008)

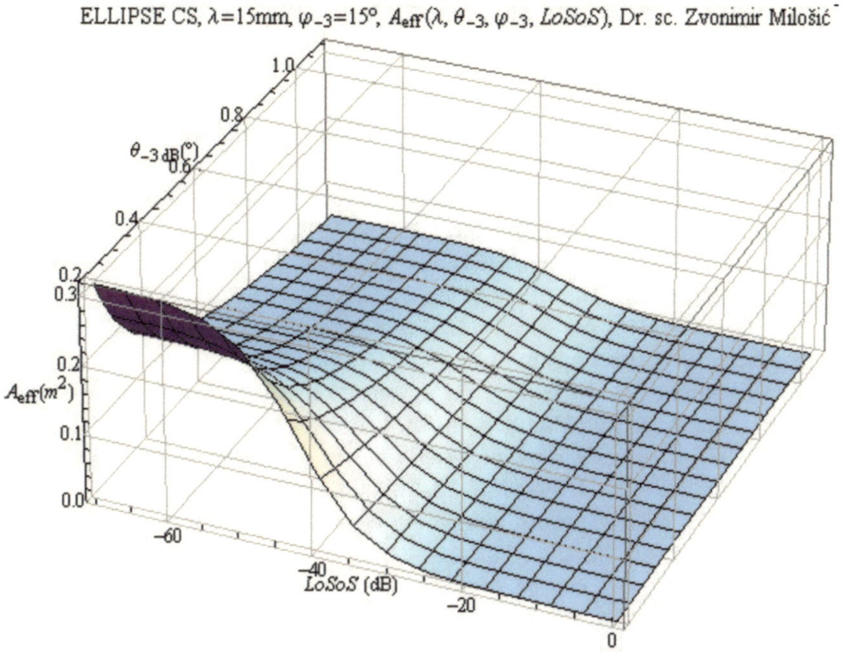


Fig. 6.3.5 Graphic presentation of an effective aperture of antenna $A_{eff}(\lambda, \theta_{-3dB}, \varphi_{-3dB}, LoSoS)$ in three dimensions at the model with elliptical cross section (Milošić 2007, 2008)

## 7. Conclusion

The presented model of vibration of medium with concentrated mechanical parameters as a starting point of analysis of transmitting or receive sensitivity of hydroacoustical transducer with mathematical solution of its differential equation is applicably carried out on the basis of the Laplace transformation of complex variable. Given analyses of antenna with concentrated mechanical parameters are in accordance with mathematical solutions by two-port network model of hydroacoustical transducer with original concentrated electric parameters and with the electric substitute of mechanical parameters inside the body, at electrical clamp on one side and on the surface of the transducer in the water on the second acoustical side.

With the analysis of the behaviour of mathematical functions of hydroacoustical sensitivity and sources of wide dispersion of phase angle of impedance of antenna elements at hydroacoustical and ultrasound transducers, we can choose the best model for optimal matching in the given sonar system. By using the ideal electric transformer models, special, original and general expressions were gained and tested in the long-time practice, we have enabled the correct computing of elements necessary for performance and the complete matching of electrical impedance at hydroacoustical antenna. In accordance with the mentioned intentions of presenting fundamental sensitivities of transducers, electro-acoustical impedance and their matching, we have presented a new important expanded and correct opinion about the fundamentals of directivity index and effective aperture of antenna in a new form of absolutely correct mathematical functions dependent on important parameter *LoSoS*. Also, all of them in two and three dimensional graphs are the best support in the building of antennas and new technologies of contemporary systems of monitoring for a world without accidents in space and, especially, in the underwater.

## 8. References

Aronov L. M., Matveev L. I. (1953); *Fundaments of hydroacoustic*, Navy Edition, Moscow, in Russian & in Croatian,

Beranek, L. Leo (1954); *ACOUSTICS*, MIT, Bolt, Beranek and Newman, Inc., Cambridge, Massachusetts, New York Toronto London, USA,

Bobber J. Robert (1998); *Underwater Electroacoustic Measurements*, Peninsula Publishing, Los Altos, California, USA,

Bogorodskii V.V, Zubarev L. A., Korepin E. A., Jakušev V. I.(1983); *Underwater electroacoustic transducers*, Sudostroenie, in Russian,

Bronstein I. N., Semendjaev K. A. (1975); *Mathematical handbook for engineers and students*, translate from Russian Danilo Blanuša, Tehnička knjiga, Zagreb, in Croatian,

Brüel & Kjær (1980); *Introduction to underwater acoustics, hydrophones – their characteristics and applications calibration technique*, Copenhagen, Denmark,

Burdic S. William (1984); *Underwater acoustic system analyses*, Prentice-Hall, Inc., Englewood Cliffs, New Jersey, USA,

Caruthers W. Jerald (1977); *Fundamentals of marine acoustics*, Elsevier Scientific Publishing Company, Amsterdam-Oxford-New York,

Evtjutov P. Alesandr, Mitko B. Valerii (1981, 1988); *Examples of engineer computing in hydroacoustics*, Sudostroenie, in Russian,

Jelaković, Tihomil (1967); *Introduction to the basics electrical engineering*, Tehnička knjiga Zagreb, in Croatian,

Jelaković, Tihomil (1973); *Transistors audio amplifiers*, Školska knjiga Zagreb, in Croatian,

Kinsler E. L., Frey R. A. (1962); *Fundamentals of acoustics*, John Wiley&Sons, Inc., USA,

Kolesnikov Aleksei Evgenievič (1983); *Acoustical measurements*, Sudostroenie, in Russian,

Loeser, T. Harrison (1998); *Sonar engineering handbook*, Peninsula Publishing, Los Altos, California,

Masson P. Waren (1950); *Piezoelectric cristals and their applications to ultrasonics*, D. Van Nostrand Co., New York, USA,

Milošić, Zvonimir (1978); *Matching electrical impedance of hydroacoustic transducers at a stable working frequency*, Elektrotehnika, XXII-1978, No. 3-6, pages 171-173, in Croatian,

Milošić, Zvonimir (1988); *Analysis of negative impact roll and pitch of ship on the measurement of its velocity with ultrasound Doppler log*, ETAN 1988 International Congress in Zadar,

Milošić Zvonimir (1990); *Physics of Ultrasound and diagnostical instrumentation in hepatogastroenterology*, Chapter I, pp. 9-45, Edited by Živković R. & Bilić A., *Application of ultrasound in clinical hepatology and gastroenterology*, Školska knjiga Zagreb, in Croatian,

Milošić Zvonimir (1993); Comments on '*Diffraction constants of acoustic transducers*', J. Acoust. Soc. Am. 36, 267-269 (1964), J. Acoust. Soc. Am., Vol. 93, No. 2,

Milošić, Zvonimir (1996); *Directivity pattern analysis of the ultrasound cone antenna by means of the model of a rigid hole circular piston in a rigid baffle*, 38th International Symposium, Electronics in Marine, Elmar June 1996, Zadar, CROATIA,

Milošić, Zvonimir (2004); *Models for parameter de-embedding of hydroacoustic antennas in underwater monitoring systems*, Dissertation, FER Zagreb, in Croatian,

Milošić, Zvonimir (2005); *Directivity index of a hydroacoustical antenna with an idealized model of a directivity pattern*, 2nd Congress of Alps-Adria Acoustics Association and 1st Congress of Acoustical Society of Croatia, 23-24 June 2005, Opatija, Proceedings AAAA 2005, ISBN 953-95097-0-X, see ending of Proceedings Acoustics'08 Paris,

Milošić, Zvonimir (2007); *The Importance of the influence of directivity index of antenna on the range at multistatic sonar systems in conditions of reverberation in the sea and with the use on radar systems*, Workbench in FGAN, pp 1-35, Germany,

Milosić, Zvonimir (2008); "*Suppression of side lobe level on the cone characteristics of the directivity pattern of an antenna as an important factor in its directivity index and effective aperture*", *1. Proceedings of the 9th ECUA*, Volume 1&2, pp. 533-538, *2.Proceedings of 2nd ASA-EAA joined conference integrated with Societe Francaise d'Acoustique 2008*, on DVD pages 4821-4826, Editor Manell E. Zakharia and co-editors: Didier Cassereau and Francine Luppe (ur.), Acoustics'08 Paris, France,

Milošić, Zvonimir (2010); *Ideal electrical transformer model in the system of impedance matching of piezoelectric hydroacoustic transducer*, Journal of Marine Sciences, Edited by University of Dubrovnik, Naše more 57(1-2) 2010, http://www.nasemore.com/sadrzaj/brojevi/57(1-2)2010/4-milosic.pdf

Rževkin, Sergei Nikolaevič (1960); *Course of lessons in theory of sound*, Edited by Moscow University, in Russian,

Scherman H. Charls, Butler L.John (2008); *Transducers and Arrays for Underwater Sound*, sponsored by ONR, published by Springer,

Smarišev, Mihail Dmitrievič (1973); *Hydroacoustic antenna directivity pattern*, Edited by Sudostroenie, Leningrad, in Russian,

Sverdlin, M. Grigorii (1976); *Applied hydroacoustic*, Sudostroenie, Leningrad, in Russian,

Sverdlin Mihailovič Grigorii (1980); *Hydroacoustic transducers and antennas*, Sudostroenie, Leningrad, in Russian,

Urick J. Robert (1975); *Principles of underwater sound*, McGraw-Hill, Book Company 1975, Science redactor E. L. Šenderov, Redactor Committee: Kolesnikov-Prostakov-Smarišev-Tarasjuk, translated in Russian,

Urick J. Robert (1998); *Principles of underwater sound*, 3rd edition, Peninsula Publishing, Los Altos, California 1998, USA,

Wilson, B. Oscar (1998); *Introduction to the theory and design of sonar transducers*, Peninsula Publishing, Los Altos, California, USA,

Wolfram Research; Europe Ltd., *Mathematica 4 & 6*, 10 Blenheim Office Park, Lover Road, Long Hanbourgh, Oxfordshire OX29 8RY, UK.; SYSTEMCOM d.o.o., certified reseller for Wolfram Research, Maksimirska 120, 10000 Zagreb, CROATIA, for Microsoft Windows 95/98/NT/ 2000/XP,

Ziomek J. Lawrence (1995); *Fundamentals of acoustic field theory and space-time signal processing*, Naval Postgraduate School, Monteray, California, 1995 CRC Press Inc., USA.

# 13

# Readout System for Medium-Sized Experiments

Stanisław Kistryn
*Jagiellonian University in Kraków*
*Poland*

## 1. Introduction

In a vast area of fundamental nuclear/particle physics investigations are performed with relatively simple setups, encompassing up to few thousands of analog data sources. Multiplicity for events in such experiments is usually of the order of few tens. On the other hand, high precision studies require accumulating of large data samples and therefore the readout system must work reliably at trigger rates between one and a few tens of thousands per second, *without* any significant dead-time. To meet these requirements it is necessary to utilize a fast bus and/or protocol for the data transmission. In contrast to the present generation of high energy physics experiments, here the usage of complicated multiplexing schemes with specially developed chips and boards as well as many-level triggering and event-building techniques is rather disadvantageous.

This Chapter describes a readout system which fulfills all the needs of moderate-size experiments and possesses a number of attractive features which allow its easy modification for specific demands. Rather than utilizing possibilities of creating electronic boards tailored strictly to the needs of a particular application, the discussed implementation is based on modular electronics, which parts are still in possession of many laboratories all over the world. In (frequent) cases, when budget limitations do not allow to follow the path of a completely new design of dedicated custom-made boards, application of older electronic modules might be the only way to successfully perform the planned measurements. In the described system use is made of CAMAC based electronics, which turns out to provide data throughput sufficient for most demanding applications. In fact, when the readout is coupled to the front-end processor via VME-bus buffers, it does not feel any speed limits present in the traditional CAMAC-based systems.

The described modular electronic system is based on the standard FERA[1] configuration, which applications in physics experiments are numerous, see e.g. (Vander Molen et al. 1991; Gazes et al. 1993; Elfman et al. 1997; Hagemann et al. 1999; Okamura 2000; Davin et al. 2001; Karpukhin et al. 2003; Loudos et al. 2004). The full power of the FERA readout system is gained by introducing an additional custom CAMAC module. In spite of its relative simplicity, the module allows to avoid the bounds imposed by the FERA standard. This includes a possibility to prolong the FERA data-bus over many crates for large setups. Configurations of the experimental apparatus require a logical grouping of the signal sources into subsystems corresponding to particular sets of detectors (wire chambers,

---

[1] FERA (in full: Fast Encoding and Readout ADC) is a trademark of the LeCroy Corporation.

trigger hodoscopes, calorimeters etc.). Use of the custom FERA Extender/Tagger module allows to divide the readout system into sections matching the detector configuration and to drive each section by a separate (differing in width or shifted in time) gate signal. In each sub-system the data are sent over a dedicated bus (at the speed of 100 ns per data word) to a pair of alternatively active buffering memories. The coordination of the full system (controlling the event cycle, switching the memories, issuing DAQ requests) is performed by a single FERA Manager, which is equipped with a logic system for distributing and multiplexing of the synchronization signals. Improvements in the FERA sector have been proposed before - see e.g. (Ordine et al. 1997; Beausang et al. 2000) for descriptions of other custom-made control modules, with functionality similar to the FERA Manager or (Sugaya & Nomachi 1999) for and auxiliary VME sequencer module. It has also to be acknowledged that at present several additional FERA-line modules are commercially available, which would allow to achieve similar functionality as the Extender/Tagger. However, the discussed *Integrated Multi-Crate FERA* readout system was the first complete solution in which possibilities of application of various gates as well as tagging of events in several sub-systems were provided in a clean way.

In the following Sections, first a short description of the standard FERA system configuration and its limitations is presented. The FERA Extender/Tagger module is then introduced and its applications in constructing more elaborate FERA systems are described. Finally, the estimations of the full system performance for a typical configuration of a moderate-size experiment are given, followed by concluding remarks.

## 2. Standard FERA configuration

Fast increase of the experimental readout electronics complexity and size, confronted with the limited speed of the data transmission over the CAMAC DATAWAY, precipitated the introduction of faster busses. One of the solutions was the FERA system, in which data from the digitizing modules are passed over a dedicated ECL data bus with the handshake taking place on another special ECL control bus. The system initially consisted of the 4300B ADC's and the 4301 FERA Driver, which mediated the data transfer to the 4302 FERA Memories (LeCroy 1983). The system was later supplemented with a number of modules (3377 TDC, 4303 TFC, 3309 PFC, various logic modules: 34xx discriminators, 45xx ECLine Logic) and in particular with the global readout controller, the FERA Manager (Watzlawik et al. 1994). FERA compatible digitizing units were produced by several manufacturers (Silena 4418/x modules, Gan'elec 812F series; recently the FERA line of modules is followed by Cheesecote Mountain CAMAC (Sumner)).

This constant growth of the FERA family indicates clearly that the system possesses a number of attractive features. In addition to the wide variety of digitizing modules and the readout speed at 100 ns per a 16-bit word, the ability to buffer the fast-readout events in the memories enables derandomization of the event rate and reduction of the dead-time by multiplexing the buffers (one is being filled over the ECL data bus while the other is readout via CAMAC). The system control is done entirely by hardware, i.e. after initialization, the synchronization of the data transmission is performed by the Manager/Driver modules and external access to the accumulated data is limited to the Memory modules at the moment of the Manager's LAM (see below). In this way hardware changes within the system are virtually decoupled from the DAQ software, requiring only small changes in the initialization routines. One should note that the total readout speed of the system is limited

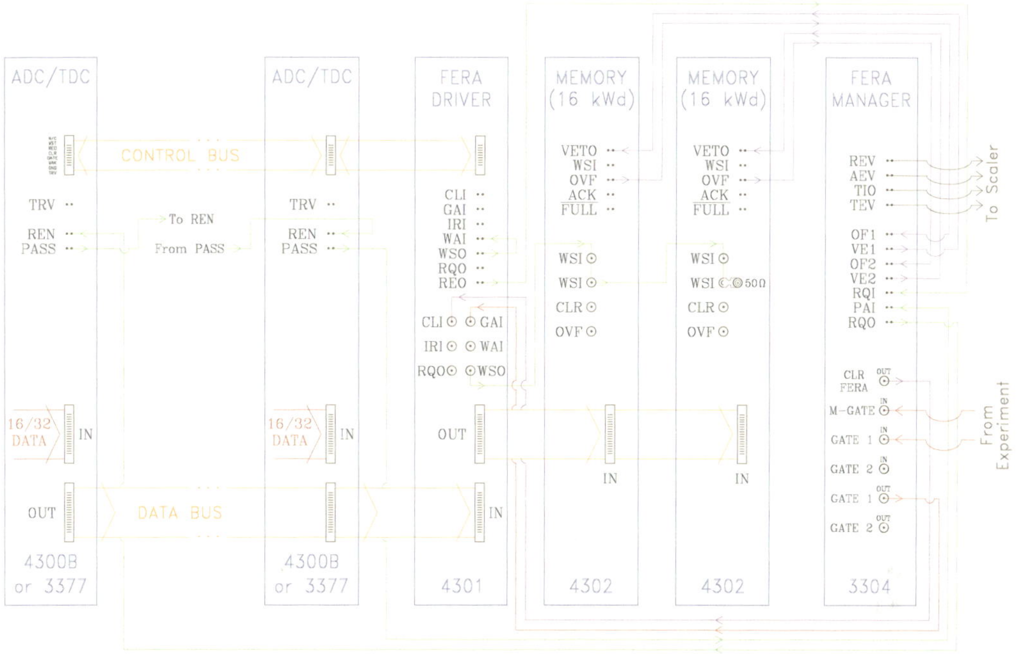


Fig. 1. Diagram of the standard FERA System interconnections.

by the CAMAC readout speed of the Memories. Therefore the overall rate capability can be further improved by replacing these by VME FERA Memories (LeCroy 1190 or CES 8170 modules).

In Fig. 1 the interconnections within the standard FERA system are presented. Several digitizing modules are chained in a readout series via the REN/PASS line and put on common control and data busses with the Driver, which converts the bussed single-ended ECL signals to true differential ones and mediates the data transfer into the Memories. Control over the memory switching and the event cycle as a whole is performed by the Manager.

### 2.1 FERA event cycle and handshake

A trigger signal from the experiment's logic system is sent to the Manager as M-GATE and starts the event cycle. The GATE signal is then sent to the Driver and distributed to all digitizing modules (ADC's and/or TDC's) in the system. If the conversion in a given module results in a valid data, that module asserts the REQ line, signaling its request for readout. Logic OR of all these signals is transmitted via Driver to the Manager. The programmed delay in the 3304 module allows all digitizing units to get ready with all their conversion before the REN signal for the first ADC/TDC is issued. Obtaining REN, the module takes control over the busses and sends the data words, strobing the active Memory with the WST line. To obtain the highest possible data throughput the Driver generates the acknowledge signal directly, without waiting for the Memory ACK (what would result in a speed reduction by a factor of 2). After the first module has sent all its data it copies REN to PASS, which sets REN of the next module. When the PASS signal of the last module in the chain is obtained by the Manager, the latter then generates a reset signal (CLR), distributed by the Driver to all modules. After approximately 2 $\mu$s the Manager is ready to accept the next event.

One more important task of the Manager is the memory switching. At the beginning of the acquisition the first Memory is enabled while the second is VETO'ed by the Manager. When the overflow mark of the Memory (e.g. 14 kWords, set by side switch) is reached, the Manager receives the corresponding OVF signal, it allows the data transfer for the current event to finish and after obtaining PASS it swaps the VETO's, thus redirecting the flow of data to the second Memory. A LAM issued at that moment by the Manager interrupts the DAQ processor and causes the data from the filled Memory to be readout via CAMAC. After emptying of the 4302 module, the processor resets the corresponding flag in the Manager's register.

### 2.2 Standard FERA limitations

With all these favorable features the FERA system nonetheless contains in its original concept two inherent limitations which pose problems when trying to use it in more complex setups.

From the discussion of the circuitry shown in Fig. 1 those two restraints became obvious:

1. The system is designed to occupy a *single CAMAC crate* (LeCroy 1983), therefore severely limiting the maximum number of readout channels.
2. A *single GATE* signal is distributed to the whole system. This restriction could lead to two kinds of problems. The measuring system might contain various kinds of detectors, like e.g. plastic and crystal scintillators, which require the integration times (gate widths) to differ by at least an order of magnitude (in the chosen example ~50 ns and ≥500 ns, respectively). On the other hand, when the readout system contains both ADC and TDC modules, timing problems can arise when the same signal has to be used as the integration gate and common start or stop signal.

Easy solutions to the above problems are biased with serious shortcomings. Simple prolongation of the ECL busses over many crates could be accepted to solve the first problem if it concerns just a few more modules. If a significant enlargement of the system is needed the long busses will lead to signal distortion and eventually to failures in the data transmission. Of course this method does not address the single-gate problem.

Apparently employing *several* systems like the one depicted in Fig. 1 would solve both problems, however a serious deficiency of such application lies in a loss of event coherency. While different parts of the experimental apparatus send their digitized data in parallel to several Memories, one is not able subsequently to reconstruct the full events, i.e. to find out the correlation between information in the sub-systems.

## 3. FERA Extender/Tagger module

The above considerations specify firm guidelines for the desired solution, which should provide means for:

- Proper *prolongation* of the ECL data bus, possibly without limits.
- Easy *division* of the whole system into sub-systems, equipped with their own Memory pairs.
- Possibility to apply *common or separate gates* within each sub-system.
- Organizing the *data transfer* to the back-end computer in a convenient structure.

These demands are fulfilled by using a custom CAMAC module installed in an extended configuration of the FERA system, which shall be called "Full FERA System". Let us first concentrate on the characteristics of the module.

Fig. 2. FERA Extender/Tagger module.

The FERA Extender/Tagger module (see Fig. 2) was designed originally at the University of Bern[2]. Additional modifications of the board to achieve the required functionality within the designed system configuration were introduced at ETH Zürich[3]. The description here is concentrated on the functions of the Extender within the FERA system, without going into a detailed discussion of its internal circuitry.

### 3.1 FERA Extender - "Separate Gates" system

When the module is used only as a data bus extender it remains a quasi-passive part of the system and does not participate in the FERA handshake. Its control bus and the REN/PASS connectors remain open. The module acts as a kind of data transmitter.

Such application of the module enables to split the ECL data bus into several independent, sequentially placed sections and allows therefore the distribution of the system over several CAMAC crates and to apply to each section an individual gate. It should be kept in mind that the gates are different in the sense of their widths and relative time shifts, they *must,* however, all be created out of the same original trigger (M-GATE) signal.

A schematic diagram of the Separate Gate system is shown in Fig. 3. Only the most relevant interconnections are shown, the other are analogous as in the standard configuration. No gate signals are indicated in the diagram - it is, however, obvious that each Driver can obtain (and in turn distribute) a GATE signal which can be unique for the given section. Some features of this configuration should be noted:

---

[2] Schemes and original design of the printed board were worked out by M. Hess, Laboratory of High Energy Physics, University of Bern, Switzerland.

[3] The author holds the permission of unlimited duplication of the board, as well as can provide details on the original Extender modifications. Their electronic realization is designed by P. Eberhardt.

Fig. 3. Schematic diagram of an example of the Separate Gate system, employing the FERA Extender/Tagger as just the data bus extender. Only the REN/PASS chain and the ECL busses are shown.

- The Extender is always the *first module* in the FERA section. Each such section is associated with a Driver - the last module within it, which mediates the handshake, receives all the data and forwards them further to the Memories.
- The Extender *receives data* directly from the Driver of the preceding section.
- Each *Driver - Extender pair* acts effectively as a *repeater*, refreshing the data word as it passes along the bus from one section to another.
- Each digitizing module in every section in turn takes control over the whole bus and must be able to strobe the Memories to accept its data. Therefore the Memories must be *strobed* by the logic OR of all Drivers WSO signals.

The Separate Gates system allows the division of the whole readout front-end electronics into sections, corresponding logically to the configuration of the experimental detection elements. There remain, however, two shortcomings which require the ability to tag events:

1. All the data flow into a single pair of Memories. For experiments containing a really large number of channels that could lead to long event cycles. It might be desirable to split the data buffering into separate parallel sections.
2. While not all detection sub-systems always deliver valid conversions the data stored in the Memories could be biased with a certain ambiguity. Consider for simplicity only

two sections: finding in the data stream (from the Memory) a sequence of data from section 1 followed by data from section 2 will always result a priori in an uncertainty as to whether these data belong to one complete event or to a series of two not-complete ones, in which the section 2 and section 1 data were respectively missing. Use of an unique event marker is therefore necessary to resolve such problems.

### 3.2 FERA Tagger

The FERA Extender/Tagger module can act as an active unit, participating in the event cycle and the FERA handshake. In this mode it inserts an *event identification* word into the data stream, acting like any other FERA-compatible unit. To work as the event tagger the Extender/Tagger module must be connected to the control bus and into the readout (REN/PASS) chain.

The event mark supplied by the Tagger is simply the event number. The module contains a 16-bit counter, which can be reset at any suitable moment (via CAMAC command or - as it is in our Full FERA system- via the front panel input) to the initial value (0 or 1, selectable by an internal jumper). During each event cycle (see below) the counter content is transferred to the Memory (with its most-significant bit being 1 or 0, again selectable by an internal jumper) and incremented. It is probably most logical to place the Tagger as the first module in the sub-system and to treat the event tag word as a "super-header", preceding the words (headers and conversions) of the digitizing modules.

The Tagger operates during the event cycle in a similar manner as the FERA ADC:

- It receives the GATE on the control bus . . .
- . . .*waits* a few $\mu$s - it emulates the conversion time in order to set the readout request signal not much earlier than the digitizing units. The delay can be adjusted by exchanging a socketed capacitor. In our application it is set to about 4 $\mu$s.
- Asserts REQ.
- After obtaining REN it *puts the counter* word on the data bus.
- At obtaining WAK it *increments* the counter and sets the PASS, transferring the bus control to the next module.

By equipping each parallel sub-system with a Tagger it becomes possible to recover the correlations between the information stored in them. Since the gate signal reaches all sub-systems (differing only in width and/or delay with respect to the Master-Gate), for a given event the Taggers will produce equal counter values in all of them, thus enabling an easy recombination of the event fragments into one full event.

## 4. Full FERA system

The last remark of the previous Section suggests an easy migration from the standard to the multi-system FERA configuration. The naive solution would consist of several copies of the standard configuration, each equipped with its own Tagger as the first module. Indeed, such a system would meet almost all requirements, in so far as its size, ability to apply separate gates and consistency in event tagging is concerned. However, this solution has one inherent *inconvenience*, connected with the fact that the event building is effectively performed in the back-end computer, after it receives all data from the FERA Memories.

A minor discomfort is posed by the fact of having many Managers in the system. The DAQ processor will have to react to several LAM's and, what is more important, perform slightly different actions at each of them.

To understand the other, really significant difficulty, consider an experiment in which in response to the trigger one sub-system receives some few tens of analog signals (e.g. calorimeter, energies and times in several elements) while in the other only very few parameters are digitized (e.g. single scintillator energy). The lengths (number of the header/data words) of the corresponding event fragments can easily differ by a factor of ten. Thus in the first system the data transfer will take place ten times more often. It is not difficult to handle these very asymmetric buffers in an off-line analysis, however in the on-line monitoring it will be necessary to temporarily store all these buffers until the one from the second sub-system is transmitted, as only then the full events can be reconstructed and sorted. Whereas it is not impossible to adopt such a scheme it would be certainly much easier to process the data coming to the back-end in a more symmetric structure.

### 4.1 Single manager control

The above considerations lead to the idea of applying a *general coordination* over all subsystems by a single Manager. The tasks it accomplishes can be summarized in the form of the basic features of the Full FERA system:

- Parallel FERA readout in sub-systems into the dedicated Memory pairs, encompassing in particular a proper coordination of the start and closing of the event cycle.
- Memory overflow in *any* sub-system is recognized by the Manager, which then redirects the data transfer in *all* of them into the complementary memory units and issues a single LAM. All the previously active Memories are readout by the DAQ processor via CAMAC while the complementary modules continue to accept data over the ECL bus.
- At any LAM the Taggers of all subsystems are reset. The event counting starts always from 1 in each block, enabling an easy correlation of event fragments.

It is obvious that in order to let the single Manager exert control over several sub-systems it is necessary to equip it with additional logic. Fig. 4 shows an example of the Full FERA system configuration (consisting of three sub-systems), with all the necessary interconnections. The FERA-compatible modules are shown as bigger rectangles while the small ones represent auxiliary logic units. The actions of the Manager can be divided into three groups:

1. Synchronization of Memory switching.
   In order to perform this task the Manager must coordinate the VETO and OVF signals of all sub-systems; also the RESET signal for the Taggers is created as the logic OR of the VETO's. The functions of the corresponding part of the logic system are:
   - Splitting the VE1 and VE2 output signals and distributing them to the appropriate VETO inputs of the Memories.
   - OR'ing the parallel Memories' OFV outputs for the OF1 and OF2 inputs of the Manager.
   - OR'ing the shaped (short) signals generated by the original veto levels of the Manager and splitting the OR for distribution to the RESET inputs of all Taggers.
2. Initiating parallel data readout.
   The Manager should take care that the request coming from any sub-system does not result in enabling the readout before all the digitizing modules are ready with their conversions. The actions performed at this stage are:
   - OR'ing all the Driver RQO signals for the Manager RQI input.

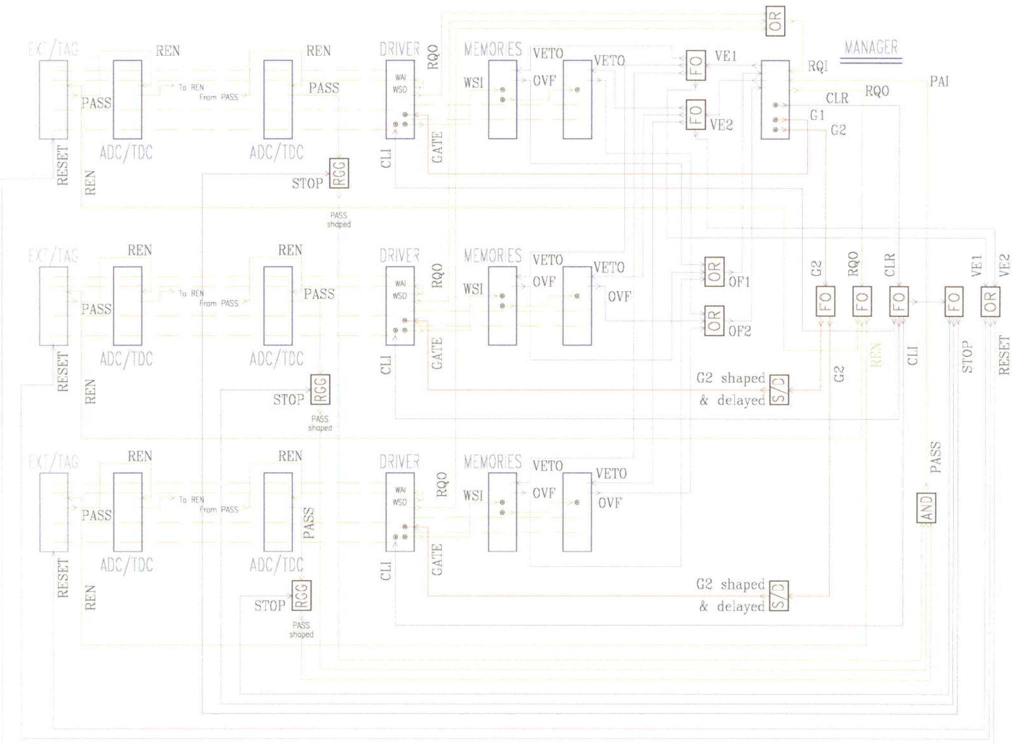


Fig. 4. Interconnections within the Full FERA system, consisting of three sub-systems. For a functional description see text. The sequence of signals relevant for the data transmission is shown in Fig. 5.

- Generating an internal delay in the Manager between obtaining the RQI pulse and setting the RQO output.
- Splitting the RQO signal and distributing it as REN to all the first modules (Taggers) in each sub-system.

3. Correlating the readout termination.
This task of the Manager is very critical for the data integrity. It must react to the PASS signals from all sub-systems in such a way that allows all the data to come to the appropriate Memories before the global clear is generated and before, at the proper moments, the Memories are swapped. The logic system must therefore:
   - Stretch the last PASS signals to cover the possible readout time span for *all* subsystems.
   - Create the logic AND of all shaped PASS signals for the Manager PAI input.
   - Split CLR output of the Manager and distribute it to all Drivers (and in consequence to all the digitizing modules).
   - Use again the CLR to re-arm the stretchers in the PASS line - since the readout time span might be quite large (even a few tens of $\mu$s), in order to avoid some overlaps between events the generated readout gates must be terminated simultaneously with the whole system resetting.

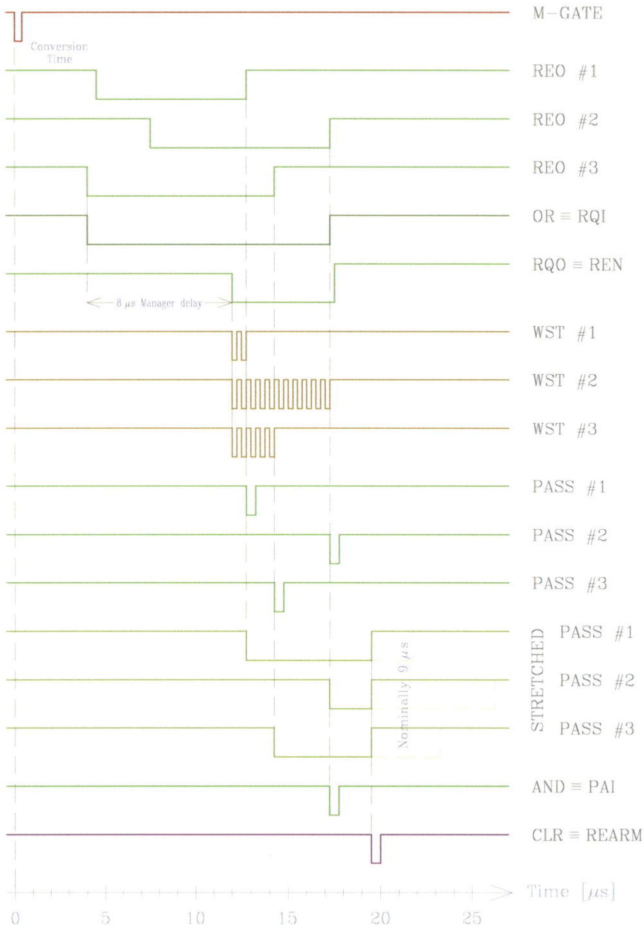


Fig. 5. FERA Readout timing - the most relevant signals for the Full FERA system shown in Fig. 4. To make the short pulses visible they are shown not to scale - the width of the M-GATE is about 50-100 ns, the write strobes (WST) are 50 ns wide with a 100 ns spacing, the PASS and CLR pulses are about 60-80 ns wide.

In addition the GATE signals passing through the Manager have to be adjusted (width and/or delay) before entering the Drivers of the individual sections. This action is again performed by the auxiliary logic.

The above list of the Manager tasks contains implicitly the types of the logic system components. The required modules include Fan-Out units, logic OR and AND modules with both, overlap and shaped outputs, shaper-and-delay units and retriggerable gate generators. Although it is possible to assemble the auxiliary logic system from commercially available modules, such a solution would necessitate the use of ECL-NIM-ECL level converters at several stages. While designing the implementation of the Full FERA system it has been decided to construct a series of CAMAC-based logic modules[4], with the

---

[4] Electrical design and mechanical construction of the logic modules used in the Full FERA system is by P. Eberhardt.

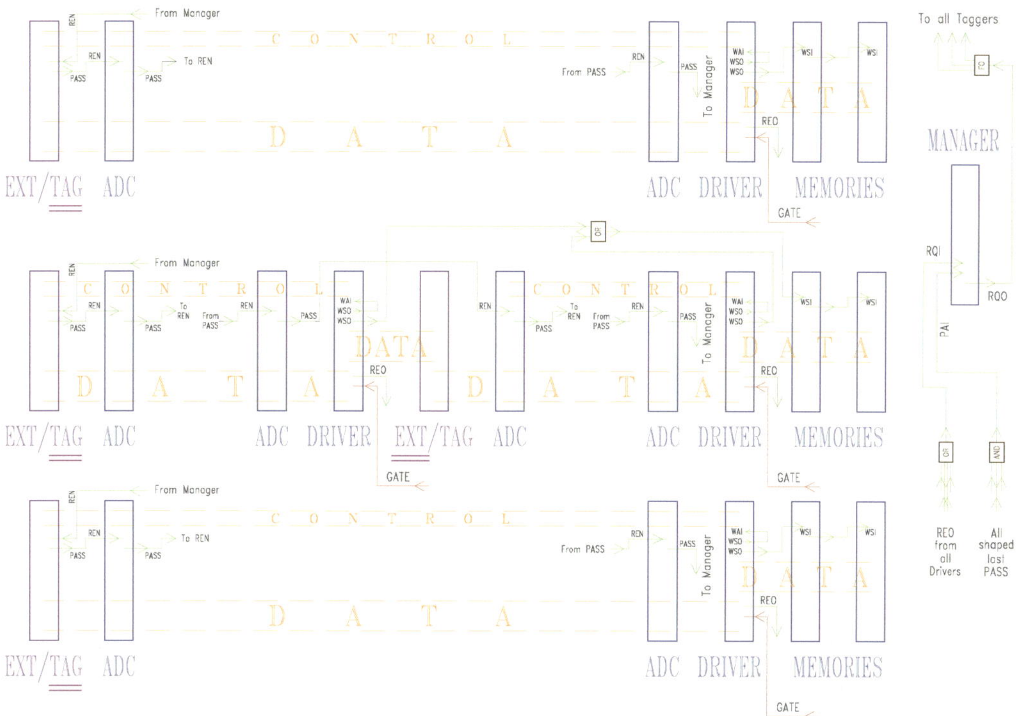


Fig. 6. Full FERA system with separate gate sections in one sub-system. Only the ECL busses and the REN/PASS chains are shown to point out the differences with respect to the configuration presented in Fig. 4.

input/output logic levels tailored to the specific demands of the FERA configuration. Using these special logic units allows to minimize the length of the cabling and make it more transparent for non-specialized users. The sequence of the most relevant FERA event cycle signals is presented schematically in Fig. 5. Again an example with three sub-systems is considered. The delay readout-request - readout-enable (RQO–REN) and the readout time span are assumed to be few $\mu$s each (cf. next Section). Please note, that the readout request signals (REO's) of each sub-system can be set at slightly different times. When using the correctly set Taggers, this spread should be largely eliminated. One can observe the action of re-arming the PASS stretchers by the global clear signal.

Of course, within the Full FERA system it is possible to apply separate gates within each subsystem - see Fig. 6. One can break the data bus in two (or more) sections, applying the Driver/Extender pairs in an analogous way as described above. It should be noted that in such a configuration the readout request signal must contain also the "middle" Driver REO output in the OR of all requests and that in the separate-gate sub-system the Memories must be strobed by an OR of all sections WSO's. The Extender/Tagger module which acts as an Extender is connected to neither the control bus nor the readout chain.

## 5. Full FERA system performance

To investigate the rate capability of the Full FERA system let us assume that the experiment contains some 1000 channels, of which about 5-10% have valid conversions for a good (triggered) event. Assume that about 60 parameters ('hits') are digitized in 20 modules for each event. Therefore at every trigger some 20 modules will prepare 4 data words to be transferred, i.e. the readout will consist of transmitting 80 Words (of 16 bit) to the buffering Memory.

The M-GATE signal defines time zero. Conversion times for various modules in the system are:

- Tagger – emulates 4 $\mu$s conversion time.
- ADC – 4 ÷ 9 $\mu$s. Assume 10 bit resolution, thus conversion time of about 4.5 $\mu$s.
- TDC – 4 ÷ (10-12) $\mu$s, depending on the number of hits.

Therefore the REQ signal will appear about 4 $\mu$s after M-GATE and one has to program ~8 $\mu$s RQI-RQO delay in the Manager. Hence, the readout starts at about 12 $\mu$s after the beginning of the event cycle.

The readout duration can be as short as few hundreds ns (with no hits and only the Tagger word present) or - for all 80 words - as long as ≥8 $\mu$s. Therefore the stretchers have to be set to ~9 $\mu$s and the transition time from REN to the PAI signal is about 9 $\mu$s.

After receiving PAI the Manager will generate CLR and after ~3 $\mu$s it will be ready for the next event cycle.

A conservative estimation for the event cycle duration is thus around 25 $\mu$s. It follows that an event rate of the order of $10^4$ per second can be processed by the system with dead-time losses of about 2%. On the scale of the experiment sizes under discussion here such performance is very attractive.

Further limitation on the rate capability comes from the Memory emptying time, a slow procedure on the CAMAC DATAWAY. It should be noted, that this could be easily improved by replacing the CAMAC Memories by their VME version, allowing for much faster data transmission - see Fig. 7 for an example of connections within such implementation.

Let us consider the restraint caused by the CAMAC readout, assuming again three FERA subsystems with the Memories set to the 14 kWords capacity. At an overflow (Manager's LAM) there is thus approximately 40 kWords to be sent over the DATAWAY. The available time for that action is determined by the speed of the Memory filling.

Assume that the DAQ processor needs as much as about 2 $\mu$s to extract one Word from the Memory and put it into the outgoing event stream. In such conditions the emptying of the whole set of 3 Memories (40 kWords) will take 80 ms, thus the maximum interrupt rate will be 12 $s^{-1}$.

Another cautious assumption concerns the memory filling - let us say that in the fastest-overflowing sub-system there are 30 Words at each event. Thus the Memory capacity corresponds to about 500 events.

By comparing the two numbers we obtain the *realistic event rate* for the Full FERA system operated in the pure CAMAC mode of about $6 \cdot 10^3$ $s^{-1}$. One should keep in mind that since the CAMAC transfer takes place every 500 events, the interrupts (LAM's) are rather derandomized and therefore this rate is processed virtually *without* any dead-time losses.

An analogous estimation for the case when the Full FERA system is equipped with VME buffer Memories of 32 kWords capacity leads, with the assumptions of 80 kWords per event and as much as 0.25 $\mu$s/word memory emptying speed, to the conclusion that the acceptable event rate (with the size as above) is around $5 \cdot 10^4$ $s^{-1}$. It is impressive, however at such load the FERA itself (readout to memories) would generate a substantial dead-time.

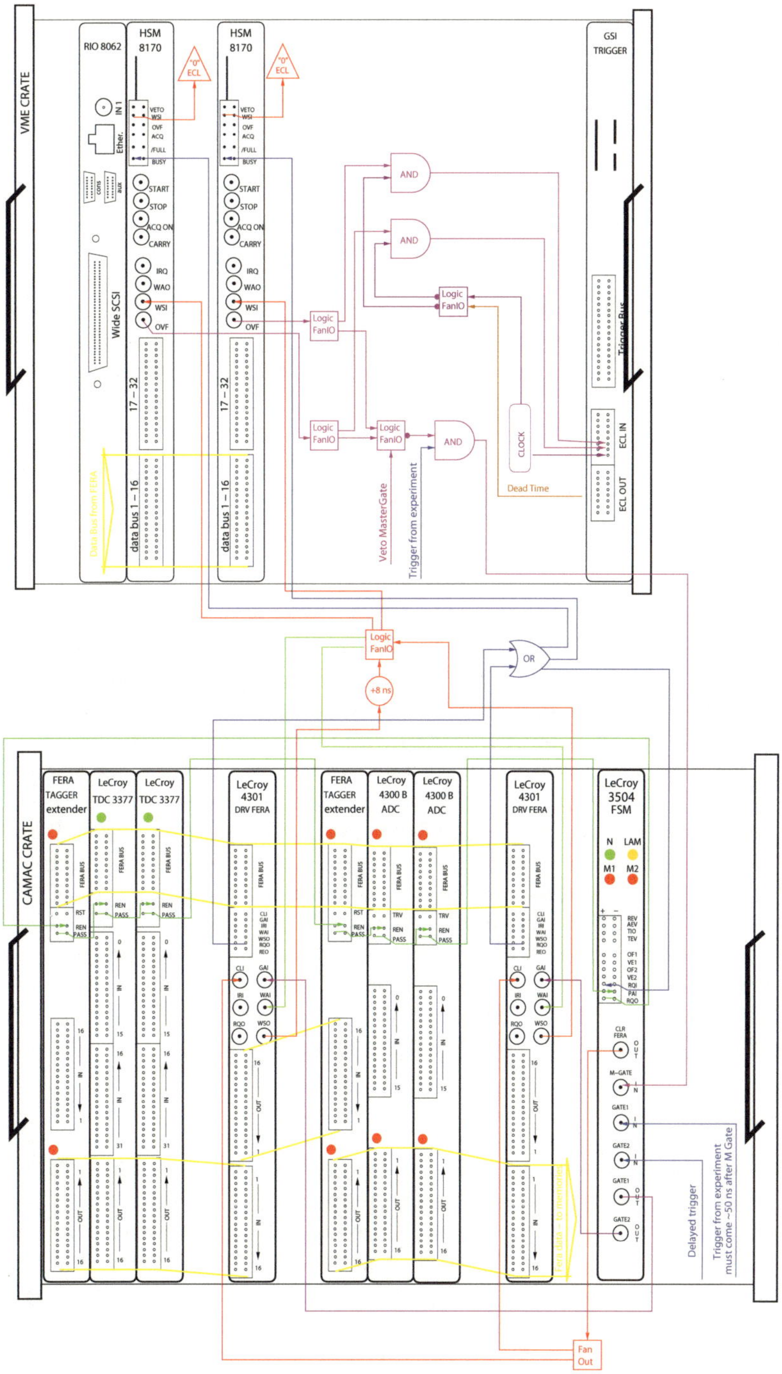


Fig. 7. Full FERA system equipped with the VME buffer Memories (here HSM 8170 serviced by a RIO2 front-end processor). The connections are slightly different than in the case of the CAMAC memories due to particularities in the requirements of the VME modules.

It is worth stressing that all the assumptions used in the above estimations are rather conservative and therefore a factor of about 2 reserve in the rate capability is most certainly incorporated. The exact number clearly depends very much on the particular experimental application. In any case, the estimated resulting Full FERA system performance is unparalleled in comparable DAQ systems.

## 6. Conclusions

This Chapter presents an important development in the area of FERA-based readout systems. A custom FERA Extender/Tagger CAMAC module is described, which offers the possibility to split FERA digitizing front-end electronics into several virtually independent sections, driven by separate, trigger-associated gates. These sections can be distributed over many CAMAC crates. The Tagger allows to fully exploit the buffering ability of the FERA system by enabling the parallel readout of several sub-systems, in which the event fragments are consistently, sequentially numbered. These fragments are then used to reconstruct full events in the back-end computer, removing the necessity to perform an on-line event building, therefore reducing the overall event readout time.
A configuration of the FERA system is presented in which a single Manager exerts control over the whole system, synchronizing the Memory readout to provide the best CAMAC data structure for the on-line monitoring software. The resultant Full FERA system can attain readout rates of about 1 MByte/s (i.e. some 6000 moderate-length events per second), which is very competitive with other comparable systems. With its extension to VME the data throughput can be as large as about 8 MByte/s (i.e. around 50000 events per second). This solution is reasonably simple but very reliable method for medium-sized experiments to upgrade and expand their readout electronics without major hardware investments. The Full FERA system has been successfully implemented in a number of recent precision experiments, in some of which the configuration has been extended to include also the generic PCOS III readout system of multi-wire proportional chambers (Barnet et al. 2000; Ban et al. 2006; Stephan et al. 2007; Stephan et al. 2009). The FERA system gains on capabilities due to now available modules, like Ortec Histogramming Memory HM413, CMCamac Driver, Memory and Histogrammer CMC203 or Wiener CAMAC-to-FERA Bridge. Logic modules based on FPGA allow to customize various functions to the FERA-compatible protocols. Examples of new implementations can be found e.g. in (Karpukhin et al. 2003; Ugorowski et al. 2006; von Reden et al. 2008). All that shows that the system is still vivid and worth considering when choosing readout/DAQ options for not-to-large experiments.

## 7. Acknowledgments

The author would like to thank at the first place the two colleagues with whom we worked at ETH Zürich on the design and tests of the system, Dr. C.P. Bee and P. Eberhardt. This work has been highly valued by the LeCroy Corporation and I have the pleasure to present the system at their headquarters (Kistryn et al. 1997). That achievement would not be possible without the contribution to the system concept of my friend and colleague, Prof. K. Bodek from the Jagiellonian University. Later steps of the system development (especially coupling of the PCOS branch and inclusion of VME Memories) and its implementation in the real experimental environment have been most efficiently assisted by two other friends and colleagues, Dr. A. Kozela from the Institute of Nuclear Physics Polish Academy of Sciences in Kraków and Dr. E. Stephan from the University of Silesia in Katowice. I wish we could follow our future team activities in equally harmonious and productive atmosphere!

## 8. References

[Ban et al. 2006] Ban, G.; Beck, M.; Białek, A.; Bodek, K.; Gorel, P.; Kirch, K.; Kistryn, St.; Kozela, A.; Kuźniak, M.; Lindroth, A.; Naviliat-Cuncic, O.; Pulut, J.; Severijns, N.; Stephan, E. & Zejma, J. (2006). A Mott polarimeter for the search of time reversal violation in the decay of free neutrons. *Nucl. Instr. Meth. in Phys. Res. Sect. A*, Vol. 565, No. 2: 711-724, ISSN 0168-9002.

[Barnet et al. 2000] Barnet, I.C.; Bee, C.; Bodek, K.; Budzanowski, A.; Danneberg, N.; Eberhardt, P.; Fetscher, W.; Hilbes, C.; Janousch, M.; Jarczyk, L.; Kirch, K.; Kistryn, S.; Klement, J.; Köhler, K.; Kozela, A.; Lang, J.; Llosa, G.; Markiewicz, M.; Morelle, X.; Naviliat, O.; Schweizer, T.; Smyrski, J.; Sromicki, J.; Stephan, E.; Strzałkowski, A.; Szeker, K. & Zejma, J. (2000). An apparatus for the measurement of the transverse polarization of positrons from the decay of polarized muons. *Nucl. Instr. Meth. in Phys. Res. Sect. A*, Vol. 455, No. 2: 329-345, ISSN 0168-9002.

[Beausang et al. 2000] Beausang, C.W.; Barton, C.J.; Caprio, M.A.; Casten, R.F.; Cooper, J.R.; Krücken, R.; Liu, B.; Novak, J.R.; Wang, Z.; Wilhelm, M.; Wilson, A.N.; Zamfir, N.V. & Zilges, A. (2000). The YRAST Ball array. *Nucl. Instr. Meth. in Phys. Res. Sect. A*, Vol. 452, No. 3: 431-439, ISSN 0168-9002.

[Davin et al. 2001] Davin, B.; de Souza, R.T.; Yanez, R.; Larochelle, Y.; Alfaro, R.; Xu, H.S.; Alexander, A.; Bastin, K.; Beulieu, L.; Dorsett, J.; Fleener, G.; Gelovani, L.; Lefort, T.; Poehlman, J.; Charity, R.J.; Sobotka, L.G.; Elson, J.; Wagner, A.; Liui, T.X.; Liu, X.D.; Lynch, W.G.; Morris, L.; Shomin, R.; Tan, W.P.; Tsang, M.B.; Verde, G. & Yurkon, J. (2001). LASSA: A large area silicon strip array for isotopic identification of charged particles. *Nucl. Instr. Meth. in Phys. Res. Sect. A*, Vol. 473, No. 3: 302-318, ISSN 0168-9002.

[Elfman et al. 1997] Elfman, M.; Kristiansson, P.; Malmqvist, K.; Pallon, J.; Sjöland, A.; Utui, R. & Yang, C. (1997). New CAMAC based data acquisition and beam control system for Lund nuclear microprobe. *Nucl. Instr. Meth. in Phys. Res. Sect. B*, Vol. 130, No. 1: 123-126, ISSN 0168-583X.

[Gazes et al. 1993] Gazes, S.B.; Perera, P.A.A. & Wolfs, F.L.H. (1993). FERA readout system for APEX. *Nucl. Instr. Meth. in Phys. Res. Sect. A*, Vol. 337, No. 1: 174–181, ISSN 0168-9002.

[Hagemann et al. 1999] Hagemann, M.; Bassini, R.; van den Berg, A.M.; Ellinghaus, F.; Frekers, D.; Hannen, V.M.; Häupke, T.; Heyse, J.; Jacobs, E.; Kirsch, M.; Krüsemann, B.; Rakers, S.; Sohbach, H. & Wörtche, H.J. (1999). A DSP-based readout and online processing system for a new focal-plane polarimeter at AGOR. *Nucl. Instr. Meth. in Phys. Res. Sect. A*, Vol. 437, No. 2-3: 459–470, ISSN 0168-9002.

[Karpukhin et al. 2003] Karpukhin, V.; Kulikov, A.; Olshevsky, V. & Trusov, S. (2003). Readout logic and its hardware implementation in the DIRAC experiment. *Nucl. Instr. Meth. In Phys. Res. Sect. A*, Vol. 512, No. 3: 578–584, ISSN 0168-9002.

[Kistryn et al. 1997] Kistryn, St.; Bee, C.P. & Eberhardt, P. (1997). An integrated multi-crate FERA readout system. *Proceedings of the Sixth International Conference on Electronics for Particle Physics*, pp. 193–207, Chestnut Ridge, May 1997, LeCroy Research Systems, ed.: Blanar, G.J. & Sumner, R.L., New York.

[Loudos et al. 2004] Loudos, G.K.; Giokaris, N.D.; Mainta, K.; Sakelitos, N.; Stiliaris, E.; Karabarbounis, A.; Papanicolas, C.N.; Spanoudaki, V.; Nikita, K.S.; Uzunoglu, N.K.; Archimandritis, S.C.; Varvarigou, A.D.; Stefanis, K.N.; Majewski, S.; Weisenberger, A.; Pani, R. & Maintas, D. (2004). High-resolution and high-sensitivity SPECT imaging of breast phantoms. *Nucl. Instr. Meth. in Phys. Res. Sect. A*, Vol. 527, No. 1: 97–101, ISSN 0168-9002.

[LeCroy 1983] FERA - Fast Encoding and Readout ADC; System Possibilities. *LeCroy Application Note* AN 4004, (1983). LeCroy Research Systems, Chestnut Ridge, NY 10977-6499.

[Okamura 2000] Okamura, H. (2000). Fast data acquisition system for the spectrometer SMART at RIKEN. *Nucl. Instr. Meth. in Phys. Res. Sect. A*, Vol. 343, No. 1: 194–196, ISSN 0168-9002.

[Ordine et al. 1997] Ordine, A.; Boiano, A.; Parascandolo, P.; D'Onofrio, A.; Campajola, L.; De Riosa, A.; Inglima, G.; La Commara, M.; Roca. V.; Romano, M.; Romoli, M.; Pierroutsakou, D.; Sandoli, M. & Terrasi, F. (1997). EBOFERA: A companion for FERA ADCs. *Nucl. Instr. Meth. in Phys. Res. Sect. A*, Vol. 390, No. 3: 366–374, ISSN 0168-9002.

[von Reden et al. 2008] von Reden, K.F.; Roberts, M.L.; Jenkins, W.J.; Rosenheim, B.E.; McNichol, A.P. & Schneider, R.J. (2008). Software development for continuous-gas-flow AMS. *Nucl. Instr. Meth. in Phys. Res. Sect. B*, Vol. 266, No. 10: 2233–2237, ISSN 0168-583X.

[Stephan et al. 2007] Stephan, E.; Kistryn, St.; Sworst, R.; Biegun, A.; Bodek. K.; Ciepał, I.; Deltuva, A.; Epelbaum, E.; Fonseca, A.; Glöckle, W.; Golak, J.; Kalantar-Nayestanaki, N.; Kamada, H.; Kiš, M.; Kozela, A.; Mahjour-Shafiei, M.; Micherdzińska, A.; Nogga, A.; Sauer, P.U.; Skibiński, R.; Witała, H.; Zejma, J. & Zipper, W. (2007). Vector and tensor analyzing powers of elastic deuteron-proton scattering at 130 MeV deuteron beam energy. *Phys. Rev. C* Vol. 76, No. 5: 057001 1–4, ISSN 0556-2813.

[Stephan et al. 2009] Stephan, E.; Kistryn, St.; Biegun, A.; Bodek. K.; Ciepał, I.; Deltuva, A.; Epelbaum, E.; Fonseca, A.C.; Golak, J.; Kalantar-Nayestanaki, N.; Kamada, H.; Kiš, M.; Kłos, B.; Kozela, A.; Mahjour-Shafiei, M.; Micherdzińska, A.; Nogga, A.; Skibiński, R.; Sworst, R.; Witała, H.; Zejma, J. & Zipper, W. (2009). Precise set of tensor analyzing power $T_{20}$ data for the deuteron-proton breakup reaction at 130 MeV. *Eur. Phys. J. A* Vol. 42, No. 1: 13–24, ISSN 1434-6001.

[Sugaya & Nomachi 1999] Sugaya, Y. & Nomachi, M. (1999). Universal I/O board for the laser-electron photons experiments at SPring-8. *Nucl. Instr. Meth. in Phys. Res. Sect. A*, Vol. 437, No. 1: 68–74, ISSN 0168-9002.

[Sumner] Sumner, R.L. *http://www.cmcamac.com/*. Cheesecote Mountain CAMAC, Pomona, NY 10970.

[Ugorowski et al. 2006] Ugorowski, P.; Propri, R.; Karamian, S.A.; Gohlke, D.; Lazich, J.; Caldwell, N.; Chakrawatrhy, R.S.; Helba, M.; Roberts, H. & Carroll, J.J. (2006). Design and characterization of a compact multi-detector array for studies of induced gamma emission; Spontaneous decay of $^{178m2}$Hf as a test case. *Nucl. Instr. Meth. in Phys. Res. Sect. A*, Vol. 565, No. 2: 657–676, ISSN 0168-9002.

[Vander Molen et al. 1991] Vander Molen, A.; Maier, M.R.; Robertson, M. & Westafall, G.D. (1991). A fast data-bus to buffer-memory interface. *Nucl. Instr. Meth. in Phys. Res. Sect. A*, Vol. 307, No. 1: 116–118, ISSN 0168-9002.

[Watzlawik et al. 1994] Watzlawik, K.-H.; Nellen, R.; Noll, T.; Karnadi, M. & Machner, H. (1994). FATIMA A data acquisition system for medium scale experiments. In *LeCroy Model 3304 FERA System Manager Operator's Manual*, LeCroy Research Systems, Chestnut Ridge, NY 10977-6499.

# 14

# Swarm Robotics: An Extensive Research Review

Yogeswaran M. and Ponnambalam S. G.
*School of Engineering, Monash University, Sunway Campus. 46150 Petaling Jaya, Selangor, Malaysia*

## 1. Introduction

Swarm robotics is a new approach to the coordination of large numbers of relatively simple physically embodied robots, that are autonomous, not controlled centrally, capable of local communication and operates based on some sense of biological inspiration (Sharkey & Sharkey, 2006a). Swarm robotic systems have become a major research area since 1980's, as new solution approaches are being developed and validated, it is often possible to realize the advantages of swarm robotic systems. Table 1 shows the key advantages of swarm

| BENEFITS | DESCRIPTIONS |
|---|---|
| Parallelism | In task-decomposable application domains, robots can accomplish a given task more quickly than a single robot by dividing the task into sub tasks and executing them concurrently. |
| Robustness | No single point of failure for the system. This is an important characteristic since many of the applications rely on continued progress even if some components in the system fail. |
| Scalability | As the swarm of robots becomes larger, its relative performance in comparison to a centralized system becomes better. |
| Heterogeneousness | Since a group of robots may be heterogeneous, it can utilize "specialists" -robots whose physical properties enable them to perform efficiently certain well defined tasks. |
| Flexibility | Easily adaptable for different applications as different applications will have different requirements, a general architecture will need the ability to be easily reconfigured for the different problems it proposes to solve. |
| Complex Tasks | Tasks may be inherently too complex (or impossible) for a single robot to accomplish or performance benefits can be gained from using a swarm of robots. |
| Cheap Alternative | Building and using several simple robots can be easier, cheaper, more flexible and more fault tolerant than having a single powerful robot for each separate task. |

Table 1. Characteristics of swarm robotic systems.

robotic systems (Cao et al., 1997; Altshuler et al., 2006; De le Torre & Stentz, 2001; Bruemmer et al., 2002): The early work on classification of research areas of swarm robotic systems was done by Dudek et al. (1993). The paper classified the areas into five areas which are swarm size, communication range, communication topology, communication bandwidth, swarm reconfigurability and swarm unit processing ability. Cao et al. (1997) presented the survey of cooperative robotics in a hierarchical way. They split the publications into five main axes: group architecture, resource conflicts, origins of cooperation, learning and geometric problems. Group architecture is further divided into centralization/decentralization, differentiation (denotes the homogeneous or heterogeneous robot groups), communication structure and modeling of other agents dimensions. Modeling of other agents dimension contains studies which models the intentions, beliefs, actions, capabilities, and states of other agents to obtain more effective cooperation between robots (Bayindir & Sahin, 2007).
Iocchi et al. (2001) presented an analysis of multi robot systems by looking at their cooperative aspects. They have also proposed taxonomy of multi robot systems and a characterization of reactive and social deliberative behaviors of the multi robot system as a whole. Rather than summarizing the research area of swarm robots into a taxonomy of cooperating systems, Parker (2003) has organized the areas by the principal topics that have generated significant levels of research. The categorization done in this paper has the main structure as in the work of Parker (2003). The research axes are biological inspiration, communication, control approach, mapping and localization, object transportation and manipulation, reconfigurable robotics, motion coordination, learning and task allocation. Each of the research axes are further separated into sub-categories for in detailed discussion.

## 2. Research axes

### 2.1 Biological inspiration

Swarm robotics and the related concept of swarm intelligence, is inspired by an understanding of the decentralized mechanisms that underlie the organization of natural swarms such as ants, bees, birds, fish, wolfs and even humans. Jung & Zelinsky (2000) described the implementation of a heterogeneous cooperative multi-robot system that was designed with a goal of engineering a grounded symbolic representation which was inspired by the communication methods employed by biological systems.
Social insects provide one of the best-known examples of biological self organized behavior. By means of local and limited communication, they are able to accomplish impressive behavioral feats: maintaining the health of the colony, caring for their young, responding to invasion and so on (Sharkey, 2006b). Labella et al. (2006) has analyzed the behavior of a group of robots involved in an object retrieval task where the robots' control system is inspired by a model of ants' foraging behaviors. The sub-tasks assigned to the robots are extracted from simple behavior of ant swarms such as search, retrieve, deposit, return and rest. Ideas inspired from such collective behaviors have led to the use of pheromones (Panait & Luke, 2004), a chemical substance deposited by ants and similar social insects in order to mark the environment with information to assist other ants at a later time.
Similarly Payton et al. (2003) and Cazangi et al. (2005) used pheromones to achieve inter-robot communication mechanism in their research. Pheromones in swarm robotics can be viewed as a mechanism for inter-robot communication that can help reduce the complexity of individual agents. Pheromone communication adopted from necrophoric bee behavior was introduced in (Purnamadjaja & Russell, 2004) to develop interaction between the

members of a robot swarm. The term "Necrophoric" signifies the removal of bee corpses from inside of the hive. Nevertheless, the introduction of pheromones has driven the research exploitation in communication and localization in the studies of swarm robotics.

A higher level of studies in this area leads to exploit the cooperation and interaction abilities in mammals. Unlike insects, mammals behave differently toward individual social partners, rather than interacting with all entities in the same way. Tomlinson & Blumberg (2002) created an interactive virtual multi-agent system based on the behavior of packs of gray wolves. Their virtual wolves are able to form social relationships with each other via the mechanism of social relationship formation involves emotion, perception, and learning.

Fong et al. (2003) have modeled their robots to adopt human's social interactions. As research progresses in this area, more sophisticated teamwork architectures are being explored into to cater the increase in problem complexity. Such sophisticated teamwork architectures was demonstrated by Kitano et al. (1998). Robocup is an attempt to foster intelligent robotics by including design principles of autonomous agents, multi agent collaboration, strategy acquisition, real-time reasoning, robotics and sensor fusion.

### 2.2 Communication

The role of communication among mobile robots remains one of the most important research issues in swarm robotics system design. When a task requires cooperation, there is a need for some form of communication between the participating agents. Cooperation work requires communication whenever one agent's actions depend critically on knowledge that is accessible only from other agents. There has been much debate about the level of communication that should be allowed between such systems. Most of the open literatures have made distinctions between implicit/indirect and explicit/direct communications. Implicit communication (also referred to as stigmergy (Trianni et al., 2004)) is a method of communicating through the environment.

Mir & Amavasai (2007) have modeled an autonomous swarm which is able to make decentralized decisions and demonstrate implicit communication. The paper also stressed that the swarm exhibits behavior based cooperation in the absence of explicit communication. White & Pagurek (1998) presented a new architectural description for an agent that is based on ants' stigmergy behavior for inter-swarm communication is introduced. Ramos et al. (2005) discusses several concepts related to self-organization, stigmergy and social foraging in animals. The paper also suggested and stressed the role played not only by the environmental media as a driving force for societal learning, as well as by positive and negative feedbacks produced by the many interactions among agents.

Pheromone signal plays an important role in communication domain as its capability of establishing communication between a sender and a receiver when there is no direct clear path between them. Pheromone communication is a type of implicit communication. There a many papers that have explored the use of pheromone signal to convey messages to other robots in a swarm such as the work by Purnamadjaja & Russell (2004) and Purnamadjaja et al. (2007). An improved form of pheromone communication method called "virtual pheromone" was used by (Payton et al., 2003; Meng et al., 2007) to employ simple communication and coordination to achieve large scale results in the areas of surveillance, reconnaissance, hazard detection, and path finding. More implementations of implicit communication in robots swarm has been reported by D'Angelo & Pagello (2005) and Bruemmer et al. (2004).

Explicit communication is the type of communication in which the robots directly pass messages to each other and/or to the human operator. McPartland et al. (2005) has made comparison between implicit and explicit communications theory by applying it to two different swarms of robot which is assigned to explore a given environment in the shortest period of time. Rybski et al. (2007) introduced and explored simple communication strategies which implemented implicit and explicit communication.

Trianni et al. (2004) studied the use of direct communication in order to achieve a reaction to the detection of a hole. Hayes et al. (2003) described a distributed algorithm for solving the full odor localization task, and shown that group performance can exceed that of a single robot using explicit communication. Christodoulopoulos et al. (2007) implemented an ad hoc wireless network communication to exchange information between all its individual agents within the swarm. Ad-hoc mode is a method for wireless devices to directly communicate with each other. Operating in ad-hoc mode allows all wireless devices within range of each other to discover and communicate in peer-to-peer fashion without involving central access points.

Communication between robots can multiply their capabilities and increase the efficiency. This has been shown in simulation and on real robots. The amount of communication has also been studied. Sometimes even little communication will enhance the performance of the system (Adolfsson, 2001). Even though there is no clear conclusion on what type of communication is better for robot swarms, but most of the current research is aiming towards implicit communication for its robust characteristics.

### 2.3 Control approach

In general, swarm robot coordination strategies assume either a centralized approach, where a single robot plans for the group, or a distributed approach, where each robot is responsible for its own planning (De le Torre & Stentz, 2001). Iocchi et al. (2001) has clearly distinguished between centralized and distributed control as:

- Centralized: the organization of a system having a robotic agent (a leader) that is in charge of organizing the work of the other robots; the leader is involved in the decisional process for the whole team, while the other members act according to the directions of the leader.
- Distributed: the organization of a system composed by robotic agents which are completely autonomous in the decisional process with respect to each other; in this class of systems a leader does not exist.

Table 2 shows the advantages and disadvantages of centralized and distributed control approach. Parker (1993) experimented on the advantages and the disadvantages of the control approaches and reported that deciding the proper balance between centralized and distributed control is the key to achieve the desired emergent group behavior in a swarm of robots. Steele Jr & Thomas (2007) introduced "Directed Stigmergy-Based Control" which incorporates the advantages of distributed control and centralized control. The aim of the paper is to stress the need of a supervisor in useful tasks that require searching large areas such as planetary science exploration, urban search and rescue, or land mine remediation.

However, both distributed and centralized control approaches have contributed individually to the study of swarm robotics and have generated interesting experimental results. Extensive studies in distributed control approaches (Spaan et al., 2006; Shen et al., 2002) lead to implementation of control laws or force laws (Gazi & Passino, 2002;

Dimarogonas & Kyriakopoulos, 2007) incorporating both attraction and repulsion features. On the other hand, centralized control approach (Li et al., 2007) has contributed in supporting several capabilities of swarm robotic systems such as hierarchical planning, concurrent planning, execution and perception, reactivity to environmental changes, error recovery, and coordination of multiple tasks.

| APPROACH | CRITERIA | DESCRIPTION |
|---|---|---|
| Centralized | Advantages | Optimal plans can be produced. The leader can take into account all the relevant information conveyed by the members of the team and generate an optimal plan for the team. |
| | Disadvantages | Strongly rely on communication. Thus, when a communication failure takes place, it results in a failure of the entire system. |
| | | A strongly centralized system can fail in accomplishing its task when its leader goes out of order. |
| | | System response to changes in the environment is sluggish since all relevant information must be conveyed to the leader before any action can be taken. |
| Distributed | Advantages | Do not have a single point of failure. The loss of a single agent will not cripple the system, as can be the case in single-agent or centrally controlled systems. |
| | | Can achieve complex results with relatively simple system design. The designer need only create simple, low level behaviors, instead of a single, computationally intense control system to govern all possible situations. |
| | | Are inherently parallel, which allows for extremely scalable systems and faster task completion. |
| | Disadvantages | Often result in highly sub-optimal solutions because all plans are based solely on local information. |
| | | Independent task execution by the system components causes problems in the area of coordination between the system agents. |

Table 2. Advantages and disadvantages of control approaches (Iocchi et al., 2001; Steele Jr & Thomas, 2007).

### 2.4 Mapping and localization

Mapping and localization is an exceedingly well-studied problem in swarm robotics which gathered a lot of research papers the last two decades. Mapping is a representation of the physical environments through the mobile robots sensory data into spatial models (Thrun, 2002). Localization is defined as finding the absolute or rational location of robot in the spatial models generated. Since the development of research in mapping and localization progressed, the problems that addresses mapping and localization has been referred to as simultaneous localization and mapping (SLAM) or concurrent mapping and localization (CML).

SLAM or CML is the problem of acquiring a map of an unknown environment with a moving robot, while simultaneously localizing the robot relative to this map (Thrun, 2002). The SLAM problem addresses situations where the robot lacks a global positioning sensor. Instead, it has to rely on a sensor (e.g., laser scanner, sonar and vision) of incremental egomotion for robot position estimation (e.g., odometry). To solve the problem of odometry in SLAM, many approaches have been made thru the application of various filters introduced in (Thrun, 2001; Se et al., 2002; Thrun et al., 2004; Howard, 2006).

There are two distinct mapping approaches available namely topological mapping and geometric mapping. A topological map is an abstract encoding of the structural characteristics of an environment. Often, topological maps (Kuipers & Byun, 1991; Fabrizi & Saffiotti, 2000; Choset & Nagatani, 2001) represent the environment as a set of distinctive places using points (e.g., rooms), connected by sequences of robot behaviors using lines (e.g., wall-following). A geometric map, on the other hand, is a representation of the precise geometric characteristics of the environment, much like a floor plan (Wolter et al., 2004). This area also covers the studies in the type of terrains (Seraji, 1999; Triebel et al., 2006) and dynamic environments (Wolf & Sukhatme, 2004).

### 2.5 Object transportation and manipulation

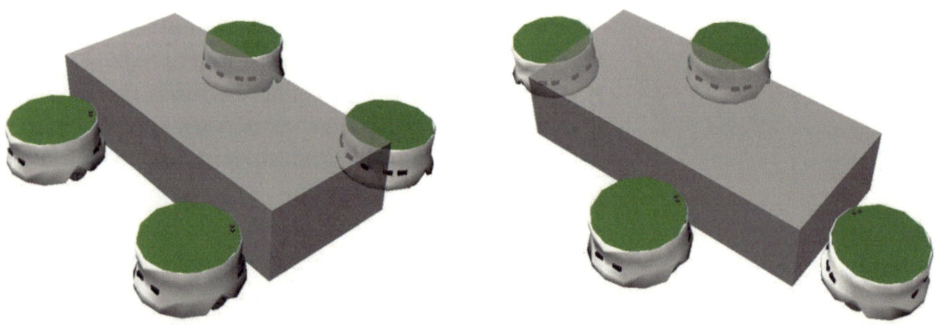

(a) Force closure. (b) Form closure.

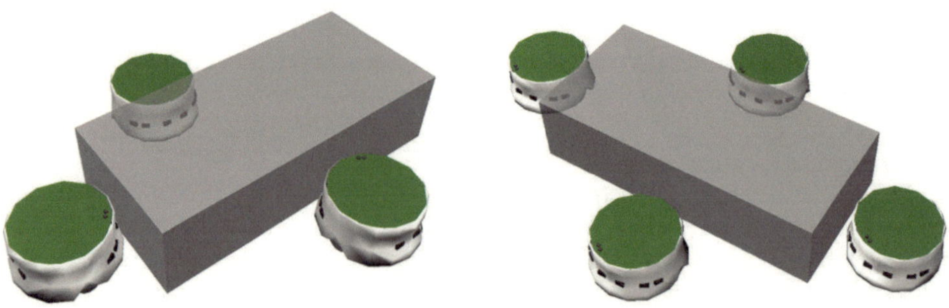

(c) Conditional closure. (d) Object closure.

Fig. 1. Closure techniques for object manipulation.

Researches in this area of swarm robotics have drafted three types object manipulation method which are namely grasping, pushing and caging. In grasping, all robots are arranged so that the total robots system is grasping the object (Wang et al., 2007; Agassounon, 2004). Grasping incorporates form closure (refer to Fig.1(b)) and force closure (refer to Fig.1(a)) techniques. Force closure is a condition that implies that the grasp can resist any external force applied to the object. Form closure can be viewed as the condition guaranteeing force closure, without requiring the contacts to be frictional. In general, robots are the agents that induce contacts with the object, and are the only source of grasp forces. Pushing (Miyata et al., 1997; Yamada & Saito, 2001) on the other hand doesn't guarantee form closure or force closure, but requires external forces to be applied to the object such as gravity and friction. For this type of object manipulation, conditional closure (refer to Fig.1(c)) is introduced. Pushing behaviors gives an advantage where any objects that can't be grasped to be moved and to perform pushing to multiple objects as well. The main difficulty on object manipulation via pushing is that the robots cannot pull the object directly when it needs to slow down or move back the object.

Caging (Pereira et al., 2003; Wang & Kumar, 2002; Wang et al., 2004) introduces a bounded movable area for the object. Then, the contact between object and robotics mechanism need not be maintained by robot's control. This makes motion planning and control of each robotic mechanism become simple and robust. This condition is called object closure (refer to Fig.1(d)). Caging has been widely used in manipulation of swarm robotics because this makes motion planning and control of each robotic mechanism simple and robust.

A leader-follower type multiple robot system was addressed by Wang et al. (2007) where the proposed system consists of a pushing leader, a robot without grasping mechanisms, and multiple follower robots. During the object transportation, a desired trajectory is given to the leader robot only, and follower robots estimate the trajectory of the leader based on force/moment from the object. In Behavior-based Multiple Robot System with Host for Object Manipulation (BeRoSH) (Wang et al., 1996), the unit which processes all common tasks is named the host. The host is incorporated into one of the robots, by giving the robot the ability to organize other robots and generate motivations/goals for the other robots. More papers reporting leader-follower implementations can be found in (GroB et al., 2006; Song & Kumar, 2002).

### 2.6 Reconfigurable robotics

Modular self-reconfiguring robotic systems or self-reconfigurable modular robots are autonomous kinematic machines with variable morphology. Beyond conventional actuation, sensing and control typically found in fixed-morphology robots, self-reconfiguring robots are also able to deliberately change their own shape by rearranging the connectivity of their parts, in order to adapt to new circumstances, perform new tasks, or recover from damage. Modular self-reconfigurable robotic systems can be generally classified into several architectural groups by the geometric arrangement of their units (Mark et al., 2007; Østergaard et al., 2006; Tuci et al., 2006).

- Lattice Architectures (refer to Fig.2(a)): have units that are arranged and connected in some regular, three-dimensional pattern, such as a simple cubic or hexagonal grid. Control and motion can be executed in parallel. Lattice architectures usually offer simpler reconfiguration, as modules move to a discrete set of neighboring locations in which motions can be made open-loop. The computational representation can also be more easily scaled to more complex systems.

(a) Lattice type. (Brandt et al., 2007)

(b) Chain type. (Yim et al., 2007)

(c) Mobile type. (Mondada et al., 2003)

Fig. 2. Architectural group.

- Chain Architectures (refer to Fig.2(b)): have units that are connected together in a string or tree topology. This chain or tree can fold up to become space filling, but the underlying architecture is serial. Through articulation, chain architectures can potentially reach any point or orientation in space, and are therefore more versatile but computationally more difficult to represent and analyze and more difficult to control.
- Mobile Architectures (refer to Fig.2(c)): have units that use the environment to maneuver around and can either hook up to form complex chains or lattices or form a number of smaller robots that execute coordinated movements and together form a larger "virtual" network.

The types of modular self-reconfigurable robotic systems reported in the gathered literatures have been classified into their architectural groups and is presented in Table 3. Self-reconfigurable robots hold potential to be able to move robotics into new areas of application. In addition to traditional mass production environments, self-reconfigurable robots may become useful in real-world environments. These environments are characterized by being unstructured, complex, dynamic, and unknown. Self-reconfigurable robots have an advantage over fixed-shape robots in these environments because of their special abilities which include versatility, robustness, adaptability, scale extensibility and even self-repair.

### 2.7 Motion coordination

Exploring into this domain, path-planning in swarm robotics has attracted a lot of attention in the past two decades. The problem of mobile robots path-planning is defined as follows: "for a given robot and an environment description, plan a route between two specific locations, which must be clear of obstacles and attend all the optimizations criteria" (Langer et al., 2007). Studies in path-planning can be divided to local path-planning and global path-planning. In local path-planning, the planning is based on the information given by sensors installed on the robot, which provide details about the unknown environment (Lei et al., 2006; Lei & Li, 2007). In the global planning case, the environment's model is precisely defined (Kang et al., 2007), and the navigation is performed with the information known in priori.

| SYSTEM | CLASS | DOF | REFERENCE(s) |
|---|---|---|---|
| CEBOT | Mobile | various | Fukuda et al. (1989) |
| Polypod | Chain | 2 | Yim (1993) |
| Metamorphic | Lattice | 3 | Chirikjian et al. (1996) |
| 3d Fracta | Lattice | 6 | Murata et al. (1998) |
| Molecule | Lattice | 4 | Kotay & Rus (1998) |
| CONRO | Chain | 2 | Castano et al. (2002) |
| Polybot | Chain | 1 | Golovinsky et al. (2004) |
| Telecube | Lattice | 6 | Suh et al. (2002) |
| Vertical | Lattice | 2 | Hosokawa et al. (1999) |
| Crystal | Lattice | 4 | Rus & Vona (2000) |
| I-Cube | Lattice | 3 | Unsal & Khosla (2001) |
| Pneumatic | Lattice | 2 | Inou et al. (2002) |
| Uni Rover | Mobile | 2 | Damoto et al. (2001) |
| M-TRAN | Hybrid | 2 | Murata et al. (2002) |
| Atron | Lattice | 1 | Brandt et al. (2007) |
| Swarm-bot | Mobile | 3 | Groß et al. (2006) |
| Superbot | Hybrid | 3 | Shen et al. (2006) |
| Catom | Lattice | 0 | Kirby et al. (2005) |
| Molecube | Chain | 1 | Studer & Lipson (2006) |
| YaMoR | Chain | 1 | Upegui et al. (2005) |
| Miche | Lattice | 0 | Gilpin et al. (2008) |
| Proteo | Hybrid | 0 | Bojinov et al. (2000) |
| ACM | Chain | various | Hirose & Mori (2004) |
| Fractum | Hybrid | 0 | Tomita et al. (1999) |
| Miniturized | Lattice | 2 | Yoshida et al. (1999) |
| Semi-Cylindrical | Hybrid | 2 | Murata et al. (2000) |
| M-TRAN II | Hybrid | 2 | Kurokawa et al. (2003) |
| RIKEN Vertical | Lattice | 2 | Hosokawa et al. (1999) |

Table 3. List of self reconfigurable modular systems (Mark et al., 2007; Jantapremjit & Austin, 2001; Østergaard et al., 2006)

The basic path-planning problem deals with static environments (Garro et al., 2007; Li et al., 2007), in which the workspaces solely containing stationary obstacles of which the geometry is known. A natural extension to the basic path planning problem is planning in dynamic environments (Van Den Berg et al., 2006; Tian et al., 2007), in which besides stationary obstacles, also moving obstacles are present. Planning in such environment is challenging as in many cases the motions of the moving obstacles are not known beforehand, so often their future trajectories are estimated by extrapolating current speed in order to plan a path. This path may become invalid when some obstacle changes its speed, so then a new path should be planned. However, there is actually no time for planning; as the world is continuously changing, the computation would already be outdated even before it is finished (Smierzchalski & Michalewicz, 2007).

Various algorithms has been introduced to tackle the problems in path-planning for example fuzzy-logics (Lei & Li, 2007), particle-swarm optimization (PSO) (Rigatos, 2008), distributed gradient (Rigatos, 2008), ant-colony optimization (ACO) (Garro et al., 2007), genetic algorithm (GA) (Lei et al., 2006), D*(Van Den Berg et al., 2006) and K-Bug(Langer et al., 2007). Most of the algorithms aim to solve the shortest path (Garro et al., 2007) problem in path-planning. Nearly all the previous work has been aimed at 2D environment; only some papers considered 3D environments such as the work presented by Kitamura et al. (1995) and Yamashita et al. (2000).

Nonholonomic path-planning is also covered in this category. Nonholonomic systems are characterized by constraint equations involving the time derivatives of the system configuration variables. These equations are non integrable; they typically arise when the system has less controls than configuration variables. For instance a car-like robot has two controls (linear and angular velocities) while it moves in a 3-dimensional configuration space (Laumond et al., 1998). Nonholonomic constraint generally exists in wheeled system. Under the nonholonomic constraint, the vehicles and wheeled mobile robots can only run along the tangential direction of trajectory within the steering angle limit, and the motion is non-slipping and pure rolling (Liu et al., 2007). In another word, the robot can instantly move forward and backward, but cannot move sideward.

Formation or pattern generation is another area in motion coordination that received a lot of author's attention. The formation generation problem is defined as the coordination of a group of robots to get into and maintain a formation with a certain shape, such as circle (Defago & Konagaya, 2002), line (Arkin & Balch, 1999) or even arbitrary shapes (Sahin et al., 2002). Current application areas of pattern formation include search and rescue operations, landmine removal, remote terrain and space exploration, control of arrays of satellites and unmanned aerial vehicles (UAVs). Bahceci et al. (2003) has divided formation generation into two groups. The first group includes studies where the coordination is done by a centralized (Belta & Kumar, 2002) unit that can oversee the whole group and command the individual robots accordingly. The second group contains distributed (Pavone & Frazzoli, 2007) strategies for achieving the coordination. Chen & Wang (2005) discussed various control strategies in formation generation such as behavior-based approach (Arkin & Balch, 1999), potential field approach (Bruemmer et al., 2002), leader-follower approach (Desai et al., 2001) and more.

### 2.8 Learning

At present most learning algorithms can be classified as supervised and unsupervised learning. Supervised learning requires the use of an external supervisor. With supervised learning the robot knows what the best output is in a certain situation as the supervisor provides the corrective information to the learner. Unsupervised learning is a method of learning with minor or without any external corrective feedback from the environment (Alpaydin, 2004). This method allows for automated design of efficient, robust controllers, which saves much design time and effort. Furthermore, it is useful for allowing robots to adapt to situations where the task/environment is unknown beforehand or is constantly changing (Pugh & Martinoli, 2006).

There are many paradigms in supervised learning that have been identified in the open literatures. Inductive learning is one of the supervised learning paradigms which is a method that generalize from observed training examples by identifying features that empirically distinguish positive from negative training examples (Mitchell & Mitchell, 1997). Decision tree learning (Quinlan, 1986), neural network learning (Pomerleau, 1990) and inductive logic programming (Konik & Laird, 2002) are all examples of inductive methods that operate in this fashion. Another well studied paradigm would be explanation-based learning (EBL) (Mitchell & Thrun, 1993) where prior knowledge is used to analyze, or explain, how each observed training examples satisfies the target concept. This explanation is then used to distinguish the relevant features of the training example from the irrelevant, so that examples can be generalized based on logical reasoning (Mitchell & Mitchell, 1997). EBL studies how domain knowledge about the function being learned can be used to speed up learning (Mahadevan, 1996). Other common paradigms that have been applied to robot learning are case-based learning (CBL) and memory-based learning (MBL) which were reported by Sim et al. (2003).

Similarly, in unsupervised learning, paradigms such as evolutionary learning and reinforcement learning (RL) received massive attention from the researchers recently. Genetic algorithms (Ram et al., 1994) and genetic programming (Koza, 1994) are the most prominent computational techniques for evolutionary learning. Evolutionary learning starts with a population of policies, and combines them to produce better policies till an optimal policy is found. The evolutionary learning paradigm is normally set with a good set of policies to start which helps to accelerate the learning process.

Reinforcement leaning (RL) (Fernandez et al., 2005) is defined as learning what to do, how to map situations to actions so as to maximize a numerical reward signal. The learner is not told which actions to take, as in most forms of machine learning, but instead must discover which actions yield the most reward by trying them. Actions may affect not only the immediate reward but also the next situation and, through that, all subsequent rewards (Sutton & Barto, 1998). Trial-and-error search and delayed reward are two most important distinguishing features of RL.

Among RL algorithms, Q-learning has attracted a great deal of attention in research. Q-learning (Yang et al., 2007; Ahmadabadi & Asadpour, 2002) is a recently explored RL algorithm that stores the expected reinforcement values associated with each state-action pair usually in a lookup table. In a survey conducted by Yang & Gu (2004) on multi-agent reinforcement learning, they have highlighted that traditional Q-learning is not directly applicable in swarm robots application as involvement of multiple robots in the environment makes the environment dynamic. Due to that reason, many researchers have put efforts to modify the Q-learning framework to suit dynamic environment involving multiple robots. Algorithms such as Minimax-Q learning (Littman, 1994), Nash-Q learning (Hu&Wellman, 2003), Friend-or-Foe Q-learning (Littman, 2001), rQ-learning (Suh et al., 1997), Fictitious Play (Claus & Boutilier, 1998), SARSA learning (Sutton & Barto, 1998) and Policy Hill Climbing (Ng & Jordan, 2000) were gathered and reported by Yang & Gu (2004).

As far as robot learning is concern, it is still at the infant stage of research and is one of the interesting and difficult machine learning problems. This domain can be further explored by exploiting more paradigms and scaling the algorithms to solve more problems related to robot learning.

### 2.9 Task allocation

Task allocation means assigning tasks among the robots in swarm in a productive and efficient manner. Task allocation must ensure that not only the global mission is achieved, but also the tasks are well distributed among the robots. An effective task allocation approach considers the available resources, the entities to optimize (time energy, quality and etc.), the capabilities of the deployable robots and appropriately allocates the tasks accordingly (Baghaei & Agah, 2002). Task refers to a sub-goal that is necessary for achieving the overall goal of the system. Tasks can be discrete or continuous and also can vary in a number of other ways, including time scale, complexity and specificity (Gerkey & Mataric, 2004).

Often in task allocation problems, the comparison between heterogeneous system and homogeneous systems are made. Heterogeneous system consists of a team of robots whose members have a difference either in the hardware devices or in the software control procedures. Homogeneous system consists of a team of robots whose members are exactly the same both in the hardware and in the control software (Iocchi et al., 2001). Such comparison results can be found in papers presented by Goldberg & Mataric (2002).

The problem of multi-robot task allocation (MRTA) has been investigated using different techniques such as physical modeling (Parker, 2002), distributed planning (Ortiz et al., 2005), market-based techniques (Dias et al., 2006), auction based techniques (Bertsekas & Castanon, 1991) and ALLIANCE (Parker, 2001). One of the first algorithms for market based solutions for the MRTA problem was described in the MURDOCH system developed by Gerkey & Mataric (2002). The implemented methodologies served as design guidelines to allow swarm robot systems to gain more efficiency.

## 3. Conclusion

A state of the art survey of swarm robotic research is presented in this paper. The research in the area of swarm in these nine research axes are critically reviewed and reported for the benefit of researchers in this field. Swarm robotic systems have a very high potential in solving highly complex tasks as they are competent of parallelism, robustness, scalability and low cost. It is clear that since the initiation of the field of swarm robotics, significant progress has been made on domains such as biological inspiration, communication, control approach, mapping and localization, object transportation and manipulation, reconfigurable robotics, motion coordination, learning, and task allocation. Most of the research conducted was based on the biological inspirations adopted from the behaviors of ants, bees and birds. Implicit communication seems to give more robustness in the communication architecture of swarm robotics. Distributed control architecture was preferred compared to centralized architecture to prevent single point failures. As far as mapping and localization is concerned, work is still being carried out to fine tune the problems faced in this domain. In object transportation and manipulation, caging is preferred over the available methods as the constraints in the domain can be reduced and kept simple. In last two decades, research in reconfigurable robotics has taken a good progress. Even so, this domain is still at its infant stage. Path-planning and formation generation is one of the main domains that received a lot of attention from the authors. A lot of new heuristics and algorithms were introduced to solve the problems in this domain. In the learning domain, reinforcement learning (RL) was given much interest by the researchers. In task allocation domain, heterogeneous and homogeneous systems are widely discussed. This domain has contributed in development of various techniques as listed in the paper.

## 4. References

Adolfsson, V. (2001). The State of the Art in Distributed Mobile Robotics.

Agassounon, A. (2004). Modeling Swarm Robotic Systems: A Case Study in Collaborative Distributed Manipulation, *The International Journal of Robotics Research* 23(4-5).

Ahmadabadi, M. & Asadpour, M. (2002). Expertness based cooperative Q-learning, *IEEE Transactions on Systems, Man, and Cybernetics, Part B: Cybernetics* 32(1): 66–76.

Alpaydin, E. (2004). *Introduction to machine learning*, The MIT Press.

Altshuler, Y., Yanovsky, V., Wagner, I. & Bruckstein, A. (2006). Swarm Intelligence-Searchers, Cleaners and Hunters, *Swarm Intelligent Systems* pp. 93–132.

Arkin, R. & Balch, T. (1999). Behavior-based formation control for multi-robot teams.

Baghaei, K. & Agah, A. (2002). Task allocation methodologies for multi-robot systems, *Technical report*, Citeseer.

Bahceci, E., Soysal, O. & Sahin, E. (2003). A review: Pattern formation and adaptation in multirobot systems, *Robotics Institute, Carnegie Mellon University, Pittsburgh, PA, Tech. Rep. CMU-RI-TR-03-43*.

Bayindir, L. & Sahin, E. (2007). A Review of Studies in Swarm Robotics, *Turkish Journal of Electrical Engineering* 15(2): 115–147.

Belta, C. & Kumar, V. (2002). Trajectory design for formations of robots by kinetic energy shaping, *Proceedings- IEEE International Conference on Robotics and Automation*, Vol. 3, Citeseer, pp. 2593–2598.

Bertsekas, D. & Castanon, D. (1991). Parallel synchronous and asynchronous implementations of the auction algorithm*, *Parallel Computing* 17(6-7): 707–732.

Bojinov, H., Casal, A. & Hogg, T. (2000). Emergent structures in modular self-reconfigurable robots, *IEEE International Conference on Robotics and Automation*, Vol. 2, Citeseer, pp. 1734–1741.

Brandt, D., Christensen, D. & Lund, H. (2007). ATRON robots: Versatility from self-reconfigurable modules, *International Conference on Mechatronics and Automation, 2007. ICMA 2007*, pp. 26–32.

Bruemmer, D., Dudenhoeffer, D., Anderson, M. & McKay, M. (2004). Components of Swarm Intelligence, *Proceedings of the American Nuclear Society 10th International Conference on Robotics and Remote Systems for Hazardous Environments*.

Bruemmer, D., Dudenhoeffer, D., McKay, M. & Anderson, M. (2002). A robotic swarm for spill finding and perimeter formation.

Cao, Y., Fukunaga, A. & Kahng, A. (1997). Cooperative Mobile Robotics: Antecedents and Directions, *Autonomous robots* 4(1): 7–27.

Castano, A., Behar, A. & Will, P. (2002). The Conro modules for reconfigurable robots, *IEEE/ASME transactions on mechatronics* 7(4): 403–409.

Cazangi, R., Von Zuben, F. & Figueiredo, M. (2005). Autonomous Navigation System Applied to Collective Robotics with Ant-inspired Communication, *Proceedings of the 2005 conference on Genetic and evolutionary computation*, ACM, p. 128.

Chen, Y. & Wang, Z. (2005). Formation control: a review and a new consideration, *2005*
IEEE/RSJ International Conference on Intelligent Robots and Systems, 2005.(IROS 2005), pp. 3181–3186.

Chirikjian, G., Pamecha, A. & Ebert-Uphoff, I. (1996). Evaluating efficiency of self-reconfiguration in a class of modular robots, *Journal of robotic systems* 13(5): 317–338.

Choset, H. & Nagatani, K. (2001). Topological simultaneous localization and mapping (SLAM): towardexact localization without explicit localization, *IEEE Transactions on Robotics and Automation* 17(2): 125–137.

Christodoulopoulos, C., Kyriakopoulos, C. & Kanatas, A. (2007). A Realistic Approach to Source Localization using a Wireless Robotic Network, *Proceedings of the 1st international conference on Robot communication and coordination*, IEEE Press, p. 46.

Claus, C. & Boutilier, C. (1998). The dynamics of reinforcement learning in cooperative multiagent systems, *Proceedings of the National Conference on Artificial Intelligence*, JOHN WILEY & SONS LTD, pp. 746–752.

Damoto, R., Kawakami, A. & Hirose, S. (2001). Study of super-mechano colony: concept and basic experimental set-up, *Advanced Robotics* 15(4): 391–408.

D'Angelo, A. & Pagello, E. (2005). Making Collective Behaviours to Work Through Implicit Communication, *Robotics and Automation, 2005. ICRA 2005. Proceedings of the 2005 IEEE International Conference on*, pp. 81–86.

De le Torre, M. & Stentz, A. (2001). A Market Approach to Multirobot Coordination, *Robotics Institute* p. 157.

Defago, X. & Konagaya, A. (2002). Circle formation for oblivious anonymous mobile robots with no common sense of orientation, *Proceedings of the secondACM international workshop on Principles of mobile computing*, ACM, p. 104.

Desai, J., Ostrowski, J. & Kumar, V. (2001). Modeling and control of formations of nonholonomic mobile robots, *IEEE transactions on Robotics and Automation* 17(6): 905–908.

Dias, M., Zlot, R., Kalra, N. & Stentz, A. (2006). Market-based multirobot coordination: A survey and analysis, *Proceedings of the IEEE* 94(7).

Dimarogonas, D. & Kyriakopoulos, K. (2007). Decentralized swarm aggregation with static communication links, *Proceedings of the 1st international conference on Robot communication and coordination*, IEEE Press, p. 8.

Dudek, G., Jenkin, M., Milios, E. & Wilkes, D. (1993). *A Taxonomy for Swarm Robots, Intelligent Robots and Systems' 93, IROS'93. Proceedings of the 1993 IEEE/RSJ International Conference on*, Vol. 1.

Fabrizi, E. & Saffiotti, A. (2000). Extracting topology-based maps from gridmaps, *IEEE International Conference on Robotics and Automation*, Vol. 3, Citeseer, pp. 2972–2978.

Fernandez, F., Borrajo, D. & Parker, L. (2005). A reinforcement learning algorithm in cooperative multi-robot domains, *Journal of Intelligent and Robotic Systems* 43(2): 161–174.

Fong, T., Nourbakhsh, I. & Dautenhahn, K. (2003). A Survey of Socially Interactive Robots, *Robotics and autonomous systems* 42(3-4): 143–166.

Fukuda, T., Nakagawa, S., Kawauchi, Y. & Buss, M. (1989). Structure decision method for self organizing robots based on cell structure-CEBOT, *Proceedings of International Conference on Robotics and Automation*, Vol. 89.

Garro, B., Sossa, H. & Vazquez, R. (2007). Evolving ant colony system for optimizing path planning in mobile robots, *Electronics, Robotics and Automotive Mechanics Conference, 2007. CERMA 2007*, pp. 444–449.

Gazi, V. & Passino, K. (2002). Stability analysis of swarms in an environment with an attractant/ repellent profile, *American Control Conference, 2002. Proceedings of the 2002*, Vol. 3.

Gerkey, B. & Mataric, M. (2002). Pusher-watcher: An approach to fault-tolerant tightly-coupled robot coordination, *Proceedings- IEEE International Conference on Robotics and Automation*, Vol. 1, Citeseer, pp. 464–469.

Gerkey, B. & Mataric, M. (2004). A formal analysis and taxonomy of task allocation in multirobot systems, *The International Journal of Robotics Research* 23(9): 939.

Gilpin, K., Kotay, K., Rus, D. & Vasilescu, I. (2008). Miche: Modular shape formation by self-disassembly, *The International Journal of Robotics Research* 27(3-4): 345.

Goldberg, D. & Mataric, M. (2002). Design and evaluation of robust behavior-based controllers, *Robot Teams: From Diversity to Polymorphism* pp. 315–344.
Golovinsky, A., Yim, M., Zhang, Y., Eldershaw, C. & Duff, D. (2004). PolyBot and PolyKinetic System: a modular robotic platform for education, *2004 IEEE International Conference on Robotics and Automation, 2004. Proceedings. ICRA'04*, pp. 1381–1386.
GroB, R., Mondada, F. & Dorigo, M. (2006). Transport of an object by six pre-attached robots interacting via physical links, *Proc. of the 2006 IEEE Int. Conf. on Robotics and Automation, IEEE Computer Society Press, Los Alamitos, CA*, Citeseer, pp. 1317–1323.
Groß, R., Bonani, M., Mondada, F. & Dorigo, M. (2006). Autonomous self-assembly in swarm-bots, *IEEE Transactions on Robotics* 22(6): 1115–1130.
Hayes, A., Martinoli, A. & Goodman, R. (2003). Swarm Robotic Odor Localization: Off-line Optimization and Validation with Real Robots, *Robotica* 21(04): 427–441.
Hirose, S. & Mori, M. (2004). Biologically inspired snake-like robots, *IEEE International Conference on Robotics and Biomimetics, 2004. ROBIO 2004*, pp. 1–7.
Hosokawa, K., Fujii, T., Kaetsu, H., Asama, H., Kuroda, Y. & Endo, I. (1999). Self-organizing collective robots with morphogenesis in a vertical plane, *JSME INTERNATIONAL JOURNAL SERIES C* 42: 195–202.
Howard, A. (2006). Multi-robot simultaneous localization and mapping using particle filters, *The International Journal of Robotics Research* 25(12): 1243.
Hu, J. & Wellman, M. (2003). Nash Q-learning for general-sum stochastic games, *The Journal of Machine Learning Research* 4: 1039–1069.
Inou, N., Kobayashi, H. & Koseki, M. (2002). Development of pneumatic cellular robots forming a mechanical structure, *International Conference on Control Automation, Robotics And Vision (ICARCV),(CD-ROM, Paper ID 1457)*, pp. 63–68.
Iocchi, L., Nardi, D. & Salerno, M. (2001). Reactivity and Deliberation: A Survey on Multirobot Systems, *Balancing Reactivity and Social Deliberation in Multi-Agent Systems* pp. 9–32.
Jantapremjit, P. & Austin, D. (2001). Design of a modular self-reconfigurable robot, *Australian Conf. on Robotics and Automation, Sydney, Australia*, Citeseer.
Jung, D. & Zelinsky, A. (2000). Grounded Symbolic Communication Between Heterogeneous Cooperating Robots, *Autonomous Robots* 8(3): 269–292.
Kang, J., Kim, S., Chung, M., Myung, H., Park, J. & Bang, S. (2007). Path planning for complete and efficient coverage operation of mobile robots, *Mechatronics and Automation, 2007. ICMA 2007. International Conference on*, pp. 2126–2131.
Kirby, B., Campbell, J., Aksak, B., Pillai, P., Hoburg, J., Mowry, T. & Goldstein, S. (2005). Catoms: Moving robots without moving parts, *PROCEEDINGS OF THE NATIONAL CONFERENCE ON ARTIFICIAL INTELLIGENCE*, Vol. 20, Menlo Park, CA; Cambridge, MA; London; AAAI Press; MIT Press; 1999, p. 1730.
Kitamura, Y., Tanaka, T., Kishino, F. & Yachida, M. (1995). 3-D path planning in a dynamic environment using an octree and anartificial potential field, *1995 IEEE/RSJ International Conference on Intelligent Robots and Systems 95.'Human Robot Interaction and Cooperative Robots', Proceedings*, Vol. 2.
Kitano, H., Asada, M., Noda, I. & Matsubara, H. (1998). RoboCup: Robot World Cup, *IEEE Robotics & Automation Magazine* 5(3): 30–36.
Konik, T. & Laird, J. (2002). Hierarchical Procedural Knowledge Learning Through Observation using Inductive Logic Programming, an Extended Abstract.

Kotay, K. & Rus, D. (1998). Motion synthesis for the self-reconfiguring molecule, *IEEE Intl. Conf. on Robotics and Automation*, pp. 843–851.

Koza, J. (1994). Genetic programming II: automatic discovery of reusable programs.

Kuipers, B. & Byun, Y. (1991). A robot exploration and mapping strategy based on a semantic hierarchy of spatial representations, *Robotics and Autonomous Systems* 8(1-2): 47–63.

Kurokawa, H., Kamimura, A., Yoshida, E., Tomita, K., Kokaji, S. & Murata, S. (2003). M-TRAN II: Metamorphosis from a four-legged walker to a caterpillar, *Proceedings of the 2003 IEEE/RSJ International Conference on Intelligent Robots and Systems*, pp. 2454–2459.

Labella, T., Dorigo, M. & Deneubourg, J. (2006). Division of Labor in a Group of Robots Inspired by Ants Foraging Behavior, *ACM Transactions on Autonomous and Adaptive Systems (TAAS)* 1(1): 25.

Langer, R., Coelho, L. & Oliveira, G. (2007). K-Bug, A New Bug Approach for Mobile Robot's Path Planning, *IEEE International Conference on Control Applications, 2007. CCA 2007*, pp. 403–408.

Laumond, J., Sekhavat, S.&Lamiraux, F. (1998). Guidelines in nonholonomic motion planning for mobile robots, *Robot motion planning and control* pp. 1–53.

Lei, B. & Li, W. (2007). A Fuzzy Behaviours Fusion Algorithm for Mobile Robot Real-time Path Planning in Unknown Environment, *IEEE International Conference on Integration Technology, 2007. ICIT'07*, pp. 173–178.

Lei, L., Wang, H. & Wu, Q. (2006). Improved genetic algorithms based path planning of mobile robot under dynamic unknown environment, *Mechatronics and Automation, Proceedings of the 2006 IEEE International Conference on*, pp. 1728–1732.

Li, M., Alvarez, A., De Pellegrini, F., Prabhakaran, B. & Chlamtac, I. (2007). ROBOTRAK: a centralized real-time monitoring, control, and coordination system for robot swarms, *Proceedings of the 1st international conference on Robot communication and coordination*, IEEE Press, p. 37.

Littman, M. (1994). Markov games as a framework for multi-agent reinforcement learning, *Proceedings of the eleventh international conference on machine learning*, Vol. 157, Citeseer, p. 163.

Littman, M. (2001). Friend-or-foe Q-learning in general-sum games, *MACHINE LEARNINGINTERNATIONAL WORKSHOP THEN CONFERENCE-*, pp. 322–328.

Liu, H., Sun, Y., Liu, Z., Yang, Q. & Lin, T. (2007). Nonholonomic Path Planning Based on Virtual Obstacle in Circuit Map, *IEEE International Conference on Integration Technology, 2007. ICIT'07*, pp. 809–813.

Mahadevan, S. (1996). Machine learning for robots: A comparison of different paradigms, *Proceedings of the Workshop on Towards Real Autonomy, IEEE/RSJ Internaltional Conference on Intelligent Robots and Systems (IROS96)*, Citeseer.

Mark, Y., Shen, W., Salemi, B., Daniela, R., Moll, M., Lipson, H., Klavis, E. & Gregory, S. (2007). Modular Self-Reconfigurable Robot Systems-Challenges and Opportunities for the Future, *IEEE Robotics & Automation Magazine* 14(1): 43–52.

McPartland, M., Nolfi, S. & Abbass, H. (2005). Emergence of Communication in Competitive Multi-agent Systems: a Pareto Multi-objective Approach, *Proceedings of the 2005 conference on Genetic and evolutionary computation*, ACM, p. 58.

Meng, Y., Kazeem, O. & Muller, J. (2007). A Hybrid ACO/PSO Control Algorithm for Distributed Swarm Robots, *IEEE Swarm Intelligence Symposium, 2007. SIS 2007*, pp. 273– 280.

Mir, I. & Amavasai, B. (2007). A Fully Decentralized Approach for Incremental Perception, *Proceedings of the 1st international conference on Robot communication and coordination*, IEEE Press, p. 10.

Mitchell, T. & Mitchell, T. (1997). Machine learning, McGraw-hill series in computer science.

Mitchell, T. & Thrun, S. (1993). Explanation-based neural network learning for robot control, *Advances in Neural information processing systems* pp. 287–287.

Miyata, N., Ota, J., Aiyama, Y., Sasaki, J. & Arai, T. (1997). Cooperative transport system with regrasping car-like mobile robots, *Intelligent Robots and Systems, 1997. IROS'97., Proceedings of the 1997 IEEE/RSJ International Conference on*, Vol. 3.

Mondada, F., Guignard, A., Bonani, M., Bar, D., Lauria, M. & Floreano, D. (2003). Swarmbot: From concept to implementation, *Proceedings of the 2003 IEEE/RSJ International Conference on Intelligent Robot and Systems (IROS 2003)*, Citeseer, pp. 1626–1631.

Murata, S., Kurokawa, H., Yoshida, E., Tomita, K. & Kokaji, S. (1998). A 3-D self-reconfigurable structure, *IEEE International Conference on Robotics and Automation*, INSTITUTE OF ELECTRICAL ENGINEERS INC (IEEE), pp. 432–439.

Murata, S., Yoshida, E., Kamimura, A., Kurokawa, H., Tomita, K.&Kokaji, S. (2002). M-TRAN: Self-reconfigurable modular robotic system, *IEEE/ASME transactions on mechatronics* 7(4): 431–441.

Murata, S., Yoshida, E., Tomita, K., Kurokawa, H., Kamimura, A. & Kokaji, S. (2000). Hardware design of modular robotic system, *Proc. of the Intl Conf. on Intelligent Robots and Systems*, pp. 2210–7.

Ng, A. & Jordan, M. (2000). PEGASUS: A policy search method for large MDPs and POMDPs, *Proceedings of the 16th Conference on Uncertainty in Artificial Intelligence*, Citeseer, pp. 406–415.

Ortiz, C., Vincent, R. & Morisset, B. (2005). Task inference and distributed task management in the Centibots robotic system, *Proceedings of the fourth international joint conference on Autonomous agents and multiagent systems*, ACM, p. 867.

Østergaard, E., Kassow, K., Beck, R. & Lund, H. (2006). Design of the ATRON lattice-based self-reconfigurable robot, *Autonomous Robots* 21(2): 165–183.

Panait, L. & Luke, S. (2004). A Pheromone-based Utility Model for Collaborative Foraging, *Proceedings of the Third International Joint Conference on Autonomous Agents and Multiagent Systems*, Vol. 1, IEEE Computer Society, p. 43.

Parker, L. (1993). Designing control laws for cooperative agent teams, *1993 IEEE International Conference on Robotics and Automation, 1993. Proceedings.*, pp. 582–587.

Parker, L. (2001). Evaluating success in autonomous multi-robot teams: experiences from ALLIANCE architecture implementations, *Journal of Experimental & Theoretical Artificial Intelligence* 13(2): 95–98.

Parker, L. (2002). Distributed algorithms for multi-robot observation of multiple moving targets, *Autonomous robots* 12(3): 231–255.

Parker, L. (2003). Current Research in Multirobot Systems, *Artificial Life and Robotics* 7(1): 1–5.

Pavone, M. & Frazzoli, E. (2007). Decentralized policies for geometric pattern formation and path coverage, *Journal of Dynamic Systems, Measurement, and Control* 129: 633.

Payton, D., Estkowski, R.&Howard, M. (2003). Compound Behaviors in Pheromone Robotics, *Robotics and Autonomous Systems* 44(3-4): 229–240.

Pereira, G., Kumar, V. & Campos, M. (2003). Decentralized algorithms for multirobot manipulation via caging, *Algorithmic Foundations of Robotics V* pp. 257–274.

Pomerleau, D. (1990). Neural network based autonomous navigation, *Vision and Navigation. The Carnegie Mellon Navlab* pp. 83–93.

Pugh, J. & Martinoli, A. (2006). Multi-robot learning with particle swarm optimization, *Proceedings of the fifth international joint conference on Autonomous agents and multiagent systems*, ACM, p. 448.

Purnamadjaja, A., Iskandar, J. & Russell, R. (2007). Pheromone Communication Simulation for Mobile Robots Using Java 3D, *6th IEEE/ACIS International Conference on Computer and Information Science, 2007. ICIS 2007*, pp. 261–266.

Purnamadjaja, A. & Russell, R. (2004). Pheromone Communication: Implementation of Necrophoric Bee Behaviour in a Robot Swarm, *2004 IEEE Conference on Robotics, Automation and Mechatronics*, Vol. 2.

Quinlan, J. (1986). Induction of decision trees, *Machine learning* 1(1): 81–106.

Ram, A., Boone, G., Arkin, R. & Pearce, M. (1994). Using genetic algorithms to learn reactive control parameters for autonomous robotic navigation, *Adaptive Behavior* 2(3): 277.

Ramos, V., Fernandes, C. & Rosa, A. (2005). Social Cognitive Maps, Swarm Collective Perception and Distributed Search on Dynamic Landscapes, *Brains, Minds & Media–Journal of New Media in Neural and Cognitive Science, NRW, Germany* .

Rigatos, G. (2008). Distributed gradient and particle swarm optimization for multi-robot motion planning, *Robotica* 26(03): 357–370.

Rus, D. & Vona, M. (2000). A basis for self-reconfiguring robots using crystal modules, *IEEE/RSJ Intelligent Robots and Systems* 3: 2184–2193.

Rybski, P., Larson, A., Veeraraghavan, H., LaPoint, M. & Gini, M. (2007). Communication Strategies in Multi-Robot Search and Retrieval: Experiences with Mindart, *Distributed Autonomous Robotic Systems 6* pp. 317–326.

Sahin, E., Labella, T., Trianni, V., Deneubourg, J., Rasse, P., Floreano, D., Gambardella, L., Mondada, F., Nolfi, S. & Dorigo, M. (2002). SWARM-BOT: Pattern formation in a swarm of self-assembling mobile robots, *Proceedings of the IEEE International Conference on Systems, Man and Cybernetics, Hammamet, Tunisia*, Citeseer.

Se, S., Lowe, D. & Little, J. (2002). Mobile robot localization and mapping with uncertainty using scale-invariant visual landmarks, *The International Journal of Robotics Research* 21(8): 735.

Seraji, H. (1999). Traversability Index: A new concept for planetary rovers, *1999 IEEE International Conference on Robotics and Automation, 1999. Proceedings*, Vol. 3.

Sharkey, A. (2006b). Robots, Insects and Swarm Intelligence, *Artificial Intelligence Review* 26(4): 255–268.

Sharkey, A. & Sharkey, N. (2006a). The Application of Swarm Intelligence to Collective Robots, *Advances in Applied Artificial Intelligence* p. 157.

Shen,W., Krivokon, M., Chiu, H., Everist, J., Rubenstein, M. & Venkatesh, J. (2006). Multimode locomotion via SuperBot reconfigurable robots, *Autonomous Robots* 20(2): 165–177.

Shen, W., Salemi, B. & Will, P. (2002). Hormone-inspired adaptive communication and distributed control for conro self-reconfigurable robots, *IEEE transactions on Robotics and Automation* 18(5): 700–712.

Sim, S., Ong, K. & Seet, G. (2003). A Foundation for Robot Learning, *The Fourth International Conference on Control and Automation*, pp. 10–12.

Smierzchalski, R. & Michalewicz, Z. (2007). Path planning in dynamic environments, *Innovations in Robot Mobility and Control* pp. 135–153.

Song, P. & Kumar, V. (2002). A potential field based approach to multi-robot manipulation, *Proceedings- IEEE International Conference on Robotics and Automation*, Vol. 2, Citeseer, pp. 1217–1222.

Spaan, M., Gordon, G. & Vlassis, N. (2006). Decentralized planning under uncertainty for teams of communicating agents, *Proceedings of the fifth international joint conference on Autonomous agents and multiagent systems*, ACM, p. 256.

Steele Jr, F. & Thomas, G. (2007). Directed stigmergy-based control for multi-robot systems, *Proceedings of the ACM/IEEE international conference on Human-robot interaction*, ACM, p. 230.

Studer, G. & Lipson, H. (2006). Spontaneous emergence of self-replicating structures in mole-cube automata, Proc. of the 10th Int. Conf. on the Simulation and Synthesis of Living Systems (Artificial Life X), MIT Press, Cambridge, MA, pp. 227–233.

Suh, I., Kim, J. & Oh, S. (1997). Region-based Q-learning for intelligent robot systems, *IEEE Int. Symp. on Computational Intelligence in Robotics & Automation*, pp. 172–178.

Suh, J., Homans, S. & Yim, M. (2002). Telecubes: Mechanical design of a module for self-reconfigurable robotics, *IEEE International Conference on Robotics and Automation, 2002. Proceedings. ICRA'02*, Vol. 4.

Sutton, R. & Barto, A. (1998). Introduction to reinforcement learning.

Thrun, S. (2001). A probabilistic on-line mapping algorithm for teams of mobile robots, *The International Journal of Robotics Research* 20(5): 335.

Thrun, S. (2002). Robotic mapping: A survey, *Exploring artificial intelligence in the new millennium* pp. 1–35.

Thrun, S., Liu, Y., Koller, D., Ng, A., Ghahramani, Z. & Durrant-Whyte, H. (2004). Simultaneous localization and mapping with sparse extended information filters, *The International Journal of Robotics Research* 23(7-8): 693.

Tian, J., Gao, M. & Lu, E. (2007). Dynamic Collision Avoidance Path Planning for Mobile Robot Based on Multi-sensor Data Fusion by Support Vector Machine, *Mechatronics and Automation, 2007. ICMA 2007. International Conference on*, pp. 2779–2783.

Tomita, K., Murata, S., Kurokawa, H., Yoshida, E. & Kokaji, S. (1999). Self-assembly and self-repair method for a distributed mechanical system, *IEEE Transactions on Robotics and Automation* 15(6): 1035.

Tomlinson, B. & Blumberg, B. (2002). Using Emotional Memories to Form Synthetic Social Relationships, *Retrieved April* 1: 2005.

Trianni, V., Labella, T. & Dorigo, M. (2004). Evolution of Direct Communication for a Swarmbot Performing Hole Avoidance, *Ant Colony, Optimization and Swarm Intelligence* pp. 130–141.

Triebel, R., Pfaff, P. & Burgard, W. (2006). Multi-level surface maps for outdoor terrain mapping and loop closing, *2006 IEEE/RSJ International Conference on Intelligent Robots and Systems*, pp. 2276–2282.

Tuci, E., Groß, R., Trianni, V., Mondada, F., Bonani, M. & Dorigo, M. (2006). Cooperation through self-assembly in multi-robot systems, *ACM Transactions on Autonomous and Adaptive Systems (TAAS)* 1(2): 150.

Unsal, C. & Khosla, P. (2001). A multi-layered planner for self-reconfiguration of a uniform group of i-cube modules, *Proc. 2001 IEEE/RSJ Int. Conf. on Intelligent Robots and Systems*, Citeseer.

Upegui, A., Moeckel, R., Dittrich, E., Ijspeert, A. & Sanchez, E. (2005). An FPGA dynamically reconfigurable framework for modular robotics,*Workshop Proceedings of the 18th International Conference on Architecture of Computing Systems*, Citeseer, pp. 83–9.

Van Den Berg, J., Ferguson, D. & Kuffner, J. (2006). Anytime path planning and replanning in dynamic environments, *Proceedings of the IEEE International Conference on Robotics and Automation (ICRA)*, Citeseer, pp. 2366–2371.

Wang, Z., Hirata, Y. & Kosuge, K. (2004). Control a rigid caging formation for cooperative object transportation by multiple mobile robots, *2004 IEEE International Conference on Robotics and Automation, 2004. Proceedings. ICRA'04*, Vol. 2.

Wang, Z. & Kumar, V. (2002). Object closure and manipulation by multiple cooperating mobile robots, *IEEE International Conference on Robotics and Automation, 2002. Proceedings. ICRA'02*, Vol. 1.

Wang, Z., Nakano, E. & Matsukawa, T. (1996). Realizing cooperative object manipulation using multiplebehaviour-based robots, *Intelligent Robots and Systems' 96, IROS 96, Proceedings of the 1996 IEEE/RSJ International Conference on*, Vol. 1.

Wang, Z., Takano, Y., Hirata, Y. & Kosuge, K. (2007). Decentralized cooperative object transportation by multiple mobile robots with a pushing leader, *Distributed Autonomous Robotic Systems 6* pp. 453–462.

White, T. & Pagurek, B. (1998). Towards Multi-swarm Problem Solving in Networks, *Multi Agent Systems, 1998. Proceedings. International Conference on*, pp. 333–340.

Wolf, D. & Sukhatme, G. (2004). Online simultaneous localization and mapping in dynamic environments, *2004 IEEE International Conference on Robotics and Automation, 2004. Proceedings. ICRA'04*, Vol. 2.

Wolter, D., Latecki, L., Lakamper, R. & Sun, X. (2004). Shape-based robot mapping, *KI 2004: Advances in Artificial Intelligence* pp. 439–452.

Yamada, S. & Saito, J. (2001). Adaptive action selection without explicit communication for multirobot box-pushing, Systems, Man and Cybernetics, Part C, *IEEE Transactions on* 31(3): 398–404.

Yamashita, A., Fukuchi, M., Ota, J., Arai, T. & Asama, H. (2000). Motion planning for cooperative transportation of a large object by multiple mobile robots in a 3D environment, *IEEE INTERNATIONAL CONFERENCEONROBOTICS AND AUTOMATION*, Vol. 4, Citeseer, pp. 3144–3151.

Yang, E. & Gu, D. (2004). Multiagent reinforcement learning for multi-robot systems: A survey, *Dep. Comput. Sci., Univ. Essex, Colchester, UK, Tech. Rep. CSM-404* .

Yang, Y., Tian, Y. & Mei, H. (2007). Cooperative Q Learning Based on Blackboard Architecture, *International Conference on Computational Intelligence and Security Workshops, 2007. CISW 2007*, pp. 224–227.

Yim, M. (1993). A reconfigurable modular robot with many modes of locomotion, *Proc. of Intl. Conf. on Advanced Mechatronics*, pp. 283–288.

Yim, M., Shen, W., Salemi, B., Rus, D., Moll, M., Lipson, H., Klavins, E. & Chirikjian, G. (2007). Modular self-reconfigurable robot systems [grand challenges of robotics], *IEEE Robotics & Automation Magazine* 14(1): 43–52.

Yoshida, E., Kokaji, S., Murata, S., Kurokawa, H. & Tomita, K. (1999). Miniaturized self-reconfigurable system using shape memory alloy, *1999 IEEE/RSJ International Conference on Intelligent Robots and Systems, 1999. IROS'99. Proceedings*, Vol. 3.

15

# Virtual Reality Control Systems

Tomislav Reichenbach, Goran Vasiljević and Zdenko Kovačić
*University of Zagreb - Faculty of Electrical Engineering and Computing*
*Croatia*

## 1. Introduction

Control systems theory and application, as engineering in general, has greatly benefited from development and progress of the computer science and technology. An exponential growth in computational power in the last few decades gave rise to new methods, algorithms and theories. Gradually, the ability to deal with more and more complex problems was within reach. Unsolvable problems, or more precisely, formerly lengthy problems, became solvable in real-time.

At the same time, the controlled systems also became more advanced and complex. Better precision and control is required within each new generation or series, this naturally leading to increased computational power requirements; thus reducing the impact of the computational power growth.

Technological advance in both hardware and software, namely in hardware graphic capabilities and complementary software, allowed creating copies of real systems and environments in the computer, and thus a new technology emerged - so called Virtual Reality.

Since the term "Virtual Reality" has different connotations in today's culture, mostly due to popular science and entertainment industry (mis)interpretations, a precise meaning and the term used in this article - "Virtual Reality Systems (VRS)" - is equivalent to the meaning conveyed by "3D Graphic Simulator". Furthermore, unless clearly specified, no clear distinction is made between the virtual reality's classes - mixed reality, augmented reality or virtuality (see Fig. 1). In general, the umbrella term "virtual reality (VR)" is used to include anything forming part of the virtuality continuum.

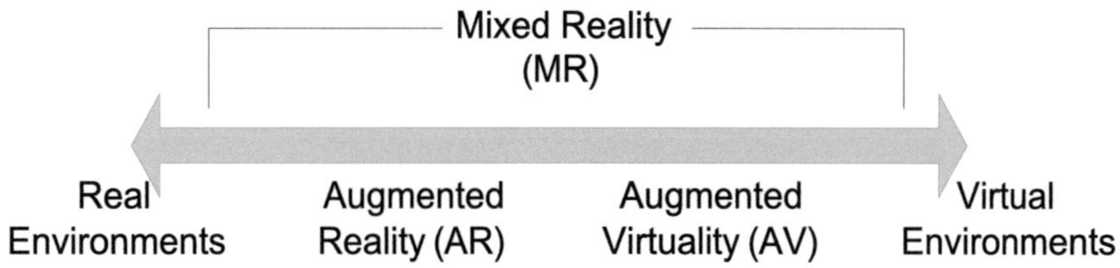


Fig. 1. Virtuality Continuum (Milgram & Colquhoun, 1999)

As the VRS turned more sophisticated due to the technological advance, new functionality became available. From the first plain 3D visualization system, subsequent major evolutionary steps are mainly: the ability to detect collisions, the introduction of physic based modeling and lately the addition of fluids, clothes and deformable bodies.

Entertainment industry embraced VRS almost from the start, but thenceforth a lot of different industries found VRS valuable, e.g. Bioinformatics (genome and protein folding research), Medicine (Virtual surgery and diagnostics, Therapeutics) and even Sociology, with virtual worlds-cultures like "Second Life" as a product and producer of culture simultaneously.

The VRS also are broadly used in control system prototyping, design and simulation. The benefits of using VRS are principally - reduced costs of development, mitigation of non-conformity and failure risks and greatly reduced prototyping and design time.

The authors became involved with VRS in control a decade ago, and continue to keep themselves engaged with VRS applications. During that time several software applications that provided the evaluation ground for new applications were developed. The aim of this chapter would be to enumerate, systematize and formalize different practices and techniques applicable to the VRS. New methodologies, showing how the VRS systems can be used complementary to the control systems, will be introduced - creating a new paradigm - "Virtual Reality Control Systems" (VRCS). Introduced methods have particularly suitable, but not exclusive application in robotics.

For the purpose of establishing the relations between virtual environments and control systems, the VRCS taxonomy is proposed, subject to the functionality available in the VRS and the way that functionality is used.

Hence, the following VRCS categories are established:

1. VRCS Visualization
2. VRCS Monitoring - Virtual sensors
3. VRCS Open loop control
4. VRCS Closed loop control

Each subsequent category adds more interdependency between the virtual and control system constituting that particular category, in respect to its antecedent.

An illustrative example for each category will be presented, with the application either in robotic arms, mobile robotics or humanoid robotics control. Data interchange between a real and a virtual system is described with an emphasis on how the data from the real system is incorporated into the VRCS.

## 2. Visualization

The first and the simplest category, in the defined taxonomy of the VRCS, is named "visualization". It is a baseline and principal prerequisite for other established VRCS categories, which are achieved simply by improving and adding features to the visualization core.

### 2.1 Introduction

Visualization itself, in general, is a technique of creating images, drawings or animations to convey information; to communicate both concrete and abstract ideas.

Visualization as a technique is not new, rather it is around 30,000 years old, dating back to the first cave wall drawings. Today, visualization has ever increasing applications in science, education, engineering, medicine, entertainment, etc. Further categorization according to the general objective in given applications is established as follows: Scientific visualization, Educational visualization, Information visualization, Knowledge visualization, Product Visualization, Visual Communication and Visual analytics ((Wikipedia, 2010)).

## 2.2 Definition

**VRCS visualization**, according to this categorization, falls into scientific visualization group. The precise definition of VRCS visualization is given with the following statement: *The use of computer-generated 3D visual representation of data from simulations or experiments to support analysis, exploration and comprehension of systems.*

In addition, for the general computer-generated 3D visualization to be VRCS visualization type, following conditions must be satisfied:

Perspective - Visualization is done in three dimensional (3D) space (with time as a fourth dimension)

Performance - Visualization execution performance is at least at the same level as the real system performance (real-time)

Model-based visualization - 3D models used are as accurate as possible or as circumstances require. (A digital construction of a real object is made directly from the available scientific data).

## 2.3 Introducing perspective

For three dimensional illusion of perception on the two dimensional screen, a proper technique for displaying depth and the corresponding mathematical method is required.

Historically, even though techniques for displaying depth in visualization were used before, it was not until Renaissance Italy that physically (optically) correct and mathematically valid technique was invented - the first major advance in scientific visualization. The first application of "true perspective" (commonly known today as geometric perspective[1] or central projection) is attributed to Filippo Brunelleschi when he painted the Baptistery of St.John in the Piazza Del Duomo in Florence. Remarkably enough, there is another reason for this application to be noteworthy in the context of this paper. As a person would stand at the exact spot where Brunelleschi painted the panel, he could observe the original scene through the tiny eyehole in the panel, or by holding the mirror in front of the panel look at the accurately drawn painting indistinguishable from the original. However, the sky was not drawn on the panel, rather coat of burnished silver was put there - creating a mirror. Consequently, a person looking would see the clouds drift across the upper part of the painting. "Here, in this calculated confusion of real world and artifice, the technological quest for virtual reality was launched."(Talbott, 1995)

The central perspective has one vanishing point where all the lines coming from the observer's viewpoint intersect. Two-point perspective exists when the picture plane is parallel to a Cartesian scene in one axis (usually the z-axis) but not to the other two axes. Therefore, there is one set of lines parallel to the picture plane and two sets of lines oblique to it, which converge to two vanishing points. Similarly, three-point perspective axes are not parallel to any of the Cartesian's three axes in the scene. In three-point perspective each of the three axes of the scene corresponds with one of the three vanishing points.

## 2.4 The graphics pipeline

The second prerequisite, for VRCS visualization class, is that the visualization performance has to be at least as fast as the performance of real system. However, it should be stressed

[1] The word "perspective" derives from the Latin perspectiva, a term adopted in the Middle Ages to render the Greek ὀπτική (optics)(Osborne, 2010).

that this only sets the minimum execution speed requirements, because in some cases we would like the virtual environment to execute the tasks as quickly as possible.
To accomplish this, rigorous mathematical method for perspective calculations is required. Subsequently, hardware capable of using that method to render virtual 3D environments is essential.
The essence of mathematical method used to describe the perspective is surprisingly simple - a 4x4 matrix. Consequently, visualization uses linear algebra and matrix multiplications for correct 3D perspective positioning, for rotations and translations in 3D space, for scaling and skewing, for projecting onto 2D surfaces, etc.[2]

### 2.5 Graphics pipeline

Basic building blocks in rendering process that creates a virtual environment are numbers. Numbers form coordinates that describe points in 3D space, which arranged create surfaces that shape a virtual world. Additionally, the points that create a virtual environment are further projected to a plane (computer screen) creating the viewpoint. The actual process and data flow is naturally more complex as the graphics pipeline takes advantage of the available hardware to process efficiently and to render scenes to a display (Walnum, 2003). Figure 2 conceptually illustrates the main components of the (DirectX) graphics pipeline.[3]

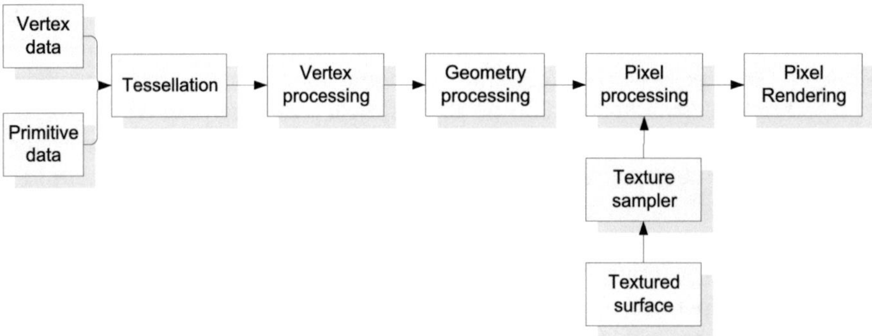


Fig. 2. Direct 3D graphics pipeline

### 2.6 Engine

Before the VRCS's (software) integral parts can be further described, concepts of engine, simulation engine and visualization engine need to be introduced.
An **engine** is general term for encapsulated block of software functionality, distinct from the user interface of that particular software. It can be either a library or collection of libraries, platform or SDK (software development kit). Engine has to provide a way to communicate with another software. Typically it is done through a dedicated API (Application Programming Interface).
**Simulation engine**, in general, is an engine with simulation functionality. Specifically, in the VRCS context, simulation engine is an engine capable of simulating dynamic systems.

---

[2] For additional reading regarding 4x4 matrix transformations in 3D perspective display, 3D rotations, translations and scaling, please refer to (Goldman, 1990),(Möller & Haines, 1999) or (Verth & Bishop, 2004).
[3] A similar process sequence is taking place in the OpenGL graphics pipeline (OpenGL is second major 3D standard along the DirectX)

**Visualization engine** is analogously an engine with visualization capabilities. Moreover, in the VRCS context it has to correspond to the previously defined requirements for the VRCS visualization. Visualization engine in normally a part of CAD software, computer games or simulation package.

Finally, an engine that possesses both simulation and visualization functionality is named **VR simulator**. During the development of the VRCS systems, a new proprietary VR Simulator was designed and developed in C++ using open-source or closed-source components, SDKs (OGRE, NxOgre, PhysX) and standards (Collada, XML, DAE) (Reichenbach, 2009).

One of the most commonly used examples of visualization engine is Virtual Reality Modeling Language (VRML) viewer. It conforms to all the requirements for VRCS Visualization and is used in many commercial products as a visualization tool. The Virtual Reality Toolbox[4] that ships with Matlab/Simulink platform is one of the examples (MathWorks, 2010).

The introduction of the VRML viewer into the proprietary platform (see (Kovačić et al., 2001) and (Smolić-Ročak et al., 2002)) for testing Flexible Manufacturing Systems (FMS) was one of our group's first forays into the field of 3D computer graphics. This typical example of the VRCS visualization (see Fig.3(a)), served as a stepping stone for next VRCS projects.

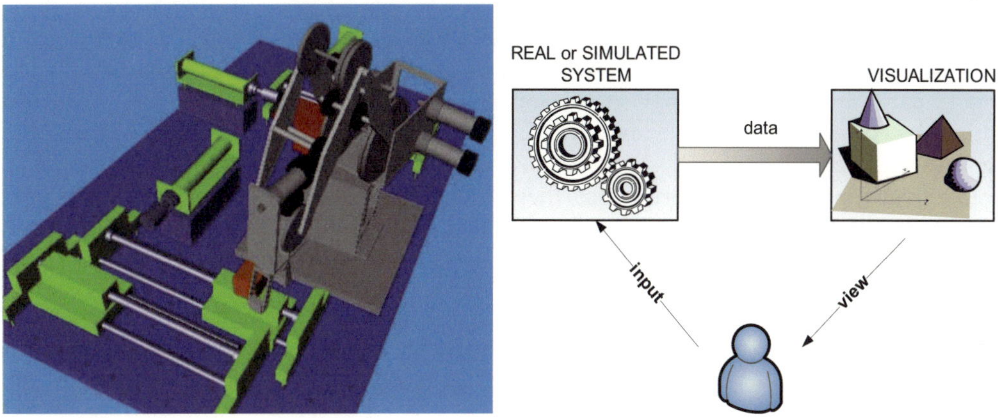


(a) VRML visualization - FlexMan (Larics (FER) -2002.)

(b) Information flow - Visualization case

Fig. 3. The VRCS Visualization

The visualization concept is shown in Fig. 3(b). The system has two main components, real or simulated system and visualization engine. Data flow is unidirectional - from real system/simulation to the visualization engine - and the visualization results (actions) are presented to the user. If no real system is present and system is simulated (within the simulation engine), one must note that this concept places no restriction on the software architecture. Simulation and visualization engine can run either in the same process, or as different processes, either on one or various machine(s), etc.

The "data" term used in the figure has broader connotations than normally associated with this word. What is communicated can be raw data in predefined format; i.e. variables, states,

[4] Virtual Reality toolbox was recently renamed Simulink 3D Animation

alerts; commands like direct function calls that manipulate objects (normally through some API) or events and messages that correspond to the particular situation occurring.
One important observation should be emphasized here. The VRCS visualization does not provide any new information, states, inputs or outputs to the particular system being subjected to the simulation or analysis. Nevertheless, there is an apparent cognitive value immediately available to the external observer performing or monitoring the undergoing simulation, through the act of observing the system behavior in a "visual" manner.

## 3. Monitoring - virtual sensor

Even though the computers have been used almost from their beginning for scientific visualization, insufficient graphics power limited their usefulness. With the general introduction of 3D hardware acceleration in mid '90, and enhancements following with each new generation, it became possible to produce more and more realistic looking visualization on a common personal computer. Apart from major advances in graphics, which exceed the scope of this paper, important step was introduction of a GPGPU (General Purpose Graphics Processing Unit) concept. This concept allows the use of graphics accelerator's massive computational power for general-purpose, in particular for real-time dynamic system simulations ("physics simulation").
In contrast to the VRCS visualization, where there was no additional logic and every action was the product of received data or command, in monitoring at least some simulation engine parts are merged with visualization engine. This integration is done preferably within the corresponding hardware (GPGPU), or with dedicated software (and paying the performance penalty).
Consequently, in VRCS monitoring case, there is additional information available to the user as a product of the visualization and simulation integration (see Fig. 4(a)). The communication between system or simulation and visualization engine is still unidirectional, as it was in the visualization case.
This additional information, representing new state, variable or an indicator of the system behavior, is something that was not previously available in the system. This information can lead to new insights, a better understanding of the system or to improved quality in the control of the system.
To help better understanding, an illustrative example of the monitoring concept is provided. The humanoid robot presented in Fig. 4(b) is modeled in detail in 3D CAD (Computer-aided- design) software. Not only is the robot's appearance data described but also its physical characteristics are specified, i.e., its links, masses, inertias, motors, etc. This physical properties are essential for dynamic system simulation. There are several predetermined points on the soles of humanoid robot's feet that are sensitive to the force exerted upon them. The resultant force and position, in respect to each sole, therefore can be calculated. This new sensor is termed **virtual sensor**, and in this particular case virtual pressure sensor. Figure 4(c) shows the resultant forces (pressure) when the lateral force is applied to the humanoid robot's body.

## 4. Open loop control

Further extension to the VRCS monitoring class, is the VRCS open-loop case (see Fig. 5(a)) where the distinction is the presence of a controller (and controller strategy in general). The prerequisite for the basic functioning of the controller is a presence of a virtual environment.

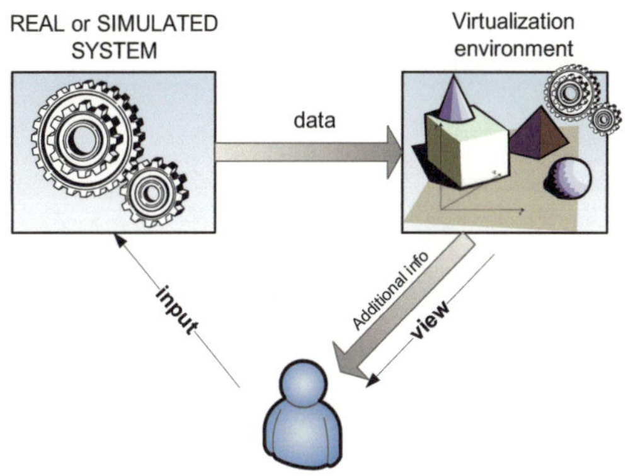


(a) Information flow - Monitoring - Visual sensor case

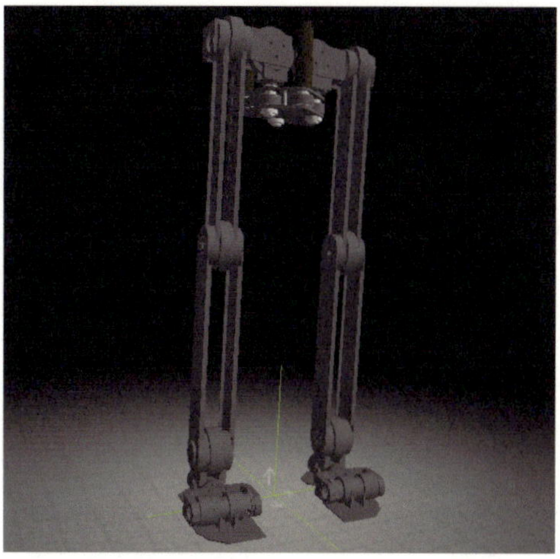

(b) Humanoid robot

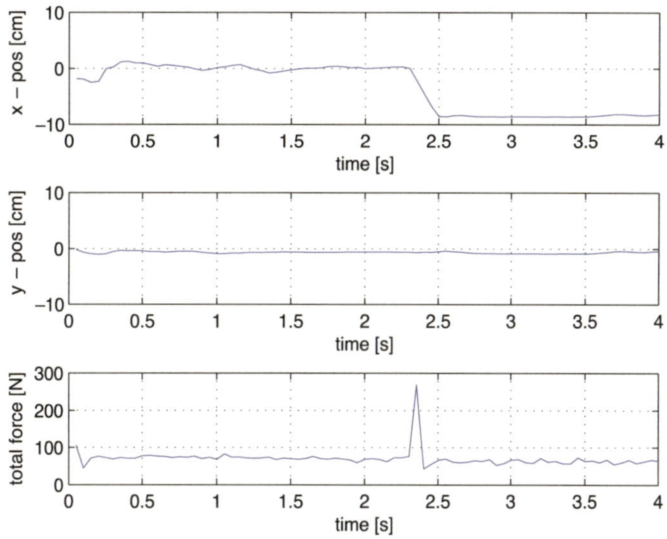


(c) Resultant virtual pressure sensor

Fig. 4. The VRCS Monitoring

Systems that fall into this category generally are remote systems that provide virtual environment of the (probably not so easy to reach) system. No other form of the feedback is available, except the supervising operator who can act only as an observer or as a man-in-the-loop control feedback.

One such example is the implementation of the Internet accessible robot control laboratory (see (Kovacic et al., 2007)) based on the use of the Matlab Real Time Workshop (see Fig. 5(c)). The developed system contains a four degrees of freedom SCARA robot, Ultimodule robot controller that communicates via TCP/IP with the server application embedded into the Simulink function block and a client web application (see Fig. 5(b)) with VRML-based GUI and Java applet for setting joint positions or tool center positions.

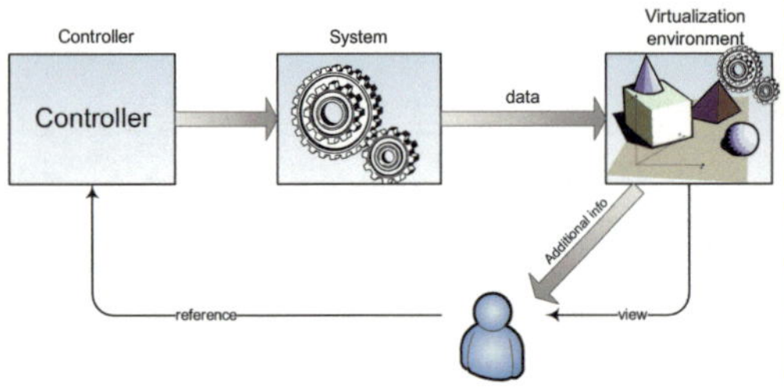


(a) Information flow - VRCS open-loop case

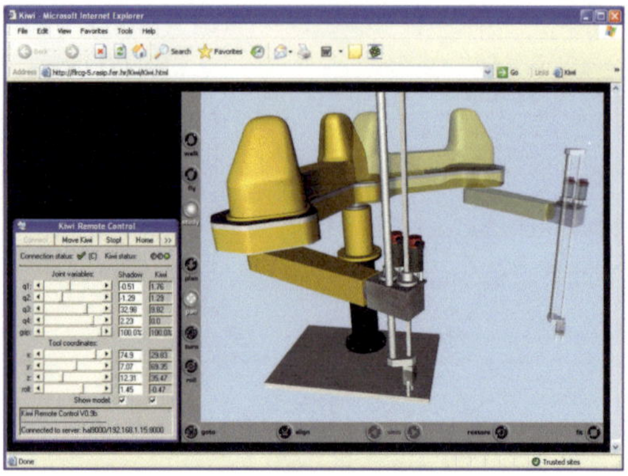

(b) The client application

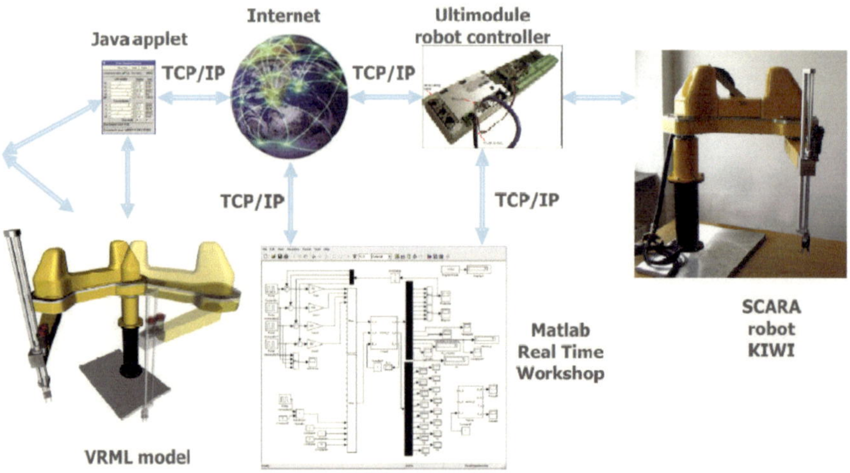


(c) Internet accessible robot control laboratory - the concept

Fig. 5. The VRCS open loop control

## 5. Closed loop control

The VRCS closed loop system is presented in Fig. 6(a). At least part of the simulation engine is bundled with the visualization engine, as was the case in the VRCS monitoring and open-loop control. Identically as in those cases, this part of simulation engine, in conjunction with the visualization engine, provides additional valuable information for the control. The improvement over the previous category, VRCS open-loop control, is that here this extra information is used as a feedback, consequently improving better control quality and responsiveness.

The closed loop can be achieved using a virtual sensor or with a help of one or two cameras (stereovision). The former one is considered next, while the later case – the usage of cameras to provide feedback – is explained in great detail in the next section. By using cameras we are thus effectively creating the feedback through augmented virtuality (See Fig. 1).

### 5.1 Collision avoidance

Another illustrative example, shown in Fig. 6(b) with two robotic arms sharing the manufacturing test bed, is the case of collision avoidance by the principle of minimal movement from the possible collision point detected using the virtual collision detection sensors. The sensors are placed along the entire robotic arm's surface thus allowing the exact collision point to be detected and the link, that is in collision, to be determined. Since that particular collision point can be evaded only by moving that link and/or links lower in the hierarchy from the colliding link, the collision evasion algorithm calculates the collision free position of the robotic arm following the principle of minimal movement of those links. The collision evasion continues iteratively until the complete trajectory is collision free (Reichenbach et al. (2006)). The resulting trajectory is shown in Fig 6(c).

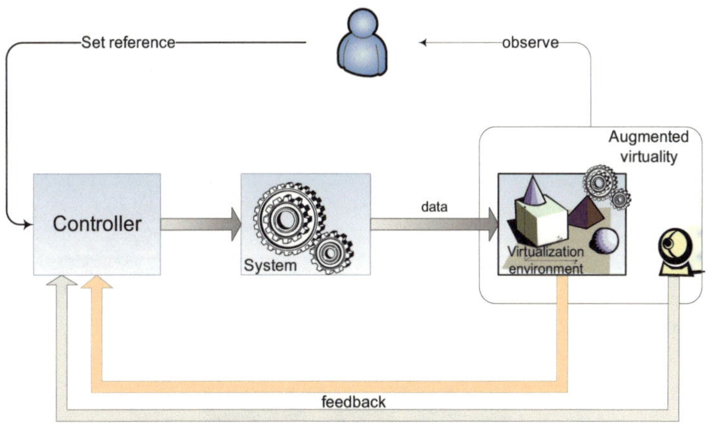


(a) Information flow - VRCS closed-loop case

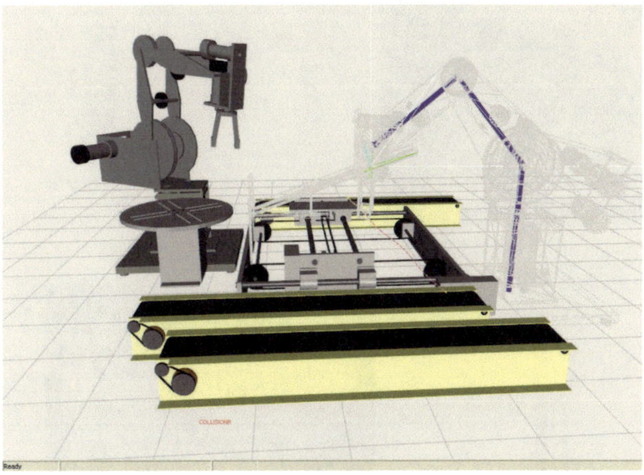

(b) FMS testbed with two robotic arm sharing the same space. One robotic arm is (will be) colliding with the gravitational buffer if the trajectory is not modified.

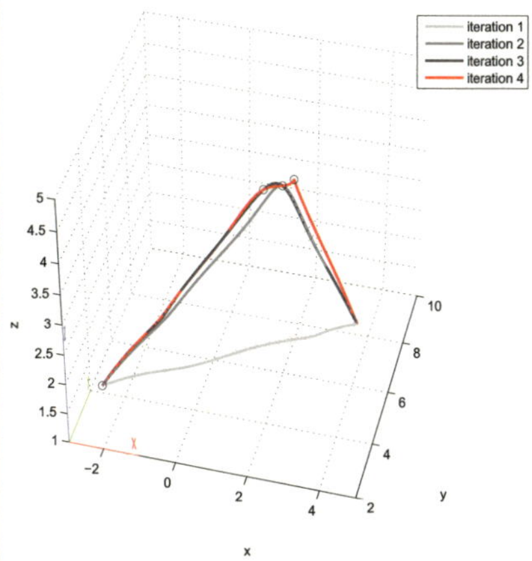


(c) Collision free trajectory and the previous iterations that led to that trajectory

Fig. 6. The VRCS closed loop control - virtual collision sensor

## 6. Virtual reality feedback

With visual sensors, providing a depth information, it is possible to identify position and pose of every actor in the virtual reality scene without the need for additional sensors. The vision-based approach for robot pose and position identification using virtual models and stereo vision in effort to match robot's representation in a virtual environment with a real one, is explained in detail.

One of the algorithms that extracts and describes local features (called keypoints) on the camera acquired image is a scale invariant feature transform (SIFT) algorithm (Lowe, 2004). Having a known 3D model of a robot in the scene and by using a SIFT algorithm, a database of robot keypoints associated with different images (views) of the robot has had to be created first (see Fig. 7). For finding the pose of the robot, keypoints of the left camera image

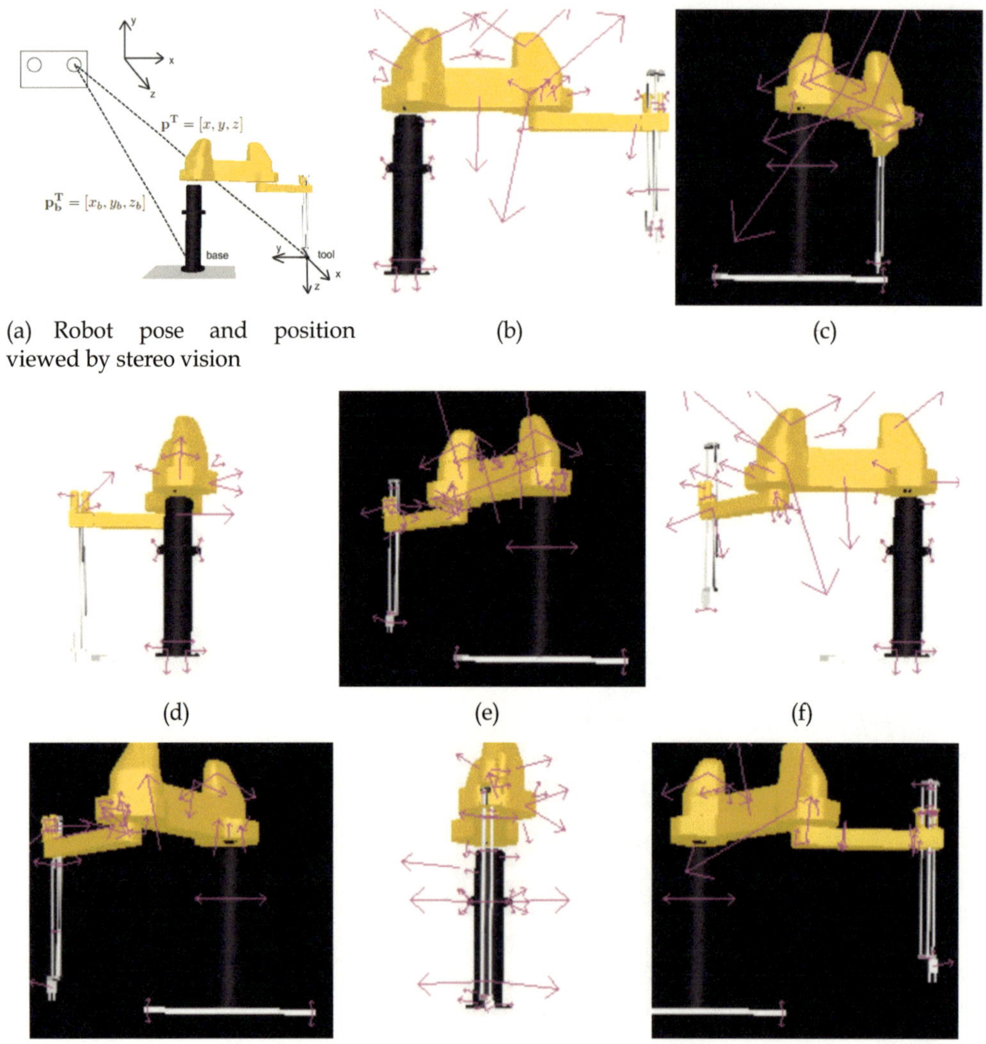


(a) Robot pose and position viewed by stereo vision (b) (c)

(d) (e) (f)

(g) (h) (i)

Fig. 7. Created base of 3-dimensional images and corresponding keypoints are first produced and then compared to the keypoints in the database. For the image pixels associated with the matched keypoints, the corresponding 3D points are calculated using a disparity map, found by dynamic programming matching algorithm (Cox, 1995), (Forstmann et al., 2004). This is possible only if a pinhole model of cameras is used, and if their intrinsic and extrinsic parameters are known (Davis, 1996). All bad points (positioned too far, too close, etc.) are discarded, while the remaining good ones are used for minimizing the distance to the robot represented with a chain of line segments. Minimization is executed by applying a Nelder-Mead simplex optimization algorithm (Mathews & Fink, 2004). Best optimization results are then compared to the image and the depth map of a 3D robot model, and the configuration with the best match is assumed to be a found pose of the robot.

### 6.1 Related work

Visual pose detection algorithms have been a subject of intensive research. From the practical point of view, few of them proved to be very effective. For example, in case of using only one camera, one can use the SIFT algorithm (Lowe, 2004) or its faster Speeded-Up Robust Features (SURF) version (Bay et al., 2006), which can extract and describe local features of image necessary to robustly find correct position and orientation of an arbitrary object, but these algorithms are not suitable for objects which change their configuration like robotic manipulators do. In most cases, the aim of using two cameras in robotic systems was to determine a position of robot's end effector, e.g. robot stereo-hand coordination for grasping curved parts (Dufournaud et al., 1998), stereo vision-based feedback (Toyama et al., 1996), aligning the end effector with object (Horaud et al., 1995), and visual servoing for precise manipulation (Jägersand et al., 1997). These approaches can give the exact position of manipulator's end effector, but they do not provide the information about positions of robot links. The method described in (Bischoff & Gerke, 2000) uses stereo vision for matching contours and critical points on both images and implements a fuzzy logic-based collision avoidance algorithm. In (Mulligan et al., 2000) the image obtained from a camera is being compared to the image from the scene model, and the difference is used for adjusting that model. In (Lawrence et al., 1989) joint angles are determined from a single image based on the positions of markers attached to robot's links. Similar problems are found in the human body pose identification. (Bernier, 2006) describes the statistical model for fast 3D articulated body tracking, (Shakhnarovich et al., 2003) shows the algorithm for the fast human body pose estimation using large base of example images. The work described in (Rehg & Knade, 1994) explains model-based hand tracking system, that can recover 27 DOF hand model from grayscale images.

### 6.2 Problem definition

Determining the pose and position of a robot by processing a stereo image requires a source of good quality video input. This is provided in the considered system by a pair of calibrated cameras located sideways to the robot and directed towards the robot. In this way, the installed stereo-vision system is able to generate fairly accurate 3D information about the elements in the scene being viewed (including a robot itself). As already mentioned, positions of elements can be obtained by producing a disparity map between the images acquired from two cameras. For this purpose, a dynamic programming stereo vision algorithm similar to one described in (Cox, 1995) and (Forstmann et al., 2004) is used.

In order to recognize the pose and position of a robot in the image, it is necessary to have its 3D model prepared and values of robot's kinematics parameters defined by a standard Denavit-Hartenberg method (Schilling, 1990).
As shown in Fig. 7(a), a position of a robot is defined as the location of a robot base $\mathbf{p_b}$ with respect to a left camera position:

$$\mathbf{p_b} = \begin{bmatrix} x_b & y_b & z_b \end{bmatrix}^T \tag{1}$$

where $x_b$ is the horizontal axis, $y_b$ is the vertical axis and $z_b$ is the axis pointing from the camera toward the object. In case that the robot position vector $\mathbf{p_b}$ is known the problem is reduced only to recognition of robot's pose.
Position of robot tool is defined as its location with respect to a left camera position:

$$\mathbf{p} = \begin{bmatrix} x & y & z \end{bmatrix}^T \tag{2}$$

The image obtained from the left camera, together with the corresponding depth map, is used to find the appropriate pose of a robot expressed in the joint space by finding joint variables:

$$\mathbf{q} = \begin{bmatrix} q_1 & \dots & q_n \end{bmatrix}^T \tag{3}$$

where $q_i$ is the $i$-th joint variable, and $n$ denotes a number of degrees of freedom.

### 6.3 Creating a database of keypoints

A virtual 3D model of a robot is used for creation of keypoints that are going to be stored in the database. The applied procedure is the following: a 3D robot model is rotated consecutively by the angle of 45°, while simultaneously joint variables are changed by one fourth of the maximal robot joint value, which results in 8 images. In the same time the color of the background is alternating from black to white and vice-versa. The same procedure is repeated four times, first for the images of 350x350 resolution, and then for images of respective height and width reduced by 20% (the reasons for varying the image size are elaborated in (Liebelt et al., 2008)). The database of keypoints is created and stored for further use for all 32 created images. Fig. 7 shows the keypoints corresponding to original 350x350 images[5].

### 6.4 Searching for robot keypoints

As mentioned above, keypoints extracted from the left camera image are compared to key-points stored in the image database. In order to make correct decision whether a given key-point $T_i$ point is valid or not, its respective nearest and second nearest neighbors $A$ and $B$ should be found. Points $A$ and $B$ are those keypoints in the same image that have the shortest Euclidean distances of their descriptors. A point $T_i$ is discarded if its nearest and second nearest neighbors satisfy the following relation (Lowe, 2004):

$$D(A,T_i) > \alpha \cdot D(B,T_i) \tag{4}$$

---

[5] It should be noted that a larger number of images being created will slow down the execution of the algorithm, while a smaller number of images will decrease the accuracy.

where $D(x,y)$ is the Euclidean distance of descriptors for two keypoints $x$ and $y$ and $\alpha$ is a distance ratio set to value 0.8 as recommended in (Lowe, 2004).

Regarding the remaining keypoints, the space coordinates are calculated with respect to the coordinate system of a left camera, using the pixel in the left camera image and the corresponding disparity map obtained by previously mentioned dynamic programming algorithm for stereo vision. In the studied system, the keypoints lying 10 m or more from the camera are automatically discarded, because for a robot that far away, the distance from the camera would be too long for reliable detection, or the number of detected keypoints would be too small for accurate pose identification.

A mean point is calculated taking into account all remaining points, and all points which are too far from the mean point are discarded. In our case, it is assumed that a point is too far from a mean point if it is located outside the area 60% larger than the maximum span $L_{max}$ of a robot. In general, $L_{max}$ is a distance from two outmost distinct points of the robot in any configuration.

### 6.5 Optimization of distance from remaining keypoints

In order to find the pose and position of a robot, a method for matching keypoints to the robot is developed. In this method robot is represented as a chain of line segments, whose points are calculated from a homogeneous transformation matrix. A homogeneous transformation matrix calculated using known robot kinematics parameters and joint variable values has the following form (Schilling, 1990):

$$\mathbf{T}_0^k = \begin{bmatrix} \mathbf{R} & \mathbf{p} \\ \boldsymbol{\eta}^T & \sigma \end{bmatrix} \tag{5}$$

where $\mathbf{R}$ is a rotation matrix, $\mathbf{p}$ is a translation vector, $\boldsymbol{\eta}$ is a perspective vector (usually null vector) and $\sigma$ is a scaling factor (usually 1).

Using (5), it is possible to determine the points of a chain that form line segments representing the robot:

$$\begin{aligned} P_{2k-1} &= P_{2k-2} + l_k \cdot \mathbf{z}_{k-1} \\ P_{2k} &= \mathbf{p}_k \end{aligned} \tag{6}$$

where $P_i$ is the $i$-th point in the chain, $l_k$ is the robot kinematics parameter representing a length of the $k$-th link, $\mathbf{p_k}$ is the translation vector, and $\mathbf{z}_{k-1}$ is the vector representing direction of $(k-1)$-st robot link, which is the 3-rd column of rotation matrix $\mathbf{R}_{k-1}$.

For a given keypoint, its distance to the nearest line segment of the robot can be calculated as follows (see Fig. 8):

1. if $b^2 > a^2 + c^2$ then $d = a$;
2. if $a^2 > b^2 + c^2$ then $d = b$;
3. else $d = \sqrt{b^2 - (\frac{b^2+c^2-a^2}{2c})^2}$

where $a$ is the length from the beginning of the line segment (point $P_i$) to the point(C), $b$ is the length from the end of the line segment (point $P_{i+1}$) to the point (C), $c$ is the length of a line segment and $d$ is a wanted distance.

The distance from a point to a chain of line segments is calculated by finding a minimal distance from that point to every line segment in the chain.

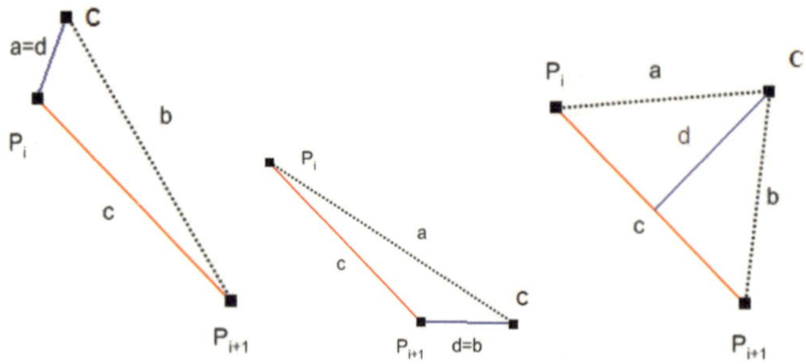


(a) $b^2 > a^2 + c^2$ (b) $a^2 > b^2 + c^2$ (c) $b^2 \leq a^2 + c^2$ and $a^2 \leq b^2 + c^2$

Fig. 8. Calculation of distance from line segment to point

It is necessary to find the pose and position of robot for which the sum of distances from points which are not discarded to a chain of line segments is minimal. This is done by using the Nelder-Mead simplex optimization method, which is performed for various initial conditions. Parameters involved in optimization are a position vector $\mathbf{p_b}$ and a vector of joint variables $\mathbf{q}$. Initial conditions for the position vector are:

1. $(x_s, y_s, z)$
2. $(x_{max}, y_s, z)$
3. $(x_{min}, y_s, z)$
4. $(x_s, y_{max}, z)$
5. $(x_s, y_{min}, z)$

where $x_s$, $x_{max}$ and $x_{min}$ are respective mean value, maximal value and minimal value of $x$ coordinates of all points, $y_s$, $y_{max}$ and $y_{min}$ are respective mean value, maximal value and minimal value of $y$ coordinates of all points, and $z$ is a minimal value of $z$ coordinates (it is assumed that the robot base is located in the bottom, which is the case for the studied robot). Initial conditions for joint variables are a combination of first three joints in which, working area of each joint is divided in 8 parts. In this way, there are 2560 initial conditions. For every initial condition 100 iterations of optimization are performed. First 30 iterations are used only to optimize the position vector of robot base, because first it is necessary to set an approximate position of the chain of line segments. Remaining 70 iterations of optimization are performed for optimizing the position vector of robot base together with the vector of joint variables.

### 6.6 Choosing the best pose and position

Twenty best results obtained by optimization from different initial conditions are then used to create the image of a 3D robot model. For each set of parameters, 3D model is set to correspond to an actual situation (the base of the robot is set to given coordinates with respect to the virtual camera and joint values are set to a given values), virtual camera is set to have identical parameters as the real one (which can be determined by calibration). The comparison is done only on the image segments where robot model is located. There are three criteria of comparison.

The first criterion compares RGB intensities of the images:

$$\begin{aligned}\Delta R &= I_{R1}^{i} - I_{R2}^{i} - I_{comp}\\ \Delta G &= I_{G1}^{i} - I_{G2}^{i} - I_{comp}\\ \Delta B &= I_{B1}^{i} - I_{B2}^{i} - I_{comp}\\ K_1 &= \frac{\sum_{i=1}^{n} (\Delta R)^2 + (\Delta G)^2 + (\Delta B)^2}{n}\end{aligned} \tag{7}$$

where $K_1$ is a value of the first criterion; $n$ is a number of points being compared; $I_{R1}^{i}$, $I_{G1}^{i}$ and $I_{B1}^{i}$ are intensities of red, green and blue channels of the image from a virtual camera; $I_{R2}^{i}$, $I_{G2}^{i}$ and $I_{B2}^{i}$ are intensities of red, green and blue channel of the image from a real camera and $I_{comp}$ is a mean value of intensity differences between virtual and real camera image segments where robot is located, used to compensate different intensities between images. The second criterion is related to the absolute sum of differences of $z$ coordinates:

$$K_2 = \frac{\sum_{i=1}^{m} \left| z_1^{(i)} - z_2^{(i)} \right|}{m} \tag{8}$$

where $K_2$ is a value of the second criterion; $z_1^{(i)}$ is the $i$-th value of $z$ coordinate obtained from the virtual image; $z_2^{(i)}$ is the $i$-th value of $z$ coordinate obtained from a disparity map of real images and $m$ is a number of points belonging to image segments where robot model is located, for which holds $| z_1^{(i)} - z_2^{(i)} | < L_{max}/2$ (it is necessary to discard points with distant $z$ coordinates, because of possible errors in the disparity map).
The third criterion has the following form:

$$K_3 = \frac{n - m}{n} \tag{9}$$

where $K_3$ is a value of the third criterion. This criterion shows the ratio between the number of discarded points and the overall number of points being compared.
An overall criterion for comparison is obtained by multiplication of criteria obtained from (7), (8) and (9):

$$K = K_1 \cdot K_2 \cdot K_3 \tag{10}$$

The entire procedure for finding a pose and position of the robot is illustrated in Fig. 9.

### 6.7 Results

The presented algorithm has been tested on a 4-DOF SCARA robot configuration. For this purpose two BTC PC380 USB web cameras anchored parallel at the distance of 10 cm were used. Prior to experiments, exact intrinsic and extrinsic parameters of cameras were obtained by calibration. During experiments, the original 640x480 image size was reduced to the 320x240 size and the images were rectified prior to starting a dynamic programming algorithm. Image size reduction is done to decrease execution time, but the cost is decreasing accuracy of an algorithm.
Experiments were conducted using two different camera positions with respect to the robot base, as shown in Table 1. Camera positions must be far enough to let the robot fit into the image frame, but still close enough for good quality of robot pose and position recognition.

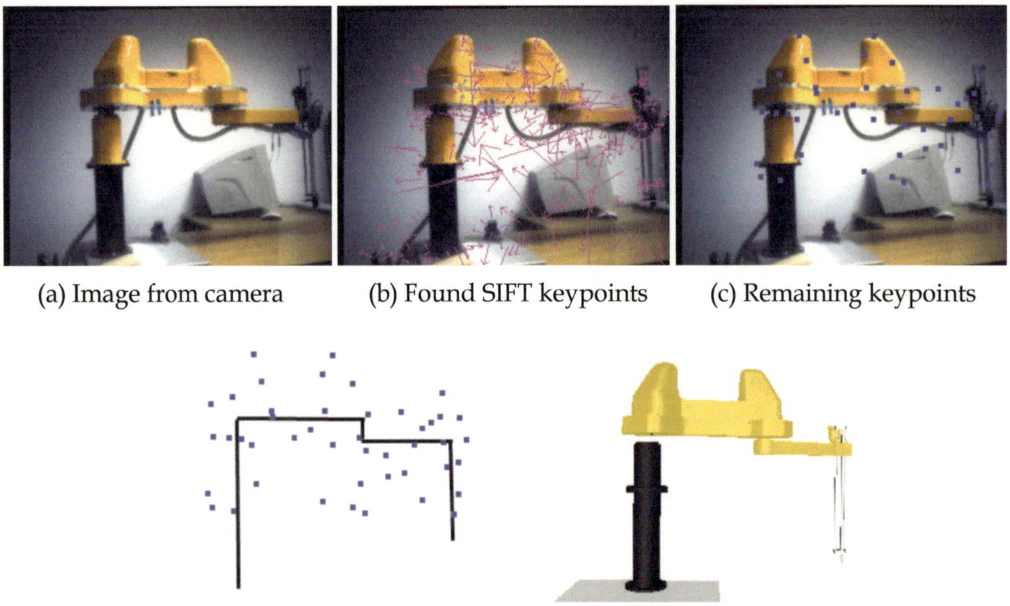

(a) Image from camera (b) Found SIFT keypoints (c) Remaining keypoints

(d) Chain of line segments (e) Recognized robot pose

Fig. 9. Searching for robot pose and position

| $x_1$ [cm] | $y_1$ [cm] | $z_1$ [cm] | $x_2$ [cm] | $y_2$ [cm] | $z_2$ [cm] |
|---|---|---|---|---|---|
| -22 | 209 | -41 | -41 | 166 | -40 |

Table 1. Two positions of robot base w.r.t. the left camera

The proposed algorithm was executed five times for 40 different robot poses, which makes a total number of 400 algorithm runs. The execution times of the algorithm were in the interval of 3-5 seconds depending on a number of keypoints found and a number of points being discarded. Using the results of the algorithm (position of robot base and values of joint variables) and by calculating direct kinematics of the robot, the assumed position of a robot's end effector has been obtained and compared to the real position of robot's end effector. The Euclidean distance between them has been taken as a direct quality measure of the result. All results having that distance greater than 40 cm were treated as inaccurate and accordingly, discarded.

The experiments have shown that 27% of the results were discarded in the first camera position, and 33% in the second one. In other words, approximately seven out of ten solutions are satisfactory. This means that good solutions prevail. But this also means that dissatisfactory solutions should be further processed to ensure constantly reliable solutions. This could be done by using some filter (e.g. a median filter) and appropriate interpolation algorithm related to prevailing good solutions.

Only the satisfactory results have been used for a statistical analysis of experiments. Table 2 shows the mean value of the distance error and the standard deviation for two respective camera positions in direction of $x$, $y$, and $z$ coordinates, as well as the overall Euclidean distance error mentioned above. Table 3 shows the mean value and the standard deviation of robot joint variables estimates error and the position of the robot base estimates error. It is

| Parameter | Mean [cm] | Deviation [cm] |
|---|---|---|
| $x_1$ | -1.3 | 7.3 |
| $y_1$ | -4.3 | 9.3 |
| $z_1$ | -1.29 | 9.13 |
| $\sqrt{x_1^2 + y_1^2 + z_1^2}$ | 13.9 | 7.35 |
| $x_2$ | 4.57 | 8.16 |
| $y_2$ | 8.45 | 8.78 |
| $z_2$ | -5.41 | 10.78 |
| $\sqrt{x_2^2 + y_2^2 + z_2^2}$ | 17.8 | 9.08 |

Table 2. Mean values and deviation of the robot tool position estimates error

| | First camera pos. | | Second camera pos. | |
|---|---|---|---|---|
| Parameter | Mean | Deviation | Mean | Deviation |
| $q_1$ | −5.07° | 22.1° | −2.62° | 13.3° |
| $q_2$ | −0.33° | 21.8° | −9.3° | 25.8° |
| $q_3$ | 0.98 cm | 9.28 cm | -0.62 cm | 10.4 cm |
| $x_b$ | -2.03 cm | 3.8 cm | -6.26 cm | 3.9 cm |
| $y_b$ | -8.69 cm | 3.9 cm | 4.32 cm | 3.9 cm |
| $z_b$ | 0.07 cm | 2.9 cm | -6.07 cm | 2.4 cm |

Table 3. Mean values and deviation of joint variables estimates error and the position of the robot base estimates error

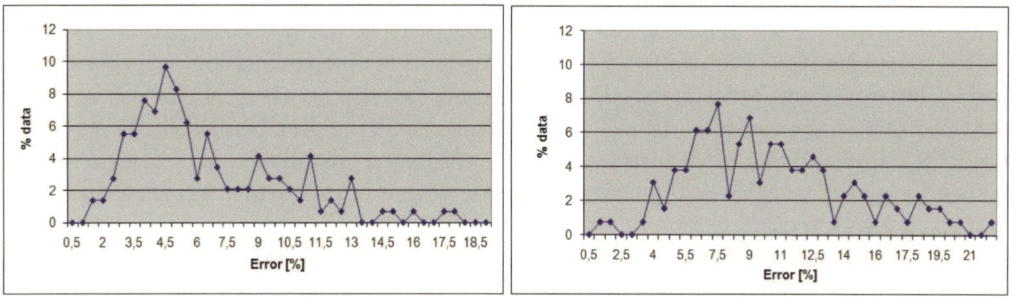


(a) first camera position (overall error) (b) second camera position (overall error)

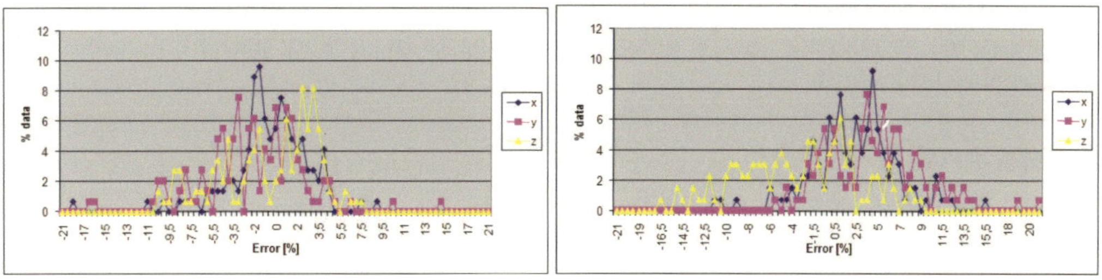


(c) first camera position (individual error) (d) second camera position (individual error)

Fig. 10. Percentage of data related to overall error and to the individual error in $x$, $y$ and $z$ direction interesting to see the distribution of results with respect to the magnitudes of Euclidean distance errors expressed relative to $\|\mathbf{p}_b\|$. Figs. 10(a) and 10(b) show the distribution of percentage of acceptable solutions having the same distance error. In the same manner, Figs. 10(c) and 10(d) show the distribution of percentage of solutions having the same distance errors along $x$, $y$ and $z$ coordinates expressed relative to $\|\mathbf{p}_b\|$. From those figures one can see that the distribution assumes the form similar to gaussian one with a center close to zero.

## 7. Conclusion

Technological advances in computing power and engineering and consequently available functionality enabled the implementation of new methodologies in control systems. The integration of computer graphics and control systems, described in this chapter, allowed for the new control system paradigm named Virtual Reality Control Systems (VRCS). The classification of the VRCS into the following categories, the VRCS visualization, the VRCS monitoring, the VRCS open-loop control and the VRCS closed-loop control, has been established and explained. Furthermore, for each VRCS category an illustrative example and its practical usage has been elaborated. The Flexible manufacturing testbed application in VRML is presented as a typical example of VRCS visualization. Virtual sensor - a humanoid robot foot pressure sensor - was introduced as the VRCS monitoring usage case. Subsequently, the Open loop VRCS control system was explained and finally a detailed consideration was given to the Closed loop VRCS case and how the visual feedback from the virtual system is established.

Having a known 3D model of a robot in the scene and by using a scale invariant feature transform (SIFT) algorithm, a database of robot keypoints associated with different images (views) of the robot has been created. By comparison of keypoints of an actual robot with the keypoints from the database, the position and pose of the robot are determined by a Nelder-Mead simplex optimization. For this purpose, a three-elements comparison criterion has been defined and best suitable parameters were determined. The comparison of the so obtained pose of the considered 4 DOF SCARA robot with the pose being directly measured has indicated that the proposed method has a precision comparable to the precision human beings have. The transfer of the estimated robot pose into the virtual model of the robot system enables use of VR feedback.

It is important to note that the VRCS principles and the methods described here are indifferent to the quality and detail of 3D models and virtual environments. The principles can be applied to various sophistication levels of simulation and virtual environment. The control quality, however, is related to both simulation and virtual environment refinements. Viceversa, the refinements can be tailored according to the quality desired, or achievable performance limitations.

## 8. References

Bay, H., Tuytelaars, T. & Gool, L. V. (2006). Surf: Speeded up robust features, *ECCV*, pp. 404- 417.

Bernier, O. (2006). Real-time 3d articulated pose tracking using particle filters interacting through belief propagation, *18th International Conference on Pattern Recognition (ICPR'06)*, Vol. 1, pp. 90–93.

Bischoff, A. & Gerke, M. (2000). Fuzzy collision avoidance using stereo-vision, *SYROCO*, Vol. 1.

Cox, I. J. (1995). A maximum likelihood n-camera stereo algorithm, *Proceedings IEEE Conf. on Computer Vision and Pattern Recognition*, pp. 733–739.

Davis, E. R. (1996). *Machine Vision: Theory, Algorithms, Practicalities 2nd Edition*, Academic Press.

Dufournaud, Y., Horaud, R. & Quan, L. (1998). Robot stereo-hand coordination for grasping curved parts, *Proceedings of the Brittish Machine Vision Conference, BMVC'98*, Springer- Verlag, pp. 760–769.

Forstmann, S., Kanou, Y., Ohya, J., Thuering, S. & Schmitt, A. (2004). Real-time stereo by using dynamic programming, *Computer Vision and Pattern Recognition Workshop*, pp. 29–29.

Goldman, R. (1990). Matrices and transformations, *in* A. S. Glassner (ed.), *Graphics Gems*, Academic Press, pp. 472–475.

Horaud, R., Dornaika, F. & Espiau, B. (1995). Visually guided object grasping, *IEEE Transactions on Robotics and Automation* 14: 525–532.

Jägersand, M., Fuentes, O. & Nelson, R. (1997). Experimental evaluation of uncalibrated visual servoing for precision manipulation, *IEEE International Conference on Robotics and Automation*.

Kovacic, Z., Smolic-Rocak, N., Dujmovic, S. & Munk, R. (2007). Matlab real-time workshop-based internet accessible robot control laboratory, *The Proceedings of the International Conference on Remote Engineering and Virtual Instrumentation REV07*.

Kovačić, Z., Bogdan, S., Reichenbach, T., Smolić-Ročak, N. & Punčec, M. (2001). Flexman - a computer-integrated tool for design and simulation of flexible manufacturing systems, *CD-ROM Proceedings of the 9th Mediterranean Conference on Control and Automation Control*, Vol. TM2-B.

Lawrence, P. D., Mackworth, A. K. & Mulligan, I. J. (1989). Patent us4826391 manipulator arm position sensing.

Liebelt, J., Schmid, C. & Schertler, K. (2008). Viewpoint-independent object class detection using 3d feature maps, *Computer Vision and Pattern Recognition*, pp. 1–8.

Lowe, D. G. (2004). Distinctive image features from scale-invariant keypoints, *International Journal of Computer Vision* 60: 91–110.

Mathews, J. H. & Fink, K. K. (2004). *Numerical Methods Using Matlab, 4th Edition*, Prentice Hall Inc.

MathWorks (2010). Simulink 3d animation, http://www.mathworks.com/products/3d animation/.

Milgram, P. & Colquhoun, H. (1999). A taxonomy of real and virtual world display integration.

Möller, T. & Haines, E. (1999). *Real-Time Rendering*, A. K. Peters. MÖL t 02:1 1.Ex.

Mulligan, I. J., Mackworth, A. K. & Lawrence, P. D. (2000). A model-based vision system for manipulator position sensing, *Workshop on Interpretation of 3-D Scenes*, pp. 186–193.

Osborne, H. (2010). The arts: Fine art, contemporary art and music - perspective, http://arts.jrank.org/pages/16368/perspective.html.

Rehg, J. & Knade, T. (1994). Visual tracking of high dof articulated structures: an application to human hand tracking, *European Conference on Computer Vision*, pp. 35–46.

Reichenbach, T. (2009). A dynamic simulator for humanoid robots, *Artificial Life and Robotics* 13(2): 561–565.

Reichenbach, T., Miklic, D. & Kovacic, Z. (2006). Supervisory control by using active virtual 3d models in-the-loop, *CCA '06. IEEE International Conference on Control Applications, Munich, Germany* pp. 1409–1413.

Schilling, R. J. (1990). *Fundamentals of robotics*, Prentice Hall, New Jersey.

Shakhnarovich, G., Viola, P. & Darrell, T. (2003). Fast pose estimation with parameter-sensitive hashing, *Ninth IEEE International Conference on Computer Vision (ICCV'03)*, Vol. 2, p. 750.

Smolić-Ročak, N., Bogdan, S., Kovačić, Z., Reichenbach, T. & Birgmajer, B. (2002). Modeling and simulation of fms dynamics by using vrml, *CD-ROM Proceedings of the b'02 IFAC World Congress*, Vol. WM2-C.

Talbott, S. (1995). *The Future Does Not Compute: Transcending the Machines in Our Midst*, 1 edn, O'Reilly & Associates, Inc.

Toyama, K., Hager, G. D. &Wang, J. (1996). Servomatic: A modular system for robust positioning using stereo visual servoing, *Proc. IEEE Int'l Conf. Robot. and Automat*, pp. 2636- 2643.

Verth, J. M. V. & Bishop, L. M. (2004). *Essential Mathematics for Games and Interactive Applications: A Programmer's Guide*, The Morgan Kaufmann Series in Interactive 3d Technology, Morgan Kaufmann.

Walnum, C. (2003). *Direct3D Programming*, SAMS.

Wikipedia (2010). Visualization (computer graphics), http://en.wikipedia.org/wiki/Visualizatio

# 16

# Real-Time Control System for a Two-Wheeled Inverted Pendulum Mobile Robot

Nawawi, Ahmad and Osman
*Universiti Teknologi Malaysia*
*Malaysia*

## 1. Introduction

The research on two-wheeled inverted pendulum (T-WIP) mobile robots or commonly known as balancing robots have gained momentum over the last decade in a number of robotic laboratories around the world (Solerno & Angeles, 2003;Grasser et al., 2002; Solerno & Angeles, 2007;Koyanagi, Lida & Yuta, 1992;Ha & Yuta, 1996; Kim, Kim & Kwak, 2003). This chapter describes the hardware design of such a robot. The objective of the design is to develop a T-WIP mobile robot as well as MATLAB™ interfacing configuration to be used as flexible platform which comprises of embedded unstable linear plant intended for research and teaching purposes. Issues such as selection of actuators and sensors, signal processing units, MATLAB™ Real Time Workshop coding, modeling and control scheme is addressed and discussed. The system is then tested using a well-known state feedback controller to verify its functionality.

## 2. Hardware development

Figure 1 show the CAD illustration of the T-WIP mobile robot towards the real hardware. The robot is equipped with two servo drives for actuation, a Gyroscope for measuring angle and angular velocity of pendulum body, and encoders for measuring the position of the wheels. Signal processing and control algorithm are distributed among three microprocessors. Two of them are used for servo drives while other one is used for stabilizing control.

Although this kind of layout enables hierarchical control design, it also complicates implementation, since processor communication must also be considered (Kim & Kwak, 2003). The T-WIP mobile robot is composed of a chassis carrying a DC motor coupled to a planetary gearbox for each wheel, the DSP board used to implement the controller, the power amplifiers for the motors, the necessary sensors to measure the vehicle's states. The battery is bolted inside the body casing and it significantly represents 30% of the total robot mass. The wheels of the vehicle are directly coupled to the output shaft of the gearboxes. The robot is control by applying a torque $C_R$ and $C_L$ to the right and left wheels respectively. Figure 2 illustrates the block diagram of the control architecture of the system.

The controller is implemented on an Embedded DSP board by Googol Technologies LTD (2007). It is a standalone motion controller based on combination of embedded PC104 main board of X86, motion control board, terminal board in one structure, and thus has the advantages of smaller dimension, less wiring, real time capability and higher reliability. It is easy to upgrade, install and maintain, and thus increase the reliability of the robot to operate under adverse industrial environments, such as humid, dust, and vibration.

Conventional inclinometers, or analog tilt sensors, typically exhibit slow response and cannot be used to track dynamic angular motion (Tsuchiya, Urakubo & Tsujita, 1999; Matsumoto, Kajita & Tani, 1993). On the other hand, angular rate sensors can be used to measure fast rotations, but they suffer from significant drift and error accumulation over time. Inertial measurement units (IMU's) can be used to overcome these limitations, but these are relatively large and expensive. As such, the FAS-G sensor from MicroStrain is used as the gyro sensor (FAS-G Microstrain, 2006).

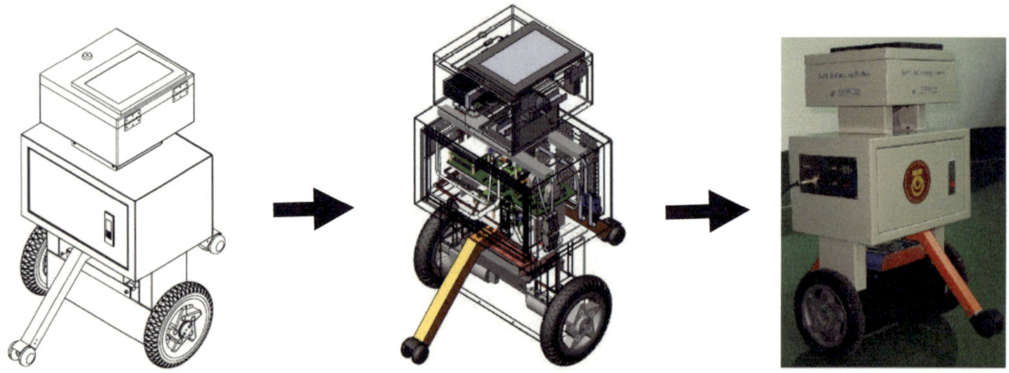

Fig. 1. CAD Illustration of T-WIP Mobile Robot towards Real Hardware

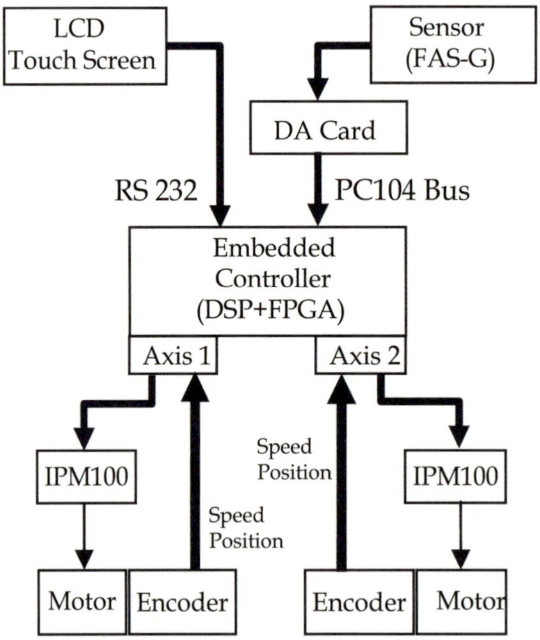


Fig. 2. Control Architecture

Employing micro-electromechanical (MEM) sensors, FAS-G consists of a combination of two low pass filtered accelerometers and one piezo-ceramic gyro. The angular rate signal is integrated internally over time and compared to the accelerometer signal to eliminate drift. The gyro output signal is an analog voltage between 0 and 5 volts corresponding to the angle of tilt. This signal is read from the Data Acquisition Card and the result is passed to PC by PC104 data bus. It was calculated that one ADC count corresponds to an incremental tilt of 0.08789°. A secondary angular rate signal is also generated by means of software computation. Figure 3 show angle of rotation for a two-wheeled inverted pendulum mobile robot in two-dimensional plane. Both geared servo motor needs to generate a very high torque. To achieve this, the IPM100 is used as the motor driver. It is basically a 36V, 3A fully digital intelligent servo drive based on the DSP controller technology. It is also embedded with the high level Technosoft Motion Language (TML) and therefore offers a flexible, compact and easy to implement solution for single or multi-axis applications with brushless and DC motors.

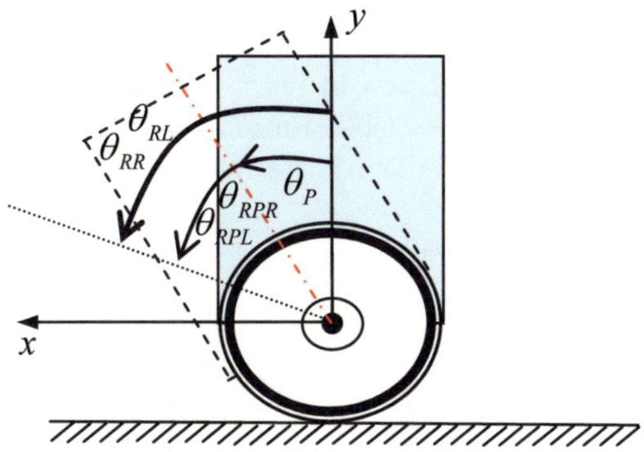


Fig. 3. Angle of Rotational

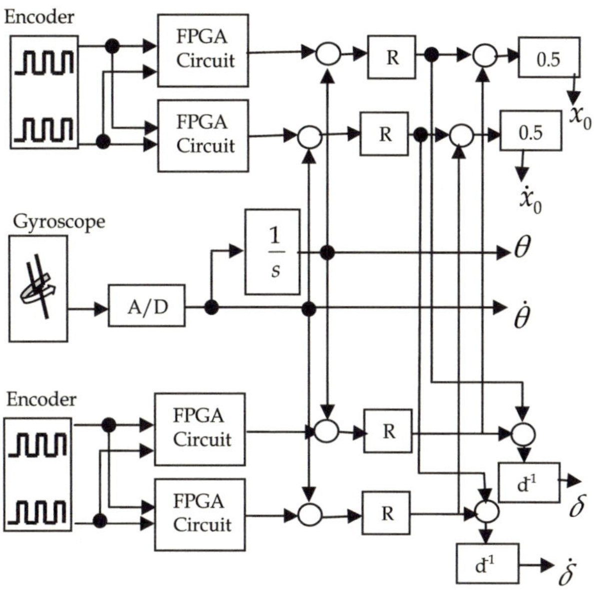


Fig. 4. Interfacing between sensor signals and the Embedded DSP board (Grasser et al. 2002)

Straight line position and speed as well as yaw angle and rate of change can be determined from the angle rotation of the two wheels ($\theta_{RR}$ and $\theta_{RR}$) with respect to the gravity. The relation of these angles with pitch angle, $\theta_P$ and the body angle, $\theta_{RPL}$ and $\theta_{RPR}$ can be referred in Fig.3. To provide information about T-WIP states for control purposes, two incremental encoders and a rate gyroscope are interfaced together as shown in Fig.4. All the interfacing is based on control structure of embedded system as seen in this figure. The embedded controller has task to monitor all feedback coming from incremental encoder. Then process the feedback to make sure T-WIP is balance at it equilibrium point. The command to embedded controller is given by IPC using C language interfacing in the Real Time Workshop of MATLAB. The IPC is running online or at the same time with system to show the real time result according to the output response needed.

## 3. Mathematical modeling

The dynamic performance of a balancing robot depends on the efficiency of the control algorithms and the dynamic model of the system (Shim, Kim & Koh, 1995;Au, Xu & Yu, 2001). By adopting the coordinate system shown in Fig.5 using Newtonian mechanics, it can be shown that the dynamics of the T-WIP mobile robot under consideration is governed by the following motion equations (1)-(15). The coordinate system for the robot is depicted in Fig.5.

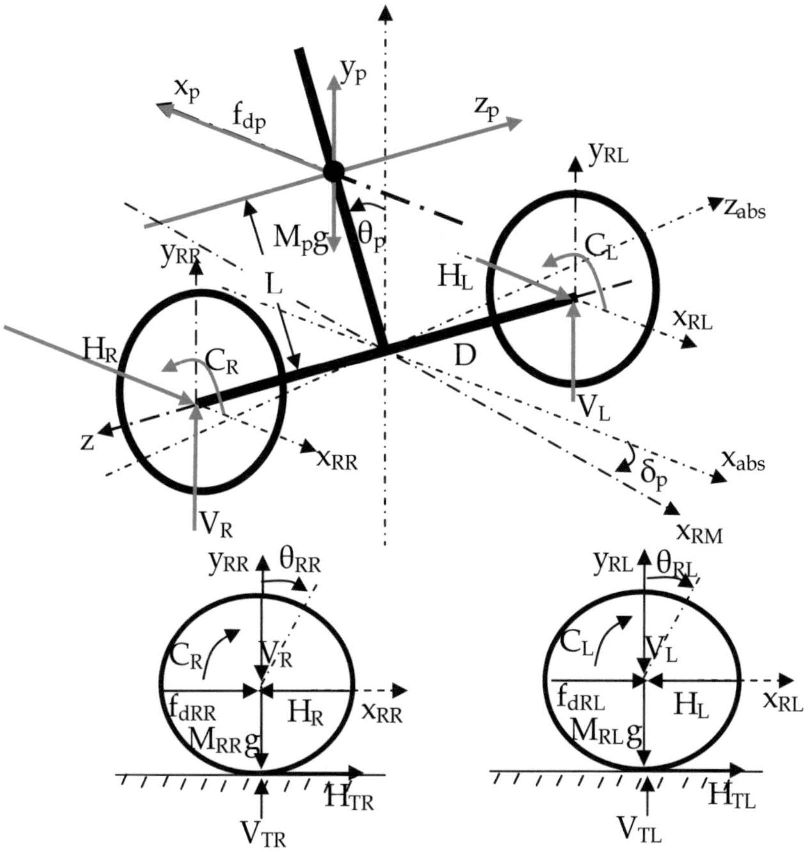


Fig. 5. Coordinate system of the T-WIP

For left hand wheel (analogous for right hand wheel):

$$\ddot{x}_{RL}M_r = H_{TL} - H_L + (f_{dRL} + f_{dRR}) \tag{1}$$

$$\ddot{y}_{RL}M_r = V_{TL} - V_L - M_r g \tag{2}$$

$$\ddot{\theta}_{RL}J_{RL} = C_L - H_{TL}R \tag{3}$$

$$\dot{x}_{RL} = R\dot{\theta}_{RL} \tag{4}$$

$$\dot{y}_p = -\dot{\theta}_p L \sin\theta_p \tag{5}$$

$$\dot{x}_p = \dot{\theta}_p L \cos\theta_p + \frac{\dot{x}_{RL} + \dot{x}_{RR}}{2} \tag{6}$$

$$\dot{\delta} = \frac{\dot{x}_{RL} - \dot{x}_{RR}}{2f} \tag{7}$$

For the chassis, the equations:

$$\ddot{x}_p M_p = (H_R + H_L) + f_{dP} \tag{8}$$

$$\ddot{y}_p M_p = V_R + V_L - M_p g + F_{C\theta} \tag{9}$$

$$\ddot{\theta}_p J_p = (V_R + V_L)L\sin\theta_p - (H_R + H_L)L\cos\theta_p - (C_L + C_R) \tag{10}$$

$$\ddot{\delta}J_\delta = (H_L - H_R)\frac{D}{2} \tag{11}$$

where $H_{TL}$, $H_{TR}$, $H_L$, $H_R$, $V_{TL}$, $V_{TR}$, $V_L$, $V_R$ represent reaction forces between the different free bodies. The robot parameters are as tabulated in Table 6.1.
Equations (1)-(11) can be represented in the state-space form as:

$$\dot{x}(t) = f(x) + g(x)u \tag{12}$$

Where $x \in \mathbb{R}^n$, $u \in \mathbb{R}^m$ are respectively the state and the control. *f(x)* is nonlinear dynamic function matrix and *g(x)* is nonlinear input function matrix. The state, *x* of the system is defined as:

$$x = [x_r, \dot{x}_r, \theta_p, \dot{\theta}_p, \delta, \dot{\delta}]' \tag{13}$$

Modifying the equations above and then linearizing the result around the operating point ($\theta_p$=0, $x_r$=0, $\delta$=0) and de-coupling, the system's state space equations can be written in matrix form as:

$$\begin{bmatrix} \dot{x}_r \\ \ddot{x}_r \\ \dot{\theta}_p \\ \ddot{\theta}_p \end{bmatrix} = \begin{bmatrix} 0 & 1 & 0 & 0 \\ 0 & 0 & A_{23} & 0 \\ 0 & 0 & 0 & 1 \\ 0 & 0 & A_{43} & 0 \end{bmatrix} \begin{bmatrix} x_r \\ \dot{x}_r \\ \theta_p \\ \dot{\theta}_p \end{bmatrix} + \begin{bmatrix} 0 \\ B_2 \\ 0 \\ B_4 \end{bmatrix} [C_L + C_R] \tag{14}$$

$$\begin{bmatrix} \dot{\delta} \\ \ddot{\delta} \end{bmatrix} = \begin{bmatrix} 0 & 1 \\ 0 & 0 \end{bmatrix} \begin{bmatrix} \delta \\ \dot{\delta} \end{bmatrix} + \begin{bmatrix} 0 \\ B_6 \end{bmatrix} [C_L - C_R] \tag{15}$$

where

$$A_{23} = g(1 - \frac{4}{3} L \frac{M_p}{X})$$

$$A_{43} = \frac{g M_p}{X}$$

$$B_2 = (\frac{4LY}{3X} - \frac{1}{M_p L})$$

$$B_4 = -\frac{Y}{X}$$

$$B_6 = \frac{6}{(9M_r + M_p)RD}$$

and,

$$X = \frac{1}{3} \frac{M_p (M_p + 6M_r)L}{M_p + \frac{3}{2} M_r}, Y = \frac{M_p}{(M_p + \frac{3}{2} M_r)R} + \frac{1}{L}$$

For simplicity, the details of equation (14) and (15) are not shown here and can be found elsewhere (Felix et al., 2002;Nawawi, Ahmad & Osman, 2007). The T-WIP balancing model, namely equation (14) will be used through out this work.

## 4. Controller design

System performance (i.e. reaction to disturbance forces, tracking of driver input, etc.) is driven by the pole placement controller. In order to test the T-WIP performance, pole-placement controllers with different poles has been applied. For a chosen pole placement, the controller's gains were calculated and implemented on the embedded board. T-WIP was then tested with the configuration and the response is then recorded by the control system. One of the tests conducted consist of an impulse disturbance force applied to a position above the center of gravity. The energy transmitted with a falling weight amounted to about 1.2 J (Baloh & Parent, 2003).

Issues like damping ratio and settling time could be clearly identified on the recorded responses and permitted an efficient fine-tuning of the system. Figure 6 shows the system's response to the above mentioned test with the initial pole placement chosen at pole [-1.5,-1.5,-0.5-3i,-0.5+3i]. Note the pronounced oscillation of the system which indicates too weak damping. Increasing the damping ratio when change the pole to [-1.5-i,-1.5+i,-3.5-5i,-3.5+5i] give the result as shown in Fig.7. It can be seen that the response improves significantly.

| Symbol | Parameter | Value/ [Unit] |
|---|---|---|
| $x_r$ | Straight line position | [m] |
| $\theta_p$ | Pitch angle | [rad] |
| $\delta$ | Yaw angle | [rad] |
| $J_{RL}, J_{RR}$ | Moment of inertia of the rotating masses with respect to the z axis | [kgm$^2$] |
| $M_r$ | Mass of rotating masses connected to the left and right wheel . $M_{RL} = M_{RR} = M_r$ | 0.420 [kg] |
| $J_p$ | Moment of inertia of the chassis with respect to z axis | 0.28 [kgm$^2$] |
| $J_\delta$ | Moment of inertia of the chassis with respect to the y axis | 1.12[kgm$^2$] |
| $M_p$ | Mass of Body | 15.0 [kg] |
| $R$ | Radius of wheel | 0.106[m] |
| $L$ | Distance between the z axis and the center of gravity of vehicle | 0.4 [m] |
| $D$ | Lateral distance between the contact patches of the wheels. | 0.4[m] |
| $y_r$ | Shift position of the wheel with respect to the y axis. | |
| $x_p$ | Shift position of the chassis with respect to the x axis. | |
| $g$ | Gravity constant | 9.8 [ms$^{-2}$] |
| $C_L$ , $C_R$ | Input torque for right and left wheels accordingly | |

Table 1. Parameters of T-WIP

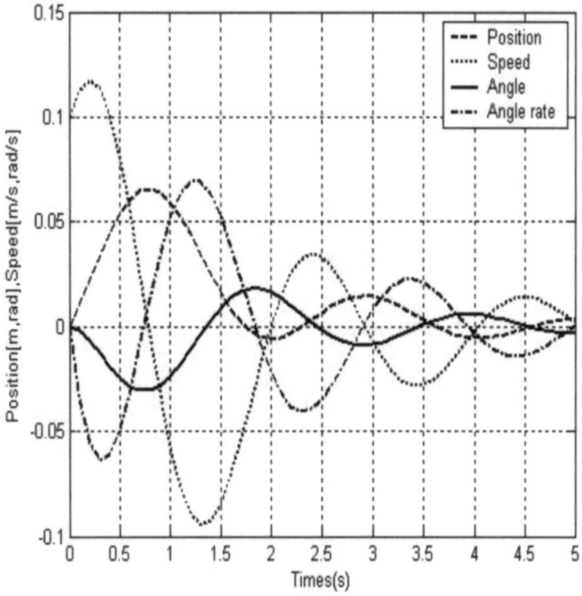


Fig. 6. Initial pole placement of the "pendulum" system and associated response to an impulse disturbance force

Now it has a harmonious catching of the disturbance force. When the force hit T-WIP, it causes the pendulum to fall forwards ($\theta_p$<0). The control system accelerates the wheels in a positive direction to catch this fall and ultimately make the pendulum fall in the other direction. A negative torque is then applied, moving the vehicle back to its original position and getting the pendulum back in an upright position. The controller task is to make sure that:

$$\theta_p \in A_s = \{|\theta_p| < \theta_m < \pi / 2\}, \text{ for a given } \theta_m > 0 \tag{16}$$

Equation (16) is representing physically problem of T-WIP, because by using these reference commands, one can safely follow a motion plan (Pathak & Agrawal, 2006). $\theta_m$ is maximum pitch angle setting for safety purpose. The pitch angle $\theta_p$ can be used as a gas pedal for vehicle and role it to accelerate and decelerate until the specified speed is attained.

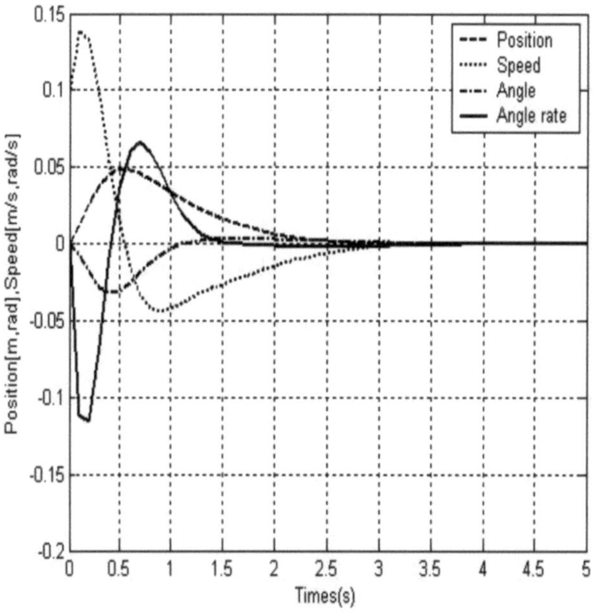


Fig. 7. Improved pole placement of the "pendulum" system and associated response to an impulse disturbance force.

Another issue that has been addressed during testing is drivability. In order to successfully improve drivability, it was characterized based on two criteria. First criteria are readouts of the system's reaction to a ramp shaped speed input and second criteria are the way different drivers felt about T-WIP handling. Combining the driver's feelings with the readouts of system behavior allowed further improvement of T-WIP control system. Figure 8 shows the system's response to a velocity ramp input with the final pole placement chosen. Note that the maximum acceleration possible is lower than the maximum deceleration. Due to the motor's speed-current characteristics, a high torque cannot be obtained when operating at high speeds (Matsumoto, Kajita & Tani, 1991). However, this is exactly what is necessary to get the vehicle back into an upright position at the end of the acceleration phase.

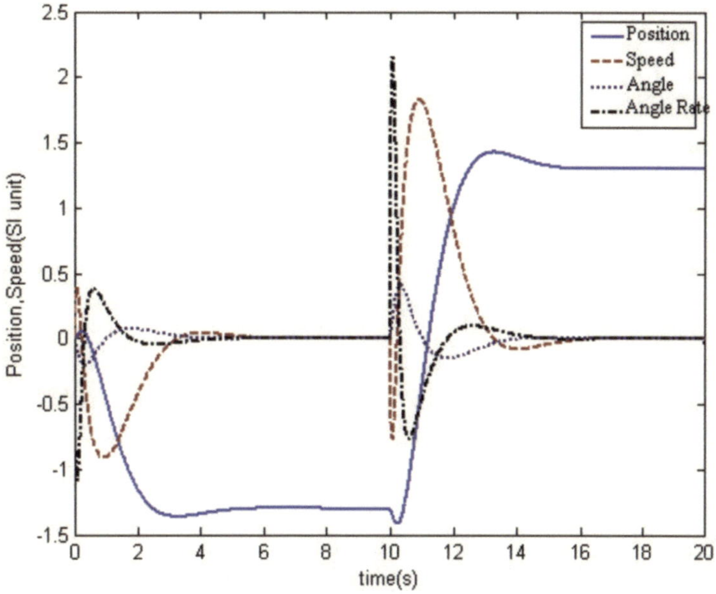


Fig. 8. Reaction to a ramp shaped speed input

Deceleration demands maximum torque at low speeds so a steeper ramp is therefore possible (Deniskina, Levi & Gurfinkel, 2001). Increasing performance with the pole placement chosen can be achieved by moving the poles further to the left, thus making the system faster. Backlash as well the maximum torque that can be transmitted to the ground (grip) prevent tuners from moving the poles past a certain limit. The used of an adaptive pole placement and nonlinear controller (depending on the system's state) would enable further improvements to the system.

## 5. Matlab™ interfacing design

The embedded control system in this work is design based on real-time workshop of MATLAB™. Hence it makes the interfacing protocol between embedded controller card and MATLAB™ is the most pivotal. T-WIP real-time balancing will be fully carried out in the Real Time Workshop of MATLAB™. Therefore it has an advantages of be intellectualized to observe the real-time results and performance of controller when be integrated with actuator. Furthermore, the controller can be redesigned expediently and repetitiously until users get a satisfactory result.

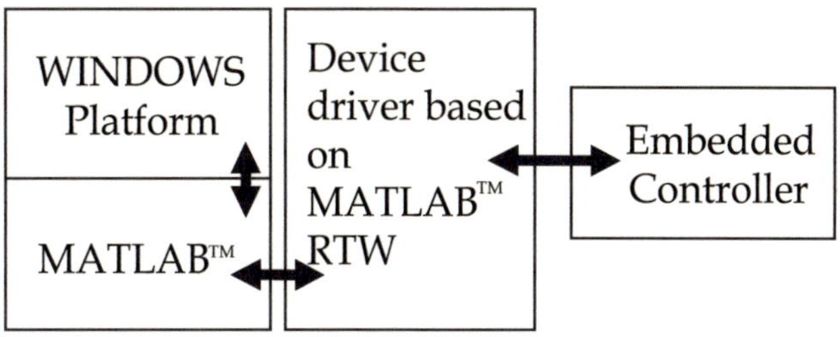


Fig. 9. MATLAB™ RTW Kernel

In the RTW (Real Time Workshop) of MATLAB™, the special real-time kernel model replaces message processing via windows as shown in Fig. 9. Hence the capability of real-time mode to gets better response is good enough.

RTW builds applications from Simulink diagrams for prototyping, testing, and deploying real-time systems on a variety of target computing platforms. Users of Real-Time Workshop can direct it to generate source code that accommodates the compilers, input and output devices, memory models, communication modes, and other characteristics that their applications may require. First step of configuration setup is to install MATLAB™ with Real-Time Windows Target and Visual C/C++ software. Then by using some command in Matlab, the Real-Time Windows Target kernel is activated together menu to select C compiler in MATLAB™.

A sampling demo of the sensor will be presented based on MATLAB™ RTW. In way to design an S-function block written in C Language, in which an S-function parameter for index of ad channels and an output should be defined. The fractional source code of GetAD.c is as follows:

```
#define S_FUNCTION_NAME   GetAD
#define NUM_PARAMS                (1)
#define AD_CHANNEL _PARAM  (ssGetSFcnParam(S,0))
#define AD_CHANNEL (real_T)mxGetPr(AD_CHANNEL_PARAM)[0])
```

After coding for GetAD.c, by using a command line in MATLAB with no errors occur, the GetAD S-function then finished generating. Then the block parameter for ad channel is configured to channel 1. Secondly another system target file GetAD.tlc need to be design which is will be saved in the same directory with GetAD.c. The main source code flow chart of GetAD.tlc is as shown in Fig. 10.

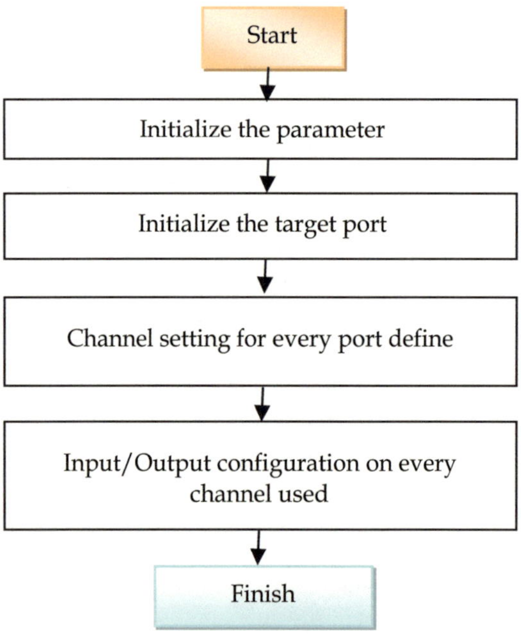


Fig. 10. Coding flowchart for GETAD.tcl

For the reference purpose, the command "_outp" and "_inp" in the target file GetAD.tlc is used for sending and receiving data between embedded controller and MATLAB™. The comand ctrl_byte=oxff , is used in GetAD.tlc file to make sure the DA card will stop find online data on the PC104 bus. GetAD.tlc then compiled and be confirmed there is no error occurs.

In simulation parameter properties of GetAD.c, category need to build as Target configuration with system target file of rtwin.tlc. This configuration is used as setting for Real-time workshop in Matlab. Then the solver options and fixed step size configuration is set with sampling time 5ms.

The file is compiled after selecting "External" mode. The output of the sensor signal can be shown in Fig. 11. The same method is using to design other S-functions models. Finally, an interface for T-WIP in the RTW of MATLAB™ is extracted. Now T-WIP test bed can be used for any type of controller as long as the structure of system remains the same. The structure of system is shown in Fig. 12.

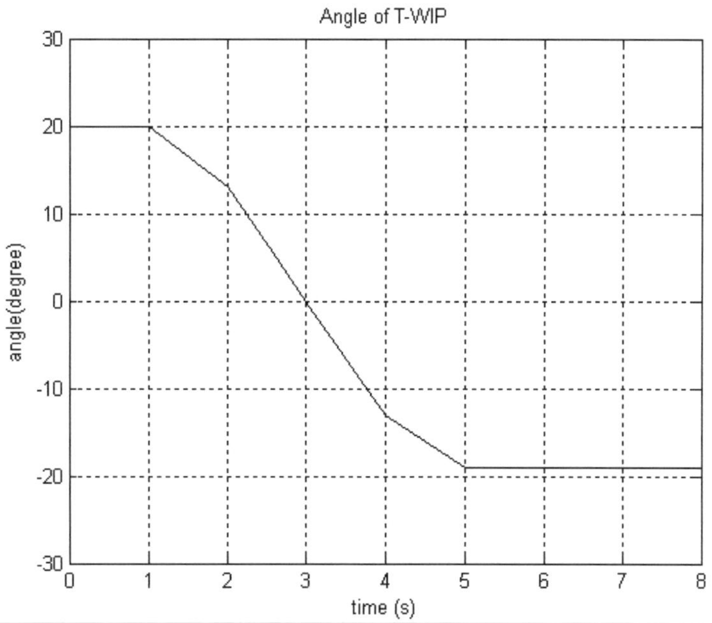


Fig. 11. Angle for sampling gyro sensor

It does consist of three main block which is Input block, controller block and Real Plant block. The input reference for speed and orientation can be replaced by desired input function while the real plant block is the actual input function is used. The real plant block is the actual plant represents the hardware of T-WIP which contains of all sensors interfacing.

## 6. Experimental result

In order to verify the developed T-WIP hardware system, the pole-placement algorithm as designed in previous section implemented as the controller. Figure 13 shows that the responses of the system closely match the simulation result in Figure 7 which demonstrates the complete T-WIP system is functioning well in close-loop system.

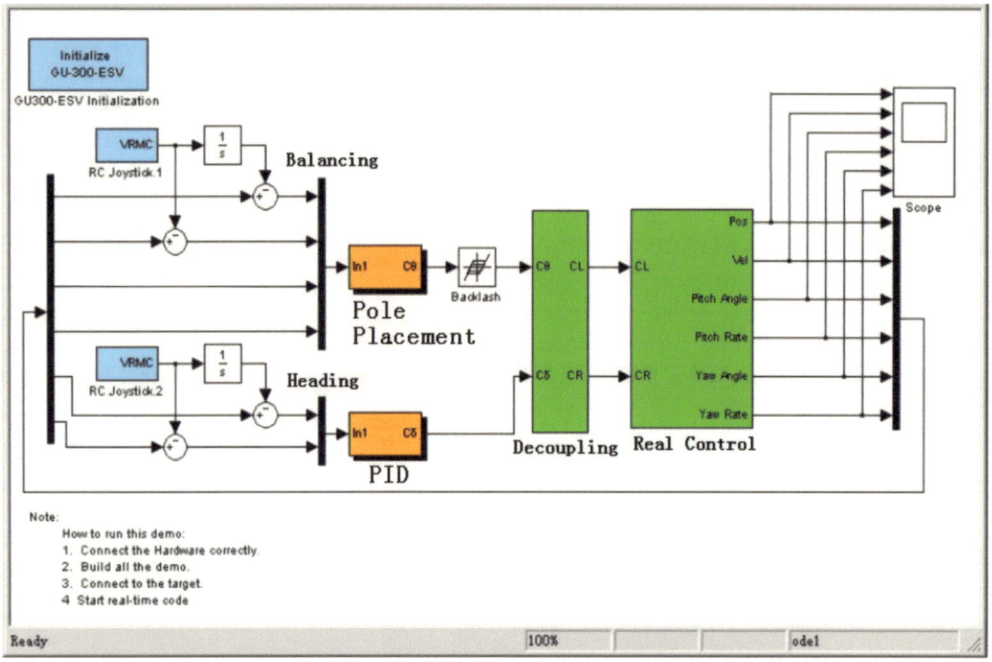


Fig. 12. Real-time control interface using poleplacement controller for T-WIP.

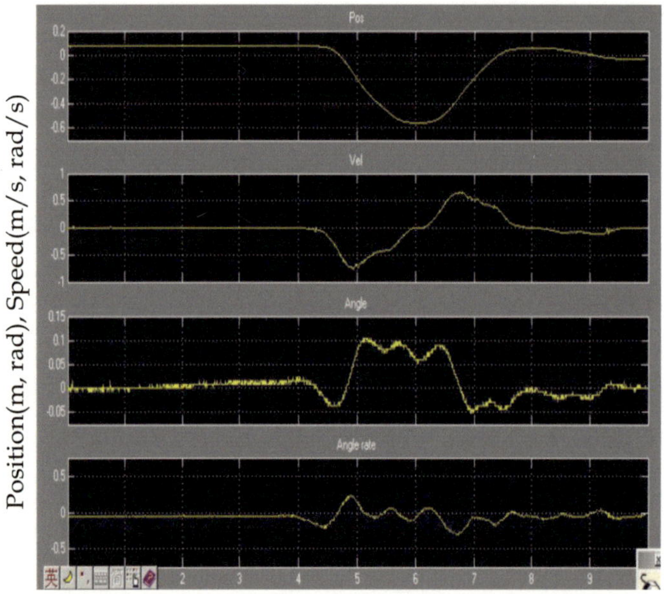


Fig. 13. Real-time control result of T-WIP output response using pole placement controller

From the Fig. 13, it can be shown that the output response for position, velocity, inclination angle and angular velocity of inclination is following the shape of simulation result. The steady state error of position and velocity is approximately zero. It also shows that the values of steady state error are about zero of the inclination angle and its velocity.

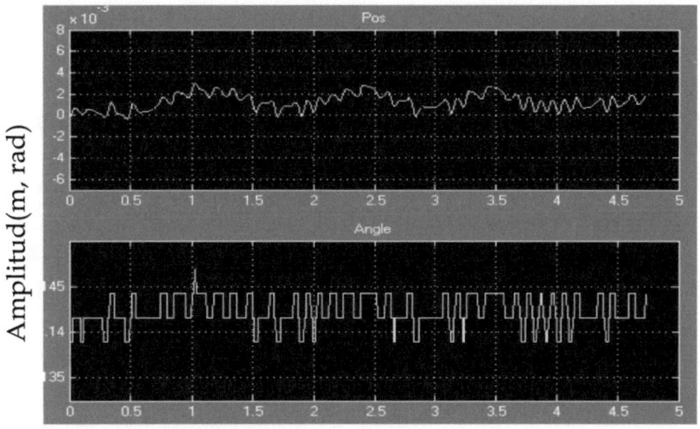


Fig. 14. Real-time control results of vibration scale for T-WIP at equilibrium

The pole placement controller seems to be capable in term of steady state error and settling time. After zooming in certain area on Fig. 13, it can be seen on result in Fig. 14, it shown that the system is in equilibrium within small range of vibration. The chassis range of vibration is about $4x10^{-3}$m and the trunk vibration range is about 0.05rad.

## 7. Conclusion

In this chapter, the development of a T-WIP mobile robot system is presented. The issues of dynamical modeling, selection of actuators and sensors, MATLAB™ based interfacing and configuration of the embedded controller, as well as the implementation of pole placement control strategy has been addressed. The embedded control system using real-time workshop of MATLAB is confirm working well and all sensors give a good feedback signal based on the response getting from the experimental work. The results from this work show that the proposed embedded design architecture based on MATLAB™ is capable of delivering the desired outcome and the T-WIP test rig is ready to be tested with a various type of controllers.

## 8. References

Au, S. K. W., Xu, Y. and Yu, W. W. K. (2001). Control of Till Up Motion of a Single Wheel Robot via Model Based and Human Based Controller. *Mechatronics.* 11, 451-473.

Baloh, M. and Parent, M. (2003). Modeling and Model Verification of an Intelligent Self-balancing Two Wheeled Vehicle for an Autonomous Urban Transportation System. *In Proceedings of Conference on Computational Intelligence Robotic and Autonomous Systems.* 15 Disember. Singapore: 1-7.

Deniskina, I. V., Levi, K. Y. S. and Gurfinkel, V. S. (2001). Relative Roles of the Ankle and Hip Muscles in Human Postural Control in the Frontal Plane Surfing Standing. *Journal of Intelligent Robot System.* 27(3), 317-321.

FAS-G Gyroscope Manual by Microstrian, available:http://www.microstrain.com/fas-g.asp

Googol Technology (HK). *All in one embedded motion controller specification.* [Online]. Available: http://www.googoltech.com

Grasser, F., D'Arrigo, A., Colombi, S. and Rufer, A. (2002). Joe: A Mobile Inverted Pendulum. *IEEE Transaction Electronics.* 49(1), 107-114.

Ha, Y. S. and Yuta, S. (1996). Trajectory Tracking Control for Navigation of The Inverse Pendulum Type Self-contained Mobile Robot. *Robotic and Autonomous System.* 17, 65-80.

Kim, Y.H., Kim, S.H., and Kwak, Y.K. (2003). Dynamic Analysis of a NonholonomicTwo-wheeled Inverted Pendulum Robot. *In Proceedings of 8th International Symposium on Artificial Life and Robotics.* 24-26 January. Beppu, Oita, Japan: 415-418.

Koyanagi, E., Lida, S. and Yuta, S. (1992). A Wheeled Inverse Pendulum Type Self-contained Mobile Robot and its Two-dimensional Trajectory Control. *In Proceedings of 2nd International Sysmposium on Measurement and Control in Robotics.* November. Tsukaba, Japan: 891-898.

Matsumoto, O., Kajita, S. and Tani, K. (1991). Attitude Estimation of the Wheeled Inverted Pendulum Using Adaptive Observer, *In Proceedings of 9th Academic Conference of the Robotics Society of Japan.* Japan: 909-910.

Matsumoto, O., Kajita, S. and Tani, K. (1993). Estimation and Control of the Attitude of a Dynamic Mobile Robot using Internal Sensors. *Advance Robotic.* 7(2), 159-178.

Nawawi, S. W., Ahmad, M. N. and Osman, J. H. S. (2007). Development of Two-wheeled Inverted Pendulum Mobile Robot. *In Proceedings Student Conference on Research and Development.* December. Kuala Lumpur, Malaysia: 153-158.

Pathak, K., Franch, J. and Agrawal, S. K. (2005). Velocity and Position Control of a Wheeled Inverted Pendulum by Partial Feedback Linearization. *IEEE Transactions on Robotics.* 21(3), 505-513.

Pathak, K. and Agrawal, S. K. (2006). Band-limited Trajectory Planning and Tracking for Certain Dynamically Stabilized Mobile Systems. *Journal of Dynamic Systems, Measurement and Control, Transaction of the ASME.* 128(1), 104-111.

Salerno, A. and Angeles J. (2003). Nonlinear Conrollability of Quasiholonomic Mobile Robot. In *Proceedings of IEEE ICRA*, 3379-3384, Taiwan.

Shim, H. S., Kim, J. H. and Koh, K. (1995). Variable Structure Control of Nonholonomic Wheeled Mobile Robot. *In Proceedings of IEEE International Conference on Robotics and Automation.* 21-27 May. Nagoya, Aichi, Japan: 1694-1699.

Solerno, A. and Angeles, J. (2007). A New Family of Two Wheeled Mobile Robot: Modeling and Controllability. *IEEE Transaction of Robotics.* 23(1), 169-173.

Tsuchiya, K., Urakubo, T. and Tsujita, K. (1999). A Motion Control of a Two-Wheeled Mobile Robot. *In Proceeding of IEEE International Conference on System, Man and Cybernetics.* October. Tokyo, Japan: 690-696.

# 17

# From Telerobotic towards Nanorobotic Applications

Riko Šafarič[1] and Gregor Škorc[2]
[1]*University of Maribor, Faculty of Electrical Engineering and Computer Science*
[2]*Resistec UPR d.o.o. & Co. k.d.,*
*Slovenia*

## 1. Introduction

During the technical evolution, telerobotic systems (see fig. 1) have lost their simple mechanical links between master and remote sites in order to operate over a grater distance and, thus, the effects of long communication delays have occured. The telerobotics projects presented in (Goldberg et al., 1995; Telegarden, 2009; Telelabs, 2009) rely on cameras to locate and distribute the robot's position and current environment to the user, via the internet. It is clear that such an approach needs a high-speed network to achieve on-line control of the robotic arm. Of course, when using the public network, the delays become unpredictable and unusably large in the case of long distance communication (space probes).
However, as the delay becomes larger, the efficiency with which operators can work decreases dramatically. This is the reason why long-range telerobotic applications also require predictive displays on the master-site and a low-level autonomy on the remote-site, in order to overcome communication delay problems (see fig. 2). Control using predictive display (Sayers, 1999) improves the teleoperational system in such a way that it provides the operator with an immediate feedback force; not with sensored force from the remote-environment, but from the model on the master-site, as shown in fig. 2 (Sayers, 1999).

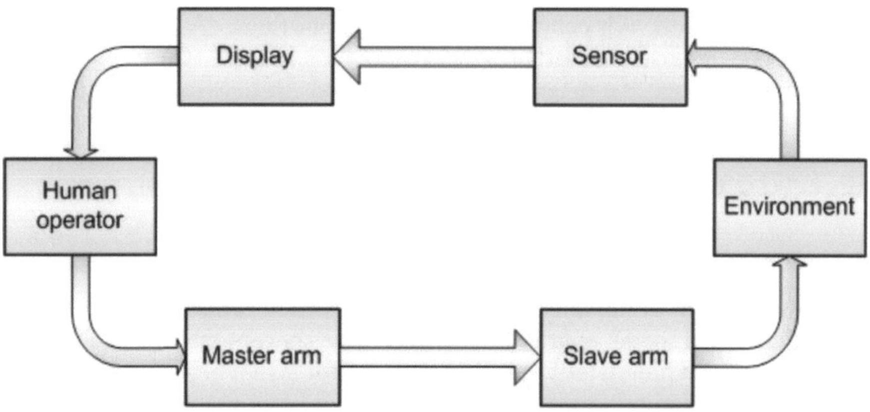


Fig. 1. Teleoperation system with a human operator in the closed feedback loop

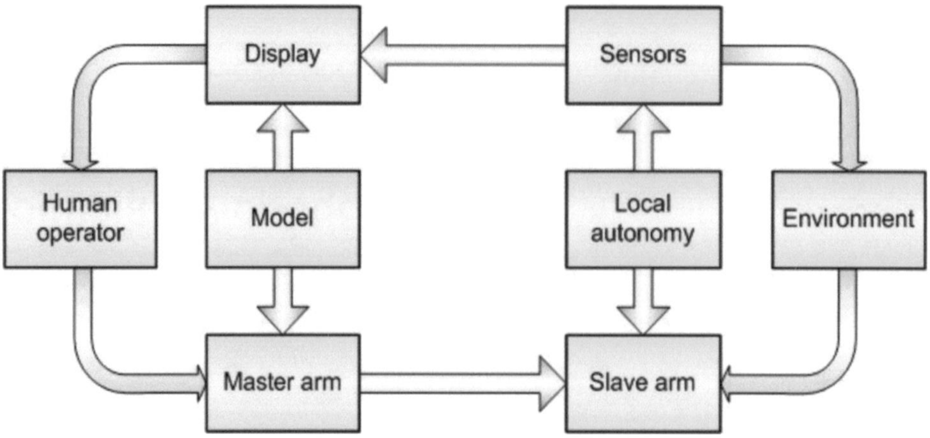


Fig. 2. Predictive display on the master side with added local autonomy on the remote site

Introducing local autonomy or increasing remote intelligence for further improvement when controlling with only a predictive display, is no longer sufficient. Of course, the goal is to ensure the remote system is able to recognize and react correctly for a few low-level problems at the remote-site. These systems allow the operator to use a more supervisory role. Added local autonomy can solve problems such as (Sayers, 1999): collision avoidance on the slave-site and, in the case of collision between the robot and environment on the slave-site, stopping the system and feeding information back to the operator in order to resolve the problem, by automatically tuning the remote robot position-controller's parameters (Čas et al., 2007)...

The aim of this paper is to present research work for developing a predictive display for telerobotic or micro/nanorobotic applications using a robotic or micro/nanorobotic arm. The remote robotic local autonomy is less precisely presented, as it is out of this paper's scope.

Rather than allowing users to interact with the laboratory resources directly, as in many of the previous examples (Goldberg et al., 1995; Telegarden, 2009; Telelabs, 2009), the reported approach requires users to configure the experiments using a simulated representation of the real-world apparatus. This configuration data is then downloaded to the real laboratory application, for verification and execution on the real device, before returning the results to the user once the experiment is complete. A virtual robot or micro/nanorobotic arm and an environment model are used instead of cameras and microscopes, in order to minimise data transmission time through the network. This means that the network speed is no longer a critical issue for the telerobotics experiment in the case of telerobotics, or in the case of micro/nanorobotic experiments when a virtual model of a micro/nanorobotic arm and its environment is used to improve 3D visualisation, instead of a microscope.

## 2. Telerobotic experiment

### 2.1 A basic description of the telerobotics virtual model approach

The telerobotics virtual model approach is based on the concept that it provides a working facility for hands-on training whilst reducing the need for actual high-cost multiple devices. It is desirable that virtual robot model simulation should be capable of execution through any standard WWW browser application (Wang et al., 2004). Standard browsers for the

VRML 2.0 language don't incorporate collision detection between shapes in the virtual world (Hudson et al., 1997). Because the adopted control strategy does not provide the remote user with immediate feedback from the actual work-cell, it is desirable that some kind of collision detection between the virtual robot and the virtual environment is created to prevent, or predict, robot collisions in the real world. This problem may be solved by building JAVA oriented collision detection software or, as decided, to use finished libraries of the complete browser and collision detection software (Fukuda at al., 2000) in the C++ language.
The telerobotic laboratory equipment includes (see fig. 4):

- a WWW network server,
- a network layer,
- a robot workcell,
- remote user personal computers, and
- a haptic device.

The WWW network server is responsible for processing requests for information by an external WWW browser, installed on the user's remote personal computer, delivering on-line documents and providing access to the robotic and control hardware. The server is implemented by currently using a personal computer, running the Windows XP operating system, and a WWW server application program.
Training operatives for working with the expensive equipment, needed for carrying out profitable work tasks (e.g. production line robots) or when the work is of a complex and safety critical nature (e.g. nuclear environments, explosive placement, surgery), has long proved problematical. The method used in some instances is that of immersive telepresence (Mair, 1999), but different approaches are needed for different sectors (Mantovani & Riva, 1999) and the equipment is often expensive and does not release high-cost capital equipment for production line usage (Bambang, 2007). In all cases, the feedback of rich data from the physical hardware site to the operator site, via the Internet or Mobile Communication links is bandwidth limited and contains uncertain delays.

### 2.2 The remote robotic arm and its environment

An approach that may bear much fruit is to use Virtual Environments for achieving a simulated hands on experience by only connecting to physical hardware for short periods of time. Engineers can use animated robotic cell activity to conduct feasibility studies on their manufacturing processes, whilst their product is still being designed. The experiences of companies with robotized production lines show that they may save up to 85 % of downtime when the robot has to be reprogrammed, and up to 50 % of programming time (Dobrovodsky et al., 2000).
The presented telerobotic experiment has many predecessors - but mostly only laboratory experiments, which have culminated in this industrial telerobotics experiment (Šafarič et al., 2001, a; Šafarič et al., 2001, b; Šafarič et al., 2003; Šafarič et al., 2005; Pačnik & Klobučar, 2006). The robotic cell of the teleoperated robotic arm cell application (an industrial welding robotic cell) is presented in Fig. 3. The Almega AX-V4 robotic arm from the OTC Daihen company was used in the presented workcell.

### 2.3 The remote robotic arm and its environment

A copy of the virtual environment has to be installed on the home client's computer. This configuration was chosen to allow various interfacing strategies to be investigated, whilst maintaining an open architecture for the future development of the project.

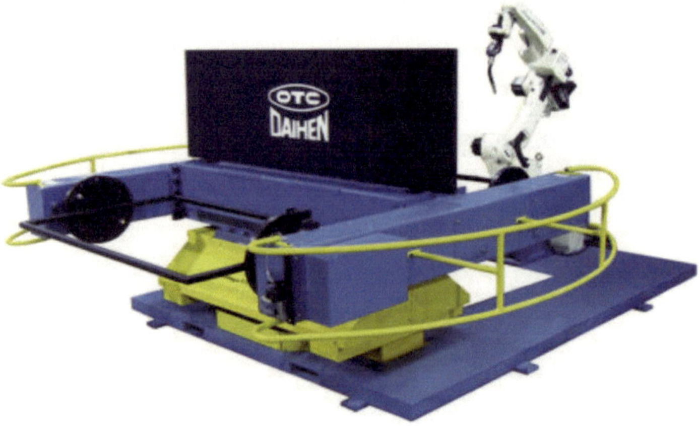


Fig. 3. Remote welding robotic arm

The user must first download and install the complete Robot Simulation application software (the teach pendant). Communication between the virtual robot model of the robotic manipulator, which is viewed by the remote user, and the control system which positions the joints of the actual laboratory-based manipulator, is achieved as follows (see also fig. 4):

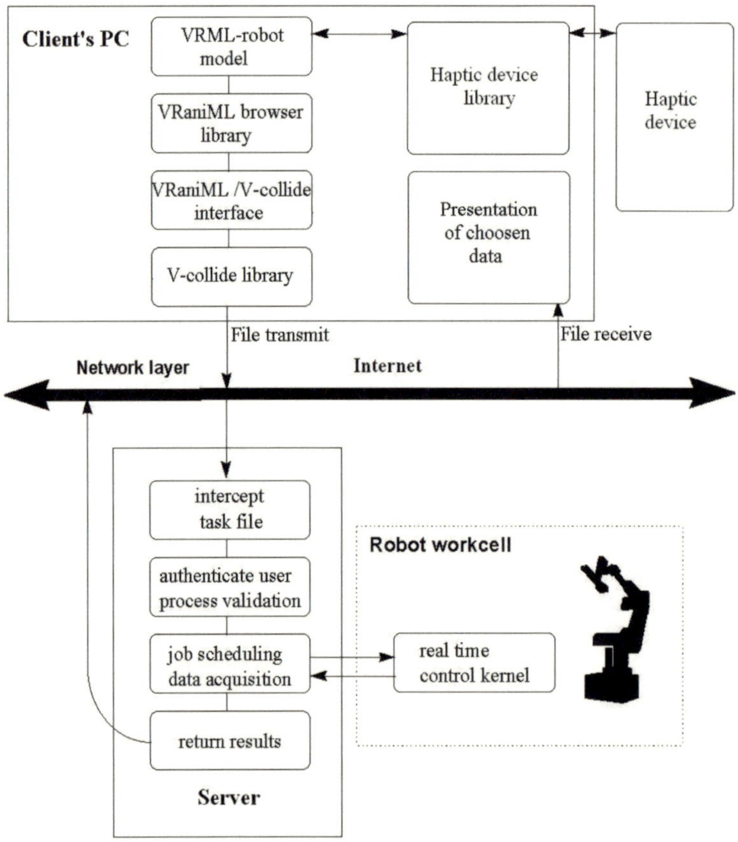


Fig. 4. The robot interface between a server and a client

- the user develops a robot task off-line within the virtual environment on the remote computer,
- collision detection checking on the remote computer; if there is collision between the virtual shapes in the virtual world of a teach pendant, then stop, otherwise proceed,
- transmission of the completed robot task file from the remote user to the laboratory server,
- authentication, error checking, and runtime scheduling of the received task file on the server,
- execution of the requested task within the laboratory workcell, and finally
- collation and return of the results to the remote user.

Of course, there were also further added improvements:

- the haptic device is introduced, so that communication between the remote user and robot is improved by the human sense of touch,
- the direct and inverse kinematic equations (Fu et al., 1987) are developed and included in the teach pendant, so that off-line programming is also possible in Cartesian coordinates and not only in joint coordinates,
- PTP movement, linear and circular interpolators are added, so off-line programming is even more accurate, especially the accuracy of its time component, and
- a set of industrial commands for the off-line programming of the Almega AX-V4 robotic arm was added to the teach-pendant, so that developed off-line programs can also be executable on the real remote arm.

Descriptions of the VRaniML/V-collide interface and VRaniML browser library are presented in (Šafarič et al., 2001, b; Šafarič et al., 2003).The VRaniML library is used as an interface between the virtual models of the robot's workcell (written in VRML language) and a teach pendant (see Fig. 5) written in C++ language. The VraniML/V-collide interface serves as an intelligent interface to prevent collision in the virtual world.

Fig. 6 presents off-line programming using the haptic device. In fact, the haptic device provides the contra force only in cases where collisions between virtual shapes in the virtual model occur: between the virtual arm itself and between the virtual arm and its static environment in the robot's virtual workcell (Friconneau et al., 2002; Dong-Soo & Seung-Chan, 2007).

## 3. Micro/Nanorobotic experiment

The micro/nanorobotic experiment is the very last in a sequence of telerobotic experiments, done in our laboratory. It is not a real telerobotics experiment, because the distance between the client's computer and a nanorobot is less than 1 metre. But the experiment could be treated as a telerobotics experiment because it connects two different worlds, the macro world of the user and the micro/nano world of the micro/nanorobot. The focus of the presented micro/nanorobotic experiment is that the user cannot see the micro/nanorobotic object's movements etc (Fukuda & Arai, 2000; Cavalcanti et al., 2004). The 3D on-line image of the gripper and the object, even with powerful microscopic visual magnification, cannot be properly seen, due to the fact that the focused images of the objects and the nano-robotic tip tool can only be seen only within a narrow vicinity (few hundred μm) of the microscope's optical lens focus. So, the same techniques as for the previously-mentioned real telerobotics experiment were used in order to make a connection between the macro and micro/nano worlds. In fact, we used the telerobotics platform developed for the

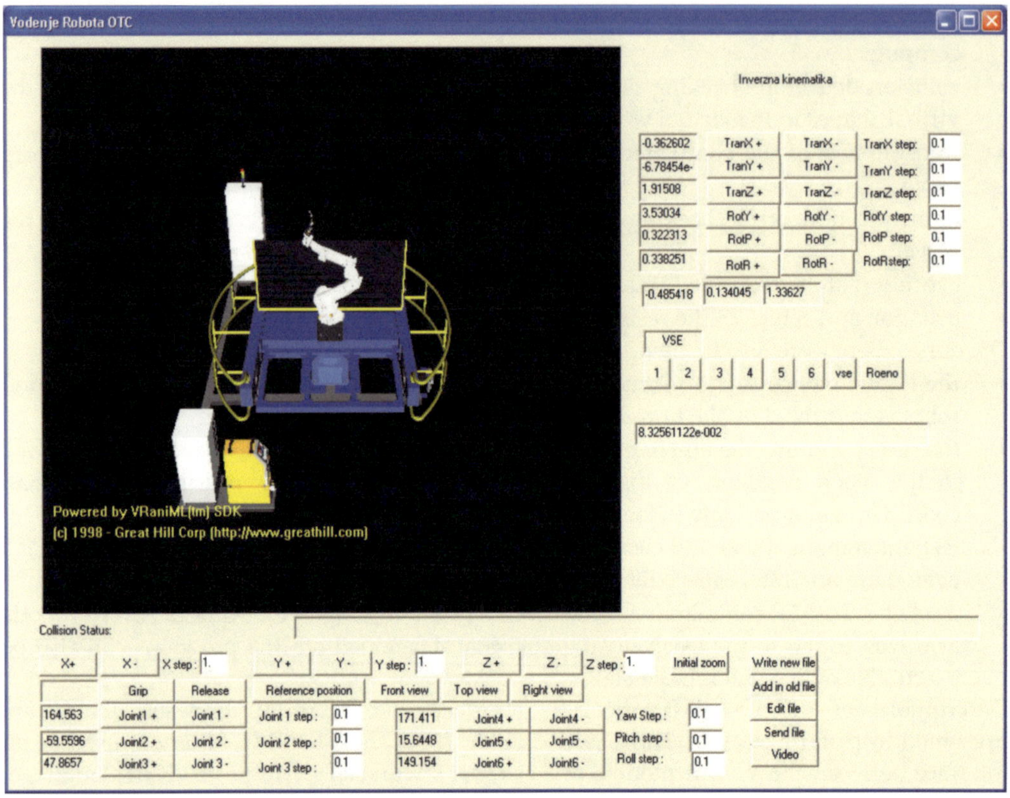


Fig. 5. Teach pendant of the telerobotic application using a haptic device

Fig. 6. Off-line programming of the telerobot using a haptic device

previously presented telerobotics experiment using a haptic device. The reason we used the haptic device is that we also like to include a sense of touch in the virtual teach pendant, in order to make communication between the human and the nanorobot easier and more user-friendly. Of course, the produced force from the haptic device is inadequate as a force produced during a collision in the micro/nano world, but it is magnified several times, so the human sense of touch can detect any collision within the micro/nano world (Dong-Soo & Seung-Chan, 2008; Cavalcanti et al., 2006). The hardware of the nanorobotic application is presented in Fig. 7.

Fig. 7. The whole micro/nanorobotic application

The micro/nanorobotic system is divided into two parts (see Fig. 8). The upper part of the figure consists of a real-time target application with a micro/nanorobotic cell: a development computer machine marked as 1, a real-time controller computer card marked as 2, and a target computer application marked as 3.

The usual notebook computer marked as 1 is used as the development computer for control algorithms and user interfaces with an installed Windows XP operating system and a LabView 8.5 software package.

The PC computer, marked as 2, executes real time control algorithms using so-called Real Time Desktop Target software. This PC runs a LabView Real Time operating system, which is independent of all the other operating systems already installed on the PC. Our real-time target PC is supported by a 7356 PCI motion-controller card from the National Instruments Company. This card is used as an interface between the control algorithm and the piezoelectric motor-power drivers. Its output has a separate reference signal for piezoelectric motor drive in regard to each axis of the controlled system for all 5 axes and is calculated by signals from the position of feedback and desired position inputs using the control algorithm. The execution time of the control algorithm is about 3 ms (National Instruments, 2009).

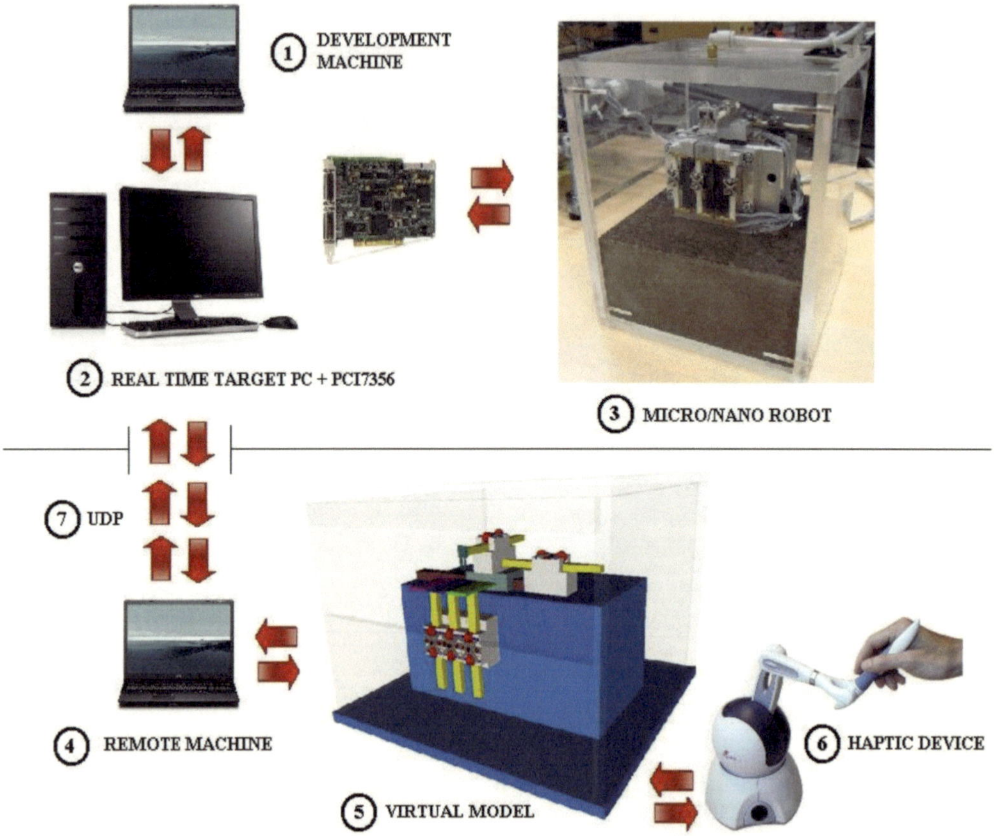


Fig. 8. Micro/nanorobot system components

The micro/nanorobotic cell, presented as 3 (fig. 8), is actuated by five linear piezo-motors produced by the PiezoMotor Upsala AB Company, where the motor movement steps can have lengths from 2 nm to 8 μm and can achieve speeds of up to 12.5 mm/s using factory-delivered demo-drive electronics (Piezomotor Upsala, 2003). The construction of the nanorobotic cell is done in such a way that two of the piezo-motors act as X/Y manipulators, and the other three are used as motion drivers for three separate serving tables within the Z axis. Positional feedback values for all axes are achieved using electro-magnetic linear encoders produced by the NANOS Instruments Company. Each encoder-set's electronics are built using magnetic scale and sensor electronics. The linear position instrument has a resolution of 61 nm with precision of +/- 0.15% (Nanos instruments, 2009). The micro/nanorobotic cell allows implementation of different micro and nanorobotic tip tools. A special two finger gripper is used temporarily for gripping objects of micro-scale sizes (100 μm to 200 μm). It is placed at the top of the Y axis (Keoschkerjan & Wurmus, 2002). The second part of the application, as presented in the lower part of fig. 8, shows a man-machine interface. It consists of a "remote computer" marked as 4, where a virtual model of the micro/nanorobotic cell, marked as 5 and a haptic-device (Phantom Omni by Sensable Technologies Company), marked as 6, have been installed. The "remote computer" is a notebook, based on the Windows XP operating system, supported by a Microsoft Visual

C++ software package and OpenHaptics software package from the Sensable Technologies Company. Both packages with the PC hardware are used for developing and executing the micro/nanorobot application. A UDP protocol, marked as 7, is used to ensure the fastest and reliable enough communication between the user and the machine.

A virtual VRML model of the micro/nanorobotic cell, marked as 5, is also included in the application, because the user does not see the target application - manipulation of the micro sized objects on all three serving tables with the naked eyes. The user doesn't have a real feeling of what is exactly happening within the target application. The virtual model gives a user 3D magnification and visualisation of the objects, including a robotic tip-tool within the target application. The virtual model of the micro/nanorobotic cell with its static macro/nanorobotic environment is updated with the on-line positional data acquired from the real micro/nanorobotic cell application. So, the user can visualise a 3D on-line image of the object's current positional situation and macro/nanorobotic tip-tool movements from different viewing points. This is needed, because otherwise we would need to use a microscope which could provide focused images of the objects and the micro/nanorobotic-tip only within a narrow vicinity (less than 500 μm if we use an optical magnification factor between 10 and 25) of the microscope's optical lens focus. The micro/nanorobot's workspace is a little less than 3 $cm^3$. The second reason for using a virtual model of the micro/nano robotic cell is for an off-line programming of it, which gives the user the possibility studying the target application program, to improve it, to test it and, after that, to send it for execution in the real-world.

The micro/nano robotic cell system uses a Phantom Omni haptic device in order to provide the user with a more realistic feeling about the situation inside the micro/nano-robot workspace. The user can control the haptic device by moving the its arm along 6 degrees of freedom (X, Y, Z, roll, pitch and yaw). Three motors are built onto the X, Y and Z axes to give the user force-feedback information as a virtual presentation of friction or space limits or collision between micro/nanorobot axes or between the micro/nanorobot tip tool with the object in the virtual world. The chassis of the haptic device has two free programmable built-in buttons which are used to grab, move, create different viewing points etc, of a single axis of the micro/nanorobotic cell's virtual model.

Fig 9 takes a close look of the current real micro/nano robotic tip gripper. It is made of so called structural glass (Keoschkerjan & Wurmus, 2002; Škorc et al., 2009) driven by a piezoelectric motor, which is situated horizontally to the vertical fingers of the gripper. The piezoelectric actuator allows the fingers to be moved approximately 100 μm. So, the gripping distance between fingers is between 100 μm and 200 μm. It was specially designed to grip and move optic fibre glass-cables with diameters between 100 μm and 125 μm.

Fig. 10 presents a screenshot of the so-called Control teach pendant or man-machine interface. This interface is divided into 7 sections:

1. The implemented VRML model of the micro/nanorobotic cell can be seen in the upper left corner of fig. 10.
2. The viewing section (right upper corner of fig. 10) is used for selecting the most appropriate viewing point for the VRML model of the micro/nanorobotic cell. Integrated virtual buttons allow the user to translate or rotate the view. A zoom function is also available within this section.
3. Manual control section (beneath the viewing section) is used for moving each axis using two virtual buttons. The first one is used for moving the axis one step forward and the other for moving one step backwards. The lengths of motor steps can be set

individually by typing the length number in millimetres in the small windows near the virtual buttons.

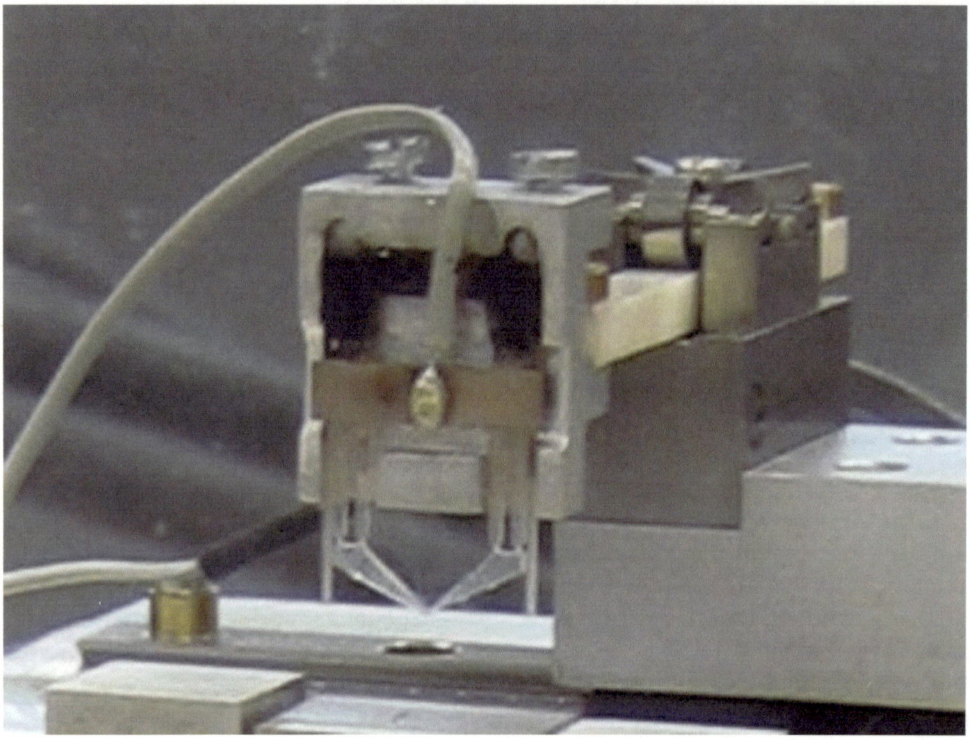

Fig. 9. Close look of a real micro/nano-robot tip gripper

4. Control of the haptic-device section (beneath the manual control section) is used for selecting the axis, which will be controlled using the haptic-device. This function is also available on the haptic-device by using one of the buttons integrated on the haptic-device's chassis. The number of the selected axis is shown within this section.
5. PTP regime control section (lower right corner of fig. 10) allows the user to load a file within the given micro/nano robotic cell program using PTP trajectory coordinates. Movements are executed sequentially, step by step, as they are programmed and written in the file. Any positional changes of any axis within the described control sections are animated in the virtual model of the micro/nanorobotic cell.
6. On-line/off-line section gives the user the possibility of simulating programmed micro/nanorobotic cell target applications before they are sent to the real micro/nanorobotic cell. Of course, this option is only provided if the off-line virtual button is selected. Here, any changes within any control-section are executed as a simulation of the micro/nanorobotic cell's virtual model. When the user enacts the on-line regime, the given changes are executed on the real machine, immediately. This off-line function is very helpful when the user programs and tests certain new trajectories in the micro/nanorobotic cell's workspace, and when it is unsure what consequences some newly-programmed movements would have (collision inside workcell space, movements outside workcell space etc).
7. The last section is the reference position section, where the user can set axis reference positions in certain specific cases, where the default given references are unacceptable.

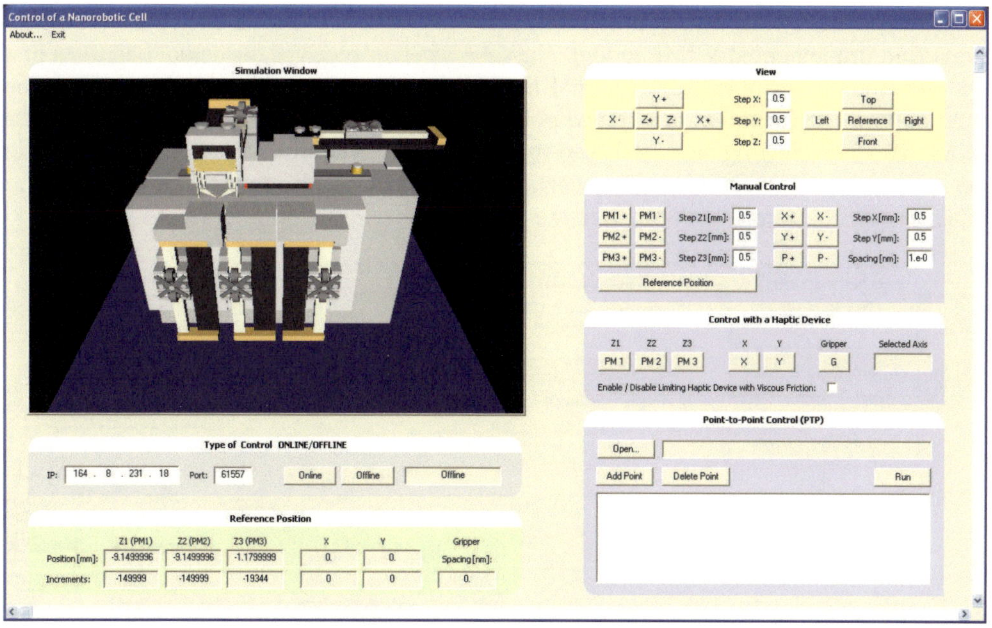


Fig. 10. The Control teach-pendant of the nano-robotic application

Another user interface, the so-called Monitoring teach pendant (see fig. 11) is built on the same basis as previously described The control teach pendant can only provide a function for axes actual positional monitoring on an already executed target application. It also has a virtual model of the micro/nanorobotic cell, so the user can visualise the real

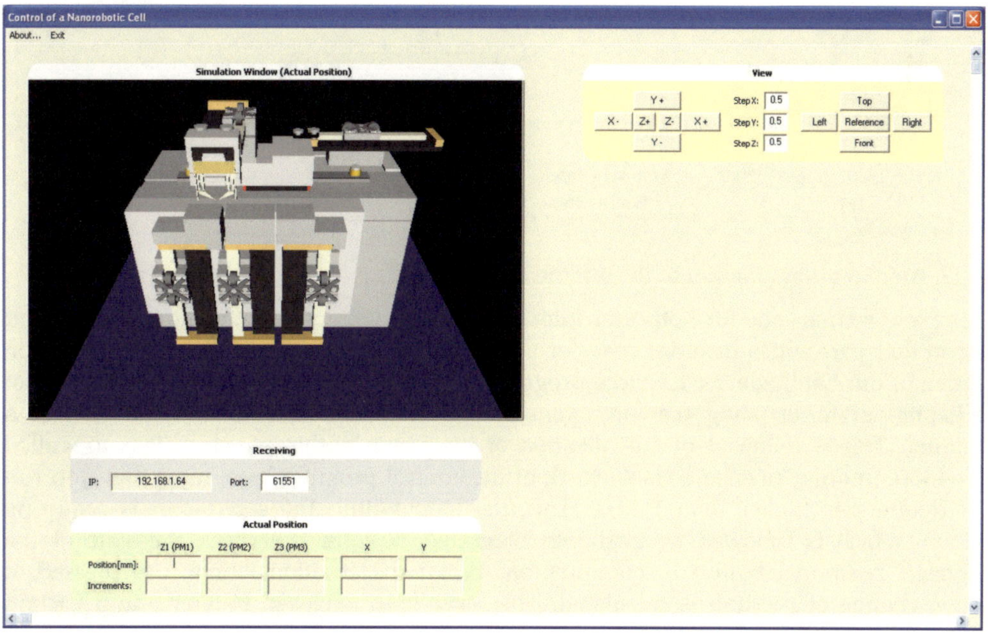


Fig. 11. The Monitoring teach-pendant of the micro/nanorobotic application

micro/nanorobotic axes, and tool movements. This interface uses a C++ built receiver to animate an implemented VRML model. The C++ receiver receives the actual positions of all five axes and the gripper from the real micro/nanorobotic cell, during the programmed target application execution, and delivers these positions to the VRML model, where they are animated. A viewing section is also available in the Monitoring teach pendant, where user can choose different angles for viewing and zooming. All other functions, which are available within Control teach pendant are disabled here.

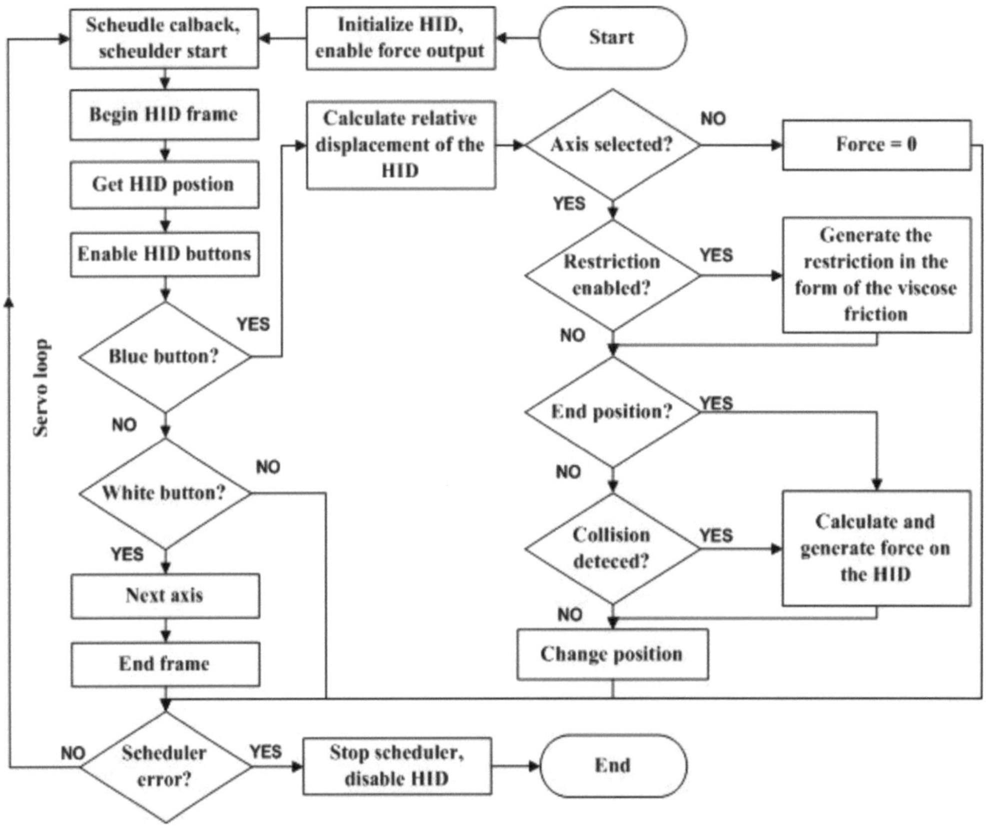


Fig. 12. An execution diagram of the remote application

A complete source code for both user interfaces is very voluminous therefore, we focused only on that part which includes code for the haptic-device. Figure 12 shows an execution diagram of our haptic-device interface program. The first program steps are initialization of the haptic-device, enabling the force generator, a schedule callback and the start of a scheduler. This is followed by initialization of the frame within which runs a so- called servo-loop. In order to ensure stable work of the control program loop, must this loop run with frequencies higher than 1 kHz. The first step within the servo-loop is acquiring position, which is followed by enabling integrated buttons. We check the state of the integrated positional button in continuation. When the positional button is pressed, a relative change of position is calculated. The servo-loop is closed by enabling a friction function and applying feedback force in case a collision has been detected. Finally we change the position of the nano-robot.

## 4. Conclusions

The chapter has presented the development of a telerobotic application using an implemented VRML virtual model. This virtual model is used for the visualisation of real-time actual or desired remote robot positional control data, and is used as a replacement for live camera pictures. The broadcasting of live camera picture over the Internet incurs long time-delays in spite of a good internet connection, which is often unavailable, for example, during rush hours.

The same "remote" techniques were also used for the next micro/nanorobotic application, where the human machine interface for connecting of macro and micro/nano worlds was presented and where a virtual model of the micro/nano robotic cell is used to improve 3D visualisation. The use of a haptic device remarkably improved the communication link between the user and the micro/nano-robot.

The main drawback of the presented methods is that they can prevent collision, or provides feeling of touch, only within predefined robotic cell and its environment, while it is very difficult or even impossible to sense or visualise so-called unknown dynamic objects (Matko & Šafarič, 2009), (Matko & Jezernik 2010).

## 5. Acknowledgment

Operation partly financed by the European Union, European Social Fund.

## 6. References

Bambang, R. (2007). Development of Architectures for Internet Telerobotics Systems, ICIUS 2007, pp. 137-142, (http://arxiv.org/ftp/arxiv/papers/0804/0804.3891.pdf), Bali, Indonesia.

Cavalcanti, A.; Freitas, R. A. Jr.; Kretly, L. C. (2004). Nanorobotics control design: A Practical Approach Tutorial, DETC2004, pp. 1-10, 2004, (http://www.nanorobotdesign.com/papers/nanorobotTutorial.pdf), Salt Lake City.

Cavalcanti, A.; Wood, W. W.; Kretly, L. C.; Shirinzadeh, B. (2006). Computational Nanomechatronics: A Pathway for Control and Manufacturing Nanorobots, CIMCA-IAWTIC'06, pp.185 - 190, Sydney, Australia.

Čas J.; Hercog D.; Šafarič R. (2007). Web based education tool for neural network robot control. International journal of online eng. Vol 3, no. 2, (http://www.i joe.org/ojs/), Vienna, Austria.

Dobrovodsky, K.; Andris, P. & Kurdel, P. (2000). A Virtual Reality Robot Workcell Simulator, Proceedings of 9th Int. Workshop Robotics in Alpe-Adria-DanubeRegion RAAD, pp. 331-336, Vienna, Austria.

Dong-Soo, K.; Seung-Chan, K. (2008). Haptic Interfaces for Mobile Devices, A Survey of the State of the Art, Recent Patents on Computer Science 2008, pp. 84-92, (http://robot.kaist.ac.kr/paper/doc/b2670_gny6c48k_PDF.pdf), ISSN: 1874-4796.

Friconneau, J.P.; Karouia, M.; Gosselin, F. (2002). Force feedback master arms, from telerobotics to robotics surgery training, CARS 2002, CARS/Springer, Zurich, Switzerland.

Fu, K. S.; Gonzales, R. C.; Lee. S. G. (1987). Robotics: Control, Sensing, Vision, and Intelligence, Mc-Graw-Hill Book Company.

Fukuda, T.; Arai, T. (2000). Prototyping Design and Automation of Micro/ Nano Manipulation System, Proc. of IEEE Int'l Conf. on Robotics and Automation (ICRA'00), pp. 192-197, San Jose, CA 95133, USA. GAMMA, (2009). http://www.cs.unc.edu/~geom/V-COLLIDE/.

Goldberg, K.; Maschna, M.; Gentner, S. (1995). Desktop Teleoperation Via The WWW, *Proceedings of the IEEE International Conference on Robotics and Automation*, pp. 654-659, Japan.

Hudson T. C.; Lin M. C.; Cohen J.; Gottschalk S.; Manocha, D. (1997). V-collide: Accelerated Collision Detection for VRML, Proceeding of VRML'97, ACM Press, C24-26, pp. 119-125, Monteray, USA.

Keoschkerjan, R., Wurmus, H. (2002): A novel microgripper with parallel movement of gripping arms, Actuator 2002, 8th International Conference on New Actuators, pp. 321-324, Bremen, Germany.

Mair, G. (1999). Transparent Telepresence Research, Industrial Robot, Vol. 26, No 3, pp. 209-215.

Mantovani, G.; Riva, G. (1999). Real Presence: How Different Ontologies Generate Different Criteria For Presence, Telepresence and Virtual Presence, Presence, Teleoperators & Virtual Environments, Vol. 8, No 5, pp. 540-550.

Nanos instruments web page (2009): http://www.nanos-instruments.de/.

National Instruments, Motion controller 7356 datasheet web page (2009): http://www.ni.com/pdf/products/us/735x.pdf.

Pačnik, G.; Klobučar, R. (2006). Parametric reconstruction of a scene from two views.: Internationale Konferenz Tagungsband REMUS'06, pp. 193-198, Niš, Serbia .

Piezomotor Upsala AB: PiezoLEGS data and user instructions(2003), 3rd edition, pp. 3- 15, Upsala, Sweden.

Sayers C.(1999). Remote Control Robotics, Springer-Verlag, New York.

Seung-Chan, K. & Dong-Soo K. (2007). Haptic and Sound Grid for Enhanced Positioning in a 3-D Virtual Environment, Oakley, I. and Brewster, S. (Eds.): HAID 2007, LNCS 4813, pp. 98–109, 2007, Springer-Verlag Berlin Heidelberg (http://www.springerlink.com/content/5r125822426634lv/fulltext.pdf).

Šafarič, R.; Calkin, D.W.; Parkin, R.M.; Czarnecki, C.A. (2001). - a, Virtual environment for telerobotics, Integrated computer-aided engineering 8: p.p. 95-104.

Šafarič, R.; Debevc, M.; Parkin, R.M.; Uran, S. (2001) - b, Telerobotics experiments via Internet, IEEE transactions on industrial electronics 48: p.p.424-431.

Šafarič, R.; Šinjur, S.; Žalik, B.; Parkin, R.M.(2003). Control of Robot Arm with Virtual Environment via Internet, Proc. I.E.E.E. 91: 422-429.

Šafarič, R.; Truntič, M.; Hercog, D.; Pačnik, G. (2005). Control and robotics remote laboratory for engineering education, International journal of online eng. 1, (http://www.i-joe.org/ojs/).

Škorc, G.; Zapušek, S.; Čas, J.; and Šafarič, R. (2010). Virtual user interface for the remote control of a nano-robotic cell using a haptic-device, accepted by Journal of Mechanical Engineering.

Telegarden (2009). http://telegarden.aec.at

Telelabs (2009 . http://telerobot.mech.uwa.edu.au

Wang, D.; Ma, X.; Dai, X. (2004). Multimedia transmission strategy in Web-based robotic system, Proc. IEEE/RSJ International Conference on Intelligent Robotics and Systems, pp:2544 - 2549 vol.3, Sendai, Japan.

Matko, V.; Šafarič, R. (2009). Major improvements of quartz crystal pulling sensitivity and linearity using series reactance, Sensors, vol. 9, iss. 10, p.p. 8263-8270.

Matko, V.; Jezernik, K. (2010). Greatly improved small inductance measurement using quartz crystal parasitic capacitance compensation. Sensors, vol. 4, iss. 10, p.p. 3954-3960.

18

# Aid for the Blind to Facilitate the Learning Process of the Local Environment by the Use of Tactile Map

Rajko Mahkovic
*University of Ljubljana*
*Slovenia*

## 1. Introduction

In this chapter we present one possibility of application of the path planning from mobile robotics of the local urban environment learning of a blind person.
The general problem of mobile robot navigation was summarized with three questions: "Where am I?", "Where am I going?", "How should I get there?" (Leonard & Durrant-Whyte, 1991). Almost identical questions were posed also in the textbook for teachers who are dealing with the blind and visually impaired (Zovko, 1994). Not surprisingly, similar to a mobile robot, in the everyday manoeuvring in the local environment the blind are forced to resolve problems of localization, orientation, navigation and moving around. Like a mobile robot, also the blind rely on *relative measurement* (e.g. "there are five steps from the house door to the street level") or *absolute measurement* (e.g. "the second crossing from the house is marked by a beeper"); that is, they rely on the sense of touch (how many steps or stairs they have already made) and hearing (sounds from the surroundings - natural and artificial markers).
Therefore, the applicability of the results from mobile robotics research seems natural also for the blind. Indeed, applications of the obstacles avoidance, localization, sensor fusion and path finding have found their use in the development for the blind. The range of equipment so far developed is from complex machines to specialized devices. The examples of the former are motorized wheelchairs, e.g. *RoTA (Robotics Travel Aid),* which are well equipped with vision, sonar, and tactile sensors. They also posses a map database system (Mori & Kotani, 1998) that is capable of guiding the blind along the road or sidewalk. However, although these wheelchairs, in fact mobile robots, are theoretically capable of guiding the blind, they are still too heavy, too big (and too expensive) to be widely accepted by the blind (let us only imagine all the raised surfaces, like stairs and sidewalks). More convenient are other devices. The portable device *NavBelt,* for example, consists of a belt with an array of eight ultrasonic sensors and a small computer worn as a backpack. After gathering the information from the sonars, the computer applies the unique obstacle avoidance algorithms and relays the data about the surrounding to the blind via stereophonic headphones (Shoval et al., 2000). Yet another device from the Mobile Robotics Laboratory, University of Michigan, is the *GuideCane,* a kind of robotic guide-dog. The blind, setting the desired direction, holds a special white cane tipped with a small mobile robot that is capable of

sensing and avoiding obstacles. After avoiding an obstacle, the mobile robot proceeds following the given direction. The blind follows the trajectory of the robot in a similar way a trailer follows a truck (Shoval et al., 2000; Ulrich & Borenstein, 2001).

Generally speaking, the main advantage that mobile robotics can offer the blind is *obstacle avoidance*, which means sensing the obstacles and planning the path around them, with respect to *conventional electronic travel aids* for the blind whose capabilities are limited to *obstacles detection*. By the name of conventional electronic travel aids one most frequently recalls (Zovko, 1998):

- The *Pathsounder,* one of the earliest ultrasonic "go-no-go" device, which informs the blind about the obstacles in the surrounding by tactile vibrations (Russel, 1965),
- The *C5 Laser Cane,* a cane equipped with three laser detectors, capable of detecting the obstacles in three directions: UP, FORWARD, and DOWN (Benjamin et al., 1973),
- The *Sonicguide,* a binaural ultrasonic aid attached to the spectacles, which encodes the distance to an object into the low frequency tone, separately for the left/right side in front of the blind, each information channel leading to left/right ear (Kay, 1974),
- The *Mowat Sensor*, an ultrasonic hand-held device that informs the blind person of the distance to the object by tactile vibrations, whose frequency is inversely proportional to the distance (Pressey, 1977).

In order to detect the obstacles, the majority of previously mentioned devices demand from the user to actively scan the environment. Another problem with the acoustic feedback devices is the interference with the sounds from the surroundings, which obstruct the blind's essential ability to orientate. In order to improve independence of the blind via active sensing, perhaps it is now time to upgrade this kind of devices with obstacle avoidance software systems from mobile robotics.

But there is yet another field of application of mobile robotics: the learning process, a sensitive and demanding process, which both the blind by birth and the acquired blind must undergo. Somewhere at the end of this learning process, there is a task where the blind must build in mind their own representation of local urban environment. This is but one of the indispensable conditions not being dependent on the help from others, that is to be able to go to school or to a job alone, to feel secure and autonomous, to take part in the social life, shortly, to be an active member of the society.

## 2. Spatial representation of the environment

In order to be autonomous in the local urban environment, for the blind, being able to build in mind their *own representation of this environment* is of the greatest importance. It means that a blind person relates all the possible markers he/she can sense (e.g. noises, smells) with spatial representation of the environment.

The results of working with sighted adults proved that the learning method when a sighted person is using a map or panoramic verbal description resulted in better coordinated spatial schemas, than the one when the space is learned through direct interaction with the environment or from a sequential verbal description (Thorndyke & Hayes-Roth, 1982). One may speculate that the more structure is 'revealed' by the learning method, the more structural spatial representation the learners are to be able to build.

As for the blind, on the other hand, the studies have pointed out that, in order to acquire, code, store and recover spatial information (e.g. Passini & Proulx, 1988; Spencer et al. 1989), they can make use of certain perceptual cues (landmarks in mobile robotics). Using those alternative strategies, the blind are able to organize the spatial information in a way that is *functionally equivalent* to that of the sighted people. However, with respect to the sighted, they do need a prolonged period of time and bigger cognitive effort.

The research with the blind has shown that tactile maps may represent useful means of providing the blind with complex spatial information about the environment (Ungar et al. 1993; 1995). To compare the effectiveness of different methods for introducing the blind to the spatial layout of urban environments, Espinosa et al. carried out two experiments. In the first, the blind learned a complex and long route through the city by direct experience, by a combination of direct experience and a tactile map, or by a combination of direct experience and a verbal description of the area. Participants who used tactile maps demonstrated significantly better spatial knowledge compared to those from the other two groups. In the second experiment, participants learned a similar route using either a tactile map or direct experience only. No significant difference in spatial knowledge was found between the two groups. The researchers concluded that the combination of direct experience and tactile maps should be employed by the orientation and mobility instructors; however, even when direct experience is impossible, an isolated use of tactile map can represent adequate means of familiarizing the blind with the environment (Espinosa et al., 1998).

## 3. Tactile maps

A tactile map is a relief map, a plastic foil, imprinted vacuumly on a metal mould with a 3D representation of an urban environment. In comparison with normal city map, a tactile map, normally of the A3 format size, contains considerably fewer information. It is also enlarged: it encompasses smaller city area than the ordinary city map. The surface of the tactile map is normally divided into levels (Fig.1), each being a millimetre or so raised over the lower one: the streets are in the lowest level, forming the channels, ground and houses are in the intermediate level, while special objects like churches or other objects of importance are represented by the highest level.

Fig. 1. Relief structure (layers) of the tactile map.

In this level there could be special map marks, or short texts in Braille letters; the signs are now more or less in accordance with the standards, which have been established recently. For the sake of clearness for the sighted people, tactile maps are coloured. The tactile maps used in this work were supplied by Geodesic Institute of Slovenia (Rener, 1993).

Practice guidelines for the design, production and presentation of tactile maps are available on the web (Gardiner & Perkins, 2002).

## 4. Tactile map monitoring system (TMMS)

We propose to extend the conventional use of the tactile maps by a system consisting of camera and the computer, named TMMS. TMMS consists of a camera connected to a computer. The camera is placed about 50 cm above the tactile map, whose field of vision encompasses a bit larger area than tactile map alone. This vision system tracks the movements of the user's forefinger while sliding all over the tactile map. In fact, it tracks only the special magenta marker, placed for the sake of quick recognition on the nail of the forefinger (Fig. 2).

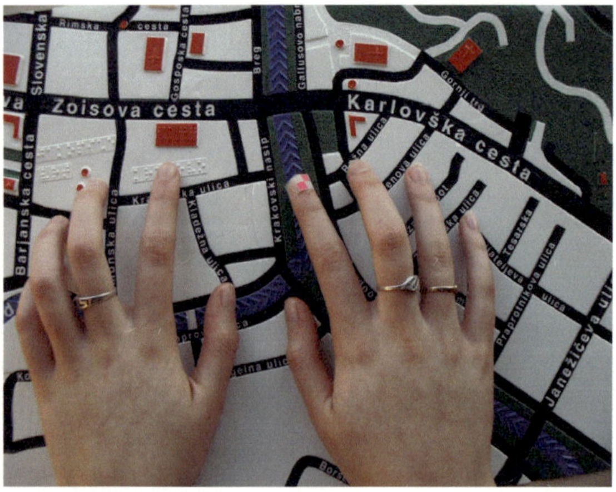


Fig. 2. The tip of the forefinger is tracked.

Although the user obviously uses all his fingers, it is only the position of the tip of his forefinger which the system regards as the *user's current position*, $P_t = (x_t, y_t)$ on the tactile map.

The TMMS expects the tactile map is always laid in front of the user like a map (north-south).

### 4.1 Tactile map description graph (TMDG)

The functionality of the TMMS is realised through the employment of a special data structure, *tactile map description graph* (TMDG), a graph where all the objects from the tactile map (e.g. houses, monuments, parks) are connected in a special way. This is the source of all the information the monitoring system is able to produce to the blind. While the user is sliding along the streets, rivers, etc., on the tactile map, the monitoring system should be able to localize his position $P$ (the *current user's position* in the TMDG) to supply him with the name of the street, river, building, or other relevant information, regardless of which specific area of the (for example) building is he currently pointing at. To capture the structure of the objects on tactile map, we use Generalized Voronoi Diagram (GVD).

### 4.2 Generalized Voronoi Diagram of the tactile map

Tactile map $\boldsymbol{T}$, formally a set of planar points, could be partitioned into set of objects $\boldsymbol{O}$

$$\boldsymbol{O} = o_1 \cup o_2 \cup \ldots \cup o_n \quad \text{for } i = 1 \ldots n$$

and the so called *free space* ***F***

$$\boldsymbol{T} = \boldsymbol{F} \cup \boldsymbol{O}$$

Sets of objects normally represents buildings, parts of parks, but also parts of rivers (e.g. from one bridge to another). The free space represents what is left, the surface you can move along, the streets, squares, etc. The objects from ***T*** are of course non-everlapping. Let $d_E(p,o_i)$ denote the minimum Euclidean distance from a point $p$ to a point in $o_i$.

Before we proceed we give the definition of the *Generalized Voronoi diagram,* GVD, of the objects on a tactile map. Let the *generalized Voronoi cell* be defined as

$$V_i(o_i) = \left\{ p; p \in \boldsymbol{T} \ , d_E(p,o_i) \leq d_E(p,o_j), \forall j \neq i \right\}$$

The collection of all Voronoi cells $V_O(\boldsymbol{O}) = \{V_i(o_i)\}$ is called a GVD generated by ***O***.

Voronoi edges and Voronoi points are defined in the same way as in the case of the ordinary Voronoi diagram. If freeform boundaries of objects in the tactile map were considered, this diagram is not easy to obtain. However, for the present purpose, it is sufficient to construct an approximated version of the generalized Voronoi diagram. Following the procedure proposed by Okabe (Okabe et al., 1992) we (a) approximate the boundary of each $o_i$ by a finite set of points, (b) construct an ordinary Voronoi diagram based on these approximation points, and (c) delete from this ordinary Voronoi diagram all the edges which were generated by the approximated points belonging to the same boundary of $o_i$. So what we have previously called GVD was actually the *approximated* version of exact generalized Voronoi diagram.

### 4.3 An example: a detail from the tactile map

We shall illustrate the procedure of generating GVD on the detail from the tactile map of Ljubljana (Fig. 3). (Presently we may also observe the simplifications of the tactile map: several buildings are represented by a single object on a tactile map -all around the map-, some streets are left out completely -in the middle, on the left and the right bank of the river-, etc. On the other side, there are some additional information such as the arrows that indicate the flow of the river, descriptions in Braille letters etc. There also existxs some inherent disproportionality: narrow streets are relatively wider on the map, etc.)

At the beginning, following the procedure of constructing approximated GVD, we approximate the boundaries of each object $o_i$ by a finite set of points. The approximated boundaries may be observed on Fig. 4, drawn by bold lines. (Notice that each object is presented by two borders, i.e. two bold lines; we will discuss the reason for that later.) Ordinary Voronoi diagram created by these approximated borders is drawn by light lines (Fig. 4a). Every light line segment on Fig. 4a consists of points, equally faraway to two neighboring approximation points which lie on the nearest boundary of some object $o_i$. Adjoining light line segments form a (convex) Voronoi cell of the ordinary Voronoi diagram. All the Voronoi points represent the complete tesselation of the tactile map. Each cell has the property that encloses the area which is nearer to some approximation point on the border of some object $o_i$ than to any other approximation point.

a) b)

Fig. 3. The same detail of Ljubljana: a) the hybrid view supplied by Google, b) section from the tactile map

a) b)

Fig. 4. Construction of the GVD: a) ordinary Voronoi diagram (light lines), b) GVD (dotted lines)

If the user's current position $P$ falls into that Voronoi cell, the corresponding part of the border may be readily identified (by that also the object the user is pointing at determined).
The third step of the construction of GVD instructs us to consider each edge in the ordinary Voronoi diagram and delete all those edges that were generated by the approximated points of the same border of the same object $o_i$. After this step only the edges generated by the borders of *different* objects are preserved in the diagram: these are the edges of the GVD. The preserved edges, hence GVD, are drawn with dotted line segments in Fig. 4b.
In the GVD, there are two types of edges: the ones that lie in the middle of the free space between two objects and the ones that pass right through the objects. The former capture the connectivity of the streets, the latter are merely information holders for buildings, rivers, parks, etc. It is clear now why every border of an object should consists of at least two parts: in this way the edges of the GVD 'enter' also the objects. Similar to an ordinary Voronoi diagram also the GVD represents the complete tessellation of the plane. It is a planar graph $GVD = \{E, V\}$ where the edges we have just described are connected at *Voronoi points*. Voronoi points, the vertices of GVD, are the positions of equal distance to at least three nearest objects in the tactile map.

#### 4.4 From GVD to TMDG

Obviously, the GVD is the essential part of the TMDG, the latter being actually the extension of the 'geometrical' data associated with the edges and vertices of the GVD with the vital information for the blind. This additional specific information is organized into three levels: elementary, intermediate and detailed. During usage the TMMS reproduce the information to the blind aurally, through the synthetic or recorded speech, or, less conveniently, written on the Braille line.
The information associated with the edges are:

- elementary - the name of the street, river;
- intermediate - the names of the streets (bridges) at the forend and at the backend of the current edge;
- detailed - the description of the pavement along the street (sand, asphalt, etc.), special sounds/smells that may be heard/scented, the description of the possible dangers (small columns, parked cars, slippery terrain, crush, etc.), the distance to the both ends of the edge, the sample of the sound recorded at the very location, the important city sights, the important personal information, etc.

The information associated with the vertices are:

- elementary - the name of the crossing, bridge,
- intermediate - navigation data (which streets are in front, behind, on the left/right),
- detailed - the complete description of the crossing (traffic light?, the description of the crossing from a pedestrian's point of view, traffic aids for the blind?), the sample of the sound from the location, etc.

The reproducing level is determined by the user and may be changed at any time.
The GVD of the detail of the tactile map may be observed on Fig. 5a. The GVD consists of two types of the edges: the ones that 'capture' the free space between two different objects, let us call them *street egdes* (drawn by continious bold line segments), and the ones that *enter* the objects, *object edges* (dashed bold line segments). There are also two types of the vertices: the ones where the street edges join together, *street vertices*, and the ones where two street edges join with the object edge, *object vertices* (we put aside the fact that generally even more

than just three edges may join at one vertex, since this situation may be avoided during drawing of the borders of objects). To the user, only street vertices are accessible, since it is there, where the stored information about the street crossings are reproduced. They are indicated by small circles on Fig. 5a. This small circles are neccessary also from practical reasons: noninterrupting reproduction of the information at some vertex would be difficult because of even small changes of $P$ (due to small movements of a forefinger) unless some tolerance circle is introduced. Despite the distinction from the user's point of view, all the edges and vertices in GVD are equivalent, however when, for example, searching a path, only street edges are considered by the TMMS.

### 4.5 Correlation between $P_t$ and $P$

In order to navigate in TMDG properly, when sliding over the objects of the tactile map, each pixel of the bitmap image of the tactile map should be in accordance with the appropriate position in TMDG. Generally, the position $P_t$ has to be transformed into $P$ by

$$P(x,y) = Tr(x_t,y_t) + Rot(x_t,y_t) + Scal(x_t,y_t).$$

The three transformations in the equation are translation, rotation and scaling of the user's forefinger position. The values needed for the transformations could be calculated from some calibrating process performed at the beginning of the usage of the tactile map. It may consist of touching the two prescribed objects in the (for example) lower left and the upper right corner of the tactile map. The existing objects of the tactile map, e.g. some monument, small building, a braille letter, or special marker could serve for this purpose.

## 5. Device - user interface

Normally, while listening to the aural information, supplied by TMMS, the user has both his palms resting or sliding over the tactile map. Yet the user also has to control TMMS by giving the commands. In this situation the TMMS is in the so called "Control mode", while, when activated at the level of operating system, it enters the "Setup mode" with the normal functionality of the keyboard. The set of active keys in "Control mode" is kept as simple as possible, nevertheless some input from the keyboard is still neccessary. Therefore, from time to time, the user has to displace his left hand (for right-hander) from the tactile map to the keyboard. The employed keys in "Control mode" are: SPACE-KEY (toggles among the operational modes, look below), PAGEUP/DOWN-KEY (rises or lowers the level of the reproduced information), ESCAPE-KEY (TMMS returns back to "Setup mode"), ENTER-KEY (TMMS stores the user's current position $P$ in the TMDG), and UP/DOWN ARROW-KEY (scrolls up and down the list of predefined locations, objects on the tactile map).

## 6. Modes of operation

As already explained, the information for the blind is held in TMDG, in fact, in the edges and the vertices of the GVD. As the blind is sliding over the tactile map, the task of the TMMS is to *determine the corresponding edge* of TMDG. To do this, the Voronoi cells of the ordinary Voronoi diagram have to be searched to find the one which containes $P$ and contributes a part of the edge in GVD. This is the central task of all the operational modes which are: Calibration, Exploration, Search and Navigation mode.

### 6.1 Calibration mode

Some technical aspects of the Calibration mode have already been described above, while the manipulating details will be omitted.

### 6.2 Exploration mode

The purpose of this mode is to enable the user to familiarize with the tactile map. The user only has to slide his/her fingers over the tactile map, and the TMMS reproduces the information about the objects the user is currently pointing at.

An example of such an exploration may be observed on Fig. 5b. The track of the movement of the user's forefinger is drawn by dashed bold line segments. For every position *P*, lying on this track, the TMMS determines a part of the corresponding edge in TMDG, aurally reproducing the available information at the selected level. The sections of the corresponding edges along the track of the user's forefinger, that are drawn by bold continuous line segments, are enumerated in increasing order. At the beginning (at the bottom, and in the middle) the Voronoi cell of the ordinary Voronoi diagram is determined in which the first *P* lies. When the corresponding object edge no.1 in TMDG is found its relevant information are aurally reproduced. As this edge also corresponds to all the successive points that are lying in the same object, the same information keeps on being reproduced every once in a while until the border of the object is reached. As the next point, representing the street, is already positioned in the channel of tactile map (the user has beforehand sensed the channel by his/her finger pad and is therefore expecting new information), the TMMS finds a new corresponding edge, no.2, which is the street edge. Following the channel of the street, he/she is continuing through the rest of the street (edge no. 2), until he/she reaches the junction of the street (a vertex in TMDG) with another. There is a continuous reproduction of the streets' and crossroads' names. Passing the junction, the user briefly follows the other street (street edge no. 3) while already exploring the next object (object edge no. 4), etc.

### 6.3 Search mode

The purpose of this mode is to help the user find the location of any desired object/location on the tactile map. The user scrolls through a list of objects/locations, that have been both predefined and added by the user him/herself, selecting one. Afterwards, while being instructed in which direction to move to find the desired object' location, he/she may slide over the tactile map in the arbitrary direction. The instructions are given by directions of eight point compass rose: N(orth), N(orth)E(ast), E(ast), etc. While advancing along the path, the appropriate information from the TMDG for the current position and a new direction are being aurally reproduced. The user may employ two strategies: he/she may either scan the area between him/herself and the selected object in order to gain the knowledge about its surroundings or approach the selected object by sliding a finger along the streets exclusively.

An example of such a search is given on Fig. 6a. The selected location is labelled by G and the user's starting position by S. The user's path (continuous bold line) reveals scanning at the beginning and sticking to the streets when close to the goal. The directions given by the TMMS are written along the path.

a) b)

Fig. 5. a) GVD of a tactile map detail: edges of the objects (bold dashed line segments) and egdes along the streets (bold continious line segments) b) Exploration mode example: the track of the user's forefinger (bold dashed lines), relevant segments of the edges in TMDG (bold continious line segments, enumerated along the movement), drawn over the objects and GVD (in light tones)

### 6.4 Navigation mode

This mode is dedicated to navigate the blind from one selected location S to the other G. This is the mode where the path from home to important everyday locations (e.g. school, bank, post office, shop, bus station, etc.) is thoroughly exercised. The TMMS determines the user's current position and instructs the user which way to take in order to move towards the goal location. Once again, the instructions are directions of eight point compass rose. As in the Search mode, the appropriate information associated with the current position in the TMDG is being reproduced aurally. In contrast to Search mode, there is also an aural reproduction of additional information whether the user's current position is *on* or *off* the proper path. The TMMS does not tolerate excursions off the proper path, so if it does happen, the user is instructed to return to the last valid position on the path.

An example is given on Fig. 6b. At start point S, the user is instructed toward N(orth) and at the first encountered crossing, toward E(ast). The goal location is G, however, at the location where the user goes off the correct path, the goal location temporarily becomes the last valid location on the path. The advancement toward G is delayed until the valid location is resumed.

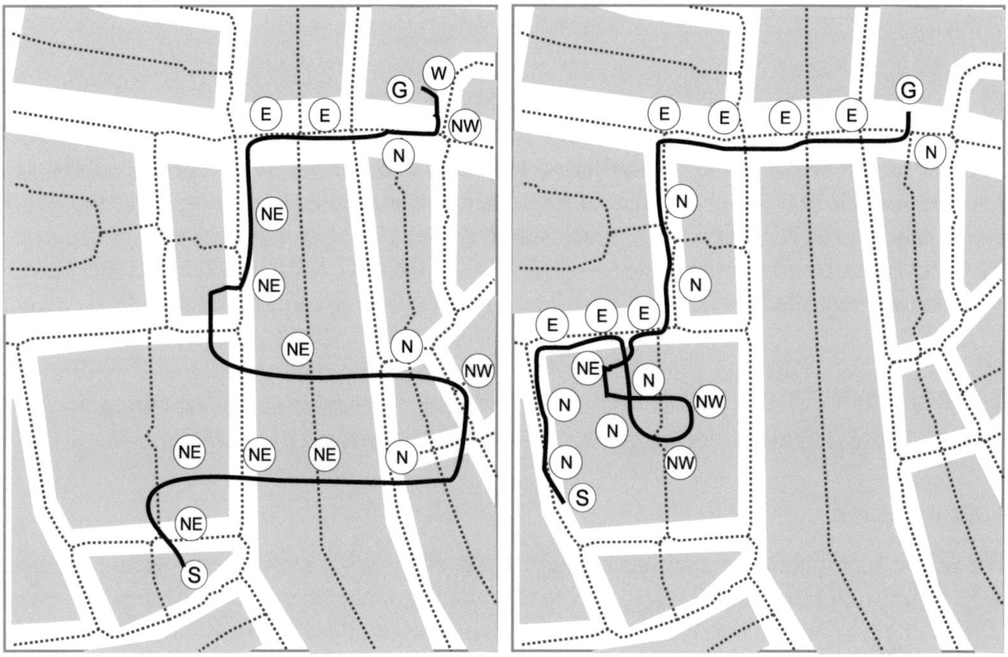


a) b)

Fig. 6. a) Search mode example: the track of the user's path from start position S to goal position G with the navigational instructions given along the path by TMMS b) Navigation mode example

### 6.5 Customizing the TMMS

Making a tactile map is not a trivial task and demands engagement of people of various professions. It is too expensive to be tailored for just one blind person. A blind person, on the other side, needs to learn about *his/her own* local environment. His/her tactile map shall include signs for *his/her* school, shop, bank, etc. Since it enables the user to store his own positions in the TMDG, which may be latter recalled and involved in the user's specific exercises of navigation, the TMMS in a way supports customization of the learning place. At those special locations on the tactile map, it would be useful to provide some tactile marks (drops of glue, stuck Braille letters). While in the "Control modes" only *the coordinates* of the user's own special positions may be stored, in the "Setup mode" also the associated information, to be reproduced later, may be added.

### 6.6 Other tactile teaching aids

Although only the tactile maps are treated in this work, any planar tactile aid may be used; e.g. the majority of the techniques for making tactile diagrams (Kermauner, 2009) produce aids suitable to be used in TMMS. For each aid, of course, its own description graph TMDG has to be made, which presently cannot be constructed by the instructors of the blind themselves. The independent production of new teaching aids at schools could be realized in the future.

### 6.7 Implementation

To construct the GVD from the tactile map, it is necessary to draw a boundary of each object from the tactile map. For the demonstrated example, this was achieved manually, although it seems possible that this process could be made automatic (after all, the mould of the tactile map is made on the CNC machine, which suggests that a suitable input for the calculation of the GVD could be obtained by the interpretation of the CNC program). Nevertheless, the information associated with the buildings and streets, held in the TMDG, should be added by hand.

The GVD was constructed by the use of the library of the data types and algorithms of combinatorial computing, LEDA (Mehlhorn & Näher, 1999); also all the searching in GVD, data structures definitions and manipulations were implemented in LEDA.

## 7. Conclusion

The research of mobile robotics has already made, and - as we may expect - is still to make even more important contribution also to developing machines, devices and aids for the blind. For example, the obstacle avoidance systems, originally developed for mobile robots, seem well suited to be incorporated into travel aids for the blind. Although most of today's dedicated mobile robots for the blind still seem too heavy, sophisticated and, first of all, too expensive, they may - as we believe - evolve into usable aids for the blind. But the mobile robotics could also participate in improving training of the blind.

The system we proposed in this work falls into this category. We further exploit the use of the tactile maps by associating the tactile information the blind gets from the tactile map with the information about the objects the blind person is pointing at. The position of the finger on the tactile map is associated with the corresponding description of the object in the information system. This description is presented to the blind aurally (the existing text-to-speech systems which involve synthetic speech have already been accepted by the blind).

The system works in three operational modes: exploration, search and navigation in which also the knowledge from the path planning is applied.

We believe the system could: (1) help the users to build in mind spatial representation of their local environment more quickly and accurately, which is essential for the blind in order to be more easily and quickly autonomous; (2) be applied whenever there is a need to associate the tactile information with aural explanation; and (3) allow for more independent learning and exercising.

## 8. Acknowledgements

The author would like to thank to Roman Rener for providing the tactile maps, to Ingrid Žolgar Jerkovič and Mirjana Hafnar for introduction to the education of blind, and to Luj Šprohar for at least partial insight of the world of blind.

## 9. References

Benjamin, J. M.; Ali, N. A. & Schepis, A. F. (1973). A Laser Cane for the Blind, *Proceedings of the San Diego Biomedical Symposium*, pp. 53 - 57, Vol. 12

Espinosa, M.A.; Ungar, S.; Ochaíta, E., Blades, M. & Spencer, C. (1998). Comparing Methods for Introducing Blind and Visually Impaired People to Unfamiliar Urban Environments. *Journal of Environmental Psychology*, Vol. 18, No. 3, pp. 277-287

Gardiner, A. & Perkins, C. (2002). Best practice guidelines for the design, production and presentation of vacuum formed tactile maps. http://www.tactilebooks.org/tactileguidelines/page1.htm (1.9.2010)

Kay, L. (1974). A Sonar Aid to Enhance Spatial Perception of the Blind: Engineering Design and Evaluation. *Radio and Electronic Engineer*, Vol. 44, No. 11, pp. 605-627

Kermauner, A. (2009). Tactile books for Blind in Slovenia, In: *The Typhlo & Tactus Guide to children's books*, Ed. Claudet, P., pp 189-204, ISBN: 978-2-916170-66-9, Les Doigts Qui Revent, Talant

Mehlhorn, K. & Näher, S. (1999). *LEDA: A Platform for Combinatorial and Geometric Computing*, Cambridge University Press, ISBN 978-0521563291 .

Mori, H. & Kotani, S. (1998). Robotic Travel Aid for the Blind: HARUNOBU-6, *Proceedings of The Second European Conference on Disability, Virtual Reality, and Assistive Technology*, pp. 193-202

Okabe, A.; Boots, B. & Sugihara, K. (1992). *Spatial Tessellations Concepts and Applications of Voronoi Diagram*, John Wiley, ISBN: 978-0-471-98635-5

Passini, R. & Proulx, G. (1988). Way finding without vision: An experiment with congenitally totally blind people. *Environment and Behaviour*, Vol. 20, pp. 227-252

Pressey, N. (1977). Mowat Sensor. *Focus*, Vol. 11, No. 3, pp. 35-39.

Rener, R. (1993). Tactile cartography: another view of cartographic symbols. *The Cartographic Journal*, Vol. 30, No. 2, pp. 195-198

Russell, L. (1965). Travel Path Sounder, *Proceedings of Rotterdam Mobility Research Conference*, American Foundation for the Blind, New York

Shoval, S.; Ulrich, I. & Borenstein, J. (2000). Computerized Obstacle Avoidance Systems for the Blind and Visually Impaired, In: *Intelligent Systems and Technologies in Rehabilitation Engineering*, Teodorescu, H.N.L. and Jain, L.C., (Eds.), pp. 414-448, CRC Press, ISBN/ISSN: 084-930-140-8

Spencer, C.; Blades, M. & Morsley, K. (1989). *The child in the physical environment: The development of spatial knowledge and cognition*, Wiley, Chichester

Thorndyke, P.W. & Hayes-Roth, B. (1982). Differences in spatial knowledge acquired from maps and navigation. *Cognitive Psychology*, Vol.14, pp. 560-589

Ulrich, I. & Borenstein, J. (2001). The guidecane-applying mobile robot technologies to assist visually impaired. *Transaction on Systems, Man, and Cybernetics - Part A: Systems and Humans*, Vol. 31, pp. 131-136

Ungar, S.; Blades, M. & Spencer, C. (1993). The role of tactile maps in mobility training. *The British Journal of Visual Impairment*, Vol. 11, pp. 59-61

Ungar, S.; Blades, M. & Spencer, C. (1995). Visually impaired children's strategies for memorising a map. *British Journal of Visual Impairment*, Vol. 13, pp. 27-32

Zovko, G. (1994), *Peripatologija I*, Školske novine, ISBN 953-160-029-5, Zagreb

Zovko, G. (1998), *Peripatologija II*, Školske novine, ISBN 953-160-131-3, Zagreb

# 19

# Cornea Contour Extraction from OCT Radial Images

Florian Graglia, Jean-Luc Mari and Jean Sequeira
*Université de la Méditerranée (Aix-Marseille 2)*
*Laboratoire LSIS (UMR CNRS 6168)*
*Marseille, France*

Georges Baikoff
*Clinique Monticelli*
*Marseille, France*

## 1. Introduction

Contour detection is part of a segmentation process. We describe a cornea contour detection approach on images from Optical Coherence Tomography (OCT). These scans present some noise due to the acquisition means. This causes the segmentation to be more difficult. OCT usually provides high-resolution images, but these pictures suffer from speckle. This multiplicative type of noise is common on such images. The elimination of this noise is thus essential before analyzing any features on the image.
The Optical Coherence Tomography is an interferometric, non-invasive optical tomographic imaging technique Huang et al (1991). Nowadays, OCT is well known, especially in ophthalmology and dermatology. This technique enables a medical examination without danger for the tissues. It is particularly used with visual examination and diagnoses. OCT approximately offers a 2-3 millimeters penetration in the tissue, which is compatible with a correct visualization of ocular tissues like retina or cornea. This technique offers live sub-surface images at near-microscopic resolution.
We study corneal images acquired by OCT. It renders radial section including iris and cornea. The cornea contour detection on this section allows ophthalmologists to measure the corneal thickness or the radius of curvature. These measurements are useful for diagnoses and for refractive surgery. Therefore the segmentation from many radial sections permits the creation of a corneal model.

## 2. Previous Work

Many techniques exist in order to detect contour on digital images. The goal of segmentation is to partition an image into sub-regions. This operation is processed according to the properties of the picture like intensity or texture. The image segmentation is typically used to locate objects or boundaries. We present in the following sections two dual methods: the edge-based segmentation and the region-based segmentation. We also analyze two others approaches: the

Active Contours and the Level Set which are continuous edge contour detector. In a last section we study the Markov models which are traditionally used for a robust-to-noise image segmentation.

### 2.1 Edge-based Segmentation

The edge-based segmentation is a first approach of image segmentation. This method seeks for variations of the intensity in an image. Thus it assumes that the sub-sections are sufficiently uniform in order to detect discontinuities.

A first approach to segment images by edge is the gradient vector. This vector gives for each pixel the difference between the pixel above and below (vertical vector), and the difference between the left and the right side of the current pixel (horizontal vector) (see Fig.1). Weight of these vectors gives the presence of edge on the pixel. The laplacian uses the derivate of this gradient to determine the location of the edge Marr & Hildreth (1980). A significant noise sensibility is the main drawback of laplacian method.

| | | |
|---|---|---|
| -1 | 0 | 1 |

| |
|---|
| -1 |
| 0 |
| 1 |

Fig. 1. Gradient kernel in horizontal direction on the left and vertical direction on the right. Kernel center is marked with grey color.

Other operations give better results with larger kernel. We can cite Marr, Prewitt (Fig.2) or Sobel. For example, Sobel Sobel & Feldman (1968) is a gaussian filtering (see Fig.3) which has a double advantage: it provides derivate like the gradient vector and a smoothing effect. This smoothing effect brings fewer noise sensibility.

| | | |
|---|---|---|
| -1 | 0 | 1 |
| -1 | 0 | 1 |
| -1 | 0 | 1 |

| | | |
|---|---|---|
| -1 | -1 | -1 |
| 0 | 0 | 0 |
| 1 | 1 | 1 |

Fig. 2. Prewitt kernel in horizontal direction on left and vertical direction on right. Kernel center is marked in grey.

| | | |
|---|---|---|
| -1 | 0 | 1 |
| -2 | 0 | 2 |
| -1 | 0 | 1 |

| | | |
|---|---|---|
| -1 | -2 | -1 |
| 0 | 0 | 0 |
| 1 | 2 | 1 |

Fig. 3. Sobel kernel in horizontal direction on left and vertical direction on right. Kernel center is marked in grey.

The Canny edge detector Canny (1986) is a two-pass process based on this Sobel operator.

The second pass uses two thresholds to determine a non-closed contour in image. In the first pass, a Sobel kernel is performed through the image. This step attenuates the most important variation in pixels intensity. After this process, the thresholding is most effective for contour detection. The Canny algorithm uses specific thresholding: hysteresis. The thresholding with hysteresis requires high and low thresholds. The high thresholding marks pixels along the contour. The hysteresis approach considers pixels with intensity between two thresholds like edge pixels in the case they are close to other edge contour pixels (superior of high threshold). Canny method and other optimal edge detectors need parameters that are unknown when dealing with OCT scans. Moreover for the specific cornea segmentation, these algorithms do not use knowledge about the cornea. Thus this method is not relevant for the OCT scans. However the hysteresis filtering is a good starting point for the elaboration of an efficient algorithm. Indeed, adding a corneal knowledge and taking into account a larger area could increase the efficiency of contour detection.
Other edge-based method uses entirely the knowledge about segmented object. The Hough transform Hough (1962) is an algorithm used for the image segmentation. The purpose of this technique is to find known shape (like line or circle) by a voting procedure. The main drawback of this method is the limited shapes it can detect. The classical Hough transform detects line and circle, and a generalized Hough detects curves and parameterized shapes. However, the cornea region has not a well known structure.

### 2.2 Region-based Segmentation

The region-based segmentation methods are dual approach of edge-based methods. In this kind of algorithms, we try to find and fix the uniform regions on the picture.
The region growing Brice & Fennema (1970), and its simplified version the pixel aggregation Gonzales & Woods (1993) are methods that merge sub-regions according to similarity in texture, color, or intensity. The pixel aggregation method is initialized with seed pixels. The algorithm merges two sub-regions (or pixels) and appends neighboring if they satisfy some user criterion. The method stops when any near regions are similar. Some important improvements of the region growing algorithm can enhance merging and segmentation result Zhu & Yuille (1995) Zhu & Yuille (1996).
The main drawback of these region-based segmentation methods in OCT scans is their incompatibility with an important noise. The region uniformity, used by segmentation methods, is broken by a significant speckle.

### 2.3 Active Contour

An efficient continuous edge detection technique is the Active Contour model, also called *snakes* Kass et al (1988). It is a framework to detect object contours from a 2D image. The aim of this algorithm is to minimize an energy associated to the current contour. This energy depends on the value of gradient (external energy) and shape-dependent parameters like curvature or elasticity (internal energy). The sum of both energies gives the edge score. With small modifications, the algorithm tries to minimize this score. The algorithm stops when a local minimum is reached, and any modification can reduce the total energy.
However, some problems occur in these methods. The main drawback is that this approach requires a good initialization. This method provides a precise contour detection only if the initialized curve is sufficiently near from the edges. Only local information along the edges are used to detect the minimum energy. In the OCT scans this initialization is relatively difficult without an a priori about the thickness and the radius of curvature of the cornea (related to the

image resolution). A class of Active Contours with shape a priori is an interesting approach to add knowledge in the detection process Gastaud et al (2004). However, the adjustments are difficult to put into practice for such specific images.
Active Contours are autonomous and self-adapting in their search for a minimal energy state. In spite of these advantages, the main drawback of these methods is the initialization of seed pixels or seed regions. In the cornea segmentation process, the Active Contour method assumes that we know the initial position of the cornea in the scan, but this is not the case for us. In the frame of a custom-built contour detection algorithm, we would like to take into account some guidance dedicated to corneal data: the stability of the thickness and the radius of curvature along the cornea.

### 2.4 Level Sets

Osher and Sethian propose Level set theory that is a formulation to implement the Active Contours Osher & Sethian (1988)Malladi et al (1995). A known limitation of the classic snakes is the use of continuous curves, without topological modifications. Level Set avoid this restriction with a two-dimensional Lipschitz-continuous function. This function has multiple level, and the evolution of level set are equivalent to the evolution of the contour. With this kind of function, the Level Set method can detect more than one boundary simultaneously, and user can initialize the algorithm with multiple contours.
The Active Contour models give fair results in boundary detection with important noise. However the same difficulties appear for Level Set with OCT scans.

### 2.5 Markov models

Koozekanani et al. proposed a Markov boundary model to extract retinal contours from radial scans of the macula Koozekanani et al (2000)Boyer et al (2000). Although scans come from OCT, this method is not applicable in the corneal region because of significant anatomical differences. It is difficult to train a new Markov model because both cornea and iris are on the scans. Moreover it could be interesting to add a priori about the cornea to the detection method, which is not possible with the proposed model. The solution proposed in this chapter is a specific algorithm, considering a priori cornea informations.

This section introduces most of the contour detection methods which bring piece of specific algorithm for OCT images. These scans have two particularities: we have some a priori information of the segmented cornea but the scans have a strong noise that complicates the majority of segmentation algorithms. Thus our specific method uses these notable characteristics with a filtering pass which minimizes the noise. We present this contour detection approach in the following section.

## 3. Contour Detection Approach

The contour detection algorithm requires three successive steps. In a first step we detect two points, which initialize the detection contour. Then some filters are applied for a noise reduction and a contrast enhancement. And finally the three-components contour detection can begin.

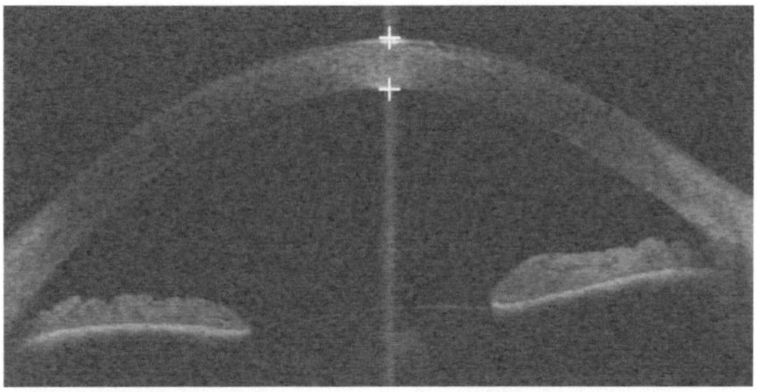

Fig. 4. A typical OCT scan. The markers show both anchor points A (the top cross) and B (the bottom cross).

### 3.1 Detection of the Top Points of Corneal Epithelium and Endothelium

The contour detection algorithm works pixel by pixel on the x-coordinate. Every pixel is found with the pixel on the left or on the right (according to the search direction). Therefore the detection of the initialization points is very important (we call them *anchor point*). The top points of corneal epithelium and endothelium are the best points to optimize the next step of the algorithm. Fig. 1 shows the two anchor points.

We conceive a robust method for the anchor points' detection. We call the top point of the corneal epithelium (the top cross in Fig. 4) the anchor point A and the top point of the corneal endothelium (the bottom cross in Fig. 4) the anchor point B. Firstly, the image is preprocessed. The aim of this operation is to obtain a better contrast and a reduction of the noise, particularly on the top of the cornea. We apply a Wiener filter to reduce the noise regions. This adaptive filter is used to reduce the background noise Lim (1990). It uses a comparison between a local variance and the background variance (noise variance). The Wiener filter moves a box over the image, and finds the local variance of each box. If the local variance is close to the background variance, a mean filter averages the box region, otherwise the filter does not blur the region (see Fig. 7). Next we apply a threshold with the maximum brightness value from background region. Finally we apply a dynamic range expansion to the image. Fig. 5 shows the result of this preprocess.

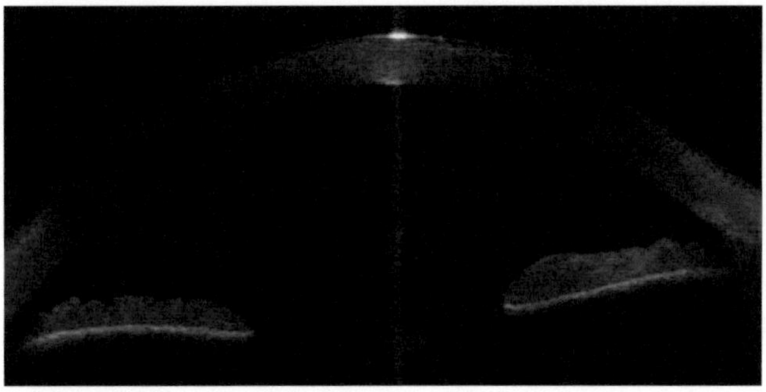

Fig. 5. The resulting image after preprocessing.

After this process, we search the y-coordinate of the anchor point A. We then compute the difference between the average of the area Z1 and the average of the area Z2, as shown on Fig. 6.

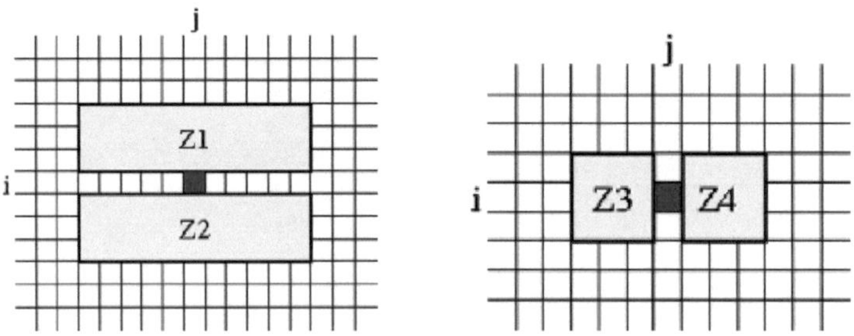


(a) Two rectangles used to compute the variation between the top and bottom areas.

(b) Two squares used to compute the horizontal variation.

Fig. 6. Both structures used to compute variations.

Then we apply this computation column by column, and we keep for every column the y-coordinate of the maximum difference. The highest y-coordinate of these maxima indicates the ordinate of the anchor point A. We now find the x-coordinate of both anchor points: we compute the difference between Z3 area and Z4 area in the y-axis corresponding to the point A ordinate (see Fig. 6). The middle of the x-coordinates upper and lower value of this difference is equal to the x-coordinate of the anchor points. In the last step, we find the y-coordinate of the anchor point B. For this, we apply the difference between Z1 and Z2 and repeat the same process as the point A. After this process we have the coordinates of both anchor points.

### 3.2 Preprocessing Functions

A strong multiplicative noise always comes with OCT scans. The speckle reduction is an important step for the quality of the contour detection algorithm. In fact this noise type creates a big luminance variation in each pixel decreasing the algorithm's quality. To obtain a correct result in the noise reduction, we apply a succession of simple filters to the image.

The results obtained by Wiener filter for the noise reduction are similar to a classic average filter. Yet the Wiener filter has an important advantage: it keeps the contour of the image intact. Fig. 7 shows an example of the application of a Wiener filter.

This filter reduces the background noise. However this noise has to be eliminated in the contour region. To do this, a sequence of classic median filters gives fair results. Contrary to average filter, the median filter preserves a precise contour, without spreading it. Thus many median filters are applied sequentially on the image after the Wiener filter, as shown in the final result on Fig. 8.

### 3.3 Contour Detection

The contour detection algorithm consists of three parts. Firstly the algorithm detects the contour pixel by pixel with the image information only. The posterior and the anterior corneal contours are detected simultaneously. Then the algorithm checks the coherence of the corneal thickness and the radius of curvature for each double pixel found. According to the relevance of the image information in an area, the contour can be more or less adjusted by these parameters.

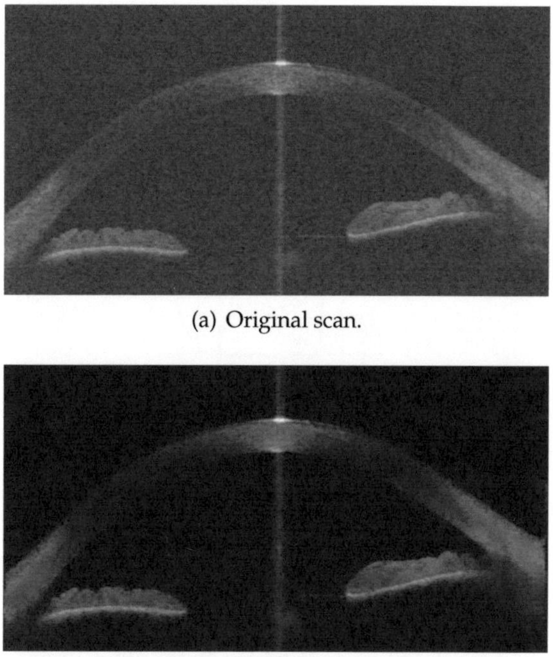

(a) Original scan.

(b) Filtered scan.

Fig. 7. The result obtained with a Wiener filter 10X10.

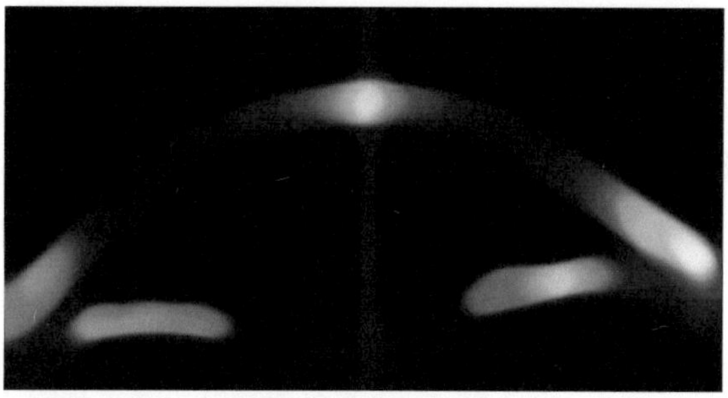

Fig. 8. Result of the preprocessing on a typical OCT scan.

**Maximization of a Difference of Luminance.**

This part is an incremental method that progresses pixel by pixel along the x-axis. The anchor points are the initial points of the first contour. The algorithm searches the left corneal contour, and then the right part. When a pixel belongs to the contour, the algorithm applies a high-pass filter on the points nearest to the contour pixel. The filter is focused on the neighborhood of the contour point. A sized neighborhood is required: five pixels above and below the contour pixel is a correct size. Then the algorithm uses two triangular areas to compute the best contour points. Fig. 9 shows the regions of interest. The next contour point is the one maximizing the difference between the mean of the upper area (Z5) and the mean of the lower area (Z6). For each pixel this difference is called *score*.

This contour detection algorithm proceeds pixel by pixel strictly with the image information.

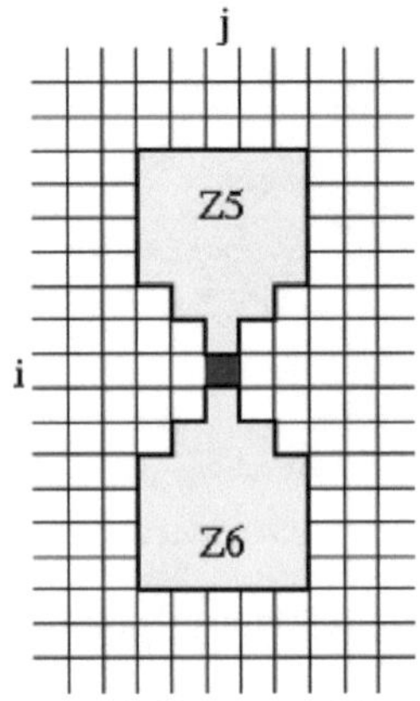


Fig. 9. The score of a pixel is equal to the difference of both shapes Z5 and Z6.

Nevertheless the OCT radial scans are of poor quality. The difference of luminance between the cornea and the background is low for many reasons. The optical coherence tomography renders a poor scan quality and the preprocessing decreases the contrast quality. For these reasons, searching the corneal contour in these scans with only the image information gives a low-quality contour. Therefore knowledge is added to the algorithm to enhance its quality.

**Variation of the Curvature.**
This step is based on the low variation of the curvature along the cornea. This global parameter influences the curve when the scores of pixels are weak. For each pixel, the contour detection algorithm mixes the pixel value obtained by the image information and an extrapolation of the previous pixels' curvature. This combination is a function of the score of the pixel.
The extrapolation of the new pixel location requires a significant number of contour pixels. Each triplet gives a contribution to a y-coordinate of the new pixel. At the end of this phase, the algorithm keeps the y-coordinate chosen by a majority of triplets.

**Variation of the Thickness.**
Like the curvature, this step is based on the low variation of the thickness along the cornea. Physiologically this thickness increases from center to periphery. However this increase is sufficiently low to consider the thickness invariant on a small length.
For each contour pixel, the algorithm sets the pixel location according to the vertical deviation of the previous contour point. This vertical deviation does not correspond to the corneal thickness (due to contours angle from x-axis), however the extrapolation is sufficient to obtain a correct result.

## 4. Results and Discussion

This original segmentation method gives significant results: the recognition phase of anchor points is robust as well as the contour detection.
The initialization of corneal epithelium and endothelium points is an essential process for the method to work correctly. A failure in this process leads to a collapse in the entire algorithm. Therefore the robustness of this step is very important in the process. On all the radial scans

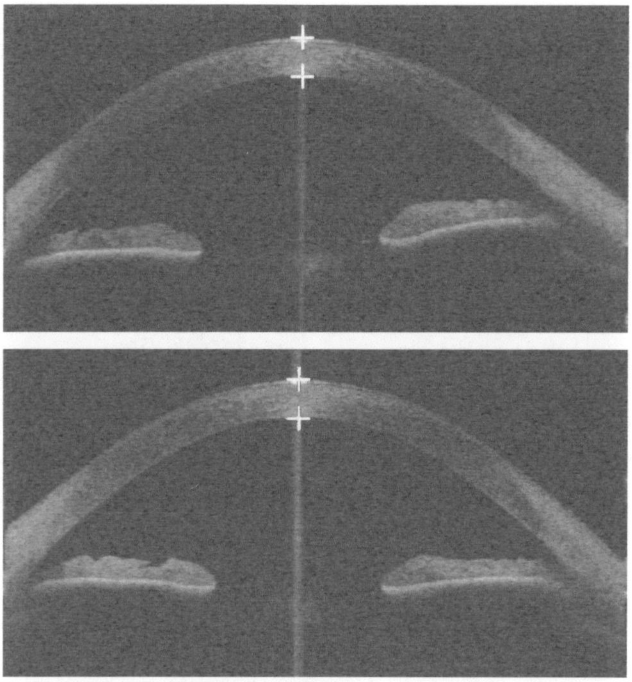

Fig. 10. Anchor points on two typical OCT scans.

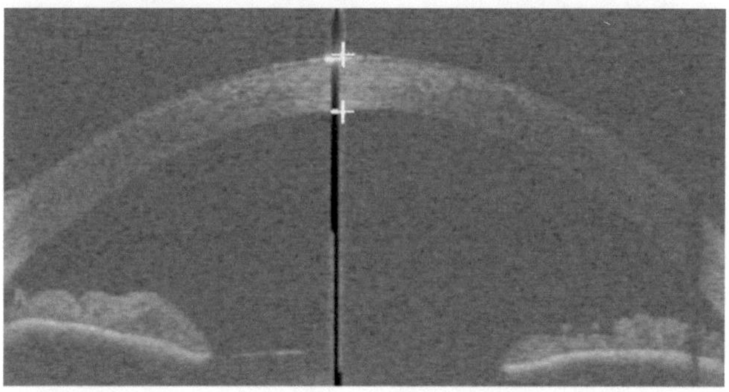

Fig. 11. Anchor points on an OCT scan with some important defects.

that have been tested, the anchor points were correctly detected. Fig. 10 shows the results for two typical scans from OCT.

Several causes (like high local saturation, eyelashes, strong noise) can degrade input images. Fig. 11 shows that the detection of anchor points succeeds even on such a deteriorated example.

Before detecting the boundaries, the noise on the images has to be reduced. This step is realized by a sequence composed of one Wiener filter and several median filters (see Fig 12).

As soon as the anchor points are correctly detected and the noise reduced, the corneal boundary detection algorithm has to go through several steps for every pixel. The first step consists in maximizing the difference between both the higher and lower zone of the pixel. This only step allows an efficient detection on most images. Fig. 13 presents two examples.

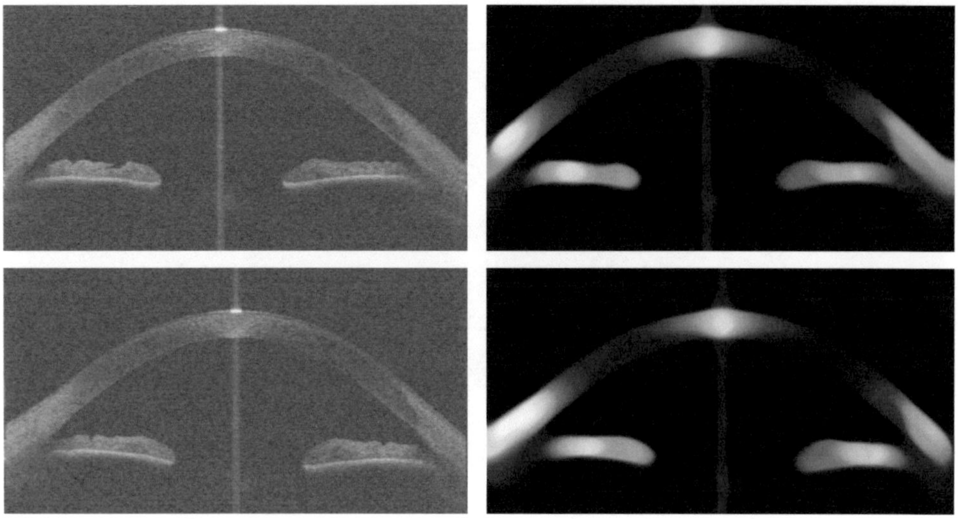

(a) Original scans. (b) Scans after preprocessing.

Fig. 12. Two examples resulting from preprocessing.

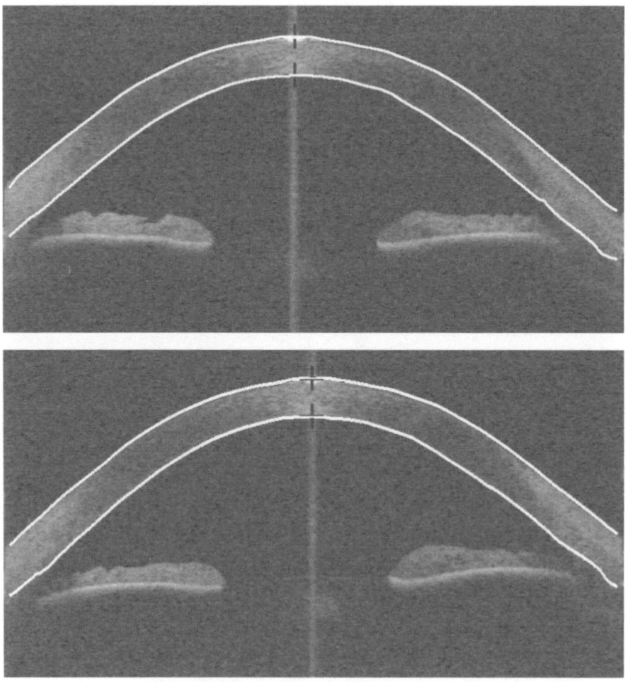

Fig. 13. Two examples of a cornea contour detected by the algorithmÕs first step.

This detection is correct for strong contrast images. However some images as shown in Fig. 14 have a lack of information at the posterior corneal level. Preprocessing allows the recovering of most image defects. For example, it is the case for the central zone of the images on

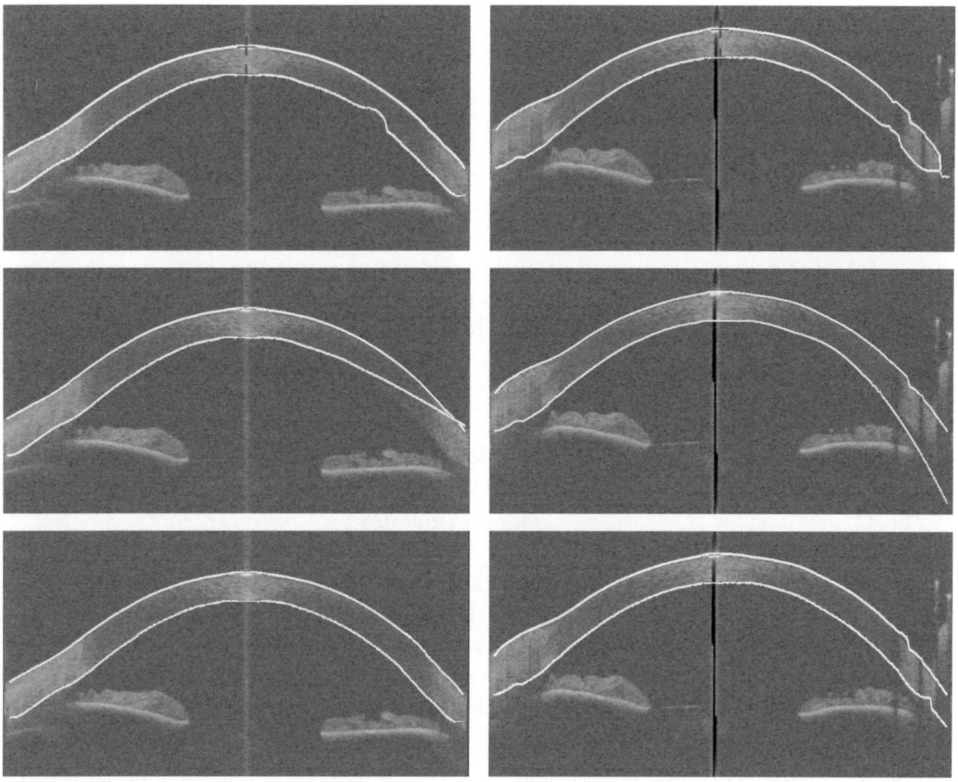

Fig. 14. Two examples (one per column) of a corneal contour. The first row shows the result of the first step: maximization of difference of luminance. The curvature guides the contours (on the second row) and the thickness refines it (on the third row).

Fig. 14. However, following the algorithm's first step we can notice sharp edges due to the presence of eyelashes.

Therefore, this step only based on the image is not enough for a correct segmentation. It is necessary to take into account some other parameters related to the cornea. The radius of curvature is the first parameter used. When the information on the image is incorrect, it is the radius of curvature that guides the detection of the corneal contour.

However Fig. 14 shows that the radius of curvature is not sufficient for a relevant contour detection. A second parameter is used for the contour detection: the corneal thickness.

## 5. Conclusion

This algorithm is an original method of contour detection using two kinds of information: local values from the image pixels, and global parameters from the contours already found. This contour detection uses a specific and robust algorithm composed of three steps: top and bottom key-vertices detection, speckle reduction and contour recognition using geometrical features of the cornea.

Ophthalmologists can use the resulting contour for visual examinations and diagnoses. As future work, we plan on developing a 3D interface based on such contours to build a 3D geometrical model of the cornea. Such a mathematical model could contribute to computer-aided measurements for prostheses design.

## 6. References

S. Osher and J. Sethian. Fronts propagating with curvature dependent speed: Algorithms based on hamilton-jacobi formulations *Journal of Computational Physics*, pp. 12-49, 1988.

S. Zhu and A. Yuille. Region competition and its analysis: a unified theory for image segmentation *Tech. Rep. 7*, Robotics Lab, Havard University, 1995.

S. Zhu and A. Yuille. Region competition: Unifying snakes, region growing, and bayes/MDL for multiband image segmentation *IEEE Transactions on Pattern Analysis and Machine Intelligence*, no. 9, pp. 884-200, 1996.

P. Hough. A method and means for recognizing complex patterns *US Patent 3,069,654*, 1962.

C. Brice & C. Fennema. Scene Analysis Using Regions *Artificial Intelligence*, pp. 205-226, 1970.

R. Gonzales & R. Woods. Addison-Wesley Publishing, 1st ed *Digital Image Processing*, 1993.

I. Sobel & G. Feldman. A 3x3 Isotropic Gradient Operator for Image Processing *Stanford Artificial Project*, 1968.

D. Marr & E. Hildreth. Theory of edge detection *Proc. of Roy. Soc.*, pp. 187-217, 1980.

J. Canny. A computational approach to edge detection *IEEE Transactions on Pattern Analysis and Machine Intelligence*, no. 8, p. 769, 1986.

Huang D; Swanson EA; Liu CR; Schuman JS; Stinson WG; Chang W; Hee MR; Flotte T; Gregory K; Puliafito CA & Fujimoto JG. Optical Coherence Tomography *Science*, Vol. 254, pp. 1178-1181, 1991.

M. Kass; A. Witkin & D. Terzopoulos. Snakes: Active Contour Models *IJCV*, pp. 321-331, 1988.

R. Malladi, J. Sethian, and B. Vemuri. Shape modeling with front propagation: A level set approach *IEEE Transactions on Pattern Analysis and Machine Intelligence*, Vol. 17, pp. 158-175, 1995.

M. Gastaud; M. Barlaud & G. Aubert. Combining shape prior and statistical features for active contour segmentation *IEEE Transactions on Circuits and Systems for Video Technology*, Vol. 14, pp. 726-734, 2004.

D. Koozekanani; K. Boyer & C. Roberts. Retinal Thickness Measurements from Optical Coherence Tomography Using a Markov Boundary Model *IEEE Transactions on Medical Imaging*, Vol. 20, No 9, pp. 900-916, 2000.

D. Koozekanani; K. Boyer & C. Roberts. Retinal Thickness Measurements in Optical Coherence Tomography Using a Markov Boundary Model *IEEE Compter Society Conf. Computer Vision and Pattern Recognition*, Vol. 2, pp. 363-370, 2000.

J, S. Lim. Two-Dimensional Signal and Image Processing, Englewood Cliffs, NJ, Prentice Hall, p. 548, 1990.

20

# Advances in Phytoremediation Research: A Case Study of *Gynura pseudochina* (L.) DC.

Woranan Nakbanpote, Natthawoot Panitlertumpai, Kannika Sukadeetad, Orapan Meesungneon and Wattchara Noisa-nguan
*Mahasarakham University,*
*Thailand*

## 1. Introduction

Phytoremediation is the process through which contaminated land is ameliorated by growing plants that have the ability to remove the contaminating chemicals. The processes in phytoremediation include phytodegradation, phytostabilization, phytovolatilization and rhizofiltration. In addition, the association of plant and microorganism in the rhizosphere seems to enhance removal of the contaminants. Although relatively slow, phytoremediation is environmentally friendly, cheap, requires little equipment or labor, is easy to perform, and sites can be cleaned without removing the polluted soil; it is an *in situ* method. In addition, precious metals, such as gold, zinc and chromium, collected by the hyperaccumulator can be harvested and extracted as phytoextraction. However, the key factor for successful phytoremediation is identification of a plant that is tolerant and suitable for each area, one which can accumulate high concentrations of the required metal. In addition, the mechanism of heavy metal accumulated in the plant should be studied before the application. Advance research in phytoremediation has been focused on the analysis of the distribution and speciation of metals accumulated in the hyperaccumulative plant by using synchrotron radiation and the techniques of micro-X-ray fluorescence imaging (μ-XRF imaging) and X-ray adsorption fine edge structure (XAFS). Expression of metal-inducible proteins in plant such as glutathione, methallothionine and heat-shock proteins have been extracted by various suitable extraction buffers, separated and purified by the techniques of dialysis, chromatography and gel electrophoresis. Then, the amino acid sequences, the crystal structures of proteins, and the status of the metal bound in the proteins have been studied. In addition, the microorganisms in the rhizosphere of metal hyperaccumulative plants have been investigated by isolating the bacteria that are tolerant to heavy metals and contain plant growth promoting properties; such as nitrogen fixation, phosphate solubilization, indole-3-acetic acid (IAA) phytohormone and 1-aminocyclopropane-1-carboxylate (ACC) deaminase production, etc. Finally, the plant design for successful phytoremediation in any contaminated area should be concerned with ground water, running off, geology and the effect of growing the plant on biodiversity. Especially, harvesting management and byproduct utilization should be studied and investigated to convince local people and government of the usefulness of phytoremediation.

### 1.1 Phytoremediation of heavy metals

Phytoremediation is a biological treatment process that utilizes natural processes harbored in (or stimulated by) plants to enhance degradation and removal of contaminants in contaminated soil or groundwater (Alvarez & Illman, 2006). Advantages and disadvantages of using phytoremediation for remediation a heavy metals contaminated area are shown in Table 1. Furthermore, the use of phytoremediation as a secondary or polishing *in situ* treatment step minimizes land disturbance. Increasing public and regulatory acceptance are likely to extend the use of phytoremediation beyond current applications (Ensley, 2000; Tucker & Shaw, 2000).

| Advantages | Disadvantages/Limitations |
|---|---|
| Adaptable to a variety of heavy metal compounds. | Restricted to sites with shallow contamination within rooting zone of remediative plants. |
| *In situ* or *ex situ* application possible with effluent/soil substance respectively. | May take up to several years to remediate a contaminated site. |
| *In situ* applications decrease the amount of soil disturbance and relatively low cost compared to conventional methods. | Restricted to sites with low contaminant concentrations. |
| Reduces the amount of waste that has to be sent to landfill (up to 95%), can be further utilized as bio-ore of heavy metals. | Harvested plant biomass from phytoextraction may be classified as a hazardous waste hence disposal should be carried out properly. |
| *In situ* applications decrease the spread of contaminant via air and water. | Climatic conditions are a limiting factor. |
| Does not require expensive equipment or highly specialized personnel, and easily implemented and maintained. | Introduction of nonnative species may affect biodiversity. Effects to food web and ultimate contaminant fates might be unknown. |
| In large scale applications the potential energy stored can be utilized to generate thermal energy. | Consumption/utilization of contaminated plant biomass is a cause of concern. |

Table 1. Advantages and disadvantages of phytoremediation for heavy metal contaminated areas (Adapted from Ghosh & Spingh, 2005; Alvarez & Illman, 2006)

Phytoremediation utilizes physical, chemical and biological processes to remove, degrade, transform, or stabilize contaminants within soil and groundwater. The mechanism for heavy metal remediation are; phytoextraction, rhizofiltration, phytovolatization, and phytostabilization, they are described briefly as following (Ghosh & Singh, 2005; Suresh & Ravishankar, 2004; Schnoor, 1997; Raskin & Ensley, 2000).

**Phytoextraction or Phytoaccumulation:** The extraction and translocation of heavy metals, in soluble form, from shallow contaminated soil to plant tissues, especially to be stored in stems and leaves (harvestable regions). Although the heavy metals are not destroyed, this approach results in considerable reduction in heavy metal mobility. Depending on the type and concentration of the heavy metals, extraction from the plant ashes for recycling purposes might be feasible. This technique is generally used for metals such as nickel, zinc, copper, lead, chromium and cadmium. Plant productivity; accumulation in harvestable portion of plant > 3 tons dry matter/acre-yr; > 1,000 mg/kg metals lightly contaminated soil near to clean-up standard.

**Rhizofiltration:** This mechanism refers to the use of aquatic plants in wetlands or hydroponic reactors. Generally, plants with large root systems are used. The submerged roots of such plants act as filters for the adsorption and absorption of a wide variety of contaminants. This mechanism is commonly used for treatment of industrial discharge, agricultural runoff, metals and radioactive contamination, with the plant densities of 200-1000 g $m^{-2}$ and hydraulic detention time of several days.

**Phytovolatilization:** The natural ability of a plant to volatilize a contaminant that has been taken up through its roots can be exploited as a natural air-stripping pump system. Volatile pollutants diffuse from the plant into the atmosphere through open stomata in leaves where gas exchange occurs.

**Phytostabilization:** This application aims to prevent the dispersion of contaminated sediments and soil by using plants (mainly grasses) to minimize erosion by wind or rain action. Plants are used to reduce the bioavailability of environmental pollutants. Conditions for optimum likelihood of success are vigorously growing roots; hydrophobic or immobile chemicals.

### 1.2 Utilization of Phytoremediation by products

In the case of phytoremediation of heavy metals, the utilization is based on hyperaccumulative plants and the phytoextraction mechanism. Where, hyperaccumulation is defined as concentration of metal in the harvestable above ground tissues of the plant, with levels in the range of 0.1-1% of the dry weight of the plant. Therefore, the phytomining and diet enrichment of trace elements in the edible parts of plants were mentioned for utilization of the byproducts (Suresh & Ravishankar, 2004; Raskin & Ensley, 2000)

Phytomining is a green technology involving the use of hyperacumulative plants to grow and concentrate a metal. The basic principle of phytomining is combined with biomass generation and its commercial utilization as an energy source, so it can be turned into a profit making operation and the remaining ash can be used as bio-ore. One approach to the post-phytoremediation strategy would be to incinerate the plants in a incinerator, resulting in ash with high metal content, and there would be no emission to the air (Ghosh & Singh, 2005; Anderson et al., 1999). The aspects of diet enrichment by trace elements such as zinc, iron and silinium in the edible parts of plants were mentioned for application as supplements in feed or biofertilizer. More than 430 taxa to date have been reported to hyperaccumulate heavy metals, ranging from annual herbs to perennial shrubs and trees. However, the chemical forms of the heavy metals accumulated in these plants have to be clearly understood before application as a supplement can be achieved (Suresh & Ravishankar, 2004; Chantiratikul et al., 2008; Ensley et al., 2001).

### 1.3 Distribution and speciation of heavy metals in plants

Plants absorb heavy metals from soil and they predominantly accumulate in the roots, then some portions are transported to other parts of the plant. Generally, the contents of heavy metals in the underground parts are higher than those found in the parts above the ground and follows a pattern of root>leaf>shoot (stem)>fruit and lateral root>main root, old leaf>young leaf (Cheng, 2003). Metals accumulated in plant tissues can cause toxic effects, especially when translocated to above ground tissues. The root epidermis served as a barrier to transport of any heavy metals to aboveground tissues. The endodermis casparian strip provided a barrier to the movement of the metals into the stele (the vascular bundles). Once in the leaves, however, metals were highest in the xylem, followed by the mesophyll and then hypodermal tissue. Concentrations of metals in the cell walls were also higher than in intracellular locations (Weis & Weis, 2004).

The distribution and accumulation of heavy metals in plants is related to plant species, element species, chemical and bioavailability, and a number of environmental conditions such as redox, pH, cation exchange capacity, dissolved oxygen and temperature (Cheng, 2003; Weis & Weis, 2004). The tolerance of plants to heavy metals and the accumulation are depended on various physiological factors such as uptake and leakage of metal ions by roots, root cation exchange capacity (CEC), phytochelatin production, antioxidative stress, carbohydrate production and utilization (Suresh & Ravishankar, 2004). Generally, the transportation of heavy metals is related to the chemical status in plants. The transport activities of the ethanol extractive and water dissoluble metals were the highest, then the sodium chloride extractive metal, the acetic acid and the hydrochloric acid extractive metal being the lowest. In spite of the chemical extraction forms, heavy metals can combine with inorganic substances (e.g. sulphides), and some small-molecular organic substances such as glutathione (GSH), oxalic acid, histidine, citrate and metal-binding proteins in the plants (Cheng, 2003). In addition, metal ion interactions might be responsible for the regulation of metal uptake and translocation, for example, free proline acts as an antioxidant in Cd stressed cells, increasing phytochelator synthesis and sequestration of Cd, ultimately leading to hyperacculation (Suresh & Ravishankar, 2004; Chantiratikul et al., 2008).

### 1.4 Metal-inducible proteins

Subsequent to metal uptake into the root symplasm, the movement to xylem involves 3 steps: metal sequestration inside root cells, symplastic transport into stele, and finally release into xylem mediated by membrane transport proteins. In addition, a mechanism of heavy metals detoxification and tolerance in plants involves the chelation of metals by organic acids, amino acids or peptides and metalloproteins (Suresh & Ravishankar, 2004; Callahan et al., 2006). Phytochelatin (PC) and metallothioneins (MT) play an important role in transport, translocation and detoxification of heavy metals (Memon et al., 2001; Cobbett & Goldsbrough, 2002).

**Phytochelatins** are a group of proteins that are inducible in plants when plants are faced with heavy metal stress. They bind to free metal ions and carry them to vacuoles, where they are no longer toxic and if the metals are essential, for plant growth, like copper and zinc, they can be utilized by the plant itself. Phytochelatins consist of 3 amino acids, viz. cysteine, glycine and glutamic acid arranged in a (γ-GluCys) n-Gly confirmation. The synthesis of PCs starts with a response to a heavy metal by the plant by activation of an enzyme phytochelatin synthase, which acts upon a glutathione substrate to produce PCs. This action continues until the complexation of metals is completed. The action of PCs on heavy metals starts with the exposure of the plant to high levels of heavy metal concentrations (Suresh & Ravishankar, 2004; Cobbett & Goldsbrough, 2002).

**Metallothioneins (MT)** resemble phytochelatins in many ways, structurally and functionally. They have high cysteine content, low molecular weight (6-7 KDa) and high metal content with coordination of metal ions in metallothionate clusters. Plant MTs are further classified into two types. The type 1 MTs have 12 cysteine residues arranged as 6Cys-Xaa-6Cys, with the Xaa consisting of approximately 40 amino acids. Type 2 MTs are arranged either as 6Cys-6Cys or 6Cys-Xaa-Xaa-6Cys formation. Even though, the exact function of metallothioneins is not clear, two theories are hypothesized. One theory says that MTs create ion storage pools for free excess heavy metal ions, which are chelated until the plant can use them, if it is an essential metal for the plant. The second theory is that MTs are transport proteins responsible for moving excess heavy metals from sites where they have built up to toxic levels to areas of the plant where they are needed (Suresh & Ravishankar, 2004; Cobbett & Goldsbrough, 2002).

The organic compounds use oxygen and sulfur groups in their structures to be bound to heavy metals; however, plants might be bound to different atoms, depending on the tissue (Cobbett & Goldsbrough, 2002; Hall, 2002). *Salsola kali*, a potential Cd-hyperaccumulator desert plant species, might synthesis phytochelatins in the stems, later coordinating the absorbed cadmium for transport and storage in leaves as a Cd-phytochelatin complex (Rosa et al., 2004). In order to understand the structure and function of these biological systems and the relationship of the metals with the proteins, a technique with high-resolution for protein separation and high sensitivity for metal analysis is required. Gel filtration, Sodium dodecyl sulfate-polyacrylamide gel electrophoresis (SDS-PAGE) and two dimension gel electrophoresis (2DE) are techniques commonly used to analyze proteins. The techniques have been applied to investigate protein detoxification of metals in both microorganisms and plants (Yoshida, et al., 2006; Sobkowiak & Deckert, 2006). In addition, X-ray absorption spectroscopy (XAS) is one of the premier tools for investigating the local structural environment of metal ions. X-ray absorption fine edge structure (XAFS) consists of two the complimentary techniques of X-ray absorption near edge structure (XANES) and extended X-ray absorption fine structure (EXAFS) (Gardea-Torresdey et al., 2005). XAFS has provided the nature of heavy metal complexes accumulated in metal tolerant and hyperaccumulating plant species, the invaluable information of metal-binding proteins, and the structure of metals-containing metalloproteins (Kelly et al., 2002; Verbi et al., 2005; Zhao et al., 2007).

### 1.5 Microorganism in rhizosphere

Although metals are essential components of microbial cells; for example, sodium and potassium regulate gradients across the cell membrane, while copper, iron and manganese are required for activity of key metalloenzymes in photosynthesis and electron transport. Perhaps the most toxic metals are the non-essential metals such as cadmium, lead and mercury. As a consequence of metal toxicity, some microorganisms have developed various resistance mechanisms to prevent metal toxicity. The strategies are either to prevent entry of the metal into the cell or actively to pump the metal out of the cell. This can be accomplished by either sequestration, active transport or chemical transformation through metal oxidation or reduction. **Sequestration** involves metal complexation with microbial products such as extracellular polymeric substances (EPS) and metallothionine-like proteins. Following metal uptake, some cells sequester metals intracellularly utilizing low molecular weight, cysteine-rich proteins called metallothioneins. The complexed metal may then either be transported back out of the cell or stored as intracellular granules. Which mechanism predominates, intracellular or extracellular sequestration, is dependent on the organism involved. **Active transport** of metals out of the cell is one mechanism of microbial resistance to metal toxicity. Highly specific efflux systems can rapidly pump out toxic metal ions that have entered the cell. Such efflux pumps may derive their energy from membrane potential or from ATP, and in fact ATP-dependent efflux pumps have been identified that are specific for metals.

**Oxidation-reduction (redox) reactions** constitute a third mechanism for microbial metal resistance. Microorganisms may either oxidize to mobilize or reduce to immobilize a metal and both reactions are used to prevent metal entry into the cell (Roane et al., 1996).
Plant growth-promoting bacteria (PGPB) have the ability to promote a plant's growth (increase biomass) and increase tolerance to toxic heavy metals by nitrogen fixation, phosphate solubilisation, sulfate oxidation and synthesis of phytohormones such as indole-3-acetic acids (IAA), cytokinins, gibberellins and aminocyclopropane-1-carboxylate (ACC) deaminase (Zhuang et al., 2007) and induced systemic resistance (ISR) mechanism in the plant. Other mechanisms are the release of antibiotics, extracellular enzymes, chemical and volatile compounds such as lumichrome that allow respiration in roots and lead to an increase in the size of plants (Mukerji, 2006). More than the plant promoting properties under stress conditions, PGPB could assist the phytoremediation process by increase the availability and mobility of heavy metals to plants through acidification, redox changes and releasing of chelating agents such as siderophores which are then transferred together with water and nutrient uptake into the plant (Jing, 2007; Khan, 2005; Zhuang et al., 2007). Some PGPB also have toxic reducing or are heavy metal resistant mechanical inducers for example extracellular polymeric substants (EPS) or polysaccharides that secreted outside the bacterial cells can modify the soil structure and induce the plants to respond to stress. This suggest that rhizosphere bacteria, especially plant-growth promoting bacteria (PGPB) that contain the properties of heavy metal resistance can increase the plants metal resistance and increase accumulation in the plants that leads to increased efficiency of phytoremediation (Jing et al., 2007; Siddiqui, 2006; Weis & Weis, 2004; Suresh & Ravishankar, 2004)
Phytoremediation is still in the research and development phase, and could be most suitable for developing countries, such as Thailand. However, there are many technical barriers which need to be addressed. Our survey in a zinc mine, Tak province, Thailand, found *Gynura pseudochina* (L.) DC. (Wan-Maha-Kan), a tuber plant in the Genera Asteraceae. It can grow in areas with high zinc and cadmium contamination and highly accumulates the metals. In addition, it can survive all year, both dry and rainy season in Thailand. The plant has a potential to be used in the phytoremediation process. However, the mechanism of zinc and cadmium accumulation have to be made clear before application. This research aimed to study the distribution and chemical speciation of the metals by transmission electron microscopy (TEM), X-ray fluorescence (XRF) imaging and X-ray absorption fine structure (XAFS), using synchrotron light source. The proteins of *G. pseudochina* (L.) DC. involved in the accumulation and tolerance of zinc and cadmium were studied by extraction and separation with SDS-PAGE techniques. A plant growth promoting rhizobacteria (PGPR) from the rhizosphere of *G. pseudochina* (L.) DC. growing in the Zn/Cd contaminated soil was isolated and studied its capability to induce phosphate solubility, nitrogen fixation, IAA and ACC deaminase production. Finally, the phytoremediation byproduct was studied for their utilization as a zinc bio-ore and phytochemical extracts.

## 2. Materials and methods

### 2.1 Plant samples

*Gynura pseudochina* (L.) DC. (Fig.1) is a member of the Asteraceae Family. It is a dicotyledon, with elliptic, coarsely dentate leaves covered with multicellular hairs, and an upright unbranched stem. The tuber has several heads near the stem apex. The flower is a long scape with an orange corolla on a short peduncle and an inferior ovary.

(a) (b) (c)

Fig. 1. Pictures of *Gynura pseudochina* (L.) DC. (a) Leaves, (b) tuber and (c) flower

Cultivation of plants and metal treatment processes were carried out in a tissue culture system to control environment conditions and decrease any effects from microorganism. In addition, propagation and experimentation using tissues derived from the same master plants, avoided the risks of variability among species. The master plant, non-contaminated shoot tips of *G. pseudochina* (L.) DC. were sterilized following the method of Gambrog (1995). The apical bud tissues were sectioned and cultured on MS nutrient agar (Murashige & Skoog, 1962). The apical bud explants were cultured at 25°C under 1,500 lux of light intensity and 12 hours photoperiod for two months. Cuttings with nodal segments from the *in vitro* shoot of *G. pseudochina* (L.) DC. with one or two buds were transferred and culture in a modified MS nutrient agar, containing indole-3-acetic acid (IAA) plus indole-3-butyric acid (IBA) (Cuenca et al., 1999).

### 2.2 Zinc and Cadmium treatment

The healthy plants were selected for Zn and/or Cd treatment under the tissue culture system. The plant samples were separately treated with 2 ml each of zinc solutions of 0 (control), 100, 250, 500, 750 and 1000 mg $l^{-1}$, or treated with 2 ml each of cadmium solutions of 0 (control), 5, 20, 50, 100 and 150 mg $l^{-1}$. The dual treatment of zinc and cadmium was carried out with various zinc concentrations containing 50 mg $l^{-1}$ of cadmium. The zinc and cadmium solutions were prepared from $ZnSO_4{\cdot}7H_2O$ (Ajax Finechem, Australia) and $CdSO_4{\cdot}8H_2O$ (Ajax Finechem, Australia), respectively. After 2 weeks of exposure to the metals, the treated plants were harvested and rinsed with an excess of deionized water before being blotted dry. The leaves were separated and dried at 80°C for 24 hours. A 0.05 g sample of each was digested following the modified method of Miller (1998); socking with 3 ml of 65% v/v $HNO_3$ for 24 hours, then heating at 150°C for 1 hour, before adding 1 ml of 70% (v/v) $HClO_4$ and heating at 215°C for 2 hours, then adding 3 ml of deionised water and boiling at 90°C for 1 hour. The digestion was analysed for zinc concentration by an Atomic Absorption Spectrophotometer (AAS) (Shimadzu AA-680, Japan). The data was analyzed by one-way analysis of variation (ANOVA). The variance and means separation were performed using the Duncan's new multiple range test (DMRT) at $p < 0.05$. Statistical analysis was performed using the SPSS Version 15.0 software program.

### 2.3 Protein samples

**One-dimensional SDS-PAGE**, the crude protein was extracted from the leaves of each treated plant. A 0.1 g (wet weight) of sample was homogenized with 400 µl of phenol extraction buffer (80% saturated phenol, 0.01% (v/v) 2-mercapto-ethanol in 12 mM Tris-HCl pH 8.0, 5 mM EDTA pH 8.0 and 10 mM KCl, pH 8.0) following the method of Sangdee et al. (2003). The crude protein was precipitated from supernatant by adding 5 volume of 100 mM ammonium acetate in 99.9% methanol then incubated at -20°C for 30 min, and centrifuged at 13,000 g for 20 minute. The protein pellet was washed with 99.96% acetone (AnalaR NORMAPUR, France) and resuspended in 50 µl of protein sample buffer (63 mM Tris-HCl pH 6.8, 2% (v/v) SDS, 5% (v/v) mercaptoethanol, 20% (v/v) glycine) and the protein concentration was determined by Bradford's assay (Bradford, 1976). Each 40 µg protein sample was fractionated by polyacrylamide gel electrophoresis, resolving gel 12% and stacking gel 5%, for 2 hours at 20 mA per gel by electrophoresis (MiniVE GE Healthcare Bio-Sciences Corp., USA). The gels were stained with Coomassie Brilliant Blue R-250 staining buffer (Bollag et al., 1996). Molecular weight of protein band was measured based on the molecular weight of two broad range protein markers of 7.1 kDa to 209 kDa and 10 kDa to 250 kDa (prestained SDS-PAGE standard, broad range, Bio-Rad, USA). The expression of proteins in SDS-PAGE was analysed by Quantity One 1-D analysis software program (Bio-Rad, USA).

**Two-dimensional electrophoresis**, a crude protein extract was extracted from the plant leaves (0.2 g) by grinding in a chilled mortar with liquid nitrogen to obtain a fine powder, then 200 µl of lysis buffer (7M urea, 2M Thiourea, 4% CHAPS, 2% IPG buffer pH 3-10, 40 mM dithiothreitol; (DTT)) was added directly to the mortar and continually ground for 30 sec. The extract was separated by centrifugation at 12000g, 4°C for 15 min. The supernatant was cleaned by 2-D Clean-up kit. Each 80 µg protein sample was isoelectric focused (IEF), fractionated on Immobiline DryStrip gel pH 3-7, 7 cm and IPG buffer for 4 hours by an isoelectric focusing electrophoresis (Ettan IPGphor II GE Healthcare, Sweden). The chemicals for 2-DE were ordered from GE Healthcare. After separating by first dimension of IEF, the strip was equilibrated in SDS equilibration buffer (50 mM Tris-HCl pH 8.8, 6 M urea, 30%(v/v) glycerol, 2%(w/v) SDS, 0.002%(w/v) bromophenol blue), before separated in the second dimension on SDS-PAGE with a 12% polyacrylamide gel for 2 hours at 20 mA per gel. The separated protein spots were visualized by silver staining (Bollag et al., 1996).

### 2.4 TEM

The samples for imaging by transmission electron microscopy (TEM) were *G. pseudochina* (L.) DC. treated with 100 mg $l^{-1}$ zinc solution, pH 5.5 ± 0.5 or watered with deionised water (control) for two months. Small sections of stem, leaf and tuber (1 mm length x 1 mm width) were fixed in 2.5-10% glutaraldehyde (v/v) in 0.1 M phosphate buffer at 4°C, pH 7.2 for 24 hours. Samples were washed 3 times for 30 minutes each in phosphate buffer before being postfixed in 1% $OsO_4$ for 2 hours. The postfixed samples were washed with deionised water 3 times for 30 minutes each, then dehydrated by ethanol series (20, 40, 60, 80, and 100%) followed by infiltration with ethanol and Spurs' resin in ratios of 3:1, 1:1 and 1:3 for 24 hours each. Embedding in Spurs' resin and polymerization was carried out at 70°C for 80 hours. Thin slide sections (60-90 nm) were prepared on a grid for viewing by TEM (JEOL JEM 2010, Japan) at an accelerating voltage of 80.0 kV.

### 2.5 XAFS and XRF imaging

Zinc treated plants were subjected to two-dimensional µ-XRF imaging and XAFS analysis. The plant samples were harvested and washed with an excess of running deionised water, before being separated into leaves, stem and tuber. A thin section of the freeze-dried sample was prepared in order to maintain its tissue structure and chemical state. The cross section of the tuber, stem and leaves were cut to a thickness of 200-300 µm using a vertical slicer

(HS-1 JASCO, Japan) and immediately put on dry ice. The sections were freeze-dried overnight using a lyophilizer (Labconco Lyph Lock 6 Freeze Dryer, USA). For bulk XAFS analysis, an amount of each freeze-dried plant part, tuber (medulla and periderm), stem and leaves, were ground and pressed into a pellet before being sealed in a mylar plastic bag (Mylar polyester film, No.100, Chemplex, USA). The whole plant treated with 1,000 mg $l^{-1}$ of Zn solution was used to prepare a crude protein pellet for XAFS analysis.

μ-XRF imaging was performed at beamline 4A, Photon Factory (PF), High Energy Accelerator Research Organization (KEK), and beamline 37XU, SPring-8, Japan. XAFS analysis was performed at beamline 12C, at PF, KEK. The XAFS analysis data was analyzed by Rigaku Rex2000 Version 2.3.2. The analytical chemicals used for reference materials were $Zn(NO_3)_2$, ZnS, $ZnSO_4{\cdot}7H_2O$, $ZnCl_2$ and ZnO. Zn-cellulose (prepared by absorption system) and Zn-cysthein (prepared by absorption system) were measured as reference materials.

## 2.6 Microbial isolation

A soil sample was collected from the rhizosphere of *G. pseudochina* (L.) DC., growing in zinc and cadmium contaminated areas. The soil sample was suspended in sterile distilled water. Bacterial isolation was carried out by spread plate techniques on nutrient agar (NA) containing Zn and/or Cd of 5, 10, 15 and 20 mg $l^{-1}$. The plates were incubated at 30°C for 3 days. Colonies with different characteristics from the Zn and/or Cd containing agar plate were picked and further isolated to single colonies on Nutrient agar containing Zn and/or Cd according to their resistant metal concentration. The isolates were given code names, for example, PDMZnCd2003 (PDM-Phadeand mining; ZnCd-agar containing Zn and Cd; 20-concentration of heavy metals in agar (mg $l^{-1}$); 03-isolate number). All bacterial isolates were Gram stained and endospore stained to confirm each isolates was not the same and pre-grouped the isolates. The isolates containing the properties of Zn/Cd tolerance and plant growth promoting were identified by API 20E biochemical test (Koneman et al., 1997) and genetic characterization.

**Genetic characterization:** Total genomic DNA of selected isolate was extracted by a modified phenol: chloroform procedure of Sambrook & Russel's (2001). Two primers of fD1 (5'-AGAGTTTGATCCTGGCTCAG-3') and rP2 (5'-ACGGCTACCTTGTTACGACTT-3') (Weisburg et al., 1991) were used for 16S rDNA (ribosomal Deoxyribonucleic acid) amplification, and nif H-F (5'-AAAGGYGGWATCGGYAARTCCACCAC-3') and nif H-R (5'-TTGTTSGCSGCRTACATSGCCATCAT-3') primer pairs (Torok et al., 1981) were used for *nif* gene amplification. Each 50 μl of polymerase chain reaction (PCR) reaction contained: 100 ng of purified total DNA, 0.2 mM of each diethylnitrophenyl thiophosphate (dNTP), 5 unit of Tag DNA polymerase (Invitrogen, USA) in 5 μL of 10x Tag buffer, 1 mM $MgCl_2$, 0.2 mM of each primer, and 35 μl sterile deionized water. Thermalcycling program for 16S rDNA amplification consisted of 1 cycle of 94°C for 5 min (denaturation), 57°C for 2 min (annealing for fD1 and rP2) and 72°C for 2 min (extension), and 29 cycles of 94°C for 2 min, 57°C for 30 sec and 72°C for 2 min, with a final elongation cycle of 72°C for 10 min (Wood et al., 1998). Amplification of *nif* gene was carried out under the thermalcycling program of 35 cycles of 94°C for 5 min, 54°C for 1 min (annealing for nif H-F and nif H-R) and 72°C for 1 min, with a final elongation cycle of 72°C for 10 min (Zehr et al., 1989). The PCR products obtained were purified with a HiYield™ Gel/PCR DNA Fragments extraction kit (Real Biotech Corporation, Taiwan) and cloned into the pGEM-T-Easy vector (Promega, Madison, Wis.) according to the protocols of the manufacturers. The plasmids were transformed into competent *E. coli* JM109 by transformation and storage solution (TSS) method (Chung & Miller, 1993). Sequencing was performed on an 3730XL DNA sequencer, monitoring the whole experimental process through Laboratory Information Magement System (LIMS), Macrogen Inc, Korea. Sequence data of 16S rDNA (1500 bp) and *nif* gene (700 bp) were compared with sequences in the National Center for Biotechnology Information data bank using the BLAST program (Altschul et al., 1997).

### 2.7 Study the plant growth promoting (PGPB) properties

All bacteria were screened for their plant growth promoting properties as measured by their IAA and ACC deaminase production, $N_2$ fixation, and phosphate solubilisation. The isolates that exhibited high heavy metal tolerance and showed plant growth promoting properties were subjected to quantitative analysis.

***IAA production:*** Bacteria were cultured in Trypticase soya broth (TSB) containing 0.2% w/v tryptophan and were incubated in the dark at 30°C for 48 hours at 150 rpm by an incubated shaker (Innova 2100 Platform shaker, New Brunswick Scientific, USA). The cultures were then centrifuged at 6,000 rpm for 15 minutes at 4°C by a refrigerator centrifuge (MX-301, TOMY, USA). The supernatants were mixed with Salkowski's reagent (ratio 2:1) and left in the dark for 20 min. The optical density was measured at an absorbance of 530 nm (Bric et al., 1991). The IAA concentration was determined by using a standard curve of authentic IAA (Sigma-Aldrich, St. Louis, MO, USA).

***$N_2$ fixation:*** One loop of each bacterial culture (24 hours old) was spotted onto N-Free agar containing 0.0025 % w/v bromothymol blue and incubated for between 1-7 days. Isolates that showed growth within 7 days and intensified the color of bromotymol blue around the colony were considered to be $N_2$-fixation bacteria. To measure quantity, bacteria were inoculated into N-free malate medium and incubated for 72 hours while being shaken. The cultures were then centrifuged at 6,000 rpm for 15 minutes at 4°C. Ammonia nitrogen ($NH_3$-N), an inorganic dissolved form of nitrogen, in the supernatant was quantitatively analysed with Nessler's reagent as described by Cappuccino & Sherman (1992). The amount of $NH_3$-H was measured against a standard curve of ammonium choride ($NH_4Cl$) (Ajax Finechem Pty Ltd, Australia).

***Phosphate solubilisation:*** One loop of each bacterial culture (24 hours old) was streaked onto NBRIP (National Botanical Research Institute's phosphate growth) agar. After incubation for 7 days, the clear zone around each colony that indicated phosphate-solubilisation was observed. The amount of soluble phosphate was measured. Bacteria were inoculated in NBRIP medium consisting of 0.5% w/v Tricalcium phosphate and incubated aerobically on a rotary shaker for 72 hours. Bacterial cultures were centrifuged at 6,000 rpm for 15 minutes at 4°C. Soluble phosphate in the supernatant was measured by the modified ascorbic acid method of APHA, AWWA (Clesceri et al., 1998). Concentration of soluble phosphate was determined against a standard curve of potassium dihydrogen phosphste ($KH_2PO_4$) (Ajax Finechem Pty Ltd, Australia).

***ACC deaminase activity:*** Bacteria were grown in TSB until late log phase and harvested by centrifugation at 6000 rpm at 4°C. Cell pellets were washed twice with DF-salt medium (Dworkin and Foster, 1958) and resuspended in DF-salt medium. The suspended cells were then added to a DF-salt medium containing 3 mM of ACC as the sole N- source and shaken at 200 rpm for 72 hours. ACC deaminase activity was measured by following the method of Penrose and Glick (Penrose & Glick, 2003).

### 2.8 Utilisation of phytoremediation by-product

The zinc accumulative plant was dried and pyrolysed in a furnace at 550°C for 4 hours to obtain ash. The 98% (v/v) sulphuric acid ($H_2SO_4$), which is used in zinc mining, was used to extract zinc from the ash. In addition, the phytochemical extraction from leaves of *G. pseudochina* (L.) DC. and the antioxidant property were studied to support a sustainable development in the zinc contaminated area. The plant from a non-contaminated side was studied in the extraction and basis data of phytochemicals. The extracts were investigated in total phenolic content (TPC) (Liu et al., 2008), total flavonoid (TF) (Yoo et al., 2008), free radical scavenging activity (FRSA) (Cotelle et al., 1996), and high-performance liquid chromatography (HPLC) by modified of the conditions of Zuo et al. (2002). Then the extracts of plants grown in zinc contaminated soil were measured to determine the possibility of zinc contaminating the extracts.

## 3. Results and discussion

### 3.1 Zinc accumulation

The concentration of zinc in *G. pseudochina* (L.) DC. leaves increased with increasing Zn levels in the treatment solution (0, 100, 250, 500 and 750 mg $l^{-1}$). The accumulations of Zn in the leaves of treated plants were 0.2-4.2 mg Zn $g^{-1}$ dry wt. (Fig. 2(a)). The plants dually treated with various zinc concentrations and 50 mg $l^{-1}$ of cadmium resulted to lower Zn accumulation in a range of 0.1-3.1 mg Zn $g^{-1}$ dry wt. (Fig. 2 (b)), compared with only Zn treatment. The amounts of Cd accumulated in treated plants' leaves are shown in Fig.2(c), the Cd level significantly increased with the increasing concentration of Cd ($p < 0.05$, $n$=8). The accumulations of Cd in the leaves of treated plants were 0.1-0.6 mg Cd $g^{-1}$ dry wt. The Cd concentration in the leaves when dually treated with various zinc concentrations and 50 mg $l^{-1}$ of cadmium resulted in higher Cd accumulation in a range of 1.0-1.5 mg Cd $g^{-1}$ dry wt. (Fig. 2(d)). The high accumulation of Zn and Cd in the leaves and the shoot, indicated the potential for application in phytoremediation (Reeves & Baker, 2000). The increase in zinc and cadmium accumulation when treated with higher concentrations of the metals was found in wheat plants, *Triticum aestivum* L.cv Klein Atalaya (Santa-Maria & Cogliatti, 1998), *Linum usitatissimum* (Chakravarty & Srivastava, 1997), gray mangrove *Avicennia marina* (Forsk.) Vierh (MacFarlane & Burchett, 2002), *Sedum afredii* (Li et al., 2006), *Brassica juncea* (Maruthi Sridhar et al., 2005), and *Potentilla griffithii* (Hu et al., 2009). The net Zn-uptake rate increased as the Zn-concentration in the growth solution increased, because the greater the external concentration of Zn, the higher were both Zn-influx and Zn-efflux (Santa-Maria & Cogliatti, 1998). In addition, the enhancement of Cd uptake under dually Zn and Cd treatment might be attributed to an altered and specialized transporter of metal ions in the plasma membrane system induced by the addition of Zn (Ebbs et al., 2009).

### 3.2 Distribution and speciation of Zn

Ultra structure studied by transmission electron microscope (TEM) showed zinc treatment might be responsible for the rough cell walls observed in stem tissues (Fig. 3(b)), and the stoma of chloroplast in leaves containing starch grains and plastoglobule (Fig. 3(d)). The rough cell walls occurred in *B. juncea* and *Armeria maritime*, when they were treated with a high zinc concentration (Maruthi Sridhar et al., 2005; Heumann, 2002). However, the complete chloroplast, containing starch grains and plastoglobule, implied that the plants still had photosynthesis system under zinc treatment (Dimassi-Theriou & Bosabalidis, 1997; Kessler & Vidi, 2007).

Conventional methods for preparation TEM samples use many chemicals to fix organelles that may cause the loss of some zinc and cadmium accumulated in plant tissues (Davies et al., 1991; Vázquez et al., 1992). In addition, using osmium tetroxide for lipid fixation caused to Os Lα signal that annoyed Zn Kα signal when measuring with TEM connecting to Energy dispersive spectroscopy (EDX) (Panitlertumpai et al., 2008). Although the zinc distribution could be due to precipitation of zinc into the tissues as zinc sulfide (ZnS) (Sarret et al., 2001; Heumann, 2002), the distribution of zinc might not reflect the real situation occurring in the plant.

Synchrotron base μ-XAS imaging shows that zinc and cadmium were transported from the root to the vascular ring of the tuber via the symplast system (Fig. 4(a)), and were then transported to the stem and leaves via the vascular bundle (Fig. 4). The combination of the

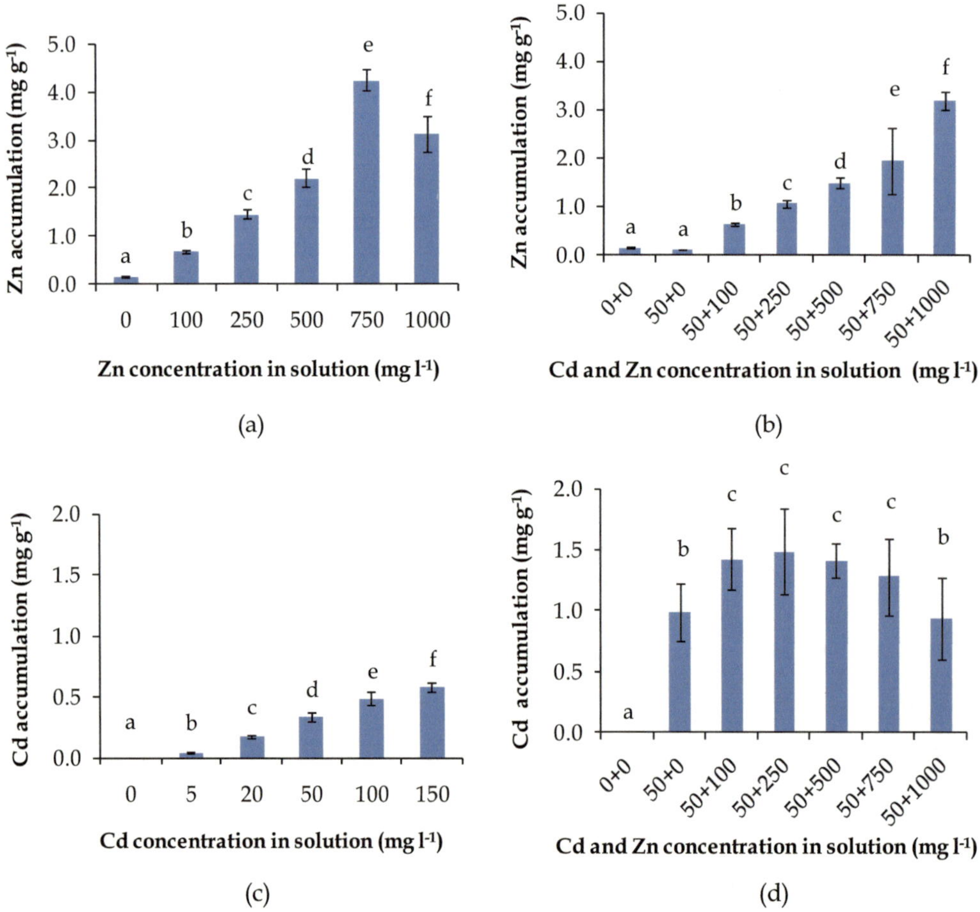


Fig. 2. Zinc and cadmium accumulation in the leaves of *G. pseudochina* (L.) DC., (a) zinc accumulation when treated with various concentrations of zinc, and (b) dually treated with various zinc concentrations and 50 mg l-1 of cadmium, (c) cadmium accumulation when treated with various concentrations of cadmium, and (d) dually treated with various zinc concentrations and 50 mg l-1 of cadmium. Means with different letters are significantly different ($p < 0.05$, Duncan's test), $n$=8.

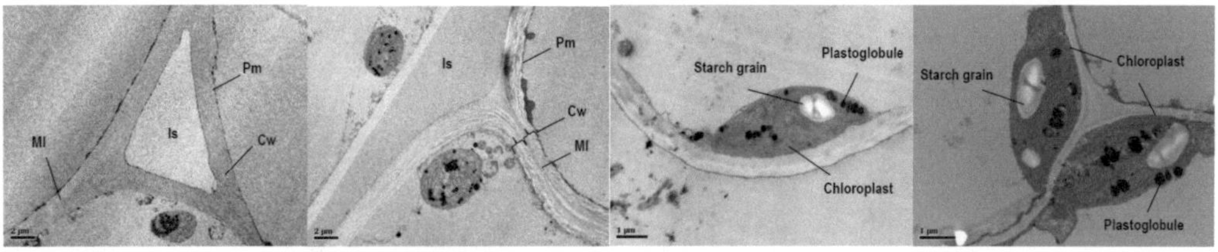


(a) (b) (c) (d)

Fig. 3. TEM images of micro-structures of stem and leaf tissues of *G. pseudochina* (L.) DC. treated with 100 mg $l^{-1}$ zinc solution (treatment) and deionised water (control). (a) stem tissues of control plant, (b) stem tissues of treated plant, (c) leaf tissues of control plant, and (d) leaf tissues of treated plant. (Is, intercellular space; Ml, middle lamella; Pm, plasma membrane; Cw, cell wall).

apoplast and symplast systems probably explained the distribution of zinc and cadmium (Karley et al., 2000). The distribution of zinc and cadmium in the stem cross section (Fig. 4 (b)) indicates major accumulated in the cortex, especially the purple colour of the parenchyma cell containing anthocyanin. The zinc and cadmium signal in the leaf cross section (Fig. 4 (c)) confirmed the transportation of zinc and cadmium from stem to leaves via xylem and vein. The relative Zn and Cd content was higher in the vein and epidermis (Fig. 4) including trichome (Fig. 5). The plant treated with a zinc concentration of 100 mg $l^{-1}$ showed the accumulation of zinc mainly in the epidermis cells (Fig.5 (b)). While treatment with a high zinc concentration of 1000 mg $l^{-1}$ showed the accumulation of zinc in trichome (Fig.5 (a)). The distribution of Zn, Fe, Cu and Mn was in the same area, whereas the distribution of K and Ca was throughout the tissues of the stem and leaves (data not shown).

Zn also hydrolyzes at pH > 7.7, resulting in hydrolyzed species that were strongly sorbed and also easily transferred in plants (Alvarez & Illman, 2006; Cheng, 2003). Zn is mainly in the acid soluble form, which is hard to be transferred in crops. The main parts of Zn in plants were seen to be low molecular weight compounds, metal proteins and free Zn, while less insoluble portions were seen to have combined with the cell wall. 58-91% of the zinc in plants was not soluble and played an important role in the physiological activities of the plant (Cheng, 2003).

### 3.3 Protein pattern

The majority of research in this area has focused so far on genes whose protein products are involved in the uptake and accumulation of metals. To investigate the effect of zinc and cadmium on the protein patterns, the crude protein extracted from the leaves of Zn and Cd treated *G. pseudochina* (L.) DC. were separated by one-dimensional SDS–PAGE. The visible differences in new and stronger protein band patterns were observed when compared with the protein pattern of control plant (0 mg metals $l^{-1}$). The protein bands of 43, 46.4, 120 and 160 kDa were observed in the Zn-treated samples, the protein band patterns as shown in Fig. 6 (a). Cd induced the synthesis of a 12.7 kDa protein (Fig. 6(b)). While, Fig. 6 (c) shows that 43 and 70 kDa proteins were induced by a combined treatment of Zn and Cd. Phytochelatins (1.5-4 kDa) and metallothioneins (8-14 kDa) have been reported to be responsible for metal tolerance in many plants (Grill et al., 1989). The expression of 70 kDa heat shock protein (hsp 70) under cadmium stress was found in *Lycopersicon peruvianum* cell culture (Neumann et al., 1994), the root of maize (*Zea may* L.) (Reddy & Prasad, 1993), and rice (*Oryza sativa* L.) (Raddy et al., 1995). Reddy and Prasad (1993) also used an *in vitro*

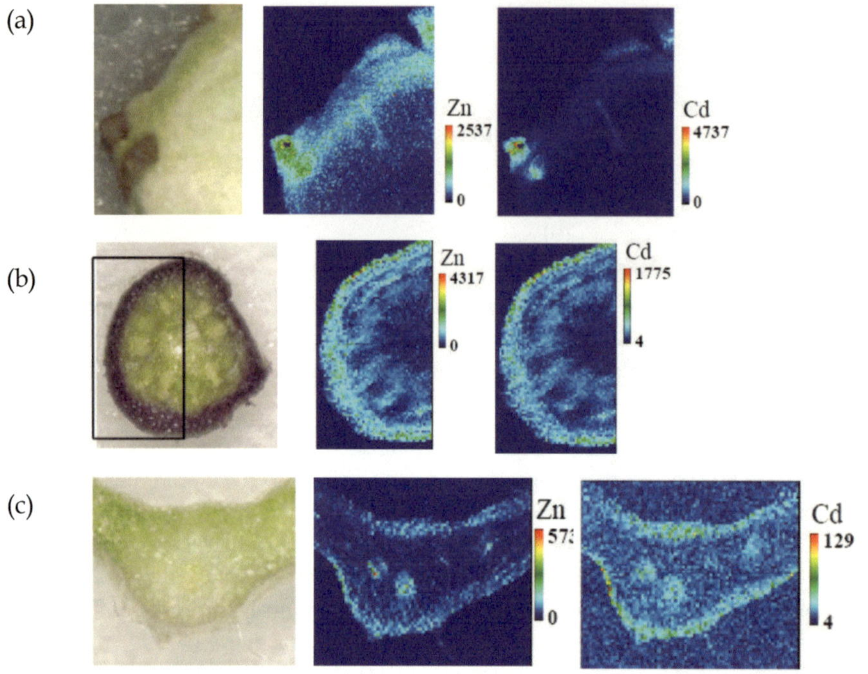


Fig. 4. μ-XRF imaging for zinc and cadmium of (a) tuber, (b) stem and (c) leaf. The red colour depicting elemental concentrations in each map are scaled to the maximum value for that map.

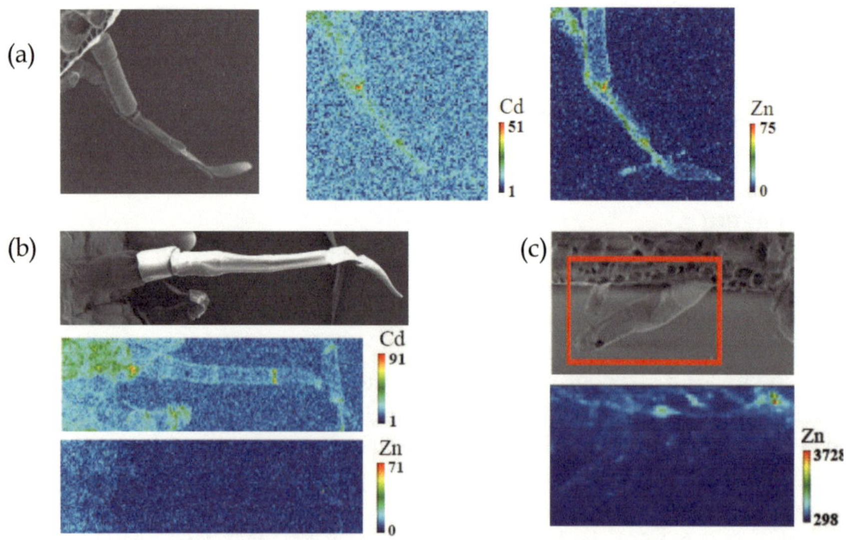


Fig. 5. μ-XRF imaging for zinc and cadmium distribution in leaves' trichomes of *G. pseudochina* (L.) DC. treated with (a) 1000 mg $l^{-1}$ zinc and 50 mg $l^{-1}$ cadmium, (b) 50 mg $l^{-1}$ cadmium, and (c) 100 mg $l^{-1}$ zinc. The red colour depicting elemental concentrations in each map are scaled to the maximum value for that map.

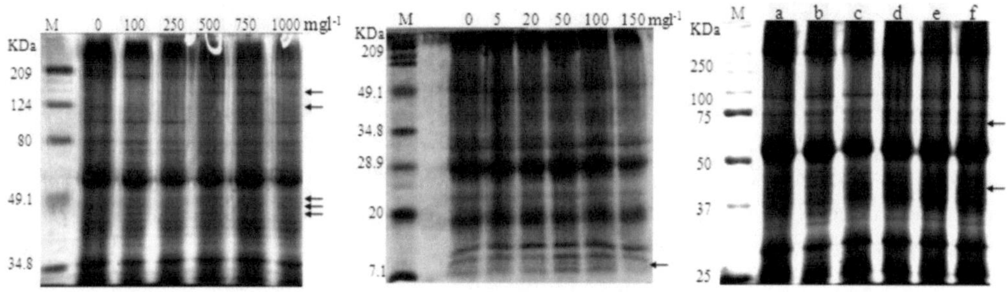


(a) (b) (c)

Fig. 6. SDS-polyacrylamide gel electrophoresis of the Zn and/or Cd treated *G. pseudochina* (L.) DC.'s leaves proteins. (a) the plants' leaves treated with various zinc concentrations, (b) treated with various cadmium concentrations, and (c) treated with various zinc concentrations and 50 mgl-1 of cadmium (Lane a= 0+0; b= 100+50; c= 250+50; d= 500+50; e= 750+50 and f= 1000+50 mg $l^{-1}$)

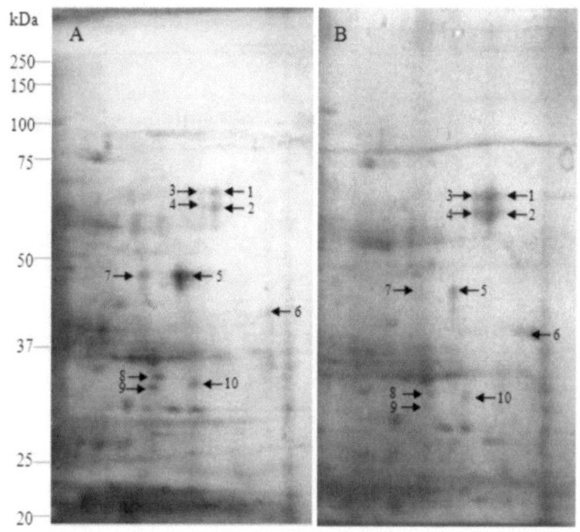


Fig. 7. Two-dimensional polyacrylamide gel electrophoresis (2D-PAGE) images of *G. pseudochina* (L.) DC. leaves protein extracts of (a) control plants, and (b) plants treatment with 50 mg $l^{-1}$ cadmium.

phosphorylation assay to show that the hsp70 was a phosphoprotein. The changes in protein patterns were analyzed by 2-dimensional gel electrophoresis (2-DE) for better separation and characterization. Ten protein spots were found to be differentially expressed in response to cadmium treatment, five proteins were markedly up-regulated (sport no. 1–4 and 6) and five proteins were down-regulated (spot no. 5 and 7-10) as shown in Fig. 7. However, the protein spots have still to be further identified by mass spectroscopy. A Cd-binding complex (Cd-BC) was isolated and purified from roots of wheat (*Triticum aestivum* L.), the molecular weight was around 10 kDa, and the composition of Glu/Gln, Cys and Gly was 4:4:1 (Cheng, 2003).

### 3.3 Speciation of Zn accumulation

The curve fitting of EXAFS oscillation yielding the coordination number (*N*) and inter atomic distance (*R*) are shown in Table 2. EXAFS structure of Zn K-edge accumulated in plant tissue was analysed in the first shell. The results showed that Zn(II) in the periderm of tuber treated with zinc was coordinated by 4.9 atoms of O with radius 2.05 A°, cellulose and pectin were the main constituents of the oxygen ligand. Zn(II) in the medulla of the tuber treated with zinc was coordinated by 2.3 atoms of O with radius 2.06 A°, cellulose was the main constituent of the oxygen ligand. In addition, there was more than one species of zinc binding with O from other sources. Zn(II) in the stem of plant treated with zinc was coordinated by 4.2 atoms of O with radius 2.14 A°, citrate and malate were the main constituents of the oxygen ligand as Zn-citrate, *N* 4.3, *R* 2.03 A° and Zn-malate, *N* 4.2, *R* 2.01 A° (Kelly et al, 2002; Straczek et al, 2008). Zn-S was coordinated by 2.4-3.1 atoms of S with radius 2.1-2.3 A°, cysteine was the main constituent of the sulfur and oxygen ligand as Zn-cysteine, *N* 4-4.5, *R* 2.34-2.35 A° (Kelly et al, 2002; Straczek et al, 2008). In addition, Zn was bound by 2.3-2.9 atoms of Cl with radius 2.1-2.3 A°. Cases of Zn-Cl have not been reported. That implied that Zn might be easily separated from Cl and dissolved as $Zn^{2+}$ ion. Therefore, the shoot parts of plants growing as zinc hyperaccumulators in the phytoremediation process should be harvested within 2 months or before falling of the leaves to prevent discharge of zinc into the environment.

| Sample | Atom type, first shell | *N* | *R* (Å) |
|---|---|---|---|
| *Model:* | | | |
| ZnS | S | 5.0 | 2.34 |
| $Zn(NO_3)_2$ | O | 6.9 | 2.09 |
| $ZnSO_4$ $7H_2O$ | O | 5.6 | 2.08 |
| $Zn(CH_3COO)_2$ | O | 2.6 | 2.06 |
| $ZnCl_2$ | Cl | 5.1 | 2.17 |
| ZnO | O | 4.4 | 1.99 |
| Zn-cellulose | O | 5.9 | 2.09 |
| Zn-cysteine | O | 4.5 | 2.11 |
| | S | 4.1 | 2.24 |
| *Sample:* | | | |
| Zn tuber-out (periderm) | O | 4.9 | 2.05 |
| Zn tuber-in (medulla) | O | 2.3 | 2.06 |
| Zn leave | O | 4.4 | 2.12 |
| | S | 3.1 | 2.23 |
| | Cl | 2.9 | 2.21 |
| Zn leave (*in vivo*) | O | 3.3 | 2.62 |
| | S | 2.6 | 2.13 |
| | Cl | 2.4 | 2.12 |
| Zn stem | O | 4.2 | 2.14 |
| Zn protein | S | 1.3 | 2.31 |

Table 2. EXAFS fitting of the reference Zn-compounds and Zn in plant samples, showing bond, coordination number (*N*) and atomic radius (*R*)(Å).

XANES spectrum of zinc on protein indicated that zinc in protein was possibly ZnS (81% fitting) and ZnO (19% fitting). The curve fittings of EXAFS oscillation are shown in Table 2. The results obtained for the first Zn-S coordination shell were 1.3 (*N*), 2.31A°(*R*). However, the first Zn-S coordination is limited by the number of free sulfur atoms on the protein and lower coordination numbers of ZnS might be due to our methodology which used a reducing agent such as mercaptoethanol ($HOCH_2CH_2SH$). It has the ability to cleave disulfide bonds so it might be decreasing the number of sulfur ligands on the protein of *G. pseudochina* (L.) DC. Ideal geometrics of zinc forms four, five and six coordinate complexes by Tetrahedral, Trigonal Bipyramidal, Square Pyramidal and Octahedral, respectively (Patel et al., 2007). Zinc was bound into cysteine residue and histidine complex by coordination of S, O and N atoms (Bracey et al., 1994). In addition, Yu et al., (2008) reported that the formation of a stable Zn tetrahedral configuration with four sulfur ligands on a protein of KTI11. Therefore, the results indicated that Zn-S coordination in the first shell for proteins of *G. pseudochina* (L.) DC. by the amino acids containing sulfur groups might be involved in zinc binding proteins such as protein content a mainly of cysteine residue and histidine. Therefore, these results indicate that protein patterns of our experiment might be zinc binding proteins.

### 3.4 PGPB properties of Zn and Cd tolerance isolates

The number of bacteria isolated from the rhizosphere of *G. pseudochina* (L.) DC). growing in zinc and cadmium contaminated soil in a zinc mining area, Phatat Phadaeng sub-distric, Mae sot, Tak province, Thailand, were 34 isolates (they were divided by NA agar plates containing Zn, Cd and Zn+Cd as 18, 10 and 6 isolates, respectively). 25 isolates were gram negative bacteria and 9 isolates were gram positive bacteria. The results indicated that 75% of the isolates were gram negative bacteria. That might be due to the cell wall structures of gram negative bacteria which are more complex and resulted in many functions to help survival in extreme environments when compared to gram positive bacteria (Willey et al., 2009; Ahmad et al., 2008). However, it depends on the kind of heavy metal, as Abou-shanab et al. (2007) found the genes that control Hg, Zn, Cr and Ni tolerance in both gram negative and positive bacteria. In nature, metal resistance-gene transformations can occur between bacteria and this mechanism is the main mechanism for bacterial resistance.

**Plant growth-promoting abilities of bacteria:** From the 34 isolates, there were 24, 24 and 15 isolates of bacteria had the properties of IAA production, $N_2$-fixation and phosphate solubilisation, respectively. The number of IAA producing and $N_2$-fixing bacteria was more than the number of phosphate solubilising bacteria. In addition, 20 isolates contained the properties of $N_2$-fixation and IAA production. These results suggested that IAA production and nitrogen fixation in free-living bacteria could be the major mechanisms needed to associate with the host plants. The large amount of IAA producing and $N_2$-fixing bacteria could be related to their plant colonization due to the mutaulism relationship between plants and bacteria (Siddiqui., 2006). For instance IAA-producing bacteria obtained tryptophan that produced by plants as an IAA precursor (Spaepen et al., 2007).

Four isolates capable of IAA production, nitrogen fixation and phosphate solubilisation were chosen for quantitative analysis of IAA production, nitrogen fixation, phosphate solubilisation and ACC deaminase activity. Table 3 shows that 4 isolates produced large amounts of IAA. The large concentration of IAA produced by IAA producing bacterial isolates might support the growth of *G. pseudochina* (L.) DC. Although, ACC deaminase production was less than that detection by measuring the amount by the α-ketobutyrate production method. High IAA production implied their ability to product ACC deaminase. The results indicated that these 4 isolates have multiple properties to promote plant growth.

| Isolates | IAA (mg $l^{-1}$) | N as $NH_3$-N (mg $l^{-1}$) | P as $KH_2PO_4$ (mg $l^{-1}$) | ACC deaminase (unit $ml^{-1}$) |
|---|---|---|---|---|
| PDMZn2008 | 275.3 | 16.2 | 13.9 | N/D |
| PDMCd0501 | 249.7 | 18.9 | 9.6 | N/D |
| PDMCd2007 | 311.3 | 12.5 | 7.5 | N/D |
| PDMZnCd2003 | 294.3 | 23.5 | 10.5 | N/D |

*N/D, not detectable

Table 3. IAA production, nitrogen fixation, phosphate solubilisation and ACC deaminase of the bacterial isolates

*Identification of bacteria*

The isolate PDMZnCd2003 was chosen for identification because of its tolerance to high concentrations of Zn and Cd (20 mg $l^{-1}$ of Zn and Cd) and its ability to produce IAA, fix nitrogen, and solubilise phosphate (Table 3). In addition, PDMZnCd2003 produced fluorescent pigments when cultured in Cd-containing medium. It is very interesting because it may be a siderophores with chelating agents for holding heavy metal ions. Moreover it could demonstrate other plant growth promoting properties that we did not test for in this study. The results of API 20E biochemical test identified that PDMZnCd2003 could possibly be *Pseudomonas aeruginosa*. The 16S rDNA and *nif* gene sequences of the isolate were compared with the sequence in Genbank according to the BLAST search tool. The organism identified from the matched sequences was *P. aeruginosa*. In addition, *Pseudomonas* sp. have been reported on heavy metals and to have chemical stress characteristics, while the bacterium has been suggested for improving phytoremediation process previously (Rajkumar &Freitas, 2008; Abou-shanab et al., 2008; Robinson et al., 2001). *P. aeruginosa* showed uranium accumulated by both passive diffusion and, in some instances, by a metabolism-dependent translocation process (Hughes & Poole, 1989; Strandberg et al., 1981), and the *Pseudomonas putida* GAM-1 was isolated as a $Cd^{2+}$-resistant gram-negative bacterium (Horitsu et al., 1986).

### 3.5 Utilization of Zn phytoremediation by product

Zinc was completely extracted from the ash of phytoremediation by-products using sulphuric acid. Therefore, the application of zinc phytoremediated by *G. psuedochina* (L.) DC. could be processed in the hydrometallurgy of zinc ore mining.

For phytochemical extracts from *G. pseudochina* (L.) DC., an extraction in a column system was carried out by a series of solvents which were hexane, ethanol, 99.8% methanol and 50% methanol, in that order. Total phenolic content (TPC) in the series of leaf extracts by hexane, ethanol, 99.8% methanol and 50% methanol were 0.74 ± 0.18, 7.94 ± 0.18, 10.24 ± 0.33 and 25.78 mg GA $g^{-1}$ dry wt., respectively. Total flavonoid (TF) in the series of leaf extracts by hexane, ethanol, 98.9% methanol and 50% methanol were 8.43 ± 7.15, 54.07, 89.07 and 138.3

mg QE $g^{-1}$ dry wt., respectively. The inhibitory concentration ($IC_{50}$) of leaves extracted by ethanol, 99.8% methanol and 50% methanol were 0.0002, 0.0028 ± 0.0001 and 0.0040 mg GA $g^{-1}$ ml reaction, respectively. The small $IC_{50}$ values indicated that the extract contained high antioxidant compounds. The HPLC chromatogram (Fig.8) shows that the most common compounds in all extracts were caffeic acid, epicatechin, rutin, myricetin, quercetin and kaempferol. The contents of rutin and myricetin were the highest in leaf extracts by ethanol as 16,592.2 ± 5216.9 and 3228.1 ± 1362.5 μg $g^{-1}$ dry wt., respectively. Whereas, the amounts of epicatechin and vanillin were highest, in leaves extracted by 50% methanol as 3592.4 ± 670.4 and 66.0 μg $g^{-1}$ dry wt., respectively. Consequently, all results clearly showed that the amount of TPC, TF and the structure of phenolic compounds in the extracts related to their free radical scavenging activity. Moreover, the leaf extracts of plants grown in zinc contaminated soil contained 0.007 ± 0.001 mg in 5 ml of methanol, which was 4% of the zinc accumulated in the leaves. In which, the zinc contaminant was within the legal level for human consumption. However, the application of *G. psuedochina* (L.) DC., growing in the zinc mine in Tak province, Thailand, which has been reported to be contaminated with both zinc (100-8,036 mg $kg^{-1}$) and cadmium (0.5-284 mg $kg^{-1}$) (Simmons et al., 2005), should be more concerned with cadmium toxicity in the biomass and by product.

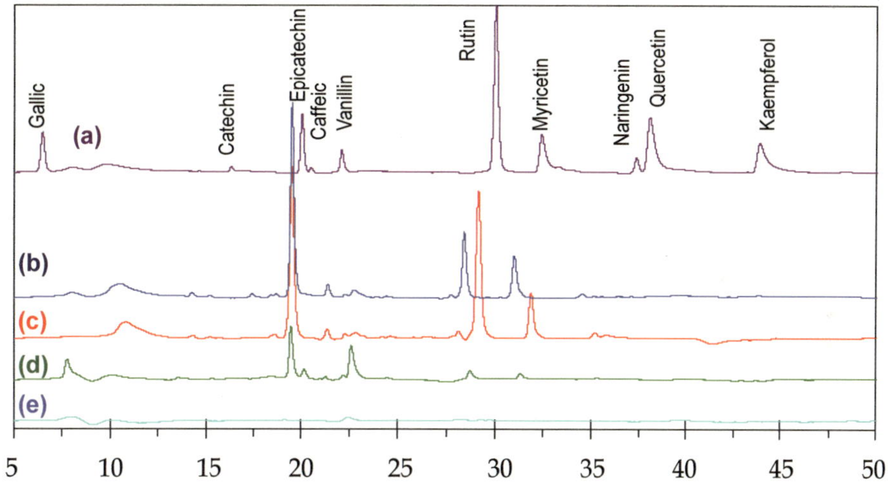


Fig. 8. HPLC chromatogram of (a) standards of polyphenol, and leaves extracts by (b) methanol, (c) ethanol, (d) 50% methanol, and (e) hexane.

## 4. Conclusions

Phytoremediation is an environmental friendly method to remediate contaminated areas. However, the mechanism of the metal accumulated in the plant should be clearly studied before application. The bacterial rhizosphere, which can stand the toxicity of the metal and contain plant growth promoting properties, should be identified to promote plant growth. Moreover, the utilization of phytoremediation byproducts have to be determined to convince people to accept the plant for accumulating toxic metals. A case study of *G. pseudochina* (L.) DC., growing in a Zn/Cd contaminated area of a zinc mine, showed that the plant has properties to be a zinc hyperaccumulator in Thailand. The mechanism of zinc accumulation involved the complexation of zinc with organocompounds, such as cellulose, anthocyanin and sulfur protein. The possible $ZnCl_2$ complex in the plant indicated that the shoot parts of the zinc accumulative plant should be harvested before falling of leaves. The bacteria isolated from the plant's rhizosphere that contained plant growth promoting properties and could grow in Zn and Cd was *Pseudomonas aeruginosa* PDMZnCd2003. The bacterium could be used to promote growth of *G. pseudochina* (L.) DC. during the phytoremediation process. Finally, for application, the polyphenolic compounds containing antioxidant properties could be extracted from the plant's leaves, then unneeded biomass should be turned to ash in an incinerator before zinc extracted using sulphuric acid as in the mining process.

## 5. Acknowledgement

Nakbanpote, W. would like to thank Synchrotron Light Research Institute (Public Organization) (GRANT 1-2549/LS01 and GS-52-M07) and Thailand Research Fund (DBG5080016) for financial support, and be grateful for ASEA-uninet (one month research scholarship) and Prof. Dr. Klaus Stolze, Molecular Pharmacology and Toxicology Unit, Department of Biomedical Sciences, University of Veterinary Medicine, Vienna, for helping in HPLC analysis. The research facilities at beamline 4A and 12C were supported by Photon Factory (PF), High Energy Accelerator Research Organization (KEK), Tsukuba, Japan according to proposal number 2008G633, and we gratefully appreciate Prof. Dr. Izumi Nakai, Assoc. Prof. Dr. Akiko Hokura, Assist. Dr.Kriengkamol Tantrakarn, and Nakai's laboratory, Tokyo University of Science, Japan, for helping research at PF and SPring-8. Natthawoot, P. gratefully thanks Junior Science Talent Project, National Science and Technology Development Agency, for grant JSTP-01-48-02R. Meesungneon, O. gratefully thanks Young Scientist and Technologist Programs, NSTDA (YSTP SP51-BT21), and National Synchrotron Research centre (GS-52-M07). Kannika, S. grateful thanks TRF Master Research Grants: TRF-MAG (MRG-WII515S097).

## 6. References

Abou-Shanab, R.A.I.; van Berkum, P. & Angle, J.S. (2007). Heavy metal resistance and genotypic analysis of metal resistance genes in gram-positive and gram-negative bacteria present in Ni-rich serpentine soil and in the rhizosphere of *Alysum murale*. *Chemosphere*, 68, 2, 360-367. ISSN: 0045-6535

Abou-Shanab, R. A.; Ghanem, K.; Ghanem, N. & Al-Kolaibe, A. (2008). The role of bacteria on heavy-metal extraction and uptake by plants growing on multi-metal-contaminated soils. World Journal of Microbiology & Biotechnology, 24, 2, 253-262. ISSN: 1573-0972

Altschul, S.F.; Madden, T.L.; Schaffer, A.A.; Zhang, J.; Zhang, Z.; Miller, W. & Lipman, D.J. (1997) Gapped BLAST and PSI-BLAST: a new generation of protein database search programs. *Nucleic acids Research*, 25, 17, 3389-3402. ISSN: 1362-4962

Alvarez, P.J.J. & Illman, W.A. (2006). *Bioremediation and natural attenuation: process fundamentals and mathematical models*, John Wiley & Sons, ISBN-13 978-0-471-65043-0, New Jersey.

Ahmad, F.; Ahmad, I. & Khan, M.S. (2008). Screening of free-living rhizospheric bacteria for their multiple plant growth promoting activities. *Microbiological Research*, 163, 2, 173-181. ISSN: 0944-5013

Anderson, C.W.N.; Brooks, R.R.; Chiarucci, A.; LaCoste, C.J.; Leblanc, M.; Robinson, B.H.; Simcock, R. & Stewart, R.B. (1999). Phytomining for nickel, thallium and gold, *Journal of Geochemical Exploration*, 67, 1-3, 407-415, ISSN: 0375-6742

Bollag, D.M.; Rozycki, M.D. & Edelstein, S.J. (1996). *Protein method*, Wiley-Liss, ISBN: 0-471-11837-0, New York.

Bradford, M.M. (1976). A rapid and sensitive method for the quantitation of microgram quantities of protein utilizing the principle of protein-dye binding, *Analytical Biochemistry*, 72, 1-2, 248-254. ISSN: 0003-2697

Bracey, M.H.; Christiansen, J.; Tovar, P.; Cramer, S.P. & Bartlett, S.G. (1994). Spinach carbonic anhydrase: Investigation of the zinc-binding ligands by site-directed mutagenesis, elemental analysis, and EXAFS. *Biochemistry*, 33, 44, 13126-13131. ISSN: 1520-4995

Bric, J.M.; Bostock, R.M. & Silversone, S.E. (1991). Rapid in situ assay for indole acetic acid production by bacteria immobilization on a nitrocellulose membrane. *Applied and Environmental Microbiology*, 57, 2, 535–538. ISSN: 1098-5336

Callahan, D.; Baker, A.J.M.; Kolev, S.D. & Wedd, A.G. (2006). Metal ion ligands in hyperaccumulating plants. *Journal of Biological Inorganic Chemistry*, 11, 1, 2–12. ISSN: 1432-1327

Cappuccino, J.G. & Sherman, N. (1999). Microbiology: A Laboratory Manual, 5th edition, Benjamin/cummings Science Publising, ISBN: 0-8053-7646-1, New York.

Chakravarty, B. & Srivastava, S. (1997). Effect of cadmium and zinc interaction on metal uptake and regeneration of tolerant plants in linseed. *Agriculture, Ecosystems and Environment*, 61, 1, 45-50. ISSN: 0167-8809

Chantiratikul, A.; Aengwanich, W.; Chinrasri, O. & Chantiratikul, P. (2008). Plasma selenium concentration and glutathione peroxidase activity in red blood cells of laying hens fed sodium selenite or zinc-L-selenomethionine. *International Journal of Poultry Science*, 7, 7, 692-695. ISSN: 16828356

Cheng, S. (2003). Review articles: Heavy metals in plants and phytoremediation. *Environmental Science & Pollution Research*, 10, 5, 335-340. ISSN: 1614-7499

Chung, C.T. & Miller, R.H. (1993). Preparation and storage of competent Escherichia coli cells. *Methods in Enzymology*, 218, 621-627. ISSN: 0076-6879

Clesceri, L.S.; Greenberg, A.E.; Eaton, A.D. (1998) Standard Methods for the Examination of Water and wastewater, 20th edition, American Public Health Association, American Water Works Association & Water Environment Federation, ISBN: 0-87553-235-7, Meryland.

Cobbett, C. & Goldsbrough, P. (2000). Mechanisms of metal resistance: Phytochelatins and metallothioneins, In: *Phytoremediation of Toxic Metals: Using Plants to Clean up the Environment*, Raskin, L. & Ensley, R.D. (Ed.), 33-49, John Wiley & Sons, ISBN 0-471-19254-6, New York.

Cobbett, C. & Goldsbrough, P. (2002). Photochelatins and metallothioneins: Roles in heavy metal detoxification and homeostasis. *Annual Reviews Plant Biology*, 53, 1, 159-182. ISSN: 1543-5008.

Cotelle, N.; Bernier, J.L.; Catteau, J.P.; Pommery, J.; Wallet, J.C. & Gaydou, E.M. (1996) Antioxidant Property of hydroxyl- Flavones. *Journal of Free Radical Biology & Medicine*, 20, 1, 35-43. ISSN: 0891-5849

Cuenca, S., Amo-Marco, J.B. & Parra, R. (1999). Micropropagation from inflorescence stems of the Spanish endemic plant *Centaurea paui* Loscos ex Willk. (Compositae). *Plant Cell Reports*, 18, 7, 674-679. ISSN: 1432-203X

Davies, K.L.; Davies, M.S. & Francis, D. (1991) Zinc-induced vacuolation in root meristematic cells of Festuca rubra L. *Plant, Cell and Environment*, 14, 4, 399-406. ISSN: 1365-3040

Dimassi-Theriou, K. & Bosabalidis, A.M. (1997). Effects of light, magnesium and sucrose on leaf anatomy, photosynthesis, starch and total sugar accumulation, in kiwifruit cultured *in vitro*. *Plant Cell, Tissue & Organ Culture*, 47, 2, 127-134. ISSN: 1573-5044

Dworkin, M. & Foster, J.W. (1958) Experiments with some microorganisms which utilize ethane and hydrogen, *Journal of Bacteriology*, 75, 5, 592-603. ISSN: 1098-5530

Ebbs, S.D.; Zambrano, M.C.; Spiller, S.M. & Newville, M. (2009). Cadmium sorption, influx, and efflux at the mesophyll layer of leaves from ecotypes of the Zn/Cd hyperaccumulator *Thlaspi caerulescens*. *The New Phytologist*, 181, 3, 626–636. ISSN: 1469-8137

Ensley, B.D. (2000) Rationable for use of phytoremediation, In: *Phytoremediation of toxic metals*, Raskin, L. & Ensley, R.D. (Ed.), 3-11, John Wiley & Sons, ISBN 0-471-19254-6, New York.

Ensley, B.D.; Elless, M.; Blaylock, M.J. & Huang, J. (2001). Nutritionl supplements, US Patent 6,270,809B1.

Gamborg, O.L. & Phillips, G.C. (1995). Plant cell, tissue, and organ culture : fundamental methods, Springer, ISBN: 3540580689, New York.

Gardea-Torresdey, J.L.; Peralta-Videa, J.R.; Rosa, G. de la & Parsons, J.G. (2005). Review: Phytoremediation of heavy metals and study of the metal coordination by X-ray absorption spectroscopy. *Coordination Chemistry Reviews*, 249, 17-18, 1797–1810. ISSN: 0010-8545

Ghosh, M. & Singh, S.P. (2005). A review on phytoremediation of heavy metals and utilization of its by products. *Applied and ecology and environmental research*, 3, 1, 1-18. ISSN 1785 0037

Grill, E.; Loffler, S.; Winnacker, E.L. & Zenk, M.H. (1989). Phytochelatins, the heavy-metals binding peptindes of plants are synthesized from glutathione by a specific γ-glutamylcysteine dipeptidyl traspeptidase. *Proceeding of the National Academy of Sciences of the United States of America*. 86, 18, 6838-6842. ISSN: 1091-6490

Hall, J.L. (2002). Cellular mechanisms for heavy metal detoxification and tolerance. *Journal experiment of Botany*, 53, 366, 1-11. ISSN: 1460-2431

Heumann, H.G. (2002). Ultrastructural localization of zinc in zinc-tolerant *Armeria maritime* ssp. Helleri by autometallography. *Journal of Plant Physiology*, 159, 2, 191-203. ISSN: 0176-1617

Horitsu, H.; Yamamota, K.; Wachi, S.; Kawai, K. & Fukuchi, A. (1986). Plasmid-determined cadmium resistance in *Pseudomonas putida* GAM-1 isolated from soil. *Journal of Bacteriology*, 165, 1, 334-335. ISSN: 1098-5530

Hu, P.J.; Qiu, R.L.; Senthikumar, P.; Jiang, D.; Chen, Z.W.; Tang, Y.T. & Liu, F.J. (2009). Tolerance, accumulation and distribution of zinc and cadmium in hyperaccumulator *Potentilla griffithii*. *Environmental and Experimental Botany*, 66, 2, 317-325. ISSN: 0098-8472

Hughes, M.N. & Poole, R.K. (1989). *Metals and Micro-organisms*, Chapman & Hall, ISBN 0412244004, New York.

Jing, Y.; He, Z. & Yang, X. (2007). Role of soil rhizobacteria in phytoremediation of heavy metal contaminated soils. *Journal of Zhejiang University: Science B*, 8, 3, 192-207. ISSN: 1862-1783

Karley, A.J.; Leigh, R.A.& Sanders, D. (2000). Where do all the ions go? The cellular basis of differential ion accumulation in leaf cells. *Trends in Plant Science*, 5, 11, 465-470. ISSN: 1360-1385

Kelly, R.A.; Andrews, J.C. & DeWitt, J.G. (2002). An X-ray absorption spectroscopic investigation of the nature of the zinc complex accumulated in *Datura innoxia* plant tissue culture. *Microchemical Journal*, 71, 2-3, 231-245. ISSN: 0026-265X

Kessler, F. & Vidi, P.A. (2007). Plastoglobule lipid bodies: their functions in chloroplasts and their potential for applications. *Advances in Biochemical Engineering/Biotechnol*, 107, 153-172. ISSN: 0724-6145

Khan, A.G. (2005). Role of soil microbes in the rhizospheres of plants growing on trace metal contaminated soils in phytoremediation. *Journal of Trace Elements in Medicine and Biology*, 18, 4, 355-364. ISSN: 0946-672X

Koneman, E.W.; Allen, S.D.; Janda, W.M.; Schreckenberger, P.C. & Winn, W.C. (1997). *Color Atlas and Textbook of Diagnostic Microbiology*, 5th Edition, Lippincott-Raven Publishers, ISBN: 0-397-51529-4, Pennsylvania.

Li, T.Q.; Yand, X.E.; Yang, J.Y. & He, Z.L. (2006). Zn accumulation and subcellular distribution in the Zn hyperaccumulator *Sedum alfredii* Hance. *Pedosphere*, 16, 5, 616-623. ISSN: 1002-0160

Liu, H.; Qiu, N.; Ding, H. & Yao, R. (2008). Polyphenols contents and antioxidant capacity of 68 Chinese herbals suitable for medical or food uses. *Food Research International*. 41, 4, 363–370. ISSN: 0963-9969

MacFarlane, G.R. & Burchett, M.D. (2002). Toxicity, growth and accumulation relationships of copper, lead and zinc in the gray mangrove *Avicennia marina* (Forsk.) Vierh. *Marine Environmental Research*, 54, 1, 65-84. ISSN: 0141-1136

Miller, R.O. (1998). Nitric-Perchloric acid wet digestion in an open vessel, In: *Handbook of Reference Methods for Plant Analysis*, Kalra, Y.P. (Ed.), 57-62, CRC Press, ISBN: 1-57444-124-8, Florida.

Menon, A.R.; Aktoprakligül, D.; Zdemür, A. & Vertii, A. (2001). Heavy Metal Accumulation and Detoxification Mechanisms in Plants. *Turkish Journal of Botany*, 25, 3, 111-121. ISSN 1300-008X

Mukerji, K.; Manoharachary, C. & Singh, J. (2006). *Microbial activity in the rhizosphere*, Spinger, ISBN: 10 3-540-29182-2, Berlin.

Murashige, T. & Skoog, F. (1962). A revised medium for rapid growth and bioassays with tobacco tissue cultures. *Physiologia Plantarum*, 15, 3, 473-497. ISSN: 1399-3054

Neumann, D.; Lichtenberger, O.; Gunther, D.; Tschersch, K. & Nover, L. (1994). Heat-shock proteins induce heavy metal tolerance in higher plants. *Planta*, 194, 3, 360-367. ISSN: 1432-2048

Panitlertumpai, N., Mongkhonsin, B., Nakbanpote, W. & Jitto, P. (2008). Zinc hyperaccumulation by *Gynura pseudochina* (L.) DC., Proceedings of Zinc processing 08, 25-26 Aug, Stamford Plaza Hotel, Brisbane, Australia.

Patel, K.; Kumar, A. & Durani, S. (2007). Analysis of the structural consensus of the zinc coordination centers of metalloprotein structures. *Biochimica et Biophysica Acta - Proteins & Proteomics*, 1774, 10, 1247-1253. ISSN: 1570-9639

Penrose, D.M. & Glick, B.R. (2003). Method for isolating and characterizing ACC deaminase-containing plant growth-promoting rhizobacteria. *Physiologia Plantarum*, 118, 1, 10-15. ISSN: 1399-3054

Rajkumar, M. & Freitas, H. (2008). Influence of metal resistant-plant growth-promoting bacteria on the growth of Ricinus communis in soil contaminated with heavy metals. *Chemosphere*, 71, 5, 834–842. ISSN: 0045-6535

Raskin, I. & Ensley, B.D. (2000). *Phytoremediation of Toxic Metals: Using Plants to Clean up the Environment*, John Wiley & Sons, ISBN 0-471-19254-6, New York.

Reddy, G. N. & Prasad, M. N.V. (1993). Tyrosine is not phosphorylated in cadmium induced hsp70 cognate in maize (*Zea mays* L.) seedlings: Role in chaperone function?. *Biochemical Archives*, 9, 25-32. ISSN: 0749-5331

Reddy, G. N. & Prasad, M. N.V. (1995). Cadmium induced protein phosphorylation changes in rice (*Oryza sativa* L.). *Journal of Plant Physiology*, 145, 1-2, 67-70. ISSN: 0176-1617

Reeves, R.D. & Baker, A.J.M. (2000). Metal-accumulating plants, In: *Phyto-remediation of Toxic Metals: Using Plants to Clean up the Environment*, Raskin, I. & Ensley, B.D. (Ed.), 193-230, John Wiley & Sons, ISBN: 0-471-19254-6, Toronto.

Roane, T.M.; Pepper, I.L. & Miller, R.M. (1996). Microbial remediation of metals, In: *Bioremediation: Principles and applications*, Crawford, R.L. & Crawford, D.L. (Ed.), 312-340, Cambridge University Press, ISBN 0-521-47041-2, Cambridge.

Robinson, B.; Russell, C.; Hedley, M. & Clothier, B. (2001). Cadmium adsorption by rhizobacteria: implications for New Zealand pastureland. *Agriculture, Ecosystems and Environment*, 87, 315-321. ISSN: 0167-8809

Rosa, G. de la; Peralta-Videa, J.R.; Montes, M.; Parsons, J.G.; Cano-Aguilera, I. & Gardea-Torresdey, J.L. (2004). Cadmium uptake and translocation in tumbleweed (*Salsola kali*), a potential Cd-hyperaccumulator desert plant species: ICP/OES and XAS studies. *Chemosphere*, 55, 9, 1159–1168. ISSN: 0045-6535

Sangdee, A.. Sirithorn, P. & Thummabenjapone, P. (2003). Virus and Viroid Causal Agent(s) of Bunchy Top and Severe Necrosis of Tomato, *Khon Kaen Agricultural Journal*, 31, 3, 161-170. ISSN 0125-2364

Santa-María, G.E. & Cogliatti, D.H. (1998) The regulation of zinc uptake in wheat plants. *Plant Science*, 137, 1, 1-12. ISSN: 0168-9452

Sarret, G.; Vangronsvele, J.; Manceau, A.; Musso, M.; Hean, J.D.; Menthonnex, J.J. & Hazemann, J.L. (2001). Accumulation froms of Zn and Pb in *Phaseolus valgaris* in the presence and absence of EDTA. *Environmental Science Technology*, 35, 13, 2854-2859. ISSN: 1520-5851

Schnoor, J.L. (1997). Phytoremediation, Technology Evaluation Report TE-98-01, GWRTAC, Pennsylvania.

Siddiqui, Z.A. (2006). *PGPR: Biocontrol and Biofetilization*, Springer, ISBN-10 1-4020-4002-4, Netherlands.

Simmons, R.W.; Pongsakul, P.; Saiyasitpanich, D. & Klinphoklap, S. (2005). Elevated levels of cadmium and zinc in paddy soils and elevated levels of cadmium in rice grain downstream of a zinc mineralized area in Thailand. Environmental Geochemistry & Health, 27, 5-6, 501–511. ISSN: 1573-2983

Sobkowiaka, R. & Deckertb, J. (2006). Proteins induced by cadmium in soybean cells. *Journal of Plant Physiology*, 163, 11, 1203–1206. ISSN: 0176-1617

Spaepen, S.. Vanderleyden, J. & Remans, R. (2007). Indole-3-acetic acid in microbial and microorganism-plant signaling. *FEMS Microbiology Reviews*, 31, 4, 425-448. ISSN: 1574-6976

Sridhar, B.B.M.; Diehl, S.V.; Han, F.X.; Monts, D.L. & Su, Y. (2005). Anatomical changes due to uptake and accumulation of Zn and Cd in Indian mustard (*Brassica juncea*). *Environmental & Experimental Botany*, 54, 2, 131–141. ISSN: 0098-8472

Strandberg, G.W.; Shumate, S.E. & Parrott, J.R.Jr. (1981). Microbial cells as biosorbents for heavy metals: accumulation of uranium by *Saccharomyces cerevisiae* and *Pseudomonas aeruginosa*. *Applied and Environmental Microbiology*, 41, 1, 237-245. ISSN: 1098-5336

Straczek, A.; Sarret, G.; Manceau, A.; Hinsinger, P.; Geoffroy, N. & Jaillard, B. (2008). Zinc distribution and speciation in roots of various genotypes of tobacco exposed to Zn. *Environmental and Experimental Botany*, 63, 1-3, 80-90. ISSN: 0098-8472

Suresh, B. & Ravishankar, G.A. (2004). Phytoremediation-A novel and promising approach for environmental clean-up. *Critical reviews in biotechnology*, 24, 2-3, 97-124. ISSN: 1549-7801

Tõrõk, I. & Kondorosim, Á. (1981). Nucleotide sequence of the *R. meliloti* nitrogenase reductase (*nif* H) gene. *Nucleic Acids Research*, 9, 21, 5711-5723. ISSN: 1362-4962

Tucker, R.K. & Shaw, J.A. (2000). Phytoremediation and public acceptance, In: *Phytoremediation of Toxic Metals: Using Plants to Clean up the Environment*, Raskin, L. & Ensley, R.D. (Ed.), 33-49, John Wiley & Sons, ISBN 0-471-19254-6, New York.

Verbi F.M.; Arruda, S.C.C.; Rodriguez, A.P.M.; Pe´rez, C.A. & Arruda, M.A.Z. (2005) Metal-binding proteins scanning and determination by combining gel electrophoresis, synchrotron radiation X-ray fluorescence and atomic spectrometry. *Journal of Biochemical & Biophysical Methods*, 62, 2, 97–109. ISSN: 0165-022X

Vázquez, M.D.; Barceló, J.; Poschenrieder, C.H.; Módico, J.; Hatton, P.; Baker, A.J.M. & Cope, G.H. (1992) Localization of zinc and cadmium in *Thlaspi caerulescens* (Brassicaceae), a metallophyte that can hyperaccumulate both metals. *Journal of Plant Physiology*, 140, 3, 350-355. ISSN: 0176-1617

Weis, J.S. & Weis, P. (2004). Metal uptake, transport and release by wetland plants: implications for phytoremediation and restoration. *Environment International*, 30, 5, 685-700. ISSN: 0160-4120

Weisburg, W.G.; Barns, S.M.; Pelletier, D.A. & Lane, D.J. (1991). 16s ribosomal DNA amplification for phylogenetic study. *Journal of Bacteriology*, 173, 2, 697–703. ISSN: 1098-5530

Willey, J.M.; Sherwood, L.M. & Woolverton, C.J. (2009). Prescott's Principles of Microbiology, McGraw-Hill, ISBN 978-0-07-128367-0, New York.

Wood, J.; Scott, K.P.; Avgustin, G.; Newbold, C.J. & Flint, H.J. (1998). Estimation of the relative abundance of different Bacteroides and *Prevotella ribotypes* in gut samples by restriction enzyme profiling of PCR-amplified 16S rRNA gene sequences. *Applied & Environmental Microbiology*, 64, 10, 3683–3689. ISSN: 1098-5336

Yoo, K. M.; Lee, C. H.; Lee, H.; Moon, B. & Lee, C. Y. (2008). Relative antioxidant and cytoprotective activities of common herbs. *Food Chemistry*, 106, 3, 929–936. ISSN: 0308-8146

Yoshida, N.; Ishii, K.; Okuno, T. & Tanaka, K. (2006). Purification and Characterization of Cadmium-Binding Protein from Unicelluar Alga *Chlorella sorokinian*. *Current Microbiology*, 52, 6, 460–463. ISSN: 1432-0991

Yu, M.; Yang, F.; Chu, W.; Wang, Y.; Zhao, H.; Gao, B.; Zhao, W.; Gao, B.; Zhao, W.; Sun, J.; Wu, F.; Zhang, X.; Shi, Y. & Wu, Z. (2008). 3D local structure around Zn in Kti11p as a representative Zn-(Cys)4 motif as obtained by MXAN. *Biochemical and Biophysical Research Communications*, 374, 1, 28-32. ISSN: 1090-2104

Zehr, J.P. & McReynolds, L.A. (1989). Use of degenerate oligonucleotides for amplification of the *nif*H gene from the marine cyanobactertium *Trichodesmium thiebautii*. *Applied & Environmental Microbiology*, 55, 10, 2522-2526. ISSN: 1098-5336

Zhao, F.J.; Lombi, E.; Breedon, T. & McGrath, S.P. (2000). Zinc hyperaccumulation and cellular distribution in Arabidopsis halleri. *Plant, Cell and Environment*, 23, 5, 507–514. ISSN: 1365-3040

Zhuang, X.; Chen, J.; Shim, H. & Bai, Z. (2007). New advances in plant growth-promoting rhizobacteria for bioremediation. *Environmental International*, 33, 3, 406-413. ISSN: 0160-4120

Zuo, Y.; Chen, H. & Deng, Y. (2002). Simultaneous determination of catechins, caffeine and gallic acids in green, Oolong, black and pu-erh teas using HPLC with a photodiode array detector. *Talanta*, 57, 2, 307-316. ISSN: 0039-9140